A
TREATISE
ON THE
BRITISH MILITARY MARTINI

THE MARTINI–HENRY, 1869–C1900

B.A.TEMPLE

&

I.D.SKENNERTON

First published 1983
by
B.A.Temple,
392 Prout Road,
Burbank, 4123,
Australia.

National Library of Australia Card Number and ISBN

ISBN 0 9596108 5 5

Sole Distributors –

Australasia

B.A.Temple,
392 Prout Road,
Burbank, 4123,
AUSTRALIA.

Canada

Fortress Publications,
P.O. Box 9241,
Stoney Creek,
Ontario. L8G 3X9
CANADA.

U.K., Europe, & Sth. Africa

Arms & Armour Press,
2-6 Hampstead High Street,
London, NW3 1QQ,
ENGLAND.

U.S.A.

I.D.S.A. Books,
1559 8 Mile Road,
Cincinatti,
Ohio. 45230
U.S.A.

Printed by – INPRINT, Brisbane, Qld.
Bound by – Book Graphics, Ferntree Gully,
Victoria.

CONTENTS

AUTHORS' NOTE

Although the British Military Martini in its common service patterns is well known to collectors and historians, some of its developmental weapons and conversions of service arms are not, so this Treatise is an attempt to portray the history of its evolution from trials weapons to the last of the service issues.

The Martini-actioned rifle as first adopted by the British service was a milestone in arms development for Britain, as it was the first breech-loader designed as such to be used in full scale issue by that service, and initially was superior to any other service arm then in use.

Predictably, as arms research and development does not stand still, the Martini lost its superiority to the small bore repeating magazine rifle, which in its turn was adopted by the British military forces. However, this was not the end for the Martini, as, after being adapted to take the magazine rifle cartridge, it soldiered on for a few more decades in a supporting role, being issued to auxiliary forces and the like.

The history of the Martini as used by the British Empire spans a period of approximately 50 years, with three basic calibres used, and quite a variety of types of weapons developed. As this makes the subject rather complex, it has been considered more convenient to separate the text into three parts, with a volume devoted to each part, complete in itself, but integrated with the whole, viz. –

Part I – The Martini-Henry, 1869 – C1900
Part II – The .40 and .303 Martinis, 1880 – C1920
Part III – Manufacture, Training Arms, and Accoutrements.

Much of the information contained in this work has been taken from official publications which had a limited circulation, and as such is publicly seen for the first time. In addition, in most instances the actual patterns of weapons mentioned were examined in conjunction with the written information, so as to confirm presented statements. In this way most speculative comment could be discarded, and the result is a coverage of Martini prototype and service arms never before attempted in a single work.

The story as presented concerns the weapon itself; how it came about, and how and why it was changed at various times. It is not the story of the British service using the Martini, and should not be regarded as such. Details of service use are only included where necessary to explain the reasons for a particular alteration to the pattern.

Often unjustly maligned by its detractors (and some of its users), the Martini was a masterpiece of design for its era, and although long gone from service use, it is still used for sporting purposes in several varieties of weapon; this Treatise is therefore dedicated to the memory of the man who designed it, the men who developed it, the men who used it, and the weapon itself.

B.A.T.
I.D.S.

ACKNOWLEDGEMENTS

Many people, both in Australia and overseas, assisted with the research for this Treatise by supplying information, or allowing inspection of weapons or items in their collections, and their contributions are gratefully acknowledged. Mention must be made of Laurie Addison, DeWitt Bailey, Mike Baldwin, Geo Battison, Geoff Bridger, Reg Chapman, John Corcoran, Frank English, Frank Garie, Bruce Hanson, Tony Harris, John Kindred, Jim Lane, Jim Lang, Gordon MacMillan, Barrie Manarey, Lionel Mundt, Denys Parker, the late Ernie Radke, Stan Robinson, Robert Shannon, Doug Smith, Bill Sykes, Keith Taylor Jnr., Bruce Tunstill, John Watts, Peter White, and Tom Williams.

Special thanks are due to the late Frank Adlam, Lord Cottesloe, the Hon. John Fremantle, the late Tom Wilson, Syd Wigzell, and Herb Woodend, for allowing access to their personal libraries and original documents; to Kevin and Janet Bestt for their hospitality and tolerance; to Ron Cook for regularly supplying pertinent information; and to Bob Richardson, who is always ready to assist.

Syd Wigzell read the manuscript and made constructive comments on it.

Staff of the following institutions were also helpful in the search for documents and weapons – The British, Birmingham, London University, Queensland University, and Science Reference Libraries; the British Patent Office; the House of Lords and Public Records Offices; the Imperial War and National Army Museums; the Infantry Centre Museum, Singleton; HM Tower of London; QAD(Ord.) Enfield Pattern Room; and Messrs. Weller and Dufty.

Text and diagrams from Patent Specifications are by courtesy of the Patent Office, and other illustrations not acknowledged are by courtesy of Her Majesty's Stationery Office and the owners of original documents published by that office. Specific weapons pictured by courtesy of their owners are acknowledged by a code adjacent to the relevant figure, in accordance with the following list –

B. Hanson, Queensland, Australia.
IWM – Imperial War Museum, London, UK.
NAM – National Army Museum, London, UK.
QAD(O) – Quality Assurance Directorate (Ordnance), Pattern Room Enfield, UK.
R. Richardson, Queensland, Australia.
Singleton – Infantry Centre Museum, Singleton, NSW, Australia.
Tower – Master of the Armouries, Tower of London, UK.
W & D – Weller and Dufty, London, UK.

To all the above, and anyone else not mentioned who helped in any way, we are deeply grateful.

B.A.T.
I.D.S.

PARTS OF RIFLE.

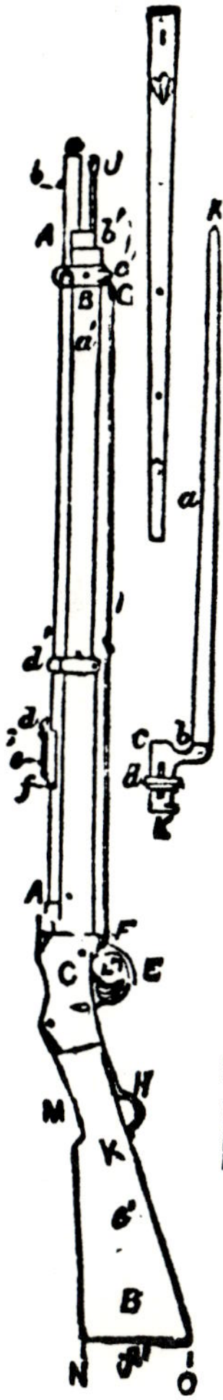

AA. Barrel
- *a.* Muzzle.
- *b.* Foresight.
- *c.* Back-sight
  - *d.* Leaf.
  - *e.* Slide, on which is a wind-gauge.
  - *f.* Bed.

BB. Stock
- *a'.* Fore-end.
- *b'.* Nose-cap.
- *c'.* Upper band.
- *d'.* Lower band.
- *e'.* Butt.
- *f'.* Butt-plate.

- *C.* Body.
- *D.* Trigger.
- *E.* Trigger-guard.
- *F.* Guard-swivel.
- *G.* Band-swivel.
- *H.* Lever.
- *I.* Sling.
- *J.* Cleaning-rod.
- K. Catch block for loop of lever.

KK. Bayonet
- *a.* Blade.
- *b.* Bend.
- *c.* Socket.
- *d.* Locking ring.

- *L.* Scabbard.
- *M.* Small
- *N.* Heel
- *O.* Toe

(*M.*, *N.*, *O.*: for drill purposes.)

PARTS OF CARBINE.

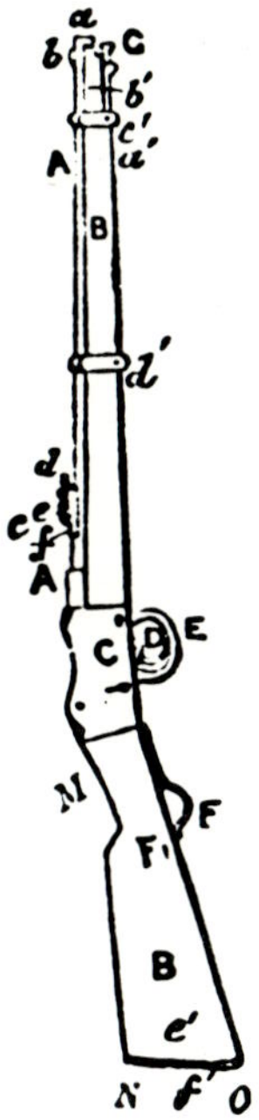

A.A. Barrel
- *a.* Muzzle.
- *b.* Foresight.
- *c.* Backsight
  - *d.* Leaf.
  - *e.* Slide, on which is a wind-gauge.
  - *f.* Bed.

B.B. Stock
- *a'.* Fore-end.
- *b'.* Nose-cap.
- *c'.* Upper band.
- *d'.* Lower band.
- *e'.* Butt.
- *f'.* Butt-plate.

- *C.* Body.
- *D.* Trigger.
- *E.* Trigger-guard.
- *F.* Lever.
- F_1. Catch block for loop of lever.
- *G.* Cleaning-rod.
- *M.* Small
- *N.* Heel
- *O.* Toe

(*M.*, *N.*, *O.*: For drill purposes.)

ABBREVIATIONS

Abbreviations used in the text to obviate repetitious designations of persons, weapons, and government depots are listed below.

More complete explanations of some of these designations will be found in the GLOSSARY, and it should be noted that the term RSAF as commonly used herein applies only to the Enfield branch of that establishment, unless otherwise stated.

Abbreviated designations of various patterns of rifles and carbines, eg – M-H CC.I – are translated thus – (M-H) Martini-Henry (CC) Cavalry Carbine (I) Mark I.

AAG – Assistant Adjutant-General
AC – Artillery carbine
Adm. – Admiral
ADoA – Assistant Director of Artillery and Stores
A-G – Adjutant-General

Brig.-Gen.- Brigadier-General
Btn. – Battalion

Capt. – Captain
C – Carbine
CC – Cavalry carbine
CE – Civil engineer
C-I-C – The Field Marshal Commanding-in-Chief
CISA – Chief Inspector of Small Arms
Col. – Colonel
Comm. – Commander
CoO – Council of Ordnance
CSA – Committee on Small Arms
CSO – Committee on Siege Operations

DAAG – Deputy Assistant Adjutant-General
DAG – Deputy Adjutant-General
DGNO – Director-General of Naval Ordnance
DGO – Director-General of Ordnance
DGOF – Director-General of Ordnance Factories
DGoF – Director-General of Fortifications
DNO – Director of Naval Ordnance
DoA – Director of Artillery and Stores
DoO – Director of Ordnance

E-M – Enfield-Martini

FRS – Fellow of the Royal Society

GOC – General Officer Commanding

I,II,&c. – Mark of weapon
IGF – Inspector-General of Fortifications
IGM – Inspector-General of Musketry
IGOF – Inspector-General of Ordnance Factories
IoM – Inspector of Musketry

LoC – List of Changes in War Materiel
Lt.-Col. – Lieutenant-Colonel

Maj.-Gen.- Major-General
M-E – Martini-Enfield
MGC – Machine Gun Committee
M-H – Martini-Henry
M-M – Martini-Metford

OC – Officer Commanding
OCO – Ordnance Consulting Officer
OSC – Ordnance Select Committee

QMG – Quartermaster-General

R – Rifle
RA – Royal Arsenal
RA – Royal Artillery
RE – Royal Engineers
RGF – Royal Gunpowder Factory
RIC – Royal Irish Constabulary
RL – Royal Laboratories
RN – Royal Navy
RSAF – Royal Small Arms Factory

SAC – Small Arms Committee
Serj. – Serjeant
SEB – Secretary, Experimental Branch
S-G – Surveyor-General
SGO – Surveyor-General of Ordnance
SOC – Siege Operations Committee
SoM – School of Musketry
SoS – Secretary of State for War
Supt. – Superintendent

WO – War Office

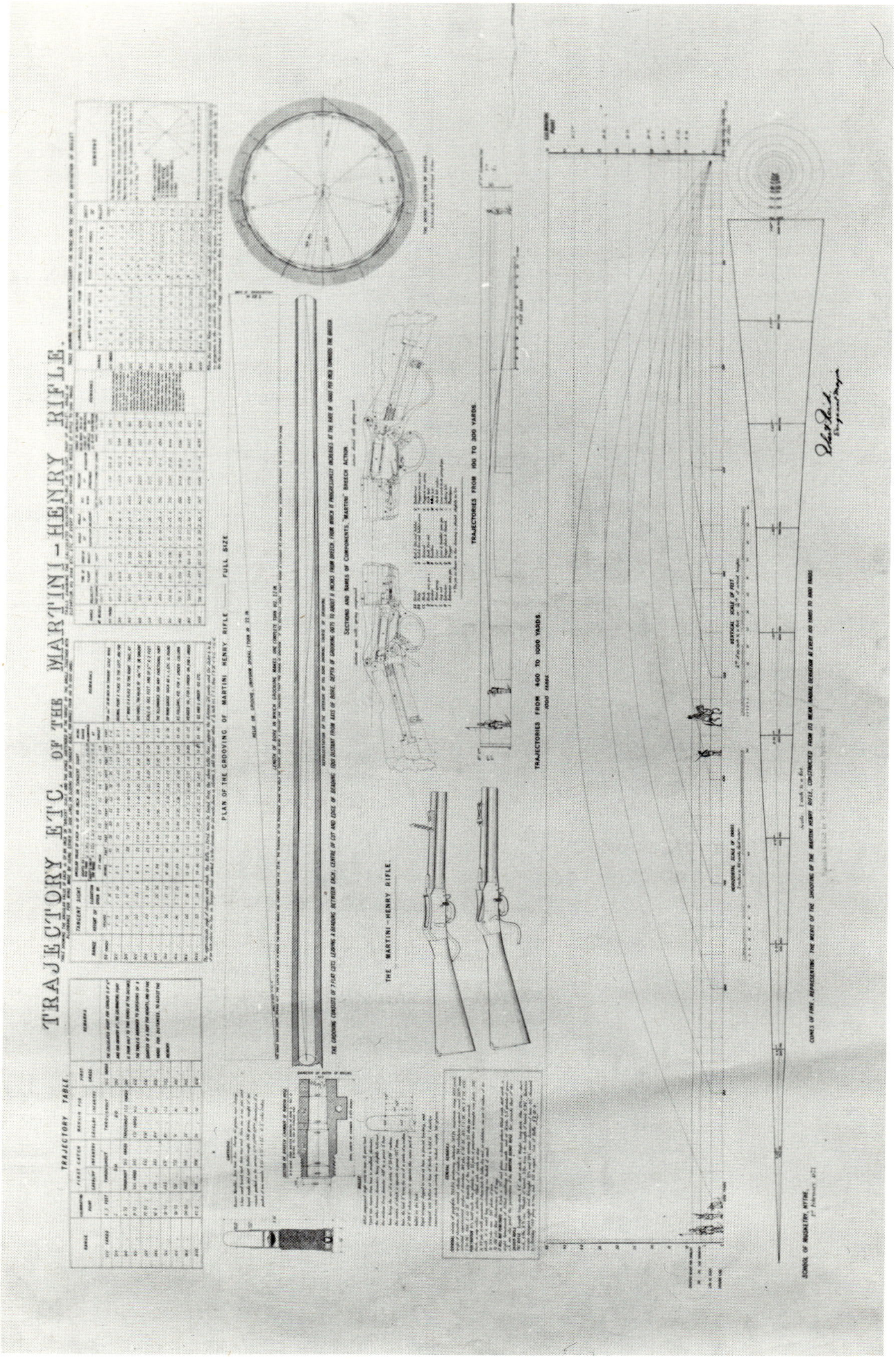

TRAJECTORY ETC. OF THE MARTINI-HENRY RIFLE.
TRAJECTORY TABLE.
PLAN OF THE GROOVING OF MARTINI HENRY RIFLE — FULL SIZE.
THE MARTINI-HENRY RIFLE.
TRAJECTORIES FROM 100 TO 300 YARDS.
TRAJECTORIES FROM 400 TO 1000 YARDS.

NAM

CHAPTER 1.

INTRODUCTION

TO understand the procedures that led to the adoption of the Martini-Henry rifle by the British service in 1871, it is necessary to go back a few years before that event to the Danish-Prussian War of 1864. In this short but decisive action the Prussians were armed with one of the first breech-loading rifles to be used to a large extent by any army – the Dreyse Needle-gun. Its impact on the battle field and on the impressions of military observers from other countries, including Britain, was such that it started a great movement towards breech-loading weapons by all the major powers of Europe and elsewhere.

That it was only an indifferent example of a breech-loader was self-evident, but it was in use in reasonable numbers, and had proven its worth sufficiently to encourage others to adopt the breech-loading principle perhaps sooner than would have been the case had it not existed at the time.

The British reaction was fairly rapid, as the then Secretary of State for War, Lord de Grey and Ripon, appointed an Ordnance Select Committee to "Report on the advisability of arming the infantry, either in whole or in part, with breech-loading arms." This committee, in its final report of 11-7-1864, stated that it considered – without reference to any particular form of breech system – it was in favour of arming the infantry wholly with breech-loading arms. This decision signalled the end of the muzzle-loader in the British service.

THE ORDNANCE SELECT COMMITTEE

To authorise the establishment of the select committee, the SoS had the following letter written, to the Military Secretary, Horse Guards –

Sir, *War Office, June 13, 1864.*

I have the honour, by direction of the Earl de Grey and Ripon, to inform you that his Lordship has had under his consideration the question of arming the infantry with breech-loading rifles; and that while it appears to Lord de Grey that there are obvious advantages in the employment of breech-loaders for certain purposes and in certain circumstances of war, practical objections of an important character and entitled to serious consideration have been urged against the general adoption of an arm of that description.

These objections relate chiefly to the danger that troops thus armed might fire away their ammunition too rapidly, and thus increase the difficulty of supplying them with ammunition during action, and render necessary the employment of a larger amount of transport than would otherwise be required.

In these circumstances he is of opinion that it would be desirable to appoint a committee of practical officers to inquire into the subject, and to report whether it would be advisable to arm the infantry, either in whole or in part, with breech-loading arms.

Lord de Grey proposes, with the concurrence of His Royal Highness the Field Marshal Commanding-in-Chief, that the committee should be composed of the following officers –

Maj.-Gen. Russell, CB
Col. Steele, CB
Col. Earl of Longford, KCB
Col. J. Clark Kennedy, CB
Col. W. Parke, CB
Col. J.M. Adye, CB, RA
Col. C.P. Walker, CB

I have, &c.,
Edward Lugard.

Col. Steele, after attending only the second meeting of the committee, had to withdraw from further attendence owing to an indisposition. He was not replaced, and the committe then met with the other members attending all meetings.

The committee met four times in all, and in the course of these meetings they interviewed several people and read extracts from letters and reports to gather evidence so as to reach a conclusion on the question put to them.

As a result of the evidence presented at these meetings the following report was drawn up, and signed by all the committee, Col. Steele included –

To the Right Honourable the Secretary of State for War.

The committee nominated by the Secretary of State for War, to consider the advisability of arming the infantry of the army, either in whole or in part, with breech-loading arms, having assembled at the War Office on the 27th June, 30th June, 5th July, and 11th July, 1864, having read and considered documents submitted to them, and having heard the viva voce statements of the following officers –

Lt.-Col. Gallwey, RE
Capt. Alderson, RA
Col. Dixon, RA
Maj. Young, RA
Mr. Burton, an American gentleman
Maj.-Gen. Hamilton, CB
Brevet-Col. Sir T. Troubridge, CB
Capt. Harrison, RA
Col. Claremont, CB
Lt.-Col. Tower

beg to report their opinion in favour of arming the infantry wholly with breech-loading arms.

The committee observe that it will be necessary to establish an efficient scheme for the transport of the first reserve of ammunition. to accompany troops on all ground, as an essential part of the system.

An abstract of the proceedings is annexed.

Signed by –

Maj.-Gen. Russell
Earl of Longford
Col. Clark Kennedy
Col. Parke
Col. Adye
Col. Steele
Col. Walker.

PREPARATIONS FOR BREECH-LOADING RIFLE TRIALS

After receiving the above report, the SoS in a memorandum dated 1-8-1864 had, in part, this to say –

This committee, composed of practical officers of varied experience, unanimously reports in favour of arming the infantry with breech-loading rifles.

The subject is of great importance, and it is desirable to lose no time in deciding what is the next step to be taken in regard to it.

Major-General Russell's committee have, in accordance with their instructions, simply reported that the infantry should be armed with breech-loaders; they have not recommended any particular system of breech-loading for adoption.

That question must now be dealt with, and it may be considered in two ways, either by itself with a view to ascertain the speediest and cheapest mode of placing a breech-loader in the hands of the troops, or in combination with other questions connected with rifles, such as the best size of bore and the best mode of igniting the cartridge, and with a view to determine what will be in all respects the most perfect arm for the use of the infantry.

The first mode of dealing with the question has the advantage of celerity; the second that of completeness.

It appears to me that an inquiry, the object of which is to ascertain which is the best arm in all respects, is of a kind which cannot wisely be pressed forward hurriedly; it must be accompanied by complete experiments and thorough trial, not only of a scientific, but of a practical kind, and will necessarily occupy a considerable time, and it would probably be more than two years before the arm ultimately selected would be actually in the hands of the troops.

It is very desirable to shorten this interval, if possible, and this can only be effected by adopting the other mode of proceeding.

In that case our course would be this; we should first adopt the readiest means now available for converting the existing arms of the service into breech-loading rifles of sufficient efficiency, and having thus armed the troops, we shoud proceed, under cover of this temporary arrangement, to enquire deliberately and fully what form of rifle would in all respects give us the most perfect military weapon.

He then outlined the measures to be adopted to select a breech action suitable for converting the muzzle-loading Enfield rifle; which measures eventually resulted in the Snider breech being used, making the Snider-Enfield, or, as it became more usually known, the Snider rifle.

The final paragraph of the memorandum then stated –

When these steps have been taken, I should be obliged to Major-General St. George if he would consider in what manner the larger inquiry as to the breech-loading rifle to be ultimately adopted should be conducted, and would let me have a full report on the subject, showing the conditions which the arm should be required to fulfil, and terms on which persons should be allowed to send in rifles for trial, &c.

In response to the above memorandum, Gen. St. George sent Minute Paper 7669/49 to the President, OSC, stating –

Now that the investigation as to the best method of converting the Enfield rifle into a breech-loader is in progress, it becomes necessary to take up the inquiry as to what form of rifle would in all respects give the most perfect military weapon. We must consider and decide upon the conditions to be laid down which a breech-loading arm should be required to fulfil, such as weight, length, calibre, method of igniting the cartridge, &c.

The committee is requested to report its opinion on these subjects and upon the whole question, and to say on what terms persons should be allowed to send in rifles for trial.

The OSC sitting in response to Gen. St. George's minute paper consisted of –

Brig.-Gen. Lefroy, RA
Capt. L.G. Heath, CB, RN
Capt. Hogge, CB, RA
Col. Younghusband, RA
Lt.-Col. Gallwey, RE
Capt. Heyman, RA, Secretary.

They considered the following questions –

1. Barrel length
2. Calibre
3. Weight of rifle, without bayonet
4. Weight of bullet, and charge
5. Cartridge, and mode of ignition
6. System of rifling, and twist.

By Committee Minute No.14,285, Report No.3,617 of 1-2-1865 they recommended as follows –

Calibre, 0.450-inch.
Barrel, length, 39 inches.
Twist, voluntary.
System of grooving, voluntary.
Musket, weight without bayonet, 9 lbs.
Bullet, weight, 480 grains.
Charge, 70 grains.
Cartridge, by preference, to carry its own ignition. (This condition was not absolutely essential to competition, but the committee remarked that every effort should be made to secure a cartridge containing its own ignition.)

THE FIRST BREECH–LOADING RIFLE TRIALS

To present the government requirements to the gun trade, so as to gain a response with breech-loading systems and cartridges, the advertisement below was published –

ADVERTISEMENT – TO GUNMAKERS AND OTHERS

1. The ultimate armament of the British infantry with breech-loading rifles having been determined upon, the Secretary of State for War is desirous of receiving proposals on the subject from gunmakers and others who may be disposed to enter into competition for the production of the best military weapon.

2. The principal elements of the new breech-loading rifle, and the conditions on which persons will be allowed to compete, are as follows –

DESCRIPTION

1. Calibre – 0.450-inches. High gauge rejecting plug, 0.453-inches.
2. Barrel – Length, 39.0 inches.
3. Barrel – Weight, 4 lbs. 8 ozs. to 5 lbs.
4. Twist – Optional.
5. System of grooving – Optional.
6. Musket, with cleaning rod or ramrod, but without bayonet – Weight not to exceed 9 lbs.
7. Bullet – Weight, 480 grains.
8. Charge – Not to exceed 70 grains J2 Government Powder.
9. Cartridge – By preference to carry its own ignition, but this condition is not absolutely essential to competition, and the Ordnance Select Committee will be prepared to consider mechanical arrangements for capping, as well as systems capped in the ordinary manner.
10. Lubrication – Wax on bullets. This is indispensible; but any other lubricant may be superadded or applied to the cartridge, if thought necessary by the competitor.

3. Competitors are at liberty to bring forward any number or form of grooves, or degree of twist in the rifling, but it is to be clearly understood that the adoption of any particular arm or system of breech-loading does not in any way imply the adoption of the system of rifling or of the ammunition which may accompany it.

4. Specifications and drawings of the methods proposed, stating the probable cost per arm, and accompanied by a finished specimen arm, with 20 rounds of suitable ammunition, should be sent to the "Director of Ordnance, War Office, Pall Mall", on or before 30th September, 1865.

5. The specifications and specimen arms will be considered by the Ordnance Select Committee and its associate members, who will select and recommend for trial such of the systems as may appear to them sufficiently promising, and each accepted competitor will then be required to furnish for experiment, at Woolwich, six arms, in strict conformity to the specimen arm submitted, with 1,500 rounds of ammunition per arm, within three months after date of demand.

6. The committee will try each selected arm with the ammunition supplied by the inventor to such extent as they may think necessary; but they will be at liberty to interchange ammunitions, and to try, at their discretion, the ammunition of one competitor, or ammunition made in imitation of it, with the arm of another. The same will apply to lubrication.

7. Each competitor will be required to disclose to the committee the exact nature of the lubrication he may employ.

8. The fittings of the musket, such as sights and bands, also the length and curve of stock, and other details not necessarily variable with the system of breech-loading, to be conformed to the service patterns.

9. A sum of £70 will be paid to each of the selected competitors, to cover the expense of the six rifles and of the supply of ammunition required.

June 21, 1865. *J. St. George, Major-General,*
Director of Ordnance.

MEMORANDUM IN EXPLANATION OF THE ADVERTISEMENT TO "GUNMAKERS AND OTHERS", JUNE 21ST, 1865.

LENGTH – I. By length of barrel 39" it is to be understood that the two following lengths are to be the same as those of the service Enfield rifle with the 39" barrel.
(1) Length from butt plate to trigger.
(2) Length from butt plate to muzzle.

RAMROD – II. Every arm will be required to have a ramrod, but the ramrod is not to be included in the fittings referred to in Section 8. It will be used chiefly as a cleaning rod, as expressed in Section 2, No.6, and may be lighter than the service ramrod.

WEIGHT – III. The limits of weight for the barrel, viz., 4.5 to 5 lbs., are intended to include any part of the breech mechanism which is attached to, and detachable with, the barrel.

BAYONET – IV. Competitors are not required to supply bayonets with the arms, but the arms are to be prepared to take a bayonet of the service pattern, except in respect to the size of the socket; and they must be fixed in the same way.

LUBRICATION – V. With reference to Section 2, No. 10, if a second lubricant is used, the committee will be satisfied with Westley Richards' No.8. Tallow, or any other animal fat is inadmissable.

VI. There will be no objection to any competitor bringing forward two descriptions of ammunition, but no more.

J. St. George, Major-General,
Director of Ordnance.

War Office, July 24, 1865.

The OSC appointed a sub-committee to examine the arms and ammunition submitted in response to the advertisement, and this sub-committee, consisting of the undermentioned officers, submitted its first report to the OSC on 27-10-1865.

Lt.-Col. Baynes, Unatt., President
Lt.-Col. Conolly, VC, Coldstream Guards
Capt. D. Thompson, 67th Regt.
Capt. Haig, RA, Secretary.

They were assisted by Mr. Gunner, Principal Inspector of Small Arms, and examined 24 systems of breech-loading small arms which had been submitted. These were – Albini; Aston; Byrnes and Benjamin; Carle; Carr; Craig; Della Noce; Henry; Hughes; Joslyn; Lindner; Luok; Mathews; Millar (2); Needham (2); Norris; Peabody; Poppenburg; Shepard (2); Snider; and Timmerhans.

Of the 24 specimen arms submitted, only eight conformed to the conditions of calibre, weight, and dimensions laid down in the advertisement, and the sub-committee commented –

The committee cannot forebear expressing their disappointment at the general inferiority of the arms from which a choice of such importance has to be made; they have however, selected the four following systems for trial, viz. – Snider; Joslyn; Henry; and Lindner.

These weapons were listed as Class 1, "Systems recommended for Trial". Put into Class 2, " Systems put aside for Further Examination", were – Byrnes and Benjamin; Millar; and Peabody. All the rest were put into Class 3, "Systems Rejected Summarily". (For full details of all weapons submitted, see Appendixes 1 and 2.)

The committee then went on to say –

Of these, Mr. Snider's is the only one which, in the opinion of the committee, approaches the degree of perfection which would justify its selection for the armament of the infantry, but they have not yet seen a rifle on this system made with all the improvements which have already been suggested by Mr. Snider himself. The systems of Henry and Joslyn are inferior to that of Snider, but appear to possess some advantages which may become further developed by experiment. That of Mr. Lindner is thought worthy of trial only because it is supposed to have received high commendation on the Continent, and is also stated to have been admitted into the Swiss Competition of Military Breech-Loading Rifles.

The reasons for rejecting the remaining 20 systems are detailed in a statement annexed.

The committee, bearing in mind that great advantages are shown in Snider's system alone, that the other systems brought forward are inferior, and that most of the leading gunmakers have not entered into the present competition, would suggest that it is well deserving the consideration of the Ordnance Select Committee and the Secretary of State for War, whether it is not desirable to postpone the present important inquiry till such time as gunmakers and others, at home and abroad, shall have further matured and developed their plans for the production of a thoroughly efficient breech-loading rifle for military purposes. This course would seem to recommend itself the more, as since the rendering of Report No.3,929, Minute 16,884, in the opinion of the sub-committee, Mr. Snider has so far improved his system that it is now an efficient means of converting the Enfield rifle, if thought desirable, the Royal Laboratory having also succeeded in making a cartridge suitable for the arm, and for military purposes generally.

The OSC accepted this report and discussed its implications, and communicated with the SoS in Report No.3,956 of 8-11-1865, with some comments and recommendations of their own.

They remarked that it was to be regretted that several eminent gunmakers failed to respond to the invitation of the government, and that they had reason to believe that some of the gunmakers were deterred from entering the proposed competition because of the limited period allowed by the terms of the advertisement for the preparation of specimen arms. They went on to say that because of the importance of the new breech-loading system, and because of the lack of a system showing the degree of perfection required, it would be desirable to postpone the enquiry to allow more time for inventors to finalise their plans which were known to be in the process of development at home and abroad.

The Snider system, however, was reserved for special consideration. An earlier version had previously been submitted for trial for the conversion of the Enfield muzzle loading rifle, but had not fared too well. The improved system submitted for the true breech-loading trials was considered eminently suitable for the Enfield conversion, so was specially recommended for further trials to that end, from which it emerged as the chosen system; and so was born the Snider-Enfield. It was not however, considered further for selection as the true breech-loader being sought, so far, in vain.

The recommendations of the OSC were approved by the SoS on 16-11-1865, and he directed that the trials of the new Snider be commenced as soon as possible. Orders were also given that the letter below be written to all the other inventors to finalise the current proceedings.

Sir, *War Office, December 12, 1865.*

I am directed by Earl de Grey and Ripon to inform you that the system of breech-loading for small arms submitted by you having been fully considered, his Lordship has decided that it is not adapted to the requirements of the service.

The specimen arm forwarded for inspection will be returned to you on your making application to the Secretary to the Ordnance Select Committee at Woolwich.

I am, &c.
J. St. George, Major-General,
Director of Ordnance.

INVESTIGATION INTO THE TRIALS

As a result of the foregoing the WO was no further advanced in its quest for a breech-loading rifle than it had been at the start, so a conference was called there on 28-11-1865, and it was attended by –

Earl de Grey
Lord Hartington
Brig.-Gen. Lefroy
Col. Dixon
Maj. Milward

After much discussion it was decided that the sub-committee was to be recalled, and in conjunction with the OSC and Col. Dixon, a series of questions was to be drawn up and sent to a number of selected gunmakers, whether or not they had entered the competition, to get their opinion on the possibility of producing a breech-loading rifle of 0.45-inch bore with ammunition containing its own ignition and fit for military use, and to gather the view of the trade upon the subject generally.

The covering letter and questions were as shown below.

War Office, December 18, 1865.

I am directed by Earl de Grey and Ripon to transmit to you, in duplicate, three lithographed papers containing queries on the subject of providing a breech-loading small bore rifle for military purposes, and to state that his Lordship would feel obliged by your giving them your early attention, returning to him one set of the forms with your replies written thereon.

I am, &c.
J. St. George, Major-General,
Director of Ordnance.

QUESTION 1.

Referring to the advertisement of 21st June, 1865, of which a copy is enclosed, will you be good enough to state, for Lord de Grey's consideration, whether there is anything in its terms or nature which had the effect of deterring you, or is likely to have deterred other leading gunmakers, from taking part in the proposed competition for the production of a small bore breech-loading military rifle; and if so, will you point out in what respect you think the terms of the advertisement open to amendment?

QUESTION 2.

If the Secretary of State should decide on issuing a fresh advertisement, what, in your opinion, is the least time that should be allowed –

(1) For the preparation of the specimen for submission to the committee?

(2) For the subsequent production of six rifles, to be submitted for trial if the system is admitted to the competition?

QUESTION 3.

Are there, in your opinion, any insuperable difficulties in the production of a breech-loading arm for general military use with cartridges containing their own ignition? Could such a cartridge be satisfactorily used with a bore of 0.45-inch, or what is the smallest calibre with which you think that such cartridges could be employed?

The inventors and gunmakers to whom the letter was addressed were –

Messrs. Swinburne and Sons, 16, Russel St., Birmingham.
Messrs. Cooper and Goodman, Woodcock St., Birmingham.
Mr. J. Turner, Fisher St., Birmingham.
Messrs. Hollis and Sons, St. Mary's Square, Birmingham.
Mr. W. Tranter, 13, St. Mary's Row, Birmingham.
Mr. G. Webley, 14, St. Mary's Row, Birmingham.
Messrs. Cock and Son, 88, Shadwell St., Birmingham.
Mr. Woodward, 16, Whittall St., Birmingham.
Mr. J. Bourne, Birmingham.
Messrs. Bentley and Playfair, Birmingham.
Mr. Westley Richards, 81, High St., Birmingham.
Mr. Greener, Rifle Hill, Birmingham.
Mr. Reeves, Charlotte St., Birmingham.
Birmingham Small Arm Company, Small Heath.
Mr. James Leetch, 19, New Church St., Paddington, W.
Mr. C. Lancaster, 151, New Bond St.
Mr. Purdy, 314½, Oxford St.
Mr. Wilkinson, 27, Pall Mall.
Mr. Barnet, Minories.
Messrs. Parker and Field, 233, High Holborn.
Mr. Daw, 57, Threadneedle St.
London Armoury Company, 36, King William St.

Mr. Mont-Storm, 3, Rood Lane.
Mr. Blanche, 29, Gracechurch St., Liverpool.
Messrs. Rigby and Son, 24, Suffolk St., Dublin.
Manchester Ordnance Company, 28, Pall Mall.
– Norris, Esq., Langham Hotel, Portland Place.
– Millar, Esq., Bethnal House, Cambridge Road.
Mr. Joslyn (Messrs. E. Newby, 31, Cheapside).
Mr. Snider, 43, Lamb's Conduit St., WC.
Mr. Needham, 26, Piccadilly.
Mr. Henry, 12, South St., Edinburgh.
Mr. Prince, 88, Piccadilly.

The OSC met on 19-3-1866 to consider the replies received from the gunmakers as a result of the letter, and by Report No.4,109 of 21-3-1866 gave their findings. Sitting on the committee were –

Brig.-Gen. Lefroy, RA, President
Capt. L.G. Heath, CB, RN, Vice-President
Col. Younghusband, RA
Col. Freeling, RE
Col. R.S. Baynes, Unatt.
Lt.-Col. Wray, CB, RA
Capt. Heyman, RA, Secretary
Capt. Haig, RA, Asst.-Secretary
Lt.-Col. Conolly, VC, Coldstream Guards
Capt. Thompson, 67th Regt., IoM

(The last two mentioned were members of the sub-committee on small arms.)

The committee, when presenting their opinions on the conclusions drawn from the views of the gunmakers expressed in the replies to the circular letter, thought it best to deal first with specific answers to specific questions, and then to offer observations on the complaints and charges against the government and the committee with which some of the makers had prefaced their replies.

In answer to the first question, three persons, Joslyn, Millar, and Westley Richards, said they did not object to the terms of the advertisement in a pecuniary sense, and three others, Howes, Norris, and Woodward, did not express any objection; all the others were unanimous in expressing in strong language their opinion that the sum of £70 was entirely inadequate to cover the cost associated with the production of six new rifles and 9,000 rounds of ammunition. The committee felt, that, considering the offer of £20 in 1864 for the conversion of six Enfield rifles into breech-loaders, and the supply of 6,000 rounds of ammunition with them, was sufficient to induce 47 competitors, including Westley Richards and Joslyn to offer their ideas, it was expected that the amount offered this time would cover selected competitors, even those ultimately unsuccessful, against actual loss; but they were quite willing to concede that the production of a new arm was a more serious proposition. It could not be the object of the government to save a few hundred pounds at the outset of such an important enquiry if the expenditure would serve a good purpose; but it was desirable not to hold out an inducement sufficient to lead speculative persons of no experience or status into the enquiry, causing delay and disappointment. The weight of trade opinion was such to convince the committee to recommend an offer of £300 to cover the supply of six arms and ammunition by each competitor selected for trial, should the advertisement be renewed.

Several persons, including Bentley and Playfair, Lancaster, Needham, and the Birmingham Small Arm Company, suggested that a definite and considerable prize be offered for the successful competitor. Needham in particular stated that the successful competitor need not necessarily be in a position to take orders for manufacture, and the committee conceded this point. They then recommended that, over and above any royalty or payment for rights of original invention, two prizes be offered –

First	....	£ 1,000
Second	....	500

to be given to the arms placed first and second in order of merit on a balance of all their qualities, whether selected in entirety or not. Partial appropriation was to be acknowledged and paid for.

Hollis urged that before advertising for a rifle, a large prize should be offered for a cartridge, and that having been determined, the arm should be designed to take it. The committee felt that this was not relevant, as Boxer's cartridge for the Snider was thought by them capable of being made in a smaller bore, and so no new cartridge was necessary.

Several expressed the thought, particularly Barnett and Sons, Birmingham Small Arm Company, Needham, Swinburn, and Westley Richards, that it should be distinctly stated beforehand what was required, and a scale of qualifications laid down. The committee objected strongly to this, as they felt it would be practically impossible to assign marks satisfactorily to different qualities, and that if they did so it would not necessarily follow that the arm which got the most marks would be the best. This system would involve a pedantic appearance of rigid comparison, without superseding the necessity for an intelligent judgement to weigh the results, and if judgement was required, it could be exercised without recourse to numerical values. Earl de Grey had decided this after an earlier representation from Westley Richards to the same effect.

Considerable jealousy of the government factory at Enfield was manifest in some answers, as was an expressed lack of confidence in fair dealing by the WO. With the former the committee had nothing to do, and on the latter, had something to say later in their report.

In reply to the second question the inference after analysis of all replies was that four months for the production of an arm in answer to any further advertisement, and three months, after examination and selection, to complete the six rifles and ammunition required, would meet the requirements of the trade.

On the third question, one had no opinion, Mont-Storm strongly objected, and Westley Richards expressed a decided preference for the capping system and paper cartridge (mainly because his patented system used them). The others were unanimous in declaring that suitable cartridges could be made, but that there were difficulties in making a small bore cartridge that had not yet been overcome. Some preferred the 0.5-inch bore, and others pressed to retain the standard bore of 0.577-inch.

(It is noteworthy, with the aid of hindsight, to observe the opinion of the London Armoury Company, who thought that with some systems in so small a bore as 0.45-inch, the great length of the cartridge might cause difficulties in loading, and Field expressed a similar view, preferring in consequence an 0.500-inch bore. In the event, both proved correct in their assumptions; but the problems caused were eventually solved without reversion to a larger bore.)

After considering the opinions presented, the committee felt that efforts to find a suitable 0.45-inch cartridge should be perservered with, and failing that, one no larger than 0.500-inch. They had already given orders earlier, from the meeting of 28-11-1865, that Col. Dixon was to make up, with or without Snider's assistance, a Snider rifle of 0.500-inch bore, with the sole object being to see whether the difficulties attached to a small bore cartridge could be overcome in one of 0.500-inch calibre.

The committee next remarked on letters received from Phelps, Lancaster, and Westley Richards, giving their reasons for not submitting arms to the competition. Their basic reasons generally arose from grievances allegedly accrued because of their treatment on other occasions of a similar nature. (Of the three, only Westley Richards will be given coverage here, for reasons which will become obvious as the history of the next series of trials is presented.)

Westley Richards made no objections to the terms of the advertisement of June, 1865, but thought it should have been more explicit, and specified the reward offered to the successful competitor. He gave other reasons for not responding to it.

Firstly, he objected to the constitution of the committee, which he alleged was composed of officers not practical and only amateurs incompetent to decide on the subjects presented to them. He also taxed them with being inventors and competitors contrary to the established rules; by taking up the crude ideas of speculators and patent jobbers (as he defined all competitors not in the gun trade), and handing them on to be perfected in government departments, who then appropriated all credit due to the inventors.

On these statements the committee remarked that it was scarcely to be expected that a disappointed inventor should express himself satisfied with the adverse opinion of any committee, and still less that he would fairly admit the merit of the invention of any rival and successful competitor.

Westley Richards went on with some general complaints about his alleged mistreatment by the government, and ended by reiterating his determination not to give the government any more information or assistance on the subject of arms.

To which the committee replied –

The assistance of Mr. Westley Richards is not indespensable, and although the absence of any gunmaker of repute from a rifle competition of national importance on imaginary and insufficient grounds is in itself a circumstance to be regretted, it is satisfactory to think that it cannot materially retard the solution of a question to which so many skilful and experienced persons are devoting their time and attention.

On the whole, these grievances seem to have arisen more from wounded pride and jealousy, rather than from any particular malice of a personal nature directed at them by the committee members, who showed a remarkable impartiality throughout the trials.

RESULT OF THE INVESTIGATION

As a result of the above inquiry, it was decided to open a new competition, with improved conditions and awards as suggested, so, to that end, the advertisement below was published –

ADVERTISEMENT.

TO GUN MAKERS AND OTHERS.

I.

The Secretary of State for War is desirous of receiving proposals from gunmakers and others for breech-loading rifles, either repeating or not repeating, which may replace the present service rifle in future manufacture.

II.

The following are the conditions considered essential in military non-repeating rifles –

(A) Weight – Not to exceed 9 lbs 5 ozs without bayonet.
(B) Length – To be 51 inches, with short stock, measured from the hollow of butt plate to muzzle.
(C) Weight of ammunition made up – Must not exceed 6 lbs 4 ozs for 60 rounds as packed for service.
(D) Cartridges – Must carry their own ignition.
(E) Sights – The foresight must be such as to admit of a bayonet being fixed according to the present system.
(F) Stock – Must be such as to carry a light metal cleaning rod, and allow a sling to be used.
(G) Recoil – Must not exceed that of the Enfield rifle by more than 10 per cent.
(H) The arm as a whole – Must be as little liable to injury by long-continued firing, rough usage, and exposure, as the naval rifle converted to a breech-loader on the

Snider system. To be capable also of being used without accident by imperfectly trained men, and of being manufactured in quantities and of uniform quality.

(I) The ammunition as a whole – Must be as little liable to injury by rough usage, damp, and exposure in all climates as the Boxer cartridge for Snider's converted Enfield rifle; also as little liable to accidental explosion as the same cartridge, and as capable of being manufactured in large quantities, and of uniform quality.

(K) Calibre – Optional.

(L) The twist and form of groove – Optional.

(M) The lock – Optional.

(N) Rapidity of fire – Capable of firing at least twelve rounds per minute without aiming, the cartridges being arranged on a table.

(O) Accuracy when fired from a fixed rest – The arm must give a mean figure of merit of not more than 36 inches at 1,000 yards.

(P) Trajectory – Not to require at 500 yards an elevation of more than 1 degree 30 minutes.

(Q) Fouling – The shooting not to deteriorate more than 20 per cent at 1,000 yards, after firing 250 rounds.

(R) Penetration – The mean penetration of five shots not to be less than that of the present sevice muzzle-loading Enfield rifle, viz, 12 half-inch elm planks, which have been soaked 48 hours in water. Distance 30 yards.

(S) Lubrication – Wax on bullets is indispensable, but any other lubricant may be superadded or applied to the cartridge, if thought necessary by the competitor.

III.

No arms will be received without the usual proof marks. Specifications, and drawings of the methods proposed, stating the probable cost per arm, and accompanied by a finished specimen arm, with 20 rounds of suitable ammunition, should be sent to the "Director of Ordnance, War Office, Pall Mall", on or before the 30th March, 1867.

The specifications and specimen arms will be considered by the Ordnance Select Committee and its associated members, who will be selected by the Secretary of State for War, and who will, after firing the 20 preliminary rounds select and recommend for further trial such of the systems as may appear to them sufficiently promising, rejecting all such as may not be considered to offer sufficient merits to warrant their being included in the competition, the con ditions of which are stated in this advertisement.

Each accepted competitor will then be required to furnish for experiment, at Woolwich, six arms in strict conformity to the specimen arm submitted, with 1,000 rounds of ammunition per arm, within four months after date of demand. Each competitor will be required to disclose to the committee the exact nature of the lubrication he may employ. A sum of £300 will be paid to each of the accepted competitors, to cover the expense of the six rifles, and of the supply of ammunition required.

The Secretary of State offers a reward of £ 1,000 for the arm which, on combinations of all qualities, is considered by the committee to be the best submitted.

A second reward of £ 600, for the arm, which, while attaining a satisfactory degree of excellence in other particulars, is selected for merit in respect to its breech mechanism.

A third reward of £ 400 for the best cartridge. The qualities which will be principally taken into consideration in awarding the prize will be, economy of manufacture, power of sustaining rough usage, freedom from deterioration in various climates, and general serviceability.

The shooting qualities of the cartridge must be fair; but as they may depend on the rifling of the arm with which the cartridge is associated, they will not be so much considered as those abovementioned.

It is clearly to be understood that under no circumstances will a competitor be entitled to more than one prize; but such prize will be irrespective of any reward which may be given to the inventor of the arm finally adopted into the service.

IV.

MAGAZINE AND REPEATING ARMS.

Magazine and repeating arms for infantry will be received and examined in a manner similar to the breech-loading rifles. They must be not less in length than 48 inches, including the stock.

The limit of weight for these arms is fixed at 9½ lbs, exclusive of the charges in the magazine.

It is indispensable that the arms be made to take a bayonet.

The Secretary of State offers a reward of £300 for the best magazine or repeating arm produced that fulfils the above conditions, and in the absence of experience does not at present define the standard of accuracy or other conditions to be fulfilled before such an arm can be adopted.

Those magazine or repeating arms which are accepted for further trial will be paid for at the rate of £60 each. This sum is to include 1,000 rounds of ammunition per arm.

V.

The Secretary of State will take care that no ingenious novelty produced in answer to this advertisement shall be adopted in the service without proper acknowledgement, and that the name of the individual with whom it originated shall be recorded in connection with it.

If the rifle to which the first prize is awarded is adopted into the service it will bear the inventor's name.

War Office
October 22, 1866.

J. St. George, Major-General,
Director of Ordnance.

CHAPTER 2.

THE PRIZE COMPETITION PRELIMINARIES

TO more readily distinguish the next series of trials for breech-loading rifles from the first series, it is intended to refer to them as the "Prize Competition", as, for the first time, a prize was offered as an inducement for more inventors to offer their designs and so allow a wider choice. That this succeeded is indicated by the number of entries received – 104 – as compared with those for the first trials, 24 only. The system eventually selected for service, the Martini, appeared for the first time in England in the Prize Competition.

(At this time, ie, early 1867, the SoS was Sir John Packington, so his name will be noted in the various references in place of Lord de Grey and Ripon, the previous holder of the position.)

To administer the prize competition a sub-committee of the OSC was formed, and called the Special Committee on Breech-Loading Arms, as authorised by the following letter –

To the President of the Ordnance Select Committee.

Sir, *21st March, 1867.*

I am directed to acquaint you that Sir John Packington has decided upon appointing a sub-committee to consider and report upon the various arms which may be submitted for trial in accordance with the terms of the advertisement issued in October last.

This committee will consist of –

Lt.-Col. H. Fletcher, Scots Fusilier Guards
Capt. Rawlins, 48th Regt.
Capt. Mackinnon, 87th Depot
Earl Spencer, KG
E. Ross, Esq.
Capt. Haig, RA, Secretary.

and they have been directed to place themselves in communication with you, with a view to the necessary arrangements being made to enable them to enter upon the duty which has been entrusted to them.

The reports of the sub-committee made from time to time for the information of the Secretary of State will be forwarded by you to this office, accompanied by such observations as the Ordnance Select Committee may think it desirable to make.

The three military members will receive 10s. a day with the personal allowance of their ranks, and the civilians £ 2.2s. a day for days upon which they may be actually employed on this duty.

J. St. George, Major-General,
Director of Ordnance.

The sub-committee, in Report No.4,612 of 11-6-1867, mentioned that 104 arms were submitted for examination in consequence of the WO advertisement of 22-10-1866. In conducting the examination they adopted the following course of action –

The arms, with their specifications and drawings were carefully examined, and a condensed description of each arm drawn up; the inventors were then asked to attend, to explain the details of their system, so that no peculiarities should escape notice.

The sub-committee then proceeded, in accordance with the terms of the advertisement, to test the general capabilities of the arms by firing them in the presence of such of the inventors as chose to attend. Two trial and eight shots were fired for accuracy at 500 yards from shoulder rest, and, immediately after, twelve rounds were fired for rapidity from the shoulder, the cartridges being arranged on a table. The option of firing was given to the inventor or his representative, otherwise a marksman from the Royal Marines was employed.

After this brief trial the arms were divided into two classes

I – Those which had complied with the terms of the advertisement (37 in number).
II – Those which had failed to do so, and were therefore ineligible to compete for the prizes (67 in number). These were set aside for consideration on their own merits.
(The arms in Class I, mentioned as being shown in Lists A, B, and C, below, are detailed in Appendix 3.)

On considering Class I in connection with the results of the trials, the sub-committee was at once able to reject 21 arms; these, with the reasons for rejection, are shown in List A.

A second examination of those systems still for consideration was instituted, resulting in the rejection of a further seven arms, shown in List B.

The remaining nine arms were placed on List C, to be given further consideration, as the sub-committee felt unable to decide upon the comparative merits of these weapons without further trial. They therefore recommended the nine systems for trial, and that each of the inventors furnish six weapons and ammunition in accordance with the conditions of the advertisement.

The nine systems carried over for the prize competition trials were – Albini & Braendlin; Burton Nos.1 and 2; Fosbery; Henry; Joslyn; Martini; Peabody; and Remington. Three of these rifles are shown in Fig.1.

The sub-committee made no further report of the Class II arms, as some were withdrawn by the inventors and had not been returned at the time of the report. They felt that some of the arms in this class warranted further trial.

No report was made on ammunition, as some patterns had been submitted independently of rifles.

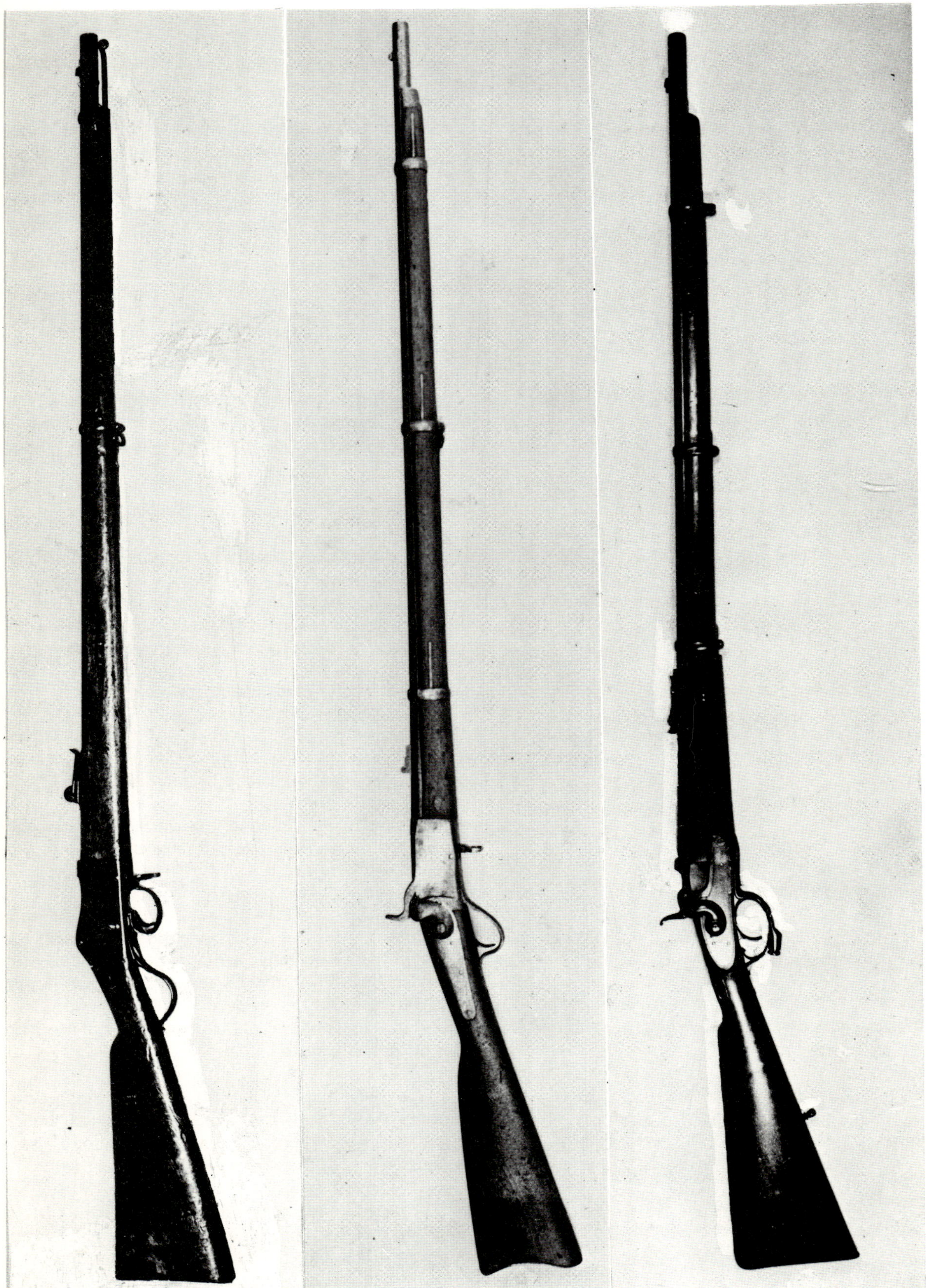

Tower B.A.T. QAD(O)

Fig. 1 – Prize Competition Rifles –
Top: Martini
Middle: Peabody
Bottom: Henry.

The report finished –

As the sub-committee consider it of great importance that the demand for the six rifles of the accepted competitors should be at once made, they have not thought it right to delay further their first report. They will send in as soon as possible their report on Class II, on the ammunition, and on the repeating arms, some of which, although not entered for the competition, have been submitted for their consideration. They append descriptions of the nine accepted arms, photographs of which will shortly follow.

This report was approved by the SoS on 19-6-1867, and the following letters were written; No.1 to the eight selected competitors; No.2 to the 18 inventors whose arms were rejected.

No.1.

Sir, *22nd June, 1867.*

I am directed by Sir John Packington to inform you that the breech-loading rifle submitted by you has been selected to compete with others for the prizes to be given by Her Majesty's Government for the best description of breech-loader announced in the advertisement issued from this office in the month of October last, of which a copy is enclosed.

You will accordingly be at liberty to send in six rifles of the precise patterns of the arms you have brought forward and 1,000 rounds of ammunition for each arm, as stated in Section III of this advertisement. They must be delivered at the office of the Ordnance Select Committee within four months from the date of this letter, and they will then be subjected to such further competitive trial as may be deemed necessary.

The sum of £300 will be paid on the certificate of the President of the Ordnance Select Committee that the rifles and ammunition have been delivered in accordance with these instructions.

I am, &c.
J. St. George, Major-General,
Director of Ordnance.

No.2.

Sir, *3rd July, 1867.*

I am directed by Secretary Sir John Packington to inform you that the breech-loading rifle submitted by you for the competitive trial of breech-loading small arms which was announced in the advertisement issued from this office in the month of October last, has been rejected as unsuitable to the requirements of the service for the reasons given overleaf.

I am, &c.
J. St. George, Major-General,
Director of Ordnance.

EXAMINATION OF THE NON–COMPETITIVE ARMS

After presenting the previously mentioned report, and therefore having a four month delay before starting the trials of the prize competition, the sub-committee turned their attention to the arms of Class II, which had been set aside for further consideration.

Originally there were 67 in this class, but an extra 16 had been sent in after the first report was completed, making a total of 83. In considering these arms the committee adopted a course identical with that pursued when dealing with the prize competition entries.

Class II, List A, shows the arms immediately rejected, 68 in number. List B, four arms, shows those which warranted a further examination, but were subsequently rejected, and List C shows 11 arms which were set aside for further consideration. (The arms in Class II, Lists A, B, and C, are detailed in Appendix 4.)

The sub-committee decided to wait until the prize competition was finalised before going any further with examination of the 11 arms on List C, being influenced by the following considerations –

1. The experience gained in the trials of the prize competition could lead to the reduction of the list of these arms, as some of the systems were partly represented among the prize competitors, so considerable expense would be saved, as six specimens were required of each system for a suitable trial.

2. Should the sub-committee recommend the purchase of six arms of each of the eleven systems, they would be unwilling to restrict the inventors to exact conformity with the specimens submitted, as thereby any improvements available would be lost. This restriction was necessary as there would then have been an unfair comparison with the arms of the prize competition, which were not allowed any such variation.

3. Some inventors had submitted arms with respect to the breech system only, and without reference to barrel, calibre, or rifling suitable for a military arm. These people professed their willingness to adapt their breech mechanism to any barrel that was approved.

The following rifles of Class II were therefore recommended to be retained until the results of the prize competition were available – Berdan; Carter & Edwards, No.3; Fosbery, No.4; Greeve & Dowling, No.4; Hammond; Needham, No.1; Poultney; Westley Richards, No.3B, No.11; Sharp; and Wilson.

With the results of the prize competition to hand, the sub-committee felt they would be in a better position to institute a final trial of all the systems that seemed suitable for military use, and so be able to recommend the best arm for the service. The sub-committee pointed out that the gunmakers did not give the terms of the advertisement full attention, as evidenced by the fact that of 120 arms submitted, only 37 were eligible to compete for the prizes. This, to a great extent, had forced upon them the course of action they had advocated, which would cause more delay; but under the circumstances they felt it was the best way the object of their investigation would be achieved.

On 24-7-1867 the SoS decided that the sub-committee's duties would be restricted to conducting the prize competition, so the examination of the balance of the arms and other matters would be referred to the OSC, who expressed their willingness to proceed with further investigations.

The report from the sub-committee on the above activities was No.4,636 of 4-7-1867, and as a result of their recommendations letters were written to the various entrants advising them of the decisions taken; Letter A to the inventors of the rejected arms; Letter B to the inventors of the arms held for further consideration.

LETTER A.

Sir, *War Office, 17th August, 1867.*

I am directed by the Secretary of State for War to inform you that the breech-loading arm submitted by you (specified in the margin) to compete for the prizes announced in the advertisement issued from this office in the month of October last, having been found on examination not to fulfil the conditions laid down, is ineligible for the competition. An extract from the report of the committee to whom the arm was referred – showing the ground of disqualification, and the objections to which it is, in their opinion, open – is given on the annexed sheet for your information.

The Secretary of State regrets that these objections are such as will preclude his further entertaining the invention.

LETTER B.

Sir, *War Office, 17th August, 1867.*

I am directed by the Secretary of State for War to inform you that the breech-loading arm submitted by you (specified in the margin) to compete for the prizes announced in the advertisement issued from this office in the month of October last, having been found on examination not to fulfil the conditions laid down, is ineligible for the competition, for the reasons given on the annexed sheet.

I am, however, to inform you that the result of the preliminary trials of your rifle has been so far favourable as to lead the committee to select it for further consideration on its own merits should you have no objection to its being reserved for that purpose. In the event of your assenting to this course your rifle will be laid aside until the issue of the prize competition is determined.

I am, &c.
T. W. Milward,
Lt.-Col. RA, Asst.
Director of Ordnance.

THE PRIZE COMPETITION

The report from the sub-committee on the conduct of the prize competition was No.4,905 of 12-2-1868, and in it were details of the various trials carried out with the nine accepted systems of breech-loading arms.

The four months allowed the entrants for preparation of the six rifles ordered for the competition having passed, the sub-committee reassembled on 29-10-1867 to start the competition, but found that all the competition arms were not to hand. The Martinis had not arrived, due to a delay in the transmission of the pattern arm to Switzerland, caused by its detention at the French Customs House, and there was also a request from the WO, on behalf of Mr. Burton, asking for a short extension of time, on the grounds that he had been required to furnish six arms each of two different patterns, making twelve in all. After consideration of the case, this request was granted.

During the delay caused by the non-receipt of the arms mentioned, the sub-committee considered and reported on some minor questions concerning some of the rejected arms as referred to them by the SoS.

They then prepared a programme of experiments for the competition rifles, to cover the various points outlined in the advertisement of 22-10-1866. These experiments were to be carried out in the following order – accuracy; rapidity of fire; recoil; penetration; trajectory; resistance to fouling; capability of resisting hard or unfair usage; increased charges; and ease of manufacture.

It was also decided at this time that six Snider naval rifles would be put through the trials parallel with the competition arms, partly because that rifle had been named in the advertisement as a standard of comparison in respect of certain qualifications, and partly to ascertain the comparative figure of merit of the government arm.

Further delays to the proceedings were caused by the preparation and trials of the fixed rests to be used for some of the tests – these rests requiring specific fittings for each system of rifle, and in one instance for each individual arm. As a result, the competition did not actually start until 28-11-1867; but it then continued without intermission up to 10-2-1868, with the exception of a ten day break at Christmas.

The inventors of the various systems were to be allowed to be present during the trials.

EXAMINATION OF THE PRIZE COMPETITION ARMS

The Burton and Martini rifles having duly arrived, the sub-committee examined all the competitive arms and ammunition, with the assistance of an armourer from Enfield, and compared them with the patterns originally submitted. The various parts of the pattern arms had been carefully stamped before issue to the makers, and the sub-committee had to satisfy themselves that the new arms sufficiently complied with the originals, in order to conform to the rules of the competition. The results of this examination were as follows –

Albini & Braendlin: The six rifles were found to be in accordance with the pattern, except that they weighed from 8 lbs 14 ozs to 9 lbs 1 oz. The pattern weighed 9 lbs 1 oz. They bore the Birmingham proof mark. The ammunition was found to correspond with the original pattern.

Specification.

Length of barrel, 32"; calibre, 0.462"; grooves, 5; twist, 1 turn in 25"; powder, 68 grains; bullet, 480 grains.

Burton Nos.1 and 2: The twelve rifles were found to be in accordance with the patterns. They bore the London proof mark. Ammunition, Boxer Pattern IV, was obtained from store.

Specification.

No.1: Length of barrel, 32.5"; calibre, 0.577"; grooves, 6, twist, 1 turn in 48"; powder, 68 grains; bullet, 480 grains. No.2: Length of barrel, 33"; other details as for No.1.

Fosbery: The rifles were found to conform with the pattern, except that they were slightly shorter (less than ¼-inch, which was apparently in the stock). The weights varied from 8 lbs 11 ozs to 8 lbs 15 ozs, the weight of the pattern arm being 8 lbs 15¼ ozs. They bore the Birmingham proof mark. Ammunition, Boxer Pattern IV, was obtained from store.

Specification.

Length of barrel, 33"; calibre, 0.577"; grooves, 3; twist, 1 turn in 31"; powder, 68 grains; bullet, 480 grains.

Henry: The arms conformed to the pattern, and bore the London proof mark. The ammunition was found similar to that first submitted.

Specification.

Length of barrel, 34.5"; calibre, 0.455"; grooves, 7; twist, 1 turn in 22"; powder, 85 grains; bullet, 480 grains.

Joslyn: The six rifles were found to be in accordance with the pattern, except that they were furnished with a rod spring and holder which were not in the pattern. The weight of the barrels also varied from the pattern (5 lbs 4½ ozs), ranging from 4 lbs 12½ ozs to 5 lbs 2¾ ozs. They bore the London proof mark.

Specification.

Length of barrel, 35.25"; calibre, 0.500"; grooves, 3; twist, 1 turn in 42"; powder, 70 grains; bullet, 394 grains.

Martini: All rifles were found to conform with the pattern, however, as there were no proof marks, they were submitted to the definitive proof at the London proof house. The ammunition was found similar to the pattern, except that the bullets were somewhat longer, with a cavity in the base instead of being flat. The copper cases were also about 14 grains lighter than those originally submitted, but had the same external dimensions.

Specification.

Length of barrel, 35"; calibre, 0.433"; grooves, 3; twist, 1 turn in 32"; powder, 72 grains (compressed); bullet, 334 grains.

Peabody: The arms conformed with the pattern except that the barrels were ½-inch too short. There were also no proof marks, so these rifles were submitted for definitive proof at the London proof house. The ammunition was found similar to the pattern, except that the cases were slightly too large to enter the chambers of the rifles.

Specification.

Length of barrel, 33"; calibre, 0.5"; grooves, 3; twist, 1 turn in 30"; powder, 60 grains; bullet, 395 grains.

Remington: The arms conformed to the pattern with some exceptions – the barrels were 1/8-inch too long; the fore-end stocks were ½-inch too long; and the stock for keeping the fore-end in position was brazed or soldered to the barrel of the pattern arm, but screwed to the barrel of the six competition arms. There were no proof marks, so the arms were submitted for definitive proof at the London proof house. The ammunition was in accordance with that originally submitted.

Specification.

Length of barrel, 35.25"; calibre, 0.5"; grooves, 7; twist, 1 turn in 30"; powder, 67 grains; bullet, 407 grains.

As the ammunition for the Martini rifle was found to differ slightly in the shape of the bullet from that originally submitted, the rifle was admitted to the competition only on the understanding that it would not be permitted to win a prize by reason of any superiority that could be attributed to the new form of bullet. (In the event, this conditional clause was rendered unnecessary by the failure of this ammunition, which in turn relegated the Martini to seventh position out of the nine entries.)

There were two types of Peabody ammunition supplied – one lot from America, the other from Birmingham. The American batch differed from the original in the shape of the bullet, so was disallowed, whilst the British ammunition, although conforming to the pattern, did not fit the chambers of the rifles. The sub-committee felt that this diversity of pattern arose from a mistake by the maker, so Peabody's agent was permitted to alter and compress the British cartridges so as to fit them to the rifles.

After the examination of arms and ammunition was finalised, the sub-committee sent a recommendation to the SoS that the sum of £300 should be paid to the competitors in accordance with the terms of the advertisement.

THE ACCURACY TRIALS

These were to be conducted as follows –

1. Four rifles of each system to be set aside for trials of accuracy.

2. If possible one rifle of each system, together with one naval Snider rifle, to be fired on each day in targets of 20 rounds; the firing to commence at 300 yards.

3. Five or more trial shots to be fired before the first target. One or more trial shots to be fired before the subsequent ones.

4. The rifles to be wiped out after every target.

5. Any one rifle attaining the necessary accuracy at any range to qualify the system to which it belonged – as far as that range was concerned.

6. The same rule to apply in the trajectory trial; and in the trial for fouling at 1,000 yards.

7. Should any system fail to attain the necessary figure of merit at any range, as prescribed in WO advertisement, the committee did not bind themselves to carry out further experiments with it.

8. In comparing the results of the qualified systems, a mean of all the targets obtained at each range would be used.

9. The order of shooting the rifles to be varied each day.

10. The five targets mentioned in the advertisement to be shot off in two day's firing if possible; two targets each on the first, and three each on the second day.

The results of the 300 yards trials are shown in Table I, the systems being placed in order of merit, and the Snider naval rifle's performance is added for comparison.

The sub-committee considered that the inaccurate shooting of the Joslyn, Martini, Peabody, and Remington rifles was apparently caused in some measure by defective cartridges.

Out of 20 targets, the Henry made 7 with a mean deviation of less than 6 inches, with each rifle achieving one or more such targets. The large mean figure of 0.85 was due to occasional wild shots.

It was noted from the summary that none of the rifles achieved the required qualification for 300 yards, viz, a mean deviation of 6 inches, and that the Fosbery, Joslyn, Peabody, and Remington rifles did not even attain the qualification for 500 yards, viz, a mean deviation of 1 foot.

The sub-committee then decided that with the latter rifles further trials for accuracy were unnecessary, and laid down the general rule that any system failing at any range to obtain the qualifying mean deviation for the next longer range, would not be tried further for accuracy.

The summary of the 500 yard shooting is shown in Table II, and again none of the systems obtained the required qualification. The Henry made six targets with a mean deviation of less than one foot, with the large figure of 1.41 again due to occasional wild shots. The five remaining systems, and the Snider, were then carried forward to the 800 yards range.

Table III is the summary of the shooting at the latter range, and three of the four Henry rifles achieved the necessary qualification for 1,000 yards, as did the No.4 rifle of the Burton No.2 system. The Henry and Burton No.2 thus carried forward to the 1,000 yards range, with the naval Snider.

As shown in Table IV, none of the rifles qualified at that range, but the Henry was noticeably far superior to the others. This superiority was attributed to the small bore and large powder charge, which gave the bullet a higher average velocity when compared with the others used.

It was remarked that, during these, and subsequent experiments, there was a liability in the Albini and Fosbery rifles to misfire, if the breech blocks were not perfectly closed with a smart movement. This was due to the direct action striker hitting the side of the hole which contained the piston, and so losing so much of its force as to render the blow of the piston ineffective.

In the Burton No.2 system, the spiral springs of some of the rifles were so weak sufficient force was not always imparted to the piston to explode the cap.

THE TRIALS FOR RAPIDITY OF FIRE

This trial was programmed as follows –

1. The entrants were to be allowed to make what arrangements they pleased to fire the rifles, so as to obtain the qualifying number of rounds per minute, viz, 12; the cartridges being laid out on a table.

2. Not more than ten trials for rapidity would be made by the sub-committee to qualify an arm; each trial to be made by serving out 13 rounds, and taking the time from the 1st to the 13th shot.

Before commencing the actual trial, the rifles were tested to see whether they would be capable of attaining the qualification. The entrants were allowed to make this trial, firing in any position they chose. All systems proved capable of qualifying.

The comparative trials then commenced, with two servicemen of proven dexterity in the use of breech-loaders being

TABLE I – Accuracy at 300 yards.

System.	Mean deviations, being averages of five targets of 20 shots each, with four rifles.				Mean of four rifles.	Mean elev-ation.
	1	2	3	4		
	ft.	ft.	ft.	ft.	ft.	o ’
Burton II	0.58	0.61	0.64	0.68	0.63	1 8
Albini & Braendlin	0.70	0.70	0.71	0.65	0.69	0 51
Burton I	0.78	0.74	0.71	0.81	0.76	1 7
Henry	0.69	0.61	0.91	1.18	0.85	0 56
Martini	1.30	0.82	0.96	1.57	1.16	0 51
Fosbery	1.12	1.41	1.21	1.18	1.23	0 59
Remington	1.39	1.88	1.50	1.53	1.58	0 53
Peabody	2.26	1.44	1.55	1.44	1.67	0 34
Joslyn	2.45	1.35	1.65	1.49	1.74	0 59
Snider naval	0.70	0.76	0.75	0.80	0.75	1 1

TABLE II – Accuracy at 500 yards.

Burton II	1.45	1.17	1.35	1.12	1.27	1 48
Henry	1.72	1.66	1.09	1.17	1.41	1 25
Burton I	1.48	1.68	1.60	1.34	1.52	1 49
Albini & Braendlin	1.50	2.10	1.21	1.30	1.53	1 27
Martini	2.00	2.06	1.72	2.27	2.01	1 24
Snider naval	1.47	1.42	1.21	1.37	1.37	1 42

TABLE III – Accuracy at 800 yards.

Henry	2.40	2.62	2.22	2.28	2.38	2 22
Burton II	3.03	3.34	3.19	2.98	3.14	3 10
Albini & Braendlin	3.15	4.18	3.11	3.40	3.46	2 36
Martini	4.47	3.92	4.24	3.53	4.04	2 33
Burton I	5.25	4.52	5.19	5.98	5.23	3 20
Snider naval	3.55	4.19	3.78	3.53	3.76	3 18

TABLE IV – Accuracy at 1,000 yards.

Henry	3.75	3.52	3.36	3.17	3.45	2 56
Burton II	6.52	5.92	5.14	5.49	5.77	4 11
Snider naval	6.95	6.51	7.07	7.15	6.92	4 24

employed. They were Serj. McCanlis, RA, and Private Crofts, RM, and each was to fire three independent series of 20 shots with a rifle of each system. Two series of comparative times were thus obtained, with a mean of the two being taken as the relative rapidity of the particular system. To show that the merits of the arms had been fully developed the entrants were also invited to fire their own system for comparison.

A summary of these trials is shown in Table V, the results being deduced solely from the trials by the servicemen, as in every instance that an entrant fired his rifle, his time was bettered by one or the other of the soldiers.

The Martini and Remington rifles were to be fired for rapidity, but the cartridges of the Martini burst repeatedly at the rim, with so great an escape of gas as to render the rifle unsafe to fire; the trials were therefore discontinued. The cartridges of the Remington were also faulty, breaking into two and sometimes three pieces, causing such delay that the trials of this arm were worthless. The Joslyn cartridges gave trouble too, jamming so tightly that its trial was

TABLE V – Rapidity of fire.

System.	Mean of three trials of 20 shots.		Mean times of six trials, 20 shots.	Calculated no. of rds. per min.
	Serjeant McCanlis	Private Crofts		
	m. sec.	m. sec.	m. sec.	
Peabody	1 17.3	1 9.8*	1 13.6	16
Henry	1 16.7	1 13.3*	1 15.0	16
Fosbery.	1 25.7*	1 23.3	1 24.5	14
Albini & Braendlin	1 33.3*	1 24.3	1 28.8	14
Burton I	1 34.7*	1 23.2	1 28.9	13
Burton II.	2 4.8*	1 24.7	1 44.8	11
Joslyn.	2 25.5†	1 40.8*	2 3.2	10
Snider naval	1 15.3	1 30.8*	1 23.1	14

†Obtained from only one trial of 20 shots.

also nearly worthless.

During part of the trials it rained heavily, and as the cartridges used were exposed to the rain, the paper on the outside of the Boxer cartridges became sodden, and on loading crumpled up, causing the cartridges to jam slightly in the chamber. This applied particularly to the Burton Nos.1 and 2, Fosbery, and the Snider. Trials affected by the rain are marked * in the table.

A further trial for rapidity and accuracy combined was then made. The target was 24 feet wide and 6 feet high at 100 yards range, and the firing was carried on for exactly two minutes with each rifle. All shots recorded struck within a width of 6 feet. The summary of results of this trial is given in Table VI.

TABLE VI – Rapidity and accuracy of fire.

System.	By whom fired.	No. of shots.	No. of hits.	Remarks
Peabody	Serjt. Mc Canlis	28	26	
Burton II.	Private Crofts	26	24	
Albini & Braendlin	Private Crofts	25	24	1 misfire
Henry	Serjt. McCanlis	25	24	
Fosbery.	Private Crofts	24	23	
Burton I	Private Crofts	20	19	
Joslyn.	Private Crofts	18	18	
Snider naval	Private Crofts	23	22	

THE RECOIL TRIALS

One rifle of each system, together with a naval Snider and an Enfield ML rifle for comparison, were fired at least three times from the OSC recoil machine.

The results are shown in Table VII, all systems attaining the necessary qualification of not exceeding the Enfield rifle by more than 10 per cent.

THE PENETRATION TRIALS

The results of this trial are shown in Table VIII, all systems and the Snider and Enfield rifles firing, with a minimum of five rounds shot.

The qualification for this trial was penetration of 12 ½-inch elm planks which had been soaked in water for 48 hours and set about ½-inch apart; the distance from the muzzle was 30 yards.

The Burton Nos.1 and 2, Fosbery, Martini, and the Snider all failed in this test. All these, with the exception of the Martini, used the government cartridge.

The sub-committee remarked that they did not attach much importance to this trial, as it was felt that the penetration was greatly affected by the extent to which the bullet was distorted by its impact on the first plank. That distortion increased with the velocity, and was affected by the distance, and the form and composition of the bullet.

TABLE VII – Recoil.

Rifle.	Reading of scale.			Mean reading	Observed pull of trigger.	Recoil.
	1st shot.	2nd shot.	3rd shot.			
	lbs.	lbs.	lbs.	lbs.	lbs.	lbs.
Albini & Braendlin	91	91	95	92.3	7.5	85
Burton I	91	91	91	91	11	80
Burton II	95	95	95	95	2	93
Fosbery	95	91.5	91.5	93	9	84
Henry	104	100	100	102	5	97
Joslyn	78.5	91	78	84.7	4.5	80
Martini	79	79	79	79	10	69
Peabody	68.5	78	81.5	76	7	69
Remington	95	91.5	95	94	10	84
Snider naval	91.5	88	91.5	90	6	84
ML Enfield	98	95	98	97	5	92

TABLE VIII – Penetration into ½-inch elm planks, soaked in water for 48 hours and set in a frame at distances of about ½-inch apart. Range, 30 yards.

Rifle.	Number of planks penetrated.					Mean penet-ration.
	1st shot.	2nd shot.	3rd shot.	4th shot.	5th shot.	
						Planks.
Remington	17	16	14	15	14¾	15.4
Joslyn	15¼	15½	14½	17¼	12¼	15.0
Henry	15¼	14¼	15¼	13	15¼	14.6
Peabody	13¼	13¾	14¼	14¼	15¼	14.2
Albini & Braendlin	13	14¼	13¼	13¼	14	13.5
Martini	11	11½	12	12¾	11½	11.8
Burton I	11	12	11½	11¼	12¾	11.7
Burton II	10¼	10¼	11	11¾	10½	10.8
Fosbery	10¼	11¼	8¾	8¾	11	10.0
Snider naval	10¾	9½	9	10½	10¼	10.0
ML Enfield	14	13	14	14½	14	13.9

THE TRIALS FOR TRAJECTORY

Only the rifles fired for accuracy at 500 yards were tested in this respect. The angles of elevation were found to be –

Martini	1 degree	11	minutes
Henry	1	12	
Albini & Braendlin	1	14	
Burton No.2	1	35	
Burton No.1	1	39	
Snider Naval	1	29	

The only systems to attain the required qualification were the Martini, Henry, and Albini and Braendlin.

THE FOULING TRIALS

As this test was to be carried out at 1,000 yards the only competitive rifles put through it were the Burton No.2 and Henry, with the Snider included for comparison only.

The programme was to be – one target shot with the arm clean; then complete 250 rounds; and then fire another target for comparison with the first one. In the event, it was carried out slightly differently, two trials being made.

1st Trial: Three targets of 20 shots each, from the fixed rests, were fired; then the remainder of the 250 rounds rapidly. A further three targets were then fired from the fixed rests.

2nd Trial: Three targets of 20 shots each were fired, then the balance of the 250 rounds were fired in alternate targets of 20 rounds rapidly, and 20 rounds marked; and in conclusion, three targets shot for comparison with the first three.

In both trials the Burton No.2 and the Snider excelled, with the shooting after 250 rounds improving rather then deteriorating. However, on the first trial the shooting of the Henry deteriorated so much it was found impossible to make any targets after the 250 rounds had been fired.

On the second trial the Henry did not show the same defect as in the first trial, and, although it did not attain the necessary qualification that the shooting should not deteriorate more than 20 per cent, yet the last of the three targets taken after the 250 shots had been fired was equal in accuracy to the first that had been made when the rifle was clean.

The results are shown in Table IX.

TABLE IX – Fouling, targets at 1,000 yards.

System.	Mean of first three targets.	Mean of last three targets.	Difference in precision after fouling.	
	feet.	feet.	feet.	percent.
Burton II –				
1st trial	5.973	5.627	+0.346	5.79
2ns trial.	5.530	4.780	+0.750	13.56
Henry –				
1st trial, mean. . . .	4.40			
2nd trial	2.78	3.58	–0.80	28.79
Snider –				
1st trial	6.09	5.67	+0.42	6.9

TRIALS FOR CAPABILITY OF SUSTAINING LONG CONTINUED FIRING, ROUGH USAGE, AND EXPOSURE

These trials were to be carried out in the following manner –

1. The rifles to be tested by throwing sand or dirt over them, with breech both open and shut.

2. To be fired after being allowed to rust.

3. To be fired with damaged cartridges, and with increased charges.

4. Strength of stock to be tested.

Sand trial: One rifle of each system (excepting the Martini) was subjected to this trial, carried out in the following manner –

1. Fine sand was thrown over the breech mechanism, the action being closed, and the hammer down. Three rounds were then fired.

2. The same repeated, with action closed and rifle at full cock.

3. The same twice repeated, with the breech action open.

All systems were unaffected when the action remained closed, and the Henry, Joslyn, and Remington worked perfectly when tested with the breech open.

With the breech open the Burton No.2, Fosbery, and Peabody were slightly affected, but with the Albini and Braendlin and Burton No.1 there was considerable difficulty in closing the breech and in placing cartridges in the chamber. In the Burton No.1 the sand entered the hinge of the breech block, impeding its working.

The naval Snider was also unaffected by the trial, except that its extraction was rendered somewhat difficult.

Exposure trial: This was carried out by firing 100 rounds from one rifle of each system, on four consecutive days, the rifles being left dirty and exposed to the weather during the intervals. The rifles, still uncleaned, were then left exposed during 14 days and nights of snow, frost, and rain, and were again fired to ascertain if they were serviceable. They were then dismantled and examined.

The following results were obtained –

Albini & Braendlin: The breech mechanism worked well throughout. On the last day much difficulty was found in placing the cartridge in the chamber, owing to an accumulation of rust. The interior of the lock and breech mechanism were in good working order.

Burton No.1: This rifle was in good working order. The interior of the lock and breech mechanism were unaffected by exposure.

Burton No.2: On the last day of the trial, when firing five rounds there were four misfires, attributed to either the weakness of the striker spring, or to the wax that had accumulated at the end of the piston. Either, or both, of these conditions would lessen the striking force of the piston. The breech mechanism was otherwise in good order; the spiral spring had been completely protected, and the sliding bolt worked perfectly.

Fosbery: The breech mechanism worked well throughout, and five shots were fired from the rifle after the exposure. On dismounting the lock it was found that the eye of the tumbler and the swivel were broken. This breakage must have occurred when the last shot was fired.

Henry: The breech mechanism worked well throughout.

Joslyn: During the trial the breech block jammed, and required so much force to open that much difficulty was found in firing five rounds. The jamming was apparently due to the cartridges bulging after firing, because of not fitting the chamber properly. The arm was not affected by the exposure. On being dismantled the wood of the stock was found to be cracked near the breech tang.

Martini: The cartridges repeatedly burst near the rim, with great escape of gas. After exposure only one shot could be fired as the extractor would not work. On dismantling it was found that the breech mechanism was clogged by rust and fouling, the latter due to the escape of gas from the burst cartridges. Before the mechanism could be taken to pieces it had to be soaked in oil.

Peabody: The cartridges occasionally burst near the rim, causing an escape of gas. Several of the cartridges had to be pushed out with a rod, as the claw of the extractor passed over their rims. This was probably partly due to the bad fit of the cartridges, and also the claw of the extractor being exceptionally short. The breech mechanism was found to be in good order.

Remington: During the trial the breech block frequently jammed, and was so hard to open that five rounds were fired with great difficulty. This defect was owing to faulty cartridges, which allowed escape of gas at the breech. On dismantling the rifle a considerable amount of rust was found beneath the hammer. In other respects the mechanism was in good order.

Snider: No.6 rifle was used for these trials, and its extractor gave occasional difficulties throughout the first trial of four days. It was thought that this problem may have been caused by a defect in that particular rifle, so Snider No.5 was also fired 400 times, to place it on a par with the other arms, so it could also be used for these trials.

The difficult extraction was subsequently found to have been caused by the cartridges, which were not of the service pattern, although the packets were so marked. This ammunition was withdrawn, and the correct pattern substituted.

On the fourth day the breech block of No.6 worked stiffly on its pin, owing to rust, and at the end of the exposure the difficulty of working had increased to the stage where the rifle was unserviceable. The breech mechanism required soaking in oil before it could be dismantled.

The No.5 rifle, which had also been exposed during the fortnight, but with its breech closed, fired five rounds without difficulty. It was clean and serviceable when taken to pieces.

THE DAMAGED CARTRIDGE TRIALS

These were performed using cartridges that were deliberately damaged by filing and piercing the heads of the cases, to ensure a considerable escape of gas, much greater than it was supposed would occur from faulty manufacture. Four such cartridges were fired in two separate trials, the damaged parts of the cartridges being placed in different positions in respect to the extractors and parts of the breech blocks.

All the competitive rifles passed this test without damage, and no breeches were blown open. The Snider had no effect from the first two shots, but on the third shot the block was partly blown open, and the base of the cartridge blown out; on the fourth shot the block was again blown open, but the cartridge remained intact.

The results of the first trial – one rifle of each system having two damaged cartridges fired from it in succession – were as follows –

Albini & Braendlin: (No.6) The hammer was blown back about 1/8-inch, paper wrapped around the breech was much blown away. Breech a little difficult to open.

Burton No.1: (No.6) The escape of gas was principally downwards, the paper was not so much blown away as with the first rifle. Breech opened easily.

Burton No.2: (No.6) Breech quite safe, opened easily, escape of gas principally upwards, as shown by blown away paper.

Fosbery: (No.6) Breech quite safe, paper was blackened on either side of the breech arrangement. The cartridge cases stuck a little tight in the chamber, and required some pressure to extract them.

Henry: (No.6) Breech action worked very stiffly after firing, apparently owing to fouling between the breech block and slot. Breech quite safe.

Joslyn: (No.5) First shot the breech block was blown slightly open, but there was some doubt whether it had been properly closed. Second shot, paper round the breech was much blown away, but the block remained closed.

Martini: (No.5) Paper much blown away, principally above the action. Quite safe.

Peabody: (No.5) Paper much blown away, principally above. Quite safe.

Remington: (No.6) Paper much blown away above. Breech opened rather stiffly after the second shot.

Snider: (No.5) First shot, breech block blown open about 1/10-inch. Second shot, breech remained closed.

The Henry and Peabody were then fired with the breech slightly open. In both cases the breech remained shut, and was quite safe.

For the second trial two damaged cartridges were fired from each rifle; the first being placed with the damaged part downwards, the second with the damaged part close to the extractor.

The results were –

Albini & Braendlin: (No.5) The breech remained quite secure during both shots. The hammer and bolt were blown back about 1/10-inch each time.

Burton No.1: (No.6) No effect either shot.

Burton No.2: (No.6) No effect either shot.

Fosbery: (No.5) No effect either shot.

Henry: (No.6) The action worked rather stiffly after the second shot.

Joslyn: (No.6) No effect either shot.

Martini: (No.6) No effect either shot.

Peabody: (No.5) No effect either shot.

Remington: (No.6) No effect either shot.

Snider: (No.5) First shot the breech block was blown open about half way, and the greater part of the cartridge case, including the solid disc at the base, was blown out at the breech. Second shot, the block was blown open, but to a lesser extent than the first shot. The cartridge case remained in the chamber.

TRIALS WITH INCREASED CHARGES

One rifle of each system was to be tested by firing one cartridge with two charges of powder and two bullets; and one cartridge with two charges of powder and three bullets.

All rifles, including the Snider, but excepting the Burton No.1, Joslyn, and Remington, stood the test without damage.

The Burton No.1 burst its barrel, but the breech was undamaged, and worked perfectly after the explosion.

The Joslyn burst at the first shot, and the breech mechanism was completely destroyed, the breech block landing about 100 yards away.

The Remington burst at the second shot, and was blown into two pieces. The barrel and part of the breech burst, so that the barrel and fore-end were separated from the action and butt. The right side plate of the breech mechanism was also blown off.

EXAMINATION FOR STRENGTH OF STOCKS

This was carried out by the Supt. RSAF, one each of the nine competitive systems being examined. His report on each system is detailed below, and taking this and other evidence into consideration, the sub-committee decided to list the rifles in the following order of merit, with those considered equal being grouped together, viz, –

Burton No.2
Fosbery

Burton No.1
Henry
Remington

Albini & Braendlin
Joslyn
Martini
Peabody

Col. Dixon's comments on the relative strengths of the stocks were –

Albini & Braendlin: The stock is in one piece, but apparently weak at the head from being cut away at back end of breech.

Burton No.1: Stock in one piece, with back action lock, which tends to weaken the hand, but otherwise it is serviceable.

Burton No.2: Stock in one piece, and equal in service to the Enfield.

Fosbery: Stock in one piece, and apparently serviceable.

Joslyn: Stock in one piece. The curve of the butt end differs so much from the Enfield as to make it doubtful whether any of the existing stocks at Enfield would serve for this arm. The construction of the stock at the head makes it weak at that point, and not so serviceable as the Snider-Enfield.

Martini: Stock in two parts. The butt piece is secured by a long bolt, but this would be insufficient to render the attachment of that piece strong enough, as there are no top or bottom plates.

Peabody: Stock in two parts. The butt piece secured by a long bolt. The strain of the stock is taken by the trigger plate. The stock is weak at head, and not considered serviceable.

Remington: Stock in two parts, but the butt piece is apparently well secured.

Henry: Stock is in two pieces, weak in head. Butt piece secure and serviceable.

EXAMINATION FOR EASE OF MANUFACTURE

The Supt. RSAF also reported under this head, but, as this report contained estimated cost of manufacture of the various systems not required under the conditions of the WO advertisement, and as it was thought that some of the inventors may have objected to publication of these estimates, the report was not published.

From the evidence contained in the report, the sub-committee decided on placing the rifles in the following order of merit, in regard to their ease of manufacture in quantity and uniform quality, those grouped together being considered equal –

Burton No.2

Joslyn

Henry
Albini & Braendlin
Martini

Fosbery

Peabody

Remington

Burton No.1

GENERAL REMARKS ON THE PRIZE COMPETITION

Before announcing their final decision in the report, the sub-committee included some general remarks on the trials, in order to explain some of their decisions, and these remarks were as follows –

GENERAL REMARKS.

The standard of excellence as measured by each and all of the several qualifications required by the terms of the War Office advertisement was proved by experiment to have been very high, and in some particulars far beyond the attainment of the five-grooved Snider naval rifle.

None of the competitive rifles reached to this standard, all, as well as the Snider naval, having failed in attaining the necessary degree of accuracy.

In rapidity, all the competitive rifles and the Snider naval qualified.

In recoil, all qualified.

In penetration, five qualified, the remainder, including the Snider naval, having failed to penetrate the required number of planks.

In trajectory, three, in addition to the Snider naval, qualified.

In fouling, the Burton No.2, and the Snider naval qualified, and it was apparent that the Henry could qualify if fired in the manner of the second trial.

In capability of sustaining rough usage, etc, all the rifles showed a satisfactory degree of excellence, and most of them appeared to be superior to the Snider naval.

In the trial with increased charges, the breech mechanism of all the rifles, excepting the Joslyn and Remington, stood the required tests.

There was considerable difficulty in instituting a fair comparison between the different breech-loading systems, owing to the great variety in ammunition and in the calibre of the arms submitted.

The sub-committee feel that unless these conditions are similar, great difficulty must always be experienced in arriving at any accurate comparison between different descriptions of breech mechanisms, for example, the celerity of loading and general manipulation of the breech mechanism is influenced greatly by the length of the cartridge, and that depends in a great measure on the calibre of the rifle, and on the charge of powder; and there is also considerable difficulty and loss of time in loading occasioned by cartridges of inferior manufacture.

The sub-committee found that the only method by which they could arrive at a just conclusion was by limiting their consideration solely to the systems as submitted to them, and to their performances during the trials, putting aside any regard to improvements of which they might be capable, and taking each as submitted with all its defects in arms or ammunition, even when these defects might have arisen from faults in the details of manufacture.

The ammunition used by some of the competitor's arms was a frequent cause of failure of the arm.

The misfires of the Albini and Braendlin rifles were partly caused by faults in ammunition, whilst the same defect was caused by unequal distribution of the fulminate in the rimfire copper cartridges used by the Martini rifles.

During the practice for rapidity and for long-continued firing, defects in the manufacture of the ammunition of the Joslyn and Remington systems became clearly apparent, and exercised a damaging influence on the rifles; whilst owing to the continual bursting of the cartridges of the Martini rifles, and the consequent great escape of gas at the breech, many of the trials with these arms were rendered hazardous, and were therefore discontinued.

During the penetration trial it was observed that none of the rifles which used the government ammunition penetrated the required number of planks, although, in the other trials the government ammunition acquitted itself well.

The sub-committee consider it due to the inventors to make these remarks on the ammunition, although they would not permit any allowance for defective cartridges to influence their judgement of the merits of the competitive arms.

Towards the conclusion of the trials a careful examination was made of the cartridges of the Henry rifle in order to ascertain whether the lubrication conformed with the terms of the advertisement, and was in accordance with the specification sent in by Mr. Henry.

Twenty bullets were sent to the Chemical Department, and a report was received from Mr. Abel to the effect that the lubrication consisted principally of tallow. A letter was likewise received from Mr. Henry describing the method he had adopted in lubricating his bullets.

The sub-committee having considered these letters, and received verbal evidence on the subject from Mr. Abel, decided that Mr. Henry's ammunition had failed to fulfil the conditions (I) and (S) of the War Office advertisement, ie, that in respect to non-liability to injury from climate it was not equal to the Boxer cartridge, and that lubrication had been applied in the sense of Par.(S) of the advertisement.

They also decided that the lubrication did not conform with its description in Mr. Henry's specifications in respect to the quantity of beeswax which had been used.

RESULTS OF THE PRIZE COMPETITION

The sub-committee then stated –

Acting in accordance with the rules alluded to in the 'General Remarks', and keeping clearly in mind the fact that none of the competitive rifles has attained the qualifications required by the War Office advertisement of 22-10-1866, and that consequently none of the inventors has claim to the prize of £1,000, the sub-committee make their report on the comparative merits of the several systems, placing them in the following order –

Henry
Burton No.2
Albini & Braendlin
Fosbery
Burton No.1
Peabody
Martini
Remington
Joslyn.

In placing the rifles in that order, the sub-committee had regarded the general results of the trials, carefully considered the degrees in which the various arms approached or surpassed the qualifications laid down by the government, and instituted additional experiments to further compare their relative merits.

The Henry rifle had most nearly attained all the required qualifications, but its ammunition was found to fail in a highly important particular.

The Burton No.2, and other arms which gave very satisfactory results in many respects, failed in a marked degree at long ranges.

As a consequence of these important failings, the sub-committee stated it did not feel justified in recommending the SoS to overlook the want of competitors of compliance with the regulations, and award the £1,000.

With regard to the £ 600 prize for the best breech mechanism, it did not appear that the reasons which disqualified the arms for the first prize applied in this instance, so the following rifles were considered eligible for the prize, and their order of merit was –

Henry
Burton No.2
Albini & Braendlin
Burton No.1

They then recommended that the £ 600 prize be given to Mr. Henry, with the comment that –

The breech mechanism combines strength, safety, and simplicity; the extractor works with remarkable regularity, and the arm can be fired with great ease and rapidity, and is not affected by rough usage.

The sub-committee then commented on some of the other arms which were not considered satisfactory for the following reasons –

The Fosbery and Peabody, on account of want of accuracy, the Joslyn, Martini, and Remington, on account of faults which were chiefly, and, in the case of the Martini, entirely owing to defects in ammunition.

The report ended –

In conclusion, the sub-committee cannot refrain from expressing their regret that no arm submitted to them should have shown sufficient merit to render its introduction into the service adviseable. The present service arm performed well during several of the trials to which it was subjected, and proved itself in many respects an efficient military weapon. They hope that the result of their future trials may enable them to recommend the introduction into the service of an arm which, while fulfilling the other requirements of a military weapon, shall be more accurate and have a flatter trajectory than the present Snider rifle.

(It is interesting to note that the system eventually adopted for the breech action of the new rifle – the Martini – did not fare very well in this competition. That the conditions were too rigid in some respects was recognised, as related in the following chapter, and under new conditions the virtues of this action were fully recognised, and so it was accepted for service.)

STANDING POSITION.—READY.

CHAPTER 3.

AFTERMATH OF THE PRIZE COMPETITION

THE prize competition, from the point of view of producing an acceptable breech-loading rifle for the British service, was actually considered a failure before it commenced, as the rigid conditions imposed for it disqualified some promising designs. Some of these were thought by the prize competition sub-committee to be worthy of further examination on their own merits, so were set aside for consideration by the OSC, as the duties of the sub-committee had been limited to judging the prize competition only.

However, on 10-12-1867 the SoS decided that the prize sub-committee should extend their examination to encompass all arms submitted to them, with a view to finding the one they could finally recommend for adoption. They then reconvened as the "Special Committee on Breech-Loading Rifles", and carried on after the prize competition had been finalised.

The experience gained in the prize competition showed the committee that most inventors of breech-loading actions had concentrated more on the mechanical aspects of the system rather than on overall design, and that the shooting qualities of the weapons thus produced were often disregarded. As a result of this approach, a variety of calibres had been presented to the committee, principally of 0.577, 0.5, and 0.45-inch bores, but none of the rifles approached the standard of accuracy laid down by the WO. This standard was readily accomplished and surpassed by muzzle-loading arms then available, and it was felt that a breech-loading arm should also be capable of equal accuracy, and that the breech mechanism could not affect the accuracy obtained, provided it could accomodate a cartridge large enough to hold an equivalent charge, etc.

It was felt, therefore, that the questions on the weight of bullet, charge of powder, cartridge case, bore and grooving, and weight and description of the barrel could be settled independently; and these points having been settled, the breech mechanisms could be more easily compared than was the case when different lengths and types of cartridges were used.

To this end the committee sought permission from the SoS to allow them to seek evidence from prominent gunmakers and others on the following subjects, to ascertain -

1. The most important qualifications for a military arm.
2. What bore, barrel, grooving, and ammunition appeared most likely to give these qualifications.
3. Whether there was a prospect of obtaining from a breech-loader as high a degree of excellence in these particulars as from a muzzle-loader.
4. What was the best mode of arriving at these requirements.
5. The method of stocking, the description of lock, and the quality of powder best adapted for a military arm.

The persons requested to assist the committee were –

Lt.-Gen. C. Hay; C.W. Lancaster; Col. H.St.J Halford; Alex. Henry; Maj. G.V.Fosbery, VC; Col. W.M.Dixon (Supt. RSAF); Col. E.M.Boxer (Supt. RL); Jas Kerr; John Rigby; J.Whitworth; Westley Richards; Capt. H.Noble, RA; F.A.Abel (Chemist, War Dept.); W.Metford; W.T.Eley; and the C-I-C.

They all, with the exceptions of Eley and Metford, gave evidence, and the majority agreed on most points raised.

All were of the opinion that the main qualifications needed for a military rifle were strength, lightness, safety, flatness of trajectory, and accuracy. Some also stressed the importance of securing a bullet of great penetrating power. To obtain these qualifications the majority recommended an 0.45-inch bore with a solid bullet of 480 grains weight, a charge of powder of 85 grains, and a centre-fire metallic cartridge case. The sytem of rifling and chambering to remain an open question.

The concensus of opinion also seemed to be that there was nothing in the nature of breech-loading arms to prevent their attaining a high degree of accuracy in shooting, but it was felt necessary that the conditions of cartridge case, bore, and weights of bullet and powder should be laid down before commencing trials for accuracy of shooting.

On the methods of stocking, description of lock, and the qualities of powder, the opinions were varied and conflicting.

As a result of the above enquiry, which corroborated opinions formed by the committee during the prize competition, they were able to decide the future course of proceedings, by separating the question of the breech mechanism from that of the barrel.

The breech system was to be decided by an open competition of all the systems that had either been or could be brought before them. The barrel was to be confined to those systems of rifling that had given the best results as muzzle-loaders, viz, those of Henry, Lancaster, Metford, Rigby, Westley Richards, Whitworth, and Enfield (as represented by Cols. Boxer and Dixon, RA).

The committee decided to lay down the length, weight, and calibre of the barrel as 35 inches, 4 lbs 6 ozs, and 0.45-inch respectively; and the weight of bullet and charge as 480 and 85 grains, respectively. The cartridge was to use the government Boxer case, and lubrication was to be pure beeswax, as the best adapted to variations of climate and storage.

It was considered preferable that for the trials of the barrels a common breech mechanism be used, to obviate any possible variations that might be caused if different breech systems were used. The Snider system was originally chosen, but as Col. Dixon advised the committee that a lengthy period would be required to produce a sufficient number of this action adapted to the 0.45-inch barrels, it was decided to adopt the Henry action instead, as it had gained a prize in the competition for the best breech action, and also was readily available.

To allow the barrel competition to proceed as planned a circular letter stating the requirements – as outlined above – was sent to the selected barrel makers, seeking their co-operation. The letter was as follows –

Ordnance Select Committee,
Royal Arsenal.
Sir, *March 9, 1868.*

The Committee on Breech-Loading Rifles are desirous of making experiments for determining the form and number of grooves and amount of twist most suitable for a military breech-loading rifle of 0.45-inch calibre.

The following elements have been chosen as the best on which to start the enquiry, viz –

Calibre	*0.45-inch.*
Barrel length.	*35 inches.*
Barrel weight not to exceed. . . .	*4 lbs 6 ozs.*
Barrel exterior at breech	*1.075-inch.*
Barrel exterior at muzzle.	*0.795-inch.*
Bullet	*480 grains.*
Powder	*85 grains, or a*

quantity of compressed powder which will give equal initial velocity.

As this inquiry has no reference to the best method of closing the breech, it has been decided that all the barrels for trial shall be fitted to Henry breech arrangements, which are now being prepared.

The committee being anxious to try your rifling in comparison with others, have directed me to inquire if you would favour them with your assistance in the necessary trials, by preparing eight steel barrels in accordance with the above conditions, and rifled in the manner which you consider best to ensure accurate shooting and freedom from fouling.

I am also to inquire upon what terms of repayment you would undertake to assist the committee in the manner indicated.

From the evidence already received, and from their own experience, the committee are inclined to prefer a bullet solid at the base, but they would not object to a slight concavity, also they have no objection to the bullet being hardened to any degree which may suit your rifling. The bullet may have cannelures or not; the lubrication must be pure beeswax, but the committee will leave it to you whether it shall be applied directly to the bullet or on a paper cap, or in the form of a wad behind the bullet, or by any combination of these methods, or otherwise.

The bullets must be secured in the cartridge cases very firmly, and by a method that could be used when manufacturing in large quantities.

The cartridge cases will be made in the Royal Laboratory, and specimens can be supplied to you to govern the dimensions of the chamber, or a gauge plug can be furnished for the chamber, which will allow for the manufacturing limits of dimensions of the cartridge.

The committee propose that four of the barrels should be chambered for cartridges made up with ordinary powder, and four for compressed powder cartridges. The former could be completed at once, as the dimensions of the cartridge are well known. The dimensions of the cartridges for compressed powder are not yet determined, but the rifling of the barrels might be proceeded with, and the chambering completed hereafter. Time being of great importance, the committee propose that all these barrels should be made to screw into one Henry breech arrangement with stock and lock, which will be supplied in the event of your being willing to afford your assistance.

The committee would be glad to have your opinion as to whether, for these experimental purposes only, the barrels should be of steel or iron, and if the weight given, viz, 4 lbs 6 ozs, could be reduced with safety.

In conclusion, I am to enquire whether any of the conditions laid down interfere with the development of your system of rifling, and if so, what alterations you would propose.

If you prefer it, the committee will undertake that the barrels shall be delivered to you bored smooth to 0.45-inch calibre, but unrifled.

The committee have no objection to the preparation of a larger number of barrels if you should require them for preliminary experiments, and would feel obliged by your including any such number in your estimate of cost, should you feel inclined to send one, and they would also wish for an estimate of time which must elapse before the barrels can be completed and delivered.

A reply is requested at your earliest convenience.

R.W.Haig, Capt. RA.
Secretary.

The letter was sent to the various barrel makers on the dates listed below –

9-3-1868	J. Whitworth, Esq.
	Westley Richards, Esq.
	C.W. Lancaster, Esq.
	W.E. Metford, Esq.
	J. Rigby, Esq.
	A. Henry, Esq.
10-3-1868	Col. Dixon, RA.
23-3-1868	Col. Boxer, RA.

Most replied in the affirmative, but Metford declined to give any assistance, and Westley Richards, although agreeing to furnish barrels, stated that he could not guarantee accurate shooting with ammunition made up as requested. Col.

Boxer also considered it undesirable to lay down specific conditions for the cartridge charge and weight and type of bullet.

After considering these objections the committee, having in mind the problems caused in previous competitions because of latitude allowed in these respects, decided that the conditions specified in the circular letter would be adhered to.

Owing to the delay anticipated before the barrels would be ready for trial, the committee proceeded to examine the breech mechanisms received, and also proceeded with trials of cartridges with compressed powder, in order to compare them with loose powder loads; however, for the sake of continuity, the barrel trials will be dealt with in this section, before giving details of the breech action trials.

THE BARREL TRIALS

The barrel trials were to be fired from fixed rests, and as far as possible under similar conditions. All used the Henry breech as specified, with some exceptions which will be described below.

The firing programme was to consist of 100 rounds fired from each of the barrels at several ranges, ie, – 300, 500, 800, and 1,000 yards, in targets of 20 shots each; two barrels firing the 100 rounds without cleaning out, and two with cleaning out after every 20 rounds, varying the barrels at each range. It had been hoped that the trials could be made simultaneously, but as the barrels were received from the makers over a period of time, this was not possible. It was then decided that if any of the systems gave nearly similar results they would then be tested together to gain a better comparison.

Four barrels were supplied by each maker who had agreed to participate, viz, – Henry. Lancaster, Rigby, Westley Richards, Whitworth, and Cols. Dixon and Boxer.

One exception not using the Henry breech was Westley Richards, who requested the committee to test a rifle with his own breech mechanism and special cartridges, in addition to the barrel sent in in conformity with the specifications laid down.

The other exception was two rifles with 0.5-inch bore barrels, rifled on the Enfield system, and fitted to Snider actions. These were sent in by Col. Dixon.

In the interval between the sending out of the circular letter and the receipt of the finished barrels, Cols. Dixon and Boxer on 20-4-1868 had made a report to the SoS in which they advocated, after a long series of experiments, a bore of 0.5-inch in preference to one of 0.45-inch, because of a greater tendency to foul in the smaller bore. This report was presented to the committee, and as it so favoured the 0.5-inch bore, the committee decided to compare the two rifles of this calibre in parallel with the Enfield barrels of 0.45-inch bore supplied under the conditions of the letter.

In conducting the trials the committee reserved the right of ceasing the trials of any rifle which showed a marked inferiority of shooting to the others, or which did not attain the standard of accuracy laid down for the prize competition.

Although the circular letter containing the conditions of entry was sent in early March, the barrels were not received by the committee from the makers until the following dates –

Henry	During the	1st	week in	June.
Whitworth	"	2nd	"	August.
Col. Dixon	"	2nd	"	September.
Westley Richards..	"	3rd	"	September.
Westley Richards*	"	4th	"	October.
Lancaster.	"	1st	"	October.
Rigby	"	4th	"	October.

*(The arm submitted with drawn brass cartridges.)

Henry's barrels were received earlier than all the others, and this was attributed to his having chambered his barrels without waiting for the gauges to be prepared at the RL, and also to his long experience with breech-loading rifles in 0.45-inch calibre.

The 500 yards range was selected as the first at which the rifles would be tried, and the actual trials commenced on 23-6-1868, with the Henry barrels being fired against the 0.5-inch Sniders – which were already available – and were continued at intervals as the other barrels came to hand. (For a description of the barrels and ammunition, see Appendix 5; and for the results of the shooting, Appendix 6.)

Two special rifles with solid drawn brass cartridges were tried at the specific request of Westley Richards, but the committee reported that the systems did not appear to have been thoroughly worked out when brought to their notice, and the accuracy achieved was not nearly equal to that from other rifles. At the same time, the type of cartridge cases submitted by Westley Richards – but which had first been brought to their notice by Gen. Berdan's agent – appeared to possess some merit, and was recommended for future consideration, should further development of it give satisfactory results. They felt that in the form presented it was not equal to the Boxer case.

On comparing the shooting at the various ranges, it was noted that the Henry barrel was superior to the others at all distances except 300 yards, at which range all were nearly equal – with the 0.5-inch bore being slightly superior. The flatness of trajectory of the Henry was considered practically equal to the other 0.45-inch calibre arms, but again was slightly excelled by the 0.5-inch bore. However, during the trials it was found practically impossible to ascertain the true trajectory when firing from the fixed rest and laying the rifle by means of a clinometer, owing to the angle of departure of the bullet being so greatly dependent on the fittings of the rest. So, experiments were subsequently carried out to find the best means of obtaining the trajectories of rifles fired from the shoulder, and these were considered successful.

To ascertain the trajectory when fired from the shoulder, of the Henry 0.45-inch, and the Snider 0.5 and 0.577-inch bores, two groups of five shots each were made by two careful shooters from each rifle at 500, 400, 300, 200, and 100 yards ranges, with the 500 yards sight. The same aiming point was used, and the means of the heights of the points of mean impact of the groups at each range above those of the group at 500 yards gave the height of the ordinates at each distance; these were then plotted out, and the curve connecting them was considered the true trajectory of each rifle. By reference to these experiments it was found that even at the shorter ranges the Henry 0.45-inch had a flatter trajectory than the 0.5-inch; and velocity experiments confirmed this conclusion.

The fouling supposed to attach to the 0.45-inch bore was not noted in the Henry, and the firing of 100 rounds without cleaning produced no deterioration in the shooting. Additional tests were made, by firing intermediate targets of 20 rounds with great rapidity, and in these the shooting improved rather than deteriorated.

It was thus confirmed that in every respect the Henry barrel was the most favourable type in 0.45-inch calibre.

REMARKS ON THE BARREL TRIALS

In their report on the barrel trials – in Minute 26,704 of 11-2-1869 – the committee paused at the above stage in the proceedings to make some general remarks on the barrel forms submitted for their consideration. They felt it would be unfair to the other inventors not to mention the latter's generally expressed opinions that the time allowed was insufficient to allow them to thoroughly work out the problem submitted to them, viz, "That of procuring good shooting from systems adapted to breech-loaders, which had shown excellent qualities when applied to muzzle-loaders." Westley Richards stated, in his answer to the circular letter of 9-3-1868, that "he did not anticipate that good shooting could be obtained under the conditions laid down therein". Lancaster and Rigby also wrote expressing their views in a similar vein. Their letters are shown below, but, in the words of the committee – "On the other hand it should be remembered that all these gentlemen had equal opportunities with Mr. Henry for investigating and working out the subject, and that his success is due, not to any sudden discovery, but to the attention he has long given to the production of breech-loading rifles adapted for metallic cartridges."

Lancaster's Letter.

151 New Bond Street, London.
Sir, September 21st.

In reply to Ordnance Select Committee letter, 16-9-68, and in reference to the interview of Thursday last, I beg to inform you that the six barrels rifled on my system for loose powder are quite ready and shall be forwarded this week.

As I had the honour of explaining personally, I have to regret that I have not been able to complete the series of trials necessary to determine the proper ammunition to be used, every trial having to be conducted by myself, no person in my employ being capable of so responsible a duty, and being unable, owing to the requirements of my private business, to devote two months undivided attention away from it, the time a proper investigation of the subject would demand. Still, permit me to assure the committee that I have, so far as was in my power, devoted myself to the purposes of the government in this matter.

If therefore it is found by the committee that through any lack of time necessary for the trials of ammunition to develop the full merits of the system of rifling the shooting is not equal to the requirements, it will be to me a matter of great regret; but I shall not the less accept any conclusion arrived at by the Committee on Breech-Loading Rifles, although I am satisfied that all things being equal, the oval bore system will hold its own with any other system of rifling as proved by 18 years continuous trials by the Ordnance Select Committee, and on service, the question of ammunition being one merely involving a certain expenditure of time, and certain facilities in conducting experiments which under present circumstances I am compelled to leave in the hands of the proper authorities.

I have, &c.,
Charles W. Lancaster.

Rigby's Letters.

24, Suffolk Street, Dublin.
Sir, 28th October, 1868.

In compliance with your notification of the 21st instant, I send to you the Henry rifle, to which I have fitted four barrels rifled on my system. I do not send any cartridges, as I am not at present prepared to submit a sample of ammunition; my experiments showing that even the best which I have heretofore tried is capable of improvement. In fact my most recent trials indicate plainly that the removal of the chief source of inaccuracy in breech-loading rifles is quite attainable, and I desire to pursue these investigations further before I submit the results to public trial.

I am, &c.,
John Rigby.

Sir, 6th November, 1868.

I have been engaged since my return here in gathering up the result of my previous experiments, and have determined the most important points. I am now most desirous to submit ammunition for my barrels, and to withdraw mine of the 28th on this subject. If the committee can possibly give them a trial, I think it will be more satisfactory than that they should have incurred the expense of my barrels, &c, without obtaining any result.

Your reply by return of post will oblige, and meanwhile I will make preparations to send in the rifle and ammunition as soon as possible after receipt of your reply.

What I would desire would be a comparative simultaneous trial with the best shooting arm you have as yet got, and I am prepared to attend personally for that purpose.

Sir, *25th November, 1868.*

I have this day received from my agent in London, a report of partial trial of barrels and ammunition sent in by me. The result is so different from that of previous ones made in Dublin, that I am certain that the ammunition sent in has been defective from want of time to prepare proper apparatus for making it. As I had not time to complete the experiments in progress, and the committee cannot further extend the time for testing the barrels, I desire that the incomplete trial may not be recorded, but that the matter may be permitted to rest on the basis of my letter of the 28th October.

I am, &c.,
John Rigby.

The success of Henry's barrel was due in some measure to his ammunition, which, although using the Boxer case, consisted of a bullet and wad unit of his own design. The ammunition was considered to have four advantages – accuracy, non-fouling, simplicity of bullet form, and great penetrating power of the bullet. A series of trials to test the penetration of the Henry bullet against those of the 0.5 and 0.577-inch bores resulted in a clear superiority for the Henry.

SUMMARY OF THE BARREL TRIALS

Having reported on the various trials and the conclusions drawn therefrom, the committee summarised the advantages and disadvantages of the Henry 0.45-inch barrel and ammunition when compared with the Snider-Enfield 0.5 and 0.577-inch rifles and ammunition as follows –

1. Accuracy. The Henry showed a marked superiority over the 0.5-inch when fired simultaneously with it; and from other experiments made, it showed a rather more marked superiority over the 0.577-inch calibre, especially at the longer ranges.

2. Trajectory. The advantage in trajectory held by the Henry up to 500 yards is shown in Table X.

3. Allowance for wind. The advantage here was greatly in favour of the 0.45-inch bore. In the simultaneous trial with the 0.5-inch bore the results shown in Table XI were obtained.

4. Fouling. There was little or no fouling observed in any of the three bores compared after firing upwards of 100 rounds each without cleaning the barrels.

5. Penetration. The results of the trials showed marked superiority of the 0.45-inch over the others; and the experiments in respect to wounds inflicted showed that the 0.45-inch was more deadly and produced more serious injuries than the other bores.

6. Form of cartridge. This was a minus for the smaller bore, as respective lengths were –

0.45-inch	3.75 inches.
0.5-inch	3.29 "
0.577-inch	2.45 "

In strength, estimated by rough usage, the longer cartridge was considered slightly inferior to the others, but all were regarded as being sufficiently strong for service use.

The results of the summary were that the Henry 0.45-inch was best adapted to the requirements of the service. Its superiority in points of accuracy, trajectory, wind allowance, and penetration, outweighed those points against it.

There remained only the questions of durability, and expense of manufacture. On the former, from the results of

TABLE X – Trajectories of trials rifles.

Snider 0.577-inch –

Safe distance for cavalry – Between 138 and 400 yards.
Safe distance for infantry - Between 92 and 438 yards.
Greatest height of trajectory – 11.9 feet.

Enfield 0.5-inch –

Safe distance for cavalry – Between 221 and 325 yards.
Safe distance for infantry - Between 123 and 406 yards.
Greatest height of trajectory – 8.9 feet.

Henry 0.45-inch –

Safe distance for cavalry – Nil.
Safe distance for infantry - Between 139 and 396 yards.
Greatest height of trajectory – 8.1 feet.

TABLE XI – Allowances for wind.

Calibre.	Range.	Wind.	Allowance for wind.	Advantage for .45-inch.
	yards.		feet.	feet.
Henry .45"	500	Fresh across range.	1.39	
Snider .5"	500	Fresh across range.	7.0	5.61
Henry .45"	800	Fresh, but not much	0.93	
Snider .5"	800	across range.	7.64	6.71
Henry .45"	1,000	Fresh across range.	13.97	
Snider .5"	1,000	Fresh across range.	28.53	14.57

the experiments, which involved the firing of upwards of 2,080 rounds from the same barrel, and from evidence received that as many as 30,000 rounds had been fired from a barrel with no indications of wear, it was clear that the Henry system of rifling was strong enough to resist wear effects from mere shooting. With regard to cleaning wear and tear, the committee felt that the Henry rifling was better able to resist these than the Enfield rifling.

With reference to the cost of rifling barrels on the Henry system, there was much conflicting evidence, but there was no reason to assume that the Henry would be more expensive than any other system.

FINAL RECOMMENDATIONS ON BARREL TRIALS

From the committee report –

In regard to both durability and cost of manufacture the committee are of opinion that the Henry barrels are adapted for military purposes, and having already reported that in other respects they appear superior to the several systems of rifling brought before their notice, the committee are of opinion that the Henry barrel, 0.45-inch bore, is that most suitable in all respects for the requirements of the service.

THE BREECH MECHANISM TRIALS

To examine the various types of breech mechanisms the committee decided on the following course of action – the arms were carefully examined, and if approved were to have 20 or more shots fired for rapidity. Then sand was thrown over the action, both open and closed, and the rifle fired without any cleaning except for what could be done with the hand. Three cartridges, purposely damaged to ensure an escape of gas were then fired, to test the safety of the arm with imperfect ammunition. If the rifle passed these trials in a satisfactory manner, and if the breech appeared suitable for military use, it was put through a course of continuous firing, being allowed to rust at intervals between the days of firing.

To justify this course of testing, the committee explained that the trial for rapidity of firing involved a test for simplicity and convenience of manipulation, and that the hurry and excitement which attended a trial for rapidity frequently developed a weakness of the action which might otherwise escape notice.

The sand trial was to simulate the conditions met in dry countries, such as parts of India. Although a severe trial, it was one that the best actions should pass without impediment. The continued firing and rust tests represented the ill-usage which arms in war may have had to endure, and, like the test for rapidity, tended to bring out any weakness that the firing of a few shots only might fail to develop.

For examination in this new series of trials the committee had before them –

1. The arms of the prize competition, viz. – Albini and Braendlin; Burton Nos.1 and 2; Fosbery; Henry; Joslyn; Martini; Peabody; and Remington.

2. Those arms not eligible for the prize competition, but put aside for further consideration, viz. – Berdan; Carter and Edwards No.3; Fosbery No.4; Greve and Dowling No.4; Hammond; Needham No.1; Poultney; Westley Richards Nos.3B and 11; Sharp; and Wilson.

3. Other arms submitted after the above arms had been reported on, but before 26-10-1868, after which date none were received, viz. – Adams; Amsler-Milbank; Bacon; Berdan (3), with a spiral spring lock, with side lock, and with sliding bolt; Benson; Braendlin-Snider; Cole (2), 0.577 and 0.45-inch; Conroy; Cooper; Chassepot; Davies; Fosbery (2), an improved 0.5-inch, and an 0.45-inch falling block; Gordon; Kerr; Money-Walker; Peabody (2), adapted for compressed powder cartridges, and with lever above instead of below, and adapted for drawn brass cartridges; Peabody-Gielgud; Peabody-Gielgud-Wessely; Prussian needle-gun; Punshon-Snider; Reilly-Comblain; Ross; Russian converted needle-rifle; Russ and Hammond (2), for metallic cartridge and paper cartridge; Roden-Snider; Stoakes (2), 0.577 and 0.45-inch; Stiff; Tranter; Wanzel; Werndle, Wilson; Witney; Wyley (2), 0.577 and 0.45-inch; and Westley Richards (4), with paper cartridge, with subsidiary lever for cocking, a falling block with metallic cartridge, and an elevating block with metallic cartridge.

The arms on List 1 had been so fully tested that no further information on them was required during the preliminary period of the new investigation. From Lists 2 and 3 a certain number were immediately rejected, and those which appeared to possess most merit, having been put through the trials listed above, were subjected to a further elimination. (The rejected arms and the reasons for rejection are shown in Appendix 7.)

The remainder, with a few arms selected from List 1, were set aside to go through the continued-firing trial.

The various eliminations were made at different times in the enquiry, and the eventual outcome was a short list of arms which appeared likely to fulfil the desired qualifications of a military breech-loader. These arms were – Bacon; Berdan; Carter and Edwards; Henry; Kerr; Martini; Money-Walker; Westley Richards (2, differing from those previously submitted); and Wilson. (For descriptions of these arms see Appendix 8.)

These breech systems were divided broadly into two groups, the block and the bolt; of which the Berdan, Henry, Martini, Money-Walker, and the two Westley Richards were block systems, and the Bacon, Carter and Edwards, Kerr, and Wilson were bolt actions.

In their report the committee observed that several of the arms on this list were placed there, not because they had proved superior to some that had gone through the prize competition trials and subsequently rejected, but because they wanted to compare them with the Henry and Martini arms, as these latter systems had been selected as possessing merits superior to those of other arms which had passed through the prize competition trials.

All the selected systems were adapted to fire metallic cartridges, but, from the results of the preliminary experiments, none was believed to depend on the strength of the cartridge case for safety, and all were thought able to withstand the explosion of a faulty cartridge. Notwithstanding this, as the arms were likely to be damaged during the course of the trials, it was decided, with the sanction of the SoS, to purchase one arm of each system.

It was now very important to fix the form of cartridge to be used in the breech action trials, as the working of some of the systems depended on the length of the cartridge to be used. This caused a point of difficulty, as the barrel trials had not been concluded, so neither the bore nor the cartridge had been definitely decided upon, and there was still some doubt whether loose or compressed powder would be adopted for the service cartridge. As the committee was unwilling to postpone the breech trials until the barrel trials were finished, it was decided to make it optional with the inventors of the breech mechanisms whether they would send in rifles suitable for an 0.5 or 0.45-inch cartridge. It was also intended that trials would be carried out under similar conditions with regard to bore and cartridge, if, after finishing the trials, the comparative merits of any of the arms remained doubtful.

As the Boxer cartridge was used in the barrel trials, preference was given to it for use in the breech trials, so it became necessary to alter two of the submitted arms – Berdan and Martini – to adapt them for the cartridge. The alterations were made at the RL by request of the committee, as the Berdan was made in America, and the Martini in Switzerland, and there were no working representatives of these makers in England. Martini's rifle was altered on the proviso he gave when entering it, ie, that it was adaptable equally to either centre or rim-fire cartridges.

Westley Richards' rifles, having been made to take a solid drawn brass cartridge, and the Money-Walker, taking the Daw cartridge, were allowed by the committee to compete with the ammunition for which they were designed.

THE BOLT ACTIONS

The committee selected these actions for trial only with considerable misgivings, as from their own observations, and from evidence received, they were inclined to believe that there was the danger in this system of a cartridge firing before the bolt had been fully closed. Against this fear were the points of easy manipulation and manufacture, and that it was used by the armies of France and Prussia. Also, in the systems selected for trial, apparently satisfactory arrangements had been made to make the arms safe.

It was decided therefore, to put the selected bolt action rifles through the same trials as the others, but with a special trial made with cartridges rendered exceptionally sensitive, to test their safety with cartridges that may have been accidentally manufactured with defects liable to make them unsafe.

The special trial cartridges were made with twelve defects, but were loaded with coal dust instead of powder. The tests included placing the cartridge in the chamber and pushing the bolt against it with considerable force; laying the cartridge in the shoe, and forcing it sharply home with the bolt. If these tests were passed, an obstruction was to be placed in the shoe or chamber – to prevent free movement of the cartridge – and the bolt then driven against the cartridge to force it into place. These experiments were intended to represent what might possibly occur on active service during rapid firing, when the soldier would naturally try to force home the cartridge with the bolt. The actions of block guns did not admit of similar experiments, but it was thought they were not liable to accidents of this nature.

The special trials were known as the Sensitive Cartridge Tests, and the various bolt actions reacted as follows –

Bacon: A cartridge containing a primer with a rounded anvil, without shoulders, was jammed in the entrance of the chamber. Force was used to push it home with the bolt, and before the bolt was closed the primer fired. It was noted that the piston had been forced out by the shock of closing and had struck the primer. A similar result was produced with a primer made with a pointed anvil, also without shoulders, but this cartridge had not been jammed in any way. Another cartridge with a similar defect was also exploded, although again not jammed in any way.

Carter and Edwards: The different types of sensitive cartridges were tried in this rifle, but none exploded. The piston was not forced forward, and the shock, which was in some cases severe, failed to fire or indent the primer. These cartridges were afterwards fired in the usual way to prove they were capable of being fired.

Kerr: A cartridge with a primer containing a long rounded anvil was jammed in the mouth of the chamber and forced home with the bolt; before the bolt was closed the primer exploded. The primer had been indented by the piston, and a similar result was obtained with a primer fitted with a pointed anvil, without shoulders.

An improved rifle submitted by Kerr was put to these tests, and in every instance the primer was indented by the piston but none was fired.

Wilson: Three sensitive cartridges were tried, and although not fired, all showed evidence of being struck by the piston.

As there had been two dangerous accidents with bolt guns during the ordinary trials, these experiments served to confirm the committee's opinion that the bolt system was not as safe as the block, and it was decided to reject from any further consideration all the bolt action arms.

The committee expressed regret for this decision, as they

felt that the Carter and Edwards and Kerr rifles possessed some excellent qualities, but there were other reasons apart from the liability or otherwise to fire sensitive cartridges, so that portion of the trial was considered closed.

(NB – In the above text, the term "piston" refers to the striker, or firing pin.)

SUMMARY OF THE BREECH TRIALS

For the sake of clarity the special cartridge tests for the bolt action arms were described in the above section, but these arms also underwent the same basic examination as the block guns, and at the same time. The results of the various trials are given below.

Rapidity trial: 21 rounds were fired from the shoulder, the cartridges being placed on a table, and the time for firing 20 rounds was obtained by observing the interval between the first and last shots, viz. –

Systems.	Fired by.	' "
Bacon 0.45-inch	Lt. Bacon	1 00
Bacon 0.45-inch	Lt. Bacon	0 58
Berdan 0.45-inch	Sjt. Bott, RM	1 10
Carter & Edwards 0.5-inch	Sjt. Bott, RM	0 51
Henry 0.45-inch	Sjt. Ward, RA	1 17
Henry 0.45-inch	Pvt. Crofts, RM	1 7
Kerr 0.45-inch	Mr. Kerr	1 15
Martini 0.433-inch	Sjt. Bott, RM	1 2
Money-Walker 0.5-inch	Mr. Walker	1 14
Money-Walker 0.5-inch with Daw ammunition	Sjt. Bott, RM	1 23
Westley Richards 0.45-inch (Falling block, solid cart.)	His foreman	1 7
Westley Richards 0.45-inch (Elevating block, solid cart.)	His foreman	1 00
Wilson 0.5-inch	Mr. Wilson	1 26

As the rifles were of different calibres, and as they all showed a satisfactory degree of rapidity, it was not thought necessary to have them all fired by the one person in order to get a more exact comparison than that shown.

Damaged cartridges: The cartridges were filed at the base and sides to ensure a considerable escape of gas. Three rounds were fired, with the damaged part of the case placed in a different position each time. As a result, the Bacon had its extractor blown away, but the others were not affected.

Sand trial: Fine sand was thrown over the action, both open and closed, and brushed off with the hand only, before firing the rifle. All the weapons passed this test satisfactorily.

Exposure test: This was conducted as follows - one hundred rounds were fired on four consecutive days, and the rifles left in the open air exposed to rain, or to water artifically applied during the intervals, the actions being left alternately open and closed. The rifles, still uncleaned, were then left exposed during three or four days and nights, and were again fired to see if they were serviceable. They were then dismantled and examined, with the following results (taken verbatim from the committee's report) –

Bacon: This rifle was not put through the exposure test, for the following reason – when Sjt. Ward, RA, was selecting some cartridges with which to try it, he placed a cartridge in the shoe and pushed it home with his thumb. He was in the act of closing the bolt when the cartridge exploded. The breech mechanism was separated from the barrel and destroyed, and that portion of the stock containing it was broken into pieces. The cartridge used was an ordinary one made in the RL. The serjeant's face and hands were slightly injured. (This accident was thought to be caused either by a fault in the catch which held back the piston, or by the blow of the bolt on the base of the cartridge.)

Berdan: In this system, unless the block be carefully closed, the hammer is apt to fall on the hinge in place of the striker. This defect was especially remarked after the first night's exposure. As the trial proceeded the breech block became jammed, and was opened with some difficulty. At the close of the trial the piston remained out, and force was needed to press it back. On being taken to pieces the side lock, as also the interior of the block, was rusty.

The quick and proper working of the breech block depends upon the hinge, (called by Gen. Berdan the "brace") which readily becomes affected by exposure.

Carter and Edwards: At the end of the exposure the bolt was set fast with rust, but was loosened with blows from a mallet, after which it moved stiffly. On stripping the gun the breech bolt and its bearings were much rusted, but the lock and piston worked well, and were comparatively free from rust.

Henry: The piston once jammed forward in the cap of the cartridge. The piston spring was found during the trial to be unserviceable, the piston remaining forward whenever pressed by the hammer. Another piston spring was substituted, one cartridge was accidentally placed in front of the extractor, and being thus held between the claw of the extractor and the end of the breech, was with difficulty forced out with a ramrod. Towards the close of this trial the piston remained out, but acted properly after a few rounds had been fired. At the end of the trial the extractor worked stiffly, and did not return of itself when the breech was opened. After oil had been applied it acted properly. On stripping the rifle the spring of the extractor was found to be broken, notwithstanding which it worked well. The spring was free from rust.

Kerr: After a considerable number of rounds, a small portion of the point of the keeper screw was found to be worn or broken by the repeated working of the breech bolt, but by screwing it a little further in, it again became serviceable. Towards the close of the trial the piston remained out, the sear spring was rusted and broken, and a new sear spring was substituted. Some difficulty was also noted in ejecting the cartridge case. This was caused by the wearing away of the head of the keeper screw, consequently there was nothing to hinder the bolt, together with the extractor holding the empty cartridge case, from being drawn back beyond the proper distance. If this was done, the base of the cartridge case caught in the shoe and did not fall out readily. On stripping the rifle there was a good deal of rust on the side lock, and the main spring was broken in two places.

This rifle was exchanged, at Mr. Kerr's request, for one he submitted with improvements, in which the keeper screw was at the side instead of underneath the breech action. This latter rifle was not submitted to the exposure tests, as, irrespective of the defect in the keeper screw, the committee had formed their opinion on Mr. Kerr's system.

Martini: During the trial several of the cartridge cases cut, and more pressure than usual was required to open the breech block. Some of the iron discs of the cartridges also broke, in which case the extraction was difficult. These defects were entirely attributable to faulty cartridges, as was subsequently proved by the substitution of a fresh supply. The arm worked well during the trial, and when stripped the breech mechanism was in perfect order, and free from rust or dirt.

Money-Walker: In firing this arm the breech block required to be closed carefully, or with a smart blow. Care was also required in pushing the cartridge home, to prevent it catching in the extractor. As the trial advanced the breech mechansim worked with difficulty, and finally could not be opened with the hand, and the rifle became unserviceable. On stripping it the parts were found rusted.

Westley Richards (Elevating block): This arm was fitted with a side extractor. During the firing of the first 100 rounds the breech action was very hard to open after each shot, but worked easily enough when there was no cartridge in the rifle; the stiffness was therefore attributed to the setting up of the brass cartridge cases, which Westley Richards stated could be improved. At the close of the trial the breech action was jammed, and on stripping the arm the whole of the breech action, including the main spring, was much rusted, and the arm was quite unserviceable.

At Westley Richards' request, this rifle was taken away and another with elevating block substituted. This arm worked stiffly, and during the first few rounds jammed, requiring blows to open the breech. This was probably owing to defects in the cartridge case, as previously mentioned. After the second night's exposure several parts of the breech action were found rusted, a few more rounds were fired, but the breech block jammed after each shot, and it was decided that it was unnecessary to continue the trial further. Westley Richards stated that by the application of a certain lubrication to his rifles, all possibility of their becoming rusted by exposure would be removed.

Westley Richards (Falling block): After the second night's exposure 50 rounds were fired, but as several cartridges burst at the rim, causing escape of gas and consequently some risk to the firer, it was decided to continue the trial for exposure without firing. At the conclusion of the trial the working of the action had not been affected by the exposure, but on stripping it all the parts were much rusted. It was also remarked that the wood of the stock on either side of the breech block was much warped and opened away from the breech action.

Wilson: During the firing of the first day, there was sometimes a difficulty in opening the breech. After the first night's exposure 60 rounds were fired, when the arm burst while being fired from the shoulder by Earl Spencer, who was slightly injured in the face. The breech bolt was blown back about an inch, and the fore part of it was bent upward and jammed. The piece of metal with lugs for taking the recoil was blown off with considerable force; it appeared to have struck the stock and glanced as the wood was dented. (This rifle exploded as it was being fired in the usual way. It was supposed that the bolt had not been secured, and that the special arrangement that was intended to prevent the piston from striking the cap until the breech was firmly closed had miscarried. The bolt only escaped being blown back into the firer's face through its being bent upwards by the force of the explosion, and so becoming jammed in the shoe of the breech action.)

After considering the results of the trials, the committee immediately rejected the Berdan, Money-Walker, and the elevating block Westley Richards, thus leaving for consideration the Henry, Martini, and the falling block Westley Richards. Of these, the Henry and Martini were considered the best, as the Westley Richards system had shown some weaknesses after the exposure test. The method of extracting the cartridge in the Martini was also preferred to that of the Westley Richards. Although Westley Richards had stated that the rusting in his action could be prevented by using a special lubricant, the committee remarked that the other systems had not used such a lubricant, and had gone through the trials without damage, so this point was not further considered.

Westley Richards made a special application on 22-10-1868 – in answer to the letter from the committee telling him of the rejection of his systems – for a trial of a new rifle similar to that rejected, and the committee was prepared to consider his request; but on 2-11-1868 he decided to withdraw from the trials and the arms were returned to him.

RESULT OF THE BREECH TRIALS

The committee was then left with two systems to choose between, the Henry and the Martini; subsequent representations had been made by Simpson (for Carter and Edwards), Kerr, Westley Richards, and Wilson, but the committee saw no reason to alter their opinions already formed on those systems.

Of the two final systems for consideration, the Martini gave the best results in the endurance trials, and showed that previously mentioned faults were caused by defective ammunition.

The just completed series of trials had been made with cartridges loaded with compressed powder charges, but it had been decided to use loose powder for service cartridges. It was thus necessary to test the Martini with cartridges loaded with loose charges, which made them longer than those used in the trials.

As it was considered that a lengthy delay would result if a new rifle was to be made by Martini in Switzerland, with Martini's approval the Supt. RSAF was asked to prepare an arm on the Martini system, to take the long 0.45-inch cartridge, and at the same time incorporate some minor alterations not affecting the principle of the breech mechanism.

This rifle was received on 21-10-1868, but failed to perfectly represent the Martini system, as was pointed out by Martini, who had in the meantime arrived in England. Its weight was in excess of that stipulated, but Martini pointed out how this could be reduced, so it was put through the series of trials again. It passed all these in a most satisfactory manner.

The rapidity, as fired by Sjt. Bott, RM, was 20 rounds in 53 seconds; and when fired by Capt. Mackinnon – after the arm had been exposed to the influence of rain or of water artifically applied for seven days and nights, and having fired 400 rounds during that period – was 20 rounds in 1 min. 3 secs. The action worked as smoothly after the exposure tests as it had done when clean, and in every instance the cartridge case was ejected.

When taken to pieces and examined, the block containing the main spring was entirely free from rust, and the other portions of the breech mechanism only slightly discoloured by it. It was now apparent that the Martini system was adapted equally for long or short cartridges, but it remained to be proved whether, with its weight reduced, and made entirely on Martini's plan it would be equally serviceable. An order for a breech mechanism, to be constructed under Martini's supervision was therefore given to the Supt. of the RSAF.

While all this was going on, Henry had submitted, on different dates, two models of proposed improvements of his breech system; one to overcome the problem of placing the cartridge in front of the extractor, and the other to remedy the liability of the piston to occasionally stick in the primer and hindering the opening of the breech block.

The committee decided to obtain one breech mechanism embodying Henry's improvements, fitted to any barrel, to compete under similar conditions with the new Martini then being made at Enfield. Henry was given the option of making the rifle himself, or having it made at Enfield, so he elected to make it himself.

COMPARISON OF HENRY AND MARTINI ACTIONS

The two new arms were received and examined. The Martini rifle made on Martini's plan was found to be within the required weight, and the Henry rifle embodied a slight alteration to ensure the withdrawal of the piston after firing.

The rifles were put through a course of long-continued firing, rough usage, and exposure, with satisfactory results. The committee had now to decide which system to select by considering the following points – safety; strength; number and simplicity of parts; facility of manipulation; and cost.

Safety: Both systems seemed secure against accidents.

Strength: Both used divided stocks, which the committee felt were stronger, and undoubtedly cheaper than full stocks. The method of attaching the stocks to the breech action in both arms seemed sufficiently strong.

Number of parts: Here the advantage was with the Martini, as its parts numbered 30, whilst those in the Henry totalled 49. (Screws and pins in both cases were counted.) Besides the greater number of detached pieces, the Henry had the manufacturing disadvantage of an extractor plate soldered on the barrel.

(For details of parts of Henry and Martini, see Figs. 1 and 2.)

Facility of manipulation: Both showed excellence in this respect, but the absence of cocking gave a slight superiority to the Martini. The Henry also still exhibited the possibility of the cartridge being placed in front of the extractor.

Cost: The advantage was with the Martini, according to evidence received.

One final question was considered – that of side locks. From experience, and evidence given, the committee were of opinion that side locks were sometimes liable to become wood bound when exposed to wet. This was impossible with the Martini action, as it was entirely contained in a metal casing.

The committee then stated –

After a careful consideration of the relative advantages and disadvantages of the two systems, and of the results of the many trials to which both have been subjected, the committee decide on giving the preference to the Martini, and on recommending it as the one best qualified for a military arm of any that has been brought before them.

COMPARISON OF MARTINI AND SNIDER ARMS

As the Snider was the standard against which the new service rifle was to be judged, the Martini was then compared with it, on the same points of comparison as with the Henry, with the following result –

Safety: The Martini was superior to the current service

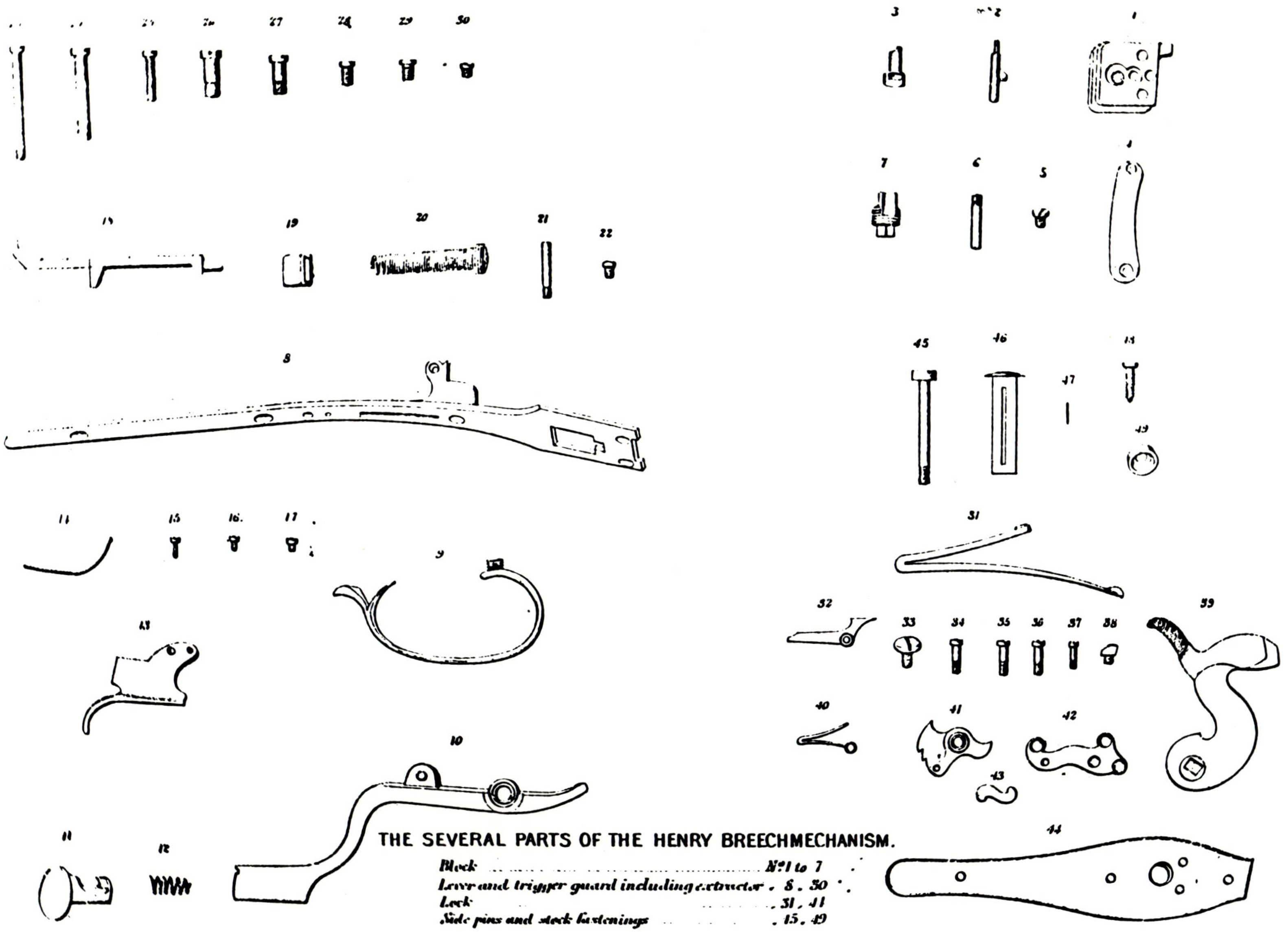
THE SEVERAL PARTS OF THE HENRY BREECHMECHANISM.
Block .... No. 1 to 7
Lever and trigger guard including extractor .... 8 - 30
Lock .... 31 - 41
Side pins and stock fastenings .... 15 - 49

Fig. 1

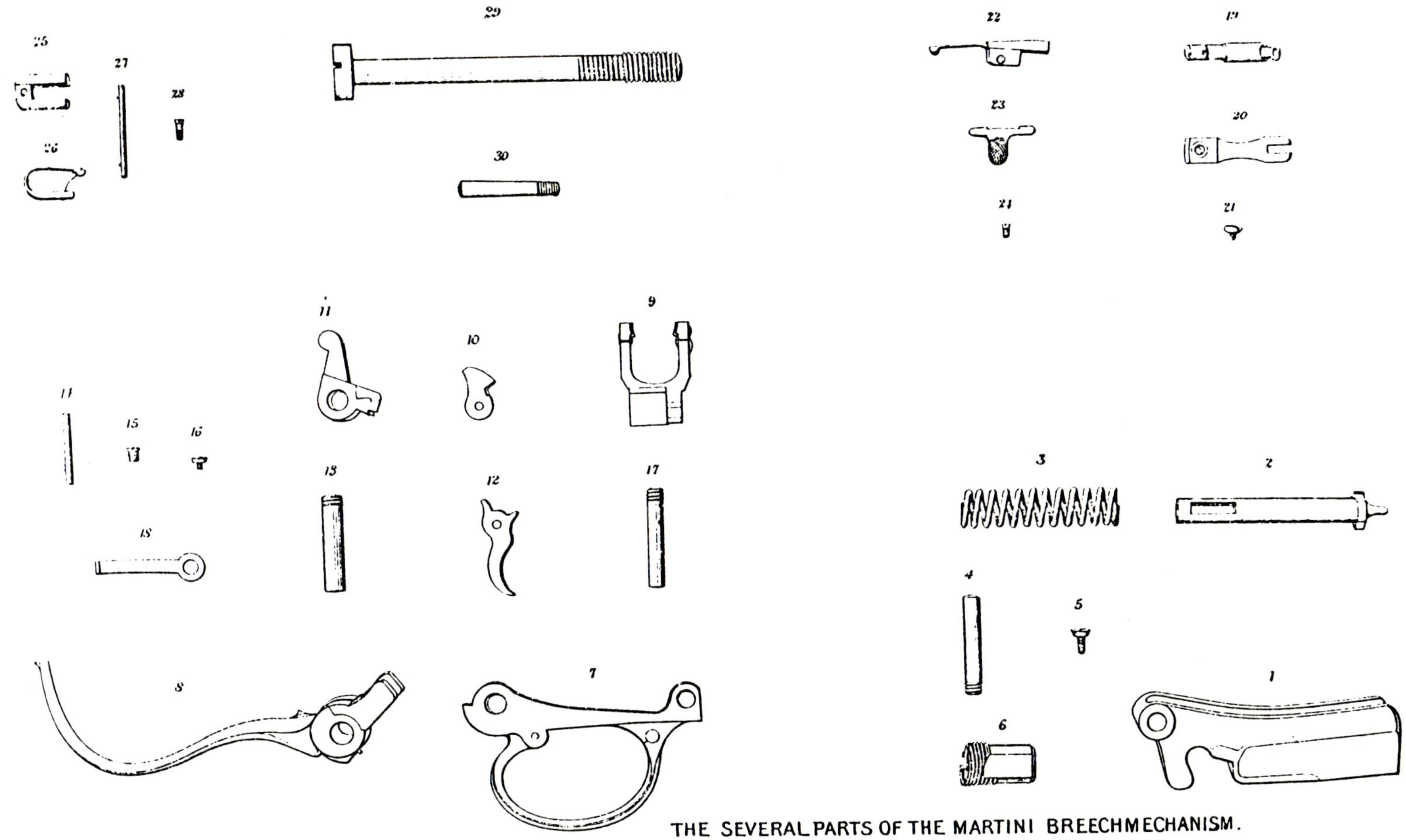

THE SEVERAL PARTS OF THE MARTINI BREECHMECHANISM.

Block	Nº 1 to 6
Lever and trigger guard including extractor	" 7 " 18
Indicator	" 19 " 21*
Safety bolt	" 22 " 24
Catch for lever	" 25 " 28
Stock fastenings	" 29 " 30

* *In the new pattern arm these three pieces have been dispensed with as the new indicator forms one piece with the tumbler pin*

Fig. 2

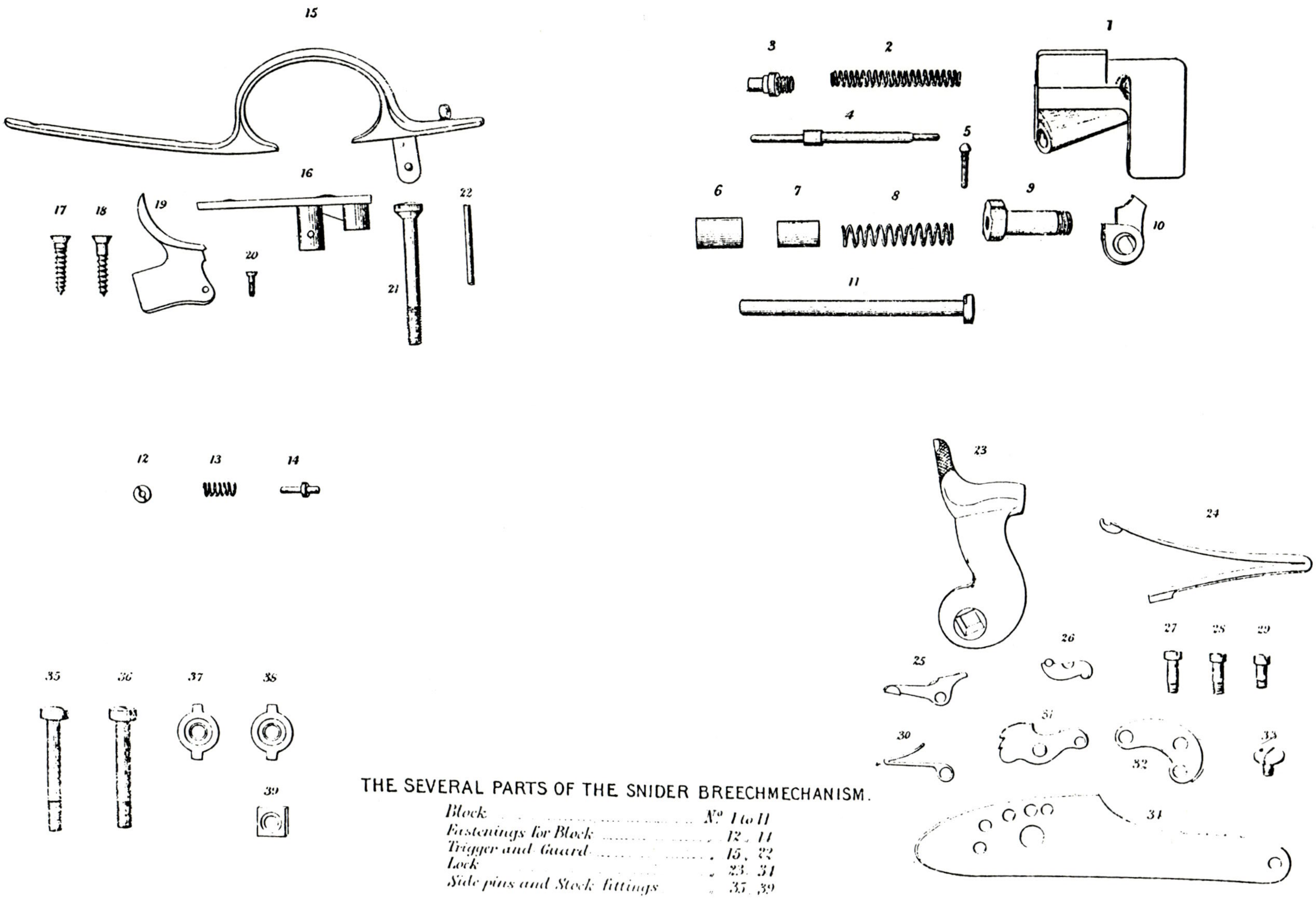

THE SEVERAL PARTS OF THE SNIDER BREECHMECHANISM.

Block	Nº 1 to 11
Fastenings for Block	" 12 " 14
Trigger and Guard	" 15 " 22
Lock	" 23 " 34
Side pins and Stock fittings	" 35 " 39

Fig. 3

Snider, which was liable to be blown open if a faulty cartridge was fired in it. The improved Snider with safety bolt was not considered safer than the Martini.

Strength: The divided stock of the Martini was considered stronger than the whole stock of the Snider, as the cutting away of the wood to take the lock was thought to weaken the whole stock. In strength of breech action, after careful comparison of the several parts, including pins, screws, and springs, the advantage was with the Martini.

Number of parts: Again the Martini had the advantage with 30 parts against the Snider's 39, and if compared with the improved Snider, 30 against 43. (The Martini later had its parts reduced to 27.) For details of Snider parts, see Fig.3.

Facility of manipulation: Once again the advantage was with the Martini, especially with a long cartridge in a small bore. The loading of the Martini was as easy, if not easier, than the Snider, and extraction was much simpler. The Snider required two actions, one for extracting the cartridge from the chamber, another to throw it out by canting the rifle to the right. The Martini performed this in one operation.

Cost: Considering the several parts, and the divided stock, the committee believed the Martini would be cheaper to manufacture than the Snider.

Finally, the same remarks concerning the side lock as made in the comparison with the Henry also applied to the Snider.

To conclude –

After a careful comparison of the merits of the two systems the committee decide on recommending the Martini system of breech mechanism in preference to the Snider system.

CHAPTER 4.

THE MARTINI–HENRY RIFLE

HAVING decided that the Martini breech and the Henry barrel were the most suitable systems of all those submitted, the committee's next step was to marry the two units, to see if the new combination would give the same results, particularly in accuracy, as those achieved during the previous trials. Accordingly, they requested the Supt. RSAF to make four arms, of which the breech mechanisms were to be made under Martini's supervision, and the barrels under that of Henry, who subsequently rifled the barrels in his own works.

The recent barrel trials had been made with Henry's system using nine grooves, but as he informed the committee that the shooting of his seven grooved barrel was equal to that of the nine groove, and that it was possibly superior in its powers of endurance and cheaper to manufacture, it was decided that two of the barrels would be rifled with seven grooves, and the other two with nine. This would allow a direct comparison to be made between the two systems.

The superintendent was also requested to fix new sights known as the "Whitworth" pattern, which had a wider space in the flap of the backsight, with a shallower V-notch. It was considered that this sight would allow the firer to take quicker and more accurate aim, particularly in bad light, than with the Snider service sight. The back sight was recommended to be set seven inches from the breech, and 26½ inches from the front sight. See Figs. 1 to 6 for comparisons of the rear sights.

The breech mechanisms were similar to the last Martini arm used in the trials, but No.2 was fitted with a slightly different safety bolt, and No.4 with an improved cocking indicator.

Two of the rifles were received by the committee about the beginning of January 1869, and the others somewhat later. Martini and Henry examined their respective parts, and expressed themselves satisfied; in Henry's case after he had rectified a slight error in the chambering.

For the shooting trials the arms were fitted into fixed rests, and shot for accuracy at 300, 500, 800, 1,000, and 1,200 yards. The trajectories up to 500 yards were also ascertained by the method previously described, and it was found that the seven groove barrel gave a lower trajectory than the nine groove, although the accuracy of the barrels was about equal. The flatter trajectory of the seven groove barrel was thought to be caused by virtue of less friction on the bullet in that barrel, as it had only fourteen bearing points as against eighteen in the nine groove barrel. For durability and cheapness of manufacture the seven groove was considered superior, so the committee recommended it in preference to the nine grooves.

Experiments were made with a lighter bullet of 380 grains in comparison with the standard 480 grains, but the lighter bullet was found to be less accurate and to have less penetrating power, with the advantages of a slightly lower short range trajectory and slightly less weight of cartridges. It was not recommended for service.

As the breech mechanism had been so thoroughly tested in the previous trials, the committee was satisfied with firing several hundred rounds to try its general serviceability and powers of endurance. Over 3,000 rounds were fired from No.1 gun, and the breech worked as well at the end of the trial as it had at the start. After 2,100 rounds the various parts had been tested for wear, using gauges, and were found to have not given way, or to show any signs of wear.

During the trials it was found that fouling forced its way into the breech action, if the primer gave way or a cartridge burst. The working was not impeded by the fouling, and from evidence from F.A. Abel, WO chemist, it appeared that the gunpowder fouling was actually a protection against rust, and there were therefore no injurious effects from it. Abel's comments on the subject are given below –

Chemical Department,
Royal Arsenal, Woolwich,
Sir, *4th February, 1869.*

In reply to your communication of the 2nd instant, I have the honour to state for the information of the Committee on Breech-Loading Small Arms, that there is, in my opinion, no likelihood of the mechanism of the Martini breech-loading system being injuriously affected by the deposition of fouling upon it.

The fouling, or powder residue, being of a powerfully alkaline nature, will not exert any corrosive action upon the metal surfaces with which it comes in contact; alkaline substances are, indeed, applied to iron and steel surfaces as protectives against oxidation.

The only circumstances under which the deposition of fouling might perhaps give rise to some injurious effect upon the mechanism, would be the keeping of the dirty arm for some time *in damp localities.*

F.A. Abel,
Chemist of the War Dept.

The only weak point that was found in the mechanism was the indicator, the spring of which broke. In No.4 arm Martini substituted a new indicator, which formed part of the tumbler pin, thereby saving three parts, and providing a unit that could not get out of order.

The trials of the four rifles combining the approved systems of Martini and Henry confirmed the committee's opinion that the arm was the best adapted for military service of any brought before them. The arm surpassed in nearly every respect that standard set by the WO advertisement of 22-10-1866, and in accuracy of shooting, flatness of trajectory, penetration, strength of barrel, simplicity, and rapidity of manipulation, excelled the Snider service rifle. The recoil

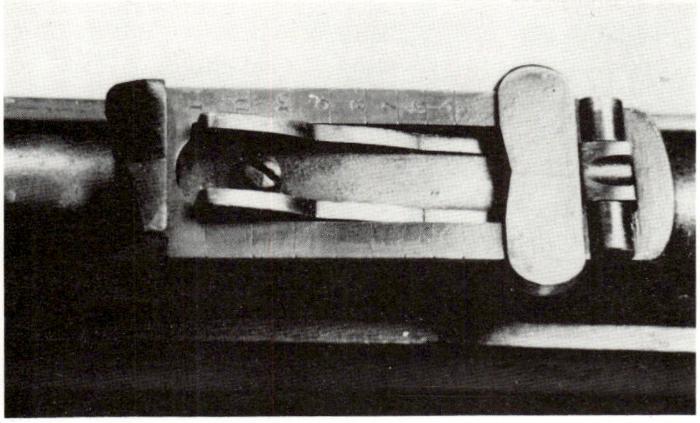

B.A.T.

Fig. 1 – Whitworth Rear Sight – Flap down.

B.A.T.

Fig. 2 – Whitworth Rear Sight – Flap raised.

W&D

Fig. 3 – Martini Rear Sight.

W&D

Fig. 4 – Martini Rear Sight.

B. Hanson

Fig. 5 – Snider Rear Sight – Flap down.

B.Hanson

Fig. 6 – Snider Rear Sight – Flap raised.

seemed about equal to the Enfield muzzle-loader.

In conclusion, the committee in their report of 11-2-1869, referring to Para.V of the WO advertisement – "That the Secretary of State will take care that no ingenious novelty produced in answer to this advertisement shall be adopted into the service without proper acknowledgement, and that the name of the individual with whom it originates should be recorded in connection with it" – were of the opinion that in the event of the arm recommended being adopted into the service, it should be called the "Martini-Henry", and so was born a famous rifle.

Both inventors were also recommended for reward for their respective systems used in this rifle.

DESCRIPTION OF HENRY'S RIFLING

Much of the success of the accuracy of Martini-Henry arms could be attributed to the barrel rifling designed by Alexander Henry, which was the result of experiments carried out during many years of long range target shooting. The basics were laid down by Joseph Whitworth and expanded on by Henry, culminating in the barrel chosen for service with the Martini action.

As can be imagined, considerable rivalry existed amongst the various gunmakers, and this often extended beyond professional bounds. Many of these makers and inventors were also quite vocal in disagreement with government officers, such as the superintendent and manager of the RSAF. In personal correspondence W.E. Metford remarked that it was commonly considered that Henry merely added small grooves to Joseph Whitworth's rifling in order to circumvent patent rights!

As issued, Henry's barrel had a nominal bore of 0.450-inch, obtained by allowing an 0.449-inch plug to run, whilst rejecting one of 0.451-inch. This bore was slightly enlarged at the breech end, so that an 0.451-inch plug would run in four inches from the breech, and one of 0.450-inch, eight inches. From this point to the muzzle the bore was cylindrical. The grooves in the tapering section were 0.009-inch deep to within one inch of the true bore, and from there to the muzzle 0.007-inch deep, giving a relieved bore of eight inches, with progressive grooves for seven inches. There were seven grooves of a right hand uniform twist, with one turn in 22 inches. The chamber was cut in the barrel, and was coned 0.018-inch to ease extraction.

The British Patent issued on this rifling was No.2802 of 1860, and the system was described as a polygonal bore, the angles of which were broken by ribs which created re-entering angles, the inscribing circle tangential to the ribs being described with the same radius as the inscribing circle tangential to the plane sides. All of which meant that the 0.030-inch wide middle portions of the grooves, and the 0.010-inch wide tops of the ribs (which formed the lands), were part of the original bore of 0.450-inch. The grooves ended up being not quite flat, but had gently sloping sides. See Figs.7 and 8 for details.

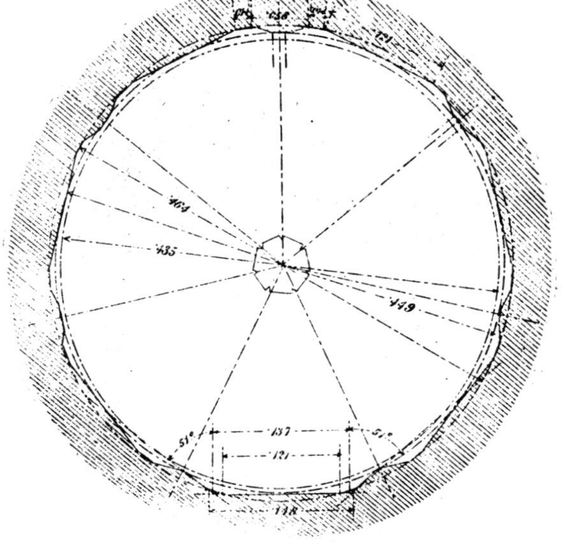

Fig. 7 – Henry's Rifling – Cross section.

EXTRACT FROM HENRY'S PATENT

A.D. 1860, 15th November, No.2802.

RIFLED FIRE–ARMS.

LETTERS PATENT to Alexander Henry, in the County of Mid-Lothian, North Britain, Gun Maker, for the invention of "IMPROVEMENTS IN RIFLED FIRE–ARMS."

Sealed the 7th May, and dated the 15th November, 1860.

PROVISIONAL SPECIFICATION left by the said Alexander Henry, at the office of the Commissioners of Patents, with his Petition, on the 15th November, 1860.

I, ALEXANDER HENRY, . . . do hereby declare the nature of the said invention for "IMPROVEMENTS IN RIFLED FIRE–ARMS", to be as follows, that is to say –

This invention relates to the arrangement and construction of rifled fire-arms, the essential peculiarity consisting in the form of the rifled bore, which includes from four to ten planes, angles, and grooves. These surfaces may be formed or arranged in various ways, and instead of relying wholly upon acute angles, semicircular or curvilinear projections may be produced upon the interior of the

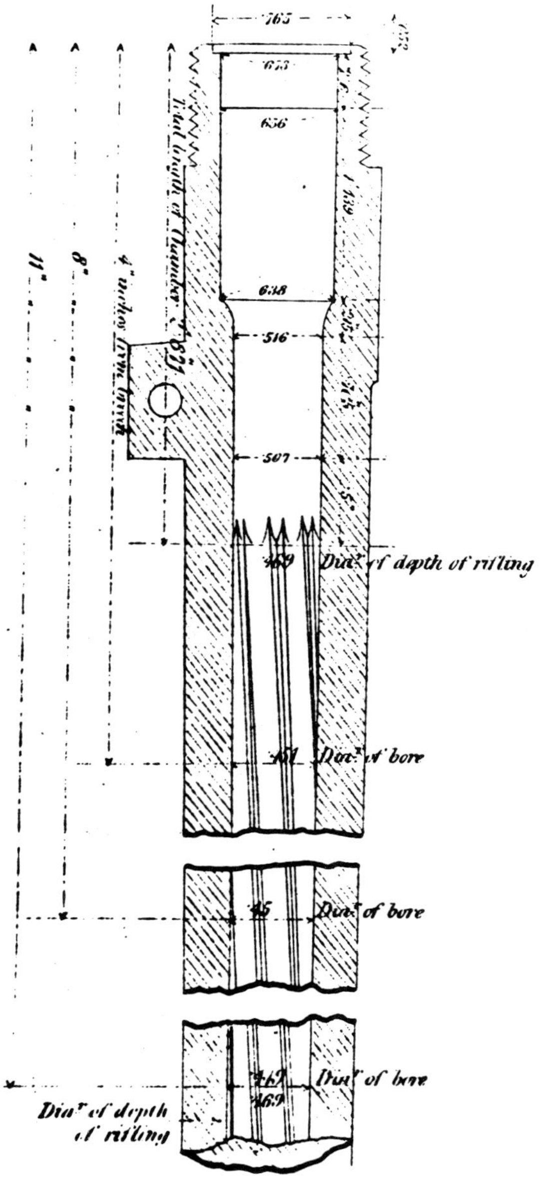

Fig. 8 – Henry's Rifling – Longitudinal section.

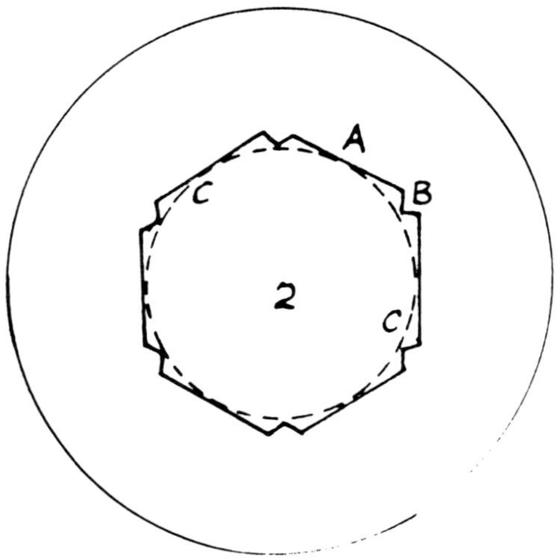

Figure 2 from Henry's Patent.

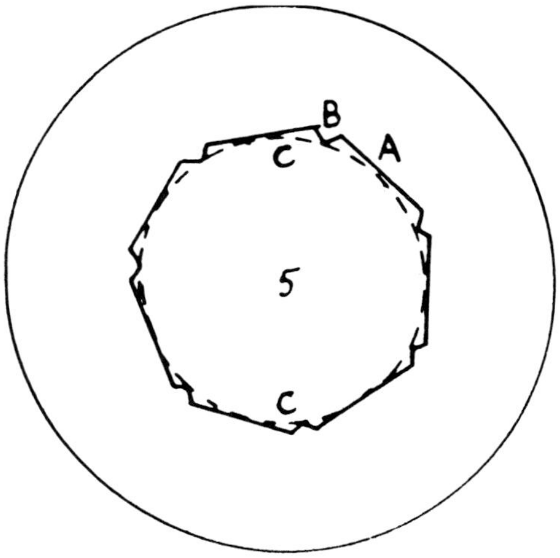

Figure 5 from Henry's Patent.

bore. In one example of the improved bore, consisting of such a combination of planes and narrow curvilinear or angular surfaces of the bore as made up of wide planes and narrow grooves admits of a plug or missile of larger size than usual, and, of course, requiring less expansion to fill the planes than one which touches the centres of the planes only, and whilst it requires less expansion there is less windage, and the planes with the grooves have more power to insure the proper rotation of the missile or ball. In other forms of bore embraced by this invention planes and internal projections, either round, square, or acute, are combined so as to afford double the number of points of bearing for the missile when in the barrel, less windage before starting it, and requiring a less amount of expansion to fill up the planes whilst there is an equal amount or more power to cause the missile to rotate.

SPECIFICATION in pursuance of the Conditions of the Letters Patent, filed by the said Alexander Henry in the Great Seal Patent Office on the 15th May, 1861.

NOW KNOW YE, that I, the said Alexander Henry, do hereby declare the nature of my said invention, and in what manner the same is to be performed, to be particularly described and ascertained in and by the following statement, reference being had to the accompanying drawings and to the letters and figures marked thereon, that is to say –

In the modification shown in Figure 2 of the accompanying drawings the number of plane surfaces A is increased to six, affording a corresponding number of bearing points to the projectile C. But there is also the bearing points obtained by the angular ridges B intervening between the planes A which fill up to a greater extent the space between the barrel and the projectile. In this way a very small amount only of expansion is required to cause the projectile to fill up the grooves of the rifling. The number of planes A in combination with the angular ridges B may be increased to twelve planes, or, indeed, to a greater number, according to the capacity or diameter of the bore of the barrel, the system of rifling being equally applicable to ordnance as to small arms.

Figure 5 is also a representation showing the rifling as composed of a seven-sided figure, with angular ridges B intervening. In this mode of rifling the projectile C very nearly fills up the whole of the bore of the barrel.

Having now described and particularly ascertained the nature of my said invention, and the manner in which the same is or may be used or carried into effect, I would observe, in conclusion, that what I consider novel and original, and therefore claim as the invention secured by me by the here-in-before in part recited Letters Patent, is the system or mode of rifling or grooving fire-arms in which a series of planes or flat surfaces are combined with angular, curved, or rectangular ridges or "lands", either intervening between the planes or intersecting the same, as here-in-before described and shown in the accompanying drawings.

In witness whereof, I, the said Alexander Henry, have hereunto set my hand and seal, this thirteenth day of May, One thousand eight hundred and sixty-one.

ALEXANDER HENRY. (L.S.)

DESCRIPTION OF THE MARTINI BREECH ACTION

The action mechanism described and illustrated here is the Mark II service pattern, as adopted in 1876 with an improved trigger mechanism. This was a reversion to Martini's original pattern, in contrast with the Mark I service rifle, which had a trigger unit designed and incorporated into Martini's breech by the RSAF.

The main difference between this action and Martini's original (described in the following section) was the squared seat on the lever axis pin for the tumbler, necessary to allow the use of the cocking indicator formed on the end of this pin. This did away with Martini's original indicator which was at the top rear of the action. See Figs.9 and 10 in conjunction with the following description.

The action consists of a body or shoe, into which is screwed the barrel, and the butt and fore-end are also attached to it. The shoe also contains the breech action, which is the mechanism for closing the breech, firing the cartridge, and extracting the empty cartridge case.

The breech is closed by a block (B), which swings on a pin (P), passing through the upper rear end of the shoe, or body, the recoil being taken by the back and sides of the body, and not by the pin. The cartridge is exploded by the striker (S), which is driven by the action of a strong spiral spring (N) within the breech block. A lever (L) in rear of the trigger guard acts by means of two horns on the breech block, so that the action of lowering the lever causes the block to fall and strike the extremity of the lower arm of the extractor (E), thus ejecting the cartridge case. With the same motion, and at the same time, the lever carries the tumbler (R) around until the trigger nose falls into the bent of the tumbler (X), and retains that component in the cocked position. The action of the lever in the above movement also draws back the striker and compresses the main spring by means of the crane (C) of the tumbler, which engages in a slot cut through the striker.

The action of the extracting lever requires special notice. It is so arranged as to give its greatest power at the commencement of the extraction, to overcome the first resistance and start the cartridge, and its greatest velocity at the end to jerk it away. Contact of the extractor arm with the falling block takes place at two alternative points; at the beginning of the extraction it acts so as to give the shortest leverage with the block and the longest with the extractor, but after the block has moved through a certain space, still continuing to bear on the extractor by the motion of the lever, the point of contact changes, so as to reverse the conditions. It is evident that when the extractor arm has become flattened, ie, lost its proper set up, the first contact does not take place, and this has been the chief cause of the alleged failures in extraction, attributed ignorantly to the cartridge.

On returning the lever to its former position, the block is raised by the horns so as to close the breech, and the mainspring is still further compressed, but the tumbler does not move; it is retained and held firmly by the trigger nose. The arm is now cocked and ready for firing.

To make the above clearer, it is as well to point out that the lever and tumbler are upon the same axis pin or spindle, which is square at the central part (A), the seat of the tumbler, and this component is incapable of rotating upon it, while the outside parts of the same pin, on which the lever works, are round, and so the lever is free to rotate on them. On lowering the lever, a projection (O) on it pushes the tumbler round until the latter engages the trigger nose, which holds it. The lever is then free to rotate on the axis pin back to its former position.

There is an indicator on the right side of the action forming part of this axis pin, which at all times shows the position of the tumbler, and whether the arm is cocked or otherwise.

On pressing the trigger to fire the arm, the trigger nose is freed from the bent of the tumbler; the striker moves forward under the action of the compressed mainspring, rotating both the tumbler and axis pin, as shown by the indicator outside, and striking the cap in the base of the cartridge.

(The above description of the operation of the Martini action is taken from official sources, such as will be noted in the various periodical books on Musketry Regulations and Treatise on Arms and Ammunition.)

MARTINI'S FIRST BRITISH PATENT

Friederich von Martini's first British patent was taken out

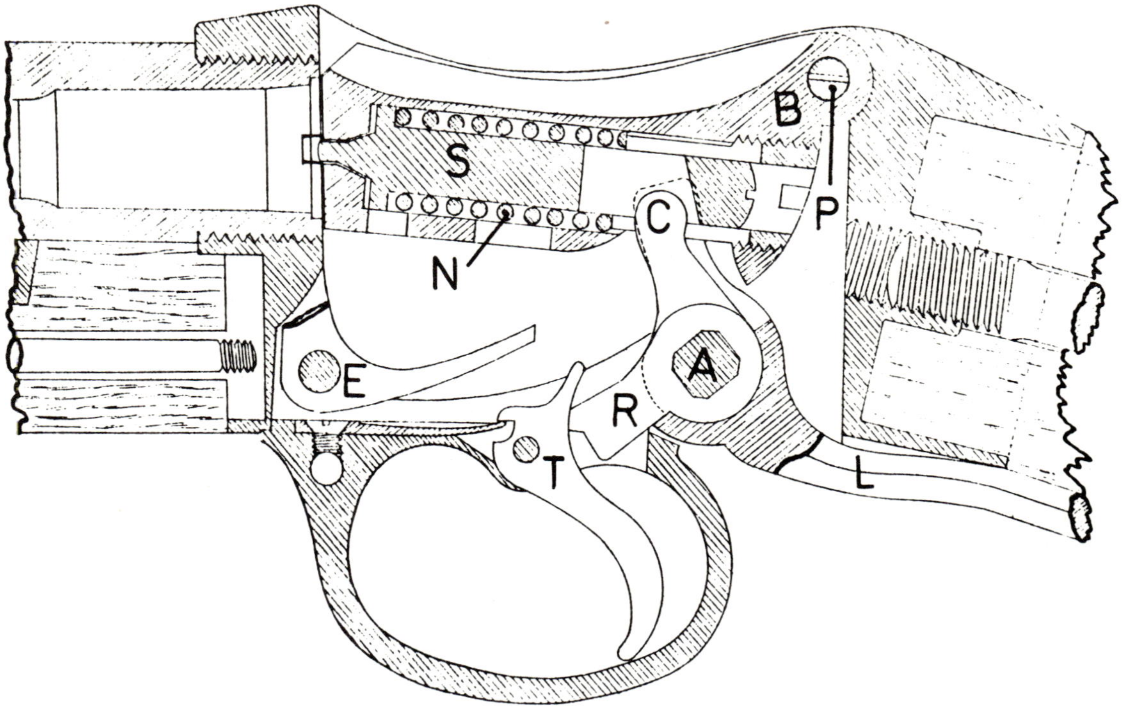

Fig. 9 – Martini Action – Closed and fired.

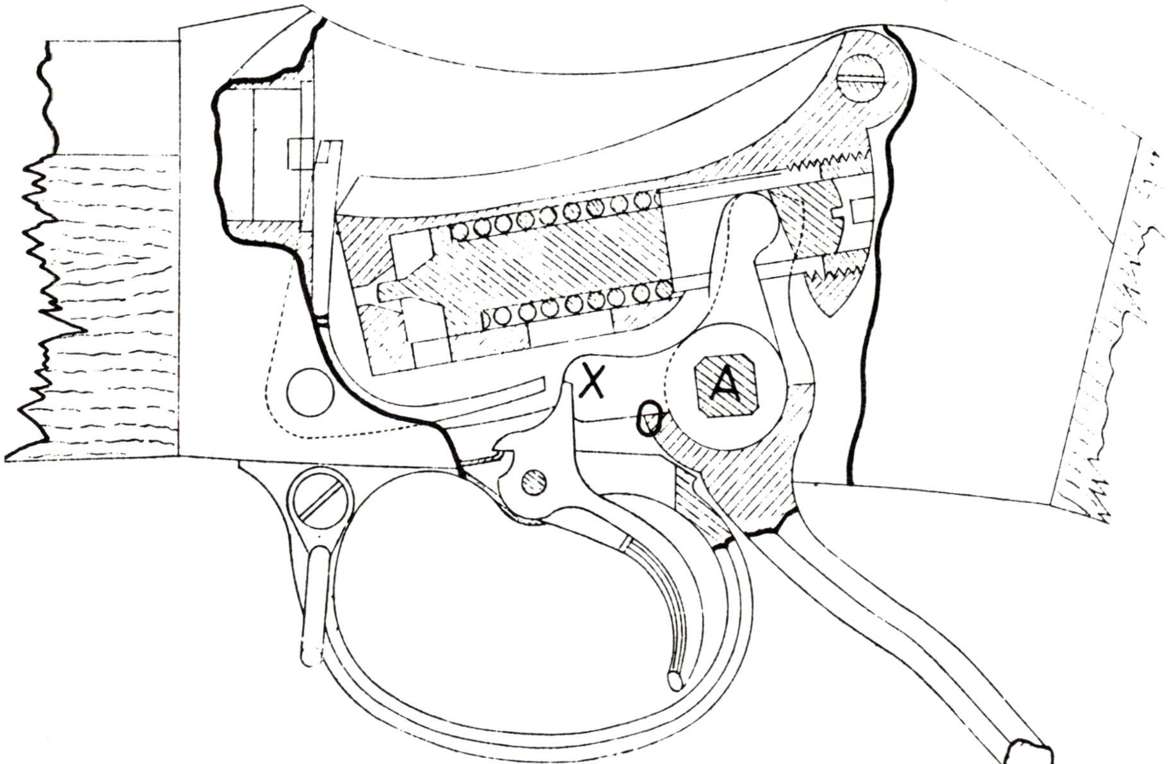

Fig. 10 – Martini Action – Open and cocked.

in 1868, presumably to give himself protection in the event, as did happen, of his action design becoming accepted for use in England. The system as described below is basically that used in his arms submitted for the prize competition and the later selection trials; alterations and improvements incorporated in the mechanism after the above trials were completed were claimed by Martini in later patents. These will be examined in a later section.

A.D. 1868, 22nd July, No.2305.

BREECH–LOADING FIRE–ARMS.

LETTERS PATENT to Clinton Edgcumbe Brooman, of the firm of Robertson, Brooman, and Company, of 166, Fleet Street, in the City of London, Patent Agents, for the invention of "IMPROVEMENTS IN BREECH–LOADING FIREARMS" – a communication from abroad by Friederich von Martini, of Frauenfeld, Switzerland.

Sealed the 1st December, 1868, and dated the 22nd July, 1868.

PROVISIONAL SPECIFICATION left by the said Clinton Edgcumbe Brooman at the office of the Commissioners of Patents, with his petition, on the 22nd July, 1868.

I, CLINTON EDGCUMBE BROOMAN . . . do hereby declare the nature of the said invention for "IMPROVEMENTS IN BREECH–LOADING FIREARMS", to be as follows –

This invention has for its object breech-loading fire-arms in which the discharge is effected by a needle or striker, and the breech bolt actuated by a lever. This arm may be constructed for exploding rim-fire and central-fire cartridges.

I proceed to describe the arm as arranged for a rim-fire cartridge. The Figure 1 is a longitudinal section of the arm with an indication in dotted lines of a second position of the lever and breech block.

A is the breech chamber which constitutes the junction between the barrel B and stock C; it consists of a rectangular metal piece in which is a parallel opening containing the moveable block D, hinged at a, *with the exploding mechanism and the extractor. The breech of the barrel is enlarged at its base to form a chamber for the cartridge. The moveable block D is raised or lowered by means of a lever E pivoting at F. The short arm L of this lever E fits into a groove formed in the block, and its extremity is rounded to permit of free movement; the block is thus supported by the lever in such a manner as to prevent all possibility of its changing its place from the force of the explosion when the arm is discharged. On the upper side of the block is a hollow which corresponds with the aperture in the barrel when it is in position for the cartridge to be placed in it. G is a lever to withdraw the discharged cartridge case; H is the exploding pin; J its spring; they are both held in position by the annular retaining screw K. The lever E is forked to receive the lever L. The longer arm of this lever L works into a groove in the exploding pin H, and the shorter arm is furnished with a projection which abuts against a stop on the lever E; it is also notched to receive the upper arm of the trigger M when it is carried back by the lever E while opening the breech, and consequently when the lever E is returned to its place and the breech closed the lever L is upheld; it again maintains the exploding pin at the same time that the spring is extended for another discharge. In causing the breech to descend by means of the lever E a shock is produced which completely removes the discharged cartridge case, the block striking against the free end of the extractor at the same time that the trigger takes into the notch in the lever L; a new cart-*

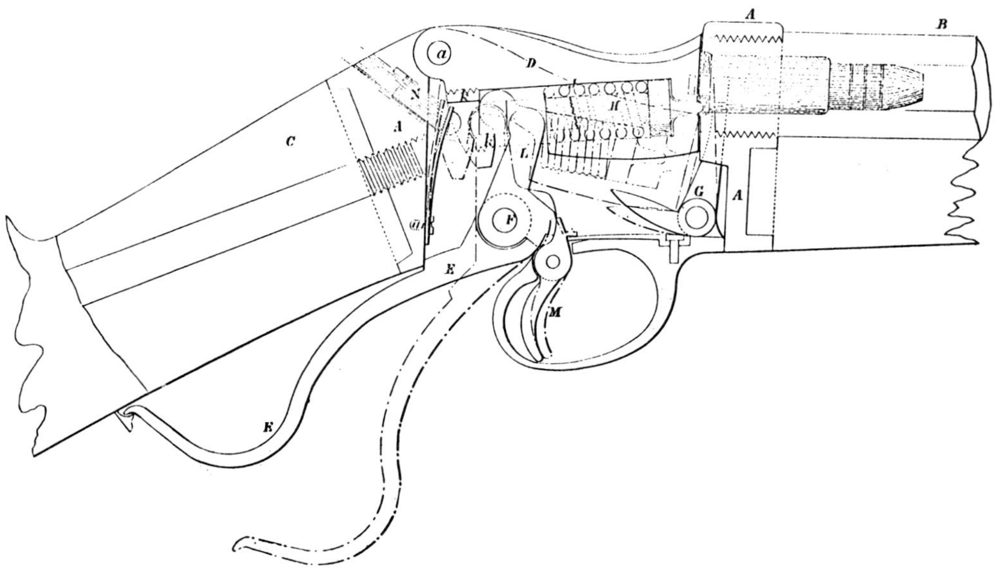

Figure 1 as referred to in Provisional Patent 2305.

ridge may then be placed in the barrel; the block is lifted by the return to place of the lever, and the arm is ready to discharge. When it is desired to uncock, the block is lowered as much as possible without however withdrawing the cartridge, the trigger is then pressed and the lever E gently returned to position. All danger is obviated in this operation in consequence of the spring of the exploding pin being free of all compression when the block is down. There is also no danger if the trigger be pressed when the breech is open, as the block rises by itself by the setting free of the exploding pin. If the arm is loaded, but uncocked, it can be cocked by moving the lever E sufficiently to withdraw the trigger from its notch and then return the lever E to its place. In order to know whether the arm is cocked or not an indicating pin N is fitted in the end of the breech chamber, which projects therefrom when the arm is cocked, and lies flush when it is discharged. A blow on this pin can never cause the arm to go off. If after the discharge has been made the cartridge case does not readily come away at the first opening of the breech it usually suffices to repeat the movement rapidly, but without pressing the trigger. If it still remains recourse must be had to the ramrod. The construction of this arm differs in many important respects from others similar to it. All the exploding apparatus is comprised in a simple pin placed in the breech. The moveable breech during the discharge is maintained in place by the lever E only, without the intervention of springs, clutches, or catches, and the short arm is so disposed that it is impossible for the block to be displaced by the force of the explosion. The exploding pin strikes against the lowest point of the rim (in rim-fire cartridges) so that it is impossible for the arm to go off until the block is in place, for it is only when the block is in position that the pin can strike the cartridge. The extractor is placed by the side of the cartridge and not above it; it bears against the breech case and forms a support for the edge of the cartridge. The spring of the exploding pin cannot have its elasticity altered, as it is submitted to a very slight pressure, and in case of breakage it can be easily and cheaply replaced. This arm unites great simplicity of construction with ease of repair, it is very durable, and little liable to damage even in the most awkward hands.

SPECIFICATION in pursuance of the Conditions of the Letters Patent, filed by the said Clinton Edgcumbe Brooman at the Great Seal Patent Office on the 22nd January, 1869.

NOW KNOW YE, that I, the said Clinton Edgcumbe Brooman, do hereby declare the nature of the said invention, and in what manner the same is to be performed to be particularly described and ascertained in and by the following statement thereof, reference being had to the drawings hereunto annexed, that is to say –

This invention relates to breech-loading fire-arms of that class in which the breech end of the barrel is closed by a block whose rear end works on a horizontal pin having its axis at right angles to the axis of the bore of the barrel, and consists in a peculiar combination of mechanism whereby the arm is made stronger, more easy to operate, simpler in construction, and more economical to manufacture than other fire-arms of its class.

Figures 1, 2, and 3 are longitudinal vertical sections of the breech portion of this improved breech-loading rifle or fire-arm. Figure 1 shews the arrangement and position of the mechanism for "rim-firing", Figure 2 for "central-firing", and Figure 3 shews the position of the breech mechanism for inserting the cartridge; Figure 4 is a transverse section of the breech mechanism through the plane x,y of Figure 2.

A is the breech frame into which is screwed the barrel B, the rear end of which is enlarged to receive the cartridge which may be of any desired shape. The barrel B is fixed to the fore part of the stock C in any ordinary manner, the "butt" end of the stock C being by preference secured to the breech frame by the screw S; D is the breech block whose upper surface is hollowed to facilitate the insertion of the cartridge into the barrel, and in the rear upper part of the block is a hinge pin on which it works. The breech block D contains the firing mechanism, which is the same (excepting as to position) for rim-fire and for central-fire, and consists of the exploding pin H, spiral spring J, tubular screw K, and tumbler lever L. The tumbler lever L at its upper end is of a circular form in one view with straight sides and takes into a mortice cut through the exploding pin H. The lower part or fulcrum of the tumbler lever L works freely upon the pin F. The exploding pin H has a rear support or bearing in the tubular screw K which is slotted to admit the tumbler L and is an abutment for the spiral spring J. The tumbler lever L has a short arm l1 provided with a ratchet tooth for the purpose of receiving the upper end of the trigger lever M which is pressed therein when in a suitable position by the spring. Below this tooth and on the same short arm is a face of metal l11 which forms an abutment for a corresponding face on the hand lever E. The trigger may be locked in position when the piece is cocked by means of a bolt inserted under the projection m11, or by any other well-known device, so as to prevent the possibility of accidental or other discharge till the said bolt is withdrawn. The hand lever E has its fulcrum F behind the trigger, and is a forked lever, that is to say, consists of a long arm to which the hand is applied and two short arms E1, E11, each of which takes into a cam recess formed in its own side of the breech block D. The form of the two recesses is the same, and is shewn dotted in Figures 1, 2, and 3; they are of irregular shape and so formed that the breech block is lowered, raised, and retained or locked by the hand lever E in the proper positions for loading and firing the piece. At N, Figures 1, 2, and 3, is shewn the indicating pin which passes obliquely upwards through the breech frame A, with whose upper surface the upper end of the pin N coincides, excepting when the exploding pin is drawn back ready for firing, in which latter position its rear end comes in contact with the front end of the pin N, thus causing its upper end to protrude above the surface of the breech frame A so as to indicate that the piece has not been discharged. G is a bell crank lever for expelling the cartridge case, and is forked at its upper end G1 so as to embrace the opposite sides of the cartridge base. The short arm G11 is at a right angle or near-

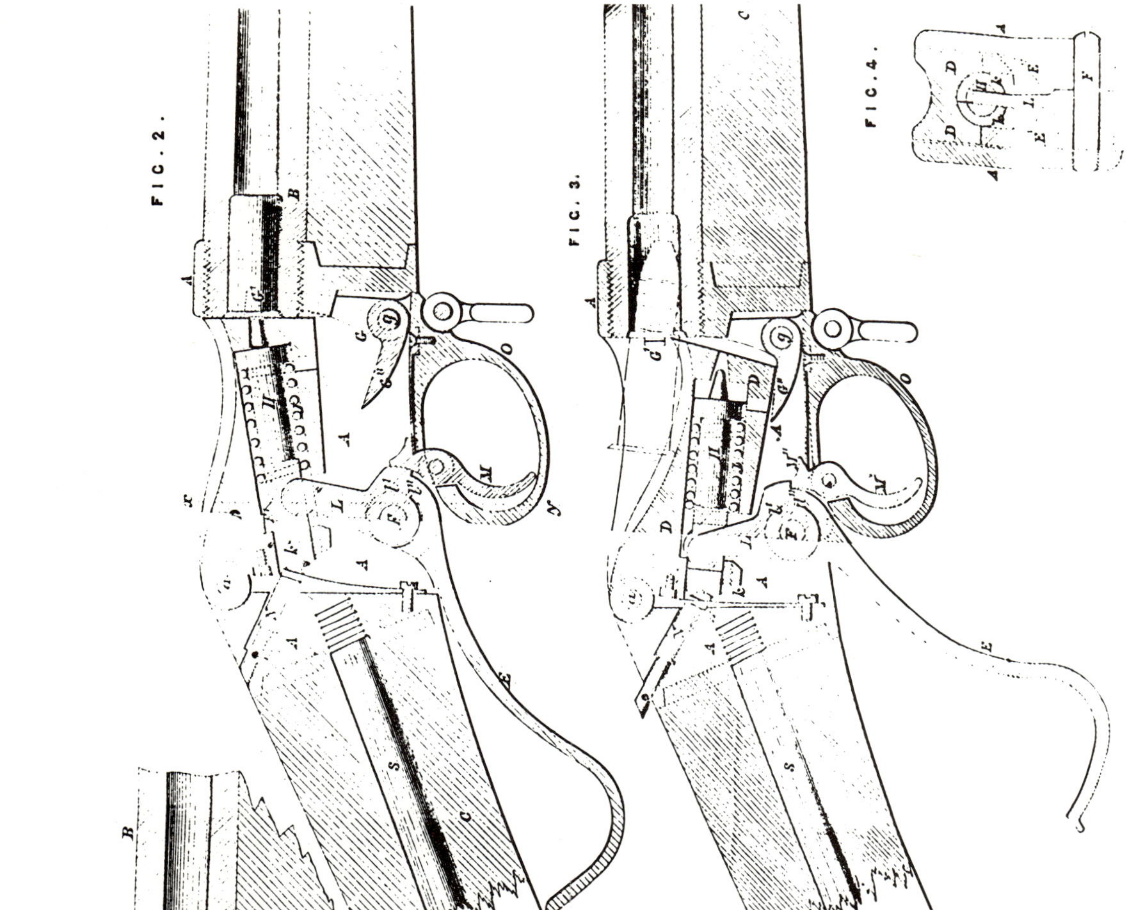

Figures 1, 2, 3, and 4 from Martini's Patent 2305.

ly so with the long arm G1, and its upper surface radiates from the fulcrum pin g. In descending the breech block D comes at first in contact with the extreme end of the short arm G11 of the bell crank lever, and causes it to turn slowly on its fulcrum pin g so as to loosen the cartridge case from the barrel, and the continued downward movement of the breech block brings its extreme end against that part of the arm G11 which is nearest to the fulcrum pin g of the bell crank lever G, thereby accelerating the speed of the lever and suddenly expelling the cartridge case. The trigger M is provided for safety with a fixed guard O as in ordinary fire-arms, such guard being fixed to the breech frame.

Having now explained the details of the mechanism of this invention in breech-loading fire-arms I will proceed to describe the operation of the same. Referring to Figure 2 it will be seen that the breech-loading mechanism is in that position which obtains when the piece has been discharged. To open the breech for a fresh cartridge the hand lever E is depressed, thus causing the upper end of the tumbler lever L to move in the direction of the rear of the arm, and to carry the exploding pin H and spring J with it until the ratchet tooth of the short arm I1 receives the upper end of the trigger lever M, as shewn in Figure 3. Simultaneously with this withdrawal of the firing mechanism from the position shewn in Figure 2 to that shewn in Figure 3 the breech block is caused to descend by the forked end E1, E11 of the hand lever E acting in the cam recesses shewn in dotted lines as before described. The parts are now in position for the insertion of the cartridge. The piece having been loaded the lever E is then to be returned to its position against the under part of the stock, which operation will cause the block to be moved upward into the position for firing, leaving the tumbler lever, exploding pin, and spring still held back by the short arm of the trigger lever. After the lever E has been returned to the position in which it is shewn in Figure 2, then on the trigger being pulled so as to release the tumbler lever L and spring the exploding pin H will be forced forward by the spring J until it strikes the cartridge so as to explode it.

And having now described the nature of the said invention, and in what manner the same is to be performed, I declare that I claim, the combination forming a breech-loading action either for rim-fire or central-fire cartridges in which the entire series of operations for opening and closing the breech, releasing and expelling the cartridge, and cocking the gun are performed by the hand of the operator on one lever, this lever being so arranged as to keep the breech block in firing position, all substantially as herein described and illustrated.

In witness whereof, I, the said Clinton Edgcumbe Brooman, have hereunto set my hand and seal, this twenty-second day of January, One thousand eight hundred and sixty-nine.

C.E. BROOMAN. (L.S.)

MARTINI Vs PEABODY

For much of its early existence (and in some instances even nowadays) the Martini breech action was given by some persons the appellation "Peabody-Martini". This was a reference to an American design of falling block rifle action which the original Martini action generally resembled. At the time neither party was overly concerned about the resemblance, as, on the first occasion the two systems were placed in direct competition the Peabody was the successful contender. That was in 1866, and the Peabody Patent owners won a contract to supply arms to the Swiss government.

Martini then proceeded to institute some major alterations into his action, including abolishing the outside lock by incorporating all the mechanism inside the action body. This new system was basically the one he presented to the Select Committee for consideration in the Prize Competition of 1867.

(The Peabody breech action of this era is shown in section in Fig.11, and this should be compared with Figs.9 and 10 to give an impression of the considerable differences between the two systems.)

When it became apparent that the Martini action was certain to be the chosen system, Peabody's agents began to attack Martini, claiming the action as their design, and demanding recognition – financial and otherwise. The following letters, printed in a prominent English technical journal are indicative of some of the acrimony that took place, albeit onesidedly, as Martini deigned to reply only once, which apparently was enough in his opinion. From *The Engineer*, 11-6-1869 –

THE MARTINI BREED.

Sir, in support of my statements which appeared in your columns denouncing the so-called "Martini" as an infringement upon the "Peabody" breech-loader, I cannot adduce better evidence than that of Mr. Martini himself, whose words I quote from a legal document, a translated copy of which is annexed, drawn up and signed by himself in 1866. He there mentions "my invention consisting in an improvement of the Peabody breech-loading system", and further on he speaks of "my Peabody gun".

After such crushing evidence I think the question of the want of originality of the so-called "Martini" is clearly established, and also its "Peabody" parentage.

H. Geilgud,
Agent, Providence Tool Company's Armoury,
3, George-Yard, Lombard Street, London, EC.
June 3rd, 1869.

DECLARATION.

I, the undersigned, Friederich Chevalier de Martini, of Frauenfeld, in Switzerland, do hereby oblige myself to cede and transfer to Messrs. James R. McDonald and Co., of Hamburg, my invention consisting in an improvement of the Peabody breech-loading system, together with my future improvements of this system; also all business transactions closed with respect to this system within three months from this date, say up to 23rd February, 1867, to be their exclusive and lawful property, on consideration that they pay to me between now and 23rd February next year, 1867, the sum of . . . payable to me at Frauenfeld in Switzerland.

Should Messrs. James R.McDonald and Co. not pay to my hands the above-mentioned amount of consideration in full within the terms specified, from any reason whatsoever, I shall be entirely free from all obligations which I have now taken upon myself, and this present document will then become null and void. On payment, however, of the above-mentioned amount of consideration in full and within the time specified I will oblige myself to execute and deliver to Messrs. James R. McDonald and Co., all documents required for a transfer to them in due form of law of

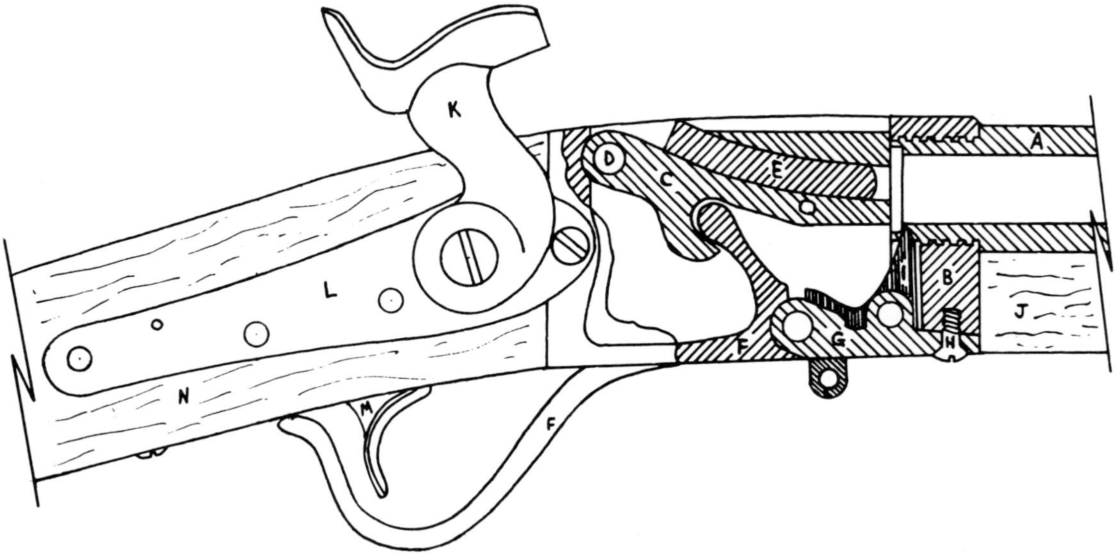

Fig. 11 – Peabody Breech Action. B.A.T.

Parts shown –

A: Barrel	**G: Action floor plate**
B: Action body	**H: Floor plate screw**
C: Breech block	**I: Extractor**
D: Breech block axis pin	**J: Fore-end**
E: Striker	**K: Hammer**
F: Lever	**L: Lock plate.**

my Peabody breech-loading system and of all business transactions closed with respect to the same within three months of this date.

Vienna, 23rd November, 1866. *(Sgd.) Fr. Martini.*

Duly witnessed, &c.

To which Martini replied (from *The Engineer*, 25-6-1869)

THE MARTINI BREECH ACTION.

Vienna, June 18th, 1869.

Dear Sir, owing to my absence from home, your letter, enclosing slip of The Engineer of 11th inst., has only just reached me. I have not now the original of the document published by Mr. Gielgud before me, but, from my recollection, I see no reason to doubt the substantial accuracy of the English translation, except as regards the important omission of the purchase money stipulated to be paid by the owners of the Peabody rifle for my invention.

The facts of the case are, briefly, these – my earliest model of a breech-action was constructed, like the "Peabody" upon the principle of a falling block. It had the ordinary side lock, but was self-cocking. This original model was presented, alongside with the Peabody, to the Swiss Ordnance Committee, sitting in Aarau in 1866. From its outward resemblance to the Peabody, although with essential differences in the combination, it was by many persons christened the "Martini-Peabody". I made no objection to this appellation, as the Peabody was up to that time the best known and most successful application of the falling block system. Moreover, the Peabody Company being able to fill an immediate order, which I was not then prepared to do, had been successful in obtaining one of some importance from the Swiss Government. That system is, however, neither peculiar to the Peabody rifle, nor is Mr. Peabody its inventor.

Among the numerous foreign officers present at Aarau was an Austrian, who requested me to make him a "Martini-Peabody" rifle, which he invited me to present in person in Vienna. In the meanwhile, further experiments induced me to change my ideas in very important particulars, and, in lieu of the pattern that had been ordered, I took to Vienna a model of the breech action which has always been known by my name alone, and the mechanical principles of which remain unchanged by my subsequent modifications of details. It was while in Vienna that Mr. Peabody's agent offered to buy my invention for the sum of 150,000F. – say, £ 6,000 – payable in three months. I believed the proposal to be a bona-fide one, and deemed the terms fair. The name was, under the circumstances, a matter of indifference to me, and the Peabody Company being themselves the purchasers, I suspected no after-thought in the use of the word "Peabody" as a generic term for falling block systems. The provisional transfer which I signed was, by its own wording, to become null and void in the case, which did occur, of the Peabody Company not carrying out their part of the contract.

I may not have been sufficiently careful as to the terms in which this document was drawn up, but I confess that I fail to see how it can be construed into a title on the part of the Peabody Company to a property which they then offered to buy for £6,000. If the document proves anything, it proves that these gentlemen distinctly recognised my undeniable title to a property for which they offered a valuable consideration.

If the owners of the Peabody Patent believe that the combination of parts which the Martini breech has, in common with theirs as it has with many others, infringes any rights of theirs, they could not have been at a loss to find the proper and obvious way of testing the question. During the two and a half years that have elapsed since the abortive Vienna negotiations, my rifle has been before the public, and numerous samples of it in constant use. It was in open competition with theirs throughout the exhaustive enquiry of the Select Committee, and the reports of the latter show that as many as five modifications of the Peabody rifle were opposed to the single model of mine. It is singular, to say the least, that the pretensions now set up were left to slumber so long, and that, instead of putting them in a tangible form, and submitting them to the decision of a competent authority, it should be preferred – without even applying to me – to prejudice public opinion by ex-parte statements and generalities in the newspapers.

You are at liberty to make such use of this letter as you think proper, although I feel bound to reiterate my firm conviction that a newspaper war does not appear to me to promise a satisfactory solution of the technical issues of a patent controversy, and I find it difficult to treat as serious claims which are put forward in that way.

Fr. Martini.

MARTINI Vs OTHERS

The Peabody patent owners were not the only detractors of Martini's system, as other inventors who had their designs rejected also reacted in an uncomplimentary manner, against both the Select Committee and Martini's breech design. The following extract from *Engineering* of 13-3-1869 mentions this, but also defends Martini against the accusations, so he did not always stand alone in defence of his invention.

THE MARTINI–HENRY RIFLE.

In recommending this new arm for introduction into the service, the committee close a long and tedious task, rendered more wearisome by the jealousies and accusations of unfairness which have been liberally made against them by disappointed competitors, and they have shown a sound judgement in the selection of a weapon which combines the qualities which they set themselves to seek. The Martini mechanism has been of course modified and greatly improved since it was first submitted to the committee; and although it of necessity has something in common with other breech-loading mechanisms of its class, it is so far superior to all others in compactness and simplicity, that no accusations of plagarism can be fairly attributed to Mr. Martini, who, while starting from the general principle of all falling block mechanisms, has shown an almost complete originality in working out the details.

The above refers to the first recommendation by the committee for adoption of the Martini after the second round of selection trials had been completed. The long chamber Martinis were then made and sent on extended troop trials, to gain experience of service use before making the final recommendation on its future. The field trials proved satisfactory, and the arm was completely recommended for service use.

Towards the end of the trials programme of the long chamber rifles the committee decided to submit the Martini action to some prominent mechanical engineers for an unbiased report of its mechanical characteristics and other relevant features. This step was ostensibly taken as a part of the test programme, but it was obviously also intended to silence those critics of the system who still persisted in denigrating the committee and the action.

The persons chosen for the examination were –

James Nasmyth, Esq., CE
Dr. Pole, CE, FRS
Edward Woods, Esq., CE
Col. Dixon, Supt. RSAF
Mr. Davidson, Manager RL
Mr. Perry of the RSAF
Mr. Martini.

The committee planned the examinations as below –

Programme for the Examination of Witnesses on the Character of the Mechanical Construction of the Martini-Henry Rifle.

The witnesses will be requested to direct their attention to the machanical arrangements of the breech-action and working of the rifle, and to state their opinions on the following points, viz. –

A. On the facility and economy of manufacture of the breech-action, in its various parts, having preference not to small supplies of hand-made arms, but to large supplies produced by machinery, at the government small arms factory, or at high-class private manufacturers, under proper supervision.

B. On the simplicity and efficiency of the breech-action generally, and of its fitness, as a whole, if introduced in rifles manufactured as above stated, to do its work in all instances with safety and regularity.

C. On the mechanical character of the various parts, viz. –

1. Of the falling block, and its power to resist the explosion of the charge without undue strain to any of the joints; and at what point or points the recoil would be transferred through the back part of the falling block.

2. Of the spiral spring and the striker, and if when combined and worked as proposed they are calculated to give an adequate and uniform blow to the detonating cap, without damage to the striker or liability in the spring to fracture or loss of power by use.

3. Of the working lever, whether it is properly placed, and if it has adequate power for its duty of lowering and raising the block, cocking the rifle as the block falls and rises, and working the extractor as the block falls, and keeping the block up to its place when firing; and whether this lever is likely to continue to do its work properly.

4. Of the centre pin upon which the lever works, and at the same time the tumbler and indicator, whether such combined use of the one pin is desirable in the view of simplicity, efficiency, and permanence, and whether the accuracy of the indicator is permanently reliable.

5. Of the tumbler, sear, and trigger, whether in their combined action they are safe and strong, and capable of proper adjustment of their bearing surfaces, to such an amount of uniform and steady pull, whether large or small, as it may be desired to give, and whether they may be expected to retain such uniform and steady pull in use.

6. Of the safety bolt, as to its simplicity, efficiency, and permanence.

7. Of the cartridge extractor, and whether by its form and the way in which it is acted upon by the falling block, it is calculated to do its work properly and permanently.

8. Of the arrangement of all the parts of the breech-action within a closed metal case, and whether such an arrangement is desirable or otherwise, having reference to compactness, strength, and protection from dust and wet.

9. Of the strength and permanence of the mode of stocking.

D. On the measure of importance of any defects which may be considered to exist, the way in which they would show themselves and after how many rounds, the facility of repair if repair should become necessary by reason of such defects, to what extent any such defects if theoretically assignable would be likely to show themselves in rifles equal in character of work to the present government rifles, well made and properly tested and inspected, how far any such defects may be inherent in the Martini action, and inseparable from it, or capable of correction without material change of design, by the fair substitution of some simple and well known form of detail.

The above programme was drawn up on 3-12-1870, and the reports of the respective engineers are given in Appendix 9. On the results of the mechanical examination *The Engineer* had this to say –

THE MARTINI–HENRY RIFLE.

The three engineers, Messrs. Woods, Pole, and Nasmyth who were called in by the government to give an opinion on the Martini-Henry mechanism, have reported favourably. They are of the opinion that to go to the flat spring for a direct action would be a retrograde step, and at least one of them has proved mathematically that a spiral spring really strikes a smarter blow than a flat spring. This disposes of the chief objection which opponents to the system have raised, but the engineers also speak well of the divided stock, which they maintain is stronger than the old form. Altogether they commend the action from a mechanical point of view. The report of this committee is now ready.

The antagonists of the action were still not satisfied, and mounted a final offensive in April of 1871, with separate attacks as outlined below.

At a meeting of the Birmingham Gun Makers' and Inventors' Club, Mr. B. Burton read a paper in which the Martini-Henry rifle was compared with rifles on the bolt system, and the following summary of the paper was presented in *The Engineer*, viz. –

From the late debate in the House of Commons arising out of Col. Barttelot's motion upon the Martini-Henry rifle, we may come to the conclusion that the above weapon is adopted for better or worse. When the government appointed the Small Arms Committee I believe the latter set about its task with a disposition to conduct the trials fairly and without undue favour. But this fairness seems to have vanished at an early stage of their proceedings. As soon as they committed themselves by selecting the Martini as the best of the arms submitted to them, so long ago as 1867, they appear no longer to have exercised their functions judicially. They became strong partisans and special pleaders for the arm of their choice, and ever after gave the cold shoulder to every invention brought before them. Their whole attention appears to have been given to patching up and remedying the very serious defects of the favourite firearm – defects which being totally ignorant of the construction of arms, they had in the first instance very naturally overlooked. They found that the gun was unsafe, liable to misfire, and very uncertain in its shooting, owing to the pull of the trigger varying from a few ounces to 25 lb. These they pooh-poohed as minor defects, and thought they could themselves easily remedy them, having at their command the best gun factory in the world, with its skilled workmen, only too anxious to do the work, and to let them have all the credit of the same. But they should have borne in mind that if an inventor, who knows all the points of his gun better than any other man, is not able to correct its defects, these are very likely to be irremediable, and inherent in the gun itself. This they soon found to be true of the Martini when they set to work on it at Enfield. With all the resources of Woolwich and Enfield at their command, the committee have succeeded in remedying one evil of the gun, the uncertainty of fire, but, in so doing they have aggravated another. With all the ingenious dodges of the Enfield artisans, the pull of the trigger in the Martini, on which entirely depends the accurate shooting of the gun, is worse than in any other existing arm, and will ever remain so. Nor is the safety of the arm now any greater. The report of the late committee records, in the first table it gives, no less than four serious accidents. The same report shows that, even in the short time the arm has been in service, the stocks have become loose, and if this has taken place in hand-made guns, it is far more likely to occur in machined ones. A further examination of the report will show that the internal parts are completely eaten up with rust, unless the arm is cleaned every time it is used.

Then there is great difficulty in putting the various parts together in the Martini, in which respects it contrasts more unfavourably with a bolt gun, which contains only about half the number of details. It is not every armourer-

serjeant who can manipulate this one. A common soldier can dismount and remount a bolt gun, even in the field, scarcely requiring a single tool for the purpose. The bolt gun will use any of the usual forms and dimensions of cartridge. It is well known that the Martini will work well with the "Boxer" only, a cartridge which must sooner or later be given up, as being far inferior to the solid metal cartridge now coming into general use, in spite of the one-sided report of the committee. Even the best form of Boxer cannot be conveniently used in the Martini, so recourse is had to the bottle-shaped, which not only weakens the barrel where strength is most wanted, but which must also increase the strain in the gun, add to the recoil, and injure the shooting; all experiments notwithstanding, which, with the committee, appear to have but one object – to support foregone conclusions.

Then in facility of manufacture, the bolt gun has immensely the advantage. The 200 Martinis made at Enfield cost nearly £15 each; the same number of bolt guns, of new pattern, can be made, and have been made, in Birmingham for £3 each. This tells its own story. Of course it is not meant to assert that this large disproportion will always exist, but there will always be a large margin in favour of the bolt gun, and when it comes to one million stand of arms (the number required for the British army) a difference in cost of £1 per arm only will make a tolerable figure. But this is not the worst. In case of emergency, the one gun can be made in any common machine shop, the Martini can only be made by the most skilled gunmakers, requiring special plant and tools, and most careful adjustment of parts. The Chassepot is a comparatively easy gun to make, and yet the French were put to their wits' end to get a supply of them during the late war, and before 300,000 Martinis could be turned out this country might be overrun from one end to the other. I might go on to show that there are several bolt guns now made that have all the advantages and none of the faults of the Martini, but this would necessitate the mention of particular guns, which might be thought invidious. Some of these may be known to the late committee, many are assuredly not, for what can they know of the hundreds of breech-loaders that have been invented during the last four years. Have they ever given them a chance? It is true that a few individuals have submitted arms during that period, notably those who had friends in the committee or influence elsewhere. But I assert, with a tolerable amount of knowledge of inventors and inventions, that there are scores of arms which have never come under the eye of the committee or the government, all of which are of newer date than the virtual adoption of the Martini, and many of which I know to be better arms. If the needlessly-hurried adoption of the Martini in this country is not to be attended with disastrous results, it will not be from any wisdom on the part of the government, who, to save themselves the bore of a little worry and controversy, are about to ignore all the inventions of the last four years.

The article further stated –

An animated discussion took place on the paper, some of the members considered that the writer had overestimated some of the defects of the Martini arm, particularly the defective stocking, which, it was thought, might be remedied; but it was agreed, on all hands that the bad and uncertain pull of the trigger was a defect inseparably connected with the principle, which it was not within the resources of the gunmaker's art to overcome. The liability of all the internal parts, with the exception, perhaps, of the spring and striker, which are, to some extent protected by the block, to be eaten away, and finally rendered unserviceable by rust was also remarked upon, as they are exposed to any gas escaping from the cap, or cartridge, to a damp atmosphere, and even to rain water.

The above dissertation was obviously in favour of the bolt action breech system, but a champion of the Westley Richards block action rifle appeared in the person of a Mr. W.P. Marshall, who had previously presented a paper (19-9-1870) in the Mechanical Section of the British Association at Liverpool on *"the Martini-Henry rifle, with the object of comparing it with that of Mr. Westley Richards"*; and who read yet another paper titled *"On the Principal Construction of Breech-Loading Mechanisms for Small Arms, and their relative mechanical advantages; illustrated by specimens of Breech-Loading rifles"* to the Institution of Mechanical Engineers on 27-4-1871. (See Appendixes 10 and 11 for details of these papers.)

These persistent polemics caused a debate in the House of Commons on the subject on 28-4-1871, but on a censure motion the outcome was a vote of 137 to 72 in favour of the committee's recommendations and report of the efficiency of the Martini-Henry rifle.

Engineering of 5-5-1871 commented as follows –

THE MARTINI–HENRY RIFLE.

The paper read on the 27th ult., at the general meeting of the Institution of Mechanical Engineers, upon breech-loading rifles, and the debate in the House of Commons the following evening upon the same subject, were evidence of the concerted endeavours of a somewhat strong party to induce the government to postpone the construction on a large scale of the Martini-Henry rifle until it had been still further reported upon in conjunction with other small arms, by a committee appointed for that purpose. . .

The opponents of the Martini-Henry rifle, and the advocates of other systems, have been, however, singularly unfortunate in their demonstration. They waited until the labours of four or five years had been finally deliberated and reported upon, until the necessary alterations at the Enfield factory had been ordered, and until the official determination had been made known for the wholesale manufacture of these weapons. Then the opponents to the measure make a final effort to postpone, for an indefinite period, the manufacture of the new arm. Why the advocates of systems other than that of the Martini-Henry chose such an unsuitable time for advancing their opinions, is not clear, but it is clear that a season so unpromising of success to their motion could scarcely have been selected. . .

The opponents of the Martini-Henry rifle, whether in the House of Commons, in the Institution of Mechanical Engineers, or in the columns of the press, are fortunately only wasting their time. It would have been a real calamity to the nation had their council prevailed, and a new delay permitted, while the weaknesses of the arm were being hunted after, and new classes tried. In fact, it would have been the story of the Special Committee over again, with another three years' work before them, the possible substitution of the Martini-Henry for a new system, and eventually a repetition of last Friday's business on the part of advocates of some other rifle, which gave promise of another advance. To suppose that the Martini-Henry is the best weapon that can ever be produced, is to assume a finality of invention and an end to progress; nay, we might admit for argument's sake, that it is possible that there exists at present a better arm than the one just finally adopted. But the line must be drawn somewhere, and having obtained a better rifle for arming our troops than any other nation possesses, we must rest satisfied. The time will come when the Martini-Henry shall be as antiquated as Brown Bess, but if we had followed the advice of the special pleaders of the period, that same venerable matron would still have been in the hands of our army, whilst committee after committee were expending their energy in overtaking the ignis fatuus *of the "best arm" which ever eluded their grasp, as it skimmed along before them upon the wings of progress.*

LYING DOWN POSITION.—PRESENT.

CHAPTER 5.

CONSIDERATION OF THE REPORT OF THE COMMITTEE ON SMALL–ARMS

THE previously mentioned report of the Special Committee on Breech-Loading Rifles, dated 11-2-1869, was presented to both Houses of the British Parliament, by command of Queen Victoria, to inform members of the progress made in the selection of the breech-loading rifle for the British service.

It was then submitted for the consideration of the CoO, which was assembled at the WO at noon, 23-3-1869.

The report was then examined on the following points —

1. Shall the report of the Committee on Small-Arms, dated 11-2-1869, be adopted?

2. Shall further experiments be made with the arm recommended for adoption, or any other?

3. If so, what shall be the nature of the further trials?

4. Shall further trial be restricted to a small number of hand made arms, or enough of the machinery at Enfield be altered to turn out a considerable number of interchangeable arms?

5. Is it expedient to invite either Mr. Henry or M. Martini to overlook the preparation of the first supply?

6. Is this the proper moment to consider the reward of the successful competitors?

As an appendix to the report, Lt.-Col. Fletcher wrote the following letter to the DGO, in order to appraise him of several points of interest not covered by the report (This is the Letter "A" referred to in Chapter 7).

Director-General of Ordnance Office,
Royal Arsenal, Woolwich, SE.
Sir, *18th February, 1869.*

1. During the long trials of the Martini-Henry, and other breech-loading arms the committee have had the opportunity of forming their opinion on several details, which, although not absolutely within the duties prescribed to them by the authority under which they have been acting, yet seem of sufficient importance to warrant their being brought to the notice of the SoS for War.

2. With respect to the rifling of the Martini-Henry barrel, the committee, as will be seen by reference to their report, consider this system of rifling to be more durable than the Enfield system, but to protect the rifling during the process of cleaning, it is recommended that a small muzzle protector, to be used when cleaning the arm, should be served out to the troops, also that a muzzle-stopper be issued, to prevent rain from entering the barrel.

3. With respect to the breech action, the committee desire to point out that although they believe the breech action of the Martini-Henry will withstand as well as any other the wear and tear of service, and is certainly stronger than that of the Snider, yet that incessant and continued opening and closing of the action for the purposes of drill, should be avoided. The drill and platoon exercise of breech-loading arms is so simple, that when once learnt, it can be kept up by means of imitating the motions of loading, instead of by continual opening and closing the breech block.

4. With reference to the Martini-Henry arm manufactured at Enfield, Col. Dixon has proposed and submitted an arm with a hole in the butt, capable of containing a jag and muzzle protector, etc. This pattern the committee approve of.

5. In regard to the safety bolt of the new arm, which does not form part of the system but has been supplemented, the committee desire to point out that it was recommended by them on the supposition that, under some circumstances, it might possibly be advisable to carry arms loaded, but they would venture to suggest that these circumstances could but very rarely occur with an arm of which the loading is so quick as that of the Martini-Henry, and that the order to unload and ease springs should follow the order to cease firing.

6. With regard to easing the spring and so letting free the piston, the committee recommend that to avoid the risk of a cartridge having been inadvertently left in the barrel the breech block should be first opened, thereby necessarily ejecting the cartridge, and the spring should be eased by pulling the trigger with the block open.

7. With regard to the carriage of ammunition, the committee would point out that, owing to the difference in the shape of the cartridges of the Martini-Henry rifle and those of the Snider, a change will have to be made in the construction of the pouches which should be so arranged as to facilitate loading.

8. In the event of the arm recommended by the committee being either served out to different regiments for trial, or being adopted into the service, the committee would suggest that copies of their report should be sent to the different regiments receiving the arms, and that the musketry instructors and armourers of these regiments should be fully instructed in the construction and manipulation of the several parts of the arm.

H. C. Fletcher,
Captain & Lt.-Colonel,
Scots Fusilier Guards,
President.

After referral of this letter to the SoS by the DGO, the former requested Lt.-Col. Fletcher to present any further points he thought would be of assistance to the Ordnance Council in their deliberations on the report. The following memorandum (Memorandum "B", Chapter 7) was then presented by Lt.-Col. Fletcher —

Memorandum by Lt.-Colonel Fletcher, Scots Fusilier Guards.

The following are the points in respect to the report of the Committee on Breech-Loading Arms which appear to require immediate consideration and decision –

1st. To fix the exact pattern of the new Martini-Henry arm. An alteration in the position of the pin on which the block swings has been proposed by Mr. Martini after communications with Cols. Dixon and Boxer; he wishes to raise the pin, placing it in an intermediate position between that adopted in the arms first made at Enfield and the last arm. The arms of both patterns have worked well, but the position as proposed appears to the committee to be the best, and Col. Dixon has been requested to construct an arm on this pattern. This arm should be examined and tested, and if satisfactory, be adopted as the sealed pattern.

The barrel of this arm should also be chambered according to the latest drawings received from Mr. Henry. The arms already tested and reported upon shoot with great accuracy, but Mr. Henry considers that the chambering (owing to an alteration made at the RL to facilitate loading) does not perfectly represent his system. The arm with barrel chambered after Mr. Henry's drawing should be tested in comparison with the arm tried and reported upon. Three days at most, after the arms have been received, would complete these trials.

2nd. The description of powder for the Martini-Henry arm should be fixed. Referring to the committee report, page XXI it will be seen that the Curtis and Harvey Powder No.6 gave better results than the service powder. It is, however, more expensive to manufacture, but Col. Younghusband believes that he can prepare a powder equally good, and costing little, if at all, more than the service powder. This powder requires trial; its shooting qualities could probably be tested in a week or ten days.

3rd. Col. Boxer should be called upon to make trial of a system for manufacturing in large quantities, and at a cheap rate, the hardened bullets employed in the Martini-Henry arm; a machine for this purpose may be required.

4th. A bayonet for the arm should be determined upon and if the recommendations of the committee be adopted, the patterns of a muzzle protector and a muzzle stopper should be fixed.

Pending the results of the experiments necessary to determine these points, a decision should be arrived at whether the arms to be served out to the troops for trial should be manufactured by hand or by machinery. In considering this point it is taken for granted that the arm recommended by the committee will be provisionally adopted, and that no fresh trials, either in respect to breech-action or barrel of rejected or new systems are contemplated. It is the opinion of the committee that the trials of hand-made arms have been sufficient, and that any further trials should be made with those manufactured by machinery. The committee's report shows the almost exhaustive trials to which the Martini-Henry arm has been subjected; they were intended to represent as far as possible the wear and tear of service. It remains to be proved whether arms made in large quantities and of uniform quality will be equally serviceable, and a decision on this point can only be arrived at with machine-made arms.

The objections to adopting this course would be the risk of failure, and consequently the risk of incurring expense without due result. If it can be shown that these risks are small, it is presumed that the principal objections will be overcome. It is believed that the Martini-Henry arm can be made at Enfield by hand for about £20 per arm. Thus, if only 200 arms were manufactured, the cost would be £4,000, and the time spent in their manufacture would be excessive. If it were determined to manufacture arms by machinery, the cost of Col. Dixon's estimate for altering the whole of the machinery for the breech mechanism would be £4,500, whilst the additional cost in rifling machines would be £1,450, making a total of £5,950. It is presumed that, if for the sake of experiment, half the machinery were altered, the cost would be about half. Thus a change of half the machinery would involve a cost of £2,975. By this machinery, according to Col. Dixon's estimate, 400 barrels per week could be turned out, and probably a proportionate number of breech-actions.

Now, supposing the arm to answer, the expense of this alteration of machinery would be covered in the manufacture of about 20,000 arms at £2.18s.9d. per arm; whilst, if the system including barrel and breech-action should fail, the whole cost involved would be £2,975 (the cost of the alteration of the machinery) plus £2.18s.9d. per arm, if a small number only were manufactured, and plus a second charge of the machinery. In fact, if the system should prove a complete failure, both in respect to barrel and breech-action, the money expended would be about £6,000. (Included in this sum would be the cost of the new rifling machines, viz, £1,450, and it is presumed that they would still be worth the greater part of this sum; thus the £6,000 might really be reduced to £5,000.) Whereas, whether the system succeeded or failed, the cost of 200 hand-made arms would be £4,000, and should the system succeed the alterations of machinery would have to be added to the £4,000 already expended. Such appears to be the money side of the question.

The time lost in preparing 200 hand-made arms, and the unsatisfactory nature of such a trial should also be considered. On these grounds the committee recommend a trial of machine-made arms.

II. In addition to these points, which require immediate consideration and decision, there are others which are touched upon in the papers referred to me with the minute of the DGO.

First is the question of the bore of the new arm. The committee unanimously decided upon the 0.45 bore. In forming this opinion, they did not so much regard the accuracy at long ranges, as the flat trajectory, the great penetration, and the nature of the wounds inflicted. The fouling and the long cartridge case were objections previously alleged against this bore. The first has been overcome, judging by the results of many trials, conducted under various circumstances. The second has been met by the employment of a breech-action which ejects a long equally as easily as a short cartridge case. The long cartridge case is also not greater in bulk or weight, and almost equally strong with the shorter case. There is another objection which applies to all changes of warlike stores, viz, the inconvenience of two or more patterns being in use in the service at the same time. This objection applies at the present time to the arms and ammunition of the English army and reserve forces, and did apply to a greater extent to the armament of the troops in the Crimea. It is therefore not an insuperable one, and the committee believe that the advantages of the small bore are sufficient to counterbalance it, and that the time has arrived to face the difficulty.

2nd. The second point is Mr. Henry's application for a new trial of his breech-action. If this were granted a door would be opened for applications from every disappointed inventor, and the results of the long enquiry of the committee would be almost worthless.

3rd. The third point is the trial of gun-cotton. Supposing gun-cotton should prove superior to powder for small arms, the difficulty attending its use lies in the alteration which might be necessitated in the form and length of the cartridge case, thereby requiring an alteration in the chambers of the rifles. The reduction in length and bulk of the cartridge case would be an advantage, and but a small cost would be involved in the shortening of the chambers if gun-cotton were introduced prior to the issue of a very large supply of arms.

The possible difficulty which might arise from a change in the form of the cartridge case, does not appear a sufficient reason for neglecting to make trial of gun-cotton as a substitute for powder.

4th. Fourthly and lastly is the question of repeating arms. No sufficiently perfect specimen of this description of arm was submitted to the committee. The Winchester repeater was reported as the best, and two improved specimens will probably shortly be transmitted from America. These should be tested in view of repeating arms being required for particular services.

1, Eaton Terrace. *H.C. Fletcher.*
March 18th, 1869. *Scots Fusilier Guards.*

The CoO committee convened at the WO consisted of –

Lord Northbrook, Under SoS for War, President
Lt.-Gen. Sir J. Hope Grant, GCB, QMG
Lt.-Gen. Sir E. Lugard, GCB, Under SoS
Lt.-Gen. Lord W. Paulet, KCB, A-G
Maj.-Gen. The Right Hon. Sir H.K. Storks, GCB, GCMG, Controller-in-Chief
Rear-Adm. A.C. Key, CB, Acting DGNO
Maj.-Gen. J.H. Lefroy, RA, DGO
Col. W.H. Halliday, IGM
Lt.-Col. H.C. Fletcher, Scots Fusilier Guards, attended for the purpose of affording explanations.

They proceeded with the questions for consideration with the following results –

Q.1 – Shall the report of the Committee on Small-Arms, dated 11-2-1869, be adopted?

The president read a summary of a letter from Westley Richards, objecting to the committee's report; a letter from Alex Henry, requesting that a trial of his breech-action should be made in conjunction with the trial of the Martini breech-action; a letter from the SoS for India, applying for a trial of the Fosbery arm; and a minute from the President of the Committee on Small-Arms on Henry's application.

Resolved. That the report of the Committee on Small-Arms be so far adopted, that no expenditure of public money be made for the trial of any other arm either for the army or navy, until trial be made of the arm recommended by the Committee on Small-Arms.

Q.2 – Shall further experiment be made with the arm recommended for adoption, or with any other?

Resolved. That further trial shall be made by the two services with the arm recommended, and that no other arm shall be issued for trial at the same time.

(Questions 3 and 4 were then discussed together.)

Q.3 – If so, what shall be the nature of the further trial?
Q.4 – Shall further trial be restricted to a small number of hand made arms, or enough of the machinery at Enfield be altered to turn out a considerable number of interchangeable arms?

(Col. Dixon was called to give evidence on certain points connected with the manufacture of arms – see below.)

Resolved. That there be no trial made of the Martini action combined with the Enfield barrel.

Resolved. That the machinery at Enfield be at once altered for the manufacture of the Martini-Henry arms at a cost, as estimated by Col. Dixon, of £ 4,500, and that 200 hand-made arms of the same pattern be also proceeded with.

Resolved. That a portion of the arms manufactured shall be of a pattern suitable for the navy.

Q.5 – Is it expedient to invite either Mr. Henry or Mr. Martini to overlook the preparation of the first supply?

Resolved. That Mr. Henry and Mr. Martini should be consulted on the change of machinery, and that they should examine and report on the first delivery of arms, each on his respective share of the arm, viz, Mr. Henry on the barrel, and Mr. Martini on the breech. (Col. Boxer was called to give evidence on certain points connected with the manufacture of the ammunition, and the committee recommended that, should he think it desirable to put up a machine for making the hardened bullets at a cost of about £ 200 he should be permitted to do so.)

Resolved. That the minor questions referring to the Martini-Henry arm, which had been alluded to in Lt.-Col. Fletcher's memorandum, be settled by the Committee on Small-Arms, which should be continued for that purpose.

Q.6 – Is this the proper moment to consider the reward of

the successful competitors?

Resolved. That the Committee on Small-Arms be directed to ascertain and report on the actual expenses incurred by Messrs. Martini and Henry, in consequence of the proceedings of the committee.

The evidence by Col. Dixon mentioned above was as follows –

1. He stated that he could not alter the machinery for making the Martini-Henry arms before the end of the present year.

2. That the alteration of the machinery would not interfere with the manufacture of hand-made arms, or with the continuation of the present rate of manufacture of Snider arms.

3. That by August next, about 200 hand-made arms could be prepared, ie, either 200 Martini-Henrys, or 100 Martini-Henrys and 100 Martini-Enfields.

4. That the alteration of the machinery, both for making the breech actions and rifling the barrels, could be made for about £ 4,500.

5. He considered that the trial of the arms in India was most important, and that that trial should have especial reference to the rusting of the barrels and the consequent wear and tear of continual cleaning.

6. He made a full statement of the reasons on which the order was based for trying the Martini breech-action with the Enfield barrel.

A brief report of the proceedings of the CoO meeting, dated 23-3-1869, was presented to the SoS, and the resolutions were approved by him on 31-3-1869, with the C-I-C concurring.

The Special Committee on Breech-Loading Rifles was dissolved on 31-3-1869, but the military members of it were retained to consider the minor questions raised in Resolution 7 above. These members were –

Lt.-Col. H.C. Fletcher, President
Capt. Mackinnon, 3rd Buffs
Capt. Rawlins, 48th Regt. (acting as Secretary).

They expressed their conclusions in a report (Report "C", Chapter 7) dated 28-5-1869, and recommended –

1. The adoption of a saw-backed sword bayonet.
2. The re-introduction of muzzle stoppers.
3. The adoption of an ebonite muzzle protector.
4. The adoption of Waltham Abbey Powder No.4, of 14 to 20 mesh.

They had no opportunity to actually test a Martini breech block with the pin in the exact position laid down by them, but as the blocks with pins above and below the position answered equally well, the committee considered that no experiments were necessary. (This would seem to indicate that the special rifle with the pin in this position, as previously requested, was not completed.)

Experiments were made to determine the exact form of lead from the chamber into the rifling of Henry barrels. The opinion was that the shooting performance of the form of lead made entirely by machinery at Enfield was equal in all respects to that of Henry's, which necessitated some hand finishing.

A sword bayonet, similar to that issued to the RIC, was shown to the committee by Col. Dixon, together with a bayonet of similar description but with a longer blade. The short pattern was selected, as, with it fixed, the rifle balanced better than with the longer pattern, and the short bayonet was more handy to carry. Although its use would reduce the overall length of the arm to about three inches less than that of the Snider long rifle with ordinary bayonet fixed, the other advantages it gave were felt to outweigh the disadvantages.

Various trials were carried out to test the efficiency of the saw back, and the committee recommended it for trial as a general purpose weapon.

The muzzle stoppers were recommended for re-issue for the following reasons –

1. Without muzzle stoppers rain or dust could enter the barrel, and consequently extra cleaning would be required.
2. If muzzle stoppers were not issued, the men would probably stop up the barrels with cork or rags, which practice would create more danger than if a recognised stopper were used. It was remarked that the bayonet could not be fixed without first removing the stopper, and if it incorporated a sight protector, the latter would be apparent when the arm was brought to the present, so would be noticed by the soldier and removed. This feature would reduce the risk attending the use of muzzle stoppers in breech-loading arms.

For the purpose of protecting the rifling during cleaning, an ebonite muzzle protector was recommended. The pattern had been fixed by the committee and a demand was made for a sufficient number to be issued with the 200 rifles being made at Enfield.

After consulting the A-G's department with reference to the best method of fixing the slings on the new rifle, the committee recommended three places of attachment; one at the top band, another in front of the trigger guard, and a third near the toe of the butt. The sling was to be usually carried between the two upper attachments, but to be capable of being lengthened and fastened to the lower attachment, to suit the soldier when on the march. The normal service swivels were adopted, although another pattern was preferred.

Experiments made with the co-operation of Col. Younghusband, Supt. RGF, resulted in the recommendation for adoption of Waltham Abbey Powder, Special No.4, as giving better results than C & H No.6, or the service powder. It was much cheaper to make than No.6, and only slightly dearer than the service powder. The committee recommended that the cartridges for the M-H rifles be made with this powder.

THE LONG CHAMBER RIFLES

As a result of the resolutions of the CoO meeting of 23-3-1869, 200 M-H rifles were ordered to be made and issued for extended trials by troops at home and abroad, so as to encompass a variety of climatic conditions and use by different branches of the services, including the navy. The arms were to be passed from regiment to regiment, fired as much as possible, taken on the march, used at drill, and subjected to as many of the vissicitudes of actual service as could be imitated or produced in peace time.

The stations selected to receive rifles for trial were – Aldershot, Canada (Quebec, Ottawa, and Montreal), Cape, Gravesend (RE), Hythe (SoM), India (to go to the three presidencies), Ireland (Dublin), Portsmouth, and the navy (9 to ships abroad). Canada and India were selected for trial as being the stations which stood in most direct opposition to each other in terms of climatic conditions.

The final disposition of the 200 rifles, with ammunition supply, was as shown in Table XII.

TABLE XII – Disposition of Long Chamber Rifles and Ammunition.

Station.	No. of rifles.	Ball.	Blank.
Aldershot.	15	30,000	15,000
Canada	30	100,380	20,500
Cape.	5	16,500	3,500
Gravesend	5	10,000	5,000
Hythe	5	10,000	5,000
India.	100	500,000	112,500
Ireland	15	30,000	15,000
Portsmouth	10	20,000	10,000
Navy.	15	46,980	1,500
Totals	200	763,860	188,000

The rifles were to be reported on by the commanding officers of the units that used them, and certain instructions and questions were framed and issued by the SoS to direct the attention of the unit commanders to the most important points on which to base their reports.

21 questions as listed below were drawn up, and the resulting reports were condensed and summarised by the committee as replies to those questions, viz., –

1. What accidents, if any, have occurred?
2. What difficulties, if any, have been found in loading?
3. What difficulties, if any, have been found in extracting cartridge cases?
4. Has the lever in any case been broken, or so bent as to impede the action?
5. Has rust been found to accumulate about the breech so as to affect its working?
6. Has the coil spring been found to become weak and inefficient?
7. Is the action of the extractor, in throwing out the empty cartridge case, considered too sudden?
8. The stock being in two parts, has it remained firm and strong?
9. Has the butt end been found to shrink or become loose from the effect of hot dry temperatures?
10. Is any inconvenience experienced from recoil?
11. Is the weight of the arm a practical objection on service?
12. Is the position of the back sight approved of?
13. How does the sword bayonet answer as a weapon of attack and defence?
14. Does it answer as an implement on service for cutting wood?
15. Are the cleaning implements (the jag and protector) found useful?
16. Is the muzzle stopper found generally useful, and is it considered desirable to introduce it?
17. Has the ammunition been found liable to become broken or damaged in transport, or when carried in the men's pouches?
18. Has any difficulty arisen from this cause in loading or extracting?
19. Is the form of cartridge convenient to use?
20. Have any of the cartridges cut around the base?
21. Have any of the caps given way?

General Observations.

As a pattern, the 200 rifles were basically a refined version of the No.4 M-H rifle (see Chapter 7), with some minor alterations to ease manufacture, and some added features for service use (eg, sling swivels). They were to use the same long cartridge case, so had a long action and chamber to accomodate it.

During the period of trial and development that led to the adoption of the first M-H pattern, various comments had been made about the length of the 0.45-inch cartridge, and this was one of the major objections raised against its use. To obviate this, W.T. Eley experimented with and eventually succeeded in developing a shorter cartridge, which held the same amount of powder charge by enlarging the body. This required a reduction of diameter at the neck, giving a bottle shape to the cartridge, which resulted in it being called the "bottle-neck cartridge".

The appelation of this round was eventually changed to "short chamber cartridge", and the original called the "long chamber cartridge". Accordingly, rifles using the respective cartridges were then designated as "long chamber" or "short chamber" rifles. The 200 rifles mentioned in this section will therefore be described as the long chamber pattern in subsequent references.

TRIALS OF THE BOTTLE–NECK CARTRIDGE

While the long chamber rifles were being produced in preparation for their trials, the DGO on 22-7-1869 suggested trials of the bottle-neck cartridge, which had recently been brought to his attention by the committee. The committee, and the superintendents of the RL and the RSAF all agreed that it would be advantageous to reduce the length of the cartridge, so on 16-8-1869 ten rifles were ordered with the chamber enlarged to take the proposed cartridge. Henry's approval was asked, and granted, for this modification.

Eight of the rifles were made using the long action already in production, and two were to be made with a short action. The eight long action rifles were distributed – 5 to Hythe, 1 to Col. Dixon, 1 to Col. Boxer, and 1 to DGO.

On 19-8-1869 another rifle was ordered from Enfield, chambered to accept a cartridge with "increased dimensions and internal lining". Although not actually specified, this cartridge seems to have been a variation of the bottle-neck round.

The trials of these weapons took place from August to October of 1869, and various types of powder were also used. A minute dated 28-10-1869 refers to reports from the RL on the shooting of ordinary and short chamber rifles and ammunition, and also on the variations of powder used, viz, –

1st Lot 9-9-1869, ordinary and short chambers.

2nd Lot 21-9-1869, enlarged and short chambers, long action rifles. Curtis and Harvey No.6 and Enfield rifle powders.

3rd Lot 14 and 15-10-1869, short chamber rifles Nos. 179 and 196. (These were perhaps the new short action rifles.)

The trials were very satisfactory, and on 9-11-1869, the DGO proposed the use of the terms "long" and "short" chamber to obviate the need to use the term "bottle-neck cartridge". The Supt. RSAF was then directed to work out the alterations and methods required to adapt the action for the new cartridge.

A minute of 24-12-1869, detailing previous events, noted official acceptance that the short cartridge was preferable to the long, and that 100 short chamber rifles had been requested for further trial. The superintendent replied that he could not make more than 20-25 due to the fact that the machinery at Enfield was being re-arranged, and the arms would in any case have to be made on the long action. He was still experimenting with the short action, as the first two "cramped the action", and he was making two more with the action ¼-inch longer. He also noted that the short action had to be more precisely made, as there had to be a dead fit between the faces of the breech block and barrel to avoid "cutting" of the cartridge case.

The two rifles with the longer short action were tested during early December 1869, as the following extracts from the Enfield Range Book show. The report is given in full, as it is pertinent to the investigations that followed in the new year, 1870. (Mr. Baker was the Range Master at the RSAF)

Memorandum for Mr. Baker.

The Manager will give you 2 Martini-Henry rifles with short actions (modified length) and the chamber cut from the laboratory tool.

Experiments.

To ascertain working of action. Fouling. Accuracy. Difficulties in extracting when the barrel is hot and cold.

Anything connected with the bottle shaped ammunition, causing either fouling, or difficulty of any nature to be noted.

The experiment is not only to find out whether the shortened action can be introduced, but whether the ammunition presents any difficulties in itself, or with said short action.

If the chamber or barrels foul, it must be specially noted whether this is caused by any defect in the barrel or in the ammunition, arising in this latter case from possibly a too great quantity of the varnish used in the cartridges.

30th Novr. 1869. *(signed) W.M.D.*

To which memorandum the Range Master replied –

Royal Small Arms Factory.
Enfield 9th Decr. 1869.

Report.

Experimental practice carried on at Enfield between 2nd and 7 both days inclusive.

First.

Martini-Henry rifle No.3 action modified length. Woolwich pattern chamber and bottle shaped cartridges.

5 diagrams of 20 shots each at 500 yards with cleaning the barrel but allowing sufficient time to elapse between each diagram for the barrel to get cool.

Diagram	*Figure*	*Corrected angle.*		
		o	'	"
1.	.80	1	19	30
2.	.87	1	19	48
3.	1.17	1	20	18
4.	1.02	1	21	30
5.	1.33	1	20	18

The breech action was then removed from the barrel. The barrel and chamber carefully examined. The chamber was found perfectly clean, and the barrel about 12 inches near the muzzle end very foul and badly leaded, and a little foul about an inch only close to the chamber.

The arm was then cleaned and a diagram of 20 shots taken at 500 yards with a figure of .77 of a foot.

60 rounds was then fired for rapidity. The barrel and chamber again examined. The barrel was very foul, and the chamber clear.

The back sight came off at the 59th round.

10 diagrams of 20 shots each was then made at 800 and 1,000 yards, 5 at each distance with the following results –

Diagram	*Figure*	*Corrected angle.*
		o ' "
1.	1.30	2 20 24
2.	2.24	2 22 36
3.	2.03	2 20 48
4.	1.96	2 23 00
5.	2.55	2 23 18

1,000 yards.

1.	3.40	3 10 30
2.	2.86	3 10 18
3.	3.62	3 10 42
4.	3.49	3 9 36
5.	2.91	3 11 18

Second.

Martini-Henry rifle No.4 action modified length. Woolwich chamber and bottle shaped ammunition carried on in the same order as with No.3 action.

500 yards.

Diagram	*Figure*	*Corrected angle.*
1.	1.21	1 20 30
2.	.98	1 19 12
3.	1.45	1 18 48
4.	1.66	1 19 54
5.	1.66	1 19 30

60 rounds for rapidity. One diagram at 500 yards. Figure 1.10.

800 yards.

Diagram	*Figure*	*Corrected angle.*
1.	1.97	2 18 00
2.	2.15	2 14 18
3.	2.10	2 14 54
4.	2.52	2 15 36
5.	2.25	2 15 54

1,000 yards.

1.	3.67	3 9 12
2.	3.27	3 8 00
3.	3.28	3 6 6
4.	2.86	3 4 12
5.	3.50	3 3 24

The report on this and No.3 barrel are identical except that the sight remained on.

The angles of elevation are above the average. This was partly attributable to the northerly direction of the wind.

The temperature ranged from 32 to 39 degrees with a cold damp atmosphere during the whole time the experiments was going on.

Throughout the experiments with these modified actions and bottle shaped cartridges /with 2 and 3 caps/ the cases extracted freely, when hot and cold. The actions worked well and alike both in quick and slow firing.

The barrels fouled and leaded very much during the practice at 800 and 1,000 yards, as will be seen by referring to the low figures of merit obtained, although the barrels were carefully cleaned and examined at these distances after every diagram of 20 shots.

Whatever may be the cause of the fouling, I do not attribute it to too great quantity of varnish used, or to the varnish at all, because the fouling was chiefly at the fore end of the barrel. Probably the cold weather acted unfavourably against the wax wads.

In cold weather such as we have had lately the beeswax wads become so hard and brittle that they cannot be expanded by the prepuce of the gases, but are actually broken up in small pieces before leaving the barrel.

This being so, there is very little to prevent the gases rushing past the bullet and fouling the barrel on every discharge, especially so after firing a great number of rounds.

I.B.Baker,
Proof Master.

FURTHER CARTRIDGE TRIALS

During the trials of the bottle-neck cartridges, the tendency had been noted for the barrels of M-H rifles to foul when fired at low temperatures, with both C & H and Waltham Abbey powders, as shown in the above report.

To investigate these problems, another committee was formed on 6-1-1870, and called the "Special Committee on Ammunition for Martini-Henry Breech-Loading Rifles".

It was composed entirely of military personnel, and carried out experiments in the small arms range at the Royal Arsenal, Woolwich, commencing 10-1-1870. The members were –

Lt.-Col. H.C. Fletcher, Scots Fusilier Guards, Pres.
Capt. R.W. Haig, RA, 7th Brigade
Lt.-Col. H. Heyman, RA, Dept. of DGO
Capt. V.D. Majendie, RA, Supt. pro tem RL

The committee reported on 25-3-1870, with the following recommendations –

1. The adoption of a powder made at the RGF, known as No.9, 20 to 28 mesh, to be designated "K".

2. The adoption, for guidance of powder manufacturers, of a specification prepared by Col. Younghusband.

3. The adoption of a hollowed beeswax wad, for lubrication, of increased thickness and diameter, for the short chamber cartridge.

4,5,6. The adoption of a short chamber cartridge, short chamber rifle, and of a short breech action.

7. The adoption, for future use with the Snider rifle, of the same powder as that recommended for the Martini-Henry, except that the grains were to be between 14 and 20 mesh, to be designated "L". Existing store of powder to be used up.

The principal experiments were made with the short chamber rifles, as, for reasons given below, the short cartridge seemed better adapted for service requirements. The standard for comparison was initially the long chamber rifle, with service cartridge loaded with C & H No.6 powder, until new combinations of powder and wads in the short cartridges gave better results; they in turn then became the standard. These experiments resulted in the committee's recommendations 1, 2, and 3.

To justify the recommendations 4, 5, and 6, they listed the advantages of the short chambered rifle and ammunition as

1. A shorter and lighter breech action.

2. Greater facility of loading.

3. A shorter and stronger cartridge, consequently one more adapted for the requirements of the service, and more convenient for carriage.

The committee remarked in the report that during the long series of experiments made with the short chambered arms, they had frequent opportunities of watching the working of both the barrel and breech-action, and also of watching the behaviour of the cartridge. The breech actions continued to work without any hitch, and showed no weakness in any of their parts.

With regard to the barrels, it appeared that several thousand rounds could be fired from them without affecting their efficiency; as an example, two arms were quoted as having fired the following number of rounds –

Rifle No.199 . . . 4,876
Rifle No.196 . . . 2,984

9,041 rounds were fired with only two misfires, of which number 8,204 were short chamber cartidges, and none of these suffered a cut or burst case.

SHORT CHAMBER RIFLE TRIALS

After reading the report from the above committee, the C-I-C requested that some rifles suitable for the short chamber cartridge might be made, and issued for trial under similar conditions to those proposed for the long chamber rifle trials.

Twelve rifles of the type had already been ordered for issue to the Wimbledon Meeting of 1870, so on 11-5-1870, a further twelve were ordered, making a total of 24 to be available for trial. (These rifles and their trials will be discussed in detail in a later chapter.)

Company Square — Preparing for Cavalry

CHAPTER 6.

THE LONG CHAMBER RIFLE TRIALS–FIRST REPORT

DURING the time the bottleneck and subsequent cartridge trials were taking place, the 200 long chamber rifles were completed, so, in November 1869 they were despatched to the stations designated to receive them. The trials of these arms were scheduled to commence on 1-1-1870, but, according to the dates on a few of the reports, trials at some stations obviously started on an earlier date. These were home stations and so the trials apparently started on receipt of the arms, which would have been before some of the overseas stations received theirs.

The intention with the trials reports was that they should be forwarded to the committee as soon as they were finalised, so that any peculiar faults of the weapons would be manifested at an early stage of the proceedings, and so could be rectified to obviate any further trouble from that weak point. That this was a sensible approach is confirmed by the early recognition of the serious fault of consistent misfiring of the trials rifles. The reasons for this problem were soon discovered and immediately corrected, so that this particular fault was practically eliminated for the remainder of the trial programme.

To examine, and advise on the reports received on these trials, and other related matters, a new committee was formed, and called the "Special Committee on Martini-Henry Breech-Loading Rifles". The Special Committee on Ammunition for Martini-Henry Rifles was dissolved on 3-5-1870, and some of its members were incorporated into the new committee, which consisted of –

Lt.-Col. H.C. Fletcher, Scots Fusilier Guards, Pres.
Capt. R.W. Haig, FRS, RA
Capt. R.T.L. Chapman, 34th Regt., District IoM
Capt. V.D. Majendie, RA, Asst. Supt. RL
Capt. J.E.F. Aylmer, Half-pay, late 8th Regt.
Lord Elcho, MP
Edward Ross, Esq.
C. Hutton Gregory, CE, appointed Sept. 1870
Lt. B de B. Tupper, RA, Secretary.

The committee's first report was presented on 12-7-1870, and contained a summary of 50 reports received from regiments in Britain and Canada, and from HM Ships. (A list of these reports and their origin is given in Table XIII.)

A summary of this first lot of reports, together with the committee's remarks on them, is given in Appendix 12, but there were also some general observations made in the report, and these will be discussed below.

The committee remarked that in nearly every instance the commanding officers and others compared the M-H with the Snider, and so based their reports on this comparison. This resulted in the general opinion that for accuracy the M-H was superior to the Snider, especially at long ranges, and for ease of operation the Martini breech was considered very satisfactory. The breech actions and barrels showed no symptoms of wear from the many and severe trials they were exposed to.

Reports from India, the Cape, and HM Ships abroad had not been received at this time, so the number of arms covered in the first reports totalled 86, from which a total of 137,308 rounds of ball, and 52,432 rounds of blank cartridges had been fired, giving an average of 1,597 rounds of ball, and 608 rounds of blank fired from each weapon. This compared well with the projected figures of 2,000 rounds of ball, and 1,000 of blank that it had been intended each arm should fire during the course of the trials.

The misfires referred to above were found to be caused mainly by weak striker springs, also by some faulty strikers. The latter defects were traced to imperfect material and bad workmanship; but the weak springs basically were the fault of the RSAF. It had been found that the misfires were more frequent in some rifles than in others, and in those rifles with a high proportion of misfires the percentage did not increase with the number of rounds fired, indicating that the striker springs were originally weak, and their strength did not deteriorate with use. The clear inference was that there was a lack of uniformity in the strength of the issued springs, and also that they were weaker than those previously used in the Martini rifles tested by the Small Arms Committee. Martini's original striker spring was of 40 lbs, although he considered one of 33 lbs to be strong enough. Hoping to lighten the pull off pressure, the RSAF employed a spring of only 26 lbs in the long chamber rifles, thus causing the problem.

It was decided to replace the issued spring with a heavier one, and so in March 1870, a supply of new springs was sent to the stations where the arms were on trial, so they could be substituted for those in use. That the new springs were effective is shown by the following: with the weak springs, 163,277 rounds of ball and blank had been fired, with 3,814 misfires, or 2.34 percent; but with the stronger springs, 26,463 rounds were fired with only 9 misfires, or 0.034 percent.

There had been complaints regarding the difficulty in loading bent cartridges, and of the paper wrapping being caught on the chamber mouth, but the committee stated that –

These difficulties have been overcome by the substitution of a shorter cartridge of a bottleneck form on which there is no paper, and which has been provisionally approved.

Similarly, complaints about the ammunition pouch, which was of a new design, were waived with the comment

The inconvenient shape of the pouch and ball bag is a matter of considerable importance which will require attention when the pattern of the ammunition is finally settled.

TABLE XIII – Origins of Reports on Long Chamber Rifles.

No. of Report.	Station.	Regiment.	Date, 1870.
1	Aldershot	67th	5 January
2	Aldershot	2nd Btn. 3rd	13 January
3	Aldershot	7th Fusiliers	13 January
4	Aldershot	2nd Btn. 23rd RWF	15 February
5	Aldershot	42nd	23 March
6	Aldershot	4th Btn. Rifle Brigade	15 February
7	Aldershot	2nd Btn. 13th	15 March
8	Aldershot	4th Btn. 60th Rifles	22 April
9	Aldershot	2nd Btn. Rifle Brigade	9 February
10	Aldershot	33rd	15 March
11	Dublin	1st Btn. Grenadier Guards	6 February
12	Dublin	1st Btn. Scots Fusilier Guards	5 April
13	Dublin	2nd Btn. 15th	5 February
14	Dublin	47th	2 April
15	Dublin	56th	4 March
16	Dublin	43rd	6 April
17	Hythe	School of Musketry	15 February
18	Hythe	School of Musketry	13 March
19	Hythe	School of Musketry	19 April
20	Hythe	School of Musketry	15 May
21	Gravesend	Royal Engineers	1 January
22	Gravesend	Royal Engineers	31 January
23	Gravesend	Royal Engineers	1 March
24	Gravesend	Royal Engineers	1 April
25	Portsmouth	2nd Btn. 2nd	31 January
26	Portsmouth	99th	3 February
27	Portsmouth	RMLI	28 February
28	Portsmouth	101st	4 March
29	Portsmouth	46th	2 May
30	Portsmouth	1st Btn. 25th	3 May
31	Quebec	69th	31 January
32	Quebec	69th	28 February
33	Quebec	69th	31 March
34	Montreal	1st Btn. Rifle Brigade	31 January
35	Montreal	1st Btn. Rifle Brigade	28 February
36	Montreal	1st Btn. Rifle Brigade	31 March
37	Ottawa	1st Btn. 60th Rifles	31 January
38	Ottawa	1st Btn. 60th Rifles	28 February
39	Ottawa	1st Btn. 60th Rifles	31 March
40	Portsmouth	HMS Excellent	31 January
41	Davenport	HMS Cambridge	29 January
42	Curragh	1st. Btn. 16th	7 May
43	Curragh	2nd Btn. 16th	9 May
44	Curragh	30th	9 May
45	Ottawa	1st Btn. 60th Rifles	30 April
46	Quebec	69th	30 April
47	Montreal	1st Btn. Rifle Brigade	30 April
48	Dublin	Inspector of Musketry	19 March
49	Portsmouth	IoM SW District	8 February
50	Dublin	Inspector of Musketry	11 May

Some objections had been made regarding the position of the back sight, declaring it to be inconvenient when the rifle was carried at the trail. The committee remarked that this complaint involved consideration of the balance, length, and weight of the arm, and that these were being reviewed as a result of the trials. They also stated that as the sights were highly approved for sighting,

No change of position which would affect the efficiency of the sights for shooting purposes could be recommended, but the committee believe that by an alteration in the balance of the arm the inconvenience complained of will be removed, the sight remaining in its present position.

To alter the balance of the arm, the committee recommended that its length be reduced, and also that the muzzle end of the barrel be lightened if necessary. The reduction in length was also thought desirable on other grounds (see Committee Remarks, Appendix 12), but, as the committee which had developed the pattern of rifle on trial had been restricted to the precise length of 51 inches, special instructions were requested as to the course to follow.

One major objection certain to be raised against shortening the rifle would be the reduction of its length as a pike. To forestall this, the committee stated that they had recommended for trial, with the extra 12 short chamber rifles, a new sword bayonet of a pattern proposed by Lord Elcho. This was a development of the bayonet currently being tested with the long chamber rifles, and was described as having a longer blade (which was better balanced and shaped for the purposes of cutting and chopping), with a longer saw, and a better handle. It was manufactured by Messrs. Wilkinson, of Pall Mall.

(In a minute of 8-9-1870 the C-I-C stated he was against reducing the length of the rifle, and the consequent use of a longer bayonet, but the committee held to their views, so the question was held in abeyance until the final discussions prior to recommending the new arm for adoption.)

Notice was also drawn to a few minor points, viz. –

1. The alteration in the form of the V of the backsight. This was recommended for trial with the short action short chamber rifles about to be issued.
2. A reduction in the size of the jag. This was recommended for the attention of the Supt. RSAF.
3. The method of cleaning the rifles. The attention of those using them should be called to this point.
4. The statement that the cleaning rod worked loose was recommended for the attention of the Supt. RSAF.
5. The inconvenient shape of the pouch and ball bag. (This was alluded to above.)

Although there were only two rifles in which the butt stock became loose, the committee proposed to carry out experiments to test the relative strengths of divided and whole stocks, and in concluding their first report, stated that they intended to await the further reports due, particularly those from India, and others on the stronger striker springs, before submitting a final opinion. Some other minor questions referred to them were to be considered and duly reported upon, as they did not want to delay any further the presentation of their first report.

THE LONG CHAMBER RIFLE AND OTHER TRIALS – SECOND REPORT

The second, and final, report of the Special Committee on Martini-Henry Breech-Loading Rifles was presented on 8-2-1871, and, for convenience and clarity, was divided into five sections –

I. The long action (ie, long chamber) M-H rifle.
II. The short action (ie, short chamber) M-H rifle.
III. The evidence on the mechanical construction of the breech-action.
IV. Alterations and improvements suggested by the results of the trials, and by the evidence.
V. Conclusion.

The long chamber rifles. After the initial summary of reports had been presented, a further 55 were received from home and overseas stations (see Table XIV for a list of the origins of these reports), and were examined and summarised in a similar manner to the first lot.

As the previous comments were strongly corroborated by the second set of reports, the committee remarked that they had very little to add to their original comments, except that the misfires had practically ceased since the substitution of the stronger springs.

The summary of these last reports is given in Appendix 13.

The short chamber rifles. As mentioned in the previous chapter, a total of 24 of these rifles had been ordered, with an original order for 12 to be issued to the Wimbledon Meeting of 1870. Subsequent trials of these weapons were quite varied, and included a series similar to those applied to the long chamber rifles, with the same 21 questions applying.

The first twelve rifles were sent to the Wimbledon Meeting of July, 1870, and some of them incorporated modifications to the sights and other small items. Two members of the committee, Capts. Aylmer and Chapman, attended the meeting to observe the behaviour of the rifles and report on them. They regarded the arms as most satisfactory, but drew attention to some small points which they felt required attention before the final pattern should be decided.

In August, 1870, a series of competitive trials was carried out at Shoeburyness, between field guns, infantry rifles, the Montigny Mitrailleur, and the Gatling gun. The infantry arms used were six Snider rifles, and six of the short chamber M-H rifles; all fired by six men from the Scots Fusilier Guards under the command of Lt.-Col. Fletcher. At these trials the M-H arms fired a total of 1,879 rounds without any defect showing in either the arms or ammunition.

22 of the arms were then issued for trial in October, 1870, to the following stations –

10 to Aldershot
4 to the Curragh
4 to Hythe
4 to Portsmouth.

The remaining two were retained by the committee for their own experiments.

TABLE XIV – Origins of Reports on Long Chamber Rifles.

No. of report.	Station.	Regiment.	Date, 1870.
51	Aldershot	4th Btn. Rifle Brigade	1 June
52	Aldershot	1/4th	31 May
53	Aldershot	42nd	13 July
54	Montreal	1st Btn. Rifle Brigade	31 May
55	Montreal	1st Btn. Rifle Brigade	30 June
56	Montreal	1st Btn. Rifle Brigade	31 July
57	Montreal	1st Btn. Rifle Brigade	19 August
58	Quebec	69th	31 May
59	Quebec	69th	30 June
60	Quebec	69th	31 July
61	Quebec	69th	31 August
62	Quebec	69th	30 September
63	Quebec	69th	4 November
64	Hythe	School of Musketry	14 June
65	Hythe	School of Musketry	16 August
66	Portsmouth	2/2nd	4 June
67	Portsmouth	2/2nd	27 August
68	Portsmouth	RMLI	30 June
69	Portsmouth	82nd	3 June
70	Portsmouth	RMA	1 July
71	Portsmouth	1/25th	2 August
72	Portsmouth	77th	1 August
73	Portsmouth	77th	18 August
74	Kinsale	1/22nd	9 July
75	Kinsale	63rd	11 July
76	Youghal	68th	1 July
77	Windsor	2/Scots Fusilier Guards	6 July
78	Windsor	2/Scots Fusilier Guards	1 August
79	Fermoy	65th	25 July
80	Fermoy	65th	13 August
81	Fermoy	89th	25 July
82	Limerick	89th	11 August
83	Buttevant	72nd	25 July
84	Buttevant	72nd	8 August
85	Palermo	HMS Lord Warden	6 July
86	Channel	HMS Minotaur	19 July
87	Nth. America	HMS Royal Alfred	6 September
88	Portsmouth	HMS Excellent	7 December
89	Plymouth	HMS Cambridge	13 October
90	Plymouth	HMS Cambridge	23 December
91	Morar	1/11th	8 October
92	Dum Dum	96th	11 August
93	Umballa	106th	27 September
94	Simla	Chief Inspector of Musketry	16 October
95	Poona	1/2nd	13 October
96	Kurrachee	66th	26 October
97	Dugshaie	1/3rd	11 October
98	Rawul Pindee	36th	10 November
99	Lucknow	62nd	17 October
100	Cork	District Inspector of Musketry	15 July
101	Cork	District Inspector of Musketry	26 July
102	Cork	District Inspector of Musketry	18 August
103	Quebec	District Inspector of Musketry	12 September
104	Dum Dum	District Inspector of Musketry	13 August
105	Lucknow	Inspector of Musketry	21 November

TABLE XV – Origins of Reports on Short Chamber Rifles.

No. of report.	Station.	Regiment.	Date, 1870.
1	Aldershot	2/22nd	11 November
2	Aldershot	2/9th	31 October
3	Aldershot	1/4th	9 November
4	Aldershot	2/17th	19 December
5	Aldershot	33rd	9 October
6	Aldershot	91st	21 December
7	Hythe	School of Musketry	14 November
8	Curragh	44th	27 October
9	Curragh	56th	25 November
10	Portsmouth	RMLI	4 November
11	Portsmouth	RMA	1 December
12	Portsmouth	82nd	7 Jan/1871
13	Dublin	Inspector of Musketry	7 November
14	Dublin	Inspector of Musketry	30 November

Fourteen reports were received on the trials of the short chamber rifles, the origins of which are shown in Table XV, and the summaries in Appendix 14. To quote the committee's report –

These reports corroborate the opinion expressed by the committee which recommended the trial, showing that in accuracy and general serviceability these rifles are equal to the long actioned arms.

The opportunity was taken during these latter trials to test a new form of back sight, furnished with a straight bar having vertical lines engraved on its rear face, instead of one with a V notch, and the rifles were accordingly fitted with these sights.

Evidence on the breech mechanism. Because of pressure by various persons interested in furthering their own designs, the committee considered that independent scientific and practical evidence should be obtained on the mechanical construction of the Martini breech-action. On 26-11-1870 the SoS approved of this proposal, so on 3-12-1870, Lt.-Col. Fletcher drew up a "Programme for the Examination of Witnesses on the Character of the Mechanical Construction of the Martini-Henry Rifle". Details of this programme were shown in Chapter 4, and, in the opinion of the committee, the evidence was conclusive as to the soundness of the mechanical principles of the breech action.

Prior to this, on 12-8-1870, orders had been given for all trials of long chamber rifles at home to cease; all weapons to be returned to the RSAF. 65 of them were selected for complete dismantling and examination by the superintendent. He reported on these arms on 30-12-1870, and this report is shown in Appendix 15.

The committee recommended on 29-12-1870 that all trials with M-H rifles should cease, and that all reports be called for. Orders were given accordingly. (The long chamber rifles in India were not affected by this order, as it was not until 26-6-1871 that the India office was informed that the M-H rifle had been adopted, and asked to withdraw from issue the 100 rifles there. They replied on 1-7-1871 that instructions for recall had been given. 36 of the arms received from Calcutta were examined by the Supt. RSAF and Lt.-Col. Fletcher, and reported on, 30-4-1872. There were no signs of wear on the surfaces which rubbed against each other in the actions, and the parts worked freely, although in many cases they were rusty and dirty. There were several misfires, which were found to be due to the rifles having the original weak striker spring still fitted. The result of this examination was considered favourable to the arms.)

Alterations and improvements. In their first report of 12-7-1870 the committee had recommended for the whole of the infantry as well as for the navy an arm 2.187 inches shorter than the original M-H. This would be the same length as the Snider rifle used by the Rifle Brigade and the navy. The committee recommended this reduction in length for the following reasons – the reduced weight and handiness of the rifle; its convenience regarding its length for military purposes, as evidenced by its use in the Rifle regiments; and the consequent abolition of the then current long rifle drill, with the establishment throughout the services of a uniform system of manual and platoon exercises. There was also the consideration of easier manufacture if only one pattern of rifle was adopted.

There had been no reason for the committee to change their views on these points, but, as they had received no definite instructions in this regard, they had made some experiments to see whether the balance of the long rifle could be improved and the weight reduced, as these were two of the objections raised against it.

To this end they consulted the Supt. RSAF and Alex Henry and the result was a barrel prepared by the RSAF six ounces lighter than the original M-H barrel, making the rifle one ounce lighter than the long Snider rifle. The balance of this rifle was better than that of the long chamber rifle, and it shot as well, but the recoil was very slightly increased. It was also found that if the back sight was shifted a half inch closer to the muzzle, the rifle could be conveniently carried at the trail. Various tests with a bayonet fitted showed the strength of the lighter barrel was sufficient for bayonet work.

While the trials of the short chamber rifles were taking place, the DoA on 7-11-1870 ordered that two of the rifles issued to Aldershot be returned to the RSAF to be shortened and the sights regraduated, previous to issue to Excellent and Cambridge with 4,000 rounds of ammunition for trial as to their relative value for sea service. The length of these rifles was the same as the naval Snider, and the weight about the same, ie, 8 lb 12 ozs. In accuracy, and flatness of trajectory, the short rifle was equal to the long rifle, and it balanced well. It was also found that by reducing the comb of the butt stock the recoil was felt less than with the original M-H. To quote the report –

The objection as to the weight and balance which has been urged against the original M-H rifle has thus been met and remedied.

The committee also remarked that experiments were still being carried out to determine whether the short rifle could not be further lightened.

(On 17-2-1871, the Admiralty, in forwarding the reports from Excellent and Cambridge on the two short M-H rifles, approved of the pattern for adoption, but recommended an alteration in the muzzle protector, as well as the adoption of a naval sword bayonet without saw back.)

The committee also mentioned a few minor alterations to the general pattern they considered necessary, such as the shape of the lever, the shape of the butt stock, and the position and form of back sight. It was also noted that other minor alterations, not involving changes of the principle of operation of the arm, might be required before the weapon was produced in large quantities. These alterations would most likely be instigated by the persons in charge of the various departments manufacturing the components of the arm.

The sword bayonet. The saw back sword bayonet issued with the long chamber rifles received the approval of the majority of the regiments that tested it, but some requested an increase in the length of the saw. A modified pattern, the Elcho bayonet, was issued for trial with 12 of the short chamber rifles, and it also received favourable comments. Its claimed advantages over the original bayonet were that it had greater power and convenience as a cutting and chopping instrument, and its increased length of saw.

Having taken into consideration the favourable reports on the original saw back bayonet, and the increased advantages of the modified pattern, the committee recommended the adoption into service of the Elcho bayonet, with some modifications to the scabbard and the method of attaching the bayonet to the rifle.

Conclusion of report. The report ended as follows –

The various trials to which the Martini-Henry arm has been subjected since issue of the report which first recommended its adoption, have now extended over a period of more than eighteen months.

The committee, after a careful review of the results of these trials, after consultation with independent scientific and practical witnesses on the mechanism of the breech action, and after full consideration of the whole question, are of opinion that the short actioned M-H rifle is admirably adapted for a military arm, and they therefore unanimously recommend its adoption into the two services.

They also unanimously recommend the adoption for use with this arm of the short chamber Boxer-Henry ammunition, and (for land service) of the Elcho bayonet.

Alterations to pattern rifle. The minor alterations to the rifle mentioned in the report were presented in an appendix headed – *Minor Alterations in the Construction of the Martini-Henry Rifle,* and were as follows –

1. Back sight. To lie back so as to touch the barrel. To be secured to the barrel by two screws as in the rifles sent to Wimbledon, July 1870. The sliding bar to be reversible, one side quite flat, the other with a very small V notch to mark the centre. A bright line to be drawn across the centre of the bar, and the spaces between this line and the side of the flap to be equally divided by bright lines not quite reaching the middle of the sliding bar. The top and bottom edges of the sliding bar to be beveled off on the side away from the eye. The sides of the sliding bar to be chequered.

2. Main lever and catch. The lever to fit close to the stock until near the end, where it projects in the form of a loop. The form of catch to be somewhat modified.

3. Form of stock. Under this head the committee recommend –

First, with a view of saving the face of the firer from a blow by recoil, that the comb of the stock should be somewhat cut away.

Secondly, a slight hollow to be cut out of the upper right rear part of the shoe to receive the thumb of the right hand when firing. This hollow should be roughened by chequering.

Thirdly, that two lengths of stock should be issued as is done at present with the long Snider-Enfield.

Fourthly, with a view to strengthening the stock the trap in the butt is to be done away with, and the stock bolt lengthened so as to bring its head into a thicker part of the butt, while the bolt itself should be made of a milder steel than that of the experimental arms, the hole to receive it being kept as small as possible; and, finally, to prevent the rifle slipping on the shoulder while taking aim, the heel plate to be roughened by chequering.

4. Trap in butt. To be done away with and the hole kept as small as possible. It is suggested that the cleaning implements be carried in one of the pouches.

5. Block axis pin. To be made of gun metal; to be a simple pin, kept in position by an eclipse or keeper screw.

6. Trigger. To lie back as far as possible and to be scored longitudinally to roughen the surface. The axis pin to be made a screw and of a stronger wire.

7. Sword. To be of the Elcho pattern and the knob of spring to be rounded off.

8. Safety bolt. Indicator to be shifted to fit the bolt when not engaged with the action.

9. Edges. All exterior sharp edges to be rounded off.

10. Cleaning rod. To be made of steel throughout, with a catch to hold under the top band by the spring of the rod itself. Head to be conical.

11. Muzzle stopper. The committee have recommended a cover in place of a stopper.

(Two other alterations were suggested by some of the witnesses, viz, the strengthening of the safety bolt, and an alteration in the form and substance of some of the screws. After consultation with the Supt. RSAF the committee came to the conclusion that it was unnecessary to accept these suggestions.

The Supt. RSAF recommended the substitution of brass for the iron furniture, but after full consideration the committee determined not to adopt this recommendation.)

THE SHORT CHAMBER RIFLE – SUPPLEMENTARY REPORT

As mentioned in the report of 8-2-1871 the committee had investigated further the possibility of reducing the weight of the short M-H below that previously attained, and on 21-3-1871 they presented a report detailing the experiments they had carried out to this end.

Trials had been performed with a barrel weighing 3 lbs 6¼ ozs, making the total weight of the rifle 8 lbs 7½ ozs, compared with 8 lbs 12 ozs, the weight of the first short rifle, and 9 lbs 7 ozs, the weight of the original M-H.

The results of the tests were –

1. Recoil. Members of the committee, and five soldiers of the Rifle Brigade, fired the arm, and its recoil was not found to have perceptibly increased. Of the five soldiers who fired it, four thought that the new rifle had less recoil than the previous pattern.

2. Accuracy. This was found to equal the previous pattern.

3. Strength of barrel. Was found to be quite sufficient. A sword bayonet was mounted and thrust into a deal board. After being twisted about until the bayonet was rendered bent and useless, the rifle was again fired for accuracy, and was found to be unimpaired.

As they felt that the importance of reducing the weight of the arm was paramount, to ease the burden of the soldier, and because of the great handiness of the lighter weapon, the committee recommended its adoption into the service, in place of the rifle of 8 lbs 12 ozs previously approved by them.

FINAL APPROVAL OF THE MARTINI–HENRY RIFLE

The CoO met on 30-3-1871 to consider the three reports of the Special Committee on Martini-Henry Breech-Loading Rifles, dated 12-7-1870, 8-2-1871, and 21-3-1871, respectively. Present were –

Lord Northbrook, Under SoS for War, President
Lt.-Gen. Sir Edward Lugard, GCB, Under SoS
Maj.-Gen. Sir H.K.Storks, GCB, GCMG, MP, SGO
The Hon. J.C. Vivian, MP, Financial Secty, War Dept.
Lt.-Gen. Sir Richard Airey, GCB, A-G
Maj.-Gen. Sir F. Chapman, KCB, IGF
Brig.-Gen. J.M. Adye, CB, DoA
Capt. A. Hood, RN, DNO
Col. W.R. Haliday, IGM

This meeting resolved –

That the short actioned Martini-Henry rifle of 8 lbs 7½ ozs, with short chambered Boxer-Henry ammunition, be adopted into the two services; and (for land service) a bayonet of the pattern proposed by Lord Elcho, and recommended by the committee.

The C-I-C concurred with this resolution, as –

Having carefully considered the report on the Martini-Henry rifle and sword bayonet Elcho pattern, I have no hesitation in recording my opinion in favour of adoption of that arm for Her Majesty's service, feeling satisfied from the trials that have been made, and the experience gained, that it is a most perfect breech-loading weapon, and well adapted for the use of the troops.

The SoS, Mr. Cardwell, on 13-4-1871 minuted *"Let the works proceed accordingly"*. On 3-5-1871, in reply to a query from M. Martini, he stated *"The rifle has been definitely adopted"*. Official letters were then writted in May 1871 to Martini and Henry, informing them of the decision, and congratulating them on the results of their efforts in producing a suitable weapon for the British service. They were also advised that the question of a reward for their ideas would receive immediate consideration.

Thus, in theory, came the end of the quest for the best breech-loading rifle for the British service – a quest which had commenced with the first advertisement to the public of 21-6-1865. It had taken nearly six years to achieve this result, but, unfortunately, the trials and tribulations of the M-H were not yet over, as will be disclosed in the following chapters.

CHAPTER 7.

THE TRIALS MARTINIS

THERE were several distinct patterns of Martini rifles tested in the selection trials from the Prize Competition onwards, before one acceptable for service was finalised. Information on some of the early examples is scanty, but a reasonably accurate description of each can be built up by a careful analysis of the information presented for each series of trials.

For the sake of convenience in describing each weapon, they will be numbered 1, 2, etc, as coinciding with the sequence of their appearance at the various trials.

NO.1 – THE PRIZE COMPETITION PATTERN

Originally presented in response to the WO advertisement of 22-10-1866, by the Prize Committee report of 11-6-1867 it was one of the nine systems selected for the Prize Competition. Six rifles of exactly the same pattern were ordered by letter of 22-6-1867 for delivery by October that year. There were thus at least seven of this particular type made, and Fig.1 shows the breech area of one of them. (For an illustration of the complete arm, see Chapter 2, Fig.1.)

By the report of 12-2-1868 the Martini was relegated to seventh position out of the nine, mainly because its ammunition was defective, and did not allow the weapon to give a full indication of its capabilities. The ammunition used was a copper-cased rim-fire cartridge, which had a habit of splitting around the base fold forming the rim.

A brief description of the rifle was given in the prize competition report, and as Martini shortly afterwards took out his first British Patent, No.2305 of 22-7-1868, we can assume that the breech mechanism illustrated therein was fairly close in design to that of the prize competition rifle.

Martini himself, in his letter seen on p.48 , stated that he had improved his original design some time in 1866, and the transfer declaration also seen on p.47 was dated 23-11-1866, ie, approximately the time that he presented his rifle for the prize competition. It is thus seen that there could be little variation in the action presented for the competition and the design shown in the patent application.

Fig.2 shows a sectional drawing of the Martini breech at this stage of its development. There are a few points worthy of mention, as being pertinent to later developments of the action, and final reversion to this pattern for some aspects of its construction, viz, –

1. The tumbler and trigger (the trigger nose had direct contact with the bent of the tumbler).
2. The cocking indicator, L, at the top rear of the action.
3. There was no safety catch
4. The lever had a large loop
5. The lever latch was outside the butt stock
6. The solid, screwed block axis pin
7. The parallel sided and screwed lever axis pin.

Specifications.

Weight: 8 lbs 15¾ ozs (4.1 kg)
Length: 51" (1,296 mm)
Barrel – Effective length: 35" (889 mm)
Calibre: 0.433" (11 mm)
Grooves: 8
Twist: 1 turn in 32"

Cartridge: Copper case rim-fire.
Total weight: 520 grains

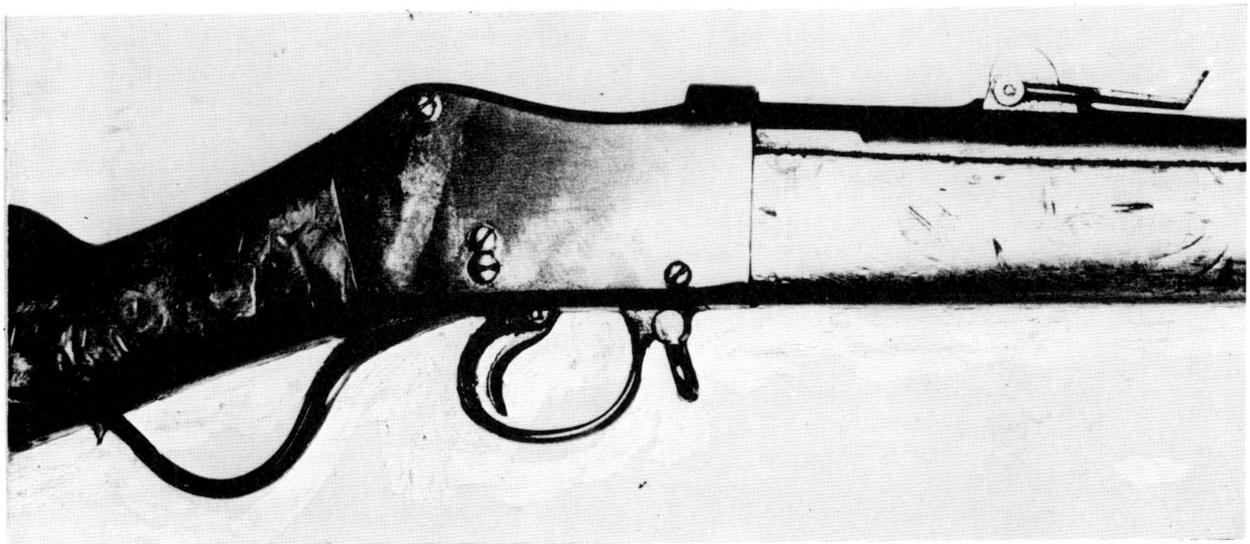

Tower

Fig. 1 – Prize Competition Rifle – Action details.

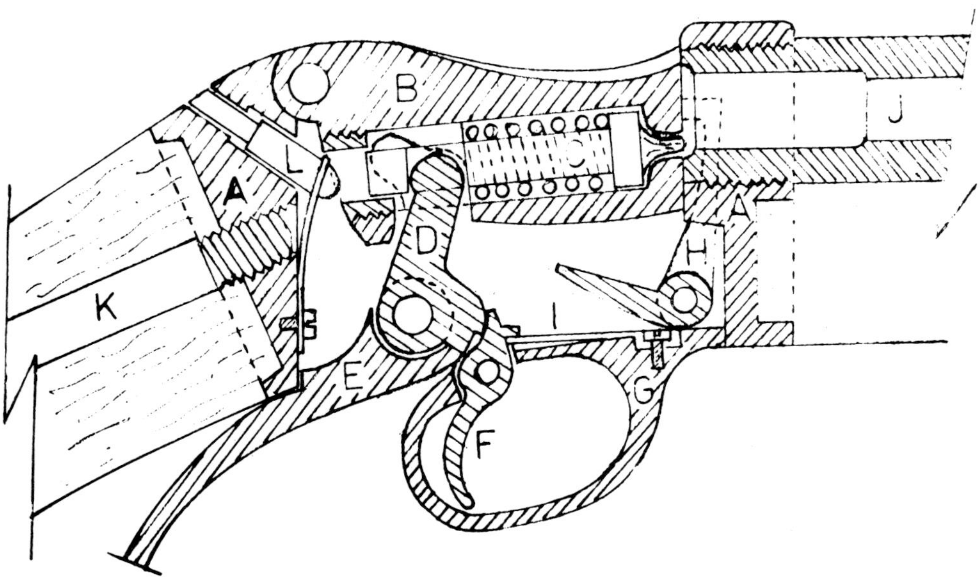

Fig. 2 – Early Martini Action – Closed and fired.

Parts shown –

A: Body, or shoe
B: Breech block
C: Striker
D: Tumbler
E: Lever
F: Trigger
G: Trigger guard
H: Extractor
I: Trigger spring
J: Barrel
K: Stock bolt
L: Cocking indicator

B.A.T.

Length: 2.292" (58 mm)
Powder charge: 72 grains BP, compressed

Bullet: Cylindro-conoidal, with 4 cannelures
Weight: 334 grains
Length: 0.94" (24 mm)
Diameter: 0.454" (11 mm)
Lubrication: 3 parts white wax, 1 part tallow

Weight of 60 cartridges packed: 4 lbs 9 oz (2.1 kg).

NO.2 – THE BREECH SELECTION TRIALS FIRST PATTERN

After the abortive prize competition came the breech selection trials, which closed for entries on 26-10-1968, and were reported upon on 11-2-1869. This series of trials had started soon after the finalising of the prize competition, and the Martini was one of the arms carried over for further consideration.

However, as the barrel accuracy trials were being carried out using the Boxer cartridge with compressed charges, it was decided that the breech systems should also use that cartridge, so it became necessary to alter the Martini from a rim-fire to a centre-fire, and adapt it for the Boxer cartridge. It is stated in the committee report that to avoid delay in this conversion – because of difficulties in getting the rifle to Switzerland for Martini to modify, and back again to England – the Supt. RL was asked to make the necessary alterations.

This raises an interesting point. In their report the committee state that, in regard to the selection trials – *As the selected arms were likely to be damaged during the course of the experiments which it was proposed to carry out, it was decided . . . to purchase one arm of each system.* This was done, and the single new specimen purchased would have been the rifle converted at the RL to take the Boxer cartridge, which indicates that it was of the same pattern as used in the prize competition, and chambered for the same rim-fire cartridge which had proved to be an abject failure at that time! If this was the case, it would appear that had the rifle been left in its original form, it would probably have again failed in the new trials, unless ammunition of an improved pattern had been provided.

Figs.3 to 6 show various aspects of the No.2 rifle, and its similarity to No.1 is evident. Noteworthy features of these arms disclosed in the illustrations are –

1. The flat fore-end retaining pin
2. Spring retained bands; and
3. "Continental" rear sight.

Also visible in Fig.4 is the cocking indicator at the top rear of the action, showing that the action is cocked.

Dimensions of this rifle would presumably be the same as for No.1.

NO.3 – THE BREECH SELECTION TRIALS SECOND PATTERN

During the barrel accuracy trials it was found that cartridges with loose powder charges were more accurate than those with compressed charges. However, the loose charge cartridges were longer than those with compressed charges, and as it was decided to test the Martini with loose charges, it became necessary to alter the action to accomodate the increased length cartridge.

The existing rifle (No.2) was not thought suitable for alteration, so the Supt. RSAF was asked to prepare a new rifle on the Martini system (Martini having been advised of this decision) to *take the long cartridge case 0.45-inch bore, and at the same time to make one or two minor alterations not affecting the principle of the breech mechanism.*

The new rifle was delivered on 21-10-1868, incorporating

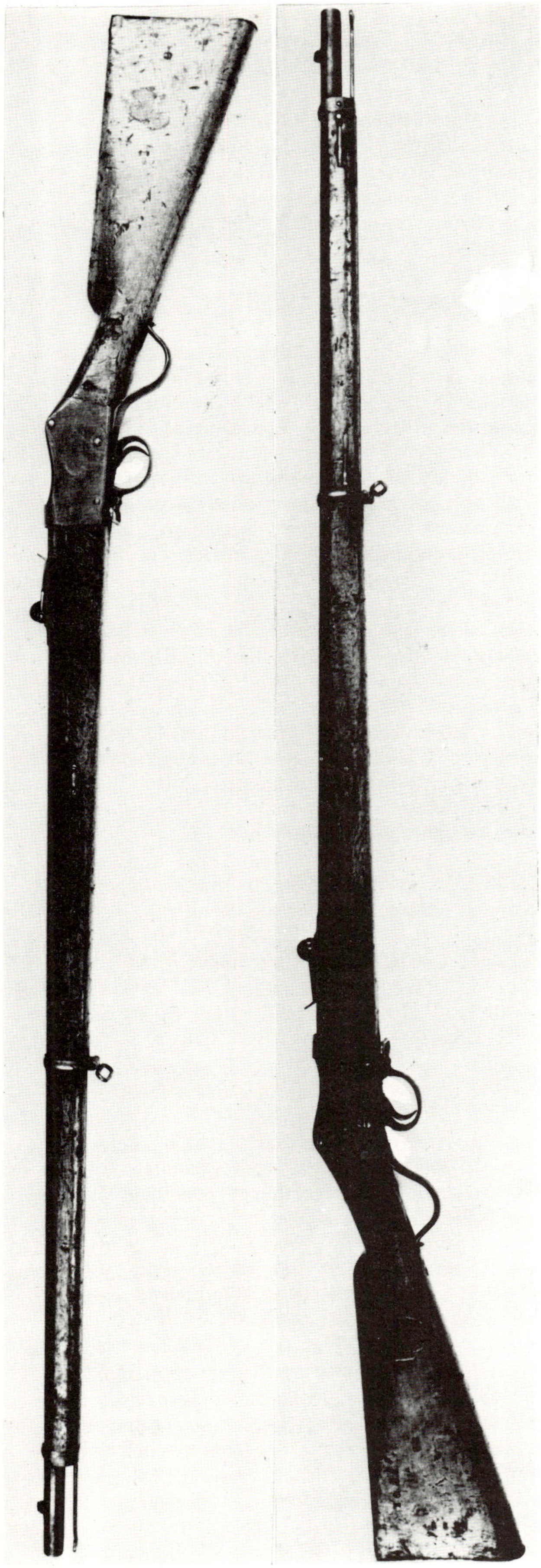

W&D

Fig. 3 – Martini Rifle, Type 2.

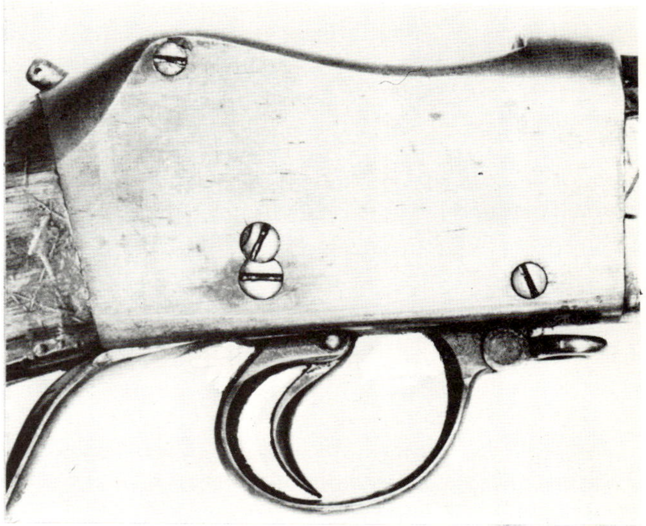

W&D

Fig. 4 – Martini Rifle, Type 2 – Action details. (Note cocking indicator.)

W&D

Fig. 5 – Martini Rifle, Type 2 – Action details.

W&D

Fig. 6 – Martini Rifle, Type 2 – Action details. (Note hole at rear of action for cocking indicator.)

the "slight improvements", which were not actually specified, but which can be easily deduced from a study of the parts drawings which were used to compare the Martini with the Henry and Snider, and from the text of the committee's report.

The parts drawing shows an extra part in relation to the trigger/tumbler unit. This was the "tumbler rest", and is the first appearance of this part, which was eventually to cause more trouble than it was worth, and so was finally discarded.

The second unit incorporated in the action was the safety bolt. In the words of the report –

It will be noticed that there is no half-cock position in the Martini system, but to allow the arm to be carried with safety when loaded and ready to fire, a locking bolt, which prevents the trigger from being pulled, has been added to Mr. Martini's original pattern. (This item caused problems too, so it also was discarded, bringing the system back to what Martini originally presented – indicating that the design was sound in the first place, and should not have been interfered with.)

Martini had arrived in England at this stage, and upon examining the rifle pointed out that it did not perfectly represent the Martini system, and was also too heavy to comply with the trial conditions. However, he showed how the weight could be reduced, and the committee accepted the rifle and put it through the same series of trials that the other rifle had performed. These trials it passed in a very satisfactory manner.

This rifle would appear to have been similar to the other patterns, but externally would have had the safety catch sliding thumb piece visible.

In comparison with the several features of the original model we now had –

1. Trigger and tumbler had added piece (tumbler rest)
2. Cocking indicator the same
3. Safety catch fitted
4. Lever the same
5. Lever latch the same
6. Block axis pin the same
7. Lever axis pin the same.

NO.4 – THE BREECH SELECTION TRIALS THIRD PATTERN

Having now tested the Martini breech with long and short cartridges, it was decided to test it with the weight of rifle reduced, and made entirely on Martini's plan. Accordingly, an order for a breech mechanism, to be made under Martini's supervision, was given to the RSAF. This rifle was to be tested against an improved Henry type rifle, to decide finally the outcome of the breech selection trials.

The rifle was found to be within the stipulated weight, and was eventually successful in the trials, being declared the best of those submitted, and passed on for comparison with the Snider.

There is scant information available on this particular pattern. It was stated to be on "Martini's plan", but still had the same number of parts as the previous pattern, and as the pattern following it also had the same number, it seems that this No.4 rifle also incorporated the tumbler rest and safety catch of No.3.

NO.5 – THE FIRST MARTINI–HENRY

After the selection of the Martini breech and the Henry barrel, the two systems had to be married to form the composite rifle that in theory would make the ultimate unit acceptable for the British service. This combination had to be tested, so four rifles incorporating the two systems were ordered from the RSAF. As Henry proposed a seven groove barrel in place of his original nine groove pattern, two of the new rifles were to have seven groove barrels and the others, nine grooves, to allow for a comparison of the two types.

Two of these rifles were received by the committee about the beginning of January 1869, and the other two later on. The rifles were numbered 1 to 4, and some slight differences were evident in the various rifles. The breech mechanisms were similar in pattern to the previous Martini, ie, Type 4, but No.5/2 had a slightly different safety catch, and No.5/4 had a different cocking indicator.

From various references we can infer that –

No.5/1 had – 1. A cocking indicator at top rear of action
2. A seven groove barrel (See Fig.7.)

No.5/2 had – 1. A cocking indicator as above
2. A nine groove barrel
3. A slightly different safety catch to the others.

No.5/3 had – 1. A cocking indicator as above (See Fig.7)

No.5/4 had – 1. A completely different cocking indicator to the others above, with a pointer on the outside of the action on the right hand side. (See Fig.8.)

These rifles all had a barrel 35" long, which weighed 4 lbs 5 ozs (1.95 kg), and was fitted with "Whitworth" sights. The overall weight of the arm was 9 lbs 7 ozs (4.3 kg).

During shooting trials of the first two rifles, the spring of the cocking indicator broke, so Martini presented a new pattern of indicator, which entailed the tumbler being keyed onto a square section of the lever axis pin, which had a pointer formed on one end. This did away with the three parts of the original indicator, and reduced the number of parts to 27. This indicator was fitted to No.5/4.

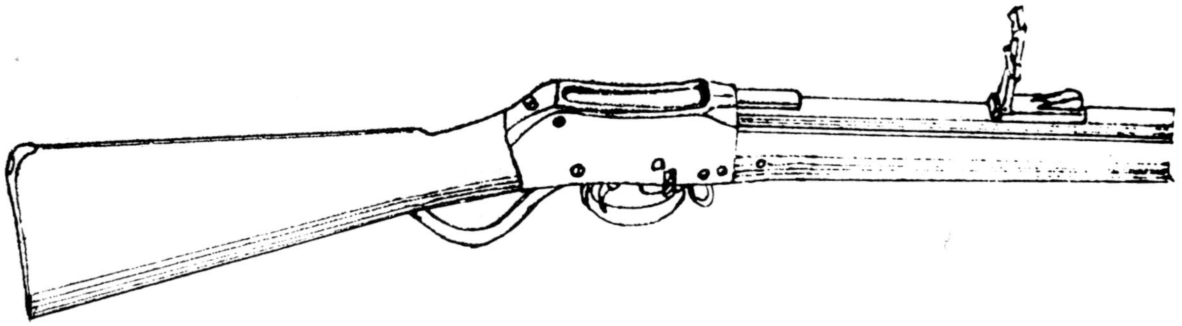

**Fig. 7 – Rifles, Martini-Henry, Types 5/1 and 5/3 –
Cocked and ready to fire.**

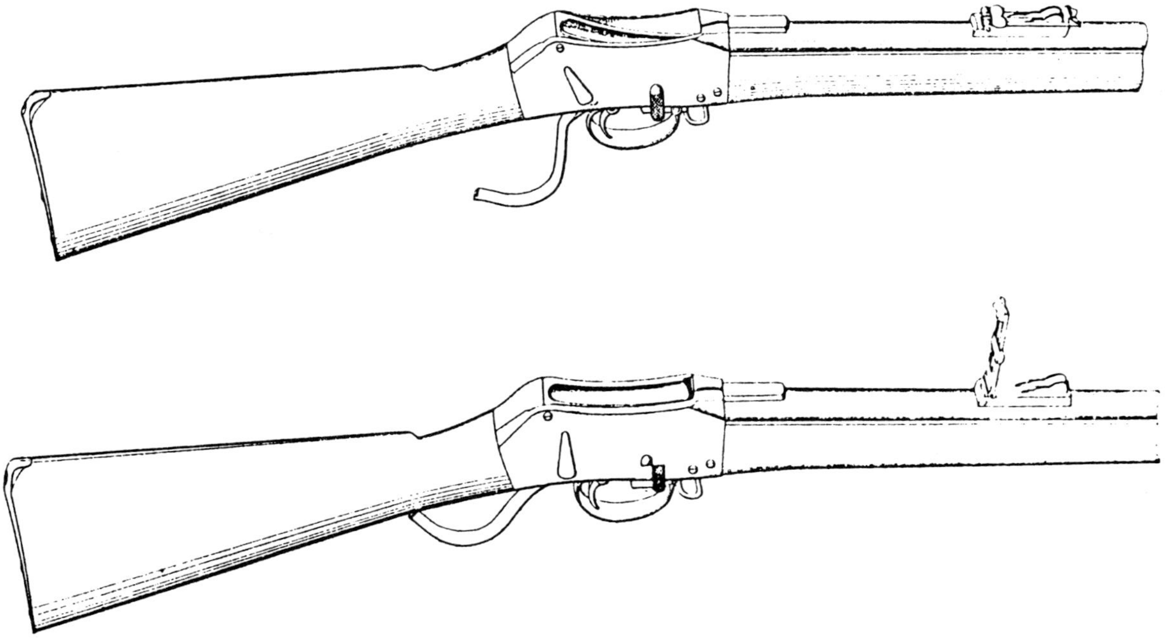

**Fig. 8 – Rifle, Martini-Henry, Type 5/4 –
Top: Open and cocked
Bottom: Closed and fired.**

the indicator was fitted to the approved pattern of the H, reference to the drawings of Figs.2 and 9 will disclose ne interesting variations, showing the development of the ion over five patterns of rifles. To quote *Engineering* of 3-1869 –

e breech mechanism had undergone several important difications in its construction since Mr. Martini first mitted the arm.

ne basic external "Martini" features retained by the M-H luded the large loop to the lever, the external lever latch, l the long comb to the butt stock. No.5/4 differed exterly from the others by having the improved cocking indicr on the right hand side of the action.

NO.6 – THE LONG CHAMBER TRIALS RIFLES

After the M-H rifle was recommended for the service by the Special Committee on Breech-Loading Rifles, the CoO on 23-3-1869 resolved, in part, *that further trial be made with the arm recommended,* and that *200 hand-made arms of the same pattern be also proceeded with.*

For such large scale manufacture – relative to previous production of trials Martinis, which had been in very small numbers only – a pattern arm was necessary, so had to be determined. A part description of this pattern arm can be built up by perusing the letter of 18-2-1869 (henceforth to be called Letter "A"), and the memorandum of 18-3-1869 (Memo "B"), presented to the CoO by Lt.-Col. Fletcher. (See Chapter 5 for the letters, memorandum, and report referred to in this section.)

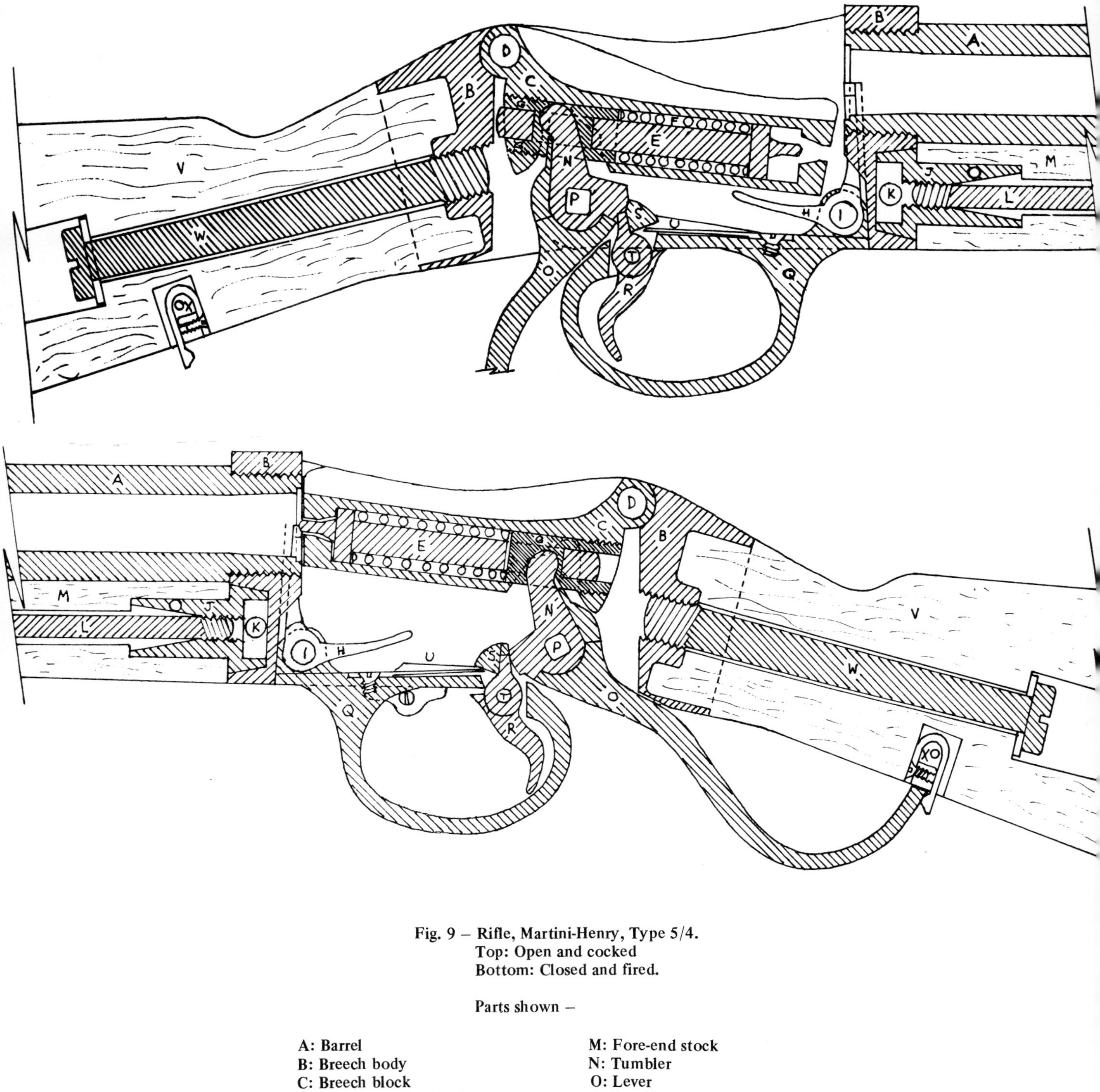

Fig. 9 – Rifle, Martini-Henry, Type 5/4.
Top: Open and cocked
Bottom: Closed and fired.

Parts shown –

A: Barrel
B: Breech body
C: Breech block
D: Breech block axis pin
E: Striker
F: Striker spring
G: Striker spring stop nut
H: Extractor
I: Extractor axis pin
J: Fore-end and rod holder
K: Fore-end and rod holder screw
L: Cleaning rod
M: Fore-end stock
N: Tumbler
O: Lever
P: Tumbler and lever axis pin
Q: Trigger guard and plate
R: Trigger
S: Tumbler rest
T: Trigger axis pin
U: Trigger and rest spring
V: Butt stock
W: Butt stock screw and washer
X: Lever catch unit.

Before proceeding with this line of enquiry, there is one point of interest in Fletcher's Memo B that requires investigation. In Point 1 he mentions Martini's desire to alter the position of the block axis pin, relative to its position in the M-H breech and that of the original trials Martinis. To quote –

The arms of both patterns have worked well, but the position as proposed appears to the committee to be the best, and Col. Dixon has been requested to construct an arm on this pattern. This arm should be examined and tested, and, if satisfactory, be adopted as the sealed pattern.

It would appear that this particular weapon was not completed, if indeed actually commenced, as the committee's report of 28-5-1869 (Report "C") stated –

The committee have had no opportunity of actually testing a Martini breech block, . . . with the pin in the exact position laid down by them, but as the breech blocks with pins placed very slightly above and below answer thoroughly well, . . . the committee consider that no actual experiments are necessary.

In the event, the pattern arm did incorporate the pin in the position designated, as authorised in a letter from the committee to the RSAF dated 8-3-1869, ie, between the dates of Letter A and Memo B.

Features of the pattern arm for the 200 trials rifles taken from Letter A are found in –

Item 2 – *It is recommended that a small muzzle protector, to be used when cleaning the arm, should be served out to the troops, also that a muzzle stopper be issued.*

Item 4 – *Col. Dixon has proposed and submitted an arm with a hole in the butt, capable of containing a jag and muzzle protector, etc. This pattern the committee approve of.*

From Memo B comes the reference quoted above on the position of the block axis pin, and from Section II – *First is the question of the bore of the new arm. The committee unanimously decided upon the .45 bore.*

Report C gives the axis pin position as referred to above; sighting, as – *The committee having made experiments to determine the sighting of the new arm, up to 1,200 yards;* the bayonet – *A sword bayonet with saw at the back, similar to those issued to the Irish Constabulary, was shown to the committee by Col. Dixon, also a sword bayonet of similar description but somewhat longer. The committee having examined the two patterns selected the first, or shorter.*

The muzzle stopper was again recommended, as – *The pattern the committee recommend is similar to that approved by the OSC, . . . but without the oil bottle. It combines a muzzle stopper with a sight protector.*

Also again recommended was the muzzle protector – *The committee recommend . . . and ebonite muzzle protector . . . to be issued with each rifle. The pattern has been fixed by the committee.*

To ascertain the best method of fixing the sling to the new rifle, the committee communicated with the A-G's department, which resulted in – *They recommend three places of attachment, one at the top band, another in front of the trigger guard, and a third near the toe of the butt. With respect to the shape of the attachments, the committee have adopted the swivels at present in use in the service, as Col. Dixon informs them that time will not admit of making a change in the pattern for the 200 arms in course of manufacture.*

To conclude – *The pattern arm approved by the committee is that of the infantry of the army. No patterns of the serjeant's and naval rifles, or of the artillery or cavalry carbine have been made. It would appear advantageous in respect to facility of manufacture that the number of different patterns in use in the service should be reduced. The pattern arm, in course of manufacture at Enfield, has the long stock and a trap in the butt, in which a jag, an ebonite muzzle protector, and three pieces of flannel (somewhat reduced in size from those issued with the .577 bore rifle) for cleaning purposes, can be carried, also the muzzle stopper when not fixed in the barrel. The committee doubt whether two lengths of stock are necessary, the long stock appearing sufficiently well adapted even for short armed men. They recommend that patterns of Martini-Henry arms, suitable for the several branches of the two services, be at once constructed at Enfield, and also that, if possible, these various patterns be reduced in number.*

The pattern arm resulting from the above was approved for sealing on 29-9-1869 (vide minute of 18-11-1869), and was formally sealed on 1-10-1869. The Pattern Book of the RSAF thus has the following entry –

Rifle, Martini-Henry.
Date of approval: 1-10-69.
Enfield No.: 8360.

Description of alterations for which the arm has been sealed as a pattern:

Original arm.

Weight of arm: 9 lb 5 oz. (As near as possible, weight of pattern arm 9 lb 5½ oz.) Vide committee letter 26-10-68.
Weight of sword bayonet and scabbard: 1 lb 14½ oz. Committee Report XXXIII.
Length of arm without bayonet: 4' 3" (The pattern is 4' 3½"). Committee letter 29-2-68.
Length of barrel: 2' 11".
Calibre: .45"
Weight of barrel: 4 lb 6 oz.
Length of pull: 14". As in committee letter 10-12-68. Committee report XXXV.
Sights, back: Whitworth, as in ditto, ditto.
Swivels: 3. As in committee report XXXIV.
Indicator: As in committee letter 15-2-69.
Position of block axis pin: As in committee letter 8-3-69.
Hole in stock, to receive: Jag, muzzle stopper, muzzle protector, and flannel (as required by committee letter 15-2-69)
Sword bayonet: Saw back. Committee report XXXIII.
Implements: Muzzle stopper and protector and jag. As in committee report XXXIII, and letters of 24-4-69, and 25-5-*

*69. (*This pattern cancelled by next pattern sealed 3-11-71.)*
Body: To be browned as approved by 7669/1952.
Chamber: For long improved cartridge approved by SoS 16-9-69.
Remarks: The length of the jam nut, length and force of coil main spring, form of striker, and hole in block and other minor points conform to No.3 pattern Martini-Henry rifle in possession of the committee, and which gave very good results in all the above essential points.

The committee particularly requested that No.3 should be taken as a guide in these particulars.

W.M. Dixon,
Col. and Supt.
24-9-1869.

Some other particulars of the standard long chamber rifle not evident from the above description included –

Block axis pin: Solid steel, screwed in
Breech block groove polished
Butt plate: Brass, with trap
Safety catch fitted to trigger.

The last-mentioned item was the same as that fitted to the M-H Type 5 rifles, as was the long comb to the butt stock, the large lever loop and external lever catch; but the cleaning rod screwed into a boss formed on the front of the action body, rather than into a separate piece pinned in position as on the former pattern. Externally, the No.6 rifle action was similar to the No.5, but could be readily distinguished from it by the lack of the extra screw in front of the extractor axis pin. Figs.10 to 14 illustrate the various features of the Type 6 rifles as mentioned here.

A final point of interest not previously remarked on in regard to this rifle was the heavily countersunk muzzle, as seen in Fig.15. This was apparently to allow the ebonite muzzle protector referred to above to seat securely on the end of the barrel, to protect the mouth of the bore and rifling when cleaning the barrel with the rod. As the ebonite protector was not proceeded with, this countersinking of the muzzle was not found on subsequent patterns of trials Martinis, and so was exclusive to this arm.

The long chamber rifles also had what was known as the long action, and this feature is important when considering the subsequent patterns of trials rifles, Nos.7, 8, and 9. (See Fig.16 for details of long chamber action.)

NO.7 – THE LONG ACTION, SHORT CHAMBER, TRIALS RIFLES

This pattern was ordered on 16-8-1869, by the authority of the DGO, to enable trials of the then new short bottleneck cartridge to be carried out. These rifles were produced by using the standard long action currently in production for the 200 No.6 trials rifles previously ordered.

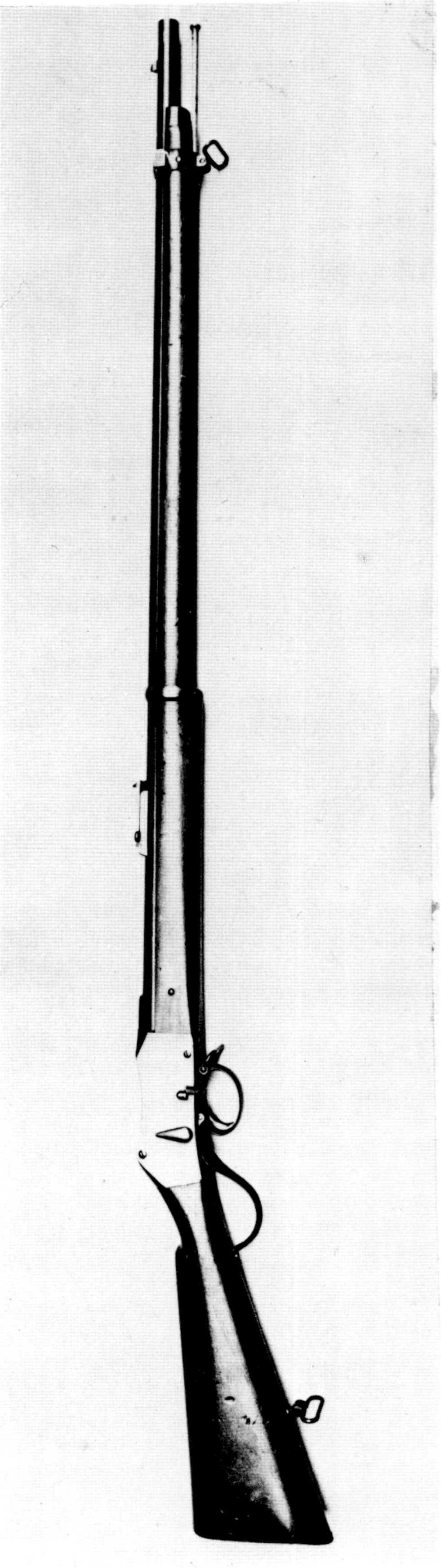
IWM

Fig. 10 – A Long Chamber Trials Rifle.

IWM

Fig. 11 – Long Chamber Rifle – View of safety catch.

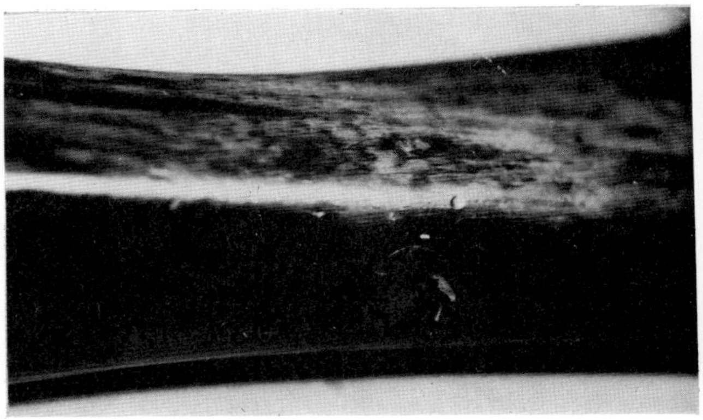

Fig. 13 – Long Chamber Rifle – Lever catch on butt stock.

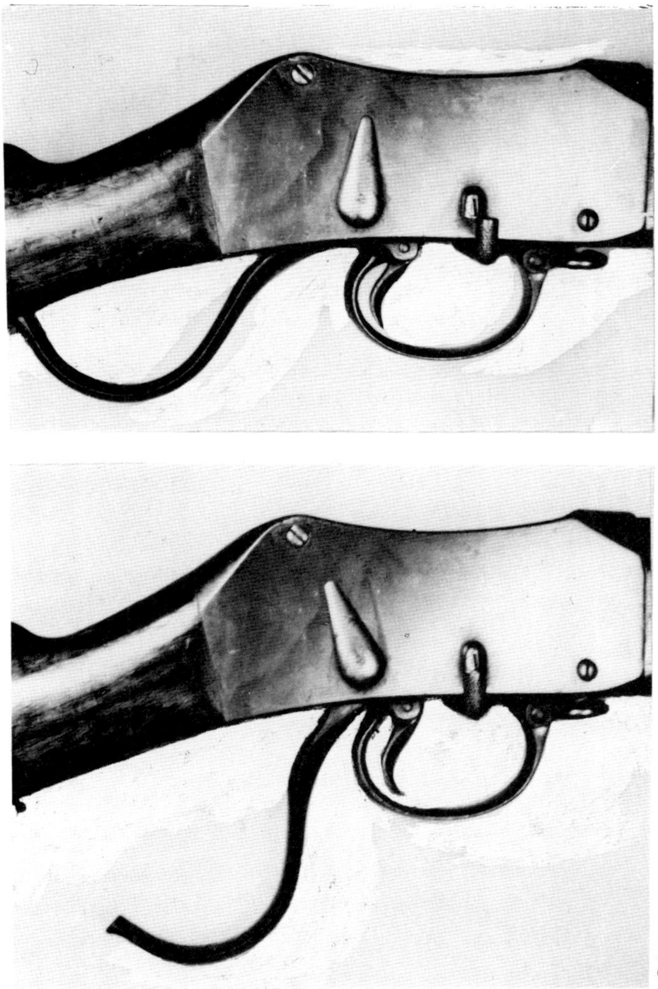

QAD(O)

Fig. 12 – Long Chamber Rifle –
Top: Action closed and fired
Bottom: Action open, with safety catch on.

IWM

Fig. 14 – Long Chamber Rifle – Front of action body, showing boss for cleaning rod.

IWM

Fig. 15 – Long Chamber Rifle – Showing countersunk muzzle.

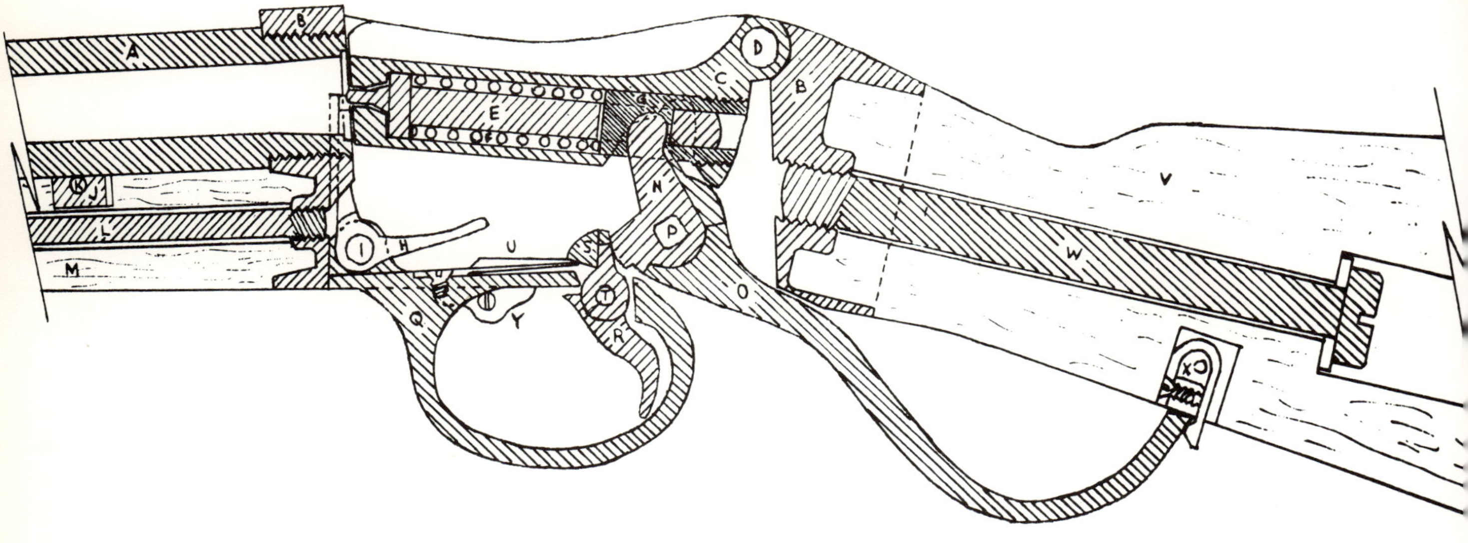

Fig. 16 – Long Chamber Rifle – Closed and fired.

Parts shown –

A: Barrel
B: Body
C: Breech block
D: Breech block axis pin
E: Striker
F: Striker spring
G: Striker spring stop nut
H: Extractor
I: Extractor axis pin
J: Barrel stud
K: Fore-end retaining pin
L: Cleaning rod
M: Fore-end stock
N: Tumbler
O: Lever
P: Tumbler and lever axis pin
Q: Trigger guard and plate
R: Trigger
S: Tumbler rest
T: Trigger axis pin
U: Trigger and rest spring
V: Butt stock
W: Butt stock screw and washer
X: Lever catch unit.

Although not specifically mentioned, it is quite likely that the other components for these pattern 7 rifles were taken out of those on hand for pattern 6, so that – apart from the different chamber and extractor to accomodate the new cartridge, and other necessary minor alterations – the No.7 rifles would have been almost identical to No.6.

Ten short chamber rifles were ordered, and eight were made to pattern 7; the remaining two were made as –

NO.8 – THE SHORT ACTION, SHORT CHAMBER, TRIALS RIFLES

No mention has been found as to why these particular rifles were made, as they were part of the order of 16-8-1869, which had been for rifles to test the short cartridge only. They were the first of the short action M-H rifles to appear, and were not entirely successful, so did not get the same exposure to the trials as the long action No.7 rifles.

As regards their appearance, it is again most likely that they used as many of the standard components as possible, so that externally, apart from the shorter action, they would have been similar in appearance to the Nos.6 and 7 patterns.

NO.9 – A LONG ACTION, SHORT CHAMBER, TRIALS RIFLE

This was ordered on 19-8-1869, ie, a few days after the No. 7 and 8 rifles. One only was ordered, to take a cartridge with "Increased dimensions and internal lining". This cartridge would appear to have merely been a Boxer cartridge with heavier construction than a normal one, so requiring a slightly larger chamber.

Apart from this larger chamber, this rifle could be assumed to be identical with the No.7 type.

NO.10 – SHORT ACTION, SHORT CHAMBER, EXPERIMENTAL RIFLES

There were two of these made and tested at the RSAF during Nov.-Dec. 1869, on the authority of the DGO, who had directed the superintendent to work out the alterations and methods required to adapt the Martini action to the new cartridge. The trials of the short cartridge were so successful it was certain to be adopted as the service cartridge, so the action could also be shortened, hence the above directive.

100 short chamber rifles had been requested, but the super-

intendent replied that it was not possible to make that many, because of machinery problems, and the fact that he was still experimenting with the short action, as the first two (No.8) "cramped the action", and so were not entirely successful. The No.10 actions were ¼-inch longer than the first short types, and were apparently successful, as no other references to the fault of "cramp" have been noted.

These two rifles would have been similar to the No.8 types.

NO.11 – THE SHORT ACTION, SHORT CHAMBER, TRIALS RIFLES

Because of the success of the short cartridge trials, but also because of some problems disclosed by those trials, a Special Committee on Ammunition for Martini-Henry Rifles was convened in January 1870, and made a report on 25-3-1870 with the remarks that *They have no hesitation, therefore, in recommending . . . the short chambered rifle as the future pattern of the Martini-Henry rifle* because of the claimed advantages of –

1. A shorter breech action
2. Greater facility of loading.

The short action recommended was in accordance with drawings submitted by Col. Dixon, which are seen in Figs. 17. As there is no mention of the arm as a whole, it is again reasonable to assume that the standard type components would be used, so this pattern of rifle would be similar in appearance to those previously produced.

Twelve of these new pattern short action short chamber rifles were ordered for issue to the Wimbledon Meeting of 1870, but after reading the report of 25-3-1870, the C-I-C requested that some of the type might be made and issued for trial by the troops. As a result, twelve more were ordered on 11-5-1870, to make a total of 24 available for trial.

The first twelve rifles – some with modified sights – were sent to Wimbledon in July, and were favourably reported upon; 22 of the 24 were sent on trial in October 1870, with the two remaining being retained by the committee for their own experiments.

NO.12 – SHORTENED AND LIGHTENED, SHORT ACTION, SHORT CHAMBER, TRIALS RIFLES

While the trials with the short chamber rifles and ammunition had been going on, the 200 No.6 rifles had been completed and issued for their trials, and early reports coming in had included some remarks that the length and weight of the arm were excessive. The navy particularly desired a M-H the same length and weight as the naval Snider, so, by order of the DoA on 7-11-1870, two of the Type 11 rifles were withdrawn from trial and sent to Enfield to be shortened and lightened for trial by the navy. The result was a rifle the same length as the naval Snider, and about the same weight, ie, 8 lb 12 oz. These rifles also had the comb of the butt stock reduced.

This naval M-H rifle, being shortened, had to have its sights regraduated because of the decreased sighting radius, and the Enfield Range Book on 16-11-1870 gave details of the new sight graduations (worked out by experiments conducted there) as –

Yards.	Inches.
200	.41¼
300	.50
400	.60
500	.73
600	.86
700	1.00
800	1.15
900	1.31¼
1,000	1.49
1,100	1.68½
1,200	1.90½

It was also mentioned that for the regraduation of the original sights, the steps were filed down, and the new marks made on the leaf of the sight.

On 17-2-1871 the Admiralty approved of this short rifle for adoption by the navy, but the committee stated they felt the weight of the rifle could be further reduced without detriment, and that they were experimenting along those lines.

NO.13 – A LIGHTENED LONG CHAMBER RIFLE

This was produced in an attempt to lighten the No.6 rifle, and improve its balance, although retaining the original length. To achieve this result the committee *tried a barrel prepared at Enfield six ounces lighter than the original Martini-Henry, making the whole arm one oz. lighter than the long Snider rifle.* A WO minute of 7-11-1870, referring to this barrel stated – *The RSAF turned down a barrel, which was chambered and screwed into an existing Martini-Henry at the RL. The weight of this barrel was 3 lb 15 oz.*

The rifle referred to in the comparison above was the Type 5, which weighed 9 lb 7 oz (4.3 kg). The subtraction of 6 oz. from this figure gives a nett of 9 lb 1 oz, against 9 lb 2 oz for the long Snider, so agreeing with the quote of 1 oz less than the latter arm.

This leads to some interesting speculation as to what type of rifle was rebarreled for this conversion. It was quoted as "an existing rifle at the RL". In view of the fact that the Type 5 weights were used in the comparison, one of those arms could have been used, and reference to the Table of Weights in Appendix 16 will show that this was highly probable. The nett weight of a Type 5 rifle was 5 lb 2 oz, as was that of the Type 13, indicating that the same basic unit was used; conversely, the nett weight for a Type 6 was 4 lb 15 oz, which shows that this was not the arm used for the conversion.

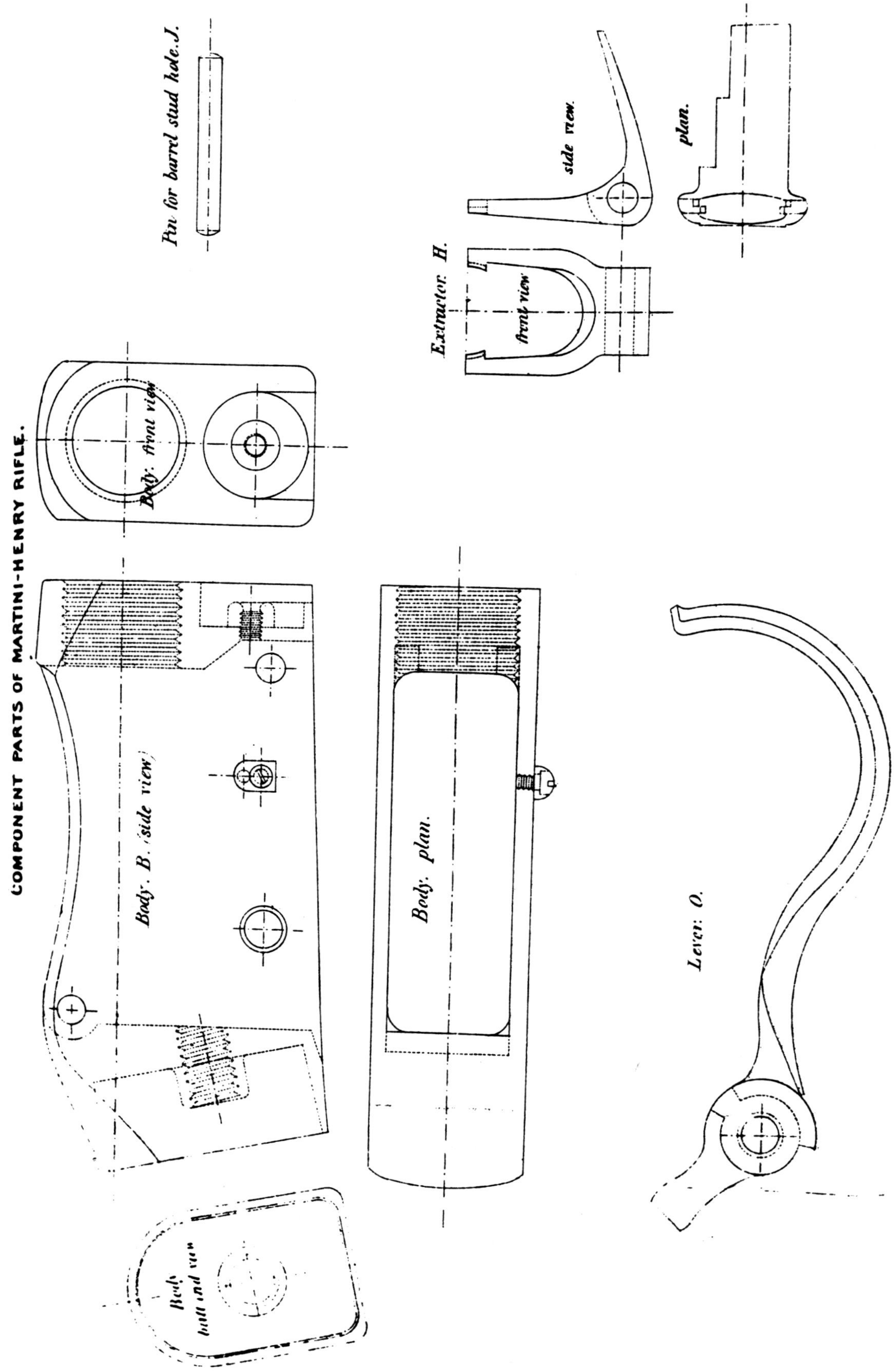

Figs. 17 (3 pages.) – Components of the Short Action Martini-Henry Rifle, Type 11.

COMPONENT PARTS OF MARTINI-HENRY RIFLE.

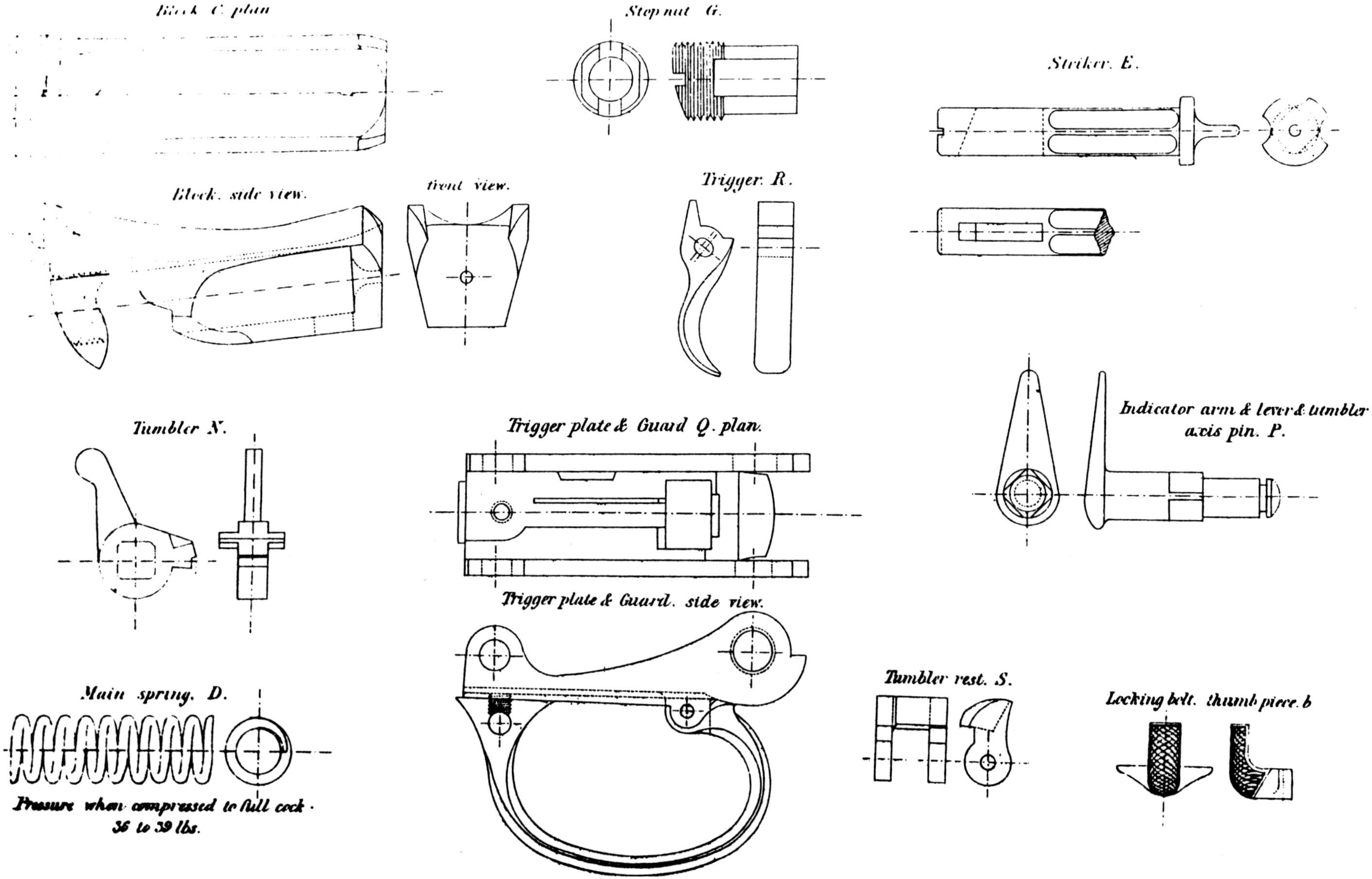

COMPONENT PARTS OF MARTINI-HENRY RIFLE.

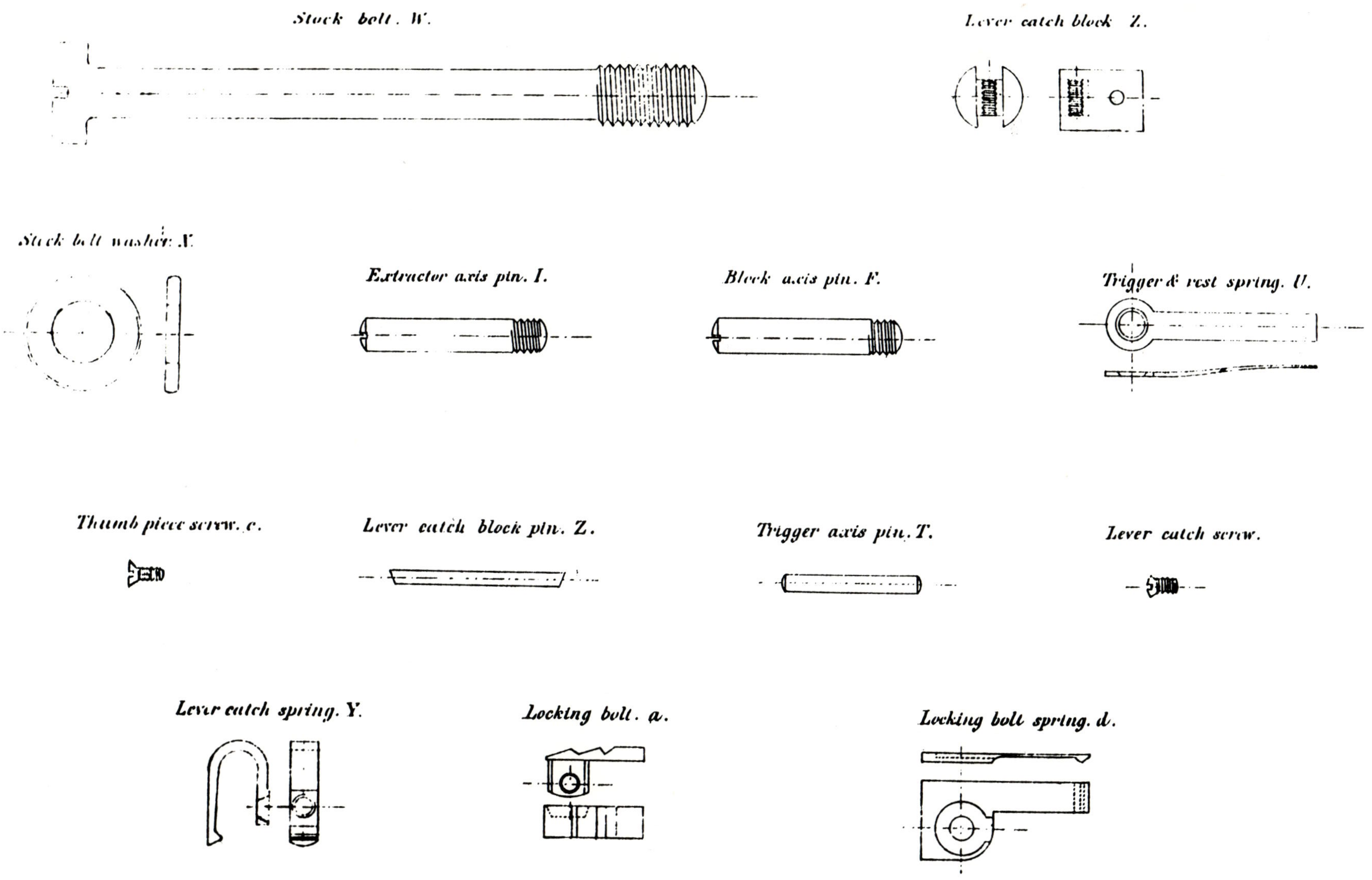

NO.14 – A LIGHTENED, SHORT ACTION, SHORT CHAMBER, SHORT RIFLE

It had been mentioned in the committee report of 8-2-1871 that after trials with the two shortened and lightened rifles (ie, the Type 12 arms), experiments were still being carried out to determine whether the short rifles could not be further lightened.

Other major alterations were also proposed, and presented in an appendix to that report. These proposals were listed in the previous chapter, and it would appear that they were incorporated into the final trials pattern rifle and tested in conjunction with the still further lightened barrel, as stated in a Supplementary Report of 21-3-1871 from the committee.

The new barrel was 3 lb 6¼ oz in weight, giving the rifle a total weight of 8 lb 7½ oz; and a stock with increased bend had also been tried.

The changes to this pattern had radically altered its appearance when compared with the preceding trials rifles, and it could thus be described as being the prototype for the subsequent service pattern arms. The most noticeable external changes that would distinguish this pattern were –

1. A reversible slide on backsight leaf
2. The lever shaped differently, ie, with a straight shank and smaller loop
3. The lever catch block of different form, and fully enclosed in the wood of the butt stock
4. A butt stock with shorter comb
5. The butt trap abolished, and the butt plate chequered
6. A small chequered hollow in the top right rear of the action body for use as a thumb rest
7. The block axis pin made of gunmetal and retained by a keeper screw
8. The trigger roughened, and its axis a screw rather than a pin
9. The safety catch indicator moved to the OFF position
10. The cleaning rod held under top band by a catch and the spring of the rod.

After the trials of this rifle the committee made some final recommendations for inclusion in the first service pattern, viz. –

1. The barrel weight to be 3 lb 6¼ oz (ie, confirmation of the trial barrel weight).

2. The stock to be of increased bend (ie, confirmation of the trial stock).

3. The thumb recess to be slightly altered.

4. Corners of the fore part of the flap of the backsight to be rounded off.

5. The lower band to be more securely fastened.

6. The hole in the head of the cleaning rod to be longer and larger.

7. The metal of the lever to be thickened near the end where it fitted into the breech action.

It is probable that this was a completely new arm, as the many changes in its components would have made it easier to produce that way rather than as a conversion of an existing rifle.

MANUFACTURE OF THE MARTINI TRIALS RIFLES

The original trials rifles, ie, Nos.1 and 2, were produced in Switzerland by, or for, Martini, and brought by him to England for the trials. However, the rifles from No.3 onwards were all made by the RSAF, during the production years 1869 to 1871, and Table XVI shows the numbers produced for this period. A comparison between the production figures, eg, Items A, B, C, etc, and the trials rifles, eg, Nos.3, 4, 5, etc, allows some of the latter to be specifically identified.

The six rifles A can be easily identified as trials patterns No. 3 (1 of), No.4 (1 of), and No.5 (4 of). The high cost of each rifle was caused by the need to supply special tools to manufacture these arms, as they were of a type never before produced at Enfield.

The 212 arms B obviously included the 200 Type 6 rifles, leaving a balance of 12 to identify. The manner of presenting the production figures seems to indicate that the B rifles were of a single pattern, so there are thus the 12 unaccounted for.

These could have been sent to the RL for cartridge trials, or to other similar places as specimens for examination and display.

There were 11 rifles C, and these were most likely No.7 (8 of), No.8 (2 of), and No.9 (1 of). These 11 rifles were all used in the bottleneck cartridge trials, for which bayonets were not necessary, so this strengthens the case for this identification, as the C rifles did not have any corresponding bayonets produced.

The increased production figures are reflected in the lower cost per unit, ie, down from around £50 each to £14 each. (Under full production the unit cost was further reduced to around £3 per arm without bayonet.)

Not identified in the production figures are the two rifles No.10, but as these were experimental, rather than trials arms, they may have been included in costs under a different heading.

The 24 No.11 rifles were produced under two separate orders, and the Elcho bayonet was intended to be used with the second order of 12 rifles, so in the production figures we find – 18 rifles D, with bayonets, etc. The first order for twelve No.11 rifles was probably in this group, leaving six to identify. The 18 sword bayonets H, were apparently for this group, although also being included in the description of them, as shown.

Conversely, the 15 rifles E, do not show bayonets, but there were 12 Elcho bayonets G, to fit them, as mentioned above. We may thus fairly assume that the second twelve No.11 rifles were in this group, leaving three to identify.

As previous patterns showed a likelihood of a number of rifles produced above that required for troop trials, the same condition could apply to the D and E rifles, so the six and three rifles respectively, could have been sent to relevant government establishments.

The No.12 rifles were modified from two Type 11 rifles, so would not show on production records.

The No.13 rifle was most likely a trials Type 5 modified, as previously described, so also would not show in the production figures.

This leaves No.14 to identify, and as it is assumed to be of new manufacture it is possible that it was one of the three rifles unaccounted for in the E group above.

TABLE XVI – Production of Martini-Henry rifles at the RSAF during the trials period 1869-71.

Year ending 31st March.	Item	Quantity produced.	Description of weapon.
1869	A	6	Rifles, Martini-Henry, specially manufactured, including costs of tools, &c, £48.18.1 each. Total cost, £51.2.11 each.
1870	B	212	Rifles, Martini-Henry, new, with steel barrels, sword bayonets, scabbards, and cleaning rods, £14.15.4 each.
	C	11	Rifles, Martini-Henry, new, with steel barrels, and cleaning rods, £14.1.8 each.
1871	D	18	Rifles, Martini-Henry, complete, with sword bayonets, leather scabbards, and cleaning rods (specimens).
	E	15	Rifles, Martini-Henry, complete, with cleaning rods (specimens).
	F	1	Rifle, Martini-Henry, sectional model.
	G	12	Sword bayonets, Elcho pattern, with leather scabbards.
	H	18	Sword bayonets, with leather scabbards (specimens).

HAPTER 8.

IE MARTINI–HENRY SERVICE PATTERN RIFLES

TH the final pattern of trials rifle accepted as the basis r the first service pattern, the development of the M-H le entered a new era, and after all the conferences, experents, trials, and alterations of pattern that had led to this ige, those concerned could be excused for thinking that re was the end of their troubles, and that full scale issue the new rifle would soon take place. This ideal situation is not to be so easily achieved however, as more trials and erations were to eventuate during the years from 1872 to 76, before a fully acceptable service pattern was obtain-.

e rifles and trials to be discussed in the following chap-s will be described as "service" rifles and trials, to more idily distinguish them from the previous competition and als rifles, although some of the so-called service patterns re never actually issued as an active service weapon.

enable the reader to understand the various arms refer-l to in the service trials and reports, brief descriptions of e service pattern arms used will be given below. Minor erations to the basic patterns will be mentioned in the xt when applicable, for clarification of changes made to e weapons which did not necessarily change the desig-tion.

IE MARK I RIFLE

cause of the several and various changes made to this irk during the years 1871-76, and because these changes eated some obvious alterations to the arm – particularly the breech action – it is necessary to describe this rifle three divisions, as Mark I, First, Second, and Third Pat-ns. These are not official designations – although the rresponding pattern arms existed – and are used for con-nience only, as some arms would not comply exactly th any one particular pattern, eg, some third pattern arms uld have features of the second pattern, and so on. This s caused by the fact that production proceeded all the ne the service trials were in progress, and so features that re eventually abolished were incorporated in some arms fore the notification to cease producing that part was ceived. Any arms not conforming to the approved pattern re theoretically altered to suit, but this was not always e case, and this can cause confusion now when identific-on of a particular rifle is sought.

e First Pattern. This was the improved version of the al trials pattern rifle, and was ordered into production by e SoS on 13-4-1871.

om WO minutes the following extract confirms the pat-n arm and accessories necessary to guide manufacture –

Patterns of the following articles were, upon recommendation of Special Committee on Breech-Loading Rifles of 26-4-1871, and with the concurrence of the C-I-C, approved by the SoS on 3-6-1871, and sealed to govern manufacture.

Rifle, Martini-Henry (long butt)
Rod, cleaning, for ditto
Short butt, for ditto
Cover, muzzle, for ditto
Jag, for ditto
Muzzle protector, for ditto
Sword bayonet, Elcho pattern
Scabbard, for ditto.

On comparison with the last pattern trials rifle (Type 14) this First pattern service rifle (NB, not actually designated as Mark I) would have had a similar external appearance and the same breech mechanism.

While the plant was being prepared for full scale manufacture of this pattern, the Supt. RSAF presented on 28-9-1871 "Certain modifications in the breech action", as devised by Artificer Todd of his department. These modifications mainly concerned the trigger mechanism, and were intended to improve the pull off of the trigger. The proposals were adopted on 21-10-1871, thus leading to –

The Second Pattern. This differed from the first pattern only in the trigger mechanism and related items, and is of interest in that its pattern arm's designation included for the first time the appellation "Mark I". See Fig.1.

A specification to govern the manufacture of this pattern by private contractors was submitted by the Supt. RSAF on 9-11-1871, and approval of it was granted on 21-11-1871.

Also, in December 1871, the superintendent asked what proportion of long and short butts were to be fitted to the M-H rifles in production. The A-G called for reports from GOC's at various home stations, and these resulted in the opinion that the existing proportions, ie, 2/3 short, 1/3 long, should be unchanged. The reports and conclusions were forwarded to the DoA on 24-1-1872, and he ordered that that proportion was to continue.

During early 1873, with trials of the second pattern rifle in progress, reports started coming in of various defects showing up, mostly concerning the trigger, block axis pin, sights, and striker. These problems led to further extended trials which eventually resulted in –

The Third Pattern. Sometimes called the "Approved Pattern", this rifle incorporated some detailed improvements on the second pattern, and *A pattern rifle, with all approved modifications, together with a jag, foresight protector, and cleaning rod, having been inspected by the C-I-C, was approved by the SoS on 17-7-1874.*

This pattern was still described as Mark I, and a WO minute of 29-7-1874 states that it was called Mark I as no rifles of the former pattern had been issued except for experimental purposes; these were to be returned to store for alteration to the "approved pattern". The designation thus required no change. See Fig.2.

On external comparison between the second and third patterns, the latter will be found to show –

Split steel block axis pin
Slightly different cleaning rod
Edges of trigger guard rounded off
Butts lengthened
Safety catch abolished
Smooth butt plate.

(The last item requires clarification: it had been decided that the chequered butt plate was unnecessary, so the roughening was abolished, and it apparently had been intended that it should be physically removed; however, the Supt. RSAF reported that its removal would make the plates too thin, so, on 4-5-1874 the DoA decided that this alteration would apply only to future manufacture, and existing stocks were to be used up. Some third pattern rifles could thus be found with the chequered butt plate, which, according to the pattern, should not have been fitted.)

The abolition of the safety catch had been specially approved by the C-I-C on 11-11-1873, and by the SoS on 18-11-1873.

On 16-1-1875 it was decided that the butt swivel was to be done away with for all corps, and on 20-1-1875 the DoA directed that the pattern arm be so altered. A memorandum from the A-G to all GOC's instructed them to withdraw the butt swivels from arms under their control. Small pegs were to be supplied to fill the holes left when the swivel was removed; these pegs were to be driven in with a little glue applied to ensure their retention. Opposition to this order came from the Rifle battalions, who wanted to remove the guard swivel instead. In March 1875, orders were given that the Rifle Brigade and 60th Rifles were permitted to keep the butt swivel, and that new arms received without it could have a swivel screwed in by the unit armourer. On 4-11-1875 the DoA directed that the altered arm should not yet be sealed, as the pattern action was under consideration. The removal of the butt swivel was recorded in minutes to allow production to proceed according to the altered arm.

The reason the pattern action was under consideration was because wider use of the Mark I Third pattern rifle had disclosed more troubles with the trigger mechanism, and a remedy was being sought. At a WO conference on 5-10-1875 the Supt. RSAF exhibited a modified breech action prepared in his department, the objects and advantages of which were stated to be –

1. Tumbler rest dispensed with
2. Tumbler rest axis screw dispensed with
3. Guard enclosed trigger, so that no sand or dust could interfere with the working of the action
4. Pull off regular, and the possibility of catching trigger nose half way in bent prevented
5. A small trigger screw which did not affect the working of the action in any way, and could not be felt in the pull off
6. The trigger spring, when fired, stood at lightest compression.

The committee recommended a trial of 1,000 arms altered to comply with the new trigger, and the necessary parts and personnel to fit them were sent to various stations to put the new trigger units into existing regimental arms. The trials commenced in late November, 1875.

The eventual outcome of the trials was that the new trigger mechanism was adopted, and together with some other minor modifications produced –

THE MARK II RIFLE

This was approved on 25-4-1877 with *Alterations in action, also browning upper surface of breech block and deepening of V notch in sight slide and leaf.* It was also intended *To govern future supply and alteration of rifles of Mark I pattern.* See Fig.3.

The conversion of Mark I rifles to Mark II pattern was achieved generally by replacing the trigger and guard unit and breech block with those of the new pattern (usually original components altered to suit), and restamping the action body to identify the new mark. Although officially only a Mark II, these upgraded arms will be referred to, for convenience of identification, as Converted Mark II rifles. See Fig.4.

Some weapons of this pattern will exhibit characteristics of Mark I Second pattern arms, as these were first elevated to Mark I Third pattern, and then to Mark II. The opportunity would have been taken on the latter occasion to rectify any small changes that may have been overlooked previously, such as removal of the butt swivel, and so on.

By the time the Mark II pattern appeared, considerable numbers of Mark I rifles had been produced, and some, generally of the third pattern, had been issued to colonial governments. As the colonies were often a considerable distance from England, with a consequent delay in communications, most of these rifles were not upgraded to Mark II immediately, and some not at all. Those that were generally had the new components put in them without the resulting change of mark being stamped on the action, and, although now of Mark II pattern, were thus still shown as Mark I.

This created a situation whereby some Mark I rifles in colonial use would have remained as an original pattern, but others, by having the trigger unit replaced, were brought up to Mark II standard. Some of the latter arms can also be found with the chequered butt plate and butt swivel, and are now a source of confusion to collectors, as they are often classed as Mark I rifles, which they obviously no

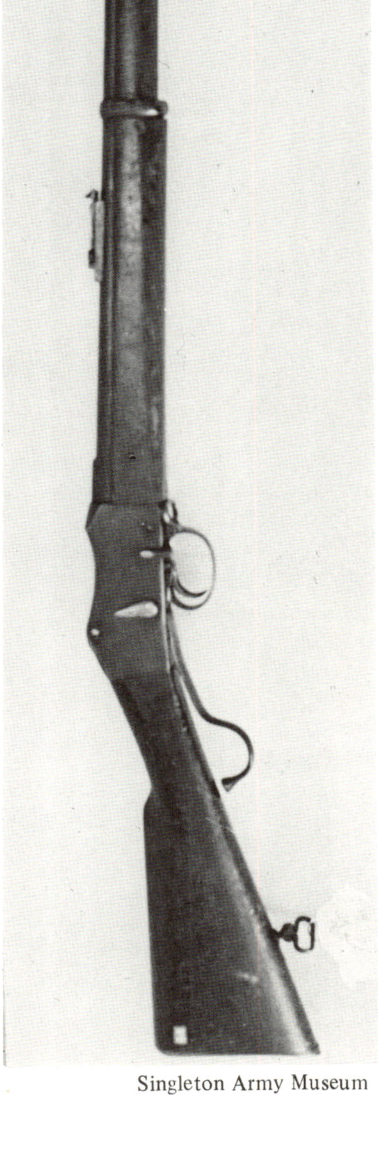

Fig. 1 – Rifle, Martini-Henry, Mark I, Second Pattern.

Singleton Army Museum

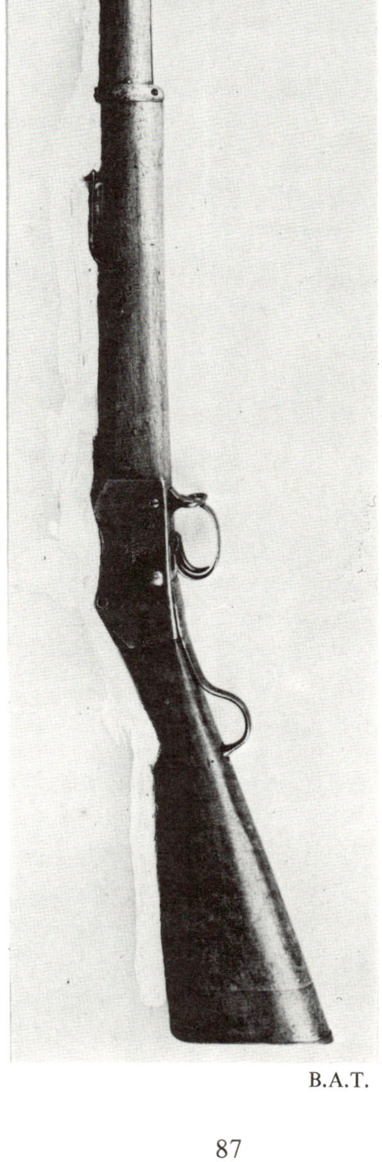

Fig. 2 – Rifle, Mark I, Upgraded to Third Pattern.

B.A.T.

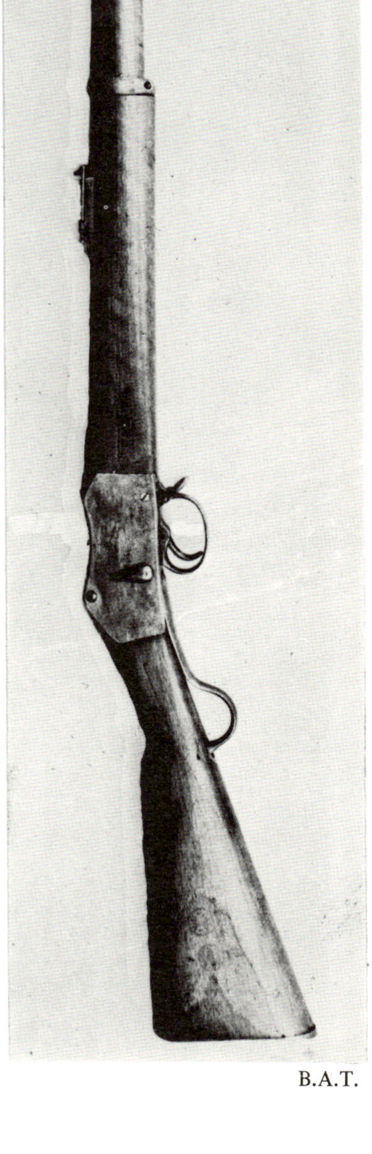

Fig. 3 – Rifle, Martini-Henry, Mark II.

B.A.T.

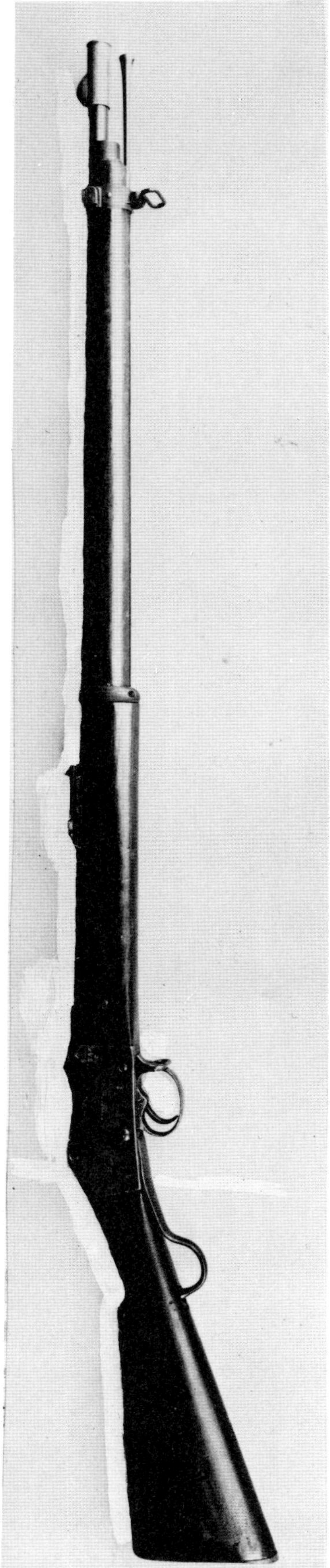

Fig. 4 – Rifle, Converted Mark II.

B.A.T.

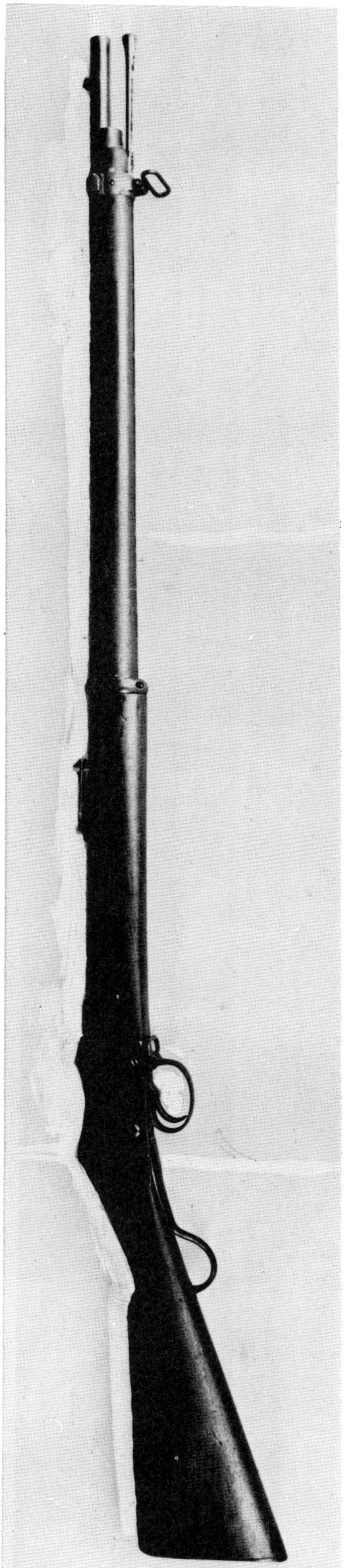

Fig. 5 – Rifle, Mark I, Upgraded.

B.A.T.

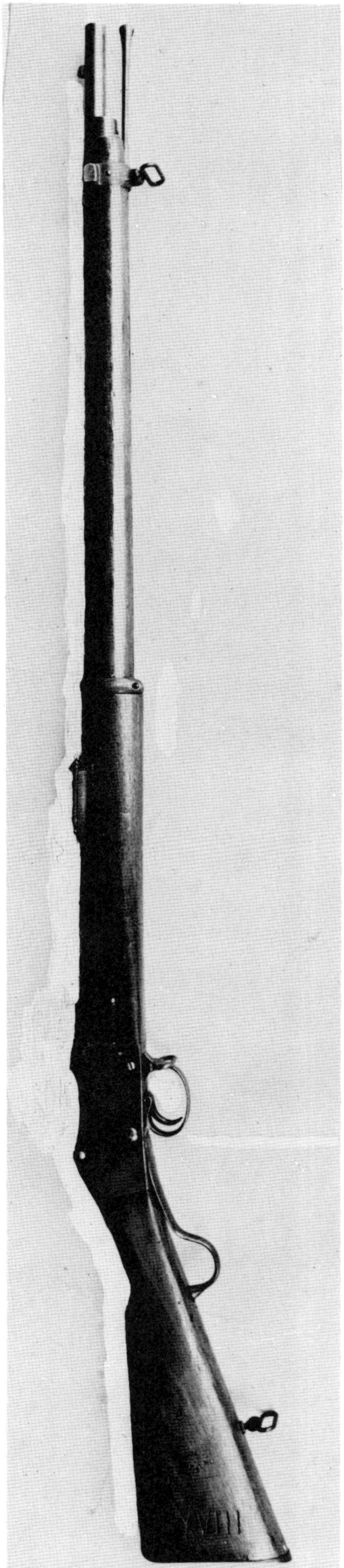

Fig. 6 – Rifle, Mark I, Interim Pattern.

B.A.T.

longer are. The best designation that could perhaps be applied to them is Mark I (Upgraded). Fig.5 illustrates one of these rifles.

Fig.6 shows a colonial weapon that escaped modification – a Mark I Third pattern with Second pattern features. It will be seen to have the solid bronze axis pin for breech block and square edged trigger guard of the second pattern, but was never fitted with the safety catch, so conforms with the third pattern in that respect. This shows that this particular rifle was made during the period after the safety catch was abolished, but before the axis pin was changed.

MARTINI–HENRY RIFLES AT WIMBLEDON

It is apparent from a study of the previous text concerning the selection trials of the M-H, that the Wimbledon Meeting of the NRA was considered to be an important event, and one that would subject rifles to a trial of accuracy and handling under conditions that would not obtain elsewhere. Each year the selection trials were under way at least a few M-H rifles were loaned to the NRA for use in the event. In each instance, where possible, the rifles would have been of the most recent pattern.

This precedent was carried on with the service pattern arms, and up to 1874 the following arms had been supplied –

1871 – 65 rifles, embodying the improvements proposed up to that date, except that they had long actions. (Trials type triggers fitted.)
6 rifles, ditto, with short actions. (Ditto.)
1 rifle of the exact pattern then approved, and fitted with an Elcho bayonet. (Mark I, First pattern.)
(The comment was made at the time – *It is believed that the whole of the above had 14-inch butts.*)

1872 – 100 rifles, short actions; 90 with 14-inch, 10 with 13-inch butts.

1873 – 120 rifles, short actions; 110 with 14-inch, 10 with 13-inch butts.

1874 – 120 rifles, short actions; 100 with 14½-inch, 20 with 14-inch butts. These rifles embodied all the various small alterations in the action recently introduced. (Mark I, Third pattern.)

The barrels were the same in pattern in all four years, weigh ing about 3 lb 6 oz.

After reports had appeared in newspapers of complaints against the M-H rifles used at the July 1874 Wimbledon Meeting, the Supt. RSAF visited Wimbledon, and made a report on his findings on 16-7-1874.

He found that one rifle had burst because a jag had been left in the barrel, which would cause an inevitable accident. The shooting of the M-H for the Queen's Prize was indifferent, yet the same rifles had shot excellently at Enfield in June, when being prepared for the event. The bad shooting was thus ascribed to atmospheric conditions and temperature. The Canadian team liked the M-H, and did not consider the recoil unduly heavy. One of them had a cut face from the recoil of a *Snider* – which accident had been reported as being caused by a M-H. Col. Fraser denied that there was any practical defect in the pull off; any variation was inconvenient only when tested for the shooting such as Wimbledon's.

The DoA wrote on 17-7-1874 to the Chairman of the Council of the NRA, asking whether any official complaints had been made, and what opinion had been formed regarding them.

A reply of 4-8-1874 stated that no reports of defects in the arm had been brought to the chairman's notice, but a variation in the pull off of the trigger had been reported, in consequence of which the usual test had been dispensed with; there was, however, no reason to doubt the efficiency of the M-H rifle.

The 65 rifles loaned in 1871 are of particular interest here, although they were not strictly of service pattern. They were originally the 65 long chamber rifles specially examined and reported on as mentioned in Chapter 6, and which were subsequently brought up to the service rifle pattern standard by having all the relevant improvements incorporated into them. An entry in the production records for the 1872 work year at Enfield confirms this – "65 Arms, repaired." They were apparently initially specifically prepared for use at the Wimbledon meeting, but were later nominated for some special service trials as detailed below.

ELCHO BAYONET TRIALS

The future employment of the Elcho bayonet – although it was approved for use with the M-H rifle, and sealed for manufacture – was in some doubt. It had originally been recommended for service use as a result of the trials carried out in 1870, during which it was well received. However, only twelve of the type had been available then, and as the SoS requested that further trials be carried out with the bayonet, the DoA on 14-7-1871 directed the Supt. RSAF to prepare 65 Elcho bayonets, to be issued to various corps at home stations together with the 65 rifles on loan to the NRA after they were returned to store by that association. All proceedings regarding demands for material and manufacture of the Elcho bayonet, were, for the duration, suspended.

The 65 rifles and bayonets were subsequently issued in September 1871 to several battalions of infantry, and the SoM. Reports from these sources also were generally favour able, and the special committee on 22-12-1871 repeated their recommendation that the Elcho bayonet should be issued with the M-H rifle.

Ten of the rifles and bayonets each were then issued to the Royal Engineers and 4th Battalion, Rifle Brigade. These trials were apparently carried out during early 1872. The report from the engineers was generally favourable, but they preferred it without the saw. The rifle brigade report of 13-3-1872 conversely was not entirely favourable, although the CO seemed to prefer it to the ordinary sword bayonet.

The DoA, submitting the reports received to date on 2-1-1872, drew attention to the increased cost of the Elcho bayonet, compared with that of the ordinary bayonet (14s. 6d to 3s 11½d). On 3-2-1872, although the C-I-C did not approve of changing the bayonets, the A-G stated that he considered the Elcho must be adopted because of the many favourable reports.

To consider the subject more fully, a meeting was held at the WO on 14-3-1872, and it was then decided that – *Having regard on the one hand to the reports from the regiments, and on the other the great increase in cost of the new bayonet over the old, the new bayonets should be supplied in the first instance to the following regiments only –*

1 regiment at the Cape of Good Hope
1 regiment at Nova Scotia

and that special instructions should be sent as to the manner of using and testing the weapons.

The regiments chosen were the 86th Foot at the Cape, and the 1st/60th Rifles at Nova Scotia. To quote – *Martini-Henry rifles with Elcho bayonets were sent for a regiment at each of the stations named above in September, 1872.*

Enfield production records for the 1873 year show that "1,473 Arms, Martini-Henry, assembled, with cleaning rods and sword bayonets" were produced; these are most probably the arms referred to above, and the rifles would have been of Mark I Second pattern.

The first report on the bayonet trials was received in November 1872, from the 1/60th Rifles at Halifax, which stated that although the Elcho was considered superior in some respects to the regulation sword bayonet with which they were normally armed, the latter was preferred as a weapon of attack and defence.

On receiving this report, the DoA on 22-11-1872 asked the WO what bayonets should be provided for the M-H rifles then in store. The S-G proposed that they should be fitted with ordinary bayonets from store, and the SoS approved of this on 27-11-1872. The C-I-C agreed with this arrangement, and it was understood that a definite decision would have to be made regarding the Elcho bayonet. In the meantime, arms made in 1873/4 were to be fitted with the ordinary bayonets, except those for serjeants, for which the ordinary sword bayonets would be issued.

The report on the Elcho bayonets sent to the Cape was not received until September 1873, and was generally favourable to the Elcho; by this time however, it was too late to have any effect on the decisions already made.

TRIALS OF MARTINI–HENRY SERVICE RIFLES

On 23-2-1872 the suggestion was made by the Supt. RSAF that as soon as a number of M-H rifles sufficient to arm a regiment was completed, they should be issued, so that any small defects – to be expected in the early stages of large scale manufacture – would be disclosed and so rectified. The DoA approved, and proposed that 20 arms each should be issued to 5 regiments, but a later decision of 5-10-1872 suspended this action; and on 12-12-1872 the DoA recommended that two infantry regiments at home should be armed with the rifles for a few months. This was approved, and the 2nd Battalion 4th Foot, and the 46th Foot were selected to carry out the trials. Bayonets to be issued with the rifles were the ordinary socket bayonet for rank and file, and the ordinary sword bayonet for serjeants. These bayonets had to be altered slightly to fit the M-H rifle.

Previous to this the S-G had, on 14-10-1872, ordered that 25 M-H rifles be issued to the SoM in order that the serjeant instructors might take them into use, and settle various points concerning drill procedures, etc.

The rifles intended for the home trials were Mark I Second pattern, and were issued to both regiments on 19-3-1873; the 2/4th received 526. After regimental markings were applied they were immediately issued.

About the time these rifles were being issued, a report was received from the 1/60th Rifles at Halifax, concerning the rifles issued to them in September 1872 for the Elcho bayonet trials. These rifles were of the same pattern as those being issued for the home trials, and some problems were beginning to manifest themselves – mainly the liability of the block axis pin to work out because of the loosening of the retaining screw, and the liability of the cleaning rods to break. The iron cup containing the spring that secured the lever under the butt was also mentioned as being too lightly constructed.

As a result of this report the IGM recommended the use of a split block axis pin of hammered brass, and a slight alteration in the swell of the cleaning rod. The Supt. RSAF was inclined to think that alterations were unnecessary, so the S-G decided on 7-5-1873 to await further reports from the trials at home.

One major fault not mentioned in the report from Halifax, but which quickly showed up at home was the tendency for the strikers to break. From a report of 21-4-1873 by the OC 2/4th Regiment –

On the first occasion of firing blank ammunition on the 17th instant with the new Martini-Henry rifles, nine strikers broke, thereby rendering the rifles quite useless for the time being; 260 men were firing on this occasion.

The 46th also reported strikers breaking, so strikers of a stronger form were supplied and fitted to the rifles in use, in early May, 1873.

Another source of complaint that became apparent was the recoil of the rifles, as in this report of 14-7-1873 from the OC 2/4th Regiment –

On the first occasion of firing . . . nine strikers broke . . . a report was made by me to the major-general, and the whole of the strikers changed for others. Since then two of the others have broken and been replaced.

The yearly course has not yet been completed . . . the shooting has not been so satisfactory as I could wish, caused chiefly, I think, by the great recoil of the weapon.

He then made a further report to the Supt. RSAF on 25-8-1873 stating –

I have to report that some of the new strikers supplied for the Martin-Henry rifles still break, also that several of the ramrods have broken during the musketry course. Several of the axis pins have been lost, owing to their getting unscrewed, and the percentage allowed to replace them is totally insufficient. Some of these axis pins have, no doubt, been lost through the men's carelessness, in which cases they will be obliged to replace them at their own expense, when we know the price, but others have been lost quite accidentally, and I can only account for it by the fact that the threads of the screws which keep the axis pins in their place have got worn loose. I have seen some of them so loose that the slightest touch will turn them.

I also wish to bring to your notice that the butt swivel screw being screwed into the stock of the rifle without any metal plate for it to be screwed in, but simply in the wood, this, by frequent unscrewing is liable to wear away the wood and thus render it loose.

Particulars as to the strikers and ramrods broken and the axis pins lost are herewith annexed.

The companies have nearly completed their annual course, and the shooting of the battalion has been bad.

Item.	*No.*	*Rifle numbers.*
Block axis pins	*6*	*444,278,157,214,354,129*
Strikers	*24*	*310,181,172,234,225,61,87, 21,91,372,153,184,458,257, 194,381,261,6,50,61,237, 257,296,430. (The last 7 broken on 26/27-8-1873.)*
Cleaning rods	*5*	*56,65,148,317,?*
Main spring	*1*	*237*
Lever catch	*1*	*362*

(The text of a report of 19-7-1873 from the 46th Regiment will be found in Appendix 17.)

On the subject of strikers generally, the Supt. RSAF had submitted a memorandum on 4-6-1873, for the information of interested persons. He stated that the breakages had occurred when snapping unloaded rifles, and that when the first muzzle-loading rifles were introduced, nipples, hammers, and main springs were continually broken from the same cause, until a snap cap was introduced. The strengthened form of M-H striker had withstood all tests, and there was no difficulty with the mainsprings, one of which was submitted as having fired 27,000 rounds without showing any alteration of form or strength.

Reports were received from the 86th Foot at the Cape (13-9-1873), and the 1/60th Rifles at Halifax (2-10-1873), on the rifles and bayonets issued to them for the Elcho trials. In these reports certain defects in the sights and minor fittings were pointed out. Both regiments spoke very highly of the rifle, but heavy recoil was mentioned. The butts were stated to be too short and too straight.

IMPROVEMENTS AND MORE TRIALS

All the above reports were considered by the Supt. RSAF, and he remarked upon them in a memorandum of 24-9-1873 to the DoA, who suggested, on 26-9-1873, that a conference should be held, at which an officer of the A-G's department, the Supt. RSAF, and an officer from the SoM should be present to discuss the subject, and submit for approval any minor changes which might be considered necessary. The S-G approved 3-10-1873.

The meeting was accordingly arranged for the 24-10-1873, and Col. Fraser's memorandum, as given below, with other papers from the IGM, was laid before the committee for consideration.

Memorandum by the Superintendent Royal Small Arms Factory on Reports of Trials of Martini-Henry Rifles by 2nd Battalion 4th Foot, 1st Battalion 60th Rifles (Halifax N.S.), and School of Musketry.

Director of Artillery, *September 24, 1873.*

I have examined the reports, and append a tabular statement extracted from them, which includes in its headings all the points touched on in the documents from Halifax, 46th Regiment, 4th Regiment, and Hythe, and I submit my remarks. The numbers of failures are given in the table whenever mentioned in the reports, but the number of rounds fired and by which the failures were elicited, does not appear in the reports. Where no mention is made of any particular point in one or other of the reports, the word "No" is inserted. (This tabular statement is given in Appendix 18.)

1. Block axis pins. The liability to get loose and drop out can be remedied by the introduction of a split pin of either metal or steel. The latter was objected to when the pin was screwed in; it then rusted. This would not occur with the split form, and steel is preferable to metal. The split pin can be readily put into the rifles already made.

2. Cleaning rods. Can be altered at small cost, so that no drawing of the head of the rod towards the body is necessary when the rod is required for use.

3. Lever catch block. I do not think any alteration is required in these. We will watch the manufacture in order that the sole may not be left too thin.

4. Strikers. Strikers of the strengthened form were sent to the 4th and 46th regiments. The metals of which they were made differed, and were differently treated in the manufacture as an experiment. Those sent to the 46th Regiment have proved satisfactory, one only breaking, and this owing to a flaw in the metal. Strikers similar to those sent to 46th Regiment should replace those in the finished rifles.

5. Recoil. The recoil is complained of as being more than with the Snider by the 46th Regiment and Hythe, and when connected with the short stock is considered by the 46th the cause of indifferent shooting. I am of opinion that the recoil is not sufficiently heavy to occasion bad shooting and agree with Hythe that a little custom with the trained soldier will get over the difficulty. I prefer the long butt.

6. Mainsprings break. The breaking of the mainsprings is, I consider, a manufacturing difficulty only, and one which it is our duty to get over. We have considerable difficulty with the tempering of the present metal, but each day will I trust, render the production more reliable. The number of failures now brought to notice is as nothing when compared with the breakages which occurred with springs and components on the introduction of the Pattern '53.

7. Barrel studs come off. One only, owing to bad brazing.

8. Trigger springs break. A similar difficulty exists as with the mainsprings, and it always has been experienced on the commencement of new work. We shall improve the manufacture.

9. Thumb-piece too far back. Appears to me to be a useless appendage.

10. Sighting. The 46th Regiment remark that it is too low at 500 and 800 yards. We find it correct from the fixed rest and shoulder.

11. Barrels heat with quick firing. I think it quite possible that the heating of the barrels on rapid firing, on a hot day especially, may prove a serious drawback to rapidity of fire. A barrel cannot be touched after five or six rounds on some occasions. A leather shield attached to the fore-end may be found a necessary addition.

12. Pull offs irregular. I cannot think there is any serious practical detriment owing to this cause. They may vary a little in use. Increased accuracy in manufacture (which is daily taking place) will do much to obviate it if indeed it exists.

13. Butt swivel screws into the wood only. It is similarly secured in rifles in the service, and no complaints have been made.

14. Butts, long or short. See 5.

15. Stock firm and strong. In spite of its being in two parts.

16. Extraction occasionally difficult. This is found to be the case with the 46th Regiment in a few instances. If the cartridge is not imperfect any mistake in extraction is due to the want of proper application of the lever in the first instance – it is simply a matter of drill.

17. Breech action impeded by rust or dirt. Appears quite satisfactory.

18. Lever broken or bent. No casualties.

19. Precision. See 5.

20. Sight. I have failed to find the defect complained of in any rifles we have examined.

No allusion is made to the locking bolt, *probably because it has not been tried to any extent. I consider it very unhandy, a man's fingers also might easily slip when adjusting it to the trigger. It is difficult, and consequently costly to make, and I think liable to get out of order. It occurs to us whether it is not now an unnecessary addition to the rifle. It does not appear in full in the report, Special Committee B.L. Rifles, on page 24, where the bolt is mentioned, why it was introduced. I learn, on enquiry, it was because the rifle was liable to fire when the butt was struck rather heavily – when the arm is "ordered" for instance.*

When this was liable to occur there was no "tumbler rest" in the action. It has been subsequently introduced and I cannot make the rifle fire with any amount of blows on the butt. I think the locking bolt might be dispensed with. If it is still retained we have a far better and cheaper arrangement, and easy of application to the rifles already made.

The engraving on the butt plates and triggers appear to me useless. On the triggers indeed it is a matter of complaint although not in these reports. It has been found to cut the firer's finger after many discharges.

If an issue of the Martini-Henry rifle is contemplated next year we should be preparing the spare parts, and the requisitions should be put forward by the control department.

It might be desirable to send the armourer-serjeants of regiments, etc., here for a 3 day course of instruction some time hence.

The suggestions as to the improved block axis pin and cleaning rod might be proved by the issue of a few to the two regiments.

G. Fraser, Superintendent,
Royal Small Arms Factories.

The papers from the IGM recapitulated the comments regarding the shooting performance of the M-H made by the regiments testing the rifles, and one minute of 3-10-1873 stated –

I can only account for the inferior shooting of the 2nd Battalion 4th and 46th Regiments with the Martini-Henry rifle, by the fact of the recoil being so great; the men in most instances fire with less confidence, and consequently at a great disadvantage; the shortness of the stock also frequently causes a smart blow on the cheek, particularly at the short distances, and this naturally increases the chances of bad shooting. Possibly as the men become more accustomed to the rifle, the shooting may improve, but I am of opinion as regards recruits, it will be a matter of great difficulty, and a very serious objection to the arm in its present state.

The precision of the rifle is undeniable.

These remarks drew this comment from the C-I-C on 10-10-1873 –

The question of recoil is so grave, and one so seriously affecting the general shooting in the army, that I wish you to confer with the Director of Artillery about it, and see what can be done to mend it.

The following extracts were taken from the minutes of the conference of 24-10-1873 at the WO. (The full minutes are presented in Appendix 19.) Present were –

Brig.-Gen. Sir J. Adye, KCB, DoA
Brevet-Col. Jenyns, CB, AAG
Brevet-Col. Radcliffe, CB, Commandant SoM
Lt.-Col. Fraser, RA, Supt. RSAF
Mr. Lewis W. Engelbach of the WO attended.

Questions connected with M-H arms were considered, and the DoA explained the current position. The several points detailed in Col. Fraser's minute of 24-9-1873 were then examined.

On the question of recoil, two serjeant-instructors from Hythe were in attendance, and were examined on that point. Also on hand were the OC 46th Regiment, and the IoM of the 4th and 46th Regiment, and these people also gave evidence.

After these examinations the committee deliberated, and confirmed their previous opinion that the complaints regard ing recoil and uncertain pull off arose chiefly from the supposed shortness of the butts, and inconvenient grip. Alterations to both were proposed.

In order to improve the grip of the right hand, a trial was recommended of a small thumb rest outside the body of the arm. A few were to be made in the first instance, and sent to Hythe for trial.

It was thought desirable to lengthen both sizes of the butts by an inch, leaving the proportions as currently issued. Numbers of the longer butts were to be sent to Hythe, 4th, and 46th Regiments for trial. The expense involved was to be reported by Col. Fraser.

Other features to be changed included the engraving on butt plates to be dispensed with, and that on the trigger modified; a few leather shields to combat barrel heating were to be tried at Hythe, as proposed by Col. Fraser; and the locking bolt was unanimously rejected. No changes were considered necessary with regard to the other minor points raised.

The recommendations submitted by the committee were –

1. Block axis pin. 4th and 46th Regiments to be supplied with split bronze and steel pins, in equal numbers, for trial and report; a few also to be sent to Hythe.

2. Cleaning rods. Some to be issued to both of the above regiments and to Hythe, as proposed by Col. Fraser.

3. Strikers. Colonels of regiments to be called upon to report carefully on the question of strikers at the end of the trial of pins and rods. Snap caps, as suggested by Col. Fraser to be tried by the 4th and 46th Regiments, and at Hythe.

4. Thumb rest. A small thumb rest to be tried on the outside of the body of the arm, to improve the grip. A few to be made in the first instance and sent to Hythe for trial.

5. Leather shields. A few to be tried as proposed by Col. Fraser.

6. Butts. Both sizes to be lengthened one inch. Proportions of each to be sent to Hythe, 4th and 46th Regiments, for trial.

7. Engraving. That on butt plates to be dispensed with, and that on triggers modified.

8. Locking bolt. To be abolished.

The C-I-C concurred in these recommendations on 7-11-1873, and they were approved by the S-G on 8-11-1873.

The question of the abolition of the locking bolt was later specially submitted, and the C-I-C highly approved of the proposal on 11-11-1873; the SoS giving his approval on 18-11-1873.

To enable the trials of the above recommendations to be carried out, the following arms and components were issued –

To Hythe,

3 rifles, with 14½-inch butts; and
3 rifles, with 14-inch butts; all fitted with thumb rests of a pattern designed at Hythe; and
3 rifles, with 14½-inch butts; and
3 rifles, with 14-inch butts; all fitted with thumb rests of a pattern designed at Enfield.

These 12 rifles embodied all the suggested alterations, and in addition the following were also sent –

18 split axis pins of metal
20 split axis pins of steel
8 cleaning rods
12 leather shields
20 snap caps.

To 2nd Battalion 4th Regiment, and 46th Regiment, each,

2 rifles embodying all the suggested alterations; and
58 split axis pins, metal
50 split axis pins, steel
48 cleaning rods
26 snap caps (2/4th)
27 snap caps (46th).

As a result of the apparent success of the strengthened strikers, the DoA on 16-12-1873 instructed the Supt. RSAF to proceed with the substitution of the new strikers for those in the arms in store; and a slight alteration in the cupping of the lever catch block in the butt. The locking bolts were also to be removed from the arms in store.

Because of the reports from regiments that the M-H rifle was undersighted, three rifles, considered by the OC 46th Regiment to be defective in this particular point, were sent to the RSAF for examination, and were reported on by the superintendent on 12-2-1874. In fixed rests, at 500 and 1,000 yards, the sighting was found absolutely correct. At intermediate ranges, with good shots firing from the shoulder, the same results were obtained, except for one rifle, which showed an inclination to shoot low, particularly at the 300 yards range. A new fore-end was fitted to it, and it then shot the same as the others. As an explanation of this behaviour, Col. Fraser remarked that, when the rifle was lightened in the last instance, the barrel was hollowed out between the breech and the muzzle, and thus rendered weak, so that, if the fore-end warped, it took the barrel with it.

On 26-3-1874, on the recommendation of the Supt. RSAF a stock bolt, slightly less finished than the original, and consequently a little cheaper to produce, was approved.

RESULTS OF THE TRIALS OF IMPROVED RIFLES

Reports on the trials of the improved arms and components were received as follows from –

IGM, Hythe, 12-2-1874
OC, 2nd Battalion 4th Foot, 17-2-1874
OC, 46th Foot, 23-2-1874.

(Copies of the reports from the OC's mentioned above can be seen in Appendixes 20 and 21, respectively.)

An abstract of comments on the several points of reference in the reports is presented below –

1. Block axis pin.

SoM: Answered admirably. The split end, ought, however, be shaped so as to fit the countersunk orifice. There appears to be no choice between the steel and metal pins.
2/4th: Steel pins stand well. None broken during the trial. Brass pins did not stand so well; two closed during trial.
46th: Have worked well; remaining firm.

2. Cleaning rods.

SoM: Answered admirably.
2/4th: Five came out during trial. This was accounted for by the top band not being sufficiently tightened up.
46th: Though preferable to previous pattern, still open to objection. There would be difficulty in accustoming men to secure it by turning, and consequently the rods would in some cases fall out, or be broken or damaged by careless manipulation.

3. Strikers and snap caps.

SoM: Not mentioned.
2/4th: Two broke.
46th: Strikers not mentioned. 100 snap caps (dummy cartridges) were tested, and appear to answer the purpose. Five were injured.

4. Thumb rest.

SoM: If no other means can be devised for bringing the trigger nearer to the thumb, the square-shaped, medium sized thumb piece (Enfield pattern), appears to be the best in every respect, it not being in the way while performing the manual exercise, while giving a sufficient purchase for the thumb of the most clumsily-handed soldier.

5. Leather shields.

SoM: The necessity for these was amply proved when twenty rounds were fired independently. It is suggested, however, that they be made of rather stouter leather, so as to be less liable to curl outwards between the straps, that they should be shortened by half an inch in front of the backsight, and lengthened by one inch at the breech end, and that oval buckles be substituted for square buckles and loop. Pattern cut in paper forwarded.
2/4th: A great improvement.
46th: Has been found completely to answer the purpose of protecting the hand from the heated barrel, but the buckle of the centre strap is objectionable. A small stud, or button, at each side of the stock might be substituted with advantage.

6. Butts.

SoM: The alteration is a decided improvement, and satisfactory. Col. Radcliffe has reason to believe that the increase in length has decreased to some extent the effect of the recoil.
2/4th: The lengthened stocks are a great improvement.
46th: The increase of length is a most decided improvement the necessity of placing the cheek on the head of the stock being to a great extent obviated, and the effect of the recoil as experienced by many men on the face thereby almost nullified.

7. Engraving.

SoM: Smooth butt plates quite as efficient as the rough-

ened ones of the old pattern, while not so likely to injure the clothing. Modification of roughness of trigger an improvement.
2/4th: Smooth butt plates answer very well. No difference between them and the roughened ones. Modified roughing of trigger is a great improvement.
46th: Smooth butt plate apparently a matter of little consequence. Modified roughing of trigger a decided improvement. If the upper side edges were also slightly rounded, it would be beneficial.

8. Locking bolt.

SoM: Not mentioned.
2/4th: It was at all times quite unnecessary.
46th: Removal highly approved of.

General remarks.

SoM: Pull off was found to be tolerably regular, and not excessive. The rifles are uniformly undersighted.

The Supt. RSAF stated on 10-3-1874, with reference to the above reports, that he would make trials with a split block axis pin with countersunk head, and would have a modified leather shield made as proposed by Hythe.

He also remarked that, considering the purpose of the cleaning rod, and the little effort that was required to secure it, he did not think the objection of the OC 46th Regiment valid; and with regard to the snap cap, if it was of no use as a drill cartridge (which point was not mentioned in the reports) it might be shortened and cheapened.

MUSKETRY EXPERIENCE WITH THE MARTINI–HENRY RIFLE

In the IGM's report on the musketry instruction of the army during the quarter ending 30-12-1873, the following remarks were made regarding the M-H rifle –

The practice made by Letter A Company, 2nd Battalion, 4th Foot, with the Martini-Henry was very bad.

The practice of the 86th Regiment had been concluded with poor results, but as the regiment had been furnished with the rifles only a few days before the course began, the men laboured under many disadvantages in firing with it. The stocks were shorter than they were accustomed to; the sighting was new to them, and the absence of a notch in the sliding bar made it difficult to get the eye well down to the back sight. The increased recoil was much exaggerated at first in the minds of the men. The rifle appears to be much undersighted. A great many strikers were broken at drill.

The Supt. RSAF remarked, on 12-3-1874, on the above –

The butts are in reality the same in length as the rifles now in the service, but the gun unquestionably comes up differently owing to its shape about the action, and there is no doubt but that the arm will be improved by the butts being made longer.

As to the sighting, the notch is on the sliding bar, and may be used, if preferred, by reversing it.

I am of opinion, that with the lengthened butt, the increased recoil is not so much as to occasion any bad results.

The remark as to undersighting is general; frequent trials at Enfield, however, do not confirm it. I am at loss to account for this reported defect, unless it be due to warping of the fore-ends, which generally bend downwards if they do warp, and they take the barrel with them. This has been found to be the case in a few instances, but it can hardly account for so generally a reported failing.

The strikers complained of as breaking have been discarded for stronger ones.

The OC 2nd Battalion 4th Foot reported to the A-G, on 18-4-1874 –

With reference to letter 7669-3112, E.9033, I have to report . . . that I should recommend the issue of the 14 and 14½-inch butts of the Martini-Henry rifles in equal proportions, one half of each.

I have further to report that the recoil with the long butt rifle is very much less than with the short butts, as the long butt keeps the man's face clear of the stock. All the NCO's and men I have questioned on the subject prefer the long stock.

CONSIDERATION OF TRIALS REPORTS, AND RECOM MENDATIONS MADE

To review the reports on the last series of trials, another meeting was held at the WO on 9-4-1874, and present were

Brig.-Gen. Sir John Adye, KCB, DoA
Col. Radcliffe, CB, Commandant, SoM
Col. Hon. H. Clifford, CB, VC, AAG
Col. Fraser, RA, Supt. RSAF
Mr. Lewis W. Engelbach of the WO attended.

The reports were read and considered in detail, and the following decisions were arrived at –

1. Block axis pin. The countersunk steel pin to be adopted.

2. Cleaning rods. The pattern as altered by the Supt. RSAF to be adopted.

3. Snap cap. The pattern submitted by the IGM to be approved, subject to any minor modifications which may be decided upon after further trial at Enfield and Hythe.

The cost would be about 4d each, but the expense would be amply covered by saving of wear and tear and injury of the strikers.

4. Thumb rest. The committee unanimously reject the proposed rest.

Trigger. To be set back a little as now proposed by the IGM with a view of bringing it more within reach, and thus facilitating the pull.

The cost of this slight alteration (which could be made without difficulty) would be about 6d per arm, but in future manufacture it would not involve any additional expense.

Trigger guard. Edges to be rounded off in the rear to prevent injury to fingers in recoil.

In discussing the question of recoil the committee thought that the IGM should be asked to ascertain whether a slight change in the position of the right hand would improve the grip of the rifle.

5. Leather shields. Pattern as altered by the IGM to be recorded, and if found absolutely necessary it may ultimately be adopted; but considering that it would be an additional article of store, costing 1s each, the committee considered that no supply should be ordered until further experience had been obtained with the arm in the hands of the troops.

6. Butts. The present lengths were 13 and 14 inches, which were issued in proportions of 2/3 of the former and 1/3 of the latter; and the committee were of opinion that the short butts should become 14 inches, and that the long butt be 14½ inches; proportions as at present.

7. Engraving. To be carried out as proposed, viz, roughening taken off the butt plates and modified on the trigger.

8. Locking bolt. Its abolition finally approved.

General remarks. The committee were of opinion that the present barrel was rather too light. Experience had shown that the fore-end was liable to warp and take the barrel with it. A small addition to the weight of the barrel would remedy this, and also probably diminish the recoil, and therefore tend to improve the shooting.

The Supt. RSAF stated that, from a manufacturing point of view, a slightly heavier barrel would be easier to make.

The committee then recommended that 50 arms should be made with heavier barrels, and that they be tried at Enfield and Hythe, and by the 4th and 46th Regiments. These rifles should have all the latest improvements incorporated, as detailed above.

Bayonets. Having carefully considered all the circumstances the committee were of the unanimous decision that the ordinary bayonet should be adopted for M-H arms with all dismounted corps carrying the rifle. The proposed arrangements were –

Infantry – Martini-Henry rifle and ordinary bayonet, all ranks.

Rifle Corps – As above.

Cavalry – Martini-Henry Cavalry carbine when approved.

Artillery: Garrison – Martini-Henry rifle and ordinary bayonet;

Horse and Field – Martini-Henry Cavalry carbine, the men to have swords.

Engineers – Martini-Henry rifle and ordinary bayonet.

Navy – To be considered.

The committee gave their reasons for those dispositions as-

1. They think that the primary object of a bayonet is for attack and defence, and that it should not be used for any other purpose. That for bush work, or other special service, special implements should be provided according to circumstances.
2. They object to the extra weight of the proposed sword bayonet and scabbard, and to its great cost.
3. They are of opinion that, considering the excellence of the Martini-Henry arm, there is no longer any reason for special corps being specially armed, and that the adoption of one universal weapon for all branches of the service, except cavalry and field artillery, will be of great advantage in every point of view.

The A-G on 4-5-1874 expressed the concurrence of the C-I-C in the recommendations on the minor points relating to the rifles, but not on those regarding the issue of bayonets. Further bayonet trials were proposed, and after some discussion it was decided that 300 M-H rifles, with 100 each of the following bayonets – ordinary pattern, Elcho pattern, and the original M-H (RIC) pattern – should be issued to the 1st Battalion Rifle Brigade for trial and report. (Enfield production records show that "112 Bayonets, sword, M-H [Irish Constabulary Pattern], with leather scabbards; and 100 Bayonets, sword, M-H [Elcho pattern], with leather scabbards", were produced during this period, indicating that the bayonets issued for trial [excluding the ordinary pattern] were new manufacture, rather than old ones re-issued.)

Upon the issue of M-H rifles to home battalions being ordered, the C-I-C stated that sword bayonets should be issued to all serjeants of the infantry and rifle corps, the rest of the line to have the ordinary bayonet. This was done when the rifles went on general issue at home.

Orders were given immediately for rifles in store to have the approved alterations applied to them, and the SoS confirmed them on 23-6-1874.

A pattern rifle, with all the approved modifications, together with a jag, foresight protector, and cleaning rod, was approved by the SoS on 17-7-1874, and sealed to govern the alteration of existing rifles. (This was the Mark I, Third pattern rifle.)

TRIALS OF HEAVY BARREL RIFLES

Having received instructions to take the necessary steps towards carrying out the recommendation of the committee of 9-4-1874 that 50 rifles be made with barrels heavier than the service pattern, and issued for trial, the Supt. RSAF reported on 29-5-1874 that he had prepared a barrel of such increased thickness as to make it 5 to 6 oz heavier than the service pattern, and to bring the weight of the M-H rifle, without bayonet, up to that of the long Snider, also without bayonet.

(If all this sounds familiar to the reader, it is indeed so. See Chapter 7, Trials rifles Types 12, 13, and 14. There are, however, also some anomalies in the officially quoted weights of the various pattern rifles when the barrel weights and overall weights quoted are compared. See Appendix 14.)

Trials were carried out at Enfield, and it was found, on placing the heavy barrel in a badly warped fore-end that the shooting was affected to the extent of 4 inches at 500 yards range, while a service barrel in a similarly warped fore-end was affected to the extent of 14 inches at the same range.

A comparison of recoil, measured on a machine at the RSAF showed that that of the long Snider was 51 lb, the M-H with heavy barrel was 57 lb, and the M-H with service barrel, 63 lb. On trying the rifles from the shoulder, no firer could detect any difference between the recoils of the M-H with the service or heavy barrel.

As these limited trials had apparently shown that the heavy barrel was a feasible proposition, Col. Fraser was directed on 9-6-1874 to proceed with the manufacture of the 50 rifles for trial, as proposed. The Enfield production records show that "50 M-H rifles, prepared with altered guards and heavy barrels", were produced. The "altered guards" presumably means that they had trigger guards with the rear edges rounded off as recommended.

The 50 rifles were issued on 6-8-1874 to Hythe for initial trials; it having been decided that they should also be sent, 25 each, to the 2/4th and 46th Foot, after Hythe had finished with them.

A report on the Hythe trials, by the IGM on 28-8-1874, stated that the rifles had been tried by men each firing 100 rounds at ranges from 150 to 800 yards. Of 39 serjeants who took part in this practice, 25 had never before fired with the rifle. No comments of any kind were made regarding the recoil, and no appreciable difference was found between the rifle with heavy barrel and the service rifle. To test this latter effect, the same men had fired 40 rounds from a service rifle for comparison. The trigger having been set back was mentioned as a decided improvement, but it was remarked that it should, if possible, be set even further back.

A report of 7-10-1874 from the IoM, 2/4th Foot, stated that the trials of the rifle were satisfactory; the increased length of the butt was an improvement, but although the increased weight of the barrel may have tended to check the tendency of the rifle to fly upwards, he could not perceive that it reduced the actual recoil against the shoulder to any extent. The excessive heating during firing had been reduced to a great extent by thickening the barrel. The OC also reported, on 9-10-1874, that the result of the trial was most satisfactory, increased length of stock and greater weight of rifle was a decided improvement, and the recoil of the arm, although still considerable, was modified.

The OC 46th Foot reported on 21-10-1874 that the increased weight of the barrel had the effect of slightly diminishing the recoil, and causing it to be less noticeable. He also stated that the pull off in the majority of the rifles was very defective and unequal, and caused dissatisfaction. He also complained of the rough finish of the triggers and trigger guards.

Because of this report the OC 2/4th was asked if the defects in the pull off had been observed in his battalion's trials, and he replied on 4-11-1874 that the pull off was very irregular, and forwarded a report from his IoM which stated that the pull off was unsatisfactory and unequal, varying in one rifle from 7 to 11 lbs, with no two consecutive pull offs being the same. This defect had been observed in all previous patterns of the M-H rifle.

In a minute of 5-11-1874 the DAG for Musketry in Ireland remarked that this defect was extremely injurious to accurate shooting.

PREPARATIONS FOR ISSUING RIFLES TO THE SERVICE

On 1-9-1874 the DoA submitted a minute to the SoS containing a precis, complete to that date, of all reports on trials of the M-H rifle, with ensuing proposals and alterations, and recommended that the rifle should be issued to the infantry in October, together with the ammunition in store, which amounted to several million rounds.

The SoS remarked on 5-9-1874 –

I think everything has been and is being done to secure that the Martini-Henry shall be issued in as perfect a condition as possible to the troops. I agree with Sir John Adye, that the time has come for the issue, and approve the course which he suggests.

The C-I-C approved on 28-9-1874 a draft General Order to the army, announcing the intended change of equipment, and instructing OC's of regiments at home to forward the necessary demands. This order was promulgated 12-10-1874, and issues of the rifles and ammunition commenced immediately.

The DoA approved on 3-10-1874 the suggestion by the Controller, Woolwich Arsenal, that packing of M-H rifles be commenced, in anticipation of demands for the supply abroad; and the A-G on 21-10-1874 agreed with the controller's proposed distribution of arms and ammunition to foreign stations, excluding India, which he submitted on 16-10-1874. The S-G gave his approval of the above proposals on 29-10-1874.

So now, three years after the definite adoption of the M-H

rifle as the service arm, it was at last issued to the troops, as the best breech-loading rifle obtainable from all those systems submitted about nine years previously. Unfortunately, its troubles still were not finished, as the wider experience gained with it in service disclosed that some of the problems previously classed as minor, particularly the trigger pull off, were potentially worse, and so further trials and changes were necessary before the rifle achieved a standard of perfection sufficient to obviate further problems of that nature.

SNAP CAPS

Because of the complaints about strikers continually breaking, a conference on 24-10-1873 recommended that 200 snap caps, as suggested by Col. Fraser, should be made and issued, 100 each to the 2/4th and 46th for trial. The reports received were favourable, but five were damaged in the 46th's trials. The IGM submitted an improved pattern to the conference of 9-4-1874, which approved it subject to any minor modifications which might have become necessary after further trial at Enfield and Hythe; its cost was estimated at 4d.

20 of the new snap caps had been issued to Hythe, and were reported upon 3-9-1874. They had been tried to the extent of 2,000 snaps, and eight were much damaged. Having been returned to Enfield, the ebonite buffers in them were replaced with new units of the same material, and the snap caps sent back to Hythe for further trial. In the meantime, manufacture for general supply was proceeded with.

The IGM reported on the trials of the improved caps on 13-11-1874. 2,000 snaps had been made; 17 had stood the test well, two or three of the ebonites were indented slightly, and three screws gave way. The strikers of seven rifles out of the 20 used for the trials were broken (one returned for examination), two of them in two places; in two cases the broken striker dropped down behind the tumbler rest and prevented the action of the trigger. The point of the striker appeared in some cases to be knocked up, and so would in time become too short to strike the cap with sufficient force to ignite it.

The Supt. RSAF remarked, on 24-11-1874, that it did not clearly appear whether 2,000 snaps were made in all, or 2,000 on each cap in 20 rifles. Assuming the latter to be the case, he thought the result satisfactory, there being but one striker broken in 5,714 snaps; he further observed that the striker sent with the report was one of the old weak patterns.

The three caps which gave way had been sent for his examination, and he reported on these on 11-12-1874. It had been found that the screws at the base would work loose in about 700 snaps, owing to the jarring received. He stated that they could be easily screwed up again if the same should occur with the caps currently being made at Enfield, which he doubted; or any armourer could easily tighten them. His opinion was that the article would prove satisfactory.

The IGM on 13-12-1874 drew attention to a catch, devised by Mr. Aston, Armourer to the SoM, for use at drill, to obviate the need for a snap cap. The Supt. RSAF reported on 16-12-1874 that the catch could be used without damage to the breech action, and that if the little action it permitted was considered sufficient for drill purposes, and if extracting drill was not thought necessary, the catch might take the place of the snap cap. He also pointed out that the catch might be used as a half-cock, remarking that this might not be considered a recommendation.

FURTHER MEETINGS AND DECISIONS

To consider reports on the heavy barrel trials, snap caps, and other matters, another conference was held at the WO on 18-12-1874, and present were –

Brig.-Gen. Sir John Adye, KCB, DoA
Col. the Hon. H. Clifford, CB, VC, AAG
Col. T.W. Milward, CB, ADC, Supt. RL
Col. G. Fraser, RA, Supt. RSAF
Mr. L. W. Englebach of the WO attended.

Several papers were considered by the committee, and the decisions below were amongst those taken –

Heavy barrels. The committee were of opinion that no further steps should be taken in this matter at present.

As regards the pull off which was complained of, the Supt. RSAF admitted there was an irregularity, but considered it not of practical importance. He said he had for some time been considering the subject, and thought the irregularity might be modified, if not remedied, by small manufacturing improvements.

Length of butts. The committee recommended that the existing proportions should be reversed as regards future manufacture, thus making 2/3 long (14½ inches) and 1/3 short (14 inches).

Snap caps. The committee recommended a trial of Mr. Aston's proposed catch, which if adopted would render a snap cap unnecessary. 12 rifles were to be fitted with it, and issued for trial for consideration and report.

The Supt. RSAF subsequently submitted a minute to the DoA on 16-4-1875, as below –

Minute of the Superintendent Royal Small Arms Factory on the Reports Generally.

Director of Artillery and Stores.

With reference to the enclosed precis of reports from Regiments, the following points appear to demand particular notice –

Undersighting. All the experience in this department, with the use of fixed rests, proves that, so fired, the rifle is not undersighted (vide report of the assistant superintendent, dated 25-3-1875).

The reports of commanding officers as to undersighting are however so numerous, that it seems desirable to ascertain what alteration to the sighting from, say, 500 yards and upwards, is best suited on the average when firing from the shoulder.

With your approval, I propose furnishing various special slides bearing distinctive numbers, and giving small differences of elevation.

One hundred of these slides to be issued to each of certain regiments selected for the experiments, which should be carried out by good and fair marksmen instructed to aim strictly by the slide, at 5, 8, 10, 12, and 1,300 yards, each man to make a target with 10 rounds at each range, the firing to be under varying conditions of weather. The mean measurement above or below centre to be recorded in each case.

Pull off. The defects in this respect are not due to any fault in the design, but to some small departures from it, such as the trigger pin being a little loose. They can always be rectified by the armourer-serjeant.

Difficulty in extraction. There would be no such difficulty if the men had experience in handling the arm, except when an old cartridge is left in the chamber some time, and the barrel, after expansion by firing, shrinks upon it in cooling; in this case, which must be rare, the rod may be required to force it out, the head of the cartridge having been pulled off.

Breaking of tumblers. This is attributed partly to inexperience in easing springs, and partly to too great hardness in some of the Birmingham supply. I don't know that any tumblers made in this department have failed, though they would be very liable to break if the action be improperly worked.

Breaking of strikers. This is mainly to be accounted for by the want of snap caps, now being rapidly supplied.

Heating of barrel. A leather guard might be provided, if necessary.

Difficulty in grasping the rifle. Some modification of the "Hythe" instructions might possibly remove this objection.

Royal Small Arms Factory. Fred. Close,
Enfield Lock, 16th April, 1875. Lt.-Col., Superintendent.

(The report of the Asst. Supt. RSAF, 25-3-1875, mentioned above, will be found in Appendix 22. It will be noted also that the above report was signed by Col. Close, in place of Col. Fraser, as Supt. RSAF, as the former had replaced the latter in the interim.)

Another WO conference was held on 24-5-1875, to consider these matters, and present were –

Brig.-Gen. Sir John Adye, KCB, DoA
Col. Radcliffe, CB, Commandant, SoM
Col. the Hon. H. Clifford, CB, VC, AAG
Col. Fraser, RA, Supt. RL
Lt.-Col. Close, RA, Supt. RSAF
Mr. L.W. Englebach of the WO attended.

The committee proceeded to consider the reports received since their last meeting, and having perused the minute of the Supt. RSAF of 16-4-1875, decided as follows –

1. Undersighting. The committee thought that an experiment should be made with a view to correcting the alleged undersighting. Trials were to be carried out at Hythe and Aldershot, those at the latter station being under the immediate supervision of the district IoM, who should be in communication with the Supt. RSAF. Five descriptions of special slides were to be prepared as recommended by the superintendent, 20 of each being forwarded to each station, 10 rounds per man to be fired at each of the five ranges specified by him.

2. Pull off. No steps appeared necessary at present, pending further experience.

3. Difficulties in extraction. No steps appeared to be necessary.

4. Breaking of tumblers and strikers. The committee, after perusing reports relative to trials of Aston's catch (there being six in favour and six against), agreed that as the present snap caps had only had a very limited trial, they should await the result of further experience, taking no further steps at present in regard to Aston's catch. The Supt. RSAF to endeavour, if possible, to improve the present snap cap.

5. Heating of barrel. No steps necessary. A leather guard had already been approved in case it was found to be absolutely necessary.

6. Grasp of rifle. The committee were not in a position to recommend any change in this respect; in fact, the question was rather for the consideration of the C-I-C.

In concluding their report the committee stated that they wished to call attention to the fact that the reports received from the troops up to that time, were, generally speaking, favourable to the Martini-Henry rifle.

The above proceedings were duly submitted to the C-I-C and the SoS, and the experiment proposed in Para.1 was ordered to be carried out.

CHAPTER 9.

SERVICE PROBLEMS WITH THE MARTINI–HENRY

SHORTLY after the general issue of the M-H at home, it was decided that a special trial should be carried out to obtain from the troops their initial impressions of it. A special army circular of 26-11-1874 authorised the expenditure of ten rounds per man at practice, for this purpose. (A precis of the reports received from home regiments is given in Appendix 23.)

The most common complaint was of undersighting, with broken strikers and tumblers common. The pull off was also complained of as being irregular, but on the whole the arm was well received. Some objections against it seemed to stem more from prejudice than from any fault of design.

However, it was not long before one particularly serious problem became obvious – premature ignition of the cartridge. This was more prevalent at overseas stations, but did also occur at home. The following reports are indicative of this occurrence –

From the OC 95th Regiment at Fleetwood, 8-1-1875 –

I have . . . to state that on the occasion of a portion of the regiment . . . firing blank ammunition with the Martini-Henry rifle . . . on closing the breech block of one of the rifles the cartridge exploded on two different occasions.

The rifle has since been examined by the armourer-serjeant, and he states that the nose of the trigger did not fit perfectly in the tumbler rest, and the trigger spring was too weak.

The Supt. RSAF commented on 9-2-1875 –

The rifle having been adjusted by the armourer-serjeant, I can only suggest that the defect was occasioned by the trigger spring screw becoming loose.

He presumed the rifle was used and acted properly on occasions previous to that on which it failed; this, again, would point to the above suggestion as defining the cause of failure.

Report from 1/4th Foot at Gibraltar, 18-5-1875 –

In two rifles it had been found that on closing the breech after firing, the striker had been released. Upon working the action several times it apparently righted itself. Experiments had been made, and it was found that if any small substance was introduced between the outer bearing of the trigger and the guard, the spring and striker were released on closing the breech. Two cartridges had been exploded in this way.

The trigger nose is too fine, and so nicely adjusted to the tumbler rest that very little will prevent it from catching sufficiently.

By cleaning the action of a rifle with a pull off like a hair trigger, the pull off was at once brought to its normal state of 8 lb.

A board of officers was convened to examine one of the rifles complained of, and after detailing the evidence, the board gave the following opinion –

The board, having most carefully examined the rifle No.145, and maturely considered the evidence produced, and having taken into consideration the substance of the report thereon made by Col. Cameron, commanding 1st Battalion 4th King's Own Royal Regiment, is of opinion that the breech action of the rifle in question is now in perfect order, except that the pull off is lighter than regulation, and that the irregularity complained of by Pvt. Upfield was probably occasioned by the presence of some foreign substance, such as grit or dust, getting into some part of the breech action, thereby preventing the trigger nose from entering the bent of the tumbler rest, and that this substance was probably ground away by the constant opening and closing of the breech, until found no longer to exist on Pvt. Upfield's return to barracks.

The board finds that the irregularities in question did not occur on the 7th instant, as stated in Col. Cameron's letter, but on some day in the month of April, and that the rifle was not sent to the armourer's shop until 9th May; it is therefore impossible, in the absence of any direct evidence as to the cause of the irregularity, for the board to come to any definite conclusion. The board finds on experimenting with several rifles, selected at hazard, that by placing a certain amount of foreign substance under the outer bearing of the trigger, a similar result is arrived at, which indeed might happen in any rifle.

With regard to this episode, the Supt. RSAF stated on 7-6-1875 –

This objectional effect of the admission of dirt, or dirt between trigger and guard, has been previously noticed. I cannot suggest any means of preventing it except calling attention to such a possibility and urging especial precautions to guard against the admission of dirt between trigger and guard.

That this problem was not always caused by dirt is illustrated by this report from the OC 1st Btn. Scots Fusilier Guards, 24-5-1875 –

A man having broken the sear spring of his Martini rifle, I find on examination that it is possible to load and fire the rifle without discovering that the sear spring is broken, and that when so loaded the slightest touch on the trigger, or a knock of the butt on the ground, will cause the rifle to go off.

On 2-6-1875 the Supt. RSAF reported, in relation to the above complaint, that it was quite true that a M-H rifle could be loaded and fired with a broken trigger spring, and that it was even liable to go off in the act of closing the block. He could not suggest any remedy, stating that the defect (such as it was) was in the construction of the action. He also considered that the accident of a trigger spring breakage would be a rare occurrence.

The DoA minuted on 7-6-1875 –

I think we need take no action at present. It is a subject which may be discussed at a future conference, with other points which may arise, when we get more experience with the arm.

The Supt. RSAF further reported on 22-7-1875 that he could not suggest any alteration but what would involve a considerable variation from the Martini design. It would take some time to perfect any change of pattern for trial, and it would have to be thoroughly experimented with before adoption. Hence no alteration in the current year's production was possible. He was of the opinion that the accident complained of (Gibraltar report 18-5-1875) had been so rare as to hardly justify an expensive alteration of the arms already issued; it might though, be as well to consider a modified design to govern manufacture after the expiration of the current year. If desired, he was prepared to submit for inspection a specimen action which would remove all possibility of such an accident. It would, moreover, simplify and cheapen manufacture, and seemed likely to be generally serviceable.

In accordance with the above comments, the DoA on 26-7-1875 minuted to the A-G that he would recommend that no steps be taken at present to meet an isolated case.

The previous complaints were, however, only the beginning, as more reports were received, with similar problems mentioned, such as this one from the IoM, Royal Marine Artillery Barracks, Portsmouth, 2-9-1875 –

In passing through the annual course of practice with the Martini-Henry rifle, lately issued to the division . . . I have found that some of the rifles explode the cartridge in the act of closing the lever.

I have further found that a great number of these rifles have been rendered temporarily useless by the breaking either of the striker or mainspring, and that the variation in the pull off ranges from 1 to 20 lb (as per inclosure).

Martini-Henry rifle, list of defects.

Number of rifles issued – 280
Strikers broken – 6
Main springs broken – 6
Trigger springs broken – 3
Pull off altered – 24.

In reply, the Supt. RSAF remarked as follows, 26-9-1875 –

The Martini-Henry arms in charge of the Royal Marine Artillery at Portsmouth, reported as defective . . . have been examined, and I find that three of them would not cock, on account of their trigger screws not fitting accurately. The same cause accounts for the irregularity in the pull off of four other rifles. These rifles were all put in perfect order by the substitution of new trigger screws for the old ones, which had, doubtless, had a great deal of wear, as it appears that the same 120 rifles are put into the hands of all recruits learning their drill at the barracks. The fact of the defects coming to light so long after the rifles have been in use would lead to the conclusion that their action was perfect when they were first issued, and that continued wear has lessened the fit of the trigger screws.

These arms should at once have been put in order by the armourer-serjeant, who, however, appears never to have had instruction in the care of the Martini rifles and so was incompetent to deal with them. This armourer-serjeant should at once be instructed at this factory.

The breakage of strikers appears to be mainly due to the arms having been much used without snap caps. A properly qualified armourer can always replace them without difficulty.

The cleaning rods were, I understand, chiefly broken by recruits when unpiling arms, great care should be enforced in practising this operation.

The breakage of other components are ordinary casualties, and can be readily made good out of the proportion of spare parts supplied.

On 27-9-1875 the ADoA observed that the defects listed seemed mainly attributable to wear, not to careless exposure or accumulation of dirt. He then asked whether this was a defect peculiar to the M-H arm.

The superintendent replied on 27-9-1875 that in this particular case the looseness of the trigger pins (which would always produce the defective action complained of) appeared to be due to wear. A small size trigger pin or a screw hole of too large a diameter would always give such results and not only with the Martini action, but also with the common lock. Dirt and grit, etc, had nothing to do with the present reported defects.

A report was also received from the navy on 21-9-1875. From HMS Excellent, Portsmouth –

1. In compliance with your memorandum of the 18th instant, . . . since the issue of the Martini-Henry rifle to this ship in April last, it has repeatedly happened that the main spring has been released on closing the breech.

2. This defect is in most cases attributable either to a weak trigger spring, or to an accumulation of rust or fouling in the notch of the tumbler rest, thus interfering with the proper bearing of the nose of the trigger.

3. It is also to be remarked that fouling (powder deposit) finds its way into all parts of the breech action, and after firing it is essential that an armourer or other skilled person should take to pieces and draw the breech action, otherwise it becomes rusty.

4. There is, however, a liability to accident in the Martini-Henry rifle to which I would call particular attention, for it is especially liable to occur on active service.

5. When the rifle is unloaded there is a small space between the frame and that part of the trigger which bears against the frame when the rifle is loaded, or the main spring drawn back; if dirt or other substance find its way into this space, the action of the trigger spring will be checked and the main spring will be released on closing the breech; this may easily be demonstrated by placing a piece of folded paper on the small space referred to, and then performing the motion of loading.

6. Attention was first directed to this defect of the rifle by premature explosion actually taking place whilst some of the men of the Excellent were firing blank cartridge in skirmishing on Whale Island; it was found that some grass had got inside the trigger guard and had been broken off in the small space referred to.

7. I have today caused a handful of sand to be poured over and around the trigger of a Martini-Henry rifle; the sand lodged at once in the small space, causing the main spring to be released on closing the breech.

8. A rifle dropped upon muddy ground may be expected to be put out of order in a similar manner.

Tabulated list of defects in Martini-Henry rifles.

Number of rifles – 600
Date received – 2-4-1875
Main springs broken – 13
Trigger springs broken – 10
Strikers broken – 5
Tumblers broken – 2
Indicator keeper screws broken – 2.

The DoA, with the approval of the S-G, on 16-9-1875 addressed the following minute to the A-G –

The subject of the effect of the admission of dirt or grit between the trigger and guard of the Martini-Henry, thus causing the pull off to be dangerously light, had been before reported but it was considered exceptional, and it was decided to wait for further experience before doing anything.

This defect has now been found to be more general than was anticipated, and an inspection of the arm will shew that, under certain circumstances, it becomes dangerous.

It may be said that although the arm has been issued for three years, and many rounds fired, no accident involving injury has occurred, but the liability remains, and the defect must be remedied.

The Supt. RSAF has suggested an alteration which would prevent the possibility of such an accident, but, though simple, it would involve a variation from the present pattern, and would have to be tried before being generally introduced.

The probability of accident with the present arm seems very small, but still it exists, and it will be for you to decide whether further instructions should be given to commanding officers on the subject of the liability of the arm to this defect when dirt or grit gets between the trigger and guard.

This prompted the C-I-C to minute the SoS on 27-9-1875

I have seen the papers on the Martini-Henry rifle, and am in great anxiety as to the defects complained of in this weapon. In my opinion no time should be lost in remedying these defects, which it is stated can be accomplished at an expense of 1s 6d per musket. It will be necessary in that case to alter the reserve arms we have got, and then to issue these as altered, calling in those now in the hands of the regiments. It is very unfortunate that the necessity for this has arisen, but I see no other mode of dealing with the case, which is of such immense importance.

PS. If the alteration could take place at the head quarters of regiments, it would of course facilitate matters greatly.

The SoS then remarked on 29-9-1875 –

The importance of remedying the defects of the weapon at once cannot be exaggerated.

A WAR OFFICE CONFERENCE AND MORE TRIALS

To consider the reports of the problems experienced with the M-H rifle in service, a conference was convened at the WO on 5-10-1875. Present were –

Maj.-Gen. J.W. Armstrong, CB, DAG
Brig.-Gen. F.A. Campbell, CB, RA, DoA
Col. W.P. Radcliffe, CB, IGM
Capt. T. Brandreth, RN, HMS Excellent
Col. The Hon. H.H. Clifford, CB, VC, AAG
Col. W.C. Bancroft, 16th Regt.
Col. Henry Kent, 77th Regt.
Col. E. Reilly, CB, RA, ADoA
Col. G. Fraser, RA, Supt. RL
Col. H.C. Fletcher, CMG, Scots Fusilier Gds
Lt.-Col. F. Close, RA, Supt. RSAF
Mr. L.W. Englebach of the WO attended.

The Supt. RSAF had prepared a memorandum on the changes to the trigger mechanism he had mentioned in a previous minute. This memorandum was tabled at this meeting for the information of the persons present.

Memorandum handed in 5th October 1875, by Lt.-Colonel Close, Royal Small Arms Factory.

20 rifles with new pattern tumbler and trigger, and altered guard, gave the following results –

1st. Tumbler rest dispensed with
2nd. Tumbler rest axis screw dispensed with
3rd. Guard encloses trigger, so that no sand or dust can interfere with the working of the action
4th. Pull off regular, and possibility of catching trigger nose half-way in bent prevented
5th. A small trigger screw does not affect the working of the action in any way, and cannot be felt in the pull off
6th. The trigger spring, when fired, stands at lightest compression.

Sand dust experiments were made with these rifles as follows –

Number of rifles tried – 20
Number of rounds fired from each rifle – 140
Number of times each arm was placed in the gun case to have sand dust blown about them – 28
Number of times placed with –
Barrel down, and butt towards the blast – 7
Barrel up, and butt towards the blast – 7
Barrel down, and butt from the blast – 7
Barrel up, and butt from the blast – 7

Results:

Number of times hard to extract out of 140 shots –
Rifle No.7567 – 20
Rifle No.8489 – 5
Rifle No.8304 – 2

Block occasionally remained down –
Rifle No.6866
Rifle No.8304
Rifle No.8058
Rifle No.8090

No other casualties occurred.

In addition to the sand dust experiments above detailed, four of the rifles, Nos.8190, 8266, 7751, and 8057, have each had 860 rounds fired from them, making altogether 1,000 rounds per arm, without their actions having been either cleaned or even examined.

The operations of extracting and loading were uniformly easy throughout the trials. The breech blocks after firing 300 or 400 rounds remained down, or did not return to the loading position, which was due to their being clogged with sand. The pull offs were regular, so far as could be detected by the usual trial with the finger. The friction of the parts from the absence of oil caused a grating noise in opening and closing the breech actions.

Mark II cartridges were used in these experiments, and no misfires occurred.

RSAF — *Fred. Close, Lt.-Colonel,*
4th October, 1875. — *Superintendent.*

The previous reports and minutes were read to the meeting by Maj.-Gen. Armstrong, who observed that the conference was assembled to consider what could be done to remedy the defects complained of in the M-H rifles in service.

Lt.-Col. Close was called upon to exhibit the modified breech action described in the memorandum. He also produced one of the rifles with the altered action, which had fired 1,000 rounds without cleaning. This rifle was taken to pieces at the meeting, and examined, and although dirt had accumulated, as might be expected from the nature of the tests described by Col. Close, the arm appeared to be in perfect working order. It was stated that the cost of carrying out the alteration in the arms in service would not exceed 1s 6d each, and the arms could be readily altered without withdrawing them from the regiments.

On being asked as to the possibility of strengthening the strikers to remedy their liability to break, Col. Close replied that this could be done if the form of breech block was also altered.

As the alteration proposed by the superintendent involved a change in the mechanism of the rifle, the chairman drew attention to the evidence given before the Special Committee on Breech-Loading Rifles in January 1871, as showing that the mechanical construction of the arm had engaged special and scientific attention at the time, which should be carefully borne in mind in considering and finally deciding on any change.

Col. Fletcher, who had been the president of the Special Committee, having been called upon for his opinion, stated that two complaints had been made of the M-H rifle –

1st. That dirt and wet might, under exceptional circumstances, enter the lock action and impede its working.

2nd. That the rifle might be rendered dangerous by the trigger being very light, or by the rifle going off unintentionally, owing to the nose of the sear failing to enter the bent of the tumbler.

He then stated that both these defects could occur with any rifle, and during the long and exhaustive tests to which the M-H had been subjected, the first defect was found to be far less likely to take place than in the Snider, whilst the second had never occurred. He therefore considered the first defect immaterial, but the second, although inherent in almost every rifle, was serious and dangerous in the M-H, owing to its being, when loaded, placed at once on full-cock. The addition of a locking bolt might reduce the danger to a minimum, but a simpler plan would be to increase the depth of the bent in the tumbler, thereby rendering the pull off longer and slower, similar, he believed, to that of the Mauser, the new Prussian rifle. There had also been complaints that many of the strikers broke when snapping the rifle. The strikers had, however, been improved in manufacture, and it might be well to ascertain if the new ones were sufficiently strong. He therefore recommended that a report on these points should be obtained, as well as on the increased safety of the rifle. Consequently, he proposed that 100 rifles with the bent deepened be sent to Hythe, and 100 to the Excellent, and that reports be called for first, in regard to the additional safety, if any, of the rifles; secondly, as to any effect that the alteration of the pull off might have upon the accuracy of the shooting; and thirdly, on the strength of the striker.

Col. Fraser, formerly Supt. RSAF, concurred in the trials of the suggestions of Cols. Close and Fletcher, but he doubted whether the latter would be acceptable with the army, on account of the long pull off. He could not concur in reintroducing a locking bolt to prevent the premature discharge of the rifle, because the bolt could only be used after the action was cocked, and the failure occurred in the act of cocking.

Col. Kent remarked on the excessive failure of strikers in

his regiment; no less than three times the regulated proportion of spare strikers having been used up in one year's practice.

Col. Radcliffe was of opinion that if any changes in the arm were contemplated, the question of strikers – which was a very important one – should be carefully considered.

Mr. Perry, the RSAF Manager, was called in, and stated that the slight alteration suggested by Col. Fletcher could be readily effected, and it would certainly remove the danger at present caused by the accumulation of grit or dust between the shoulder of the trigger and the guard; but other difficulties might arise.

As regards strikers, Mr. Perry explained that the best material was used, but the metal deteriorated by the frequent and heavy blows (120 lbs); there were no means of enlarging the striker or strengthening it without altering the action. But there had been some imperfections in manufacture, especially in some of the trade arms, which had now been remedied.

The committee then deliberated, and agreed to recommend as follows –

1. 1,000 rifles to be altered according to the plan proposed by the Supt. RSAF, which had already been since tried at Enfield. The necessary parts could be prepared in about a month, and fitted at the head-quarters of the regiments selected.

Full and careful trials were to be made, and reports rendered on forms specially prepared, which would include an enquiry in regard to strikers, respecting which there had been frequent complaints.

2. 200 rifles to be prepared with the slight alteration suggested by Col. Fletcher. These could be altered almost immediately, and should be issued to Hythe and Excellent, and reports called for as recommended by Col. Fletcher.

The SoS approved these recommendations on 20-10-1875, the Supt. RSAF having already been given instructions to proceed without delay.

FLETCHER'S TRIGGER TRIALS

The 200 rifles with Col. Fletcher's proposed alteration were reported ready on 26-10-1875, and instructions for their trial were prepared; but in discussions that had taken place after the meeting of 5th October, it was thought desirable that the shoulder of the trigger be removed. Col. Fletcher had also decided to make a trial of arms with the trigger shoulder filed off, and, if this was successful, he would consider it preferable to the deepening of the tumbler notch.

He accordingly had two rifles of the Scots Fusilier Guards altered, one with shoulder of trigger rounded, the other with it cut completely off. Another rifle was altered at Woolwich by the Secretary of the Experimental Branch and 100 rounds were fired from it with no problems.

Col. Fletcher's trials consisted of pouring sand into the actions, one dry, one oiled; here also with no problems. The rifles were then forwarded to Enfield, where trials showed that in the rifle with the shoulder removed the block did not return to the loading position, which was considered a defect that would be exaggerated if the trigger guard had been of the old form intended for the locking bolt, of which 140,000 were in use (ie, in second pattern rifles upgraded to third pattern). When this action was tested with mud it became so clogged it could not be pulled off without extreme force.

On 11-11-1875 The DoA directed that the old trigger guard be tried. One was tested with the shoulder of trigger removed. As usual, sand was thrown over the action, and although it kept on working, sand and dirt were found to have worked their way inside, mainly through the slot left by the removal of the locking bolt.

The trials to this stage seemed successful, but the Supt. RSAF objected to the alterations from a mechanical point of view, so these trials were called off. However, the A-G and the SGO both agreed that the 200 rifles with the altered bent were to be kept on hand until the trials of the new trigger components had been carried out.

PREPARATIONS FOR ENFIELD TRIGGER TRIALS

For these trials the actions were altered as follows –

1. The shoulder of the trigger was removed, and that portion of the trigger rounded off concentrically with the axis of the trigger pin.
2. A knuckle piece was riveted and brazed onto the trigger guard; its inner surface closely fitted to the rounded portion of the trigger.
3. The tumbler rest and axis pin were dispensed with.
4. The lower arm of the tumbler was lengthened, and a bent cut therein, in which the nose of the trigger rested.
5. The under surface of the block was recessed, in order to allow free play of the lengthened tumbler.
6. The pressure of the trigger spring on the trigger was somewhat reduced.

The objects in view when these alterations were designed were –

1 and 2. The removal of the liability to accidental explosion in closing the action, through the admission of sand or other foreign substance.

3 and 4. The furnishing of a simple and effective method of working the action in the absence of any support given by the shoulder of the trigger.

5. Became necessary as a result of the increased length of the tumbler arm.

6. A better proportioning of the two pressures on the trigger, so as to secure greater regularity in the pull off.

The forms issued to the regiments testing the components

provided for reports to be made under the heads shown below, viz, –

1. State the number of rounds fired from each rifle; and, if possible, the number of times the gun has been snapped.

2. Describe briefly any special tests you may have applied to the arms, and their results.

3. State whether the alterations have obviated the danger of an accidental discharge of the gun arising from a sudden jar or from dirt having entered between the trigger and lock plate, or from both causes combined.

4. State whether the alterations have improved the pull off either in regularity or other respects, or have had any prejudicial effect with regard thereto.

5. State whether during the trials any strikers have broken, and if so how many, specifying whether in firing, in snapping without a snap cap, or in snapping with a snap cap.

6. Express your opinion on the arm generally.

The new components were ready by 15-11-1875, and four skilled mechanics proceeded to the following stations to fit the units to the requisite number of arms of the selected regiments –

Aldershot – 250 sets for 5 regiments, to be selected by GOC.
London –
50 to 2nd Btn. Scots Fusilier Guards
50 to 2nd Btn. Coldstream Guards
Chatham –
50 to 2/16th Regiment
50 to 3rd Btn. Rifle Brigade
Woolwich – 50 to 77th Regiment
Hythe – 50 sets
Portland – 50 to 102nd Regiment
Pembroke – 50 to 95th Regiment
HMS Excellent – 100 sets
Curragh – 50 to 2/17th Regiment
Fermoy – 50 to 2/8th Regiment
Cork –
50 to 1/12th Regiment
50 to 1/23rd Regiment
Buttevant – 50 to 82nd Regiment
Total – 1,000 sets.

The following letter of instructions, together with an explanatory memorandum and the form of report to be used, was issued from the A-G's office to the various OC's on 16-11-1875.

In consequence of certain complaints having been made as to the occasional liability of the Martini-Henry rifle to accidental discharge on the action being closed, owing to the accumulation of dirt or grit over the shoulder of the trigger, orders have been given for . . . rifles belonging to your regiment to be fitted with certain modified components as described in the enclosed memorandum.

The opportunity has been taken to simplify the action to some extent, and you are requested to have the arms thoroughly tried; and to report upon them on the accompanying form.

A competent person from the RSAF will attend to fit the new parts, and 20 rounds of ball ammunition per man will be issued, on demand, for the purpose of this trial, and a further supply, including blank cartridge, may be obtained as required.

E. R. Greaves, Colonel,
Asst. Adjutant-General.

(The explanatory memorandum mentioned above listed the alterations to the action as given in Items 1 to 6 at the beginning of this section.)

RESULTS OF THE TRIGGER TRIALS

During early December 1875 the reports on the new components began coming in, and it was apparent that the number of rounds fired, and special tests applied, varied considerably.

Regarding the liability of the rifle to accidental discharge, the reports were unanimous that this problem had been obviated by the new components. The main object of the trials had thus been achieved.

With the exception of two at Hythe, no strikers had been broken, and as special attention had been directed to these, this result was also very satisfactory.

An abstract of the reports was prepared, and is given below: the original reports can be seen in Appendix 24.

1. 2nd Btn. Coldstream Guards (4-12-1875): 50 rounds each from six rifles; pull off more regular; the arm is now a most serviceable and superior weapon.

2. 2nd Btn. Scots Fusilier Guards (8-12-1875): 100 rounds from each; two fired over 400; besides other severe tests; pull off more regular; arm greatly improved.

Suggests case-hardening of upper surface of breech block, and something to remedy injury to men's coats by blueing of trigger guard coming off.

3. 102nd Fusiliers (8-12-1875): 20 rounds from each rifle. Breech action considerably improved, also the pull off; grip still imperfect.

4. 95th Regiment (11-12-1875): 20 rounds. Pull off improved; the arm is now most satisfactory.

5. 82nd Regiment (11-12-1875): 30 rounds. Arm much improved, also the pull off, which was very regular. If barrel or bayonet was lengthened, and some protection afforded to the hand from heated barrel, the arm would be very effective.

6. 1st Btn. 23rd Regiment (20-12-1875): 30 rounds. Unfavourable report. Arm too complicated; pull off unsatisfactory.

7. 2nd Btn. 8th Regiment (21-12-1875): 20 rounds. The arm is a good, serviceable, and handy weapon. The pull off is much more regular and uniform.

8. 1st Btn. 12th Regiment (21-12-1875): 30 rounds. A first rate arm, and would work well on service, but there is

a want of uniformity in the pull off.

Another report from the same regiment says that the pull off is perfectly regular.

9. 2nd Btn. 17th Regiment (23-12-1875): 20 rounds ball, besides blank. Pull off more regular, but the lock is still too complicated, sights defective, and the rifle does not balance well at the slope.

10. School of Musketry (28-12-1875): 20 rounds. Satisfactory, considering severity of tests, but the striker is the weak point of the arm; pull off varied in some cases.

11. 2nd Btn. 16th Regiment (29-12-1875): 40 rounds. Pull off somewhat "dragged", but not complained of. The arm is a little too complicated for the ordinary soldier; bayonet too short; absence of half-cock a great disadvantage.

12. 3rd Btn. Rifle Brigade (1-1-1876): 40 rounds. Pull off improved, and the alterations of the arm very favourably thought of, but further trial necessary before expressing a decided opinion.

13. 77th Regiment (1-1-1876): 20 rounds. The alteration seems to be an improvement, but the pull off has varied a good deal, and is otherwise unsatisfactory.

14. HMS Excellent (5-1-1876): 20 rounds and more. Trial not completed to date. Half of the arms varied in the pull off. It is thought to be a great defect to have to employ an armourer to strip the action when necessary for cleaning.

15. 106th Regiment (7-1-1876): 40 rounds. The arm is improved, but the pull off is very irregular, and undersighting is still complained of. The barrel, after a few rounds of rapid firing becomes too hot to hold.

16. 2nd Btn. 6th Regiment (8-1-1876): 20 rounds. The lock action is much improved, also the pull off; extractor too weak.

17. 1st Btn. 15th Regiment (8-1-1876): 20 rounds. The alterations are real improvements, and the pull off is more regular.

18. 1st Btn. 9th Regiment (11-1-1876): 40 rounds. Pull off more regular. The rifle, as altered, superior to any arm yet introduced into the service.

19. 2nd Btn. 11th Regiment (11-1-1876): No firing as yet, but innumerable snapping, besides other tests. Pull off much improved. Arm considered almost perfect. 25-1-1876, 20 rounds have now been fired with satisfactory results.

An extra report was received from Excellent, dated 1-2-1876 –

1. Number of rounds fired. Over 33,000 were fired, and, in addition, the 100 arms were snapped above 41,000 times.

2. Special tests. 77 rifles were exposed to damp and foggy weather (with one wet night) for 72 hours, they were then fired with 20 rounds of ball each. When examined, 20 were found to have a clean breech action, the remainder were more or less dirty.

Two of the above 77 arms were then taken at random, and after being snapped 200 times each with snap caps, and 200 without, 100 rounds of ball were fired from each. Extractors of both arms worked badly towards the end of the practice, and pull off increased from 10 to 16 lbs. Rifles were then left out, uncleaned, in a damp and foggy night; next day snapping and firing 100 from each was repeated; extractor so faulty that the cleaning rod and jag had frequently to be used to force out the empty case. Pull off, which at beginning of second day's practice had decreased to nearly its original state of 10 lbs, increased again during firing to about 16 lbs. Lever worked stiffly throughout the two day's firing and snapping.

3. Accidental discharges. There were no accidental discharges.

4. Pull off. Pull off appears to increase during firing; but, after a considerable interval, it reverts nearly, but not quite, to original strength. Pull off still deficient in regularity; but in no case has it decreased appreciably.

5. Strikers. None broken.

6. Shooting. Very good. Danger arising from premature explosion appears to be removed.

7. Enumerates defects as follows –

> *1. Liability of lock action to rust.*
>
> *2. Difficulty of discovering whether a striker is broken.*
>
> *3. Liability of extractor to rust and fail in its action.*
>
> *4. Cleaning rod useless without a jag, which is liable to be lost on service. If extractor fails and jag is not forthcoming, the rifle is temporarily disabled.*

Sea air, combined with dampness of decks, tend to produce more rust in lock action than when rifles are kept in barracks.

The experience on board the Excellent seems to point to necessity of special provision for preventing lock action rusting on board ship; no rifle can be considered an efficient naval weapon which necessitates frequent taking to pieces of the lock action.

The Supt. RSAF on 24-1-1876 presented the following memorandum to the DoA –

Observations on the Foregoing Reports, by the Superintendent, Royal Small Arms Factory.

The new construction appears to have removed all danger of accidental discharge on closing the block, at the same time giving security against accidental explosion from jolts and jars after the block has been closed.

The statements and opinions as to the regularity of the pull off are somewhat conflicting; 13 CO's reporting favourably on it, the remainder either giving qualified approval or disapproval.

Most of the rifles adversely reported upon have been very carefully tested under my directions. The results of the testing of the arms from Excellent, and from the 77th and 106th Regiments, speak uniformly in favour of the principles of the new construction. This would leave only four questionable reports out of 20. One of the four (from 2/16 th Regiment) says nothing against the irregularity, but merely that the pull off is somewhat dragged but not complained of. Two of the remaining reports, viz, from the School of Musketry, and from the 1/23rd Regiment, do not appear to be of so serious a character as those dealt with above.

I have no doubt that any exceptional variations in the weight of the pull off will be found to proceed from rust, or from some small manufacturing irregularities (as in the case of the rifle from the 77th Regt.), and not from defect of design. These triggers and tumblers were all finished by hand, thus admitting of greater irregularity in form than when turned out by machinery, as they will be if the pattern is adopted.

I gather from these reports that with only one exception, all the objectionable pull offs have been in excess of the regulation maximum; the dangerously light pull off not unfrequently objected to with the present service action would appear therefore to have been got rid of.

Of the 1,000 strikers on trial only two have broken. The trials however have varied greatly, and in no case have been sufficiently exhaustive to sanction a reliable opinion of the durability of this component. They are made with the greatest care from the most suitable class of material hitherto found, and no pains are being spared to yet further improve its quality. But I am strongly of opinion that the peculiar form of the striker, and of the recess in the block into which it is thrown, taken in conjunction with its weight and velocity, give rise to a set of conditions which are likely to destroy it under less work than the ordinary hammer and nipple and some other forms of striker are capable of enduring.

I have endeavoured to improve it by thickening the point, but without any very marked success, and I do not consider this method of strengthening it worth further trial.

I have subsequently tried various forms of strikers with loose pins. One of these, which has given good results, I am prepared to submit, and if an improved striker is deemed necessary, would propose this one for adoption. Three strikers of this form have been snapped, each about 50,000 times, without snap caps, and are quite uninjured.

These strikers give promise of being far more reliable than the present ones, but the striker will continue to be the component most likely to injury owing to the hard usage thrown on them in snapping and firing. Notwithstanding the not unfavourable opinions expressed as to the present strikers, they are yet undoubtedly the most vulnerable part of the action.

The chief faults and suggestions noticed under the head of general remarks, including those on the unaltered arms, are as follows –

Heating of barrels. The only means of affording protection is by some such shield as has already been tried.

Shortness of bayonet. The reports on the long bayonet are generally favourable.

Upper surface of block should be dulled. I think this most desirable.

Blueing of guards comes off on tunics. This is in great measure due to the position of guard. As a matter of fact, it is rather the action of the metal itself rather than the blueing.

Thumb piece too high. Is this very important?

Ridges wanted on levers. Ditto.

Foresight liable to injury from bayonet. I do not see how this can be.

Danger in carrying the rifle at full-cock. There is some risk no doubt, but no more than with the common lock. The necessity too for marching with loaded rifles must be of less frequent occurrence with the present means of quick loading. If, however, the re-introduction of a locking bolt or half-cock stop is decided upon, I can submit designs.

Jar of trigger. This will be remedied in the new action when the parts are more accurately made.

Slight drag of trigger. Many think this rather advantageous. It is certainly not a serious objection, and it cannot be dispensed with in the new action.

Flap of back sight liable to be bent. I think this should be provided against by the drill regulations.

Rifle is undersighted. This has been proved, but the cause of the error lies in the manner of holding the arm and not in the sighting. I have nothing to add to my former proposals.

Extraction difficult. Mainly due to the jerk not being sharp enough. Occasionally if an empty cartridge is left some time in the bore after much firing it will stick. To prevent this the old cartridge should be extracted immediately after firing.

Sight lines rust and become obliterated. Remedy this by the use of the sight line tool.

Rod holders break. Some of these, made at Birmingham, were hardened by mistake, hence the complaint.

Rods get loose. Because the top band is not screwed up.

Notch of back sight should be deepened. This can be done on new caps.

Notch on sliding bar should be deepened. This can be done on new slides.

Flaps should not fly back. This is a great safeguard against its destruction.

Rod breaks. This is generally from want of care in unpiling arms, &c.

Action admits dirt. A leather guard might be found advantageous, especially for use on board ship.

Cleaning rod injures bore. The sight protector which I recently submitted for trial would effectually remedy this most serious evil.

Some further remarks were made by the superintendent on the irregular pull offs complained of by some regiments.

77th Regt. 8 rifles were received at Enfield on 22-1-1876, about which complaints of irregular pull off had been made. On being carefully tested seven of them gave the following weights: 8, 7, 7½, 7½, 8, 9, and 8 lbs respectively. The eighth, No.169, had the service pattern action, and should not have been sent. Of the seven experimental actions, only one exceeded the regulation weight; this was No. 666, and on examination its action was found to have a slight defect in the form of the tumbler, on the removal of which by a file, the pull off was at once corrected to 6 lbs. The discrepancies between the above readings and those reported by the OC were considered to be caused by differences in the manner of using the tester.

106th Regt. The assistant superintendent visited Aldershot on 17-1-1876, and reported the following results of pull off tests, carried out in his presence –

In ten rifles the pull off had not altered since issue.

In 22 it was slightly increased by ¼ to ½ lb.

In 13 it was slightly lessened by ¼ to ½ lb.

In one (No.79) it was excessive by 2lb. The parts of this rifle were taken to Enfield for examination. The superintendent in forwarding this report on 18-1-1876, made the following observations –

By this report it would appear that the record of the pull offs, as made by the armourer-serjeant of the regiment after the conclusion of the trials, is not reliable; that in only one case (No.79 rifle) has the pull off varied more than half a pound; that, of the whole number tested, there are only 3 altogether (including No.79) which exceed the prescribed maximum limit; 2 of these by a quarter of a pound only, and No.79 by half a pound. The tumbler and trigger of this rifle have been brought back by Major King-Harman for special examination, but I should wish the entire rifle to be sent also, to test it under the original conditions. There are several minor disturbing causes which are elements of error in indicating the weight of the pull off, and which are liable to affect the readings to the extent of a ¼ or ½ lb. And even supposing that the readings were absolutely true, I should deem those variations of no importance which are confined within the maximum and minimum regulation weights, viz, 6 and 8 lbs inclusive. On the whole, therefore, the state of the pull offs in the above arms is satisfactory.

HMS Excellent. The superintendent reported on 22-1-1876 – 25 rifles received from Excellent were carefully tested, and in nine of them the maximum weight of 8 lb was found to be exceeded.

One action gave 20 lb pull off
Two gave 14 lb ditto
Two 13 lb ditto
One 12 lb ditto
One 10 lb ditto
One 9½ lb ditto
One 9 lb ditto.

Eight were simply cleaned, and then gave the proper weights, ie, between 7 and 8 lbs inclusive.

One with a 14 lb pull off was found to have a broken mainspring, which should have reduced it.

The excessive weight in all the actions was entirely due to a quantity of rust which had accumulated on the components. One sample action was sent to the DoA as a fair specimen of the state in which they had been received for testing.

The superintendent commented –

It is astonishing that they should have got into this deplorable condition in so short a time. Either they must have been intentionally rusted by way of testing them severly, or else it would appear that the Martini-Henry action is not adequately protected against the corrosive influence of salt air, spray, etc. Frequent cleaning and oiling of the components in such cases is absolutely necessary. I fear that this has not been done, and I understand that the ship's armourer of the Excellent has had no proper instruction in the present arm.

The remaining 14 rifles had given the regulation weight when first tested, but were all rusty, although not generally as bad as the other nine. The varying pull offs complained of were thus fully accounted for.

RESULT OF SIGHTING TRIALS

In accordance with the recommendations of the WO conference of 24-5-1875, three descriptions of slides (A, B, and C) for the backsights of M-H rifles were sent in June 1875 to the SoM for trial. None were sent to Aldershot, as the range and targets there were not considered suitable for the trial.

The Commandant of Hythe reported on 17-9-1875 that the small number of trials had not given trustworthy results, particularly for the longer ranges. Extensive trials would have been required for better results. He forwarded a survey showing the average elevation found practically required by various regiments, which, although showing great variations, proved that all agreed that the regulation sighting was too low. From the average it appeared that a sliding bar, giving .060 more than the regulation elevation, would give very nearly the average extra elevation required. He remarked, however, that the difference between rifles manufactured at Enfield, Birmingham, and London, were such that it would not be possible to obtain more than an approximation of the correct elevation with any rifle with any sliding bar of the present pattern.

It was difficult to adjust the sliding bar accurately when the rifle was undersighted, as the line on the flap was then hidden by the bar. He forwarded two sliding bars (D and E), altered from the regulation pattern, which allowed adjustment without difficulty for the regulation sighting, or for any height from one to eight hundredths of an inch above it.

The Supt. RSAF commented on this report on 6-12-1875 that it was evident that for use by the troops some increase in the height of the slide was necessary, although theoretically the sighting was known to be correct. He considered the design D would be highly suitable for experienced marksmen, but in the hands of the ordinary soldier would be likely to mislead him; and he did not believe it necessary in practice.

He submitted that a further and more extended trial should be made with two dimensions of the slide E, one giving an increase of .060 and the other .080 inch above the present heights for ranges of 500 yards and upwards. He thought it would be desirable that each regiment going through next year's course in Great Britain should be furnished with a proportion, say 20 of each, and should especially report on them at the end of the practice season.

The DoA considered it unnecessary to take any further steps in the matter until the trials of the new components were reported on. The A-G concurred 17-12-1875.

CONSIDERATION OF TRIALS REPORTS

A conference was called at the WO for 28-1-1876, to peruse reports of the various trials resulting from the recommendations of the previous conference of 5-10-1875. Present were –

Maj.-Gen. J.W. Armstrong, CB, DAG
Brig.-Gen. F.A. Campbell, CB, RA, DoA
Col. W.P. Radcliffe, CB, IGM
Capt. T. Brandreth, RN, HMS Excellent
Col. W. Bancroft, 16th Regt.
Col. Henry Kent, 77th Regt.
Col. G. Fraser, RA, Supt. RL
Col. H.C. Fletcher, CMG, Scots Fusilier Gds.
Lt.-Col. F. Close, RA, Supt. RSAF
Lt.-Col. C.M'c. Cotton, 20th Hussars
Brevet Lt.-Col. T.D. Baker, CB, AAG
Mr. L.W. Engelbach of the WO attended.

This committee, after careful consideration of the reports and papers presented to them, agreed to report as below –

1. New components. The committee considered them satisfactory, both for land and sea service, and recommended that the arms be altered accordingly. They also recommended that the upper surface of the block be dulled, as proposed by Col. Fletcher.

2. Strikers. The committee proposed to wait on the result of the current year's practice with the present form of striker, before recommending the adoption of a new one. They also recommended that a severe test of the striker proposed by the Supt. RSAF be made, in such numbers and in such manner as could be arranged with the A-G and the Admiralty.

3. Locking bolt or half-cock. The committee agreed to reserve their opinion on this question for the present.

4. Sighting. They recommended a further trial of slides for backsights, as proposed by the Supt. RSAF, and that the notches of the backsights and sliding bars be deepened in future manufacture, as recommended by the superintendent.

5. Leather shields. They were of opinion that these were not required, either for the protection of the hand from heated barrels, or for preventing the admission of dirt into the action.

6. Pull off. Extraction of empty cartridge cases, &c. The committee attentively considered the reports of the Supt. RSAF in regard to the complaints of variable pull off. They observed that the dangerously light pull off complained of had been entirely remedied, and they saw no need for any further orders on the subject.

As regards extraction of empty cases, this did not seem to be sufficiently provided for in the drill, and the committee wished to draw attention to this point.

The complaints respecting flaps of backsights, rods, rod-holders, &c, were considered of minor character to be dealt with as they arose. No general instructions on the subject were considered necessary.

7. Lengthened bayonet. They did not feel justified in recommending the adoption of this bayonet, and suggested that further trials should be made with it during the ensuing drill season.

8. Breech-loading carbine. The committee recommended further trials; 500 M-H's to be prepared with the new components, and with such improvements as may be possible in sights and other details.

The proceedings of this conference were referred to the A-G on 2-2-1876, for the consideration of the C-I-C. The A-G replied on 14-2-1876, that under the circumstances of this report, and the opinions submitted by various CO's, the C-I-C proposed to accept the M-H rifle, with the alterations of the components, etc, as the arm for the service, although he could not forbear expressing his regret that no means for a half-cock could be applied to the lock, and would wish this opinion to be borne in mind, in the event of its being possible, at any future time, to devise a remedy.

The SoS approved on 16-2-1876, and the Supt. RSAF was directed on 19-2-1876 to note the decision and prepare new patterns.

Orders were also given in regard to the sight slides and carbines, and steps were taken in connection with recommendations in sections 2 and 6.

FINAL SIGHTING TRIALS

In accordance with the decisions made on the recommendations of the WO conference of 28-1-1876, the Army Circular shown below was sent to selected regiments to authorise the trial of the new rear sight slides.

Martini-Henry Rifles, Slides for Backsights.

1. Complaints having been made as to the alleged under-sighting of the Martini-Henry rifle for ranges of 500 yards and upwards, and it having been ascertained, by careful experiments from the fixed rest at the RSAF Enfield, that the sighting is theoretically accurate; it has been decided that a course of experiments shall be carried out, under the direction of officers commanding regiments, for the purpose of ascertaining what increase in the height of the slide of the backsight, for ranges mentioned above, will give most satisfactory results when firing from the shoulder.

2. For this purpose two patterns of slide have been prepared, marked respectively E and F, a proportion of each which will be issued to the several regiments, &c, in which the experiments are to be carried out.

3. These slides have portions both of the notched side and of the flat side of the bar, cut away at the ends, so that by using the bottom edge of the slot thus produced, instead of the original line of the bar, when adjusting it for a specified range, a slight increase in elevation is given.

4. In the pattern marked E, the increase in the height of the slide, when adjusted as above, is .060 inch, and in the pattern marked F, it is .080 inch.

5. Practice will be carried on at a range of 500 yards, and such other ranges above that figure as may be available.

6. The men selected for the practice must be good shots, and it is essential that they aim dead on the point intended to be hit, making no allowance either for wind or under-sighting, care being taken that the point chosen be such that all the hits may appear on the target.

7. Ten rounds will be fired from each rifle at every range, half with slides marked E, and the remaining half with slides marked F. The practice with both patterns of slide to be carried out, as far as possible, at the same time, and under exactly similar conditions.

8. The diagrams of practice to be carefully prepared, under the direction of the officer appointed to carry out the entire series.

War Office. June, 1876.

As a result of these trials a slide with a height adjustment of .060 inch was adopted. It was sealed as a pattern with the Mark II rifle on 25-4-1877, and incorporated the deepening of the V notch as previously approved. The deepened notch was also applied to the sight cap, and then became the standard form for all subsequent M-H rifles, until the introduction of the Lewes sights on the Marks V and VI rifles.

KNEELING POSITION.—PRESENT (First Motion).

CHAPTER 10.

THE EVOLUTION OF THE MARK II RIFLE

THE M-H RII was the first service pattern considered free from major defects, because the several and various alterations made to the Mark I rifle during its first years of service caused that arm to progress through first, second, and third patterns, which culminated in the Mark II as incorporating all the improvements in the one arm.

The changes were gradual in some instances, allowing features of one pattern to be included in the next because of manufacturing processes, and the list below indicates some of those changes, but not necessarily in the chronological order in which they actually appeared –

1. Safety bolt and spring – abolished.
2. Gunmetal solid block axis pin and keeper screw – abolished.
3. Steel split block axis pin – substituted.
4. Striker – strengthened.
5. Butts – lengthened.
6. Cleaning rod – altered.
7. Chequering on butt plate – abolished.
8. Butt swivel – abolished.
9. Rear sight – altered.
10. Trigger mechanism – altered.

All the above, together with others not mentioned, are described in detail in Chapter 30, but the following sections show how each arm concerned was affected by the abolition or alteration of the various components. (For previous descriptions of rifles Marks I and II see Chapter 8.)

SERVICE RIFLE MARK I, FIRST PATTERN

This was the first model approved for full scale production, the pattern being approved on 3-6-1871, as shown in the following entry from the Pattern Book of the RSAF –

Rifle, Martini-Henry.
Approved: 3-6-1871.
Description: Prepared in accordance with instructions received from SAC 18-1-71, E.No.12079 8/6; 18-1-71, E. No.12089 8/6; 4-2-71, E.No.12167 8/6; 12487 8/6; and 21-3-71, E.No.12511 8/6 (Long butt).

It is doubtful whether any were actually produced, apart from pattern arms, and it is even difficult to ascertain how many of the latter were made. There was obviously one in the Enfield Pattern Room, and it is stated that at the 1871 Wimbledon meeting there was, among others, "1 Martini-Henry rifle of the exact pattern then approved, fitted with an Elcho bayonet." It is difficult to conceive that this would be the Pattern Room sample, so it could have been an extra weapon, giving at least two made. It was not stated if this rifle was fired at Wimbledon; it may have been for display only, to show what the new service rifle looked like.

The dimensions of the first pattern rifle, without bayonet were –

Overall length:
Long butt – 4' 1" (1,244 mm)
Short butt – 4' 0" (1,219 mm)
Overall weight – 8 lb 7½ ozs (3.8 kg)
Barrel weight – 3 lb 6¼ oz (1.5 kg)

Before many were actually produced, the trigger mechanism was changed, so this first pattern was superseded by the

SERVICE RIFLE MARK I, SECOND PATTERN

This was listed in the Enfield Pattern Book as –

Rifle, Martini-Henry, Mark I.
Approved: 3-9-1872. E.No.16234 8/6.
Description: Sealed in substitution of pattern approved 3-6-1871, in consequence of a modification in the trigger arrangement approved 21-10-71 (14238 8/6).
(This rifle had a short butt.)

There was a total of 69 parts in this pattern, listed below for reference.

1. Barrel
2. Action body (or shoe)
3. Breech block
4. Striker
5. Striker spring
6. Striker spring stop nut
7. Stop nut lock screw
8. Breech block axis pin
9. Axis pin stop screw
10. Extractor
11. Extractor axis pin
12. Trigger guard and plate
13. Trigger
14. Trigger axis screw
15. Tumbler rest
16. Tumbler rest axis screw
17. Locking bolt spring
18. Trigger spring
19. Trigger spring screw
20. Tumbler
21. Locking bolt
22. Locking bolt thumb piece
23. Thumb piece screw
24. Locking bolt indicator
25. Indicator screw
26. Lever
27. Lever and tumbler axis pin
28. Axis pin stop screw
29. Foresight
30. Back sight base
31. Back sight base screw
32. Back sight spring
33. Spring and base screw
34. Back sight leaf

35. Back sight leaf cap
36. Leaf cap screw
37. Back sight slide
38. Back sight leaf pin
39. Barrel stud
40. Fore-end retaining pin
41. Stock, fore-end
42. Fore-end nose cap
43. Nose cap screw
44. Cleaning rod stop
45. 46. Cleaning rod stop screws
47. Upper band
48. Upper band pin
49. Upper band swivel
50. Upper band swivel screw
51. Swivel screw lock nut
52. Lower band
53. Lower band screw
54. Lower band pin
55. Trigger guard swivel
56. Trigger guard swivel screw
57. Butt swivel
58. Butt swivel pin
59. Butt swivel screw
60. Stock, butt
61. Stock, butt, bolt
62. Stock, butt, bolt, washer
63. Butt plate
64.65. Butt plate screws
66. Lever catch block
67. Lever catch spring
68. Lever catch block pin
69. Cleaning rod.

Figs.1 and 2 show two views of the action mechanism of the second pattern rifle, and points of interest in the drawings are –

1. The original striker with thin nose
2. The tumbler rest in trigger mechanism
3. View (A) showing the safety bolt engaged with the trigger.

The dimensions of this pattern, without bayonet, were the same as those for the first pattern.

SERVICE RIFLE MARK I, THIRD PATTERN

Listed in the Enfield Pattern Book as –

Rifle, Martini-Henry, Mark I.
Approved: 17-7-74.
List of Changes: No.2659.
Description: Sealed to govern the alterations in above, viz, trigger set back, block axis pin altered, and locking arrangement dispensed with.
Remarks: To govern alterations of existing rifles.

It was officially introduced for service in LoC Para.2659 of 1-10-1874 as –

Rifle, Breech-loading, Martini-Henry, Mark I.
Jag, Mark I, for ditto.
Protector, foresight and muzzle, Mark I, for ditto.
Rod, cleaning, Mark I, for ditto.
Bayonet, Mark I, for ditto.

Patterns of the rifle and articles for use therewith, above-mentioned, have been sealed to govern supplies.

The Martini-Henry is a breech-loading arm on the falling block system.

The action consists of –

Body	*Trigger spring*
Block	*Tumbler*
Main spring	*Tumbler rest*
Striker	*Trigger guard*
Stop-nut	*Extractor*
Lever	*and*
Trigger	*Indicator.*

With the corresponding screws and pins.

The barrel is made of steel.

The stock is in two parts – "Butt" and "Fore-end". The butts are of two lengths, viz, – 14" and 14½".

The rifle is sighted to 1,400 yards.

Weight of barrel – 3 lb 6 oz (1.5 kg)
Weight of rifle (without bayonet) – about. 8 lb 12 oz (3.9 kg)
Length of barrel – 2' 9.22" (842 mm)
Length of rifle (without bayonet):
Short butt – 4' 1" (1,244 mm)
Long butt – 4' 1½" (1,257 mm)

The bayonet is simply the Pattern '53 bayonet altered in the socket so as to fit the barrel of the Martini-Henry rifle.

Martini-Henry Rifle, Mark I, Third Pattern – Parts List.

On comparison with the parts list of Mark I, Second pattern it will be seen that the total number of parts has falled by 7 to 62. This was caused by the abolition of the safety catch unit, and the block axis pin changed from a solid to a split pin. The seven parts deleted were (with reference number of the original in the second pattern parts list in brackets)

1. Axis pin stop screw (9)
2. Locking bolt spring (17)
3. Locking bolt (21)
4. Locking bolt thumb piece (22)
5. Locking bolt thumb piece screw (23)
6. Locking bolt indicator (24)
7. Indicator screw (25).

Parts of the third pattern rifle (Items marked with * are illustrated in Fig.3) –

1. Barrel*
2. Action body*
3. Breech block*

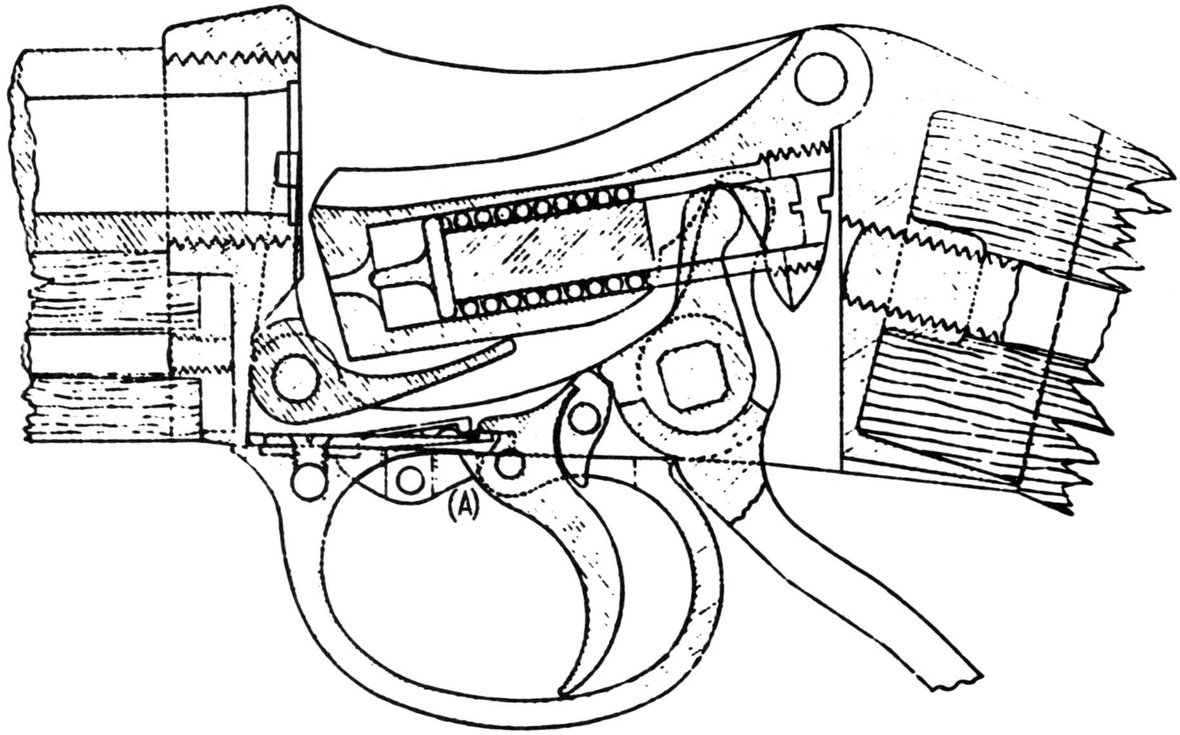

Fig. 1 – Rifle, Mark I, Second Pattern, Action Mechanism – Open and cocked.

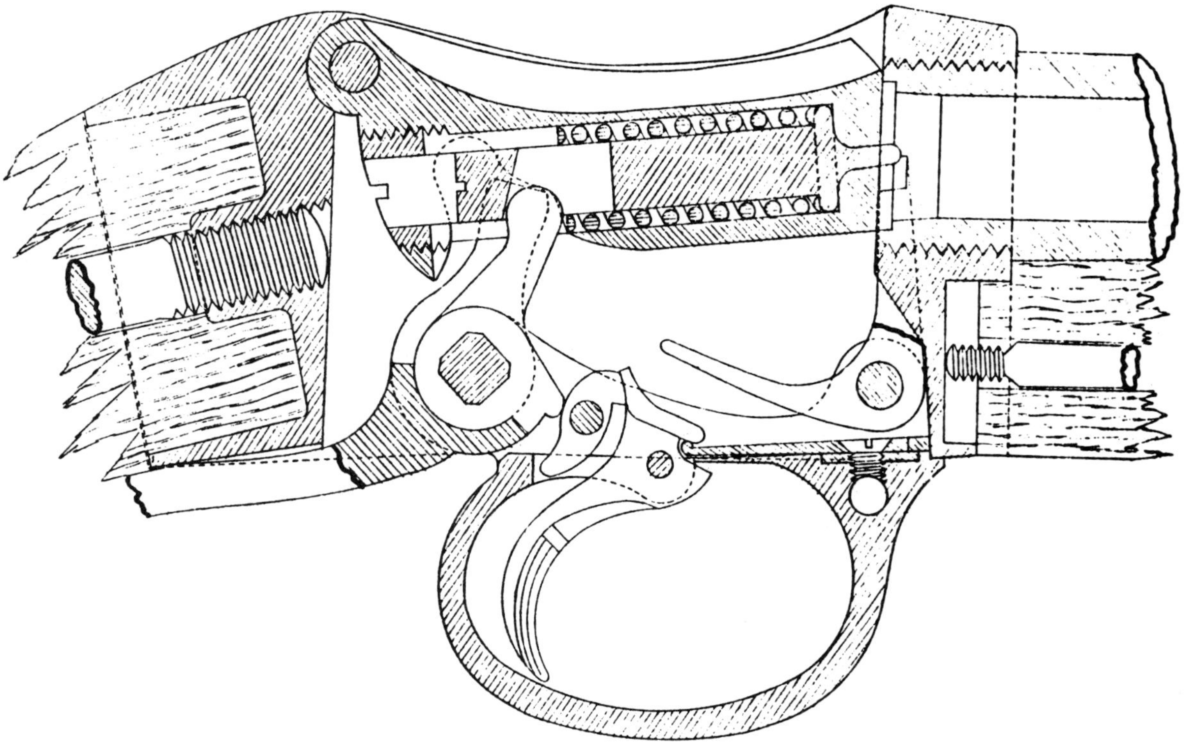

Fig. 2 – Rifle, Mark I, Second Pattern, Action Mechanism – Closed and fired.

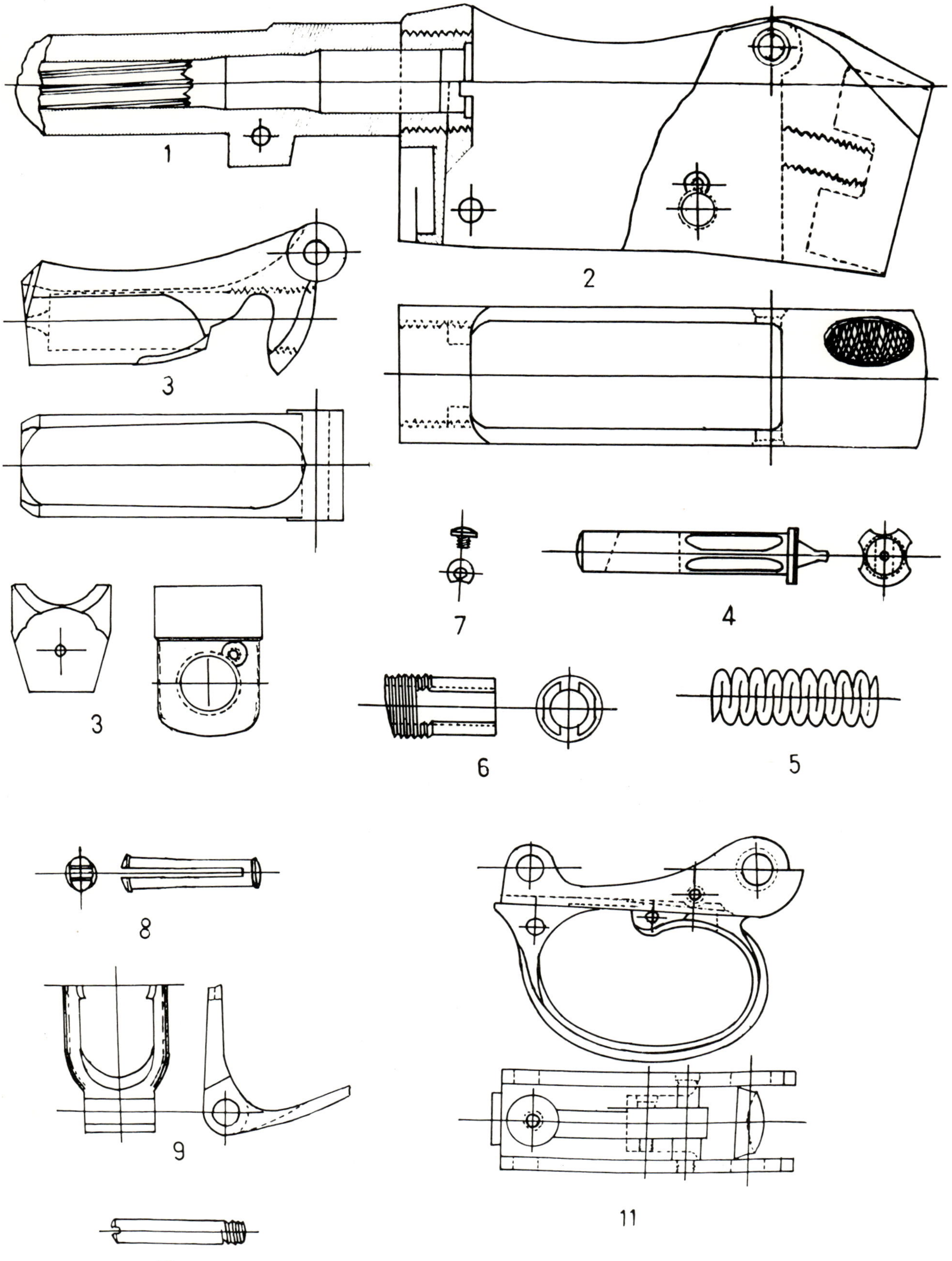
1
2
3
3
7
4
6
5
8
9
11
10

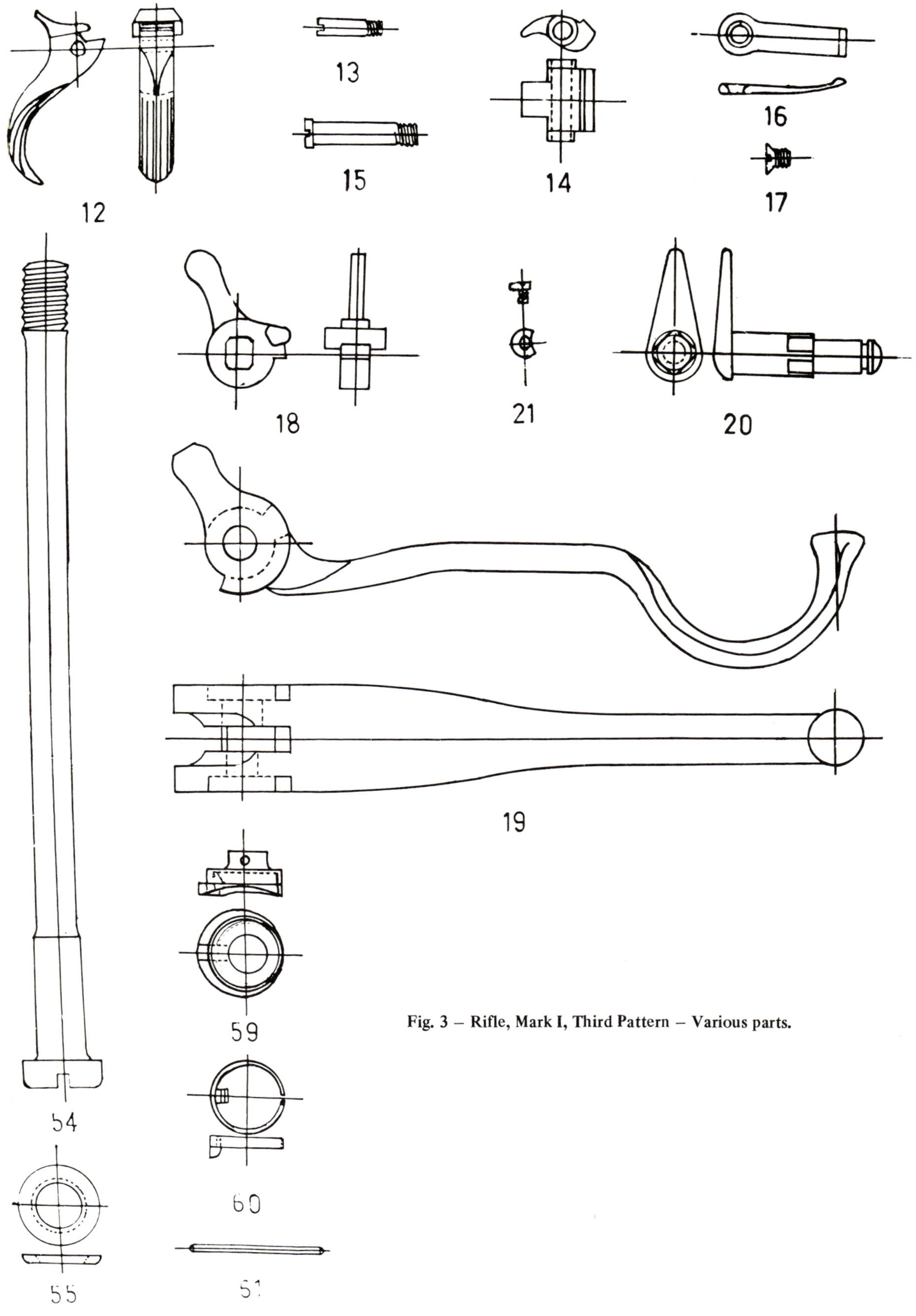

Fig. 3 – Rifle, Mark I, Third Pattern – Various parts.

4. Striker*
5. Striker spring*
6. Striker spring stop nut*
7. Stop nut lock screw*
8. Breech block axis pin*
9. Extractor*
10. Extractor axis pin*
11. Trigger guard and plate*
12. Trigger*
13. Trigger axis screw*
14. Tumbler rest*
15. Tumbler rest axis screw*
16. Trigger spring*
17. Trigger spring screw*
18. Tumbler*
19. Lever*
20. Lever axis pin and indicator*
21. Lever axis pin stop screw*
22. Foresight
23. Backsight base
24. Backsight base screw
25. Backsight spring
26. Spring and base screw
27. Backsight leaf
28. Leaf cap
29. Leaf cap screw
30. Leaf slide
31. Leaf pin
32. Barrel stud
33. Fore-end retaining pin
34. Fore-end, stock
35. Fore-end, nose cap
36. Nose cap screw
37. Cleaning rod stop
38.39. Rod stop screws
40. Upper band
41. Upper band pin
42. Upper band swivel
43. Swivel screw
44. Screw lock nut
45. Lower band
46. Lower band screw
47. Lower band pin
48. Trigger guard swivel
49. Swivel screw
50. Butt swivel
51. Swivel pin
52. Swivel screw
53. Butt, stock
54. Butt, stock, bolt*
55. Stock bolt washer*
56. Butt plate
57.58. Butt plate screws
59. Lever catch block*
60. Catch spring*
61. Catch block pin*
62. Cleaning rod.

Fig.3 illustrates some of the parts of the Mark I, Third pattern rifle, and in view of the changes made to a couple of them, it is interesting to note that the striker shown (It.4) is of the later strengthened pattern, whereas the butt stock screw (It.54) is of the early pattern which was replaced in March 1874 by a cheaper unit. The new bolt was turned to shape at the end parts only as necessary, instead of all over, as the pattern illustrated was; this resulted in a saving of ½d per unit, and was proposed by the Supt. RSAF. The DoA approved its manufacture on 26-3-1874.

SERVICE RIFLE MARK II

The Pattern Book entry for this arm was –

Rifle, Martini-Henry, Mark II.
Approved: 25-4-77.
List of Changes: No.3193.
Description: Altered in action, also browning upper surface of breech block and deepening of V notch in sight slide and leaf.
Remarks: To govern future supply and the alteration of rifles of Mark I pattern.

It was introduced for service in LoC Para. 3193 of 1-11-1877 as –

Arms, Interchangeable, Rifle, Breech-loading, Martini-Henry, with cleaning rod, (Mark II).

A rifle of this description has been sealed to govern future manufacture, and the alteration of rifles of Mark I (2659).

This arm differs from the previous pattern principally in having the components of the action modified, as below described, with the object of obtaining a more regular pull off of the trigger, and of removing a liability to accidental discharge, caused by dirt becoming deposited between the trigger and the trigger guard of the action.

The alterations in the action are as follows –

The tumbler is of a new pattern, acting directly on the trigger, the tumbler rest and screw have been abolished.

The trigger is of a new pattern.

The trigger guard has a shield covering the trigger knuckle.

The block has a slot cut through the underside to allow for the play of the tumbler.

The extractor has the sides of its lower arm parallel throughout.

The following alterations have also been introduced in Mark II rifles, viz, –

The groove on the upper side of the block is browned instead of being bright.

The V notch in sight slide has been enlarged and deepened, the slide being correspondingly deepened so as not to affect the sighting.

The notches in the cap of the sight leaf are of a similar form to those on the slide.

The rifle is not fitted with a butt swivel, the use of such swivels having been abolished in March 1875, except for Rifle Regiments, in which the use of the swivel is retained.

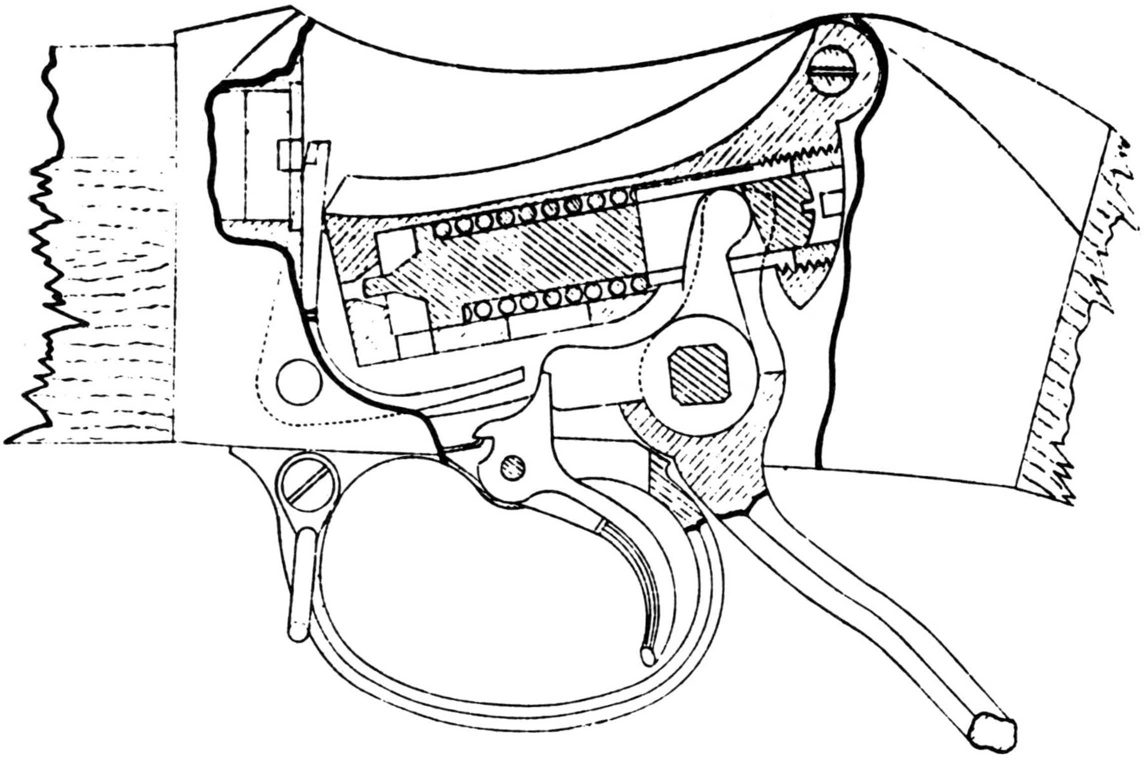

Fig. 4 – Rifle, Mark II, Action Mechanism – Open and cocked.

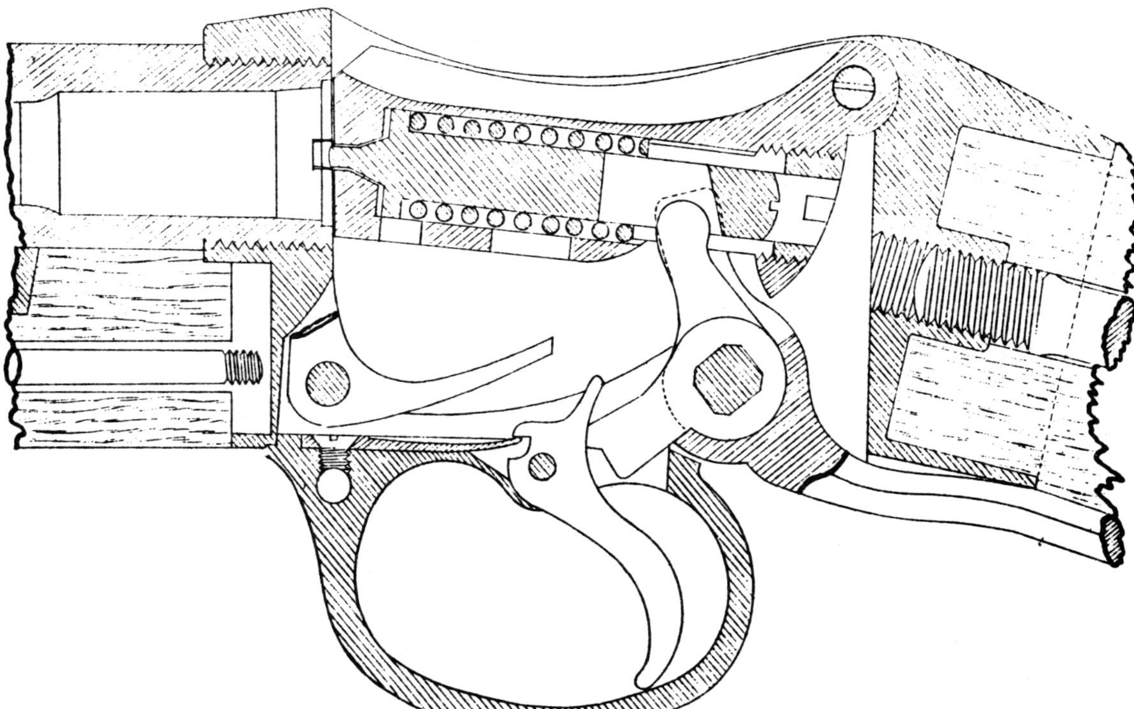

Fig. 5 – Rifle, Mark II, Action Mechanism – Closed and fired.

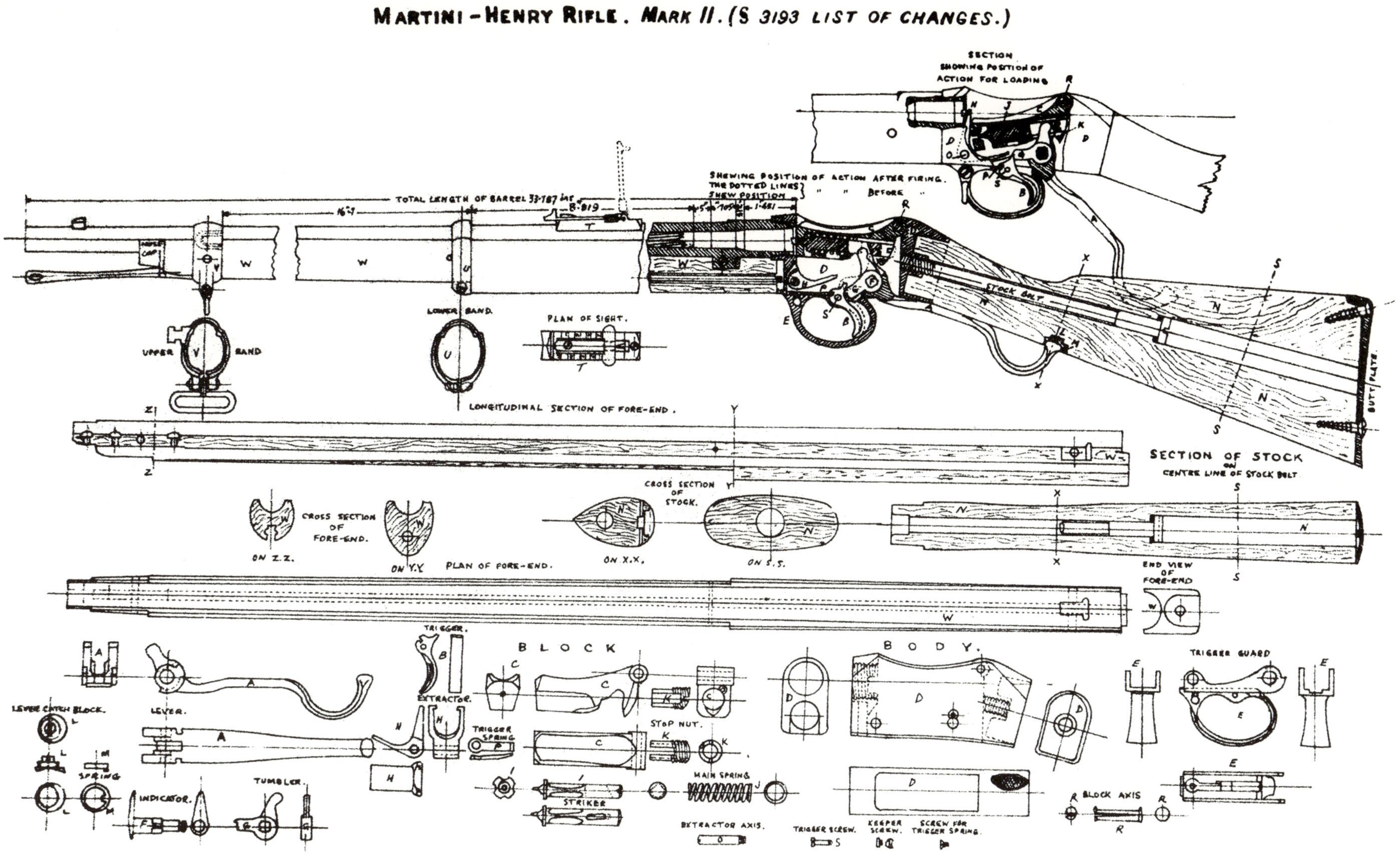

Fig. 6 – Parts of Rifle, Mark II.

There was also a new cleaning rod adopted in late 1876, and this rod, the Mark II, would have been sealed as part of the Mark II rifle, so on external comparison with the Mark I third pattern, the Mark II would show –

No butt swivel
Smooth butt plate
Different trigger unit
Different cleaning rod
Trigger guard with rounded edges at rear
Back sight with deeper notches.

Figs. 4 and 5 show the action mechanism of the Mark II rifle, in which will be noted the strengthened striker.

During the initial few months of its manufacture, the Mark II rifle was not made in any great quantity by the RSAF, as is shown by the production figures for the 1878 year – "11,053 Arms, assembled, with cleaning rods." Although this figure could have included Mark I Third pattern rifles it is unlikely that it did so, as the changes in the parts as a prelude to the Mark II pattern had been approved before the start of the new production year, so it would have been possible to plan the manufacture of the new pattern rifle to commence with the coming production period, ie, 1st April 1877 to 31st March 1878.

There were possibly several reasons for this drop in output including –

1. The concentration on production of the then new M-H CC, as it was considered imperative to manufacture a large quantity as quickly as possible to arm the troops (25,000 were made in this period); and

2. The absorption of plant and personnel in the alteration of Mark I rifles to Mark II pattern. Although not perhaps a major job, this alteration did involve a greater amount of work than did the earlier modifications, and noted in this period is – "125,771 Rifles, Martini-Henry, altered."

For the 1879 year there were 45,600 Mark II's produced, and for 1880, 33 only. This latter low figure was caused by the adoption of the Mark III rifle in August 1879, resulting in the cut back of Mark II production at the RSAF.

The Mark II pattern was, however, carried on in production by the trade, as this course obviated any great alteration in their machinery such as a changeover to the Mark III would have occasioned. Thus 6,000 Mark II's were supplied in the 1880 year, and contracts for Mark II rifles were given to the BSA Co in 1886 and 1887 for 10,500 and 53,100 respectiv-ely. These were to be produced at the rate of 400 per week, and the last delivery under these contracts was made in June, 1890.

Fig.6 shows various parts of the Mark II rifle.

Dimensions of the Mark II rifle –

Overall length:
Long butt – 4' 1½" (1,257 mm)
Short butt – 4' 1" (1,244 mm)
Barrel length – 2' 9.187" (842 mm)
Overall weight:
Long butt – 8 lb 10½ oz (3.8 kg)
Short butt – 8 lb 8 oz (3.8 kg)
Barrel weight – 3 lb 6 oz (1.5 kg).

CHAPTER 11.

THE DEVELOPMENT OF THE MARTINI–HENRY CARBINE – THE TRIALS PATTERNS

THE development of the M-H carbine paralleled that of the rifle by having a series of trials weapons before the service pattern was eventually adopted, but, during their trials, the various carbine models had the improvements of the rifle action incorporated into them, so that mechanically the carbine was spared many of the teething troubles that had plagued the rifle.

As with some of the Martini trials pattern rifles, information on the Martini trials carbines is also sparse, and few specimens seem to have survived. For this reason the same procedure will be followed as used in Chapter 7, ie, numbering each type, and describing it from clues in official text where possible.

THE FIRST TRIALS PATTERN

By early 1871 the first service pattern of M-H rifle was established, so the Special Committee on Small Arms requested on 8-2-1871, authority to shorten one of the existing short action trials rifles held at Enfield to the length appropriate for cavalry, to allow experiments to be carried out. The DoA approved this request on 13-2-1871.

On 9-6-1871 the Supt. RSAF submitted one specimen each of artillery and cavalry carbines of the M-H rifle type, with a sword bayonet for the former. The artillery carbine had the same muzzle diameter as the rifle, so could mount the rifle sword bayonet, which is apparently what was supplied with it.

Both carbines had the first pattern of short breech action, but the butt stocks were of the latest pattern, so the wood was slightly higher than the rear end of the action. New sights were fitted, similar to those of the rifle, but smaller in dimensions. Apart from the obvious special fittings for the relevant service use, these two specimens had much in common, and will be generally described before their individual features are presented.

They were stated to be of "M-H rifle type", with sights of "rifle type", only smaller. This seems to indicate that both were full stocked, and generally would have resembled a shortened rifle. A comparison of their quoted weights, which shows a difference of only ¾ oz bears out this assumption.

Because of the type of action used, these carbines would have had the safety catch on the action, and most probably a chequered butt plate.

To ascertain which of the "existing short action trials rifles" were used, we should refer to Chapter 7 where these are described. There were four possible sources for the actions – Rifles Nos.8, 10, 11, and 12. No.8 seems unlikely, as this type was "not successful"; there were two No.10 rifles, which were retained at Enfield for experiments, and so could be the two actions used. The No.11 rifles were made in reasonable numbers, and are also a possibility. The two No.12 rifles were modified from No.11 arms, so can be classed as that type, thus leaving Nos.10 and 11 as the likely sources. In any case, with the apparent willingness displayed by the RSAF staff to use existing experimental arms as the basis for other weapons, it is not difficult to see why some of the trials pattern arms are no longer in existence.

The Cavalry Carbine. This was made to the same length as the Snider CC, ie, 3' 0¾", and would not have had provision for either bayonet or sling. An entry in the Enfield Range Book, dated 9-6-1871, gave its weight, with leather sight cover, as 7 lb 8 oz. It was fired on the range for trial and sight graduation, as the Range Book entry below shows –

Measurements of the sighting of the first M-H Cavalry Carbine.

No.1 pattern ammunition.

Yards.		
100	.24	Measured in front of the sight.
200	.30	
300	.36	
400	.41	Measured at the back of the sight, and on the flat of the barrel.
500	.49	
600	.585	
700	.69	
800	.81	
900	.93	
1,000	1.06	
Front sight	.27	

I.B. Baker.
Proofmaster.
RSAF Enfield,
1-6-1871.

There was no mention of this carbine in the Enfield production figures, but, as it used parts of an existing rifle, and the butt from the current service pattern, it is quite likely that other standard parts were used, so its cost would be mostly accounted for by money already spent. Any further development costs could have been paid for from a contingency fund.

The Artillery Carbine. In keeping with the trend set by the CC, the artillery pattern was made to the length of the corresponding Snider carbine, ie, 3' 4". It was fitted to take the standard rifle sword bayonet, so probably used a standard rifle top band. It would also have been fitted with sling swivels. The Enfield Range Book entry of 9-6-1871 also gave the weight of this carbine as –

Weight of the M-H Artillery carbine	7 lb	8½	oz.
Weight of sword and scabbard	2	1½	
Total.	9	10¼	
Weight of sword	1	8	

The sighting measurements were also given –

Measurements of the sighting of the first M-H Artillery Carbine.

Yards.		
100	.29	Measured in front of the sight.
200	.36	
300	.44	
400	.525	Measured at back part of the sight and on round part of the barrel.
500	.615	
600	.715	
700	.820	
800	.935	
900	1.055	
1,000	1.185	
Front sight	.25	

I.B. Baker.
Proofmaster.
RSAF Enfield,
25-5-1871.

This carbine also did not appear in the production records, and similar conditions as for the CC could apply to it.

The Supt. RSAF recommended that should it be decided to adopt a length of carbine suitable for both services, the artillery length should be selected. If one length only was adopted, that arm could be used by either service simply by the use of a top band with or without the bayonet bar on it as required, and this would simplify production.

Neither of the arms submitted could be sealed, as the action was not of the latest pattern.

The committee reported on 22-2-1872 with the results of the trials of these carbines, which were very satisfactory. They nearly approached in accuracy the shooting of the standard rifle, and recoil was not excessive. As the accuracy of both carbines was practically equal, it was considered that both patterns could be the same length, and unless it was thought necessary that artillerymen should be able to fix a bayonet, the committee saw no reason why one pattern should not be adopted for both services.

However, the accuracy was so good, the committee thought it worth considering whether the carbine could also be used by the engineers, as it was convenient to carry, and adapted for men working in close confinement. If it was used for this purpose it would be necessary to fit a sling, so the stock would have to be full wood, and the arm adapted for a bayonet. In this case it would be a question whether to arm the artillery with this or the CC.

For cleaning purposes a jag string and flannel was recommended, and these should be carried in a pouch or in a trap in the butt.

The committee finally stated that if their recommendations as to the CC were approved, a pattern arm should be prepared, and that if two descriptions of carbine were decided upon, patterns of each should be prepared, and special trials carried out by the relevant services.

THE SECOND TRIALS PATTERN

As a result of the above report, the C-I-C on 26-3-1872 approved of the RA and RE being armed with the same carbine, and patterns of

1. A carbine for cavalry; and
2. A carbine for artillery and engineers, with sword;

were ordered to be prepared.

They were submitted by the committee on 25-11-1872 for inspection, and the A-G on 18-1-1873 notified the approval of the C-I-C, but remarked that the CC would not fit into the existing carbine bucket, because of its cleaning rod. Reference to Table XVII (Items A and B) will show that these arms were listed in the production figures for the 1873 year as –

"2 Arms, assembled, artillery carbine pattern"; and
"2 Arms, assembled, cavalry carbine pattern".

Their costs indicated that they were new weapons, and presumably made from parts of the current service rifle. They would thus have had the safety catch and chequered butt plate.

The committee had recommended that both patterns of carbine be of the same length, and the Supt. RSAF further recommended that of the artillery carbine. Although not specifically mentioned, it could thus be assumed that the No.2 carbines were all of the same length; and, in appearance, similar to No.1. This is confirmed by the statement that the CC would not fit into the existing bucket because of "its cleaning rod".

After some brief trials of these carbines objections were made to the poise of the arm – it being badly balanced, and uncomfortable to grip – so the DoA suggested that the papers should be returned to the A-G, and that, should the C-I-C desire it, a few arms might be made for trial by a cavalry regiment. He also observed that as it was advantageous to have as few patterns as possible, when the cavalry weapon was decided upon, it might be considered whether the artillery and engineers could not also adopt it.

On 8-2-1873 the A-G stated that the C-I-C had examined the proposed M-H carbine, and considered the Snider better adapted for cavalry use. He proposed that a few modified M-H carbines should be made for trial; but, if the Henry barrel could be altered to fit the Snider action, a few arms on that principle could also be made for trial.

The Supt. RSAF reported on 13-2-1873 that the alterations to the M-H carbine could be made, but the Snider action was not suitable for the M-H cartridge. The C-I-C suggested that a carbine be made for trial with the alterations proposed by the superintendent, and the S-G approved 1-3-1873, and orders were given accordingly, resulting in –

THE THIRD TRIALS PATTERN

This weapon was submitted for inspection on 15-5-1873, and was listed in production figures for the 1874 year as – "1 Arm, assembled, cavalry carbine pattern". See Table XVII, Item C. It used the standard rifle action, with safety catch, but incorporated several of the features proposed by the superintendent, such as –

1. The grip made smaller by altering the shape of the metal body.
2. Balance improved by tapering the barrel to the muzzle.
3. Cleaning rod placed in butt.
4. Stock at muzzle made the same as Snider.
5. Trigger guard and butt plate made from brass instead of iron.

It thus seems to have resembled the Snider CC in general appearance. Its high cost reflects the extra work necessary to make the above changes.

After preliminary trials at Woolwich it was sent to Hythe for trial against the Snider CC at 300 and 500 yards. The old pattern carbine was also used in these trials, and the new arm was found better at 300 yards, but worse at 500. With the new pattern the recoil was felt to be excessive, and the barrel heated so rapidly the grip was interfered with. The C-I-C decided on 10-10-1873 that the carbine as then made could not be adopted because of its excessive recoil, and that a method of reducing this should be sought.

REDUCED CHARGE AMMUNITION FOR CARBINES

The Supt. RSAF observed on 27-10-1873 that to modify the recoil of the M-H carbine there seemed no alternative but to lessen the charge of the cartridge, either by reducing the weight of powder and retaining the same bullet, or by reducing both the powder and bullet weights. He was directed on 30-10-1873 to confer with the Supt. RL, and carry out preliminary experiments, retaining the existing form of chamber.

The two superintendents reported on 15-12-1873 that careful experiments had been made, and it was found that by using a bullet of 380 grains and a powder charge of 70 grains the recoil was reduced by the proportion of about 120:94. The shooting at 500 yards was very good, but declined proportionately at longer ranges. They stated that a cartridge suitable for this reduced load would require considerable alteration in the form of the chamber, or the service cartridge and chamber could be retained, with the excess space in the cartridge case filled with cotton wool, or some similar substance.

Neither cartridge of the types described would be suitable for use with the standard rifle, so the necessity for retaining the service chamber would disappear, and they remarked that there seemed to be no special reason why the carbine, if adopted, should not have a special chamber and ammunition for it alone.

They concluded by suggesting that as the Snider carbine in use was satisfactory for the requirements of the cavalry and artillery, it be continued in use, and the question of a M-H carbine be allowed to rest until the necessity for new arms became more apparent.

The DoA did not agree with those suggestions, and decided to continue experiments with the M-H carbine, using the existing chamber and cartridge case, but with a reduced charge. The advantage claimed for this arrangement was that in emergencies the carbine could use rifle ammunition and vice versa. On 29-12-1873 the A-G notified the C-I-C's concurrence with this proposal.

A carbine sighted for a 70/380 gr. cartridge was received from Enfield on 23-3-1874, with 100 rounds of ammunition, for trial. It was not stated whether this was the No.3 specimen resighted, but as no mention was made of another new arm being assembled, it most likely was that arm altered as necessary.

The trials results were good, and the weapon was submitted by the DoA for the C-I-C's inspection on 8-5-1874, with the remarks that should it be desirable to order a trial in a cavalry regiment and at Hythe, a few could be made for that purpose. The C-I-C approved on 11-5-1874, and on 17-5-1874 orders were given for six carbines to be made.

Although it was May before the C-I-C inspected this carbine and approved of further trial, that possibility had already been anticipated, as the Supt. RSAF had earlier stated that if the carbine was approved for the reduced charge cartridge he would prepare one, without the safety bolt, for sealing. The DoA on 11-4-1874 had requested that the safety bolt be removed, and asked when carbines could be ready for trial at Aldershot and Hythe. The superintendent replied that six arms could be completed within one month of the return of the pattern arm.

THE FOURTH TRIALS PATTERN

For the next pattern carbine the superintendent proposed three of the last type, and three with rifle bodies and the trigger set back as recently recommended for the rifle action; however, it was pointed out to him that it was very desirable there should be only one form of body, and the ordinary iron mountings could be used instead of brass.

The six carbines were reported ready on 21-7-1874, and were made with two patterns of body; one special, as in the last carbines tried, and the others the same as the standard rifle action. The stocks were in the proportion of two long and one short.

Most official references indicate that only six of this pattern were made, but the Enfield production figures for the 1875 year show –

"6 Arms, assembled, cavalry carbine, with cleaning rod"; and

"1 Arm, assembled, cavalry carbine, without cleaning rod";

thus giving a total of seven arms. See Table XVII, Items D and E.

Both lots of carbines were made to the same order number, No.262, so can be assumed to have been made at the same time. The odd arm could be the one fitted with the special body, leaving the six with standard bodies. There would thus be an extra standard arm, and this could have been the pattern for the others, as it was mentioned that the superintendent, if required, could prepare such an arm, without the safety catch, for sealing as a pattern to govern the supply of arms for further trial.

The general appearance of the six Type 4 carbines would appear to have been similar to that of the Type 3, with the special Type 4 being practically identical, but for the absence of the safety catch.

They were issued to the 19th Hussars for trial, with 1,000 rounds of 70/380 gr ammunition, as ordered on 16-7-1874, and were subsequently to go to Hythe for further trial. The OC 19th Hussars presented his report on the trials on 26-8-1874, remarking that accuracy was satisfactory, and recoil very slight. The 14-inch stocks were preferred; there were no objections to the iron mountings; but the rough thumb piece was considered useless. The pull off was considered too heavy.

For the Hythe trials, a further 1,000 rounds of 70/380 gr ammunition was supplied, and because of considerations involving the manufacture of two types of ammunition, a batch of 500 rounds of the "light" rifle round then under trial, ie, 80/410 gr, was also sent for comparison.

On 26-10-1874 the IGM reported on the Hythe trials, and the results, as regards accuracy, were slightly in favour of the carbine cartridge. With recoil it was stated *the very slight recoil with the carbine ammunition was remarkable, whereas with the rifle ammunition it was excessive.*

A further trial was made with similar cartridges, and the IGM reported the results on 19-11-1874. The accuracy was slightly in favour of the heavier ammunition, but *the recoil was certainly greater with the rifle ammunition, but not of sufficient consequence to cause any inconvenience.*

THE FIFTH TRIALS PATTERN

At a WO conference on 18-12-1874, called to discuss various matters concerning the M-H rifle, it was decided that as it was desirable to have further trials with the carbine, 50 should be made, with bodies the same as the rifle, and with ordinary mountings.

The trials reports on these weapons complained that the foresight was too coarse, and that an arrangement to carry a one-piece cleaning rod was required. The Supt. RSAF replied that *if the foresight was made sharper it would cut the carbine bucket* (indicating that the foresight was a block and barleycorn similar to that on the rifle) and, *To carry a cleaning rod without joints, the carbine would have to be full stocked* (indicating that the No.5 pattern still carried the short rounded fore-end of Snider pattern).

This new pattern was apparently not much changed in appearance from the No.4 types with standard action, and was listed in Enfield production for the 1876 year (Table XVII, Item F) as –

"50 Arms, assembled, cavalry carbines".

For the proposed trials the ammunition to be used was the light rifle pattern, ie, 80/410 gr. The A-G approved 1-2-1875, and the arms were issued on 31-5-1875 to Aldershot, with 50 rounds per man to the following units –

17 to 14th Hussars
17 to 20th Hussars
16 to 21st Hussars.

Reports from these units were received as follows –

1. 14th Hussars (5-8-1875): The shooting of the M-H carbine is generally much more accurate than that of the Snider, particularly at the longer ranges. It is accurately sighted up to 300 yards, but is 40 yards oversighted at 400 yards. This error increases in a ratio of 10 yards for every 100 yards up to 1,000 yards, the 900 yards sight giving the correct elevation for 1,000 yards. The recoil is no greater than that of the Snider. Suggest a slight alteration to the bucket will be necessary to admit of the M-H carbine being carried in the bucket now in use. The sighting is too coarse to admit of an accurate aim being taken at the long ranges; and to this cause rather than to any defect in the arm itself, or in the ammunition, ought the falling off in the shooting at 900 and 1,000 yards be attributed.

2. 20th Hussars (30-7-1875): With regard to the accuracy of the M-H carbine, at the short ranges, ie, from 100 to 400 yards they are very accurate, but after that distance they are oversighted as much as 80 yards at 900, and 100 yards at 1,000. The sights are too coarsely made, the foresight being so thick that it is very difficult at the longer distances to get a sufficiently fine sight; the back sight is too close to the breech, so much so that when firing with the flap up, the eye is so close to the sight that it causes it to appear all blurred, which of course increases the difficulty of aiming. The barrel is considered very good. The stock shape at the breech is not liked; it is not comfortable or easy to hold, either at the shoulder or at the trail, and the way the carbine balances adds to this. In firing, the shape of that part prevents any grasp of the small of the butt, which is absolutely necessary in firing mounted, where the man has only

one hand free to hold the carbine. After firing about 15-20 rounds the recoil is very considerable, and the barrel becomes so hot one can scarcely hold it. Suggest that the sights be altered, the foresight being made finer, and the back sight made much smaller and neater, the notch in it being more clearly defined, and also that it be placed at least an inch further along the barrel from the breech. Also suggest that some means of placing the carbine at half-cock be adopted, for without it it is considered dangerous for a mounted man; and also that something be done to prevent the simple pressing of the trigger closing the breech and firing the carbine. A cleaning rod should also be attached to the carbine.

3. 21st Hussars (25-7-1875): Reports that, up to 400 yards in no way superior in accuracy to the Snider carbine, but beyond that range much more accurate. Extreme accurate range 900 yards. At distances above 400 yards the carbine is oversighted about 80 yards; on the carbine the correct elevation has been marked on the back sight with sealing wax, but it is very difficult to ensure the same elevation owing to the want of finish in the sights, as the foresight is so coarse that at long ranges it covers nearly the entire target, and the notch of the backsight is frequently not in the centre as marked by a silver line. The recoil is nothing to speak of. The pull off (from 8 to 9 lb) is too great for fine shooting; it also varies considerably. Suggest that the grasp of the small of the butt is too large for a man to hold and fire mounted with one hand; as a cavalry soldier does not require to use his carbine as a pike or club, strength is not required, but lightness. The carbine balances at the trail very badly. The back sight should be placed 2 inches more forward. The space between the thumb and trigger is too great. In firing, the forefinger is often severly pinched between rear of trigger and trigger guard. A bolt for half-cock is necessary for a mounted man, and an arrangement for carrying a cleaning rod.

The above reports were referred to the Supt. RSAF who responded on 9-9-1875, stating that as regards the sighting, the arms were inadvertently sighted for the 70/380 gr cartridge, instead of for the 80/410 gr, and that this could be easily corrected.

With reference to the other points raised, he stated that the back sight could be moved forward, and the front sight filed to a sharper edge, but in that case it would be liable to cut the bucket, and would also soon wear blunt. The size of grip was due to the form of the action, and could not be avoided. It could not be made to handle well at the trail, as the heavier part was behind the hand, nor to carry well at the shoulder because of the lever position. The firing off when the trigger was pressed and the lever open was considered to have been already avoided by the introduction of a stronger cap. An arrangement for locking the action at cock could be introduced, but not a half-cock. To carry a cleaning rod without joints the carbine would have to be full stocked, which would of course add to the weight.

He finished by commenting that if the objections that had been made as to the shape of the action, etc, were of vital importance, and, as they could not be got over, it might have been as well to consider the "Lee Modification" of the M-H, which did not have these defects.

(Note: No details of the "Lee Modification" have been found, so a description unfortunately cannot be given.)

THE SIXTH TRIALS PATTERN

Another WO conference was held on 28-1-1876 to examine the M-H rifle situation, and the carbine was also discussed, with the result that further trials were recommended, and that 500 carbines were to be prepared with the new action components (ie, Mark II trigger mechanism), and with such improvements as were possible to the sights and other details.

A WO minute of 4-3-1876 requested the Supt. RSAF to have 450 of these carbines ready for trial as soon as possible and on 31-3-1876 another minute, apparently in reply to a query from the superintendent, asked if the 50 carbines (Type 5) previously tried could be altered to the new pattern. These had been returned to the Tower after the trials, and it had been thought they could be modified in accordance with the trials recommendations and re-issued.

On 6-6-1876 the Supt. RSAF forwarded for inspection a modified design of cavalry carbine, and proposed the adoption of this pattern for the 500 ordered. It incorporated –

1. Cleaning rod removed from butt to fore-end
2. Full stock fore-end
3. Method of attaching fore-end was altered so as to occupy less space for admission into the bucket
4. Foresight made finer, and protected with wings
5. Backsight advanced, and attached by a new method which dispensed with soldering, so permitting easier repair
6. Head of cleaning rod reduced, for use in extracting empty cartridge cases.

Although not mentioned in the above list of improvements, a half-cock arrangement operated by a thumb piece on the right hand side of the action was also incorporated in this pattern. See Figs.1 and 2, in which this unit will be noted in two positions, ie, ON and OFF.

Fig.1 shows the action in detail, which, on comparison with the rifle action, discloses some interesting variations. It will be noted that the cocking indicator is smaller than those previously used, and the lower front corners of the action are markedly rounded off. The indicator was made smaller to allow clearance with the thumb piece when the action was cocked; and the front corners were rounded off to allow the action body to blend with the fore-end, which was lighter in construction than that for the rifle, to allow it to fit more easily into the bucket. (See Item 3 above.) These last two features were carried on to all subsequent original M-H carbines, and the smaller cocking indicator was also used on all subsequent original M-H rifle patterns.

On 15-6-1876 the SoS approved this carbine for production

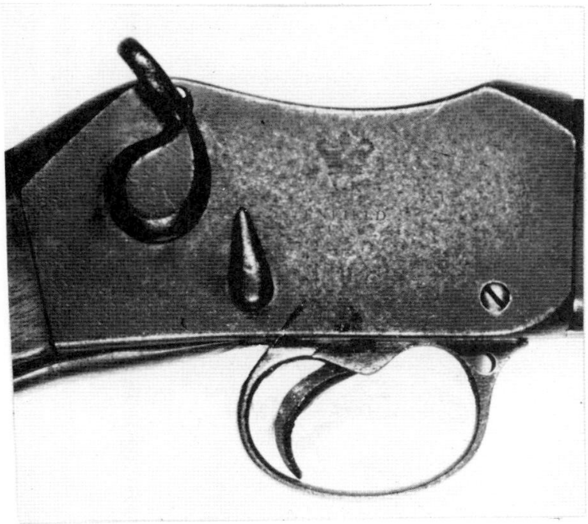

QAD(O)

Fig. 1 – Trials Carbine, Sixth Pattern – Action details. (Note thumb-piece in OFF position, and small indicator necessary to clear thumb-piece.)

and on 16-6-1876 the superintendent stated that the 50 older pattern arms could not be altered to the new pattern. It was then ordered that they remain in store, and the order for 500 was to be filled by the new pattern.

These were produced in the 1877 work year as shown in the table, Item G, and it was proposed on 15-11-1876 that some of them be issued to the artillery for trial, so the distribution was planned as –

50 to each of 7 cavalry units	350
100 to the Royal Artillery	100
25 to the SoM	25

giving a total of 475, and no mention has been found as to the allocation of the remaining 25.

The reports on the trials of the Type 6 carbines declared the half-cock arrangement dangerous, and the thumb piece weak. The front sight wings also needed to be widened. However, the carbine generally was approved of.

On 23-7-1877 the C-I-C approved the abolition of the half-cock arrangement, and after the front sight had been modified, the carbine was approved for service on 24-9-1877, and thus became the first Service Pattern M-H Carbine.

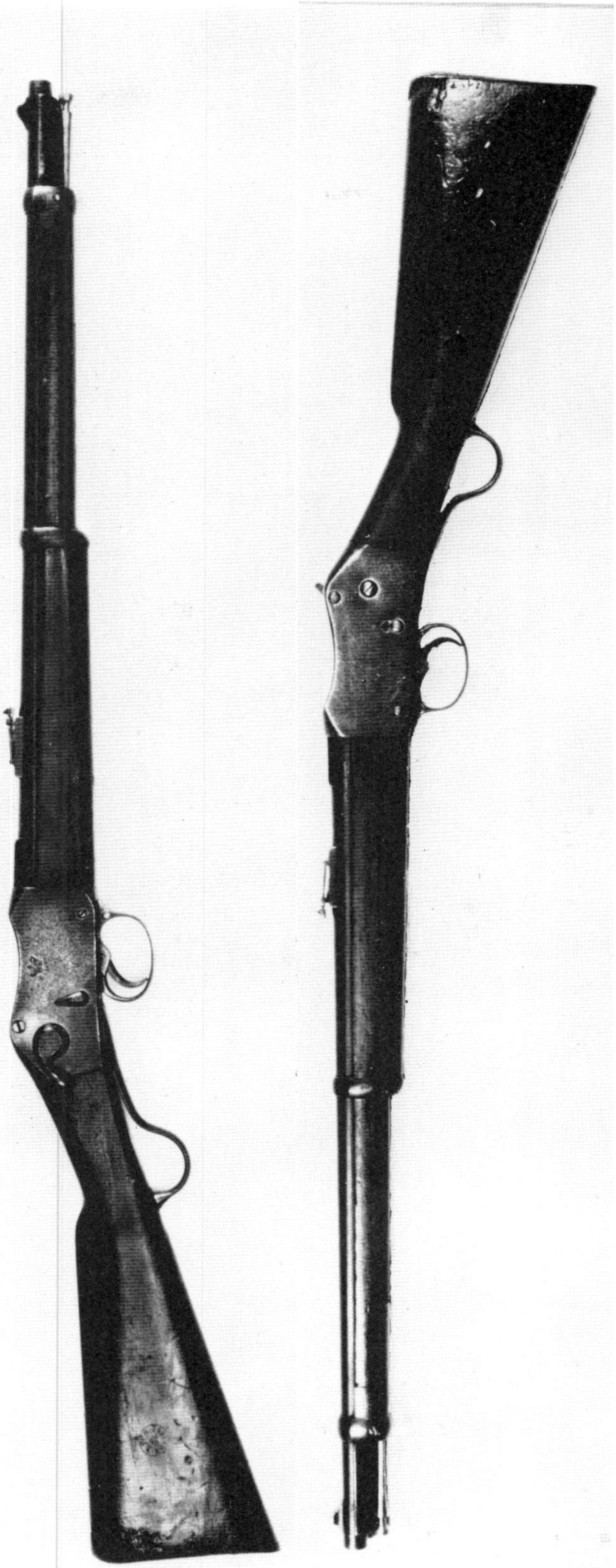

IWM

Fig. 2 – Trials Carbine, Sixth Pattern –
Top: Right hand side, showing half-cock thumb piece in ON position
Bottom: Left hand side, showing retaining screw for half-cock unit between the block axis pin and indicator axis retaining screw.

TABLE XVII – Production of Martini-Henry carbines at the RSAF during the trials period 1871-77.

Year ending 31st March	Item	Quantity produced.	Description of weapon.
1873	A	2	Artillery carbines, patterns, £ 9.9.1 each. (Type 2)
	B	2	Cavalry carbines, patterns, £ 11.11.2 each. (Type 2)
1874	C	1	Cavalry carbine, pattern. £ 28.0.1½. (Type 3)
1875	D	6	Cavalry carbines, with cleaning rod, £ 3.16.11 each. (Type 4)
	E	1	Cavalry carbine, without cleaning rod, £ 3.13.6. (Type 4)
1876	F	50	Cavalry carbines, assembled, £ 2.14.11 each. (Type 5)
	G	500	Cavalry carbines, assembled, £ 5.9.4½ each. (Type 6)

CHAPTER 12.

THE DEVELOPMENT OF THE MARTINI–HENRY CARBINE – THE SERVICE PATTERNS

THE initial development of the M-H carbines, as far as mechanical details of the breech system were concerned, followed that of the rifle, as any improvements effected to the rifle action were not incorporated into the carbine until its next trials pattern appeared. This created the effect of the carbine always lagging behind the rifle in the development of the breech system.

However, with the adoption of the first service pattern carbine, this trend was reversed, as some apparent, and not so apparent, modifications were incorporated into the action with the introduction of this arm. Some of these modifications had actually been introduced with the sixth trials pattern carbine, but the first service pattern was the unit which embodied all the changes, and, as the approved action pattern, served as the basis for all subsequent new M-H carbine and rifle patterns in the British service.

THE FIRST SERVICE PATTERN

This was a direct development of the sixth trials pattern carbine, and was approved for service on 24-9-1877 as the "Arms, Interchangeable, Carbine, Breech-loading, Rifled, with Cleaning rod, Martini-Henry, Mark I". It will be noted that it was not described as a CC, as at this stage it was intended that the artillery should also use it, in conjunction with a side arm – swords for garrison artillery, sabres for horse and field artillery.

The weapon was listed in the Enfield Pattern Book as –

Carbine, Martini-Henry, Mark I.
Date of approval: 24-9-1877.
No. of para. LoC: 3215.
Description of alterations: Form of stud of fore-end altered by authority 20-8-1880.
Remarks: Originally "Cavalry, and Horse Artillery, and Field Artillery". Changed to "Cavalry" only.
From DGOF 17-11-1887. Screws in butt plate to be brass.

(NOTE: The fore-end hook modification will be described in a later chapter. The brass screws for butt plate were the result of the adoption of the E-M rifle; however, this modification was not carried out on production models of the carbine.)

The pattern for this carbine was sealed on 26-11-1877, and it was introduced into service by LoC Para. 3215 of 1-12-1877 as –

Arms, Interchangeable, Carbine, Breech-loading, Rifled, with Cleaning rod, Martini-Henry, (Mark I).

A pattern of this arm has been sealed to govern manufacture.

The diameter of the bore and the rifling of the barrel are the same as in the Martini-Henry rifle, and the general construction of the breech mechanism is the same as the rifle.

Ammunition of a special pattern (3220) is intended to be used with the carbine, but the barrel of the latter is so chambered that the rifle ammunition may be fired from it if necessary.

The carbine is sighted to 1,000 yards. (Note: This is on the leaf; the maximum sighting range over the leaf cap is 1,180 yards.)

The arm is full stocked; the fore-end being attached to the body by means of an iron hook, called the "fore-end hook", which is secured to the former by two screws, and engages in the latter.

Several parts of the carbine are common to it and the rifle. Particulars on this point will be included in revised "Instructions to Armourers" about to be issued.

The foresight is similar to the rifle, but finer, and is furnished with a "wing" on each side to protect it from injury.

The bed of the back sight is held on by a dovetail in front, and a single screw in rear, without solder.

Weight of barrel – 2 lb 4¾ oz (1.0 kg)
Weight of carbine complete – 7 lb 8 oz (3.3 kg)
Length of barrel – 1' 9.375" (543 mm)
Length of carbine complete – 3' 1.687" (957 mm)

The improvements made to the carbine action included –

1. The attachment of the fore-end by a hooked tang in place of the barrel stud and pin
2. The cocking indicator was made smaller
3. The barrel at the breech end had two "lumps" instead of the one previously used
4. A new breech block and striker unit was fitted, to obviate the striker breakages.

The parts common to it and the Mark II rifle were –

(a) Trigger guard and mechanism
(b) Extractor and axis pin
(c) Lever
(d) Butt and associated furniture
(e) Block axis pin.

(Full details of the improved Items 1 to 4 are given in Chapters 30 and 31.)

The carbine was ordered into immediate production after being sealed, and in the balance of the 1878 production year 25,000 were made. This figure was achieved towards the end of the year, and even allowing for some prior preparation, is indicative of the capacity of the RSAF to produce a large number of weapons quickly.

This carbine as originally produced differed in minor details from later weapons of the same designation, and will be referred to here as the First pattern (see Fig.1), although in this instance there was no official recognition of any differences between it and subsequent production arms, such as had occurred with the Mark I rifle. There is also a proviso with the first pattern carbine similar to the Mark I rifles, in that some of the later alterations would have been applied to the earlier arms, and so would submerge their identity; however, some of the first patterns still exist, because of the same reasons as previously mentioned, viz, supply to colonial governments, and so not subsequently elevated in pattern.

On 18-4-1879 a leather rear sight cover was approved for the carbine, and this required two screws to be fixed in the fore-end. These were added to the sealed pattern, and fitted to all subsequent arms, but some of the original batch missed having them installed. See Figs.2 and 3.

These screws created a problem in service, by catching on the users' clothing, so the following paragraph (3566) was issued in LoC's on 1-8-1879 by approval of 3-7-1879 –

Carbines, Breech-loading, Martini-Henry.

Heads of screws for back sight covers, to have edges rounded off.

Complaints having been received as to the sharpness of the edges on the abovementioned screws, it has been decided that in future the edges shall be slightly rounded off.

The alterations will be applied to carbines in possession of the troops by regimental artificers, without charge against the public. The screws of carbines in store will be altered before issue.

The second pattern's main difference from the first was in the form of the fore-end hook, which was altered by approval of 14-8-1880: and later, on 12-8-1882, a sling with steadying strap was approved for the cavalry carbine, as it had then became named. This sling unit was introduced by LoC Para.4152 of 1-11-1882, and this led to a butt swivel being fitted. See Fig.1. This again could have been added to earlier arms, but not always, as a comparison of the arms in Fig.1 shows. The first pattern there is dated 1877 and has none of the later modifications applied, so is obviously one of the first production batch. It was issued by the South Australian Colonial government, which explains why it retained the original configuration. The second pattern carbine had all the modifications fitted, so the difference is readily apparent.

A short time after the introduction of the first service carbine, the decision was made that a version should be produced for use by garrison artillery units, with the Horse and Field Artillery to still use the original patterns. The DoA on 7-5-1878 accordingly decided that the description of the original carbine should be altered to "Arms, Interchangeable, Carbine, Breech-loading, Rifled, with Cleaning rod, Martini-Henry, Cavalry, and Horse and Field Artillery".

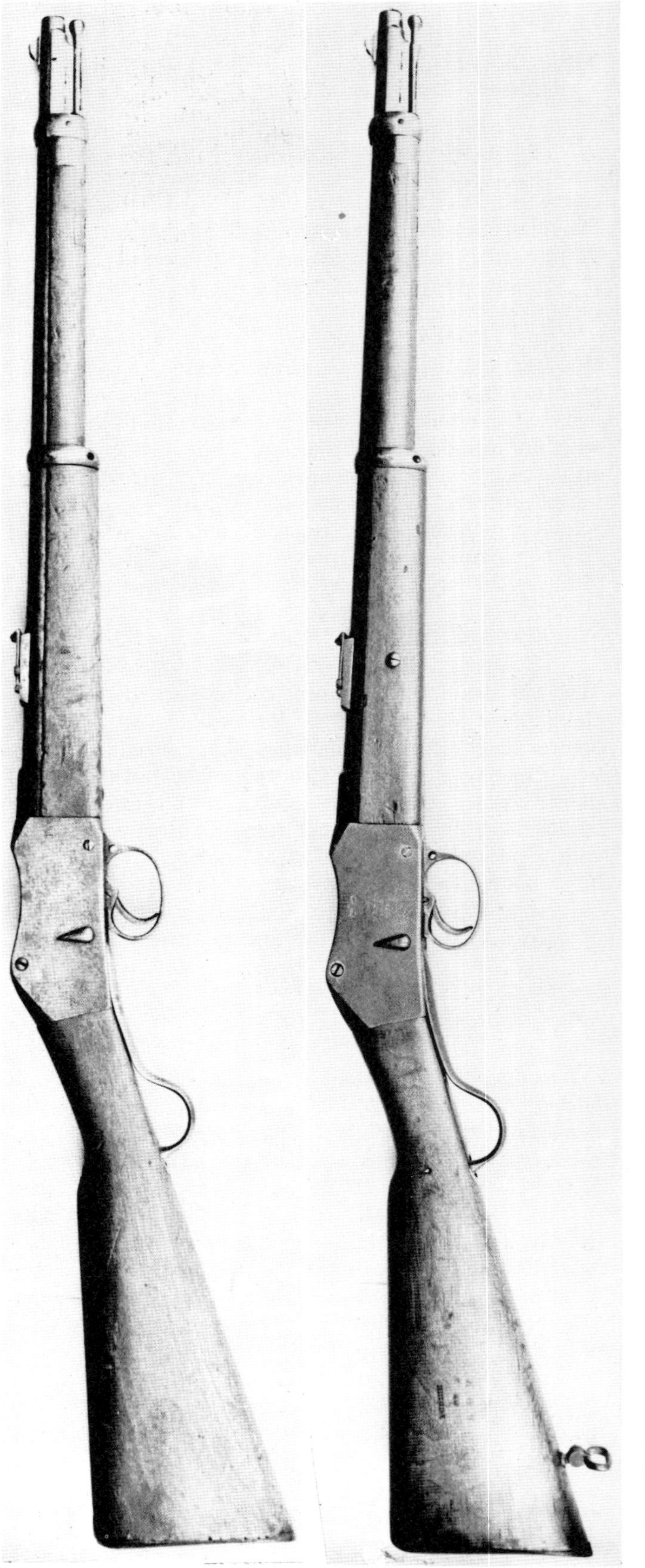

B.A.T. B.A.T.

Fig. 1 – Service Cavalry Carbine –
Top: First pattern
Bottom: Second pattern.

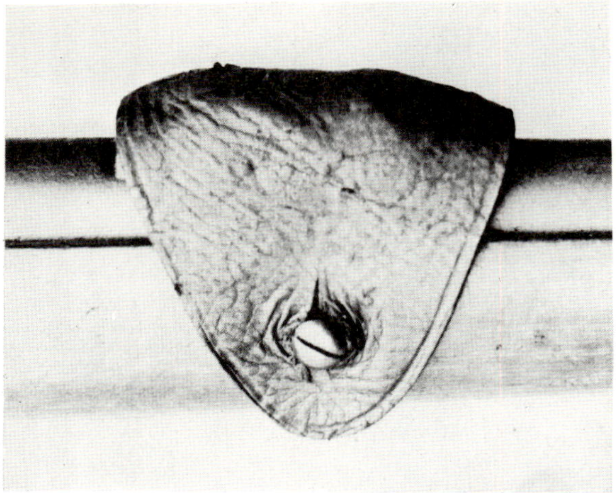

B.A.T.

Fig. 2 – Cavalry Carbine – Rear sight cover fitted.

B.A.T.

Fig. 3 – Cavalry Carbine – Rear sight, and cover screw.

However, on 20-1-1879 the DoA then proposed that the horse and field artillery should have the same carbine as the garrison artillery, and that two patterns of carbine would be issued – one for cavalry, the other for artillery. It was then decided to alter the description of the first carbine to "Cavalry" only, by deleting the words "and Horse and Field Artillery" from its description, so that, just over one year after its introduction, it finally became known as the Martini-Henry Cavalry Carbine.

The final designation for this carbine came with the introduction of the M-H AC in LoC Para.3615 of 1-11-1879, which stated in part –

The carbine mentioned in 3215 and 3566 will in future be designated – Carbine, Breech-loading, Rifled, with Cleaning rod, Martini-Henry, Interchangeable, Cavalry, with Cover, leather, backsight.

THE GARRISON ARTILLERY PATTERN

On 3-11-1877 the DoA advised the Supt. RSAF that probably about 20,000 M-H carbines would be made in the coming work year (ie, 1-4-1878 to 31-3-1879) for the artillery. As it was desired they mount a bayonet, he was asked if the stock of the current sword bayonet could be utilised for this purpose. In response, the superintendent on 20-11-1877 presented a CC altered to take the common yataghan bayonet, but he stated that the fittings for this bayonet necessitated an alteration of form of the nosecap, cleaning rod, and upper band from those of the cavalry carbine, so that, as a consequence, the interchangeability with that arm was sacrificed. He also stated that he thought the combination was too short as a pike, and likely to be dangerous to the user; so recommended that the sword bayonet be issued as a side arm to be fixed only in an emergency. On 8-1-1878 the DAG of Artillery concurred; but the arm was still to be produced with bayonet fittings, to use the yataghan bayonet bushed in the muzzle ring to fit the smaller muzzle of the carbine.

Figs.4 show comparisons between the nosecaps and associated fittings of the cavalry and garrison carbines, and it will be seen that to fix the bayonet the top band of the latter had to be moved lower on the fore-end, hence the alteration to the nose cap. The shank of the cleaning rod head also had to be shortened, to allow clearance for the muzzle ring of the bayonet, and this feature is also noticeable. Also to be noted is the lack of sling swivels on the garrison carbine, as these were not required for that branch of the service.

On 9-4-1878 this new carbine was approved as "Arms, Inter changeable, Carbine, Breech-loading, with Cleaning rod, Martini-Henry, Garrison Artillery, Mark I", and the sword bayonet as "Arms, Interchangeable, Parts of, Bayonet, Sword, Breech-loading carbine, Martini-Henry, Garrison Artillery". On 24-4-1878 the DoA advised that no bayonets would be provided at present.

This arm was listed in the Enfield Pattern Book as –

Carbine, Martini-Henry Mark I, Garrison artillery. With cleaning rod.
Date of approval: 9-4-1878.
Remarks: The upper band, nosecap, screws, and cleaning rod differ from those of the cavalry, the fore-end is slightly altered to receive the same. This is to admit of a sword bayonet being fixed when necessary.

(Because of the introduction of this carbine, the DoA decided on 7-5-1878 that the description of the carbine in LoC 3215 should be changed. The Supt. RSAF was directed to alter the descriptive label of the pattern arm accordingly. He replied on 9-5-1878 that this had been done.)

There was only one arm of this new pattern produced during the 1878 year, and it was listed in production records as –

"Carbine, artillery, Martini-Henry – 1 Arm, assembled,

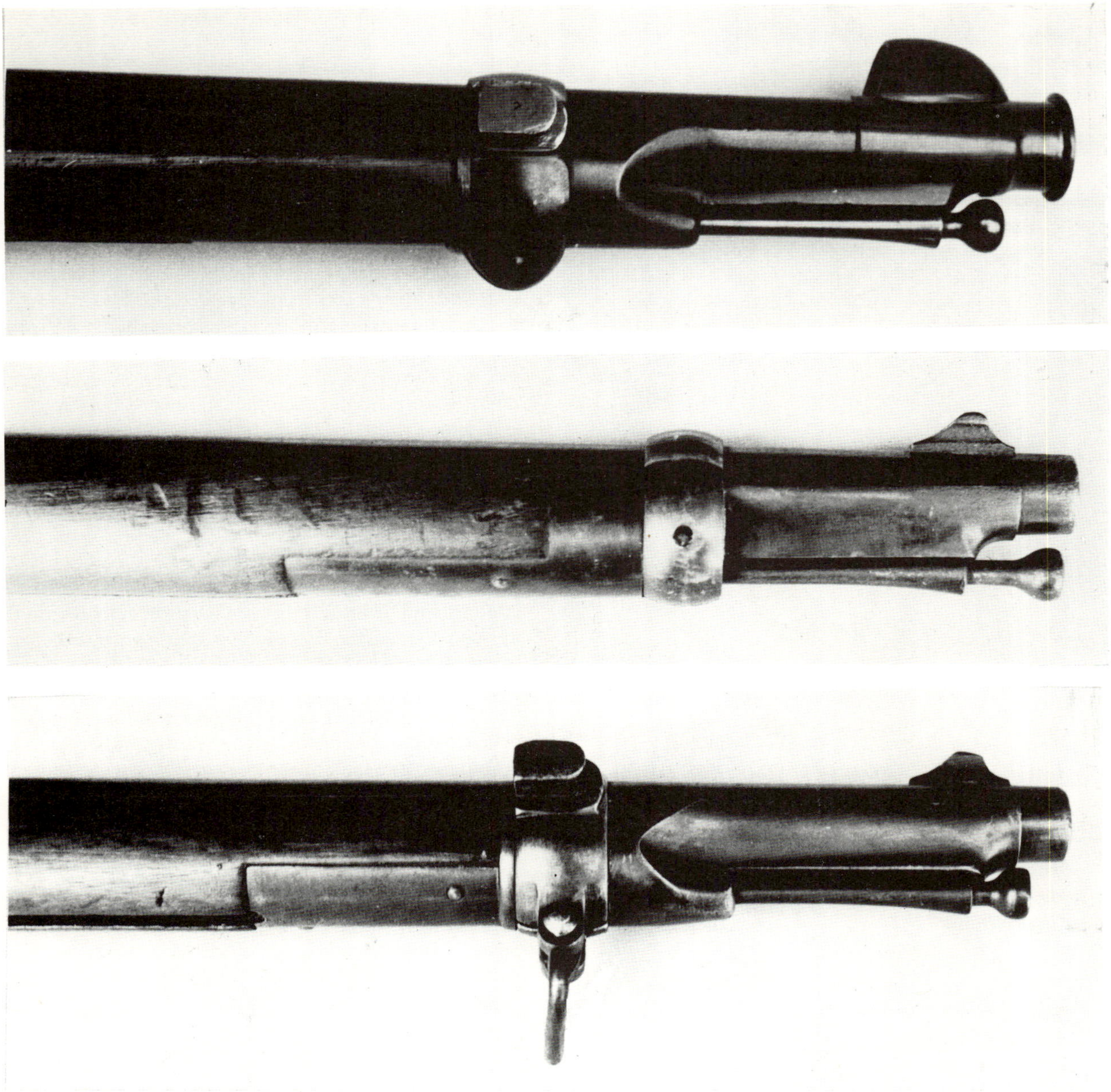

QAD(O)

B.A.T.

B.A.T.

Fig. 4 – Carbine Fore-end Fittings –
Top: Garrison Artillery
Middle: Cavalry
Bottom: Artillery, Mark I.

with cleaning rod, pattern."

This could have been the specimen presented by the superintendent on 20-11-1877.

In a minute of 22-5-1878 it was stated that the DoA had informed the SGO that as 25,000 M-H carbines had been produced, he hoped these would be available for garrison, as well as horse and field artillery units. It was decided, how ever, that supplies to the garrison units would be suspended for one year, and they would retain the Snider carbine. It was then found that there were not enough Snider carbines for this purpose, so it was recommended that 5,000 M-H carbines with artillery attachments and sword bayonets complete, be made at Enfield.

On 23-5-1878 a further minute stressed that a decision on the above recommendation was urgent, and the proposal was accordingly approved.

THE FIRST PRODUCTION ARTILLERY CARBINE

The carbine urgently requested on 23-5-1878 was produced in the 1879 work year as – "Carbine, Artillery, Martini-Henry – 5,001 Arms, assembled, with cleaning rods." They were made to Order No.195, which, together with the urgent requisition, indicates they were made sometime in the middle of 1878, and this is important in view of subsequent events.

No specific example of this batch of arms has been identified, so its exact configuration is not known. It is thus unfortunately necessary to speculate to some extent in describing it.

The order for these arms stated "with artillery attachments, and sword bayonets complete", indicating that it was fitted with sling swivels, so could not be made to the garrison pattern as that arm did not have sling swivels. The extra arm could thus have been the pattern necessary to guide the manufacture of the 5,000 arms ordered, as was the usual practice.

So, although not made to the actual garrison pattern, this artillery carbine probably used that arm as its basic form, but with the addition of sling swivels; and, if this was the case, it would then resemble the later approved AC, and indeed, may have served as the basis for this subsequent arm.

That it did not differ from the standard carbine to any great extent is indicated by two entries from the 1879 production figures; under the heading "Carbine, Artillery, Martini-Henry" is shown –

> "New pattern upper bands for swivels (O/No.187)
> New pattern upper band screws (O/No.188)."

These were the only special parts necessary to allow the use of sling swivels, as the actual top band swivel, and butt swivel complete, would have been standard rifle items, and so readily available.

As no other special parts were mentioned, the inference from the above is that the first production batch of M-H AC was made to the GA pattern, but with a special top band to allow the fitting of sling swivels, and, in view of subsequent events, the GA carbine as such was produced as a pattern arm only.

The DoA proposed on 20-1-1879 that the horse and field artillery should have the same carbines as the garrison artillery, and that field batteries should have the sword bayonet. It was considered more convenient to have only cavalry and artillery carbines, and to alter the description on the pattern arm of LoC 3215 to "Cavalry" only. It was then decided on 19-3-1879 that the word "Garrison" should be removed from the description of the AC, as it was now to be issued to horse and field artillery. On 20-3-1879 the DoA stated that a new pattern of AC was being prepared, and this was approved on 21-7-1879 as "Carbine, Breech-loading, Rifled, with Cleaning rod, Martini-Henry, Interchangeable, Artillery, Mark I".

It will be seen from the above paragraph that the first batch of AC was produced approximately one year before the approval of the carbine officially designated as Artillery Mark I, and, as it was stated that "a new pattern of artillery carbine" was being prepared – and eventually adopted – and as this new pattern was fitted with sling swivels, it is

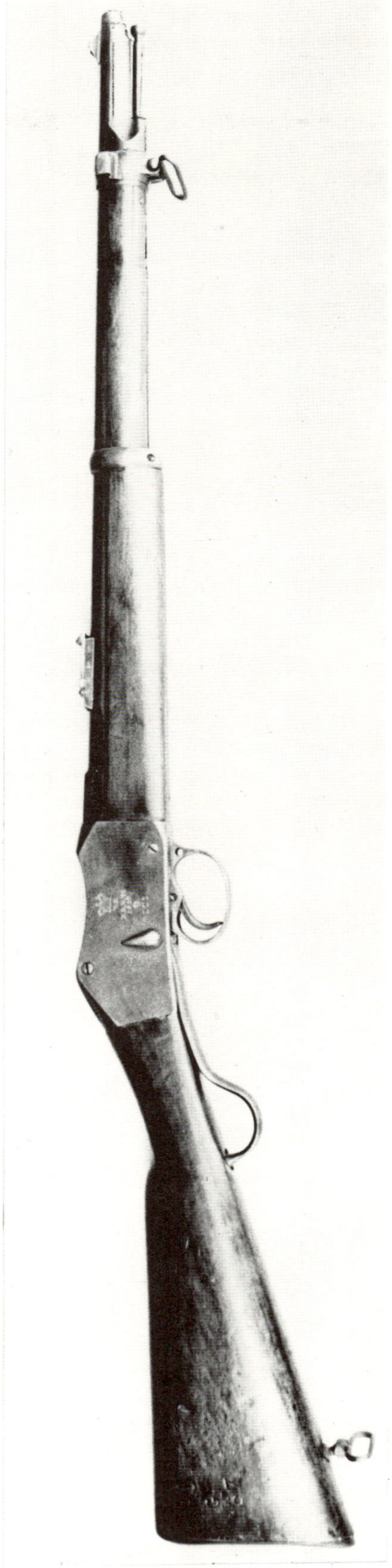

B.A.T.

Fig. 5 – Artillery Carbine, Mark I.

likely that the new pattern was very similar to the first production version, and so replaced the swivel-less GA model as the pattern to govern manufacture of all subsequent AC of original M-H type.

THE ARTILLERY CARBINE, MARK I

The new pattern AC was listed in the Enfield Pattern Book as –

Carbine, Martini-Henry, Mark I, Artillery.
Date of approval: 21-7-1879.
No. of para. LoC: 3615.
Remarks: Form of stud of fore-end hook altered by authority 20-8-1880.
From DGOF 17-11-1887. Screws in butt plate to be brass.
(Note: The same remarks apply in this latter instance as for the CC.)

Its introductory paragraph in LoC's was 3615 of 1-11-1879 as follows –

Carbine, Breech-loading, Rifled, with Cleaning rod, Martini-Henry, Interchangeable, Artillery, (Mark I).

A pattern of the abovementioned article has been sealed to govern manufacture.

The carbine differs from the cavalry carbine (3215) in the following particulars only –

The nosecap is altered in form and size to take an upper band with bar, for the sword bayonet; the front edge of the bar is rounded off to prevent injury to the hand when the arm is held at the "order".

The carbine is fitted with swivels for a sling.

The upper band swivel is the same as that of the Martini-Henry rifle.

The butt swivel, also similar to that for the Martini-Henry rifle, is placed 2¼ inches from the toe of the butt.

The cleaning rod is shortened to allow the hilt of the sword bayonet, when fixed, to clear it, and the head is cupped to prevent injury to the striker point should the rod be dropped into the bore head first.

Weight of barrel – 2 lb 4¾ oz (1.0 kg)
Weight of carbine – 7 lb 10½ oz (3.4 kg)
Weight of carbine with bayonet fixed – 9 lb 4¾ oz (4.1 kg)
Length of barrel – 1' 9.375" (543 mm)
Length of carbine – 3' 1.687" (957 mm)
Length of carbine with bayonet fixed - 5' 3.375" (1,610 mm)

The foresight and muzzle protector used with the carbine is that mentioned in 3216.

Fig.5 shows a specimen of this carbine, and Figs.4 a comparison of nosecaps and fittings of the GA and AC. It will be noted from the illustrations the only differences between the two are the upper band and head of cleaning rod; so by the substitution of these two items, and the addition of a butt swivel, the garrison pattern is readily converted into an AC I pattern. The interim production version was probably similar in appearance, but may have used the GA cleaning rod.

Fig.6 illustrates the various parts of AC and CC Mark I.

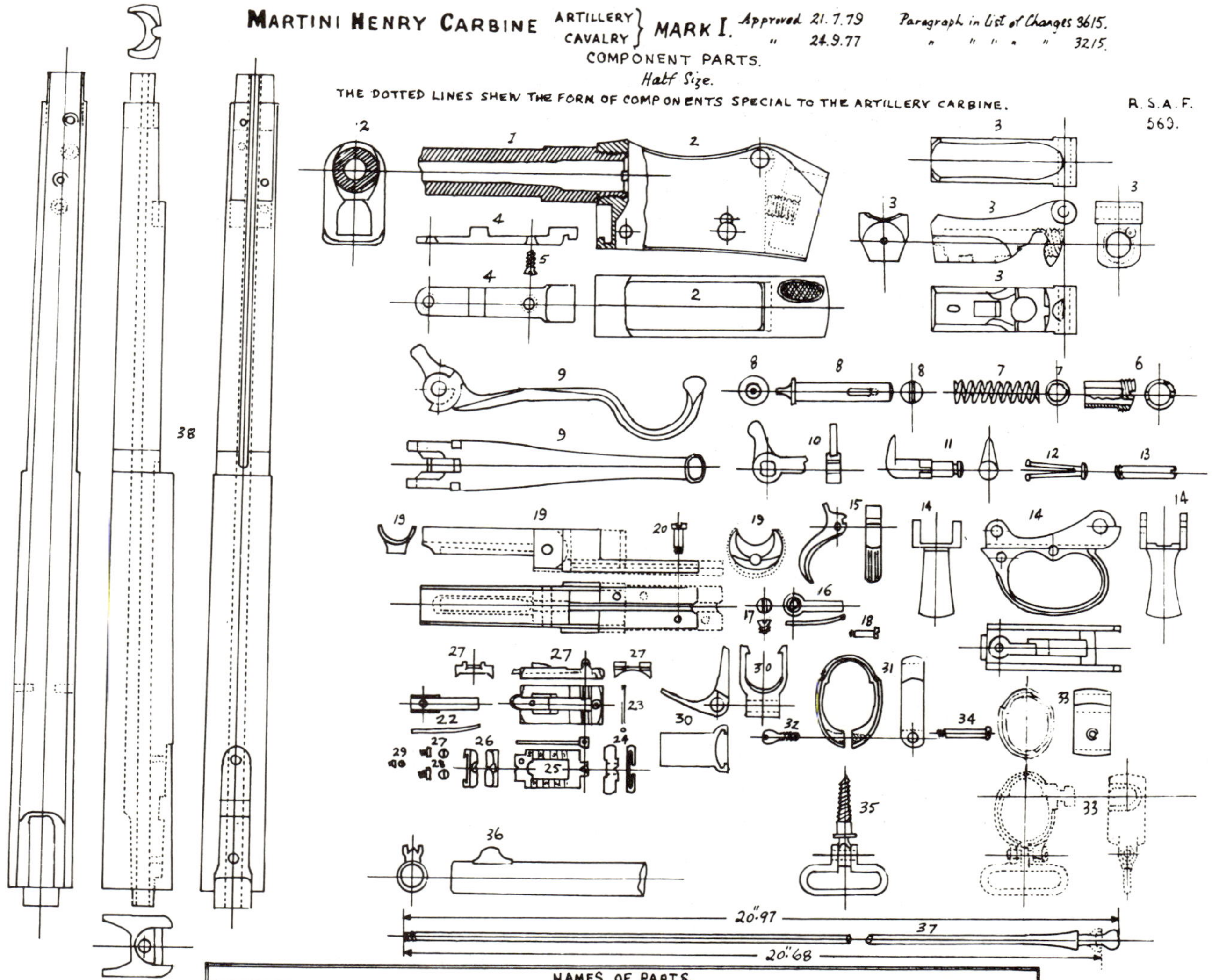

NAMES OF PARTS.											
1.	Barrel.	8.	Striker.	15.	Trigger.	22.	Sight spring.	29.	Screw, sight cap.	36.	Sight, fore.
2.	Body.	9.	Lever.	16.	Trigger spring.	23.	" axis pin.	30.	Extractor.	37.	Rod, cleaning.
3.	Block.	10.	Tumbler.	17.	Screw, trigger spring.	24.	" slide.	31.	Band, lower.	38.	Stock, fore-end.
4.	Hook.	11.	Indicator.	18.	Screw, trigger.	25.	" leaf.	32.	Screw, band, lower.		
5.	Screw, hook.	12.	Block axis.	19.	Nose cap.	26.	" cap.	33.	Band, upper.		
6.	Stop nut.	13.	Extractor axis	20.	Screw, nose cap.	27.	" bed screw.	34.	" " screw.		
7.	Main spring.	14.	Guard, trigger.	21.	Sicht bed.	28.	" spring "	35.	Swivel, butt.		

Note: For butt end of stock with its fittings, see "Rifle lithograph".

Fig. 6 – Parts of Artillery and Cavalry Carbines.

NAM

A Corporal of the 14th Hussars, armed with a Martini-Henry Cavalry Carbine.

CHAPTER 13.

CARBINE CONVERSIONS

DURING the initial years of the M-H service carbine production, various changes were made to the arms and their nomenclature, because of differing ideas on their service employment – caused by the vacillation of the higher command when considering the use of bayonets by the various artillery corps.

References to some aspects of this situation were made in the previous chapter, but a re-presentation will clarify the position, and also be of assistance when interpreting the reasons for some of the conversions of carbines as outlined in this chapter.

The first production carbine was not fitted for sling or bayonet, as it was basically a cavalry pattern, to be carried in a bucket. The initial batch of these arms was of a large number, and it was desired that they be rapidly introduced into service with as many units as possible.

These were essentially mounted units, and as horse and field artillery were in this category, they too were to be issued with the carbine, and in lieu of a bayonet, be equipped with side arms.

The garrison artillery, not being mounted, was not included in the above classification, and, as it was felt necessary that their carbine mount a bayonet, a special pattern with this capability was designed for them. As it was not necessary to sling it, no swivels were provided. It would appear, however that no allocation was made for the manufacture of the GA carbine, as none, apart from the pattern arm, were made during the first production year of the M-H carbine.

The DoA then requested a supply of the ordinary carbine for the garrison artillery, but was told that those units would not be supplied for at least a year, so would retain Snider carbines. It was then found that there were not enough Snider carbines for that supply, so a batch of M-H carbines, specially adapted for artillery use, with sling and bayonet fittings, was ordered.

The design of this latter carbine apparently caused a change of opinion again, as the DoA then proposed that the horse and field artillery should have the same carbine as the garrison artillery, and field batteries should have a sword bayonet in lieu of a side arm. The original carbine was then designated as the CC. After changes to the pattern arm, the other carbine was redesignated as AC. This meant that the CC was the pattern without swivels or bayonet bar, whereas the AC had both these fittings.

CONVERSIONS OF CAVALRY CARBINES

The initial batch of cavalry carbines was 25,000 produced in the 1878 work year to O/No.143, but, in the same year

B.A.T.

Fig. 1 – Converted Cavalry Carbine.

is found the entry "76 Arms, assembled, Carbine, Martini-Henry, altered". This activity was to O/No.3888 – a later number than that for the production of the arms – so it presumably refers to weapons from that batch. What was altered is not known, but the costing of the job shows that for each arm the material cost 6d, and labour, 4s 6d; indicating that what was done was a labour intensive change of a small item/s. It could thus have been the replacement of some part with one of a new pattern, or something of a similar nature that did not change the character of the arm.

The next conversion took place in the 1879 year, to O/No. 419 as –

> "Carbines, Artillery, Martini-Henry, converted from Carbines, Cavalry, Martini-Henry; 1,059 with swivels, 701 without swivels."

These will be referred to as carbines A and B respectively. A cost analysis shows that materials cost per arm was – A, 1s 7d; and B, 1d; and labour – A, 6s 9d; and B, 6s 1d; again showing a labour intensive replacement of small items only.

Fig.1 shows a carbine that is considered to be a Type A; and Fig.2 shows its fore-end fittings, ie, a standard CC nose cap, but with a special top band fitted with a sling swivel – which, together with a butt swivel, form the only variation from a standard CC, and so is in keeping with the analysis above.

Fig. 2 – Converted Carbine – Fore-end fittings.

To complement the above features, two other entries for the 1879 year should also be examined. These are shown under the heading "Cavalry carbine, Martini-Henry" as –

> "1,100 special swivel band screws (O/No.203)
> 1,100 special upper band swivels (O/No.204)"

As a unit the cost was about 6d each, and as 1,059 conversions as a figure is just short of 1,100, it is probable these screws and swivels were for the Type A carbines, with an allowance for spare parts, as was the usual practice.

Two other items were necessary for this conversion – an upper band, and the butt swivel (a standard pattern as issued on the M-H rifle). Costing of standard carbine upper bands shows approximately 9-10d each; a butt swivel, about 2-3d; so the combined cost of all pieces necessary is (in d) 6+10+3 = 19d, or 1s 7d, which agrees with the material cost quoted for the conversion.

As these carbines were for artillery, with no bayonets, and were to be slung, they were apparently intended for use by mounted units equipped with side arms; but after the approved AC became readily available, would have been withdrawn and issued elsewhere. One batch of 20 arms of this pattern was sent to the NSW colonial government in 1879, to fill an order for M-H carbines placed two years previously. Because of the demands of the regular British service, any colonial orders had to wait until the former were satisfied, so that, when these non-regulation arms became available, they were used to fill this particular colonial order to save further delay.

The precise modifications carried out on the Type B carbines are not known, but at 1d for material, it would appear that only a very minor part was affected, so the basic configuration was probably unchanged. If this was the case, it leads to speculation as to why it was designated as an AC, but this may have been done to keep the books tidy – ie, carbines used by artillery units must be AC.

The Type B carbines were probably intended for mounted infantry units; carried either in a bucket, or racked on the limbers, and would later have been replaced by the approved AC, as was done with the Type A carbines.

During the 1880 work year some apparently similar conversions took place as – "523 Carbines, Cavalry, altered to Carbine, Artillery, Martini-Henry (O/No.357)". Material cost was 8d per unit, with labour, 5s 6d; so the same conditions of a labour intensive replacement of a small part still applied.

One other activity that same year is perhaps not in the nature of a conversion from one pattern to another, but is of interest, ie – "3,900 Carbines, Artillery, new, altered (O/No.365)". This again was a labour intensive alteration, but not to the former degree, as material cost was 9d, and labour, 1s 11d. Again, what was done is not known, but, as the first production batch of the approved AC was made during that year, to O/No.147B (ie, an early order in the year), it could be possible that some of the arms first made did not conform exactly to the finally approved pattern, hence the necessity for alteration.

CONVERSIONS OF RIFLES TO CARBINES

A new series of M-H carbines commenced in 1892 with the appearance of the M-H ACII – a converted arm made by reducing the M-H RII in length to that of the standar carbine. What corps this new carbine was intended for is not known, but, as the horse and field artillery were to be armed with 0.303-inch carbines from this period onwards, it is possible that it was intended initially for issue to garrison artillery, until the latter arms became available for them too.

The garrison artillery was armed with the M-H ACI, but as most suitable arms of the type were being used for conversions to M-M patterns, these would have been withdrawn from service, and a replacement would be required. As the mass-production of M-H arms had ceased with the adoption of 0.303-inch weapons, the only means of obtaining more carbines quickly was by converting rifles, so this was done, with the M-H ACII resulting. (However, a note has been found in Enfield records to the effect that the above designated pattern arm was "Special for issue to schools", and dated 1896; but, because of that date, this apparently only applied to the final batch of 1,000 arms of the type produced during that work year, presumably for issue to school cadets.)

The thought may have occurred to the reader that it would have been simpler just to convert the rifles into the 0.303-inch arms, and leave the carbines untouched; but that would not do: the basic patterns were different, and, in any case, for first line use the latest patterns and newest arms were converted initially, and the older arms of earlier patterns, later. In this instance, as it was not intended as a first line weapon, the new pattern carbine was converted from second class weapons of an obsolescent pattern, and so utilised stocks of arms that were lying idle in store, thus giving them another term of service.

Another converted carbine has also been noted in official documents – the M-H ACIII – which is an oddity, with sparse information on it available. It is shown on a "List of Small Arms in British Service, 1910", and is stated therein to be "Converted from Rifle, Martini-Henry, Mark III, and barrels from Carbine, Martini-Henry, Mark I". It was thus obviously intended to utilise the stocks of barrels taken from the M-H carbines when they were converted into 0.303-inch patterns, but it is doubtful if in fact any of the Mark III pattern were made, apart from prototypes. No mention has been found of any in the Enfield production records, and only two proven specimens are known to exist. (This carbine will be described in detail, below.)

THE MARTINI–HENRY ARTILLERY CARBINE MARK II

Fig.3 shows this weapon, which was produced in quantity, and, although there is no mention of a pattern arm in the Enfield Pattern Book, its specification to govern the conversion was approved on 16-6-1892.

The conversion consisted generally in shortening the original barrel and reducing the resultant muzzle diameter to normal, shortening the fore-end and moving the shoulders down, fitting a brass marking disc and standard swivel to the butt, fitting new sights, and supplying a new cleaning rod. The part specification below lists original and new parts used in this alteration. Fig.4 shows the fore-end fittings after conversion, and it will be noted that the fore-end stops about one inch (26 mm) from the muzzle.

As there were no wings to the foresight, a muzzle and foresight protector was provided, and this was special to this

B.A.T.

Fig. 3 – Artillery Carbine, Mark II.

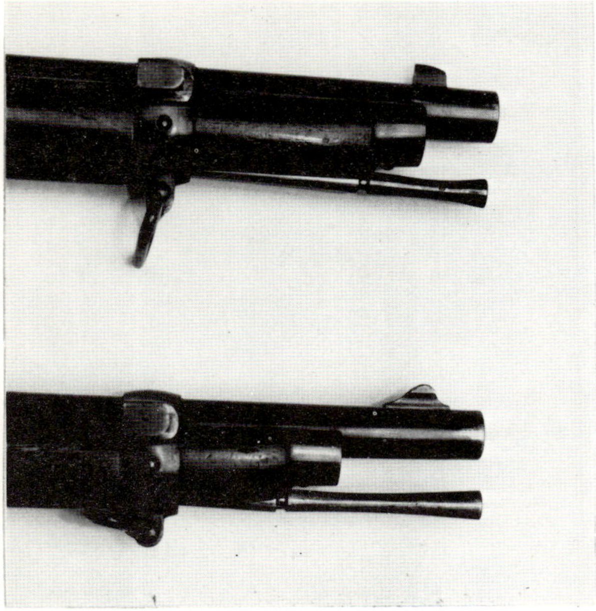

Fig. 4 – Artillery Carbines, Marks II and III – Comparison of fore-end fittings.

carbine, being known as the Pattern "C", approved for sealing as a pattern on 4-8-1892 (see Chapter 33).

As this conversion used second class arms, most specimens examined had been made from Mark II Converted rifles, so will exhibit features of those arms, and, in keeping with their second class status as a carbine, most were later relegated to drill purpose arms, for use by cadet forces and the like. When the carbine was used for this purpose the brass butt disc was usually replaced by one of steel.

Production records show for the 1892 year – "40 Carbines, Martini-Henry, Artillery Mark II, converted from rifles", and, "1 Drawing of Carbine, Artillery, Martini-Henry Mark II, Converted". This was the first production batch, and in the following years the numbers gradually increased to 7,367 in 1893, and 30,000 in 1894. There were no conversions of this pattern in 1895, but a final batch was made in 1896 of 1,000 arms, making a total production of 38,407, compared with 57,208 M-H ACI made at Enfield before manufacture of that pattern ceased there.

Dimensions of the M-H ACII were –

Overall length – 3' 1.687" (957 mm)
Barrel length – 1' 9.437" (544 mm)
Overall weight – 7 lb 9 oz (3.4 kg)
Barrel weight – 2 lb 5 oz (1.0 kg)

SPECIFICATION FOR MARTINI–HENRY CARBINE, ARTILLERY, MARK II

CARBINE, ARTILLERY, MARTINI–HENRY, 0.45-INCH, MARK II. L.

Converted from Rifle, M.H, Mark II.

Specification to Govern Conversion and Inspection.

Approved 16-6-1892.

The carbine to be in general accordance with the sealed Pattern, governed by the conditions laid down herein, or the sizes shown on the accompanying drawing.

. . .

Contractor will be supplied with Mark II 0.45 M.H. rifles. He will utilise the components shown on List "A", and will return those shown on List "B" to store, replacing them by others of his own manufacture.

. . .

List A, showing parts of Mark II 0.45 M.H. rifle to be used in the conversion –

*Barrel**	*Upper band**
Barrel stud pin	*Upper band screw*
Barrel stud stop	*Nut, upper band screw*
Block	*Striker*
Block axis pin	*Stock bolt*
Body	*Stock bolt washer*
Butt stock	*Stop nut*
Butt plate	*Stop nut keeper screw*
Butt plate screws	*Spring, main*
Extractor	*Swivel, upper band*
Extractor axis screw	*Trigger*
Guard	*Trigger screw*
Indicator	*Trigger spring*
Indicator keeper screw	*Trigger spring screw*
Lever	*Tumbler*
Lever catch block	*Nose cap**
Lever catch block spring	*Nose cap screw*
Lever catch block pin	*Rod holder*
*Lower band**	*Rod holder screws*
Lower band screw	*Pin, upper band*
Lower band pin	*Fore-end stock**

**These components will require altering to suit the convert ed arm as follows –*

Lower band will be altered to suit larger diameter of barrel
Upper band will be altered to suit larger diameter of barrel
Nose cap will be altered to suit larger diameter of barrel
Barrel will be shortened and muzzle reduced to size; back sight screw holes plugged
Stock, fore-end shortened and band shoulders moved further back; lower band pin hole plugged, and holes bored for upper and lower band pins, nose cap seating and rod holder seating cut
Stock, butt drilled for swivel and marks obliterated. (Note: Although not mentioned here, the seating for the butt marking disc would also have to be machined into the butt, and the disc screw hole bored.)

. . .

List B, showing the new components to be supplied by the contractor . . . –

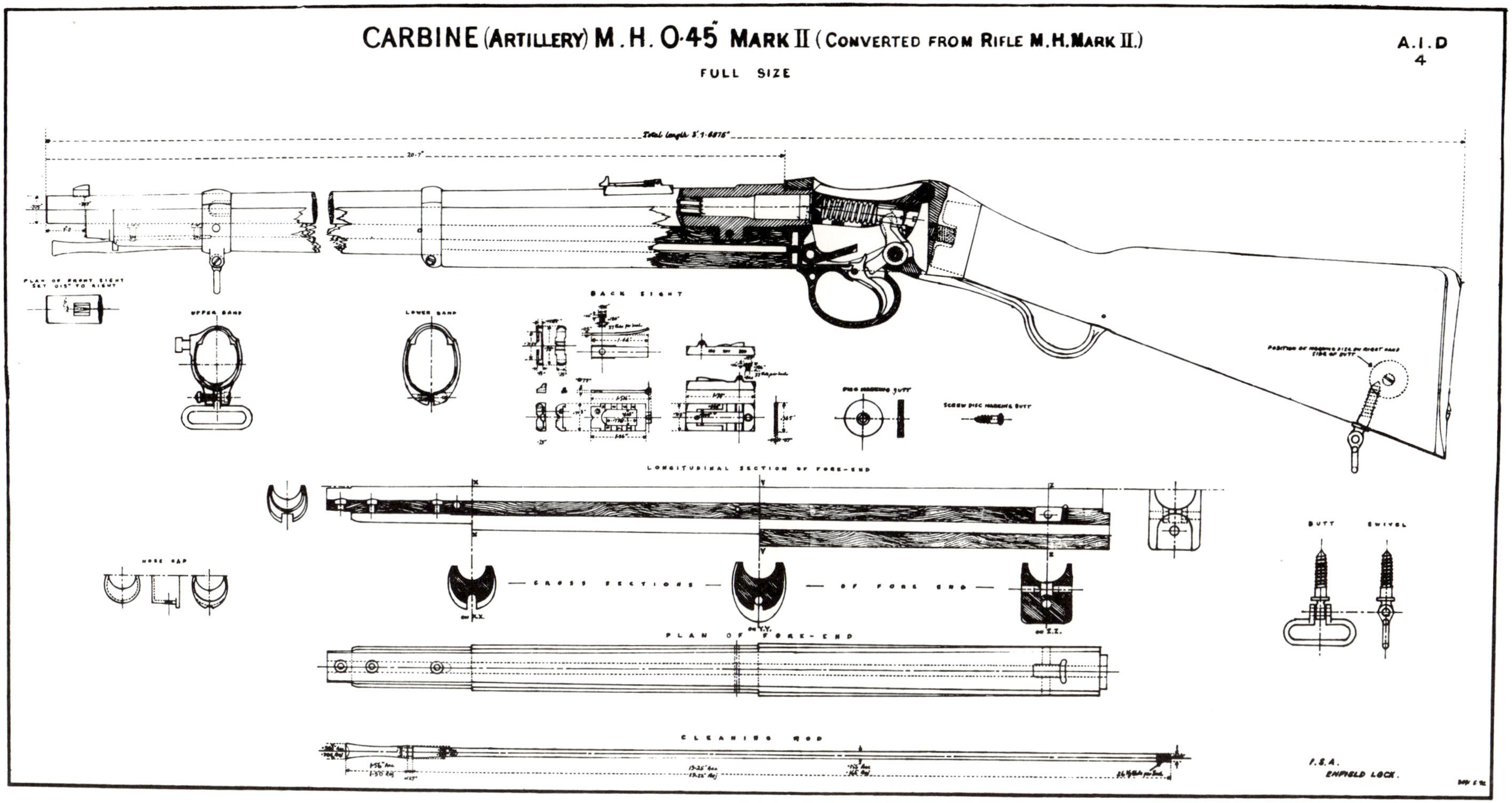

Fig. 5 – Artillery Carbine, Mark II – Specification drawing.

Disc, marking.butt	*Screw, marking disc*
Swivel, stock, butt	*Screw, sight bed*
Sight bed	*Screw, sight cap*
Sight cap	*Screw, sight spring*
Sight slide	*Cleaning rod*
Sight spring	*Jag*
Sight leaf	*Pin, back sight leaf*
Sight, front	

Fig.5 shows the Specification Drawing for this arm.

(The salient points only of the above specification are given here. Full details of representative specifications will be presented in a later chapter of this study.)

THE MARTINI–HENRY ARTILLERY CARBINE MARK III

This arm, shown in Fig.6, was officially described as being a conversion from the M-H RIII, but with a carbine barrel rather than a cut-down rifle barrel. However, an examination of both known specimens shows that in each instance the carbine action was also used. Although this action was of the same type as designated, ie, one able to accept a fore-end hook, it was nevertheless a variation from its official description, and this anomaly is only one of a few exhibited by this arm.

It cannot be stated with any certainty whether or not the Mark III carbine was contemporary with the Mark II, but it was similar in appearance, and converted in a similar manner. Even so, there were differences in details, and most parts were not interchangeable between the two.

In the Mark III conversion the barrel retained its original winged foresight, but the back sight was the same as that fitted to the Mark II. The original rifle fore-end was shortened, and the bands moved down as for the Mark II, but there the similarity ended. Fig.4 shows a comparison of the fore-end fittings of ACII and III, and it will be noted that the fore-end of the latter ended nearly 2 inches (50 mm) from the muzzle, against 1 inch for the former. This created a variance in the cleaning rods, as, although of the same length of 21 inches (533 mm), neither was interchangeable because of the position of the rod holder groove. This was different in each instance because of the unequal distances of the rod holders from their respective muzzles. See Fig.7 for a comparison of the cleaning rods.

Why the Mark III fore-end was not made similar in length to that of the Mark II, so allowing the use of a common rod, is another anomaly of this arm, as there does not appear to be any obvious reason why this could not have been done.

The muzzle protector, on the other hand, even had the fore-ends been of the same length, could not have been made as a common item, as the muzzle diameters were different, consequent on the use of the carbine barrel in the Mark III. The protector as a result was special to this pattern, and designated Pattern "D", sealed on 24-5-1893. See

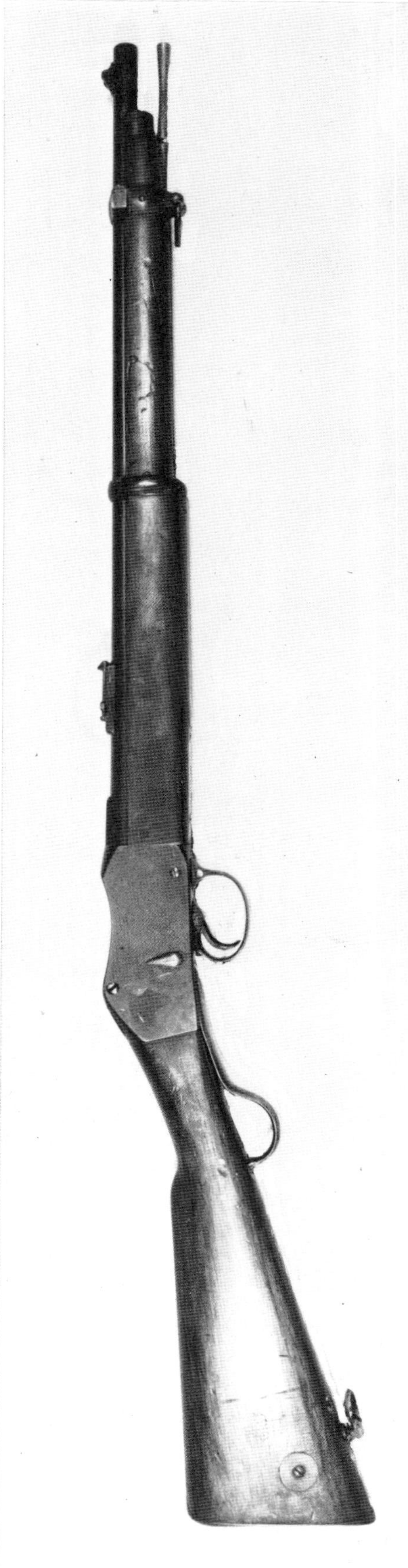

Tower

Fig. 6 – Artillery Carbine, Mark III.

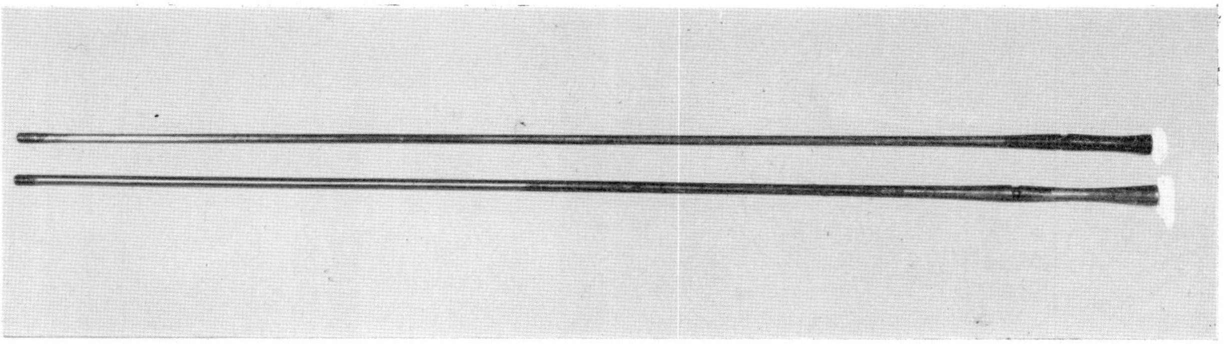

Tower

Fig. 7 – Artillery Carbines, Marks II and III – Comparison of cleaning rods.

Chapter 33.

The remainder of the conversion was straight-forward, with a brass marking disc and swivel fitted to the butt as before.

The Mark III does not show in Enfield production records, and, although it could have been produced elsewhere, this seems unlikely. The BSA and LSA Co's did not do conversion work, and the HRB Co who did, were busy with M-M conversions, so would not have been in a position to work on these special arms.

It is probable that this pattern was developed as an arm that could be made if a demand arose, and it would have been produced cheaply by utilising stocks of parts on hand from converted and condemned arms. Apparently this demand did not arise, so only the prototypes were made.

The dimensions of the ACIII were –

Overall length – 3' 1.687" (957 mm)
Barrel length – 1' 9.375" (543 mm)
Overall weight – 7 lb 7 oz (3.3 kg)
Barrel weight – 2 lb 4¾ oz (1.0 kg)

CHAPTER 14.

THE MARTINI–HENRY RIFLE, MARK III

THIS pattern was a logical follow-on from the carbine, using the improved action mechanism and the fore-end hook as introduced with that weapon. It also incorporated some modifications to the rear sights, but in general appearance was similar to the RII. It did not entirely supplant the earlier pattern in service use, as for some years after the introduction of the Mark III, the Mark II was still being produced by private contractors, as mentioned in Chapter 10. See Fig.1 for illustration of the Mark III rifle.

The RIII pattern was approved on 22-8-1879, and was listed in the Enfield Pattern Book as –

Rifle, Martini-Henry, Mark III.
Date of approval: 22-8-1879.
Description of alterations for which the arm has been sealed as a pattern: Form of stud of fore-end hook altered by auth ority 20-8-1880.

It was introduced for service by LoC Para. 3998 of 1-3-1882 as –

Rifle, Breech-loading, with Cleaning rod, Martini-Henry, Interchangeable, (Mark III).

A pattern of the abovementioned rifle has been sealed to govern future manufacture. It differs from Mark II (3193) in the following particulars –

Backsight bed: This is made 0.125" longer in order to give more support to the leaf and cap. The backsight bed is soldered on the barrel in such a position that when the leaf is raised it is inclined to the left at an angle of 1 deg 6 min with the vertical line through the axis of the bore. This inclination is intended to correct the permanent deflection due to the rifling.

Backsight spring: This is made 0.125" longer.

Barrel: The barrel has a double lump at the breech end, one projection on the upper, and one on the under surface, as is the case with the Martini-Henry carbines. A similar lump is on the Mark II rifle barrel, but only on the upper surface of the breech. This allows a better bearing to be obtained when the barrel is "breeched up" to the body, and gives additional strength to the chamber. The barrel stud is dispensed with.

Body: Is recessed in front to take the fore-end hook.

Block: Is made wider at the front to make it steadier when firing, and is the same as that for the Martini-Henry carbines. The diameter of the striker hole in the face is increased 0.002".

When fitted with a Mark II stop nut and striker it can be used with a Mark II rifle, but not otherwise.

All blocks for Martini-Henry rifles or carbines will in future be made of this pattern.

Fore-end: Is made 0.312" longer and is recessed to

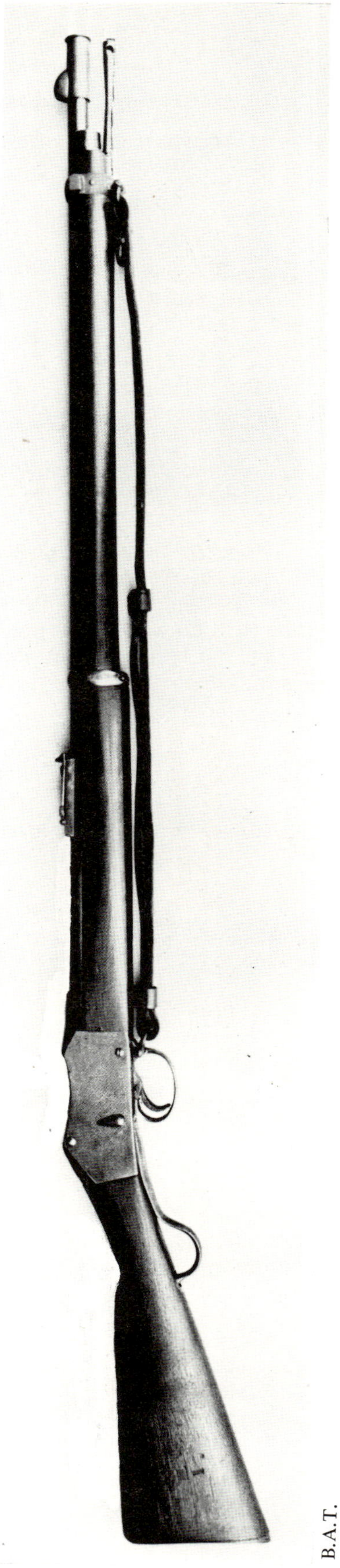
B.A.T.

Fig. 1 – Rifle, Mark III.

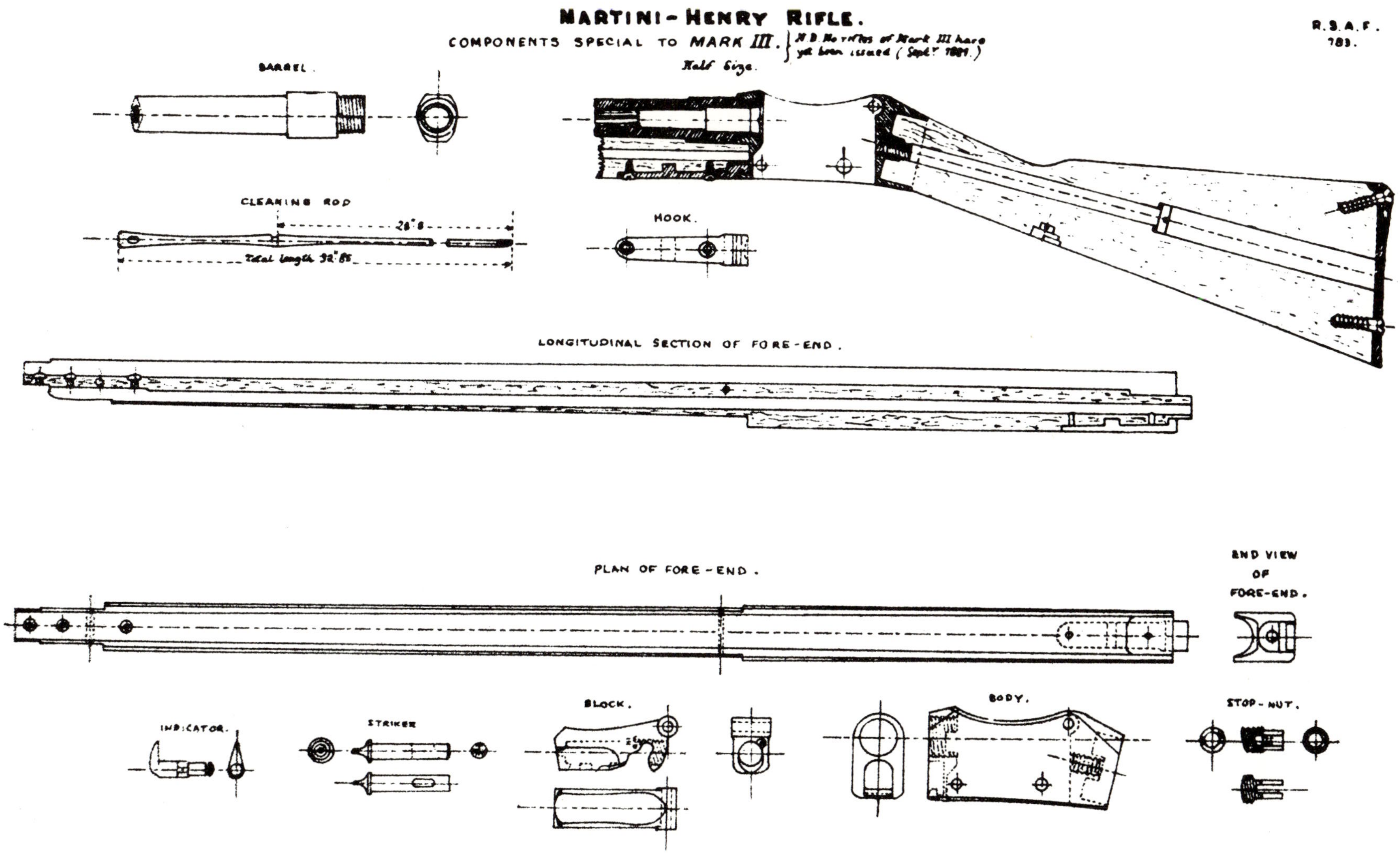

Fig. 2 – Components Special to Rifle, Mark III.

take the under lump on the breech of the barrel. It engages in the body by means of a fore-end hook, which is attached to the fore-end by two screws. The barrel stud stop, and the barrel stud pin are dispensed with.

Hook, fore-end: Is the same as that on the Martini-Henry Carbine, Mark I.

Indicator: The head is made smaller and is the same as in the Martini-Henry carbines.

Stock bolt: The shank is of the same diameter throughout. It is interchangeable for all Martini-Henry arms, and all bolts for such arms will be made of this pattern in future.

Stop nut: The hole in the stop nut is increased 0.010" in diameter. It is the same as in the Martini-Henry carbines. It can only be used in the Mark III block.

Striker: The diameter of the point is reduced 0.002". The shank of the striker, which is cylindrical, is increased in diameter 0.010", and the slot is reduced in width 0.010", in order to give strength to the sides of the slot. The diameter of the collar is increased to 0.560" to make it a sliding fit in the spring chamber of the block. This causes the striker point to be guided clear of the sides of the striker hole in the face of the block. It is the same as for the Martini-Henry carbines. It can only be used with a Mark III block.

Snap caps are not required for this pattern.

The cleaning rod is Mark II (2956).

The maximum and minimum weights of the rifle vary as much as 12 oz, according as the stock is made of heart or sap wood, but the average weight is about 9 lbs.

In the "Instructions for Armourers", issued with Army Circulars, 1st October, 1881, at pages 3 and 4, there is a table showing what spare parts will interchange between the Martini-Henry Rifles Marks II and III, and the Martini-Henry Carbines, Cavalry and Artillery patterns, and the components special to the Mark III rifle are shown in Plate III, appended to those instructions.

ALTERATIONS TO THE SERVICE RIFLE PATTERN

It will be noted in the above description that several changes were made in the Mark III pattern, when compared with the Mark II, and these also are described in detail in Chapter 30, whilst Fig.2 shows the parts special to the Mark III rifle, mentioned as Plate III above.

Dimensions of the RIII were –

Overall length:
    Long butt – 4' 1.5" (1,257 mm)
    Short butt – 4' 1" (1,244 mm)
Barrel length – 2' 9.187" (842 mm)
Overall weight:
    Long butt – 9 lb 1 oz (4.0 kg)
    Short butt – 8 lb 13½ oz (3.9 kg)
Barrel weight:
    Bare – 3 lb 6 oz (1.5 kg)
    With backsight – 3 lb 7¼ oz (1.5 kg)

CHAPTER 15.

MARTINI–HENRY RIFLES, MARK IV

THE history of this mark of M-H rifle could be classed as a continuation of the evolution of the E-M rifle, which had been developed as a replacement for the former arm. The E-M was an improved Martini-type arm, in 0.4-inch calibre, and had been produced in quantity during the 1887-88 work years. However, as its development had taken longer than anticipated, it was rendered obsolescent by the advent and adoption of the 0.303-inch magazine rifle into the British service.

The magazine rifle brought another type of ammunition into service, so, if the E-M had also been issued, its cartridge would have been an additional pattern to supply, making a total of three calibres necessary to supply the needs of the infantry – 0.45-inch M-H, 0.4-inch E-M, and 0.303-inch magazine rifle. This did not include the 0.577-inch Snider ammunition, which was still in demand for volunteers, etc, so four types were actually involved. This number was considered excessive, and it was decided that at least one type of ammunition would be dispensed with for infantry use, so because the 0.303-inch was the latest design, and there were many more arms in 0.45-inch M-H calibre than in 0.4-inch, the last-mentioned cartridge was selected.

The decision to restrict the use of the 0.4-inch cartridge meant that about 65,000 finished E-M rifles were rendered unusable by the infantry; so too were components for many thousands more rifles in various stages of manufacture at Enfield, unless some way could be found to utilise those rifles and components.

As the magazine rifle was not yet ready for production, and as there had been a demand for more Martini rifles for the service – which was the reason the E-M had been produced in such quantity – it was decided to put the E-M rifles into use by converting them into 0.45-inch arms, and at the same time utilise the components of the unfinished arms of that pattern by making enough new weapons to use them up, and subsequently achieve a production total of 100,000 arms.

In WO minutes 33/47 (1888) it is stated that on 17-6-1887 the Supt. RSAF reported that it would cost 5/- per arm to convert the E-M to 0.45-inch calibre. A proportion of barrels, not exceeding ten percent, would probably be spoiled in the operation.

To prove the conversion a prototype Mark IV rifle was prepared, using an E-M RI Second pattern as its base, but with an 0.45-inch barrel with block foresight fitted in place of the original. (Note: It is possible that a standard M-H rifle barrel was used in this instance, as the actual conversions retained the original ramp foresight.) The butt of this new rifle was marked on the left hand side *TO TAKE M.H. CARTRIDGE*, and approval of the converted arm was given

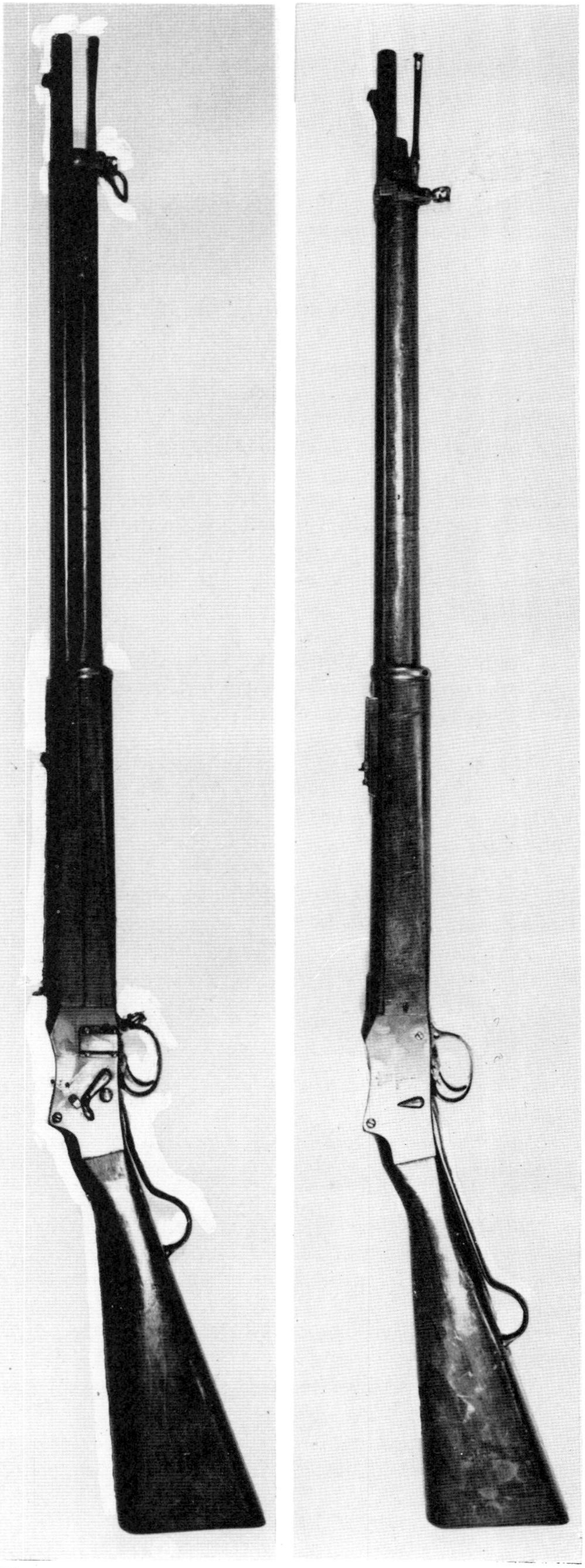

Tower Tower

**Fig. 1 – Enfield-Martini Rifles, Mark I –
Left: First pattern
Right: Second pattern.**

on 15-9-1887.

The converted rifle was given the designation M-H RIV, and was made in three patterns – A, B, and C – necessitated by the nature of the arms being converted or made from parts, as the E-M had been produced as two patterns, viz, Mark I, First and Second patterns. Fig.1 shows these two arms, and the differences between them will be readily seen. The conversions were catalogued as –

Martini-Henry Rifle, Mark IV;

Pattern A: To govern alteration of Enfield-Martini, Mark I, First pattern.

Pattern B: To govern alteration of Enfield-Martini, Mark I, Second pattern.

Pattern C: To govern manufacture of new weapons from parts on hand, or of new manufacture.

For the A and B patterns the conversions included reboring and rifling the barrel, and this resulted in the barrel losing about 0.125" of its length, to 33.062"; whereas the C's barrel, being new made, was to the standard length of 33.187".

One feature of the E-M second pattern rifle incorporated into the converted arms was the lengthened lever, which was intended to give better extraction.

The M-H RIV was entered in the Enfield Pattern Book as –

Martini-Henry Rifle, Mark IV, A, with cleaning rod.
Date of approval: 15-9-1887.
LoC Para: 5603.
Martini-Henry Rifle, Mark IV, B, with cleaning rod.
Date of approval: 15-9-1887.
LoC Para: 5603.
Martini-Henry Rifle, Mark IV, C, with cleaning rod.
Date of approval: 15-9-1887.
LoC Para: 5603.

It was introduced into service by LoC Para.5603 of 1-1-1889 as follows –

Rifle, Martini-Henry, (Mark IV). With cleaning rod.

Patterns of the abovementioned rifle, distinguished respectively as A, B, and C, have been sealed to govern the completion of a certain number of rifles under manufacture.

These rifles differ from Mark III (3998) in the following particulars, viz, –

The body is reduced at the top of the socket in order to give better grip to the right hand.

The block is reduced in thickness, and the angle on the underside is altered, so as to allow of the use of the modified form of extractor.

The extractor is of stronger form, and is ½" longer than Mark III (4793). It has a slot cut in the tail to admit of its passing on each side of the trigger.

The lever is lengthened 3" so as to increase the power of extraction.

Extractor.

Half size.

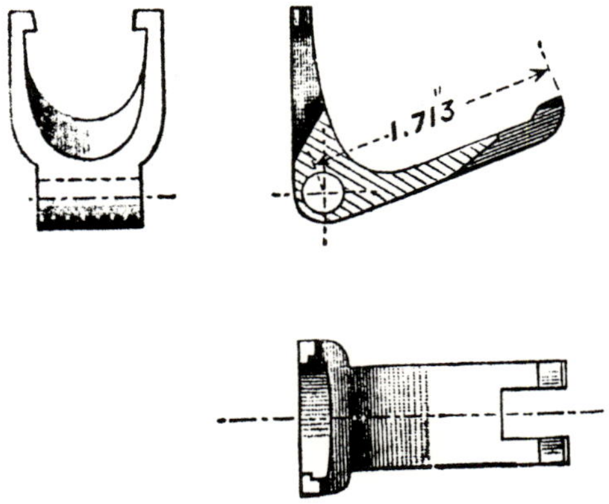

The butt stock is narrowed, and is cut so that the butt plate is at an angle of 84½ degrees with the line of sight instead of 86 degrees as in Mark III.

The butt plate is narrowed, and has a brass liner between it and the stock to prevent corrosion.

The butt screws are made of brass for the same reason.

The lever catch block is made of gunmetal.

The nose cap and rod holder are combined.

The cleaning rod has no cam, but has a recess cut round it at 3¾" from the head, which engages with the rod holder, the shape of the head being slightly altered. The rod is disengaged from the rod holder, for the purpose of withdrawal, by being sprung outwards.

The sighting is the same as in Mark III rifle, except that the rifles distinguished as B and C have the block of the front sight furnished with an inclined plane, as shown in the drawing annexed.

Front-sight.

Full size.

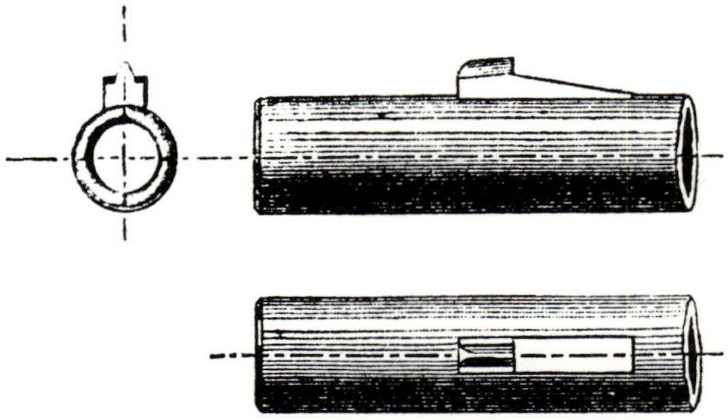

A and B rifles have the barrel 0.125" shorter than Mark III or C Mark IV. A rifles have a slightly shorter knox form on the barrel.

Mark IV rifles are fitted to take the sword bayonet, Pattern 1887 (5604), but not the triangular bayonet.

The undermentioned parts are special to Mark IV rifles other parts being interchangeable with those of Mark III, viz, –

Body

Block
Extractor
Front sight
Lever
Butt plate, with brass liner
Butt stock
Nose cap and rod holder, combined
Cleaning rod.

THE MARTINI–HENRY RIFLE, MARK IV, PATTERN A

The basis for this conversion was the E-M RI, First pattern, which on examination (see Fig.1) is found to exhibit certain features not usually found in British military Martini arms. These features were peculiar to this pattern (and some developmental trials arms), and included an action with safety catch and loop for quick loader; short range sights on top of the nocksform; top handguard; cut-away fore-end exposing most of the barrel; top band with bayonet bar on the bottom; and a special cleaning rod. To obviate rust problems the butt plate was separated from the wood by a thin brass plate, and the butt plate screws were also of brass. The lever catch block was gunmetal, and the lever was of the same length as those fitted to M-H arms.

The conversion of this rifle into a M-H RIV Pattern A (Fig. 2) involved a major reconstruction, as the only original parts usable were the butt and its associated furniture; the breech block and trigger guard unit; and the barrel. Everything else was replaced by new parts of the E-M second pattern or M-H type.

The conversion programme consisted of –

Barrel – Rebored and rifled to 0.45-inch Henry pattern which involved cutting about 0.125" off the breech end to remove the original extractor notches; the thread was extended to the original length, and the barrel rechambered to the new form.

The short range back sight was removed and replaced by a small plate brazed on top of the nocksform. See Fig.3.

The rear sight was replaced by a unit of M-H RIII pattern.

Action – Body replaced by one of the second pattern. Action parts replaced by those of the second pattern where necessary. See Fig.4.

Furniture – Lever catch block repositioned in the butt to accept the long lever; and the original catch position plugged. See Fig.5. (On 21-9-1887 the DoA had approved this conversion on 20,423 butts of E-M RI First pattern, to allow them to be used for the M-H RIV.)

Fore-end and bands replaced by those of the second pattern.

Second pattern cleaning rod fitted. See Fig.7.

Enfield production records show the production years and numbers of E-M RI First patterns made each year as –

1887 – 21,725 Arms, assembled, with cleaning rod
1888 – 7 Arms, assembled, with cleaning rod

thus giving a total of 21,732 produced. The conversion figures then show –

1888 – 21,185 Arms, assembled, with cleaning rods, Mark IV, altered from Enfield-Martini First pattern; and
1889 – 570 Arms, assembled, with cleaning rod, Mark IV, altered from Enfield-Martini First pattern

giving a total of 21,755, which is 23 arms above the figure produced. This is not a large discrepancy, and may have been accounted for by the use of old parts found in store, and which had not previously been assembled into complete arms.

THE MARTINI–HENRY RIFLE, MARK IV, PATTERN B

This rifle, Fig.6, was converted from the E-M RI Second pattern which was similar in appearance to the M-H RIII. Some parts of the second pattern, such as the butt and its furniture, and breech block and some action parts were the same as the first pattern's, whilst others were interchangeable with those of the Mark III, so the conversion was rather simple when compared with that of the first pattern. The programme in this instance consisted of –

Barrel – Rebored and rifled to 0.45-inch Henry pattern which involved cutting and rethreading the breech end as above, so the nocksform and barrel lost about 0.125" as a result.

The rear sight was replaced by a unit of M-H RIII type. All other parts were unchanged.

As the A and B patterns were of the same overall length, and used the same parts, the easiest way to identify the particular pattern is by comparing the foresights. Fig.7 shows the fore-end fittings of both patterns after conversion, and the different types of sight will be noted; also the E-M second pattern cleaning rod. However, it has been suggested from examination of B pattern arms that new parts were sometimes used in the conversions, presumably to replace unserviceable items, and if a new barrel was so used, it would have been of the usual length, so a B pattern in this instance would agree in length with the C,rather than with the A pattern. Notwithstanding this, the number of arms was unaltered, as the production figures for manufactured and converted arms agree exactly, viz –

1887 – 21,487 Arms, assembled, with cleaning rod, 2nd Pattern
1888 – 21,415 Arms, assembled, with cleaning rod, 2nd Pattern; thus giving a total of 42,902 arms made, and

1888 – 3,040 Arms, assembled, with cleaning rod, Mark IV altered from Enfield-Martini, latest pattern; and
1889 – 39,862 Arms assembled, with cleaning rod Mark IV altered from Enfield-Martini, latest pattern

giving a total of 42,902 conversions, which agrees with the

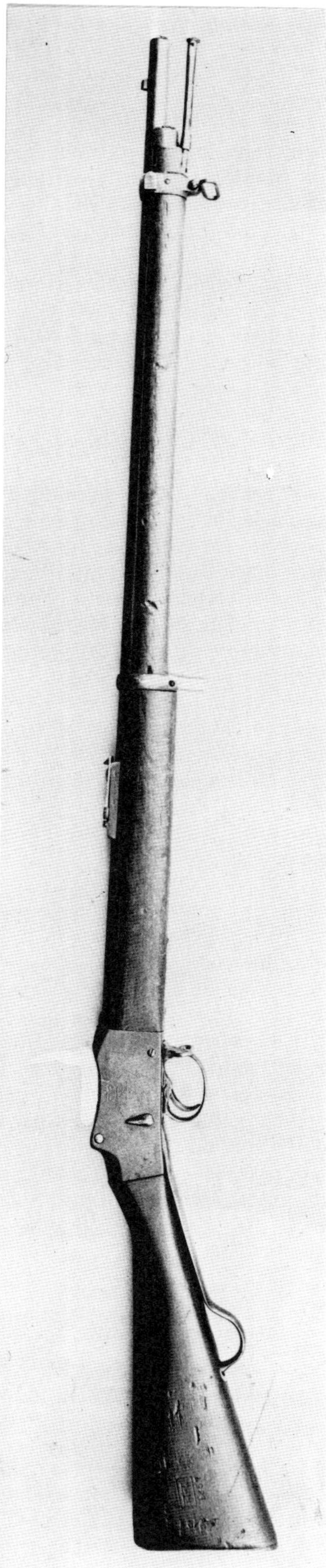

B.A.T.

Fig. 2 – Rifle, Mark IV, A Pattern.

B.A.T.

Fig. 3 – Rifle, Mark IV, A Pattern – Nock's form.

B.A.T.

Fig. 4 – Rifle, Mark IV, A Pattern – Action details.

production total.

The dimensions of Mark IV A and B were –

Overall length:
  Long butt – 4' 1.375" (1,254 mm)
  Short butt – 4' 0.875" (1,241 mm)
Barrel length – 2' 9.062" (840 mm)
Overall weight:
  Long butt – 9 lb 2 oz (4.1 kg)
  Short butt – 9 lb 0 oz (4.0 kg)

THE MARTINI–HENRY RIFLE, MARK IV, PATTERN C

Made entirely from new parts, this pattern (Fig.8) resembled the B in all respects, and could only be distinguished from it by the lengths of barrel and nocksform (which in the new rifle were of the same length as the Mark III rifle),

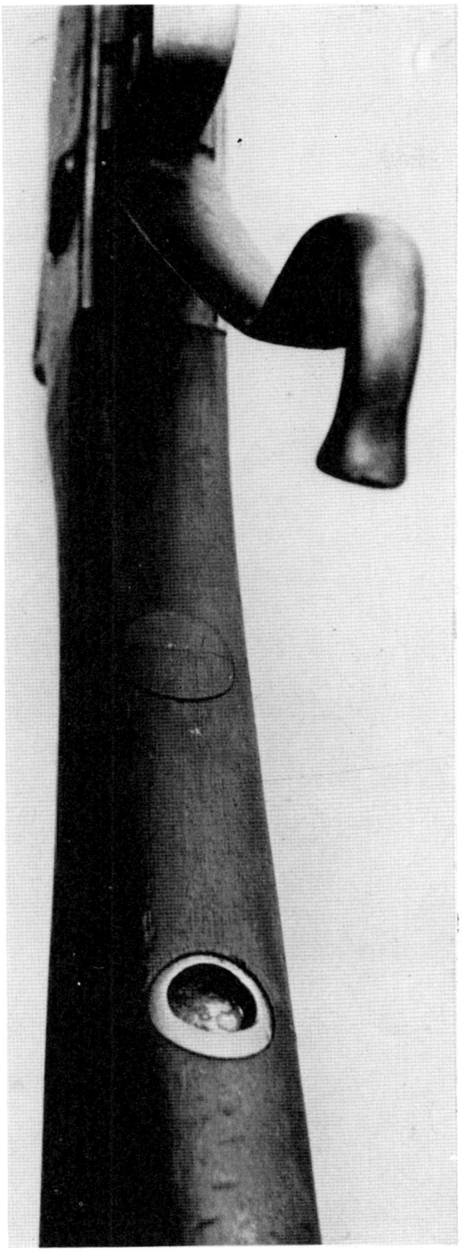

B.A.T.

**Fig. 5 – Rifle, Mark IV, A Pattern –
Butt, showing relocated lever catch block.**

and the action markings (which will be described in a later section). Fig.9 shows the nocksforms of the two rifles – the B will be seen to be shorter as described above.

The C pattern rifles were manufactured as –

1888 – 16,203 Arms assembled, with cleaning rods, Mark IV
1889 – 19,141 Arms assembled, with cleaning rods, Mark IV

giving a total of 35,344 made.

The total production of all patterns of M-H RIV was thus 100,001 arms.

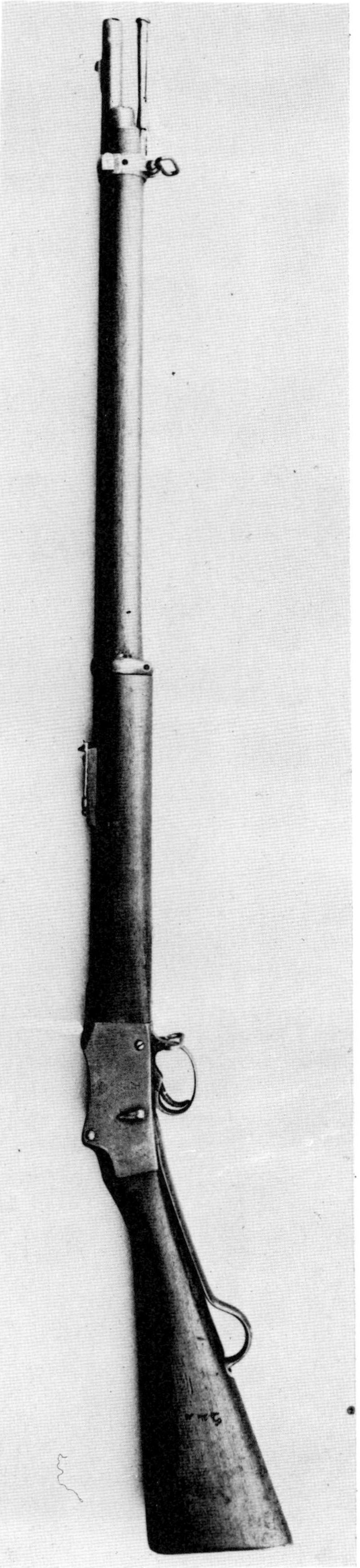

B.A.T.

Fig. 6 – Rifle, Mark IV, B Pattern.

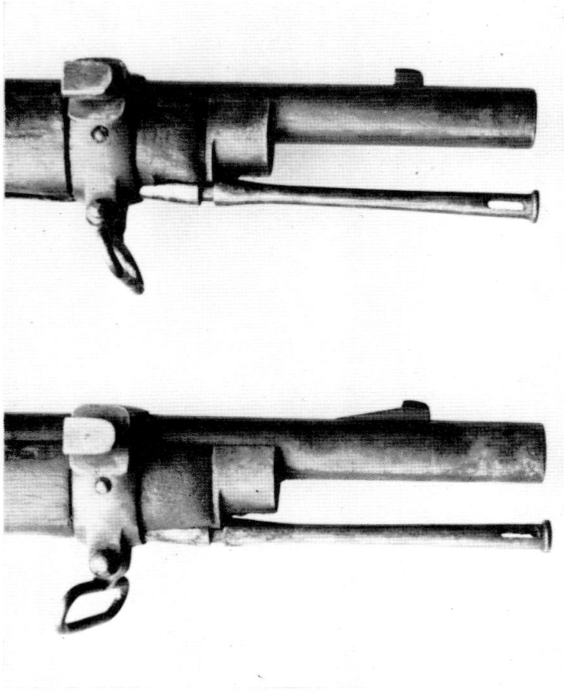

B.A.T.

Fig. 7 – Rifle, Mark IV, A and B Patterns –
Fore-ends, showing different foresight blocks.

The dimensions of C pattern were –

Overall length:
Long butt – 4' 1.5" (1,257 mm)
Short butt – 4' 1" (1,244 mm)
Barrel length – 2' 9.187" (842 mm)
Overall weight:
Long butt – 9 lb 2 oz (4.1 kg)
Short butt – 9 lb 0 oz (4.0 kg)

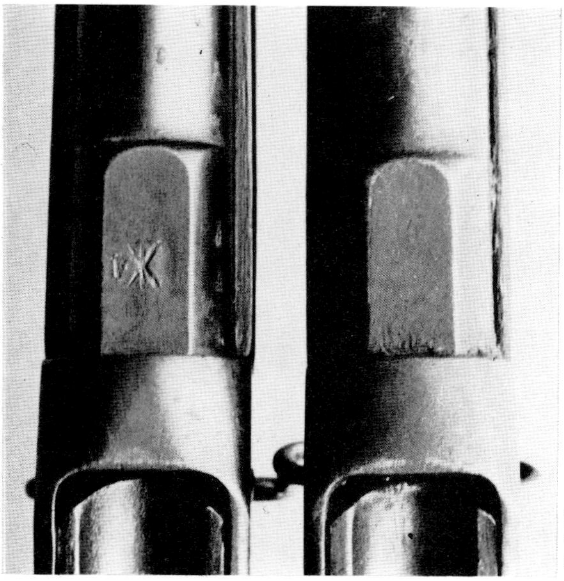

B.A.T.

Fig. 9 – Rifle, Mark IV, Nock's Forms –
Left: C Pattern
Right: B Pattern.

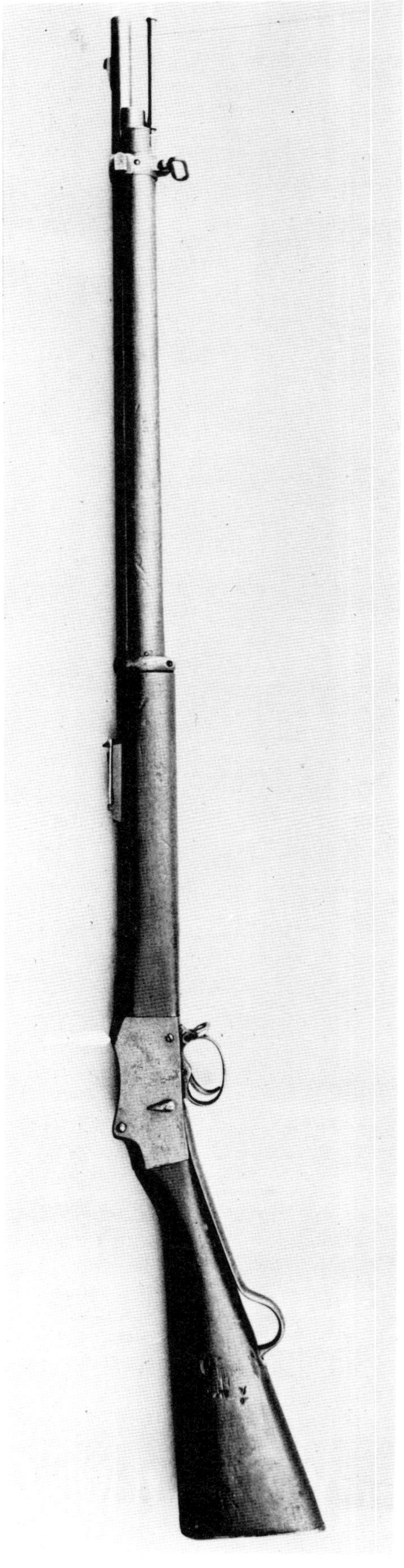

B.A.T.

Fig. 8 – Rifle, Mark IV, C Pattern.

THE ORIGINAL MARTINI–HENRY RIFLE MARK IV

The Mark IV designation applied to the three patterns approved on 15-9-1887 was actually the second time it had been used for a M-H rifle – the first time being in 1881 for a variant of the standard rifle. This briefly came about in the following manner.

In late 1880 the decision was made to appoint a Committee on Martini-Henry Rifles and Ammunition to look into various aspects of the service use of these items, and report accordingly. This committee first met on 18-1-1881, and one decision taken was to try the 0.45-inch solid case Gatling gun cartridge in the M-H rifle, by bushing the chamber to accept that round. This was proposed because there was no solid case cartridge available for the M-H chamber form, and it was thought desirable that a solid case round should be available for use in that rifle.

Approximately 50 rifles were bushed and issued for trial, during April-May 1881, with favourable results regarding accuracy, loading, and extracting, but with above average numbers of mis- and hang-fires. These were eventually attributed to the thicker primer of the machine gun cartridge, which the rifle striker spring was not strong enough to indent fully each time. The Gatling cartridge was prone to misfires in any case, and it was thought necessary to rectify this problem before the final decision to bush all rifles in the service could be made.

However, on 26-8-1881, the Supt.RSAF suggested that if it was intended to adopt the Gatling form of cartridge for the M-H rifle in future, it would be advisable to chamber the rifles about to be made to take the Gatling instead of the service cartridge. This would save the cost of bushing in the future, and the rifles would have solid instead of bushed chambers.

He then requested authority to chamber rifles under manufacture to take the Gatling cartridge, with the comment that if it was eventually decided not to bush the rifles, the chambers could be easily enlarged to take the service cartridge. This action was approved by the DoA on 5-9-1881, and it was then decided on 1-10-1881 that the rifles so chambered should be distinguished as the M-H RIV.

In the meantime, the Gatling cartridge was undergoing modifications to its base and primer, with a new pattern resulting. As the rifle could be fitted to take one pattern of cartridge only, the Supt. RSAF reported in November 1881 that because of this anomaly, it would not be desirable to issue the rifles with a chamber form that would accept unsuitable cartridges only (ie, the original Gatling round), and also, there was the possibility of a new rifle and cartridge being introduced in the near future, so alteration of the existing rifles was not justified under the circumstances. He accordingly requested that his previous recommendations be put aside.

The committee met on 30-11-1881, and discussed the super intendent's report, agreeing with his conclusions. They then recommended that no further steps be taken towards bushing the present M-H rifles, pending the introduction of the new rifle.

The SoS approved the decision on 16-1-1882, and so ended the brief life of the first M-H RIV.

CHAPTER 16.

0.303-INCH MARTINI–HENRY ARMS

AFTER the acceptance for the British service in late 1888 of the 0.303-inch magazine rifle, it was decided that the M-H should also be produced in that calibre, to obviate ammunition supply problems. To that end, a series of arms consisting of conversions of basic M-H patterns was planned and these conversions were initially to consist of rebarreled M-H RII and III, and the M-H CCI. The new 0.303-inch barrels were to be rifled on the Metford system as used in the magazine rifle. The altered arms were to be designated as –

Martini-Henry Rifle –
Mark V (ex RIII);
Mark VI (ex RII); and
Martini-Henry Cavalry carbine Mark II (ex CCI).

Pattern arms were made under those designations.

During 1891 it was decided to alter the nomenclature of the magazine rifle to include the names of the designers of the action and barrel form – as had been done with the M-H – so the magazine rifle became "Rifle, Magazine, Lee-Metford, Mark I". It was then obvious that the converted M-H arms using the same barrel would also require a change of nomenclature, so this was accordingly altered to –

Rifle, Martini-Metford –
Mark I (ex M-H RV);
Mark II (ex M-H RVI); and
Carbine, Martini-Metford, Cavalry, Mark I (ex M-H CCII).

All these changes of nomenclature were approved 8-8-1891.

In a minute of 30-10-1891 the DoA stated that the SoS had approved the rifles and carbines with Martini actions and 0.303-inch barrels being called rifle and carbine, Martini-Metford, and he then directed that the sealed labels on the M-H RV and VI be altered in accordance with the decision recorded above. The CISA replied on 2-11-1891 that the sealed labels had been altered. (Although not mentioned, that for the carbine was also changed.)

As the pattern arms of the M-H 0.303-inch conversions – and some production weapons – were completed before the nomenclature change, it is intended to describe them below as they would have appeared in their original form. Some alterations to the pattern were made after the nomenclature change, but these will be described in a later chapter.

THE MARTINI–HENRY RIFLE, MARK V

This pattern (Fig.1) was to be produced by converting M-H RIII; the conversion including the fitting of a new barrel, breech block, and various related items (see Specification below). The barrel, and the fore-end and its furniture were

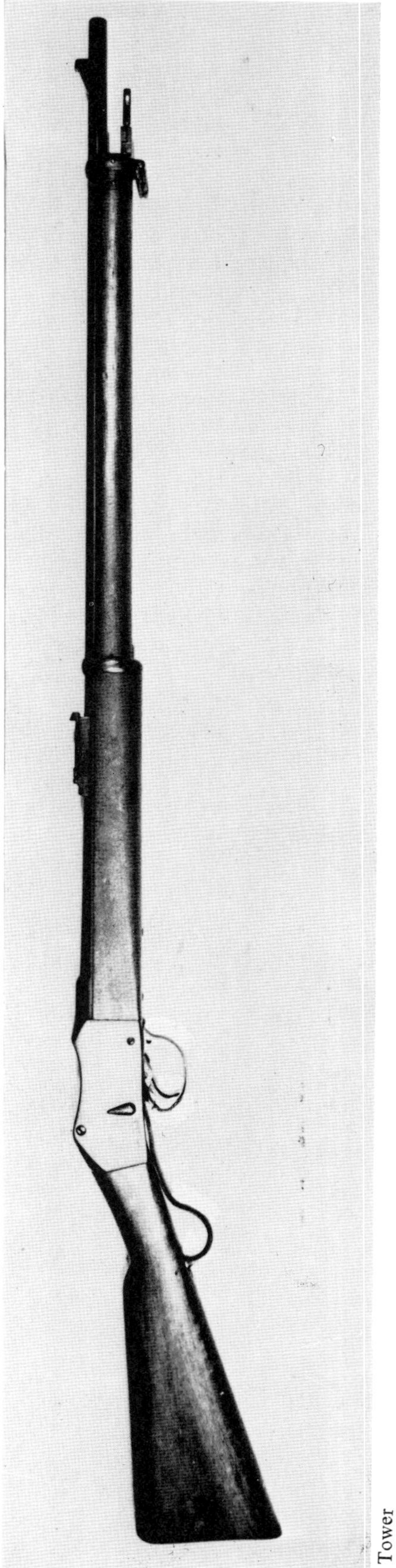
Tower

Fig. 1 – Rifle, Mark V.

patterned on those of the magazine rifle, so the same Pattern '88 sword bayonet was to be used. The M-H RV barrel, as it was kept to the same length as the original Henry barrel, was longer than that of the magazine rifle.

Fig.2 shows the fore-end fittings, in which will be noted the nosecap, incorporating the bayonet bar; the top band with two swivels, one for sling, the other divided for piling arms; and the cleaning rod end. The rod was retained by being screwed into a rod nut brazed onto the end of the fore-end hook.

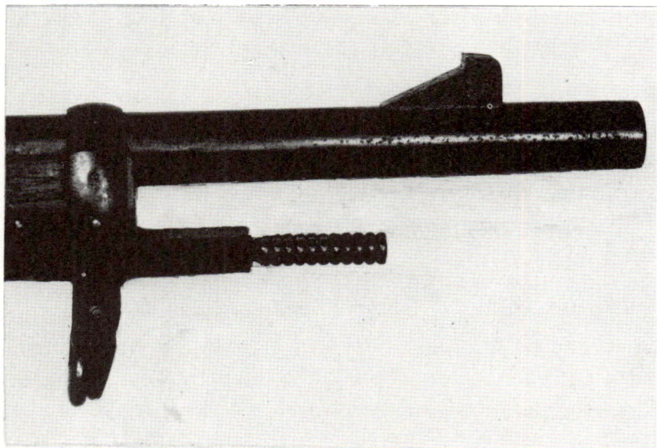

Fig. 2 – Rifle, Mark V – Fore-end fittings. Tower

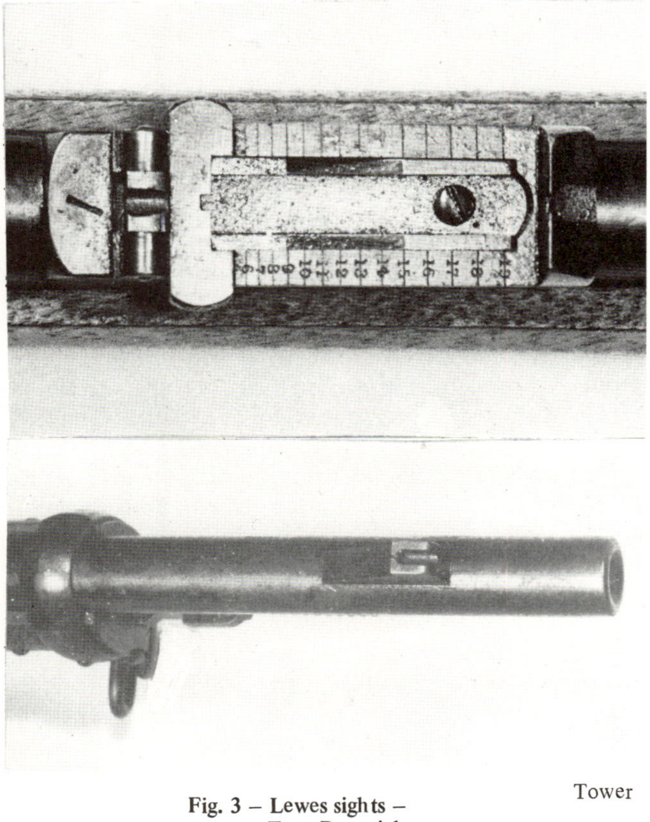

Fig. 3 – Lewes sights –
Top: Rear sight
Bottom: Front sight. Tower

Another feature of the magazine rifle used by this arm was the Lewes sighting system, as seen in Figs.3, and in the Specification drawings. This system was copied from the French and consisted of a square notch rear sight, and a square topped foresight cut with a narrow groove. The backsight leaf was graduated to 1,900 yards, and was intended for black powder cartridges.

This pattern was noted in the Enfield Pattern Book as –

Rifle, Martini-Henry, Mark V (.303). Converted from Mark III.
Date of approval: Approved by SoS 30-7-1889.
Remarks: Nomenclature altered to Martini-Metford, Mark I, by WO papers 8-8-1891.

Its dimensions were –

Overall length – 4' 1.75" (1,263 mm)
Barrel length – 2' 9.25" (844 mm)
Overall weight – 8 lb 12½ oz (3.9 kg)

The specification to govern conversion and inspection of this rifle was approved on 18-2-1890, but it is unlikely that any weapons apart from pattern arms were actually converted. The Enfield production records for the 1890 year show

> "6 Rifles, Martini-Henry, Mark III, fitted with .303-inch barrels and jags, long butt. With drawings and specifications."

It is fairly safe to assume that these were the first of the RV and, for lack of evidence to the contrary, were probably the only arms of the type to be made. At least two specimens still exist, and these do not show any designation of the new mark, only the original M-H RIII markings on the right hand side of the action body.

SPECIFICATION FOR MARTINI–HENRY RIFLE, MARK V

MARTINI–HENRY RIFLE, MARK V, .303", CONVERTED FROM MARK III, 0.45-INCH.

Specification to Govern Conversion and Inspection.

Approved 18th February, 1890.

The rifle to be in general accordance with the sealed pattern, governed by the conditions laid down herein, or the sizes shown on the accompanying drawing RSAF/1231.

. . .

Contractor will be supplied with Mark III 0.45" M.H. rifles. He will utilise the components shown on List "A", and will return those on List "B" to store, replacing them by others of his own manufacture, except in the case of mainsprings, which will be supplied by ordnance factory.

. . .

List A, showing the parts of Mark III M.H. rifle to be used in the conversion –

Block axis pin	*Lever catch block pin*
Body	*Band, lower, screw*

Butt	*Band, lower, pin*
Butt plate	*Stock bolt*
Butt plate screws	*Stock bolt washer*
Extractor axis screw	*Stop nut keeper screw*
Guard	*Trigger*
Guard swivel	*Trigger screw*
Guard swivel screw	*Trigger spring*
Indicator	*Trigger spring screw*
Indicator keeper screw	*Tumbler*
Lever	*Hook, fore-end**
Lever catch block	*Hook, fore-end, screws*
Lever catch block spring	

**This component will be altered to receive the rod nut.*

List B, showing the new components to be supplied by contractor . . .

Barrel	*Band, lower*
Block	*Swivel, piling*
Sight bed	*Rod nut**
Sight cap	*Extractor*
Sight leaf	*Cleaning rod*
Sight slide	*Jag*
Sight spring	*Pin, upper band*
Sight, front	*Pin, back sight leaf*
Striker	*Screws, nose cap*
Stop nut	*Screw, sight cap*
Nose cap	*Screw, sight bed*
Band, upper	*Screw, sight spring*
Band, upper, swivel	*Screw, band, swivel*
Band, upper, nut	*Fore-end***

**The rod nut will be brazed to the fore-end hook, supplied to contractor, vide List A.*
***The fore-ends will be supplied (in the rough) from the Government Stores on repayment, if required, contractor paying carriage.*

(The usual Course of Inspection and Proof followed.)

The specification drawing is shown in Fig.4.

THE MARTINI–HENRY RIFLE, MARK VI

Originally intended to be produced by converting M-H RII in a manner similar to that of the RV, the RVI differed from the latter by retaining an appearance resembling the original M-H arm. This was achieved by making the new 0.303-inch barrel to the same profile as the Henry barrel, and utilising most of the original furniture. The RVI thus mounted the standard M-H rifle sword bayonets, but could not use the socket bayonet because of the form of the foresight block. The sights were of the Lewes pattern (see Figs.3). Fig.5 shows the prototype Mark VI rifle (see text below), and Fig.6 the fore-end fittings. The M-H type band and nosecap will be noted; also the Lewes foresight block, and 0.303-inch type cleaning rod head. Although the fore-end retained the M-H rod holder, the 32.75" long rod screwed into a rod holder nut set into the face of the action body. It would appear that the original rod holder was retained to protect the rod groove from injury when withdrawing or replacing the rod.

There is some confusion as to the date of approval of the Mark VI as a pattern. In its original form it was intended as a conversion of existing arms, but, as it was found there was still a demand for new M-H RII at the time of its inception, it was subsequently produced as a new arm in its own right, using RII components where possible. This led to its being approved again, as a new made weapon, and the Enfield Pattern Book has this entry –

Rifle, Martini-Henry, Mark VI (.303").
Date of approval: 10-1-1890. Sealed 18-6-1891.
Remarks: Sealed in substitution for previous (hand made) pattern. Nomenclature altered to Martini-Metford Mark II by WO papers 8-8-1891.*

*This refers to the prototype mentioned above. This had been hand made as a pattern to govern the conversions, but it was superseded by the pattern listed in the Pattern Book, as this later pattern was intended to govern the future manufacture of the arm. There is an entry in the Enfield production records for the 1889 work year which could indicate the prototype RVI. Under the heading of "Repairs and conversions" is – "1 Arm, assembled, with Martini-Henry stock and action, chambered to take Rubin rimmed cartridge." (The 0.303-inch British cartridge was earlier known as a "Rubin" type, as it was based on the Swiss cartridge of that name.)

The specification to govern manufacture and inspection of the RVI was approved on 7-1-1890, but the order for production had been given previously on 2-5-1889, so it will be noted that the arm had been in production for some months before the pattern arm and specifications were officially approved. The date of approval for the converted arm is not known, if indeed there was one.

All RVI were manufactured by the BSA Co to an order for 9,600 arms. The company at the time was producing M-H RII under a WO contract, and instructions were given to the company on 2-5-1889 by the Director of Army Contracts that that number of arms was to be made in substitution for a similar number of the M-H rifles currently on order. An extra 5/- per rifle was allowed for the change in pattern. As the company was not set up to produce 0.303-inch barrels, arrangements were made for the RSAF to supply 3,000 barrels to enable the manufacture of the RVI to proceed without delay. The following entry in Enfield records for the 1890 year shows this supply – "3,000 barrels, bored and rifled to .303", Martini-Henry rifle, for BSA and M Co."

Fig.7 shows the action and butt of a new production arm compared with the prototype converted weapon. It will be noted that the prototype carries the original action markings and no butt roundel, whereas the production model has normal pattern markings and a butt roundel.

(As an aside here, a note has been found in Enfield records to the effect that "[the Mark VI] rifles were made at Birmingham from sealed pattern M-H RII components, and do not agree in a few minor details with those made at

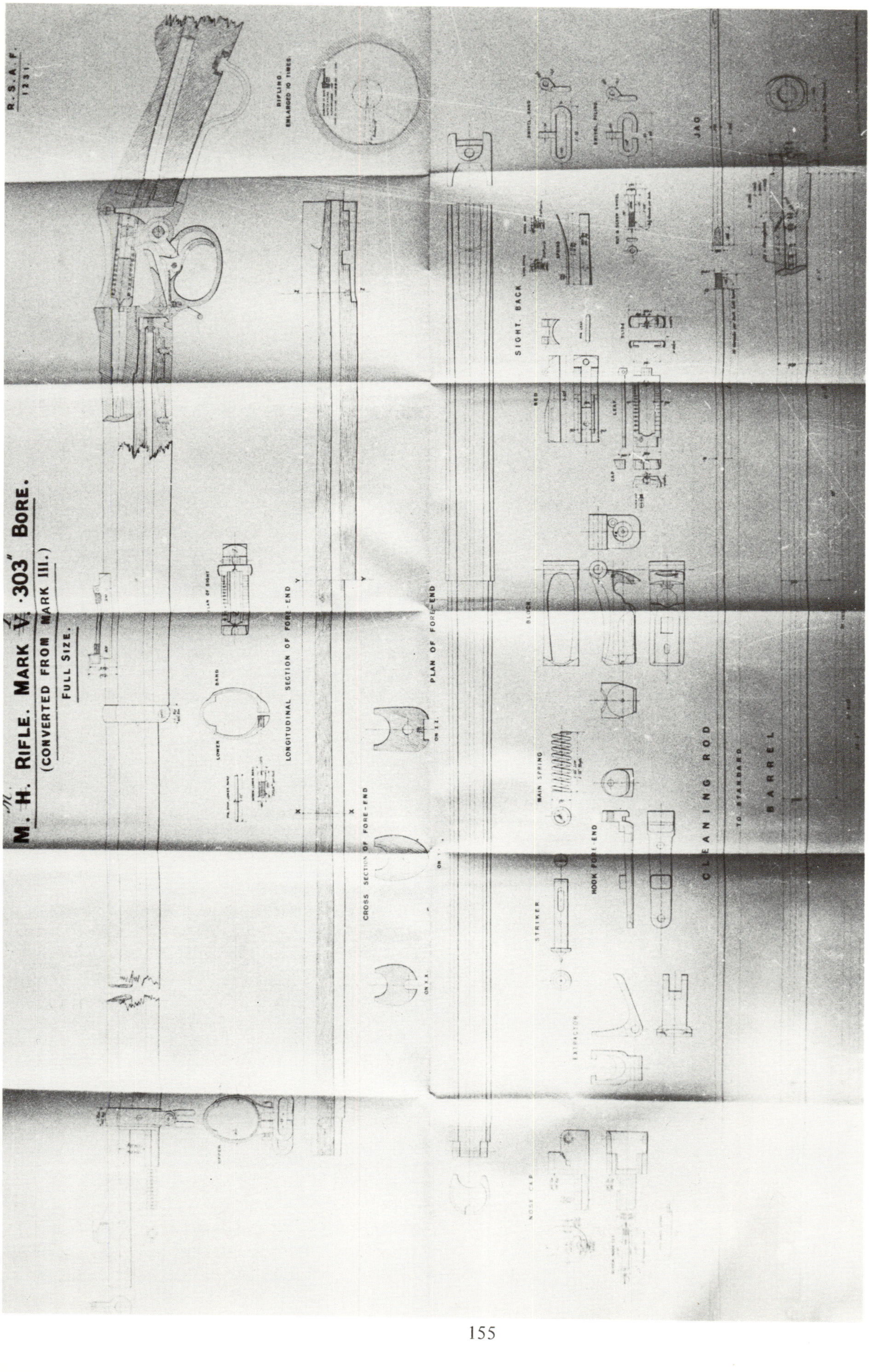

Fig. 4 – Rifle, Mark V – Specification drawing.

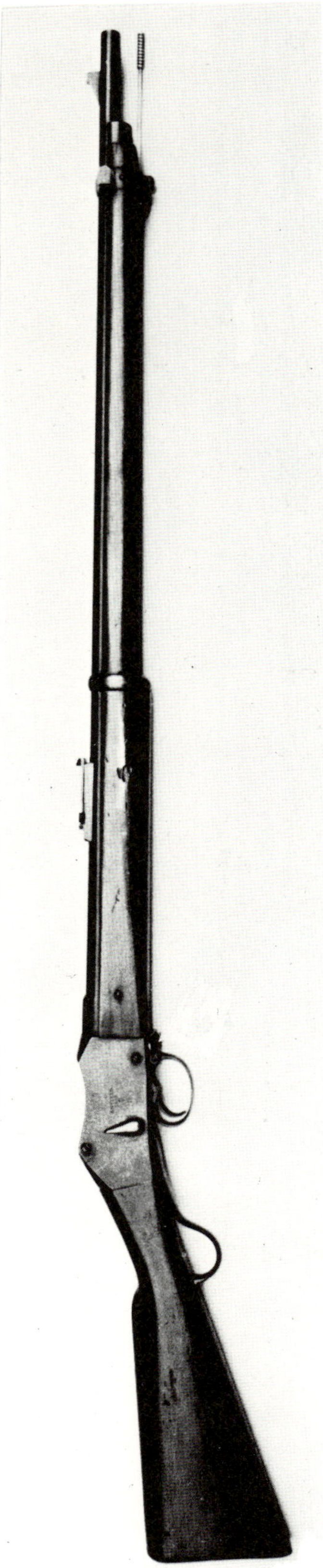

QAD(O)

Fig. 5 – Rifle, Mark VI, Prototype.

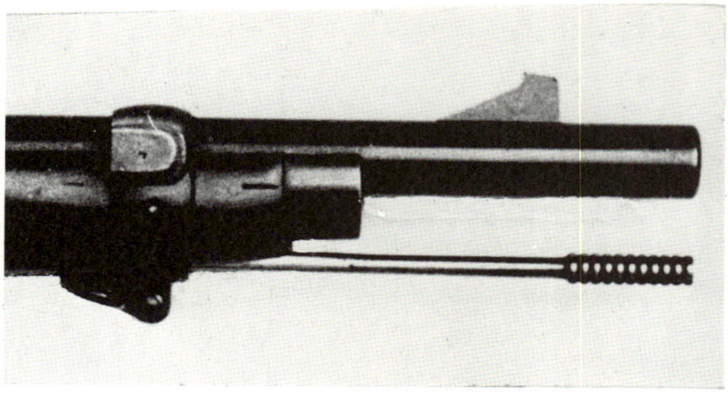

QAD(O)

Fig. 6 – Rifle, Mark VI – Fore-end fittings.

Enfield."

The exact meaning of this statement is obscure, as an examination of production rifles of this pattern disclose that the only apparent deviation from the RII pattern in the relevant parts is in the form of the indicator, which in all instances noted has been of the Mark III pattern with small head. See Fig.7.

However, the statement did say that the differences were "minor", and the different indicator is brought to your attention mainly because it is visibly out of context for the pattern, and no logical explanation has been given for its use, as the correct indicator should have been readily available.)

The Mark VI, or M-M RII as it was later named, was issued mainly to the colonies, and, for all the haste to get it into production, about one half of the arms of this pattern that were made were still in store in 1892, as the following production entry for that work year shows – "4,940 Martini-Henry Mark VI rifles, altering chambers at Weedon."

One reason for the delay in issuing these rifles could be the circumstances leading to the entry in the Enfield Experimental Range Book of 26-9-1890, which stated that 25 M-H RVI had been received on 28-7-1890 for testing. The sighting was found very unsatisfactory, being nearly 300 yards undersighted at 500 yards range. The rifle was declared unfit for issue, and it was recommended that it should be laid before a committee for investigation.

The above seems to indicate that an initial issue of the RVI had been made, and service use had shown that it was badly sighted, hence the tests. As the error was found, the remaining unissued rifles could have been held in store pending rectifications. The sighting of all 0.303-inch British service arms reverted to the standard barleycorn foresight and V notch backsight after the Lewes sights were officially abolished in early 1892, so the Mark VI rifles would have had the sights altered then, and so could be issued at last.

The dimensions were –

Overall length – 4' 1.75" (1,263 mm)
Barrel length – 2' 9.25" (844 mm)
Overall weight – 9 lb 11 oz (4.3 kg)
Barrel weight – 4 lb 4 oz (1.9 kg)
Weight, with bayonet – 11 lb 6 oz (5.1 kg)

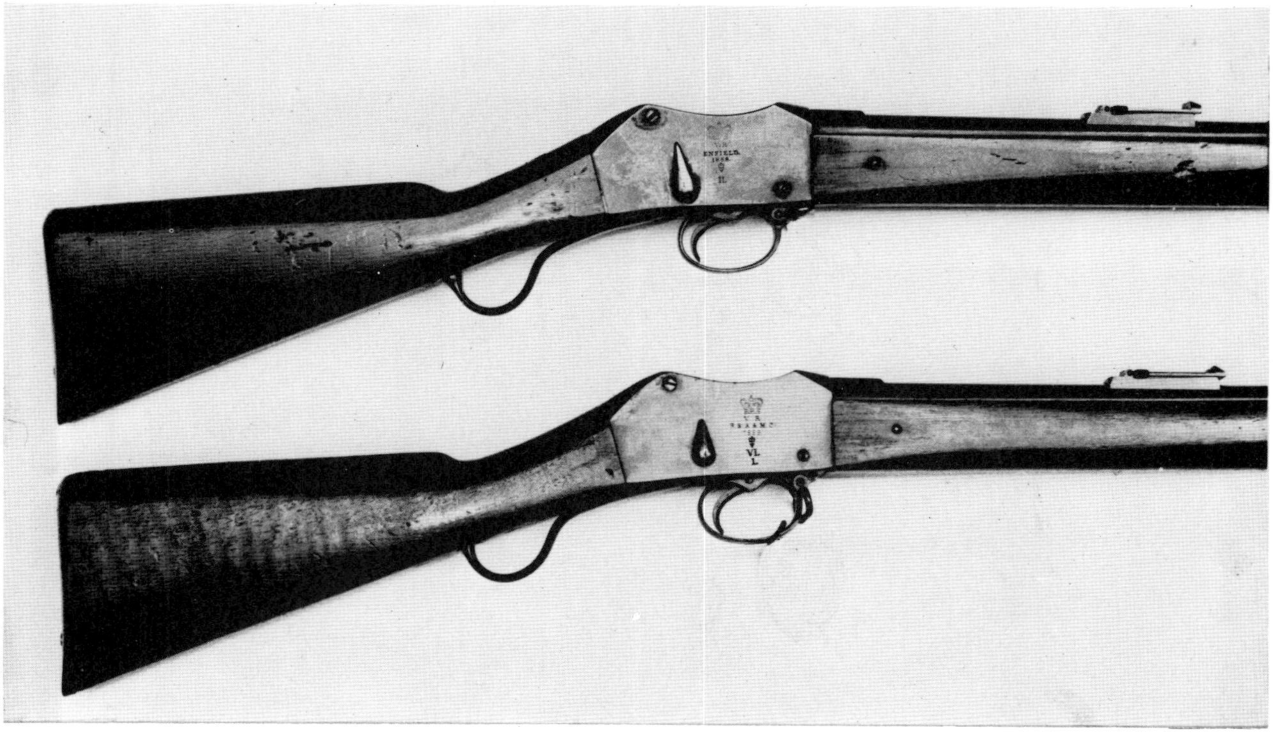

QAD(O)

Fig. 7 – Rifles, Mark VI –
Top: Prototype
Bottom: Production version.

SPECIFICATION FOR MARTINI–HENRY RIFLE, MARK VI

MARTINI–HENRY RIFLE, MARK VI, .303-INCH.

Specification to Govern Manufacture and Inspection.

Approved 7th January, 1890.

The rifle to be in general accordance with the sealed pattern, governed by the conditions laid down herein, or the sizes shown on the accompanying drawing, RSAF/1232

. . .

List showing the parts which will be common to Mark II, 0.45" and Mark VI, .303", Martini-Henry rifles –

Block	*Band, upper, swivel, screw, nut*
Body	*Band, lower*
Butt	*Band. lower, screw*
Butt plate	*Band. lower, pin*
Butt plate screws	*Stock bolt*
Extractor axis screw	*Stock bolt washer*
Guard	*Stop nut keeper screw*
Guard swivel	*Trigger*
Guard swivel screw	*Trigger screw*
Indicator	*Trigger spring*
Indicator keeper screw	*Trigger spring screw*
Lever	*Tumbler*
Lever catch block	*Rod holder*
Lever catch block spring	*Rod holder screws*
Lever catch block pin	*Barrel stud stop*
Band, upper	*Barrel stud pin*
Band, upper, pin	*Nose cap*
Band, upper, swivel	*Nose cap screw*
Band, upper, swivel, screw	

List of parts special to Mark VI, .303" M.H. rifles.

Barrel	*Extractor*
Block	*Cleaning rod*
Sight bed	*Jag*
Sight cap	*Pin, backsight leaf*
Sight slide	*Rod nut*
Sight spring	*Screw, sight cap*
Sight, front	*Screw, sight bed*
Striker	*Screw, sight spring*
Stop nut	*Fore-end**

**The fore-ends (in the rough) will be supplied from the Government Stores, on repayment, if required, contractor paying carriage.*

(The usual course of Inspection and Proof followed.)

The specification drawing is shown in Fig.8.

0.303-INCH MARTINI–HENRY CARBINES

The history of the 0.303-inch M-H carbines is rather involved when compared with that of the 0.303-inch rifles, and is made so because of an overlap into the period when these arms were redesignated as M-M. The basic patterns were developed under the M-H designation, but, with one exception, they were adopted and sealed as M-M. The exception was the M-H CCII, entered in the Enfield Pattern Book as –

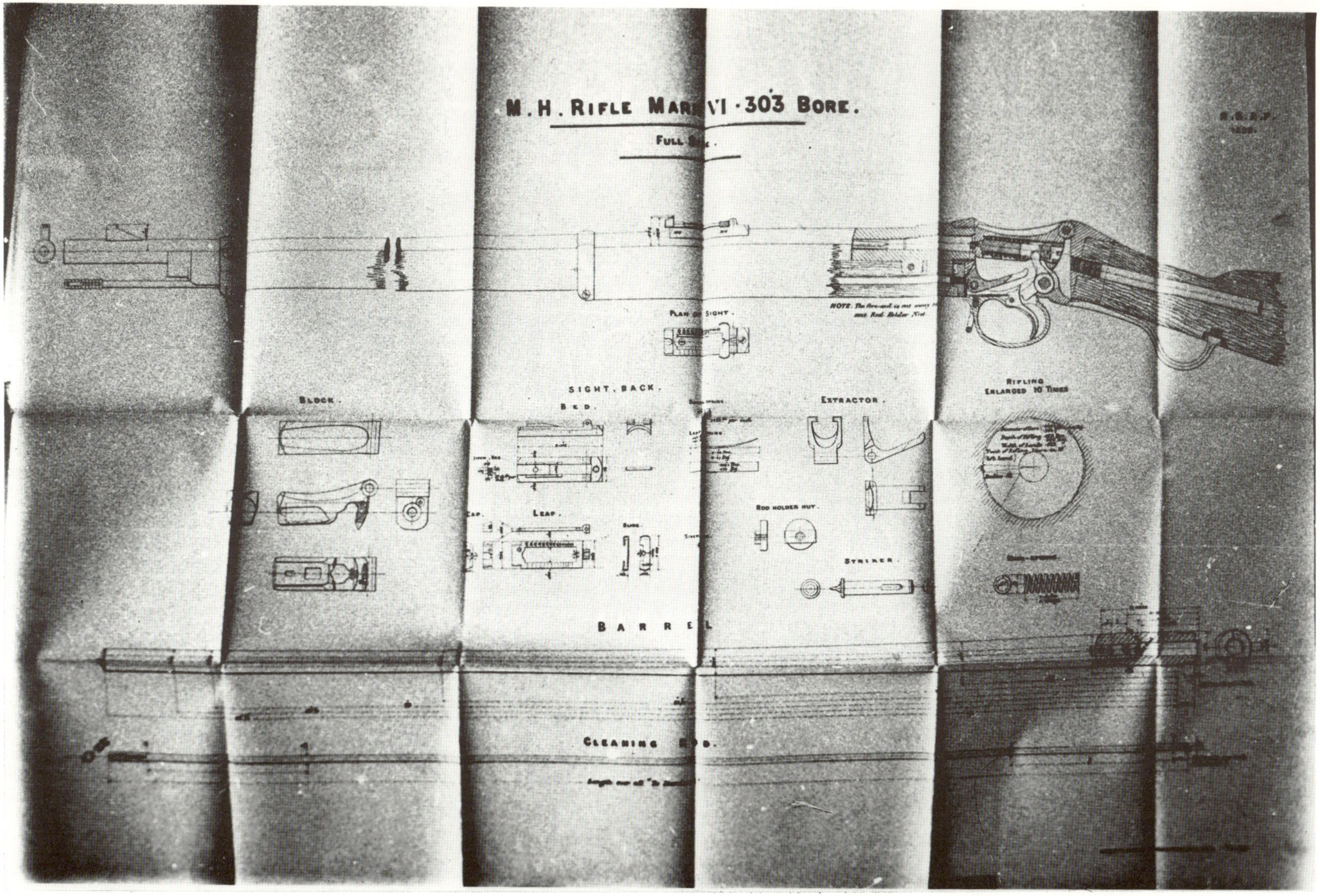

Fig. 8 – Rifle, Mark VI – Specification drawing.

Carbine, Martini-Henry, Cavalry, .303, Mark II.
Date of approval: 1-5-1891.
Remarks: The nomenclature of this carbine altered by WO papers 8-8-1891.

The development of the 0.303-inch Martini carbines started in July 1889 when the C-I-C decided that – as a result of the adoption of the magazine rifle for the infantry – it was essential that the cavalry and horse and field artillery should be able to use a common ammunition with the infantry. He proposed that the cavalry be armed with a magazine carbine, and the others, a single loading carbine of the same calibre. As it seemed there was no probability of a suitable magazine carbine being developed for some time, it was decided that, in the interim, patterns of single loading carbines for both cavalry and artillery should be produced. A programme for developing and testing prototypes for these arms was accordingly instituted.

PROTOTYPE CARBINES

The prototype Martini carbines in 0.303-inch calibre resulting from this programme are shown in several references in the Enfield production records for the work years shown –

1890 –
  3 Carbines, Artillery, Martini-Henry, converted to .303-inch
  3 Carbines, Cavalry, Martini-Henry, converted to .303-inch, with backsight cover
  2 Drawings, Martini-Henry Carbine converted to .303-inch, Cavalry and Artillery (RSAF/1233 and 1234).
1891 –
  1 Carbine, M-H, converted to .303-inch, Artillery
  1 Carbine, M-H, converted to .303-inch, Cavalry.
1892 –
  1 Carbine, M-H, altered to .303-inch, Artillery
  1 Carbine, M-H, altered to .303-inch, Cavalry
  2 Drawings completed, as regards sighting, for Specifications, Carbines Cavalry and Artillery, .303-inch, M-H Converted.
  2 Drawings for Specifications of Carbine, Cavalry, M-H, Mark III.
  1 Drawing of Carbine, Cavalry, M-H, .303-inch, Mark III, converted from Carbine, Artillery, .45-inch, Mark I. (This drawing was RSAF/1231, dated 30-12-1891.)

It would appear that no actual example of the CCIII was produced at this point, but as it obviously existed as a design study that reached the specification stage, it was most likely ready for a sample prototype about the time the nomenclature was changed, and it was indeed later produced as a M-M.

As indicated by the nomenclature these arms would have all been M-H, because even those shown in the 1892 figures could have been completed before the August change of name, as that work year started on the first of April, ie, several months before the name change.

Although one only of these prototype carbines achieved an official designation (viz, the CCII), they were all given a preliminary designation as M-H CCII (Drawing RSAF/1233), and CCIII (Drawing RSAF/1351); and M-H ACII (Drawing RSAF/1234).

After the change to Metford designation, these three patterns ended up as M-M CCI and II, and ACI, respectively.

None of the prototypes has been sighted to allow a positive description to be given, but from a study of the relevant drawings, which were amended in detail only, and the subsequent patterns of M-M carbines, a reasonably accurate representation of each can be given as –

M-H CCII: A simple conversion of the CCI, consisting mainly in having the barrel replaced by one of 0.303-inch calibre but of the same profile, so that the original fore-end and furniture could be used with a minimum of alteration. See Fig.9.

M-H CCIII: A similar conversion of the ACI, with similar comments.

M-H ACII: Conversely, was a conversion of the ACI using the action and butt only, the replacement barrel, fore-end, and furniture resembling those of the magazine rifle, so that all were to be new-made parts. As the muzzle profile and nosecap were the same as for the latter rifle, this carbine was to mount the same bayonet, ie, the Pattern '88 sword bayonet.

(These arms will all be described in greater detail as M-M in the relevant chapter.)

The above 0.303-inch carbines, in keeping with the Martini rifles of that calibre, were fitted with the Lewes sights, which were eventually discarded. As a conversion programme for carbines had been commenced in 1891, it became necessary to change the drawings of the two specifications already completed (RSAF/1233 and 1234), to include the sighting changes, as indicated in the 1892 reference. The new sighting, however, was not entirely satisfactory, and it was not until April 1892 that the pattern arms were fully approved for service and conversion. By that time the arms were M-M, so the subject will be more fully discussed in the section on those arms.

THE MARTINI–HENRY CAVALRY CARBINE, MARK II

This was the only 0.303-inch carbine to be actually named and produced as a M-H. It was approved on 1-5-1891, but kept its name only until August that year, when it was renamed. There were thus a scant three months during which it was known as a M-H. The contract to convert these arms was given to the HRB Co of London some time in 1891, but as the exact date is not known, or when production actually commenced, just how many, if any, were made as M-H is also not known.

The order was for 12,000 arms to meet immediate requirements, and the weapon shown in Fig.9 is one of this batch, but, although actually a M-M, it would indicate the appearance of the M-H CCII.

The carbine's dimensions were –

Overall length – 3' 1.625" (956 mm)
Barrel length – 1' 9,375" (543 mm)
Overall weight – 8 lb 1½ oz (3.6 kg)

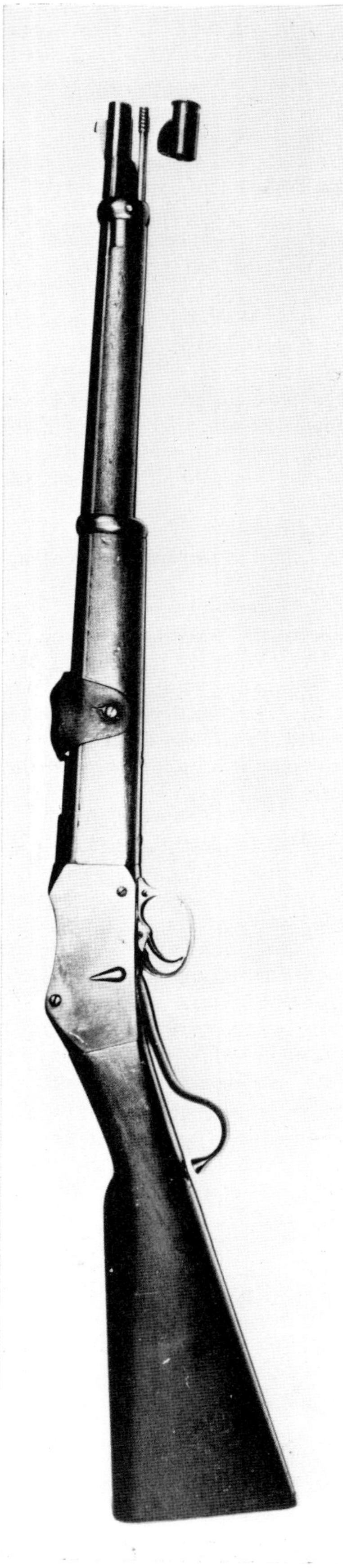

QAD(O)

Fig. 9 – Cavalry Carbine, Mark II.

NAM

A dismounted Lancer at Skirmishing Practice, armed with a Martini-Henry Cavalry Carbine.

APPENDIX 1.

Being details of weapons submitted in response to the WO Advertisement of 21-6-1865; showing the classifications allocated by the sub-committee, and their remarks thereon.

CLASS No.1

Systems Recommended for Trial.

Mr. Jacob Snider. Small bore breech-loading rifle adapted for central fire cartridges on the Lefauchex principle.

1. WO by minute 9-10-65. Forwards for committee's consideration, a letter, 5-10-65, from Mr. Snider, together with a specimen arm, in an unfinished state, but in accordance generally with the terms of WO advertisement.

He requests that this specimen arm may on no account be shown to any person connected with the gun trade. In a few days he will forward drawings and name the cost price at which such guns can be supplied.

The breech-closing arrangement of this rifle is similar to that of the Enfield rifles converted to breech-loaders by Mr. Snider.

2. Mr. Snider attended 20-10-65, and submitted for the committee's consideration a small bore (0.45-inch) rifle on his system. The stock, lock, and fittings are identical with those of the Enfield rifle, and the exterior dimensions of the barrel also correspond with those of the Enfield barrel. The rifle may therefore, in some respects be considered a converted Enfield rifle.

Remarks: For trial.

Mr. B.F. Joslyn, by Mr. E.H. Newby. Breech-loading rifle for metallic cartridges.

WO by minute 9-10-65. Forwards ... a letter, 30-9-65, from Mr. Newby, stating that he has delivered to the OSC a specimen Joslyn rifle with 10 metallic cartridges. The six arms that will eventually be required are nearly ready for delivery.

The specimen rifle has been received by the committee, it does not conform to the dimensions laid down in WO advertisement.

Remarks: An improved cartridge, made with two diameters, had been prepared since this rifle was last considered. Recommended for trial.

Mr. A. Henry, of Edinburgh. Breech-loading rifle adapted for metallic central fire cartridges.

WO by minute 9-10-65. Forwards ... a letter, 29-9-65, from Mr. Henry, with a description of his breech-loading rifle; also a specimen rifle, not in accordance with the dimensions of WO advertisement.

The breech of this rifle is opened and closed by a slide and lever similar to that of Sharp's rifle, but the shape of the slide is altered so as to force home the cartridges, and a hook is added for withdrawing the empty cartridge cases. Two photographs of the rifle are forwarded. No ammunition forwarded.

Remarks: Recommended for trial.

Mr. E. Lindner, of New York. Small bore breech-loading rifle.

WO by minute 9-10-65. Forwards ... a letter, 30-9-65, with specifications, drawings, model arm, and two specimen cartridges from Mr. Lindner. He states that he has conformed to the dimensions of WO advertisement as far as facilities would permit. The ordinary nipple and cap with flanges are used with this rifle. The breech is closed by a plunger, which screws into its place, and is easily freed, as half the screw thread is cut away, so that a quarter turn opens and closes the breech. There is a short lever attached to the plunger for making this quarter turn with. The chamber of the gun is much larger than the bore, the diameters being nearly –

Chamber . . . 0.58-inch
Bore 0.41-inch

The cartridge is of peculiar construction, having a papier mache sabot at the base, with the percussion cap countersunk in it, so that the cartridge is first made use of as a handle with which to place the cap on the nipple. There is a nipple shaped projection on the end of the plunger or breech plug, which fits the hole from which the cap has been taken, and when the gun is fired the sabot is forced hard back on it, so that on withdrawing the plunger the sabot comes with it.

Mr. Lindner also describes a needle gun of his invention, but no specimen is submitted.

Remarks: This system is recommended for trial solely in consequence of the committee understanding that it has received high commendation on the continent, and has been submitted to the Swiss Competition for Military Breech-loaders.

CLASS No.2

Systems Set Aside for Further Examination.

Messrs. Byrnes and Benjamin. Small bore breech-loading rifle.

WO by minute 9-10-65. Forwards ... a patent specification, 31-12-63, of Messrs Byrnes and Benjamin's breech-loading rifle, together with specimen arm and ammunition.

The rifle is identical in principle with those submitted minute 12,805, and it is stated that it can be used indifferently with cartridges with or without a wad at the base. The rifle is in accordance with the dimensions of the WO advertisement. Ordinary percussion caps are used.

Remarks: In this system the breech is closed by a plunger somewhat similar to that of Westley Richards, but is has the disadvantage that any dirt or fouling getting under the plunger cannot be removed without taking the breech arrangement to pieces, and would prevent the breech from closing, and render the arm useless. The cartridge is identical with that of Westley Richards.

Mr. J. Millar. Small bore breech-loading rifle adapted for metallic cartridges.

WO by minute 9-10-65. Forwards ... a letter, 30-9-65, from Mr. Millar, with three specimen rifles and a few cartridges, also a rough drawing and description of the system.

All three rifles are adapted for metallic cartridges with fulminate in the rim of the base. In one of the specimen arms the ordinary form of lock is used, but in the two others a spiral spring presses a piston forward on the rim of the cartridge when the trigger is pulled. The bores of the three specimen arms are 0.450-inch in diameter, but in other respects they do not entirely accord with the dimensions laid down in WO advertisement.

Remarks: Of these three rifles, No.1 and 2 are of the same principle. The manipulation of the breech-closing arrangement is difficult, and the spring catch in all three rifles for withdrawing of the empty cartridge case after firing does not take sufficient hold of the rim of the cartridge, and moreover, the wear of this catch would render it inefficient.

Mr. Henry O. Peabody, of Boston, Massachusetts. Breech-loading rifle.

WO by minute 25-9-65. Forwards ... a letter, 23-9-65, from Mr. Anthony, together with a printed description and specimen of the "Peabody Breech-loading Arm".

It is adapted for the use of metallic cartridges, with fulminate in the rim of the base of the pattern so much used in the United States, and especially by Mr. Joslyn. The working of the breech is somewhat similar to that of Mr. Sharp's rifle. The empty cartridge case is withdrawn after each shot by a simple mechanical arrangement which is worked by the lever, which opens and closes the breech. The calibre of the specimen arm is 0.50-inch, and length of barrel 36".

Remarks: This rifle is open to most of the objections of other American rifles adapted for metallic cartridges. It is heavier than the weight specified in the WO advertisement. The stock is made in two pieces, and the breech action is liable to be fouled by dust and grit.

CLASS No.3

Systems Rejected Summarily.

Mr. E.C. Shepard. Breech-loading rifles for metallic cartridges.

WO by minute 9-10-65. Forwards ... a letter, 29-9-65, from Messrs. Shepard and Newton, describing four different systems of breech-loading rifles adapted for metallic and pasteboard cartridges. They are all modifications of the system submitted as applicable for conversion of the Enfield rifle.

He states that 20,000 carbines are being made for the United States Government on plan No.1, which is adapted for metallic cartridges with fulminate in rim of base. Plan No.2 is adapted for central fire cartridges similar to those of Snider's system.

Rifles on Plans 4 and 5 are being constructed by the Belgian Government. Drawings only of these rifles are forwarded.

It has been found impossible to make guns of the exact calibre specified in WO advertisement within the prescribed time, and therefore the specimen arms of Plans 1 and 2 must only be looked on as models of the systems proposed to be used. 20 central fire cartridges for Plan No.2 are forwarded.

Remarks: Mr. Shepard submits four systems of construction, all strongly resembling each other in principle, but only specimens of two systems before the committee can alone be considered. Of these, No.1 is a very clumsy contrivance, having none of the merits of the original system proposed by Mr. Shepard. The action of the lock is awkward, the hammer requiring to be pulled back to too great a distance. The method of withdrawing the empty cartridge case is also unsatisfactory, necessitating an extra motion and the existence of an additional spring. This rifle has also the disadvantage that any dirt falling between the hammer and the breech stopper would render it unserviceable until taken to pieces and cleaned. No.2 is free from this latter defect, but the lock is very poor. The stocks of both, from being cut in two, are so much weakened as to render them unserviceable for use with the bayonet.

Mr. S. Norris, United States. Small bore breech-loading rifle for metallic cartridges.

WO by minute 9-10-65. Forwards ... a letter, 30-9-65, from Mr. Norris, stating that the rifle he had intended to submit has not yet arrived from America, but he forwards one, with a packet of ammunition, on the same principle, which has been patented in this country by Mr. W.E. Newton, 18-1-65. The rifle is adapted for the use of a metallic cartridge with fulminate in the rim of base. The breech action bears some resemblance to that of Mr. Shepard's rifle. Specification and drawings forwarded.

Remarks: This system is open to the same objections as No.

1 of Mr. Shepard, viz, that any dirt falling into the space between the hammer and breech stopper would render the arm quite unserviceable. The stock is also weakened by being cut in two.

Mr. T. Craig. Breech-loading rifle adapted for the use of the central fire Lefaucheux cartridge.

WO by minute 9-10-65. Forwards . . . a description, 30-9-65, with drawing by Mr. Craig, of his system of breech-loading rifle. It is adapted for the use of a central fire cartridge similar to Snider's. The striker which fires the cartridge is worked by a spiral spring. A specimen arm is forwarded, together with a packet of suitable ammunition.

Remarks: The breech closing arrangement of this rifle has too many parts, and is too complicated for military service. The care necessary in placing the cartridge exactly in the proper position when loading would prevent its being fired with any degree of rapidity, and is a sufficient cause for rejecting it.

Mr. J. Needham. Breech-loading rifle for metallic cartridges.

1. WO by minute 12-10-65. Forwards . . . . a letter 10-10-65, from Mr. Needham, with a specimen rifle carbine and cartridge. The cartridge is identical with that of Snider's system. The lock and piston for striking the cartridge are contained in the breech stopper, which is worked by a lever and to which is also fixed an arrangement for withdrawing the cartridge case a short distance after being discharged. The act of closing the breech by means of the lever at the same time cocks it ready for firing.

Mr. Needham forwards a metallic cartridge of a different description, but sends no rifle for which it is adapted.

2. Mr. Needham attended 20-10-65, and submitted a second rifle on his system, but not in accordance with WO specifications. Like the first it is adapted for metallic cartridges. The breech stopper, with lock, hammer, trigger, and trigger guard work on a hinge below the barrel, the action of opening and closing the breech being similar to that of Sharp's rifle. In opening the breech the cartridge case of the previous round is withdrawn by a catch.

Remarks: Two systems of breech-loading rifles are submitted by Mr. Needham. The lock mechanism in both cases is too complicated for a military arm, and the stocks are too much cut away and weakened.

Mr. W.J. Mathews, of Birmingham. Breech-loading rifle adapted for central fire Lefaucheux cartridge.

WO by minute 9-10-65. Forwards . . . a letter 4-10-65, from Mr. Mathews, with patent specification, 30-11-64, together with a specimen rifle and packet of ammunition. The rifle is somewhat similar to that of Mr. Snider, and is adapted for the same kind of cartridge. The method of withdrawing the old case is different, the cartridge being caught on both sides and being drawn fairly back. The breech stopper has an action similar to the chamber of Storm's rifle. The dimensions of specimen rifle do not correspond to those of WO advertisement.

Remarks: This rifle, adapted for a cartridge similar to that of Snider's system, and firing by a piston in the same manner, is in other respects inferior. The special method of with drawing the cartridge case for which Mr. Mathews takes credit is a slower process than with Snider's system. As Mr. Snider's plan invariably succeeds in withdrawing the cartridge, the supposed improvement of having a double claw for the purpose is more than counterbalanced by the increased number of motions necessary in loading.

Captain Albini, Italian Army. Breech-loading rifle for metallic cartridges.

WO by minute 9-10-65. Forwards . . . letters, 30-9-65, and 7-10-65, from Mr. Roberts, with specimen rifle and self-igniting cartridges on Captain Albini's patent principle.

The rifle is in accordance with dimensions laid down. The breech action is exactly the same as that of the rifle submitted by Captain Albini, Minute 14,220, but the method of firing is different. In place of the nipple is a vertical piston with a spring to sustain it, the inner end of this piston strikes a percussion arrangement at the base of the cartridge.

The cartridge is peculiar, having a copper cup and a brass cap holder at the base. The brass cap holder consists of a transverse tube with a copper cap at each end, and a wire between them, a communication hole from the centre leads to the cartridge. The point of the plunger is fitted to receive the brass cap holder, and to retain it in such a position that the piston will strike the uppermost cap. The fore part of the cartridge is of paper, of the same consistency and thickness as that in Westley Richards' cartridges.

The estimated price of making these rifles in large numbers is£3 each.

Remarks: The breech-closing arrangement of Captain Albini's rifle resembles that of a rifle previously submitted, Minute 14,220. Escape of gas at the breech is in the present case prevented by the use of a special and complicated cartridge having a copper cup at the base, and a metal cap holder. This complication of the cartridge and the necessary loss of time in loading are sufficient reasons for rejecting this rifle.

Mr. Poppenburg, by Messrs. Benson and Co. Needle gun.

WO by minute 9-10-65. Forwards a letter . . . 30-9-65, from Messrs Benson, together with description, drawings, specifications, and pattern needle gun, with ammunition on Poppenburg's principle. The action of the needle is similar to that of the Prussian needle gun, but the method of closing the breech resembles that of Storm's system. A chamber opens sideways on a hinge by means of a spring, the back of the chamber is perforated to admit of the passage of the needle. The rifle is made in accordance with the dimensions of WO advertisement.

The bullets have a copper cap placed in a cavity at the base, and the needle advancing through the powder strikes the cap and ignites the charge.

The estimated cost of these rifles is –
For quantities under 5,000 . . . . £ 6 each
For quantities above 5,000 . . . . £3 each.

Remarks: The opening of the breech is entirely dependent on the action of a spring, which in the specimen arm before the committee is most uncertain. The cartridge case is made of prepared combustible paper or calico. The breech action is much too complicated, and liable to accident for a military arm.

Mr. J.F.C. Carle, of Hamburg. Improved needle gun.

WO by minute 21-10-65. Forwards a letter, 19-10-65, from Mr. Beckwith, with drawings, descriptions, specimen arm, and 20 rounds of ammunition of an improved needle gun invented by Mr. Carle. In opening and closing the breech the whole barrel is made to move back and forward, and when forward the weight of the front part lifts the breech up sufficiently clear of the stock for loading. The lever which moves the barrel back and forwards is underneath the stock in front of the trigger guard. It has to be moved through a half circle. This lever also cocks the gun.

The ammunition consists of a paper cartridge with felt wad at the base, the fulminate being on the inner side of the wad in a little metal capsule placed in the centre of a papier mache wad. The needle therefore has only to penetrate a little more than the thickness of the wad at the base of the cartridge.

The inventor is not prepared to state definitely what the cost of manufacture would be, but is of opinion that it would not much exceed that of the present Enfield rifle.

Remarks: The break off in the barrel of this rifle renders it quite unfit for military purposes. The manipulation of the breech action is also very difficult, and would be almost impracticable to a mounted soldier. It is very liable to strain when the breech is open.

Mr. Charles A. Luok, of Suhl, Prussia. Improved needle gun.

WO by minute 21-10-65. Forwards a letter, 9-10-65, from Mr. Luok, offering a newly invented needle gun to the British government. He enumerates the advantages which it has over the needle gun, viz, lightness, simplicity, strength, applicability to the conversion of existing rifles of any description, &c, &c. He also offers on conditions of secrecy to disclose the secret of the fulminating composition in the Prussian needle gun cartridge.

No specimen is submitted. The estimated cost of conversion to this system is £1 per arm.

Remarks: The absence of a specimen rifle and the vague explanations of Mr. Luok are sufficient reasons for rejecting this system.

Lieut. G.S. Hughes, 3rd Manchester Volunteers. Small bore breech-loading rifle (Muir's Patent).

WO by minute 9-10-65. Forwards a letter, 19-9-65, from Lt. Hughes, forwarding a specimen rifle on Muir's patented system, which he wished to enter in the forthcoming competition. The rifle does not agree in dimensions with the terms of the WO advertisement except as regards the diameter of the bore.

It is adapted for the use of a paper cartridge and ordinary percussion cap. The breech is closed by a stopper, worked by a small lever behind the hammer. The fore part of the plunger or stopper falls down when the breech is open, and is raised and pushed a very little forward by the action of the lever when closing the breech. No specimen ammunition forwarded.

Remarks: Breech arrangement not sufficiently secure. It is evidently inferior to Westley Richards' system, the cartridge requiring to be pushed quite home into the chamber before the plunger or breech plug can rise to close the breech.

Mr. E. Della Noce. Small bore breech-loading rifle.

WO by minute 9-10-65. Forwards a letter, 29-9-65, with description and drawing, also a model arm received from Mr. Della Noce, agreeing in some respects with the terms of the WO advertisement. The rifle is on the same principle as that proposed for the conversion of the Enfield rifle by Mr. Della Noce, Minute 15,457. He states that the cost of this rifle would be from 6 to 8s greater than that of ordinary arms.

Remarks: The only peculiarity worth noticing in this rifle is the ingenious method of capping already reported on by the committee, Report No.3,777, Minute 15,618. This system of capping, however, necessitates a very indirect communication from the nipple to the chamber, and would be very likely to cause misfires. The construction of the lock is special, and was reported against in the abovementioned report.

Mr. Carr. Patent breech-loading small arm.

WO by minute 9-10-65. Forwards a specimen breech-loading rifle on Carr's Patent principle. The breech of this rifle is closed in a manner similar to Wilson's or Green's method. The ordinary percussion cap is used. The specimen rifle does not correspond to the dimensions laid down.

Remarks: The breech of this rifle is closed in a manner somewhat similar but not so secure as Wilson's system reported on in Report No.3621, Minute 14,414. A cartridge similar to that of Westley Richards' would have to be employed, and as it appears in every way inferior to that system, which is already to a considerable extent in the service, the committee cannot recommend a trial.

General Timmerhans, of Liege. Breech-loading rifle.

WO by minute 9-10-65, forwards a book by Gen. Timmerhans, on the subject of small arms, published in 1865, and containing a description of his system of breech-loading for rifles. A specimen rifle with 20 cartridges is also forwarded. This rifle does not correspond to the dimensions prescribed by WO.

Remarks: The breech closing arrangement of this rifle is not so simple as that of many other systems (Westley Richards' included) in which the breech is closed by a bolt or plunger. The interrupted screw is very liable to wear.

Mr. C.P. Aston. Breech-loading rifle.

WO by minute 28-10-65, forwards a letter, 24-10-65, from Mr. Aston, together with a specimen rifle of his invention, which he states is similar to that approved as a military arm by the French government. The rifle is similar to that of Prince, the whole barrel sliding forward from the breech by the action of the lever. The rifle in no way corresponds in dimensions to the figures of WO advertisement. The ordinary nipple and cap are employed.

Mr. Aston states that from 31 to 35 rounds can be fired in one minute from this rifle. No description or specimen of the cartridge is sent.

Remarks: This rifle is identical in principle with that proposed by Mr. Prince in 1858, and reported on unfavourably by the Small Arms Committee, 10-8-58, on WO papers, 81/W/82. The fact of it being necessary to move the whole barrel in the stock for the purpose of loading is a sufficient reason for rejecting it for military purposes. Considering that a percussion cap is employed, the rapidity of fire stated by Mr. Aston appears to the committee altogether unattainable.

APPENDIX 2.

Being notes of examination of the under-mentioned breech-loading arms referred to as Class 1 and 2. To be annexed to the report of the sub-committee submitted on 27-10-1865. (See Chapter 1.)

Name of Inventor	Weight of arm complete	Weight of barrel and action	Remarks
	lbs. ozs.	lbs. ozs.	
Snider	9 0	4 11¼	This arm is manufactured in a sound workmanlike manner, the construction of which is well adapted for the Enfield machinery, and would be cheaply made. The conditions of the advertisement appear to be adhered to.
Henry	9 0	5 1	This arm is manufactured in a workmanlike manner, but more like a sporting gun than a military arm; the lock is special, similar to the Westley Richards' now being made at Enfield. The stock is cracked near the end of the lock, and appears to have been glued. The construction of this arm appears complicated and less suited to the Enfield machinery than the Snider arm, and more expensive to make. The conditions of the advertisement appear to be generally adhered to.
Joslyn	8 13	4 15	The manufacture of this arm, so far as the barrel and breech arrangement is concerned, is sound and workmanlike. The lock is very inferior, and the stock has been mended at the end of breech. The construction is entirely American, and no attention has been paid to the conditions of the advertisement. The system, if approved, could be made more suitable to the Enfield pattern and machinery.
Lindner	10 15½	6 6	This arm is manufactured in a workmanlike manner upon the Swiss system. The stock is very much cut away at the head, and is quite unserviceable. The conditions of the advertisement have in

					no way been adhered to.
Brynes & Benjamin	9	5	5	13¾	This arm is manufactured in a sound workmanlike manner, and could be readily made by the Enfield machinery, which would require some alteration and adjustment. The construction appears simple and secure. The conditions of the advertisement appear to be generally adhered to, with the exception of the weight.
Millar	9	0½	4	7½	This arm is manufactured in a workmanlike manner, but the stock is broken near the head, where it is very weak, and it is not serviceable. The breech arrangement appears doubtful as to its proper working. The conditions of the advertisement appear to be adhered to.
Peabody	9	12¼	–	–	This arm is manufactured in a sound workmanlike manner, the breech arrangement appears complicated and expensive to manufacture. The construction is such as to necessitate the adoption of a back action lock, and would require much special machinery to make it. No attention whatever has been paid to the conditions of the advertisement.

APPENDIX 3.

Being the details of weapons considered eligible for consideration for the Prize Competition, having complied with the terms of WO Advertisement of 22-10-1866; showing the classifications allocated by the sub-committee, and their remarks thereon.

CLASS I. LIST A.

Systems Summarily Rejected.

J. Boucher – The extractor of this rifle is slow in its action, and any accumulation of sand or dirt at the bottom of the shoe is pushed forward by the extractor, and is likely to obstruct its action, and prevent the closing of the breech.

Lt. F. Bacon, RMA – The incomplete state of this rifle, and the difficulty of loading, are sufficient to warrant its rejection.

Carter & Edwards, No.2 – The extractor is uncertain in its action, and there are frequent misfires.

E. Colley – This rifle shows a decided want of accuracy with the ammunition sent in. There is nothing to prevent the cartridge being pushed beyond the reach of the needle during the action of loading, or the cartridge may be shaken forward by a violent jerk when the gun is carried loaded.

Callisher & Terry – This rifle needs to be held firmly and in a horizontal position whilst loading, to prevent the breech block from closing, or the cartridge from falling out on the ground; it also appears that the prevention of the escape of gas in front of the chamber depends on the accurate fitting of two surfaces which are liable to become worn or rusted.

H. Dines – The sub-committee do not consider the bolt at the side a sufficient substitute for the half-cock position of an ordinary lock. The rifle can be fired before the breech bolt is securely fastened. The spring at the side which holds the tail piece of the breech bolt is delicate and uncertain in its action.

T.A. Edgley – The bolt which is intended to secure the breech bolt at the time of firing does not answer its purpose. Should any accident happen to the spring which works the stud of the extractor, the rifle would be rendered unserviceable. The extractor is also found to jam if the rifle be held muzzle upwards whilst opening and closing the breech. The trial was not completed, as the breech block was blown violently open, and some pieces of the cartridge were driven into Mr. Edgley's face.

C. Fougeroux – The breech mechanism of this rifle failed in its action. In firing for rapidity the extractor broke off, and the trial was discontinued.

Gray – The sub-committee think that the breech arrangement of this rifle is simple and strong; the cartridge however, is liable to be placed in front of the extractor, in which case the breech cannot be closed, and considerable difficulty is experienced in withdrawing the case.

A. Henry, No.3 – A separate motion is required to extract the cartridge, which prevents sufficient rapidity of fire from being attained.

Le Penotiere – The rapidity of fire of this rifle is satisfactory. The shooting was extremely inaccurate. There was an escape of gas at the breech, and the number of springs in the breech mechanism is objectionable.

Pringle – In the trial for rapidity, the firing was very slow, and the sub-committee do not think it likely that the necessary rapidity could ever be attained. The mechanism, although ingenious, would not be likely to stand rough work.

R. Punshon – Mr. Punshon claims to have improved the Snider rifle, but his bolt for securing the breech block was out of order, and the breech could not be opened. The mechanism does not appear to the committee to be an improvement on the Snider rifle.

Roden-Snider, No.2 – This is on the same principle as No.1 (placed in List B), but inferior in its accuracy.
No.3 – The shooting of this rifle is extremely inaccurate, and the extractor failed to act properly.
No.4 – Great force is required to withdraw the cartridges, which rendered the rapidity of fire unsatisfactory.

Captain Selwyn, RN – The performance of this rifle was unsatisfactory, both as regards accuracy and rapidity. The mode of extraction failed. The sub-committee attribute these failures to defects in the system.

Westley Richards, No.2 – No proper trial could be made, as the chamber was unsuitable for the cartridges sent with this rifle.
No.3 – The piston or striker was too long, sometimes withdrawing the wad. In firing for rapidity, owing to this defect in the arm, the trial was discontinued.
No.4 – Withdrawn from competition.

Wollemann – The operation of loading was rendered slow by part of the paper case being left in the barrel, and part adhering to the needle.

CLASS I. LIST B.

Systems Rejected After Further Examination.

J.R. Cooper – There appears to be considerable jar on the extractor in closing the breech of this rifle. The rim and body of the cartridge being exposed, renders the firing with damaged cartridges dangerous.

Major Fosbery, VC, No.2 – This rifle is nearly identical with No.1 which has been placed in List C.

A. Henry, No.1 – This rifle is identical in principle with No.2, placed in List C, differing from it only in calibre.

Krutzsch – The working parts of the breech mechanism of this rifle are too much exposed, and are therefore liable to become rusted or clogged with dirt.

Roden-Snider, No.1 – The breech block is liable to be blown open with a defective cartridge. It is necessary to turn the rifle over to throw out the cartridge. The cartridge needs to be pushed completely home into the chamber, before the breech block can be closed.

W. Soper – The performance of this rifle, both for accuracy and rapidity, was very satisfactory, but the sub-committee consider the breech mechanism to be too complicated. The safety catch to the trigger is not a satisfactory substitute for the ordinary half-cock.

W. Tranter – There is no half-cock or equivalent safety catch to this rifle, which could not, therefore, be placed in the hands of untrained men without risk of accident. In its present condition this rifle does not conform with the conditions of the WO advertisement.

CLASS I. LIST C.

Systems Accepted For The Prize Competition.

Albini & Braendlin – The rifle is adapted for central-fire metallic cartridges, calibre 0.462-inch. The breech block, which closes the breech, works on a hinge, in the same manner as the chamber of the "Storm" rifle. A piston, with spiral spring, passes through the axis of the breech block, and serves to communicate to the cartridge the blow which it receives from behind from a bolt worked by the lock. This bolt, which thus fires the gun, at the same time prevents the breech block from being blown open by an accidentally unsound cartridge. The breech action is made on a shoe, which afterwards receives the breech end of the rifle barrel.

Remarks: 26-4-67, trial shooting for accuracy and rapidity of fire. The cartridges were easily withdrawn, and no delay or accident took place throughout the trials. The rifle was fired by Mr. Braendlin, who pointed out that the rapidity of fire would be increased by tapering the cartridges.

29-6-67, a large bore 0.577-inch rifle was brought by Mr. Braendlin, having the cartridge chamber more tapered than he finds it possible to do with the small bore rifle owing to the form of the cartridge. 12 rounds were fired in 51 seconds by Mr. Braendlin.

J.H. Burton, Rifle No.1 – Has a cast steel barrel; it is adapted for the central-fire Boxer cartridge, calibre 0.577-inch. The breech block works on a hinge under the barrel by means of a handle in front of trigger guard. The cartridge is exploded by a piston in breech block and ordinary lock. The piston has no spring, but is withdrawn by the action of opening the breech. The breech can be opened without raising the hammer, but the hammer must be raised afterwards before it can be closed again. The rifle cannot be fired unless the breech block is well home.

Remarks: 26-4-67, trial shooting for accuracy and rapidity of fire. The breech arrangement worked well, with no misses. Mr. Burton fired 12 shots in 57 seconds. When firing for rapidity, the ejected cases did not invariably go through the hole in the stock made for their passage.

J.H. Burton, No.2 – It is also adapted for the Boxer cartridge; the breech is closed by means of a sliding bolt worked by a lever handle; the cartridge is exploded by a piston within the breech bolt. The rifle cannot go off unless the breech bolt is in the firing position. Calibre 0.577-inch.

Remarks: 26-4-67, trial shooting for accuracy and rapidity of fire. The breech arrangement of this rifle worked well. 12 shots were fired by Mr. Burton in 1 minute 2 seconds.

Major Fosbery, VC, Rifle No.1 – Is adapted for central-fire metallic cartridge, but with a slight alteration, self-consuming paper cartridges might be used. The breech is closed by means of a block which works on a hinge at the breech end of the barrel, in the same manner as the "Mont Storm" rifle. The breech is opened, and the empty cartridge case extracted by the act of drawing back a rod attached to the right side of the barrel. The cartridge is exploded by means of two pistons, the one passing through the centre of the breech block, and the other acting as a striker, which also serves to secure the breech block, and prevent it flying up in case of any escape of gas. There is a stud in the shoe which greatly facilitates the ejection of the empty cartridge case. The lock is in the centre of the stock and is of simple construction. Calibre 0.568-inch.

Remarks: 2-5-67, trial shooting for accuracy and rapidity of fire. No accidents or delay. Major Fosbery fired 12 shots in 50 seconds.

A. Henry – It is adapted for the Boxer cartridge. The breech is opened by means of a breech block, which works vertically by the movement of a lever under the stock; this lever, when the rifle is loaded, is fastened by a catch under the trigger guard. The cartridge is exploded by a piston passing diagonally through the breech block, and driven by a common lock. The empty cartridge case is extracted by the same movement that opens the breech. Calibre 0.453-inch.

Remarks: Fired for accuracy and rapidity, 8-5-67. 12 shots in 57 seconds.

B.F. Joslyn, by E.H. Newby – The rifle is well adapted for a copper rim-fire cartridge. but can be equally adapted for central-fire. Calibre 0.500-inch. The rifle is closed by a breech block opening laterally on a hinge, which is hollowed out so as to fit over a collar at the end of the barrel; the recoil is thus taken on two bearings. A spring piston passes through the breech block and is driven by the hammer of an ordinary side lock. The extractor is worked by a screw thread on the hinge joint of the breech block.

Remarks: 8-5-67, trials for accuracy and rapidity of fire. Mr Newby attended, and his friend Mr. Bird fired the rifle throughout the trials. Rifle worked well and gained 12 shots in 47 seconds.

F. Martini – Rifle is adapted for a copper rim-fire cartridge, but can be equally adapted for central-fire. Calibre 0.433-inch. The rifle is closed by a breech block, which falls and rises on a hinge, and is worked by a lever in rear of the trigger guard. The method of opening and closing the breech is similar to that of the Peabody rifle. The breech block contains a spiral spring and piston for striking the cartridge. The action of opening the breech throws out the empty cartridge case by means of a lever extractor, and at the same time cocks the rifle. The ordinary lock is entirely dispensed with. The rifle is placed on half-cock, or rather in a position of safety, by pushing forward the lever rather slowly, so as not to throw out the cartridge, and pulling the trigger while the breech is partly open. Another slow motion of the lever re-cocks the piece.

Remarks: 14-5-67, trials for accuracy and rapidity of fire, by Private Bristow, RM. After the 8th and 9th shots for accuracy some force was required to withdraw the cartridge case. 12 rounds fired in 48 seconds, by Private Bristow, who was not well acquainted with the manipulation of the rifle.

H.O. Peabody – The rifle is adapted for a rim-fire metallic cartridge. Calibre 0.500-inch. An iron breech frame closed at the sides unites the barrel with the stock. In this is placed the breech block, working on a pivot fixed at the rear and moved by means of a lever which forms the trigger guard when the rifle is ready for firing. In the upper side of the breech block is a groove, which coincides with the bore of the barrel when the breech is open. The extractor is in the form of a lever, which is moved by the breech block, and throws the cartridge case clear of the rifle when the breech is opened. The breech is secured by a lever affixed to the lower side of the block, and worked by a spring which presses it against a strong pin. The block carries a striker driven by the hammer of a common side lock, which explodes the cartridge.

Remarks: 14-5-67, trials for accuracy and rapidity of fire, shot by Sgt. Bott, RM. Breech worked well, and 12 rounds fired in 53 seconds by Sgt. Bott, who was unacquainted with the rifle, and did not, therefore, attain the highest rate possible.

S. Remington – Rifle adapted for a copper cartridge, either central or rim-fire, there being a duplicate breech piece. The breech piece or block works on a transverse pivot below the barrel, and is secured by the hammer of a central lock, the hammer being also the tumbler of the lock. Calibre 0.500-inch. Mr. Remington claims as advantages of this sytem, simplicity of construction and of action, combined with great strength. The surfaces in contact are few and well protected.

Remarks: 14-5-67, trials for accuracy and rapidity of fire, shot by Mr. Kerr on behalf of Mr. Remington, with both central and rim-fire cartridges. With central-fire cartridges the rims of some of them were found to be too small, and allowed the extractor to pass over them. 12 rounds fired in 50 seconds. With rim-fire cartridges, 11 rounds fired in 40 seconds.

APPENDIX 4.

Being the details of weapons ineligible for the Prize Competition, showing the classifications allocated by the sub-committee, and their remarks thereon.

CLASS II. LIST A.

Systems Summarily Rejected.

Antoine – There is no proof mark on the breech arrangement. The sub-committee are not satisfied with the safety of this rifle; and since the workmanship is very rough, and it can be fired when unbolted, they rejected it without firing.

Allemans & Barelli – Rifle is overweight. The needle is liable to accident. If the cartridges be not pushed far enough into the chamber the breech block cannot be closed without injuring them. There is nothing to prevent them from being pushed beyond the reach of the needle either in the process of loading, or by a jerk when the rifle is loaded.

Armstead – Rifle is too short. There are no proof marks, and Mr. Armstead declined to fire it.

Appleyard – Rifle was too late for competition. During the firing the cartridge was placed in front of the extractor, and the rifle was disabled.

Bacon, No.1 – Rifle is overweight. The shooting, both for rapidity and accuracy, was good, but the complicated nature of the breech mechanism and extractor, and their liability to injury, render it unsuitable as a military arm.

John Bensun & Co, Nos.1, 2, and 3 – Rifles are too short. There are several good ideas embodied in their breech action, but they appear to have been hastily manufactured, and the inventions are as yet in an incomplete state.
No.4 – Rifle is too long. The extractor, similar in principle to No.2, breaks the cartridges.

Bier – Rifle is overweight and too long. The block, which contains two chambers, is liable to jam, and the operation of cocking is difficult to perform. The rifle was not fired, as there were no proof marks.

Bridges – Rifle was too late for competition. The cartridges did not fit the chamber, and therefore a proper trial could not be made. Mr. Poultney stated that he would submit another rifle, with which the ammunition could be fired.

Carter & Edwards, No.1 – Rifle is overweight. From a defect in construction it could not be fired.

Craig, H – Rifle was too late, having been taken away to be proved. The breech mechanism was insecure, and was blown open after every shot. There was an escape of gas. The system is not considered applicable for military purposes.

Craig, T - Owing to a wrong address having been sent by Mr. Craig, he was prevented from attending the trial of his rifles.
No.1 – Rifle was too late for competition. Only one shot was fired, followed by two misfires. The action of the extractor is unsatisfactory. There appears no likelihood of attaining the proper rapidity.
No.2 – Too late for competition. No cartridges were sent in with it, but from examination made, the sub-committee are of opinion that the breech mechanism is not adapted for military purposes.

Cyliax – Rifle was too long. It is identical with No.2 rifle sent in by Mr. Tanner, and is rejected for similar reasons.

Davis – Rifle has no proof marks, and is too long. As it is in an unfinished state, and there were no cartridges, it was not fired.

Elliott – Rifle is too short. There is no half-cock, and the breech arrangement is exposed to rain. Delay in loading is likely to occur if the cartridge is placed in front of the extractor.

Flachat – Rifle is too short. The cartridge case burst, being unsupported by the extractor; two small pieces of the case were blown back into the face of Private Croft, and the trial was discontinued.

Fougeroux, No.1 – Rifle is overweight, and too short. After a misfire, on opening the breech, the cartridge was broken open, the powder was scattered in the shoe, the bullet remained in the barrel, and the base and body of the cartridge in the chamber. Mr. Fougeroux explained that this might be avoided by using the ramrod. The rapidity of fire was not sufficient.

Fosbery, No.3 – Rifle was too late for competition. It is identical with No.4 in principle, but proved itself inferior in shooting qualities to No.4, carried on to List C.

Greve & Dowling, No.1 – Rifle is too short.
No.2 – Rifle is too heavy and too short.
No.3 – Rifle is too short.
The rifles were withdrawn by Messrs. Greve and Dowling, and were not fired.

Girvan – Rifle is too heavy, and there are no proof marks. The sub-committee did not consider it safe to fire.

Glisenti, No.1 – Too late for competition. It could not be fired, as there was no ammunition.
No.2 – Too late for competition. The system could not be thoroughly tested, as the india-rubber wads at the base of the cartridge were too large, and prevented the breech being closed. It does not appear applicable to military purposes.

De Grelle, the "Loron" – Too late for competition. It could not be fired, as no ammunition was sent. The breech mechanism appears too complicated for military purposes.

Halliday – Rifle is too heavy. It was not in a sufficiently finished state to admit of any judgement being given on the merits of the principle.

Hahn – Rifle too long. It could not be fired, and Mr. Hahn withdrew it, stating that it was only a rough model. It was subsequently tried, but having failed again, was withdrawn.

Hookham – Rifle was in an unfinished state, and was withdrawn by the inventor.

Isherwood & Warry – Rifle is too long. The extractor requires to be pushed entirely back after each shot to enable the breech block to be opened; it also causes delay in the cartridge case being taken from the shoe. In the trial one cartridge case split, and was extracted with difficulty, and another jammed, and required a ramrod to withdraw it.

Jaspar – Too late for competition. It could not be tried, as no ammunition was sent. The system appears inapplicable for military purposes.

Jerome – Too long. The firing was extremely inaccurate. The cartridge jammed so as to render great force necessary to close the breech block.

Julien – Rifle is overweight. There is considerable ingenuity in its breech mechanism. The extractor is not satisfactory in its action. The safety catch is not a sufficient substitute for half-cock.

Kilbee – Rifle is overweight. The extractor failed to remove the cartridge cases, which jammed, and required a ramrod to force them out.

Kuberick – Too long. It was fired with metallic cartridges, but there was great escape of gas, and it was considered unsafe. The rifle was then tried with india-rubber cartridges, but they were found to be too large for the chamber.

Little, Walker, & Money – Rifle was too late for competition. It was not fired, as there were no proof marks. It was then withdrawn.

Lintott – Rifle too late for competition. It had been separately considered, as it was merely a modification of the government arm, and has been specially reported on.

Mappin, Nos.1, 2, and 3 – All were too short. The extractor did not work well, the cartridges having to be withdrawn by hand. No.2 could not be fired. No.3 being almost identical with No.1 was not fired.

Mercier, Nos.1, 2, and 3 – All are too short. They were withdrawn and so not fired.

Needham, Nos.2 and 3 – No.2 is too short and was withdrawn by Mr. Needham. No.3 was rejected as being in an unfinished state.

Prince – Too long. The shooting was extremely inaccurate. The breech mechanism is not considered sufficiently strong for military purposes.

Poilvache – Too long and heavy. As the cartridges would not explode the trial was discontinued.

Reeves, No.1 – Rifle too long.
Nos.2 and 3 – Both too short. All were withdrawn, and Nos.4 and 5 substituted.
No.4 – The system is somewhat similar to the Snider rifle, but is not so quick or convenient. The extractor works very badly.
No.5 – The cartridge can be placed in front of the extractor, and the firing for rapidity was not satisfactory, great exertion in the manipulation being necessary.

Robert – Too long and heavy. Part of the india-rubber washer was blown away, great escape of gas ensued, and the rifle was rendered unserviceable; the breech block however, appears to be very firmly secured.

Russ & Hammond, Nos.1 and 2 – Both rifles too long.
No.2 – The small bore rifle, failed on account of the cartridge heads breaking off. Judging of the system from the trial of the large bore rifle (No.1), the sub-committee are of opinion that when shut the breech arrangement is very secure, but that considerable force is required to close and open the breech block. The general working of the extractor is inconvenient.

Westley Richards, No.1 – Too heavy. The chamber was not adapted for the cartridges.

Schneider – Rifle is too short and has no proof marks. It was fired by Mr. Schneider, but the rapidity was very unsatisfactory, as the paper of the exploded cartridge needed picking out after each shot.

Selwyn – Rifle too late for competition. The trials (as of the one previously tried, and referred to in the first report) were unsatisfactory, both as regards accuracy and rapidity. The mode of extraction failed.

Syme – Rifle too long. The cartridges fitted the chamber so badly that a piece of wood was required to push them home. Most of them burst at the rim on being fired. The cases were extracted with difficulty, and the rapidity was therefore unsatisfactory.

Tanner, Nos.1 and 2 – Both too long. The firing was very inaccurate, and on account of the great difficulty in loading, owing to the grease of the cartridges obstructing the breech mechanism, the necessary rapidity could not be attained.

Tronchon – Too short, and having no proof marks was not fired; but it is considered inferior to many others.

Whitwortn & Co. – Rifle is over weight. It was withdrawn at the request of the company.

Wollemann, No.2 – Too long and heavy. There was great difficulty in opening and closing the breech, and also much escape of gas.

Wright – Too late for competition. It was not tried, as there were no proof marks, and only one cartridge was sent.

Wyley – Too late for competition. The breech bolt is liable to be detached from the rifle in opening the breech. The cartridge can be placed in front of the extractor.

CLASS II. LIST B.

Systems Rejected After Further Examination.

Cornish – Rifle too short for competition. Two trials were made and the extractor was not found to work satisfactorily.

Henry, No.4 – Rifle was too short for competition. The action of the extractor is awkward in comparison with that of some of the other rifles. Two trials were made.

Laloux – The breech of this rifle is closed by a sliding bolt. Its construction is simple, but there are others on a somewhat similar principle which the committee prefer.

Westley Richards, No.5 – Too late for competition. It is made on a somewhat similar principle to the rifles with the jointed breech block (placed in List C) and as the latter rifles are preferred, this will not be considered further.

CLASS II. LIST C.

Systems Retained For Further Consideration.

Berdan – Messrs. Kerr state that Berdan's system is available for making new arms, as well as for conversions. They have failed for want of time to prepare new arms, and there fore submit a converted long Enfield. Points of excellence claimed – cheapness of conversion. A simple direct action in making up new arms. The block will push the cartridge home, though nearly half an inch from its proper place. No spiral spring required for striker. (This appears not to be the case with arms submitted.) Stock not cut away.

The arm submitted has had the second proof in the usual way, but as the barrel did not have the first proof applied again, previous to conversion, it could not be stamped with out having the first heavy proof charge tried in it, which it was thought would be unadvisable, as it might strain the arm.

Construction of breech: Breech block on being opened folds over barrel. Back sight consequently moved forward. Extractor worked by action of breech block. Exploded by spring piston. Common lock and hammer. The arm is adapted for Boxer cartridge.

Remarks: 26-4-67, trials for accuracy and rapidity of fire, shot by Mr. Kerr on behalf of Col. Berdan. No misses or misfires. Breech arrangement worked well, and 12 rounds fired in 57 seconds. Service Boxer Pattern III used.

Carter & Edwards – Rifle is adapted for Boxer cartridge. The breech is closed by means of a sliding bolt worked by a lever handle. The case of the discharged cartridge is thrown out by the act of drawing back the breech bolt to load. This rifle is an improvement on those originally submitted, the pistons of which were found to be too short.

Remarks: 12-6-67, trials for accuracy and rapidity of fire, shot by Private Croft, RM, using Boxer cartridges, Service Pattern III; 12 rounds in 44 seconds.

Fosbery – Rifle is adapted for central-fire metallic cartridges, but with slight alteration, self-consuming paper cartridges might be used. The breech is closed by means of a block, which works on a hinge at the breech end of the barrel, in the same manner as the chamber of the "Mont Storm" rifle. The breech is opened, and the empty cartridge case extracted by the act of drawing back a rod attached to the right side of the barrel. The cartridge is exploded by means of two pistons, the one passing through the centre of the breech block, and the other acting as a striker, which also serves to secure the breech block, and prevent it from flying up in case of any escape of gas. The rifle is similar in principle to the one accepted for the competition, but it is a small bore, calibre 0.451-inch.

Remarks: 5-6-67, trials for accuracy and rapidity of fire, all shot by Major Fosbery. Several misfires occurred, but, with one exception, they fired on the 2nd or 3rd trial. RL cartridges used. 12 rounds fired in 59 seconds, using Boxer-Eley cartridges.

Greve & Dowling – Rifle adapted for central-fire metallic cartridges. The barrel is enlarged at the breech by an open cylinder containing large slots. The breech is closed by a sliding cylindrical bolt, moved and secured in a similar manner to that of the Prussian needle gun. The extractor is attached to the lower part of the bolt, by which it is moved, and it is returned by a spring. The bolt contains a spring piston, terminating behind in a nut or thumb-piece, by which it may be drawn back. The spring which drives the piston is compressed when the bolt is pushed forward.

Remarks: 5-6-67, trials for accuracy and rapidity of fire. Accuracy shots fired by Private Croft. Rapidity, 12 rounds in 52 seconds, shot by Mr. de Castro on behalf of the inventors. The inventors pointed out that the muzzle of the rifle should not be held too high while extracting the empty cart ridge cases.

Hammond (by Mr. W.H. Grenelle) – Rifle is constructed for copper rim-fire cartridges. The breech is closed by means of a block, which works from right to left on the small of the stock as a pivot. The cartridge is exploded by a spring piston in the breech block, which is struck by a hammer in the centre of the stock.

Remarks: 8-5-67, trials for accuracy and rapidity of fire, shot throughout by Mr. Daw. Two shots missed the target. Rapidity, 12 shots in 1 minute 1 second. The cartridge case was easily withdrawn, but required a touch of the finger to complete the extraction.

Mr. Grenelle expressed himself dissatisfied with the results, which did not fulfil his expectations. He took away the rifle to have it adapted for central-fire cartridges, and will then resubmit it for consideration on its own merits.

20-6-67, further trials for rapidity, Mr. Grenelle and Mr. Daw attended, the cartridges used being on Daw's patent. Mr. Daw fired 12 rounds in 1 minute 5 seconds, and a second 12 by Private Croft in 1 minute 4 seconds. The cartridges required to have their extraction completed by hand. The cartridges fitted the chamber easily both before and after being fired.

Needham – This rifle is adapted for the Boxer central-fire cartridge. The barrel is prolonged at the breech by a cylinder open at the right side. The breech is closed by a block opening out laterally on a vertical pivot at the fore part of the open cylinder. The extractor is a lever of the first order on the vertical pivot, and is worked by the action of opening the breech. A piston passes through the axis of the breech block, and is forced forward by a peculiar wedge-shaped hammer, worked by a common lock. The hammer also answers the purpose of a locking bolt, and prevents the breech being blown open.

Remarks: 20-6-67, trials for accuracy and rapidity of fire, all shot by Mr. Needham. The cartridges were easily extracted after firing. 12 shots in 59 seconds, without accident or delay.

Poultney – Rifle is adapted for central-fire metallic cartridges. The breech block works on a hinge under the barrel, by means of a lever handle, which also serves as the trigger guard. The cartridge is exploded by a piston in the breech block, and ordinary lock. The cartridge case is thrown out in the act of opening the breech.

Remarks: 5-6-67, trials for accuracy and rapidity, shot by Capt. Bridges. 12 rounds fired in 59 seconds by Mr. Poultney. No accidents throughout the trials.

Westley Richards, No.11 – This rifle has a Whitworth barrel, and is adapted for a self-consuming central-fire paper cartridge, with a perforated felt wad at the base. The breech is closed by a plunger attached to a lever similar to that of the Westley Richards capping breech-loaders at present in the service, but a piston passes through the plunger, and communicates the blow from the hammer to the base of the cartridge.

Remarks: 5-6-67, trials for accuracy and rapidity. Accuracy shot by Private Croft, and rapidity by Westley Richards' foreman. 12 shots in 46 seconds. 1 cartridge hung fire, and in another instance the trigger was pulled when the rifle was at half-cock, which occasioned a trifling delay.

Westley Richards, No.3 – Adapted for special Westley Richards central-fire metallic cartridges, with paper ends for carrying the bullets. The breech block is in two pieces hinged together; the hinder part having a lever attached to it by which the breech is opened. The block when closed resembles a dovetail, the metal at the rear end of its bed being undercut to receive it.

Remarks: 5-6-67, trials for accuracy and rapidity of fire, by Private Croft, and Westley Richards' foreman. 12 shots in 1 minute 29 seconds; 1 misfire. Cartridges rather difficult to extract. Several cartridges rather tight to withdraw, and all the caps blew open backwards when fired.

Sharp – Rifle is constructed for metallic cartridges with ignition in the rim. It has no rod. The moving parts to operate the arm are only three, viz., lever, slide, and extractor. The breech is closed by means of a lever forming the trigger guard. The breech slide being spheroidal in shape, admits of using the cartridges with ease if the heads vary in thickness, which they all do more or less as stated by Mr. Kerr.

Remarks: 17-5-67, trials for accuracy and rapidity, all shot by Mr. Kerr. Breech arrangement worked well. 12 rounds fired in 51 seconds by Mr. Kerr, who did not appear to work the rifle quite so quickly as might have been done.

Wilson – The rifle is a needle gun adapted for a paper cartridge, with india-rubber or felt wad at the base, a short distance in front of which is placed the fulminate in a copper cap. Mr. Wilson stated that the cartridge is only one half the weight of the Boxer round, and 50 percent cheaper. The needle of the rifle is driven by a riband spring, which he prefers to an ordinary spiral spring.

Remarks: 20-6-67, trials for accuracy and rapidity. Mr. Wilson fired for accuracy, and one cartridge missed fire, although the needle pierced the fulminate in the cap. 12 shots were fired in 44 seconds by Private Croft. One cartridge broke in loading and was not fired. Two cartridges were dropped on the ground during the trial and were picked up by the man firing. There was a slight escape of gas at the breech.
Second trial for rapidity: The first shot missed fire, and the trial was re-commenced. 6 shots were then fired in 25 seconds by Private Croft, then followed two misfires, and the trial was discontinued.

APPENDIX 5.

Being details of the barrels and ammunition for the trials commencing 23-6-1868.

BARRELS of uniform weight and length. Weight 4 lb 5 oz, length 35 inches.
AMMUNITION, Boxer cartridge case; Powder, Curtis and Harvey's No.6, 85 grains (except in .5-inch Enfield).

HENRY

Bore –

Diameter: .45"

Twist: 1 turn in 22", uniform

Grooves: 9 flat cuts. leaving a beading between each, centre of cut and edge of beading equidistant from axis of bore.

Cartridge –

Length: 3.76"

Weight: 718 grains

Description: Bullet held in by being crimped after insertion; one jute wad next to powder, then wax wad, then one or two jute wads, then bullet.

Bullet –

Length: 1.27"

Diameter: .45"

Description: Compressed bullet, solid, slight cavity in rear, of 12 parts lead, 1 part tin; it tapers from base to smallest diameter, the sides between diameters being slightly hollowed, head conoidal; paper wrapper dipped in wax at base. Weight 480 grains.

ENFIELD

Bore –

Diameter: .5"

Twist: 1 turn in 28", uniform

Grooves: 5 segmental grooves, width of lands and grooves equal or .157 each, depth progressive from .005 to .012.

Cartridge –

Length: 3.288"

Weight: 670 grains

Charge: 80 grains FGR

Description: Case choked into rear cannelure of bullet; cotton wool between powder and bullet.

Bullet –

Length: 1.21"

Diameter: .498"

Weight: 440 grains

Description: Compressed cylindro-conoidal, five saw-shaped cannelures filled with wax; pure lead, deep cavity in base with clay plug, hollow head, turned over with thin lead.

ENFIELD

Bore –

Diameter: .45"

Twist: 1 turn in 20 ", uniform

Grooves: 6 segmental grooves, depth progressive from .015 to .004.

Cartridge –

Length: 4"

Weight: 715 grains

Description: Case choked into rear cannelure, a plain wax wad with a little French chalk in it, between powder and bullet.

Bullet –

Length: 1.425"

Diameter: .449"

Weight: 480 grains

Description: Compressed cylindro-conoidal, 12 parts lead, 1 part tin, eight cannelures filled with wax, cavity in base with clay plug.

RICHARDS

Bore –

Diameter: .45"

Twist: 1 turn in 21", uniform

Grooves: Polygonal, eight cuts.

Cartridge –

Length: 3.65"

Weight: 730 grains

Description: Bullet not secured in case, plain wax wad between powder and bullet.

Bullet –

Length: 1.256"

Diameter: .44 to .45"

Weight: 485 grains

Description: Compressed solid bullet, 95 parts lead, 5 parts tin, tapering from base and head; conoidal paper wrapper, dipped in wax at base, and half wax, half WR No. 8 supperadded.

LANCASTER

Bore –

Oval, No.1 –

Diameter: Major axis .466", minor .451"

Twist: 1 turn in 36" at breech, 1 in 20" at muzzle

Semi-oval, No.2 –

Diameter: Major axis .460", minor .450"

Twist: As above.

Cartridge

Length: 3.82"

Weight: 720 grains

Description: Bullet not secured in case, plain wax wad between powder and bullet; both bullets were tried with plain wax. and both with wax between millboard wads.

Bullet –

No.1 –

Length: 1.315"

Diameter: .45"

Weight: 480 grains

Description: Compressed solid bullet, 100 parts lead, 5 tin, 5 antimony; six round cannelures, paper wrapped, no lubrication; cylindrical with ogival head.

No.2 –

Length: 1.276"

Diameter: .45"

Weight: 477 grains

Description: 4 round cannelures, slight cavity at base, otherwise as above.

WHITWORTH

Bore –

Diameter: .45"

Twist: 1 turn in 20", uniform

Grooves: Hexagonal.

Cartridge –

Length: 3.86"

Weight: 722 grains

Description: Bullets not secured in case, wad of lubrication between powder and bullet of wax and small portion of Price's mixture.

Bullet –

Length: 1.42"

Diameter: .443"

Weight: 480 grains

Description: Compressed, pure lead, cavity at base and in point, wood plug in point; cylindro-conoidal; dry paper wrapper.

RIGBY

Bore –

Diameter: .451"

Twist: 1 turn in 20", uniform

Grooves: 8 grooves of equal depth from breech to muzzle so formed as to leave 8 narrow lands or ridges with rounded edges; greatest depth of grooves .005".

Cartridge –

Full details not ascertained. Bullet wrapped in two folds of thin paper.

Bullet –

Length: 1.25"

Diameter: At base .448". At .75" from base, .440".

Weight: 480 grains

Description: Cylindro-conoidal, flat base, hardened lead.

APPENDIX 6.

Being a summary of the shooting of the various barrels in the trials commencing 23-6-1868.

NOTE: In the trials the mean deviations on target were taken as the averages of five targets of 20 shots each from each barrel. Two barrels were cleaned out between targets and two were left uncleaned. In the tables below, these mean deviations are designated as –

A – Cleaned
B – Uncleaned
C – Cleaned
D – Uncleaned

ACCURACY at 300 yards.

System.	Mean deviations.				Mean elevation
	A	B	C	D	
	feet	feet	feet	feet	o ' "
Enfield	.62	.51	.61	.61	0 35 42
Henry	.62	.47	.68	.63	0 38 3
Lancaster (1) . . .	–	–	–	–	– – –
Rigby (1).	–	–	–	–	– – –
Westley Richards (1)	–	–	–	–	– – –
Whitworth	.52	.64	.63	.62	0 40 10
Snider .5" (2). . .	.59	.59	–	–	0 30 28

(1) These rifles were first fired for the sake of convenience at the 500 yards range, and as the results were not sufficiently good they were not fired at this distance.

(2) Only two barrels were submitted, and it was thought better not to fire a larger number of rounds from these barrels than from those of the other systems. Vide note at 500 yards.

ACCURACY at 500 yards.

Enfield	1.27	1.20	1.03	1.11	1 8 25
Henry	1.06	1.07	0.90	1.06	1 8 42
Lancaster (1) . . .	1.08	–	–	–	1 19 20
Rigby (2).	2.34	–	–	–	1 17 0
Westley Richards (3)	1.39	1.30	–	–	1 17 41
Whitworth	1.07	1.51	1.09	1.30	1 12 3
Snider .5" (4). . .	1.02	1.13	1.16	1.11	1 5 17

(1) As before mentioned, Mr. Lancaster submitted two descriptions of barrel and four of ammunition. The results of only one of each are given in the table, viz. – Semi-oval barrel, No.1 bullet, and with wax wad only – those from the other combinations not being sufficiently satisfactory to warrant a continuation of the trial.

(2) It was not considered desirable to continue this trial, as the results were not satisfactory. Figure shown is average of four targets.

(3) Only one barrel submitted, which was fired twice.

(4) As only two barrels were submitted, they were fired at this range twice over.

ACCURACY at 800 yards.

Enfield	2.47	2.08*	2.94	2.42	2 2 23
Henry	2.39	1.85	2.30	2.35	2 3 57
Lancaster (1) . . .	–	2.14	–	–	2 15 57
Rigby (2).	–	–	–	–	– – –
Westley Richards (3)	–	–	–	–	– – –
Whitworth	2.91	3.11	4.48	2.94	2 4 36
Snider .5" (4). . .	3.01	2.46	–	–	2 13 40

*Mean of four targets, as the rest was unsteady during the fifth target.

(1) Vide remark at 500 yards to explain only one barrel being taken on.

(2) The remark at 500 yards range.

(3) The shooting of this arm was not considered sufficiently good at 500 yards to warrant its being carried on to the other ranges, especially as Mr. Westley Richards, who was present, expressed his dissatisfaction at the result of the shooting.

(4) Vide remark at 300 yards to account for only two barrels having been fired.

ACCURACY at 1,000 yards.

Enfield	3.93	3.55	4.74	4.15	2 46 21
Henry (1).	2.65	3.33	2.59	3.12	2 47 4
Lancaster. . . .	–	4.65	–	–	3 5 0
Snider .5" (2). . .	3.96	4.90	–	–	3 23 19

(1) Men were working behind the butt during the firing of the Henry rifle, and consequently it was necessary to make the point of impact lower than usual, in order to prevent the chance of a shot going over the target. Thus misses (short) occurred in shots which would otherwise have hit the target, and the average was consequently deteriorated.
(2) Vide remark at 300 yards.

APPENDIX 7.

Being the list of arms rejected from the Breech Action Selection Trials, and the reasons for rejection.

Adams, 0.577" – In the damaged cartridge trials the breech block of the rifle was blown open, and the cartridge case blown out to the rear.

Amsler-Milbank 0.45" – In this rifle the cartridge can be placed in front of the extractor.

Berdan 0.45" (with spiral spring lock) – The breech block of this rifle was not properly secured to the barrel, which prevented the proper working of the breech mechanism.

Berdan 0.45" (with side lock) – Unless carefully shut, the hammer of this rifle falls on the hinge that closes the breech instead of on the striker. The quick and proper working of the breech action depends upon the hinge called the 'brace' which at once becomes affected by exposure to weather. The piston is liable to become fixed out by rust.

Berdan 0.45" (sliding bolt) – This rifle was submitted after the committee had decided from previous experiments to reject all sliding bolt guns as being liable to accident with over-sensitive cartridges.

Benson – If dirt or sand enters the shoe of this rifle it causes misfires, and even prevents the bolt from entering the aperture in the block. The working of the breech mechanism is slow.

Braendlin-Snider – In this rifle there is a liability to misfires when sand or dirt clogs the breech, and prevents the bolt fairly entering the hole in the block. Other methods of securing the breech block are preferred.

Cole 0.577 and 0.45" – These rifles were not fired as they bore no proof marks. It is possible to place the cartridge in front of the extractor.

Conroy 0.577" – The breech mechanism is more complicated than that of many other rifles. The rifle is a large bore, and consequently has a shorter cartridge than could be used in a small bore. It is doubtful whether the extractor would answer with a long cartridge.

Cooper 0.577" – In this rifle the breech block is kept open by a spring, which is always in a state of tension when the breech is closed. There is a liability to misfires.

Chassepot – There were continued misfires with this rifle, and considerable fouling about the point of the breech bolt. The india-rubber wad in the percussion cap was almost invariably left in the rifle after discharge, and was also blown into the breech bolt, thus clogging the needle. After a misfire the ramrod has to be used to push out the cartridge. (In some Chassepots shown to the committee on a subsequent date, which were stated to be of more perfect make, these misfires did not occur, but after a few rounds some difficulty was found in forcing the cartridges into the chamber.)

Davies – The breech mechanism of this rifle is more complicated than that of other systems, and the manipulation is slower.

Fosbery 0.5" (elevating block) – In the sand trial this rifle worked with difficulty. A touch of the finger is required to complete the ejection of the empty case.

Fosbery 0.45" (falling block) – In this rifle the extractor occasionally failed to withdraw the empty case, owing, as stated by Major Fosbery, to defective chambering. The breech cannot be closed after sand has been thrown on it.

Gordon – This rifle is a modification of the Snider system. Rifles, in many respects resembling it, have been reported on.

Gielgud (Peabody) 0.45" – Mr. Gielgud withdrew this rifle, on being informed that other systems, on somewhat similar principles, were preferred to it.

Larsen 0.45" (4 rifles) – One rifle of this system was fired (due precautions being taken) with the breech lever not quite home, the escape of gas destroyed the stock and rendered the arm unserviceable. All the rifles appear liable to an accident of this kind.

Money-Walker 0.5" – By exposure to weather the breech mechanism of this rifle is liable to become jammed and unserviceable. A smart blow is necessary to ensure the breech mechanism being closed.

Mabbutt 0.577" – The breech block is liable to fall down while the empty case is being thrown out.The manipulation is slow. Sand or dirt entering the hole which contains the plunger causes difficulties in opening the breech block.

Newark – The breech mechanism of this rifle is a modification of the Snider principle. The method of bolting down the bolt in this rifle appears simple. The wood of the stock is more cut away than is the case in an ordinary Snider block. The committee recommend that it should be brought under the notice of the Supt. RSAF Enfield.

Needham 0.577" – Although the breech mechanism of this rifle is strong, it is not so handy as others.

Peabody 0.5" (with trigger guard lever, adapted for Boxer compressed powder cartridges) – In this rifle the breech action jammed during the rapidity trial, which had to be discontinued. The breech mechanism worked stiffly.

Peabody 0.45" (modified Peabody with lever above, adapted for Berdan central-fire cartridges) – The committee had before them rifles which they preferred to this. Mr. Gielgud accordingly withdrew it.

Peabody-Gielgud-Wessely – This rifle became unserviceable when sand was thrown on the open breech. The breech action is simple and strong. Mr. Wessely withdrew the arm stating that it was not a perfectly finished specimen.

Prussian needle gun – The breech mechanism of this rifle was slower and more difficult of manipulation than that of many other arms brought before the committee. The rifle is liable to the objections of arms using the paper cartridge. There was a great escape of gas at the breech.

Punshon-Snider 0.577" – The extractor of this rifle jammed when sand was thrown on the breech mechanism. After firing, the hammer frequently passed over the catch of the bolt, and so failed to release the spring which holds down the breech block. The breech was blown open by a damaged cartridge.

Reilly-Comblain 0.577" – The committee made no experiments with this arm as they had before them systems of breech mechanism which they preferred.

Ross (P. Campbell) – No ammunition was submitted with these rifles. Other systems are preferred.

Russian converted needle rifle 0.577" – This rifle became unserviceable when fine sand was thrown over the breech arrangement. There was great difficulty in withdrawing the cartridge after a misfire.

Russ & Hammond 0.577"; and 0.45" (paper cartridge) – These rifles are slow in manipulation, although their breech mechanism is strong. Other systems are preferred.

Roden-Snider – With this rifle the jerk which is required to eject the empty case renders the breech block liable to fall over, the ocking bolt appears to be inferior to other systems of securing the breech block.

Stoakes 0.577" – The piston of this rifle being broken it could not be fired, and there was no suitable ammunition wherewith to try the small bore barrel.

Stoakes 0.45" – The breech mechanism is liable to be rendered unserviceable by sand or dirt entering the several parts. There were no proof marks on the rifles.

Stiff – This rifle was not submitted until the committee had expressed an opinion adverse to sliding bolt guns generally. They have before them other rifles on the bolt system which they prefer.

Tranter 0.577" – This rifle became unserviceable when sand was thrown over the breech mechanism.

Wanzel 0.45" (1); and 0.45" (2) – There is a liability to mis fires and failure in extraction of the cartridge cases in these rifles. Other systems of breech-loading are preferred.

Werndle 0.45" – In this rifle the action of the extractor is uncertain. Dirt or sand thrown over the breech arrangement prevents it from working.

Witney – Dirt or sand entering the working parts of the breech action renders the gun quite useless. It is capable of being fired rapidly when in good working order.

Wyley 0.577" – These rifles were received after the decision of the committee against bolt guns. They have rifles before them on the bolt system which they prefer.

APPENDIX 8.

Being the list of arms retained for the Breech Action Selection Trials, with a description of each system.

Bacon – This rifle is adapted for the Boxer cartridge. The breech is closed by a sliding bolt worked by a lever handle. The explosion is caused by a direct action piston driven by a strong spiral spring in the bolt, which also does the duty of a sear spring. The action of pushing forward the bolt and closing the breech, compresses the spring, and when the handle is turned down the arm is ready to fire. The empty cartridge case is withdrawn from the chamber and thrown out in drawing back the bolt to open the breech.

Berdan – This rifle is adapted to Berdan central fire drawn brass cartridges. The barrel and shoe are in one piece. The breech is closed by a block which folds forwards on a hinge over the chamber. The explosion is caused by a loose piston passing diagonally through the block, driven by the hammer of a common side lock. The breech is opened by raising and swinging forward the breech block; in doing so, the extractor spring is compressed and at the end of the motion is suddenly released, causing the empty case to be flipped out. A brace working in a mortice in the block, the rear end of which has a curve struck from a centre below the axis of the rifle, falls in shutting down the block into a corresponding curve in the shoe, and effectually prevents the possibility of the breech being blown open by a damaged cartridge.

Carter & Edwards – This rifle is adapted for the Boxer cartridge. The breech is closed by a sliding bolt, worked by means of a lever handle curved down so as to lie when shut against the side of the stock, and prevent an unsightly appearance and the chance of catching in the clothes or accoutrements. The cartridge is exploded by means of a direct acting loose piston passing through the bolt, and driven by a hammer and flat spring in the centre of the stock. This piston has a head, the inner face of which is cut in an incline, there being a similar incline on the heel of the bolt; it is of sufficient length to strike the cartridge only when the inclines coincide, and this can only occur when the handle of the bolt is turned down in a position of safety. In turning the bolt for the purpose of opening the breech, the piston head, which travels in a groove in the shoe, is unable to turn with it, and is consequently forced back and the piston withdrawn. In drawing back the bolt the breech is opened, and the hammer pressed down to full cock, the cartridge case is withdrawn into the shoe, and thrown out by a slight cant of the rifle. When the bolt is pushed forward and the handle turned down into its place, the rifle is ready to be fired. The lock arrangement is in five pieces, is very simple and strong; it can be carried at half-cock, and is provided with a safety bolt.

Henry – This rifle is adapted for the Boxer cartridge. The breech is closed by means of a breech block which works vertically by the movement of a lever, which is fastened by a catch under the trigger guard; the same movement causes the extractor to eject the empty cartridge case. The cartridge is exploded by a piston passing diagonally through the breech block, and driven by a common side lock and hammer; on raising the hammer the piston is withdrawn by the action of a spiral spring. Mr. Henry has another system of withdrawing the piston which dispenses with this spring, the piston being withdrawn by the act of opening the breech.

Kerr – Rifle is adapted for the Boxer cartridge. The breech is closed by means of a sliding bolt, worked by a lever handle. The cartridge is exploded by a direct acting piston which is driven by a common side lock, and so arranged that it cannot be struck by the hammer until it is in a position of safety. On raising the hammer the piston is withdrawn by means of a spiral spring. Mr. Kerr, however, states that this spring could be dispensed with. The discharged cartridge case is withdrawn from the chamber on drawing back the bolt, and is thrown out by giving the rifle a slight cant to the right. There is a slight incline in the fore end of the shoe which gives to the bolt, in shutting and opening, a screw motion, the effect, in the first instance, being to gently but firmly press home the cartridge, the shock being taken by the shoe, and thereby the risk of an accidental explosion diminished; in the latter to facilitate the extraction of the empty case.

Martini – Is adapted for the Boxer cartridge. The breech is closed by a block which swings on a pin passing through the upper rear end of the shoe, the recoil being taken by the shoe. The cartridge is exploded by a direct action piston which is driven by the action of a strong spiral spring within the breech block. This block is acted on by a lever to the rear of the trigger guard. The act of pushing the lever forward causes the block to fall, the spring to be compressed, and the empty cartridge to be thrown out to the rear; on drawing back the lever, the block is raised so as to close the breech and the arm is ready to be fired. It can be placed at half-cock, and it is also provided with a safety bolt.

Money-Walker – Is adapted for central fire metallic cartridges. The breech is closed by means of a block, working on a pivot or centre which passes through it and the sides of the shoe, and which takes the whole recoil. The fore part of this block contains the lock, and the rear part serves as a lever handle: on raising the handle the fore part of the block is depressed, thereby opening the breech, compressing the spring which drives the piston, and causing the extractor to eject the empty case; on lowering the lever the breech is closed, and the arm is ready to be fired.

Westley-Richards No.1 – Is adapted for a central fire metallic cartridge. The breech is closed by a block swinging on a pin which passes through the upper rear end of the shoe. The lock is contained in the block. By pushing forward a lever which is fastened by a catch to the trigger guard, the block is lowered and the flat spring compressed, which acts on a hammer striking upwards and against the base of the piston which, when the block is opened, is always withdrawn, and a continuation of the motion causes the extractor, which is part of this lever, to withdraw the cartridge case: on drawing back the lever, the block is raised and the rifle is ready to fire.

Westley-Richards No.2 – Is adapted for central fire metallic cartridges. The breech block consists of two main parts connected by a hinge, and the whole fastened by a hinge to the upper part of the shoe, where the barrel is screwed in. The block which closes the breech contains the lock and piston; the other, or tail piece, is the lever by which the action is opened; when shut, this tail piece rests against the curved end of a corresponding curve in the shoe, both struck from a centre below the axis of the rifle, and thus making the action secure. The breech is opened by raising the tail piece and continuing the motion so as to fold over the barrel the two pieces composing the action; in so doing, the spring which drives the piston is compressed, the piston withdrawn, and the extractor caused to withdraw the case. In closing the breech, the block containing the lock is first lowered, and a continuation of the motion shuts the tail piece into its place; the rifle is then ready to be fired. A more perfect description of these systems could have been given had they not been withdrawn by Mr. Richards.

Wilson – Adapted for the Boxer cartridge. The mechanism is on the bolt system. The breech is closed by pushing forward the bolt with the ball of the hand, and when in its place is secured by two lugs on a moveable collar, which are forced into corresponding slots in the shoe, by means of a spring in the shoe-cap. The explosion is caused by a direct acting piston within the bolt, which is driven by a spiral spring: on withdrawing the bolt, the empty case is extracted and thrown out.

APPENDIX 9.

Being the oral and written statements of the Mechanical Engineers as requested by the Special Committee on Martini-Henry Breech-Loading Rifles.

William Pole, Esq, FRS, as questioned by the committee 4-1-1871 (in part) –

Q.7. Have you examined the mechanism of the Martini action, in connexion with this programme? – I have.

Q.8. Have you prepared any written statement of your opinion with reference to the questions contained in this programme? – I have.

Q.9. Will you be so good as to read it to the committee? – I will do so with great pleasure. . .

Having reference to the programme issued by the committee I find it most convenient to begin with the Division C, "On the mechanical character of the several parts", and I will remark on the several subdivisions seriatim.

C.1 – On the falling block, and its power to resist the explosion of the charge.

It is a necessary condition of the contrivance of a radially moving block for closing the breech, that the main centre at its back end on which it moves must be, not in a line with the axis of the barrel, but a certain distance above it.

This position of the centre not only allows the block to fall clear away from the end of the barrel, but when it rises again, causes its face to press against the barrel end, so as to ensure close contact. In fact it is to the raised position of the centre that the efficiency of this ingenious mode of closing the breech is chiefly due.

But it is in consequence of this construction that the block has no *point d'appui* to resist the recoil of the explosion, placed immediately in the position where it would be most effective and most properly situated, namely, in a *direct line with the axis of the barrel.*

The raised main centre will take a large share of the resistance, but the recoil, acting below it, will give the block a tendency to fall, or rotate round its centre. This tendency is diminished by a circumstance which I shall hereafter explain; but treating it now as simply the result of the statical action of the force of the recoil, it would require to be resisted by some external support placed below the block. In the Martini-Henry rifle such a support is formed by the tooth or short lever which actuates the block, and which after forcing it up to its proper closed position wedges itself under a notch made in the block to the purpose, and so offers the required resistance to the recoil.

The proportions of the resistance, which, according on the resolution of the forces, would be taken by the main centre and by the external prop respectively, may be easily calculated. I find that in the short action rifle, estimating the force of recoil of the cartridge as 100, the resulting pressures would be, on the support = 38½, and on the main centre = 98, the latter acting in a direction slightly upwards, at an angle of about 23 degrees with the line of the barrel.

There is however, another important element affecting the equilibrium of the block, namely, the resistance in action offered by the *friction of the base of the cartridge case* on the block face. The effect of the recoil is to press these surfaces together with great force, and so to cause a considerable obstacle to their sliding on each other, which they must do if the block moves. The value of this resistance may also be estimated, and I find that if the coefficient of friction be greater than 1/7th (which it will be in the ordinary condition of the surfaces) the block will have no tendency to turn or fall even if the lower support be removed.

The chief resistance, namely on the main centre, is not taken by the centre pin, but is thrown entirely on a solid knuckle joint of about ½-inch diameter. This abuts directly on a strong solid part of the lock-case, which is firmly united to the barrel; so that the system of forces is selfcontained, and the entire mass of the iron work of the gun is brought by its inertia to resist the blow. The duty of the centre pin is reduced to acting as a centre of motion.

Any pressure coming upon the supporting arm would be carried down to the strong centre pin of the main handle, and so transmitted to the solid metal of the case; but, as previously explained, this pressure is much reduced, if not removed altogether, by the friction against the block face.

To show that this friction really acts in this way a remarkable experiment has been tried at Enfield, which was repeat ed yesterday in my presence. The spring steel pin of the handle centre was taken out, and a soft lead pin substituted and the gun was then fired twice with ball cartridge and then examined; the lead pin came out with perfect ease, and exhibited no mark of the contact of the prop, showing unmistakeably that the latter had sustained no strain from the recoil. The pin will be produced here today. A further proof was afforded, in the same experiment, of the direct back action of the recoil by taking out the main centre pin of the block, and cutting away the upper part of the knuckle socket, so leaving the hinder end of the block quite free to move upwards, and fly out of the case. But when the gun was fired the block did not stir, showing that the effect of the recoil was transmitted almost directly backwards, without any material tendency to force the block either in an upward or downward direction. It is worthy of remark that the original Peabody falling block, the type of all the modern ones, had no lower support; from which it is to be inferred that the direct action of the recoil was known to the inventor of that gun.

C.2 – On the lock action proper, the spring and striker, &c.

It must be admitted that the Martini lock action is a considerable innovation on the old plan, and it will throw light on the comparison between the two to inquire into the nature of the circumstances that have determined the change.

In all ordinary percussion firearms as made down to a few years ago, the fulminating cap has been placed on an external nipple; and no more convenient mode of striking it could be devised than a direct adaptation of the old flint lock, by substituting for the flint foreceps a solid hammer moving round an arc as before. In order to give this radial motion, and so produce thereby a forcible blow, the most expedient means was to use a spring of flat form, which could lie conveniently against the lock plate; this spring being connected by a link and internal lever to the axis of the hammer.

It would seem therefore, that this form of main spring and its somewhat complicated and indirect connexion with the hammer were determined entirely by, as they were admirably adapted to, the old position of the detonator outside the gun. It is at least difficult to see how, under this condition, any other form of spring could have been advantageously used, or how it could have been made to act more directly on the striking body.

But the invention of the breech-loading cartridge, with a detonator at its centre, introduced a new fundamental condition for the striking apparatus. It was evidently possible to adapt something to this which should be more simple, more compact, and more direct in its action than the old apparatus; and for this object nothing could be more appropriate than a spiral spring, actuating a straight striker, both placed immediately behind the centre of the cartridge, and having their line of motion directly upon the point to be struck. It was only necessary so to arrange the breech-closing apparatus as to give room for such a spring and striker in the line of the barrel, and the lock action was at once obtained in the simplest manner.

The inventors of the French Chassepot and the Prussian Nadelgewehr, as well as the designers of other breech loading central fire rifles seized upon this idea, which has also been adopted by M. Martini.

The arrangement of this striking action, so simple in its construction, so direct in its action, and so secure and shelt ered in its position, is altogether so admirable, and, to use an untranslateable German word, so *Zweckmassig* that I can hardly understand the proposal to substitute for it the more cumbersome, complicated, indirect, and exposed mechanism of the old lock, which was intended for and adapted to an entirely different set of fundamental conditions. I conceive such a substitution would be mechanically a retrograde step, which could only be justified by the exist ence either of some great defect in the new lock, or of some great superiority in the old one. It is therefore, desirable carefully to compare the principles and practical action of the two, in order to see if any such reason for the change can be found.

It has been said that the effect of the spiral spring is more in the nature of a pressure than a blow, but this assertion does not seem to be tenable in the present case. The principle of action is alike in each variety. In the act of cocking the hand furnishes a quantity of mechanical power, or "work" which is employed to overcome the resistânce of the spring through a certain space, and which remains stored up in the spring so long as it is held by the detent in its full state of compression. When the spring is let go, as it finds little or no resistance, it flies back, and during this action the work stored up in it is employed in giving *velocity* to the striker or hammer and other parts moved, so that by the time it has arrived at the end of its stroke, the power or work originally put into the spring by cocking has (with some small deductions for friction, etc) become converted into the *vis viva* of the moving parts; and finally, when these parts are brought to rest by striking the cartridge, this amount of power or work is given out upon the fulminating cap, causing its ignition.

The amount of power or work employed, and the consequent dynamic power of the blow, are capable of easy determination. I have endeavoured to estimate them in the short action Martini, and to compare the result with that in the service Snider-Enfield. Taking the data furnished me by Col. Dixon, (the resistance of the Martini spring I have taken at 40 lbs, that of the Snider spring at 56 lbs, both at full cock) I find in the Martini action the quantity of work is = about one unit (ie, what would be equivalent to raising 1 lb 1 foot high) whereas in the Snider it is about 1.68. Hence the dynamic power of the blow in the Snider is two-thirds greater than in the Martini, which is reasonable, as in the former it is more indirect in its action, and has to pass through the medium of the long oblique piston with its strong spring, whereas in the Martini the whole power stored in the spring, with the exception of a very minute friction, is discharged directly upon the detonator.

It is further possible, knowing the weights of the parts in motion, to calculate, by the laws of dynamics, the *velocity* with which, in each case, the striker impinges on the cartridge. In the Snider this comes out under 30 feet per second whereas in the Martini, from the lighter mass in motion, the velocity is nearly 35 fps. (Col. Dixon has confirmed this result, not only by calculation, but by an interesting experiment. He has let the striker fall from various heights upon a cap, and has found that when the height is such as to give a velocity of about 35 fps, the cap is fired with the same certainty as in the gun.) So that, although the dynamic force of the blow is less, the striking velocity is greater; or in other words, instead of being, as has been asserted, analogous to a dead pressure, the Martini spiral spring really strikes a smarter blow than the old lock action.

But after all the efficiency of the blow is really a question for experiment. Repeated trials will show whether, with a certain strength and range of spring, the ignition is certain; and if so, nothing farther is wanted. If on the other hand misfires are found to occur, the strength or range of spring will require further increase until the requisite certainty is ensured. The foregoing calculations are only useful as showing the erroneous nature of the objections to the Martini action on the supposed ground of a difference in the nature of the blow.

It remains to say a few words on the chief practical points in the lock action.

First, as to the nature of the spring. It is objected that the spiral spring is less trustworthy than the flat one; but I cannot think that there is any good ground for such an assertion. The spiral spring is a form which has been used long enough, and often enough, to prove its efficiency. Two well known examples of its extensive use may be mentioned, one on the largest, and the other on the most delicate scale, namely, the railway buffer, and the chronometer balance spring. Between these there are all sorts and sizes of spiral springs, used in all sorts of ways. Almost all complicated and delicate machinery abounds in them, and without them many mechanical contrivances would be almost impracticable. At Enfield there are machines containing spiral springs, each of which makes nearly a million strokes per week; and yet these have worked for years without requiring repair or giving any trouble, and without losing power. One large application illustrates the *permanence* of the strength, namely, the Salter's Spring Balance, which is seen upon every safety valve of railway locomotives. If the force varied with the age or use of the spring the thing would be useless and untrustworthy, but it is not found so. The spiral spring is probably the simplest, cheapest, and most easily made of all forms, and I know of no reason why it cannot, by goodness of material, and care in manufacture and tempering, be given as great a degree of perfection and permanence as any other kind of spring. One of its greatest advantages is its independence, requiring no fixed abutment as the flat lock spring does.

In the Martini rifle the spring and striking action are completely housed, not only within the general external case, but also further within the internal falling block, a very great protection, as is shown by the admirable way in which these arms appear to have stood the tests of exposure. It is asserted as a counter-vailing disadvantage, that the parts within the block are liable to get fouled or clogged up with dirt or oil; but I am not aware that this is shown by experience, and the facility of cleaning would be, I should think, an answer to the objection.

C.3 – On the duties and action of the main handle.

I believe this is usually called the lever, but I call it the main handle, because there are so many levers in the motion, that it is perhaps a better distinguishing name. The main handle has three duties to perform, viz. –

(A) To raise and lower the breech block
(B) To cock the lock action
(C) Indirectly to actuate the cartridge extractor.

The last of these will be noticed under head C.7. It is only necessary here to speak of the other two.

(A) Action of the main handle in lowering and raising the breech block.

The motion of the breech block is effected by a short arm fixed on the handle, and engaging in a notch in the block; this arrangement is in duplicate, one arm and notch actuating the block on each side.

This arm is usually called a lever; but I am inclined to infer from its peculiar form, that the inventor had in his mind the idea of causing the two members, the block and the handle, to rotate together by toothed gearing, one tooth of which (being sufficient for the small angular motion required) is represented by the arm in question. In order to show that, I have made a diagram with an imaginary continuation of the teeth (see Plate I). This is the arm as existing in the Martini-Henry rifle, and I have drawn those dotted teeth in order to show that it really is one tooth out of several, of which one tooth is sufficient to communicate the small motion which is required.

This view of the case aids materially in judging of the mechanical fitness and merit of the arrangement, inasmuch as the communication of angular motion by toothed gearing is a very common and approved contrivance; and the adaptation of it by a single tooth to a slight motion, assumes a more legitimate character than if the arm were treated as a mere short arm, without any special design.

At a certain point of the upward motion of the block the tooth enters a side recess, and gradually fixes itself firmly under the block so as to form the support to it when it has arrived at its proper position for firing. This has been mentioned under a previous head.

It is, I believe, said that it would be more advantageous to communicate motion to the block at a point farther from the main centre and nearer to its front end. There is no doubt that a force so applied would exert a greater power over the angular motion of the block; but the question here would arise, whether such an increase in power is warranted? For it is evident that if the present arrangement is sufficient for all the reasonable requirements of the arm, no departure from it, on the ground of a mere hypothetical superiority, would be any advantage.

In the ordinary normal action of the gun, there is certainly no sign of insufficiency of power, the movement of the block, in both directions, being easy and certain. It can only be to meet abnormal and exceptional cases that an increase of power would be required. I have no means of judging what cases of this kind might arise; I can conceive that the sides of the block or of the external case, or both, might become rusted or dirty, when the block would be difficult to move; and I have also heard that great power might be wanted to raise the block in order to force home a sticking cartridge. The probabilities of these or other such contingencies arising and the necessity of providing for them, are questions I must leave for the consideration of the committee. All I can say is that the present is a good mechanical arrangement; it is part of a general design pre-

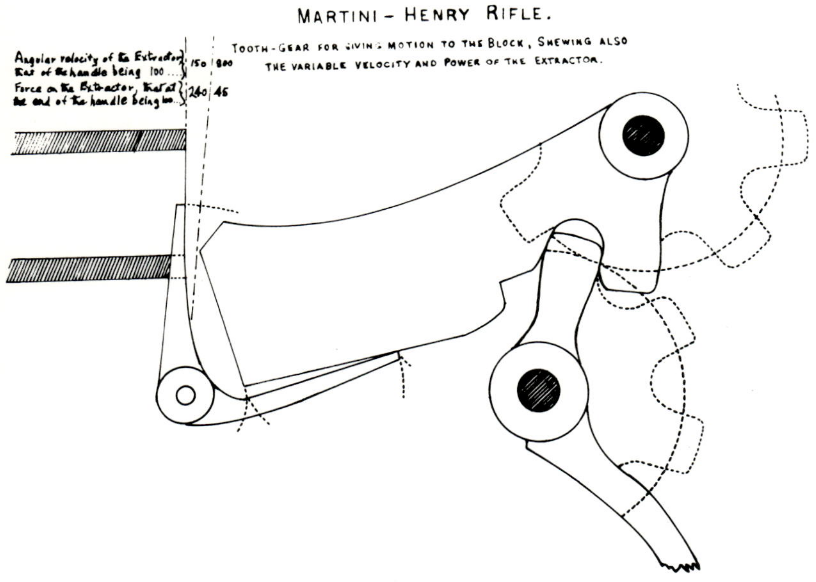

Plate I of Professor Pole's Statement.

senting, as a whole, great advantages; and unless satisfactory proof can be brought of its practical insufficiency there would seem no satisfactory ground to warrant its condemnation.

In raising the block the tooth has to overcome a resistance arising from the force of the main spring, which (as hereafter explained) it has to compress to some extent to complete the cocking. This resistance is felt most strongly when the tooth is about to slide into its final bearing. It is objected that under this force the friction of repeated use would tend to wear away the tooth and notch; the result of which would be that the block would not be brought up to its proper position. No doubt the force acting on this point is considerable, but as the parts will of course be either made of steel or case hardened (which is the same thing as far as the surfaces are concerned) and so the friction will, under ordinary circumstances, be kept down by regular cleaning and oiling, no considerable wear should occur. Besides, a careful examination of the action will show that the heavy friction will come only on the front corner of the tooth, and on a small projection that it works on; and that even if these parts wear away a little, the *top surface* of the tooth and its corresponding face in the block (on which the final position of the block really depends) will remain unaffected the only result of the wear being a little change in the velocity of motion, a little tardiness in coming up to its place, which is quite immaterial. However, as the absolute tightness of the fit of the block face against the barrel is not essential with the new cartridge, the only evil of the block not fully rising would be that the striker would impinge a little too low, and if this happened to such an extent as to cause a misfire, the defect would be at once discovered, and a remedy might be easily applied, by either slightly drawing out the tooth, or substituting a new one. It would I think be easy by a slight modification of the top of the tooth to make it self-adjusting if necessary.

It has been further objected that the wear of the axis of the main handle would also produce similar evils, but this with hard surfaces would be unlikely to occur, and if it did the remedy would be as easy as in the former case.

These questions of wear should however be submitted to practical trial, which would soon show the value of any objections made in relation thereto. I have been shown a rifle which is said to have passed a very large number of rounds, 30,000 I think; and on the most careful examination of the parts I can find no trace of any wear. Some of these parts will be produced here today. (NOTE: In a footnote in the original text it is stated this rifle had probably fired about 10,000, not 30,000, rounds.)

(B) Actions of the main handle in cocking.

The cocking is done by the same motions which activate the block, and it is worthy of remark that by a very ingenious arrangement the work is divided between the two motions, forward and backward. This diagram (Plate II) shows the three positions: first after discharging, secondly with the block lowered, and thirdly with the block raised again and the gun cocked.

In the first or forward motion of the handle (lowering the block) the upright arm of the tumbler, which is actuated by a shoulder on the handle, pulls back the striker, compressing the spring by about 3-10ths of an inch, the tumbler, striker, and spring being all held in position by the tumbler rest having caught under the upper notch or "bent" of the tumbler.

When the handle is moved backwards (raising the block again) the striker and fore end of the spring are held in position by the tumbler independently of the position of the block, but the stop or resisting base at the back end of the

Process of Cocking.

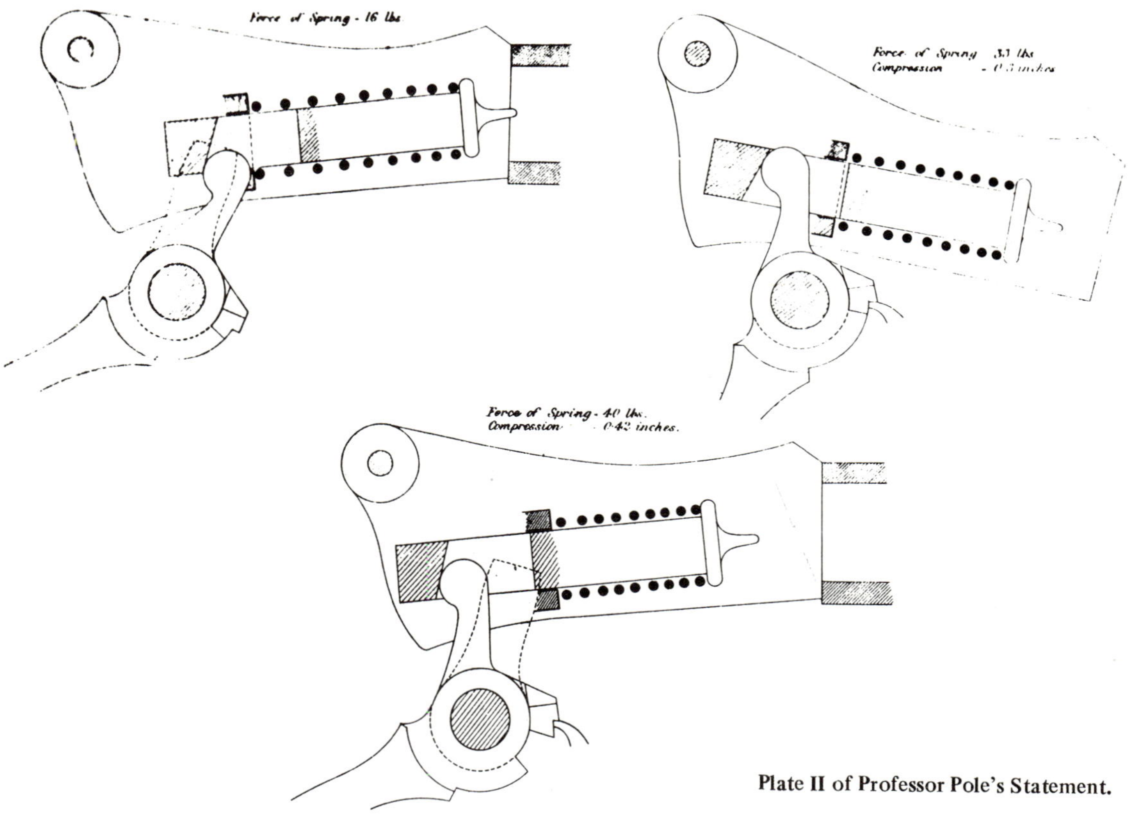

Plate II of Professor Pole's Statement.

spring (which is fixed to the block and moves with it), is caused to move forwards, shortening the distance between it and the fore end of the striker and thus compressing the spring about 1-8th inch more.

If by mistake the shooter pulls the trigger while the block is down, no harm will be done, for the spring will raise the block to its place again, and as it has not been fully compre ssed, and as it has work to do in raising the block, it will probably not have power enough to fire the cartridge.

C.4 – On the centre pin of the main handle.

This pin is a very ingenious part of the mechanism; it has several duties to perform. In the middle of its length it carries the tumbler of the lock action, which fits on a square part of the pin, and consequently whenever it is moved the pin revolves with it.

On each side of this come the jaws of the main handle, serving to raise and depress the block; these are perforated with round holes and turn on the pin.

Outside these come the two sides of the trigger guard, which the pin passes through and serves to fasten into the general frame. Beyond these again the pin passes through the two walls of the main case.

On one end of the pin, outside the case, is fixed a pointer, called the "indicator", this is in one piece with the pin, and as the pin must always move with the tumbler, the position of the external indicator will always show whether or not the gun is cocked.

The pin is kept in its place by what is called an "eclipse" screw, an ingenious and effective contrivance, which allows the pin to turn without the danger of working loose, which would arise if it were fastened by an ordinary thread or nut.

None of the various offices of the pin interfere with each other, and this pin is efficient for all. It is strong and of large diameter, and is, I believe, made of hard steel.

C.5 – On the trigger action.

The trigger action as now made in the Martini-Henry rifle, is peculiar, and differs from every other action I have seen. Although exceedingly simple in construction, its modus operandi requires careful attention thoroughly to understand, and is not easy to describe. It will facilitate the description to state certain facts communicated to me by Col. Dixon as to the history of this part of the mechanism.

In its original state, the action consisted merely of a simple trigger prolonged upwards, the top of which engaged in a notch or "bent" of the tumbler, and was liberated, discharging the gun, by the pressure of the finger below.

This exceedingly simple arrangement was however attended with some disadvantage in consequence of the great pressure of the spring on the bent or notch of the tumbler, which amounted with a 40lb spring to about 75 lbs. If the line of the bent or notch was radial, that is to say, in a line with the centre of the tumbler, the pull necessary to detach it was found too heavy, and if this was eased by inclining the line of the bent the gun was unsafe and liable to go off if struck on the ground.

To remedy this, Col. Dixon devised the present solution. In it the tumbler rests securely on a piece separate from the trigger and analogous to the ordinary sear, and which in this gun is called the "tumbler rest".

The trigger is made to move on its centre pin with a slotted hole, the long axis of this slot being inclined at a particular angle, and when the gun is cocked the trigger is quite loose, playing about in its slot, and not touching either the tumbler rest or the tumbler.

When however the pressure of the finger is applied, the trigger, pressing the inclined surface of the slotted hole against the centre pin, rises, and its top-end engages under a second notch in the tumbler below the main bent, and as the finger pressure increases, an upward force is exerted on the tumbler, thus relieving the tumbler rest from a portion of the weight it previously sustained. At the same time the trigger acting as a simple lever, its upper end presses horizontally outwards against the tumbler rest, and when the latter is sufficiently lightened the trigger end forces it away, disengaging it from the bent and discharging the gun.

It might be said that this action is only relieving the tumbler rest of a weight to put it directly on the end of the trigger, and that no good is done; but that is not so, for this reason – the weight relieved from the tumbler is taken on the upper end of the trigger; but the surface of the latter is considerably inclined, so that it will slip away with ease; and it is found, I believe, that by altering the angle of this surface the discharging pull may be adjusted and made lighter or heavier at pleasure.

I find by calculation that a pull of 8 lb on the trigger will give an upward force of about 24 lb, so reducing the pressure on the tumbler rest from 75 to 51 lb. It also gives an outward horizontal thrust against the tumbler rest of about 14 lbs, which is ample to disengage it from the friction of the bent. The usual pull I believe varies from 4 or 5 lbs according to the state of lubrication of the surfaces. (See Plate III.)

I learn that in an ordinary Snider lock, the pressure on the bent is about 36 lbs, and it has been urged that the pressure in the Martini, being so much greater, gives a tendency to a more rapid wear, by which the original adjustment of the pull of the trigger will be disturbed, and the action become untrustworthy.

The value of this objection will depend on the original strength, hardness, and accuracy of the parts and likewise on the care bestowed on the use of the gun. If the parts are strong and hard, and are kept clean and well oiled, I should not think that they would materially suffer under long use;

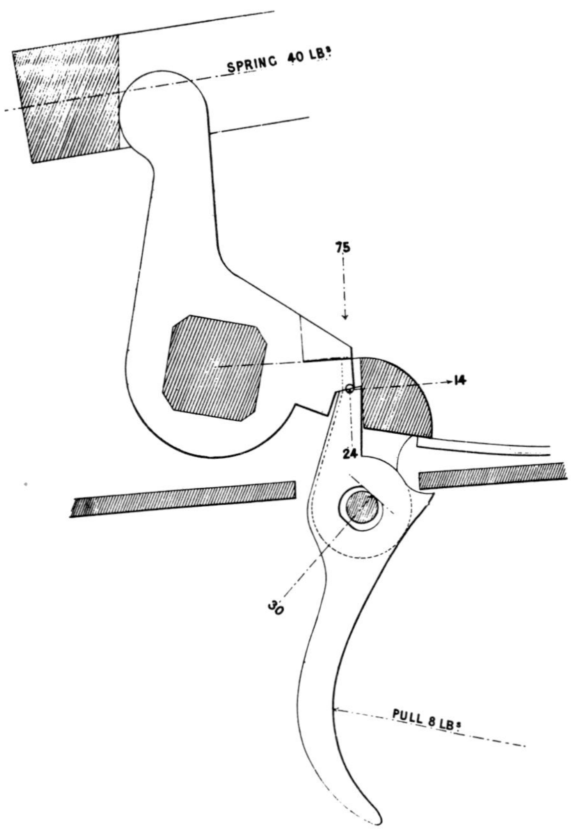

Plate III of Professor Pole's Statement.

but this is perhaps a matter for practical trial. In the gun shown to me which had passed such a large number of rounds no trace of wear on these parts was perceptible. The parts will be produced here today.

I cannot see any ground of objection to any other part of the apparatus, all the directions of the pressures and bearing parts appearing to me properly and mechanically adapted for performing their duty.

The action undoubtedly requires accuracy in the manufacture, but this condition must always be expected with arms of such precision and perfection as that now in question, and it is for the purposes of obtaining such accuracy as I understand the beautiful contrivances of the Enfield manufactory have been in good measure designed. Moreover, some of the parts seem a little delicate, but they are well protected, and they are capable of being strengthened, and the bearing surfaces increased if necessary.

The looseness of the trigger when the gun is at full cock, and its slight tendency to rise, when first pulled, appear to be liked in practice as being analogous to the ordinary design.

C.6 – On the safety bolt.

This appears to be made on a good principle, namely that of inserting a bar under the tumbler rest, which, as long as it is kept there will effectually prevent the gun from going off. But the mechanism is delicate, and might be liable to get out of order, or be cogged up with dirt. Moreover, it works at a disadvantage by the power being applied considerably out of the line of motion, which throws an oblique strain on the parts. Probably this part of the apparatus would admit of improvement.

C.7 – On the cartridge extractor.

The cartridge extractor appears well designed; it acts on two opposite sides of the cartridge, thus getting a better hold on it than the Snider, which acts on only one side.

The action of the extracting lever has a feature which is very ingenious and effective. It is so arranged as to give its greatest power at the commencement of the extraction and its greatest velocity at the end. The advantage of this is evident; for the greatest force is exerted to start the cartridge, while after this first resistance is overcome the slightly conical shape purposely given to the chamber allows it to move easier, and then it is more important to give it a high velocity in order to jerk it clear away. The manner in which these varying effects are produced will be explained by the diagram. (See Plate I.)

The horizontal arm of the extracting lever is acted on by the contact of the lower side of the falling block, but this contact takes place at two alternative points. At the beginning of the extraction it acts so as to give the shortest leverage with the block and the longest with the extractor, but after moving through a certain space the point of contact changes, so as to reverse the conditions.

I have calculated the force and velocity in both positions. At the commencement of the extraction, supposing the force applied at the end of the handle be = 100, then (neglecting friction and the resistance of the spiral spring) the force on the cartridge will be about 240; also supposing the angular velocity of the handle = 100, that of the extract ing lever will be = 150. But when the cartridge has been moved through a space of about 1/16th of an inch, the conditions change; the force becomes reduced to 45, and the velocity increased to 800.

The action of the extractor does not begin until the handle has nearly finished its stroke, and it is principally worked by a jerk, in which, however, the changes abovementioned do not fail to tell.

C.8 – On the closing case.

The arrangement by which all the machinery of the lock and breech action, except the trigger, is enclosed in a metal case, appears to me to be very beneficial in reference to compactness, strength, and protection from external injury or from dust and wet.

This, however, involves the condition that as the parts are concealed from ordinary view they must be easily taken out for examination and cleaning, and that condition is complied with. It requires a little "knack" to get the breech block out and in again, but this is soon learned, and then the operation of taking the whole action to pieces and putting it together again is quick and easy.

C.9 – On the stocking.

The question of the strength of the stocking is rather a question for experimental trial than for pre-judgement. I presume that the condition of enclosing the whole breech action in a metal case must necessarily involve the separation of the wooden stock in two parts, but I do not think the continuity in the ordinary gun adds much to the strength, as the wood is so cut to pieces about the lock.

It is possible that the present mode of attachment may be somewhat weak when strained flatwise, but it can be so easily strengthened in this or in any other direction that it appears unnecessary to consider this matter further.

The three other points *A, B, D,* need very little remark.

A – On the facility and economy of manufacture.

This is rather a question for the authorities at Enfield, but having visited the establishment there and seen the high degree of perfection arrived at in the processes of manufacture of small arms, I see no reason to doubt that the Martini action can be made at such an establishment with facility and accuracy and at a reasonable cost.

B – On the simplicity and efficiency of the breech action generally.

This will probably have been sufficiently dwelt upon under head C.

As a whole the Martini breech action appears to me exceedingly simple and perfectly efficient, and I cannot see any reason why, with ordinary care, the efficiency should suffer by use in any climate.

The enclosing case protects the action against external violence, and as to internal derangement by dirt or rust, this can be guarded against by a moderate amount of examination and cleaning, which in any arm of precision must be required to a greater extent than with the old rough firelock.

D – On the measure of importance of any defects in the Martini action.

This has also been anticipated under head C, but it may be worth while to recapitulate the chief points to which it would seem desirable to direct attention.

The first is the mainspring. The proper strength and range of this which will suffice to give certainty of the fire having been determined by experiment, such precautions must be adopted in the manufacture as will ensure uniformity of strength and permanence of elasticity. This is only an ordinary manufacturer's problem, and with the ability and experience to be found at Enfield, or in any of the larger gun factories, it can be easily and certainly solved. And when this uniformity and permanence are attained, from the extreme simplicity of the lock action, there would appear to be little chance of any derangement. If a spring should break a new one can be inserted in two or three minutes with the greatest ease, and at an insignificant cost.

As to the tumbler and trigger action some of the parts are rather delicately made in the specimens I have seen, and might, perhaps, suffer if forced by rough hands, when anything went wrong in the use of the arm; but they would easily admit of strengthening, and there is nothing in the nature of their action to lead to derangement. The question as to the probable wear of the bent and tumbler rest has already been remarked upon.

The motion of the block by the handle and tooth appears scarcely liable to derangement. The question of probable wear as effecting this has also been considered.

The sufficiency of power to move the block in extraordinary cases will be settled by practical judgement as to the nature and degree of probability of such cases.

The safety bolt and the strength of stocking will probably receive further consideration.

There are also some minor points about the construction, such as the form and strength of screws, &c, which may perhaps be improved.

Great attention should, I think, be devoted to the facility of getting the action to pieces and putting it together again. This is not only the condition which allows the whole to be enclosed, but it is all important as regards the prevention of derangement or interruption of the action by dirt, rust, or clogging. With this view every fastening screw should be strong, perfect, and free in its action, and the parts should be so arranged as to leave no doubt or possibility of mistake in coming together. I may add my opinion that the superintendent of the small arms factory should have no difficulty in meeting these requirements.

If all these things are attended to, and the parts are as well made as might be expected from the general excellence of the Enfield manufacture, I cannot, for my own part, see anything but a favourable prospect for the success of the arm.

Edward Woods, Esq., CE, as questioned by the committee, 4-1-1871 (in part) –

Q.41. I presume that you have before you the programme for the examination of witnesses on the mechanical construction of the Martini action? – Yes, I have that before me.

Q.42. Would you wish to bring before the committee a written statement in connexion with this programme, or would you prefer that the committee should ask you questions about it? – I have prepared a written statement, and perhaps it might facilitate the expression of my views if I read it, and I shall be very happy to answer any question that may arise upon it.

Q.43. Would you be so good as to read it to the committee?

Letter A.

Having carefully examined the breech action, and having seen the machinery and appliances at the small arms factory at Enfield for the manufacture of breech actions, I am of opinion that the Martini-Henry rifle breech action can be manufactured with facility and economy by machinery properly arranged for the purpose, whether at the government small arms factory, or any higher class private factory.

Letter B.

My examination of the mechanical character of the various parts as applied under the head C, and my investigations at the small arms factory, Enfield, have led me to the conclusion that the Martini breech action generally is of a very simple and efficient character, and that such action if introduced in rifles properly manufactured will do its work in all climates with safety and regularity.

Letter C.

1. Falling block. The falling block is of simple construction, affording great facility for the introduction of the cartridge, and is in itself sufficiently strong for transmitting the pressure on to its joint and support.

The principal part of the pressure produced by the explosion of the charge is transferred to the joint at the back, such joint being composed of the rounded end of block as an axis, and the corresponding socket in the body or case; in combination with the block axis pin and the holes in which this is inserted. The pressure is mainly taken by the knuckle joint, the fit of the pin being purposely made a little slack.

Taking the force of the recoil as 100 acting in the line of axis of the barrel, and measuring the moments round the joint of the block (see Plate IV), I find the resultant pressure acting on the joint to be represented by 98, such pressure being transmitted in a line inclined 20½ degrees to the axis of the barrel, and passing within the surfaces of the knuckle joint. Hence ample provision is afforded, irrespectively of the block axis pin, and irrespectively of the friction of the parts, for resisting the tendency of the pressure to force the knuckle end of the block out of the socket. I consider that adequate support is afforded to the block by the short arm of the lever below it.

C.2 – The spiral spring and striker.

The action of the spring and striker is calculated to give an adequate and uniform blow to the cap. Spiral springs of the required strength and dimensions, are, if made of proper

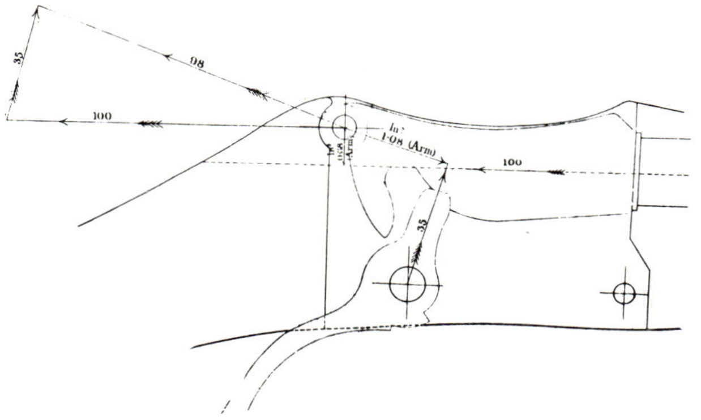

Plate IV of Mr. Wood's Statement.

material, and when adjusted for permanent set, as little liable to fracture or loss of power as are springs of any other form, provided they can be kept from rusting.

The spiral spring is effective in striking the sharp, quick, blow wanted for ingnition of the cap, and can by trials be readily adjusted to produce such blow, the effect in this respect being analogous to that of the ordinary lock spring, inasmuch as the force of the spiral spring imparted to the striker throughout its "stroke" (of .42-inch) is engaged in the production of accelerated motion and storing up of *vis viva* to be momentarily expended in the blow on the cap. A pressure ranging from 40 lbs to 18 lbs appears to be sufficient.

The concentric combination of spiral spring and striker, the one within the other, and both within the cylinder of the block, is a simple and compact arrangement, affording the parts protection from dust and dirt. Thus enclosed it would seem probable that the usual periodical overhaul and cleansing of the action would suffice to keep it in good working order.

A spiral spring is more likely to have its power impaired by rust than an ordinary spring, on account of the large surface of metal exposed compared with the weight of the material. The plunger of the striker being guided by the cylinders in which it works, the striking point is directed accurately into and through the hole in the block face, and therefore cannot fail to hit the centre of the cartridge, assuming the block to be brought up to its correct place.

The motion of the striker in a straight line admits of great strength being given to the block face, as an increase of length given to the hole (determined by the requisite thickness of the face plate), does not affect the action of the striker, whilst it increases the strength of the block to withstand the pressure, and conduces to prevent enlargement of the hole.

C.3 – The working lever.

The working lever possesses adequate strength for the performance of its various functions, viz, lowering, raising, and supporting the block, cocking the rifle as the block falls and rises, and working the extractor.

Taking the force of the recoil at 100, (see Plate IV) and measuring the moments round the joint of the block, the abstract pressure on the end of the lever acting in a line drawn from the middle of its end through the centre of its axis pin is represented by 35, assuming there to be no friction. When the block is up to its place for firing, the short arm of the lever is subject only to a compressive strain, and consequently the pressure is transmitted through it without inducing a transverse strain, and in the most favourable manner for preventing injury to the fibre of the iron, whilst the pressure passing from the lever arm to the body is conveyed into a strong and well-supported centre pin.

The friction produced by the jamming of the cartridge case after explosion, added to that occasioned by the pressure of the block on its axis of motion, must materially reduce the downward pressure on the lever arm.

That such is the case was amply proved by experiments I witnessed at Enfield on 2-1-1871, in company with Col. Dixon, Professor Pole, and Mr. Nasmyth, when the Martini-Henry rifle was fired off several times in succession after removing the block axis pin altogether and substituting a lead pin for the steel pin of the lever axis, and filing away the top part of the socket of the block joint to a surface at right angles to the axis of the barrel. Under these circumstances the gun was fired without causing any disturbance of the block, and without producing any sensible impression on the lead pin.

The point of greatest wear is the *edge* of the tooth or cam which operates on the inclined curved surface of the block in raising the same; but the parts of the surfaces of the tooth and the block on which the accuracy in keeping the block up to its place depends, are seen to be subject to very little wear and tear, the work of lifting the block having been done *before* the flat end of the lever arm slips into its place of rest under the corresponding ledge in the block.

If the working parts are well case hardened there is every reason to believe that the lever will be likely to continue to do its work properly in all respects. A Martini-Henry rifle, which was said to have fired 30,000 times (10,000), was submitted at Enfield for our inspection. The action was taken to pieces in our presence and on submitting them to the standard gauges no sensible wear could be detected.

The compression of the main spring is effected by two movements of the lever, viz, those which are incidental, first, to the lowering, and secondly, to the raising of the block; the last operation simultaneously placing the gun at full cock.

C.4 – The centre pin of lever, tumbler, and indicator.

This is a strong pin, and I see no objection to placing the lever, tumbler, and indicator to work on it. By such combin ation a simple, compact, and I consider, durable arrangement of parts is effected, enabling several important movements to be accomplished by one pull of the hand.

The action of the indicator being a direct function of that of the lever and tumbler, all being connected with the same shaft or pin, it cannot fail to indicate correctly, whether to sight or touch, the state in which the gun is as to being cocked or otherwise.

C.5 – The tumbler, sear, and trigger.

The tumbler, sear, and trigger may in their combined action be rendered safe and strong, and appear to be capable of adjustment on their bearing surfaces to any desired pull, say within the prescribed limits of from 6 to 8 lbs.

The retention in use of a steady pull will depend on the maintenance of uniform power in the main spring, on the durability of the engaging surfaces, viz, the noses and rests, and on the good fitting of the axis, holes, and pin.

The original adjustment of the trigger with its oval hole for the axis pin, in its connexion with and relation to, the tumbler, is one of some delicacy requiring great accuracy in the construction, but this once effected the mechanism may be expected to be efficient and durable. It would contribute to the durability if the axis pin of the trigger were made of a greater diameter.

C.6 – The safety bolt.

I am of opinion that the locking bolt, with its thumb piece, screw, and spring, is of somewhat too delicate a construction, and that in ordinary use and when the parts are clogged with oil or dust, the bolt may be liable to stick. Such will most likely occur if the soldier should not be in the habit of systematically using the locking bolt.

C.7 – The cartridge extractor.

The form and application of the extractor seems to leave nothing to be desired. The double blow struck on the lower arm of the bent lever by the descending block, first at the long leverage, giving great power to draw the cartridge case; and secondly, at the short leverage, giving velocity and consequently a sharp jerk to the loosened case, serving to completely throw it out, is eminently effective.

C.8 – The closed metal case.

I am of opinion that the closed case affords great strength and reliability to the parts of the breech action, making this, so to speak, a self-contained piece of mechanism, and tending to promote its durability. Doubtless, dust and damp will find their way into the case, but experience alone can determine whether to an extent likely to cause failures in firing. The rubbing surfaces will, to a great extent, keep themselves clean by use, and there is plenty of room within the case for the dirt thus thrown off the working parts to rest quietly until it is removed at the ordinary period for overhauling the action.

C.9 – The mode of stocking.

In principle I see no objection to the divided stock, whatever objection there may be attaching to the mode of fixing the butt end to the body of the breech action. The fixing of this certainly appeared at first sight rather weak. When at Enfield on the 29th of December last I witnessed some trials made by Col. Dixon to determine the relative strength of the Martini-Henry and Snider stocks, and will describe the results. The muzzle end was placed in a ferrule swivelling on a pivot, the gun was elevated and allowed to descend through a space of 4 feet 5½ inches, and to fall upon a cast iron anvil plate, supported by a wooden block below. The guns which were tried were a Martini-Henry which had been returned from Canada, and an ordinary Snider, which Col. Dixon provided. The blow produced no disturbance of the stock in either case. We tried the locks afterwards, and they worked perfectly free, and in fact no damage was apparent to either, with the exception of a little bruise on the edge of the end of the butt. These trials, as far as they went, showed the Martini-Henry stocking to be as strong as that of the Snider. The Snider stock afterwards proved to be weak at the point where the lock is inserted, as much of the substance of the wood there is removed.

I would here explain another experiment Col. Dixon made, using each arm as a sort of club, and dashing the butt end against a wooden block. In both cases he broke the stocks with apparently equal blows as far as one could judge by the efforts he appeared to put into his blows. The Martini-Henry broke first through the "hand" or small part of the stock, one of the fractures commencing at the point where the head of the bolt was screwed up against the washer, and another fracture commencing at the insertion of the lever catch. Upon the second trial of the Martini-Henry, the butt came out of the socket altogether, the steel bolt having broken short off through the screw just at the place where it screwed into the boss. The Snider broke to pieces through the lock, in fact, the whole of the wood was crushed through the lock. The Snider stock thus proved to be very weak at the point where the lock is inserted, so much of the substance of the wood being there removed. The Martini-Henry gave way either in the hand of the stock, by the wood breaking across, or by the butt coming out of its socket through the fracture of the bolt.

That completes my observations on mechanical construction and the only further observation which I have put down is this, and in reference to Letter D, that the defects which I have noticed in commenting upon the mechanical character of the various parts are defects of detail, being neither inherent in, and inseparable from, the Martini-Henry action, and appear to me to be capable of correction without material change of design.

James Nasmyth, Esq., as questioned by the committee, 4-1-1871 (in part) –

Q.75. I presume you have looked at the programme for the examination of witnesses on the mechanical construction of the Martini-Henry rifle? – I have.

Q.76. Have you prepared a paper in answer to any of the questions? – Yes: they are rather laconic answers to the various questions, but I daresay they are subjects for extension if it may appear desirable to the committee to question me further.

Q.77. Will you be so good as to read the paper to the committee, and you can enlarge upon any portions of it to which you wish to draw particular attention, and the committee will also have an opportunity of examining you on any portions of it? – Yes, I shall be happy to do so.

My answer to Question A is this: All the parts of the Martini-Henry rifle, as submitted to my inspection, appear to me capable of being manufactured by appropriate machinery with as great economy and with as small an amount of hand-work, fitting, and special adjustment of parts as in the case of the Enfield or other rifles as made at the government small arms factory, or any other first-class manufactory.

Upon Question B my answer is: Taken as a whole I consider the general construction and details of the Martini-Henry rifle to be simple and efficient, and likely to perform the required duty in all climates with durability, safety, and regularity.

On Question C I say: As to the mechanical character of the various parts, they are in themselves of an ordinary nature, and are likely to perform their respective functions in an effective and durable manner. What I mean by ordinary nature is, there is no absolute novelty in the mechanical details; they are all well understood forms and parts, and there is nothing very special in them.

With regard to C.1, I reply: The form and arrangement of the falling block I consider to be well adapted to resist the explosion of the charge without any undue strain on any of the joints. The position of the falling block when subjected to the action of explosion is most favourable to its capability of resisting its violence. The recoil of the falling block is transferred to the general body of the rifle at the hinge joint at the rear end, where it abuts on to a corresponding recess in the action box, from whence the recoil is transfered to the entire mass of the rifle in the most favourable manner for the safe absorption of the recoil by the inertia of the rifle. The hinge or joint pin at the rear end of the falling block is purposely fitted loose so as to save it from any direct or destructive injury by the immediate violence of the explosion. The substantial and intimate union of the breech action box with the barrel and other parts of the rifle lends the entire inertia of the mass of the rifle into play, and so renders the concussion practically harmless to the general structure of the rifle.

With regard to C.2: I am of opinion that the spiral spring and striker may be confidently relied on to perform their respective duties effectually and permanently.

My reply to C.3 is this: So far as I am capable of judging, the working lever is placed in a suitable and convenient position, and has at the same time ample power for performing the duties assigned to it, and with every reasonable probability of doing so without undue wear and tear.

With regard to C.4: I see no practical objection against employing the centre pin of the working lever to serve the combined purposes referred to in this question. The permanence of the parts it actuates and their efficient action are not interfered with by the combination in question, while simplicity is much enhanced.

As to C.5: I consider that the tumbler, sear, and trigger are sufficiently strong for the durable performance of their respective functions.

To C.6: The safety bolt appears to perform its duty in a satisfactory manner, but I consider that some improvement may be made in it as regards the substantiality of some of the details, so as to render durability and faithfulness of action.

To C.7 my answer is: The cartridge extractor appears to me to perform its function with certainty and durability.

With regard to C.8: I consider that the mode in which the parts of the breech action of the Martini-Henry rifle are enclosed in a metal case, while securing their efficient action, at the same time importantly contribute to their preservation from the injurious action of dust, wet, or other causes of derangement or decay, while it affords a simple and substantial means of preserving the exact relative position of the parts, and yet presents no difficulty to their inspection when such may become desirable.

With regard to C.9: The mode of stocking appears to me to be at once simple and effective; if however, an increase in the depth of the socket in the rear of the breech action box could without inconvenience be made, it would materially add to the firmness of the hold of the stock when subject to violence. It would also, with this object in view, be well to make the bolt head hole in the body of the stock as small as possible in diameter.

As respects Question D: I do not see any special cause to anticipate undue deterioration of the parts of the Martini-Henry rifle, with the exception of the doubtful substantiality of the parts of the safety bolt as referred to in answer to No.6. All its parts and details appear to me to be well contrived and adapted to the performance of their respective duties and to be easily get-at-able for inspection, cleaning, and repairs, or substitution of new parts when such may become requisite. With due care in the selection and treatment of the best class of materials wrought into parts by the aid of those mechanical means by which accuracy and identity of corresponding parts is secured, I consider the Martini-Henry rifle as submitted to me, to be likely to yield in all respects permanent and satisfactory results.

APPENDIX 10.

Being an abstract of a paper titled *The Comparative Merits of the Martini Rifle and the Westley Richards Rifle and Ammunition*, read before the British Association by its author, Mr. W.P. Marshall, on 19-9-1870. (Details from *Engineering*, 27-4-1871.)

The author stated that more than five years had elapsed since a government commission reported unanimously in favour of arming the whole British infantry with breech-loading guns; and in 1865 a government advertisement invited patterns for the proposed arm. A committee of investigation examined these patterns, and at the end of 1868 they recommended the adoption of the Martini breech mechanism, with the Henry rifling and the Boxer ammunition.

The breech-loading arrangements in this combination were considered by practical men to be mechanically defective, although the bore of the barrel, the turn of the rifling, and the weight of the bullet gave the best results as regards accuracy, trajectory, penetration, and rapidity of fire. The principle of the falling block in the breech action, which was a previous American invention, was generally admitted to be the best that had been suggested, and so far the arm justifies the decision of the committee. The faults said to exist in it were in the spiral striking spring, the lock arrangements, the lever, the stocking, and the ammunition. All these were said to be defective in principle, that they could not answer when made in large quantities, although a few rifles might be so made that no great fault should be detected in a limited trial while the arms were new. It was considered, however, that to adopt such a rifle would not be a mechanical credit to the country. Since the end of 1868 the committee has been endeavouring to perfect the arm, and several patterns of it have been made at Enfield, but it still retains its inherent defects and objectionable features.

At this point a description of the mechanism was introduced, and illustrated by pattern models and enlarged sectional drawings. The most important of the defects were said to be in the following points:

1, the position of the lever which elevates and depresses the block and also holds it in position; 2, the percussion arrangement for igniting the cap; 3, the form of mainspring; 4, the position of the sear, the shape of the bent in the tumbler, and the position and length of the trigger; 5, the bolt for supplying the place of half-cock; 6, the mode of stocking.

The author claimed that the whole of these defects had been overcome in the Westley Richards rifle by the application of the ordinary hammer, spring, sear, tumbler and trigger, which are the same as those used in the old gun lock, and are well known mechanical arrangements that have stood the test of experience ever since percussion guns were invented. These points of construction, like those of the Martini-Henry rifle, were fully described and illustrated.

The paper then proceeded to say that the points at issue with regard to the mechanical construction of the two arms had been submitted to some of the most eminent engineers (Mr. Hick, MP, Mr. Penn, Mr. Barlow, and Mr. Greenwood) in the form of six questions about the relative mechanical merits of rifle A and rifle B, the former being a Martini-Henry and the latter a Westley Richards. The questions were as follows –

On comparing A and B, which of the two breech mechanisms do you consider is constructed on the best mechanical principles, and best adapted to perform the work required of it? No.1. Which is the best position for the lever used for elevating and depressing the block, and also for holding it in position? No.2 Which is the best arrangement for imparting the blow required to ignite the percussion cap? No.3. Which form of spring do you consider most likely to retain its power, with the least liability to deterioration; No.4. Which is the best position of the sear and pin upon which it turns to make a well-shaped bent in the tumbler, by which a steady and uniform pull can be obtained, so necessary in a rifled arm? Which shaped bent is best adapted to resist wear, and to keep to the weight it was originally made. The weight of the mainspring must be considered a very important element in the work which the sear nose will have to perform. It must be borne in mind that the bent and sear nose in these arms will have much more wear and tear than the top bent in an old gun lock on the muzzle-loading principle. No.5. Which is the simplest and most serviceable arrangement of bolt for supplying the place of half-cock in an ordinary gun? No.6. Which is the strongest and best mode of stocking?

On every one of these points all the engineers who were consulted assigned the palm of superior merit to B, and that without any doubt or hesitation.

Messrs. Penn, Barlow, and Greenwood make a joint report, simply answering the questions and stating the reasons for their opinions; but Mr. Hicks reports separately, and has appended the following rider to his answer –

In conclusion I beg to remark that, although in the hands of an ordinary user of the weapon A, much inferiority of action would not at first be felt, it is so liable to deterioration and change in power to cock and discharge as to lead to serious inconvenience in a very short time, even if it did not become altogether useless. Whereas in B the general mechanical arrangement and application of the various parts are so far superior and the liability to derangement so remote that I cannot conceive any competent judges disagreeing on the subject.

Having stated these facts, the author went on to argue that, as the two kinds of rifle appeared to admit of equally safe and expeditious handling and to be of equal shooting power the question between them resolved itself into one of mechanical construction. The military members of the committee had done their work well, the distinctive military requirements were satisfied by either weapon, and accuracy of shooting had probably reached its limit. What was now wanted was a fresh and independent committee, containing some experimental mechanical engineers, for the purpose of determining points of mechanism only. There was however, another question of almost equal importance, and that was the question of ammunition.

The first pattern of Boxer cartridge recommended by the committee had been withdrawn, and another, that was no better was substituted for it. This had the great fault of having a case larger than was required to contain the proper charge; and the common solid brass cartridge case, now in general use in America and other countries, would in many respects be preferable to it, especially because it can be readily obtained in large quantities; because its adoption would leave the chamber of the rifle of a minimum size, and because the cases can be filled over and over again, and their use would thus be a source of great pecuniary saving to volunteers.

The joint answers to the Questions 1 to 6 above, were as follows –

Q.1. The lever as applied in breech arrangement B is far better than the one at A. It has greater power to elevate and depress the block, and will hold it much more firmly in position; there will also be less wear on the bearing surfaces, as it has so much less work to do. The end of the lever in lock A has to cock the gun by forcing the block up against the weight of a heavy mainspring.

The lever in A has also the disadvantage of having two arms to fit, both of which should bear equally against the block.

Q.2. B is the best arrangement. The hammer travels over a space of 1½ inches, it requires a light spring only, and, from the spring acting on the short arm of a lever delivers a sharp quick blow. It is an old and well-known mode of ignition, employed in all percussion guns; it has been found from long experience to answer better than any other arrangement. A is precisely the reverse of the above. The hammer or striker travels over a very short space, being only from 1/4 to 3/8 of an inch, and is actuated by a short, stiff, spiral spring, requiring to be 40 lbs at cock to ignite the cap. The spiral spring is more suited to resist compression than to impart a blow. The percussion arrangement is very inferior to that employed in B, and not at all suitable for a Military Gun Lock.

Q.3. The spring in lock B is an old and well-tried spring; it has been used with complete success ever since percussion guns were invented, and long before. No other spring has been found to retain its powers so well, or to suffer so little deterioration; it should, therefore, not be abandoned without very strong reasons. The short, stiff, spiral spring, like that employed in lock A, has too short a range of action, it produces pressure rather than impact, and is much more liable to deterioration than the old gun lock main spring. We therefore consider the spring in lock B is the best.

Q.4. The relative position of the pins, and the form of notch of the bent, and the sear nose, in the lock B, are the same as those in an ordinary gun lock; they have been arrived at after long experience, and are universally admitted to be the best form to ensure a good pull of the trigger; experience has shown that they cannot be improved upon.

In lock A, these arrangements are altogether departed from; the position of the pins, and the form of notch of the bent are entirely changed, and not calculated to ensure the same good pull of the trigger as in lock B.

The sear has also the great disadvantage of having three bearing points, which cannot fail to cause much labour, and must require good workmanship to get all three points to bear equally. It is not suitable for a military lock. The committee should examine some practical lock-maker on this point if they have any doubt.

Q.5. The bolt in the arrangement B is of the simplest possible construction; it is all outside, and is easily seen. It works on a segment of a circle, so that a considerable leverage is obtained for moving it, and it is not liable to stick or to have its action impeded by rust.

The bolt in arrangement A works on straight flat surfaces, has a small projection to lay hold of, without any leverage, and would be liable to become stiff and disabled.

The bolt itself in arrangement B is the best.

Q.6. The mode of attaching the butt to the body of the breech in arrangement A, by fitting the end into a shallow box, and then passing a screw through the other end of the butt into the bottom of the box, is most objectionable, and unsound in principle.

If the screw, from any cause, should become slightly bent, it cannot be unscrewed.

The stock in arrangement B is of the ordinary kind; it has been long in use in military arms, and is known to withstand the usual rough usage of the service.

APPENDIX 11.

Being an account of a general meeting of the Institution of Mechanical Engineers on 27-4-1871, at which Mr. W. P. Marshall read a paper, of which he was the author, on *The Principal Constructions of Breech-Loading Mechanisms for Small Arms, and Their Relative Mechanical Advantages; Illustrated by Specimens of Breech-Loading Rifles.* Details are from *Engineering*, 5-5-1871.

The writer stated that the general adoption of breech-loading small arms had caused a number of mechanical contrivances to be brought out of great ingenuity and interest for overcoming the difficulties met with in obtaining a satisfactory breech-loading action. The principal objects to be effected were: 1. To open and restore the breech of the gun rapidly and securely by a simple and convenient movement of the hand without removing it from the trigger and without shifting the hold of the gun by the other hand. 2. To extract the empty cartridge case or previous charge by the same movement as the opening of the breech so as to present an open barrel ready for instant reloading. 3. To have the whole mechanism of a simple, strong, and durable character, free from the risk of derangement, either by accident, long wear and tear, rough usage in active service, exposure to wet or sand, or fouling by long continued firing. In the case of military guns, the latter requirements were of special importance, as the whole value of a breech-loading gun, on account of rapidity of fire, would be outweighed by any increased liability to failure in action. When the formidable and conflicting character to these requirements was considered, it would be seen how much mechanical skill was involved in the very complete and successful manner in which the whole had now been accomplished.

Breech-loading guns were first adopted by the Prussian army, the celebrated needle gun having been in use for more than twenty years, while for many years it had been the universal arm used by that army. Although breech-loading carbines had been in use for fourteen years to a limited extent for the cavalry in England, it was only since 1866 that the principle had been adopted for the army generally. Breech-loading carbines were adopted for the cavalry solely for the purpose of overcoming the difficulty of loading whilst on horseback.

The writer, after having described the various breech-loading guns, including the needle gun, Chassepot, Albini-Braendlin, Werndl, Henry, Soper, Westley Richards, Sharps, Snider, Remington, Berdan, &c; went on to consider the gun which had been selected for adoption in the British army after a long investigation and practical trial.

The Martini-Henry is a compound of two independent constructions – the Martini breech action and the Henry rifled barrel. The Henry barrel, by Mr. Henry, of Edinburgh, is a modification in rifling of the Whitworth polygonal barrel, being cut with seven equal sides instead of six, and having a small projecting angular rib in each of the angles of the poly gon, the diameter of the bore being the same at the centres at the sides, and the summits of the ribs. The bullet employ ed – a plain cylindrical one – fits close at those fourteen points around the circumference. The effect of the firing is to "upset" the base of the bullet slightly, and to cause it to lay hold of the ribs sufficiently to produce the rotation of the bullet. The amount of twist in the rifling is one turn in 22 inch length.

The Martini breech action, by M. Martini of Switzerland, is a modification of the Peabody breech-loader, which is an American invention, and has been in partial use in the United States since 1865. The principle of action is the use of a longitudinal falling block to close the breech. This block is hinged on a transverse pin at the back end, and falls at the front end sufficiently to clear the opening of the barrel. The upper surface of the block is hollowed out so as to allow a free entrance for the cartridge into the barrel in loading the gun. The breech block is lowered and raised by means of a curved lever, which forms the trigger guard when closed ready for firing, the block being lifted by an arm entering a notch in its underside. The hammer is an external cock at one side, propelled by an ordinary flat main spring, and the blow of the hammer is conveyed to the base of the cartridge by a striking bar sliding in a curved groove in the side of the breech block, the cartridge being one of rim-fire class, exploded by a blow at the edge of the base.

The extractor is a bent lever which is struck by the breech block when lowered, and is made to jerk the cartridge case out. The cocking of the gun has to be effected by a separate movement of drawing back the hammer.

In the Martini breech action the hammer and striking bar of the Peabody have been replaced by a direct-acting striker impelled by a spiral spring, the whole being contained within the breech block, and the gun being cocked by the act of opening the breech; in other respects the mode of working the block and actuating the extractor is the same as the Peabody gun. The action of the falling block has been found thoroughly satisfactory, having been found to withstand successfully the extremes of heat and cold and exposure in wet and dry climates.

The mechanical principle of a falling block hinged in a rifle breech is such that the whole of the strain for the explosion is received by the cylindrical hinge socket within which the tail end of the breech block rests; and as this forms the end of a solid wrought-iron box within which the breech block works, the strain is resisted by the whole strength of the sides of the box. The hinge pin of the block is made an easy fit within its socket, so that it does not receive any strain from the explosion, the whole being borne by the cylindrical abutment. This has been proved by the substitution of a soft lead pin at the joint, when it was found that the pin was not marked by the explosion, thus evidencing the absence of all strain.

There are however, mechanical details that are objectionable in the Martini lock action. One of a very serious character arises from the substitution of a spiral main spring with direct action in place of the ordinary flat gun-lock spring acting through a variable lever. There is no material difference as regards the spring itself between the two constructions, either in strength, durability, or rate of deflection, but in their suitability to the present purpose, the difference is remarkably great.

The force that is required to explode the detonating cap on the base of the cartridge has been found by actual experiment to be equal to a velocity of 35 feet per second. The spiral spring of the Martini lock is necessarily very short, being confined within the limits of the breech block and the length of its stroke is consequently less than ½-inch, being only .42-inch, and as the velocity of the striker is only the same as that of the spring, the pressure of the latter has to be increased to a sufficient amount to produce the required velocity of 35 fps at the end of the stroke. This requires an average pressure of 28 lb throughout the stroke of .42-in, and is found to necessitate a spring having a pressure of 40 lb at the beginning and 16 lb at the end of the stroke.

The practical objection is in the circumstance that the whole pressure of the compressed spring has to be supported upon the end of the trigger or "sear nose" when the gun is at full cock, and the trigger has to be "pulled off" under the pressure in the act of firing the gun. The leverage of the spring over the sear nose being nearly double (1.9 times), increases the pressure of 40 lb to as much as 75 lb upon the sear nose, and this result is unavoidable on account of the limited space available above the level of the trigger.

This pressure of 75 lb is very greatly in excess of that in ordinary gun locks, and makes the pull of the trigger too stiff. The pull is limited to 8 lb, a heavier pull disturbing the aim, and from 3 to 5 lb is the pull preferred for match shooting. A lighter spring was at first tried, but it was found liable to misfire; then an inclined bearing face for the sear nose was tried to ease the pull off, but this was found dangerous from the risk of the trigger going off and firing the gun if jarred by a sharp blow of the stock upon the ground.

The difficulty has been met by Col. Dixon, Superintendent of the government small arms factory at Enfield, by an ingenious arrangement of a double catch for holding the springs, one with a square nose for holding securely while the gun is in full cock, and the other with an inclined nose, to which the pressure is partially transferred in the act of firing. They consist of two separate catches working independently upon the same centre; the upper one, called the "tumbler rest", has a bearing face square to the radius, so as to hold the spring securely without any tendency to shift under a jar. The lower one, which is the end of the trigger, has an inclined bearing face, but hangs loosely at first without any pressure, as its centre is made with an inclined slot hole. When the trigger is pulled, a portion of the pressure is expended in sliding the trigger obliquely up the inclined slot of its centre bearing, and causes a vertical pressure at its upper end, which takes off part of the pressure of the spring for the bearing of the upper tumbler rest. As the pull upon the trigger continues, a greater portion of the total pressure is transferred from the upper square bearing to the lower inclined bearing until at last the resistance to the trigger is overcome, the two catches are pulled off together, and the gun is fired. The contrivance fully answers the purpose when properly made, and whilst clean and well lubricated, but it introduces into the lock a piece of delicate fitting of a very exceptional character, as a very nice adjustment of the various parts is required in order that during the pull off all may work harmoniously together.

The mechanical question is, whether this objectionable complication is unavoidable, or whether by the use of a different kind of spring it can be obviated, without sacrificing any of the good points in the breech action.This appears to have been thoroughly and satisfactorily accomplished in the Westley Richards lock, in which exactly the same breech action is obtained with an ordinary flat gun lock spring, and the trigger action and pressure upon the sear nose correspond to those in the ordinary gun lock action, which has been proved by general practice to be satisfactory and durable, and to retain an uniform steady pull off.

The breech block is the same as in the Martini gun, but is raised and lowered by a lever acting at the front end, and supporting the block as a strut at the point furthest from its centre of motion. The lever fits close to the trigger guard, when the breech is closed, and is held by the pressure of a spring at each extremity of its motion. The hammer moves in a hollow in the underside of the breech block, striking the cartridge through a small hole in the centre of the face of the block. The hammer is cocked by the action of the lever in opening the breech, the arm of the lever carrying back the hammer, compressing the main spring, and leaving the hammer caught upon the sear or catch, which is released by an ordinary trigger. The cartridge extractor is a finger acted on by a shoulder on the breech lever, which has power to start the extractor and jerks out the empty case clear of the gun.

The breech block being lifted from below, becomes jammed between the end of the barrel, and the rear abutment, if forced above its final position, and there is consequently no risk of the breech being blown open by the explosion, and any risk of the breech block dropping is prevented by the firm support of the lifting lever, which acts as a strut underneath. The action of this falling block is therefore thoroughly satisfactory, and mechanically good, and it has the advantage of presenting no projection for the gun when open.

In this lock the spring pressure averages 31 lb, and ranges from 43 to 19 lb, being nearly the same as the Martini spring, which averages 28 lb, ranging from 40 to 16 lb; but the leverage at which the flat spring acts is only about half that of the sear nose (1:1.8 times) instead of being nearly double (1.9 times), as in the Martini lock, thus giving a pressure on the sear nose of only 24 lb at full cock, instead of 75 lb, as in the Martini lock. An ordinary square nosed sear is consequently used, and an easy trigger pull obtained with a secure hold of the spring, and the pull is not affected by rust or want of lubrication.

The propelling pressure of the spring measured at the striking point is only an average of 8 lb throughout the stroke, instead of 28 lb as in the Martini lock, but the length of stroke being four times as great, the same velocity is obtained at the moment of striking, or about 35 fps. in each case.

The ordinary gun lock swivel action is employed for regulating the propelling effect of the spring upon the hammer, by means of an oblique connecting link, which by its change of inclination during the stroke, reduces the effective leverage of the spring as its compression increases when putting it to full cock. The varying pressure on the spring during the stroke of the hammer is thus greatly modified, so that, although the spring presses with double the force at the beginning than it does at the end of the stroke, the propelling force on the hammer is considerably less at the beginning than at the end, and consequently the pressure on the catch of the trigger action is considerably less than the average pressure throughout the stroke. This pressure on the sear at full cock amounts to only 13 lb instead of 75 lb as in the Martini lock. It thus appears that in the Martini by the introduction of a spiral spring instead of the ordinary flat gun-lock spring, a serious mechanical difficulty is caused, which is only got over by the addition of a piece of apparatus of an exceptionally delicate nature, and requiring an extreme nicety of adjustment to be constantly kept up, in order to ensure its continued efficiency of action. But it also appears that the whole of this difficulty and complication is unnecessary and can be avoided by simply adhering to the ordinary flat gun-lock spring, and action, and trigger, and that this can be done without in any degree interfering with the advantages of the breech action.

On the contrary, in the Westley Richards arrangement some valuable advantages are gained. The lifting lever acting upon the free extremity of the breech block is a better arrangement than lifting the block near its centre of motion as in the Martini, since the wear will be less in consequence of the diminution of pressure, and will not so much affect the accurate lifting of the block. The position of the lever in front of the trigger guard, and fitting down close to it when closed, is more convenient, and requires less change from the position of firing than is the case with the Martini lock, where the lever is situate behind the trigger guard. The position of this latter lever, too, is found to interfere with the proper grasp of the stock in bayonet exercise, and it is proposed to extend it still further back.

There is likewise an objection to the method of fixing the stock into the body of the breech action in the Martini, which is done by making a shallow socket in the rear, into which the butt of the stock is fixed by a long steel screw passed through a longitudinal hole in the stock. The ordinary mode of having two long straps upon the rear with a transverse screw through the stock is pursued in the Westley Richards gun, and it is a question whether this is not preferable, as sometimes through the shrinking of the wood, the stock of the Martini gun becomes loose in the socket, and in the event of the screw becoming bent the stock must be sawn off for getting it out.

The conclusion arrived at, therefore, is that, although in the Martini-Henry rifle, the principle of closing the breech by a falling block enclosed in a mortised breech, and also the bore and turn of the rifling are thoroughly satisfactory, and well suited for adoption by the army, yet the details of the lock action in this gun involve serious mechanical defects, which, however, can be readily corrected by employing the ordinary principle of construction of gun-lock action, confirmed by long experience, and this can be effected without any detriment to the principle of closing the breech while very decided advantages can be gained as regarding other points.

The chairman then invited discussion of the paper, with the following resulting –

Mr. Soper of Reading, said he was sure that he could only add a very few remarks in regard to breech-loading guns, to the very full and valuable statements laid before them in the paper that had just been read. Having studied the subject very closely for the last nine years, and practically for nearly the whole of his life, he had of course passed through many different systems, and he had arrived at the conclusions that there were certain definite principles that should be borne in mind when working out any system of breech-loaders if they wished to have a good weapon. One of the most essential features of a good breech-loader was that the person who fired the rifle under all circumstances should be perfectly safe. In his experiments he had tried various systems of closing the breech, and he found from experiment that no better system of preventing escape of gas from behind and through a defective cartridge used in the gun, than allowing the block to swing at right angles to the bore, so that it might pass readily into its socket or chamber, and act as a valve in the same way that the cartridge acted as a valve inside the barrel when it did its duty. This gave a great advantage over the Prussian and Chassepot needle guns. In these there was no valve provided. The consequence was that they frequently had a great escape of gas, and the firers were thereby injured in some cases, and in other cases they were merely frightened, so that they did not make effective work with their rifles. Having gone on somewhat further in experiments with breech-loading arms he had come to the conclusion that the valve must be inserted in the rifle to form a new joint at every charge. He had tried various patterns of cartridge, some of them acting remarkably well after five, six, and some of them twenty times reloading. It was well known that cases did occur in which a cartridge was defective, although supposed, when placed in the rifle, to be a good and serviceable cartridge. Therefore it seemed to him that to have a good breech-loading rifle they wanted something that would leave the men – the firers – in a perfectly safe position, and to allow a defective cartridge being in the rifle without danger. Speaking of the Martini gun, which had passed through many trials, he might remark that very few men would like to fire the Martini with a damaged cartridge. He was perfectly aware that the cartridge being a good one and fixed in place they could not blow the breech down; but the breech working on a pin at right angles to the line or axis of the barrel and falling down in the line of the barrel, must leave a certain space between the sides of the breech shoe of the breech block for it to work in, in order to get freedom of action. At the back of the rifle there was an open space between the breech block and the breech shoe. As a necessary consequence there must be freedom for the block to work in. As these gaps were in a direct line with the barrel, should there be an escape of gas it rushed immediately into the face of the firer. The pin being at right angles with the line of fire, and the block falling down in line with the axis of the fire, involved the necessity of having a small space left between that block and the shoe, in order to allow facility of working. Then if there were room for working, there should be room for the gas to escape also, in case of an imperfect cartridge being accidentally used. And as they were in that position in firing (illustrating the position) they would observe that the eye of the firer was immediately in line with the two lines through the block of the breech. It seemed to him that no man in his senses would like to fire a gun with a defective cartridge in it, having the eye immediately in line with these points. He pointed out all this to show why he had gone to a block mounted in the position adopted in his own rifle. It was mounted on a pin running parallel to the axis of the bore, and making the

WESTLEY RICHARDS'
PATENT CENTRAL-FIRE BREECH-LOADING MILITARY & SPORTING RIFLE.

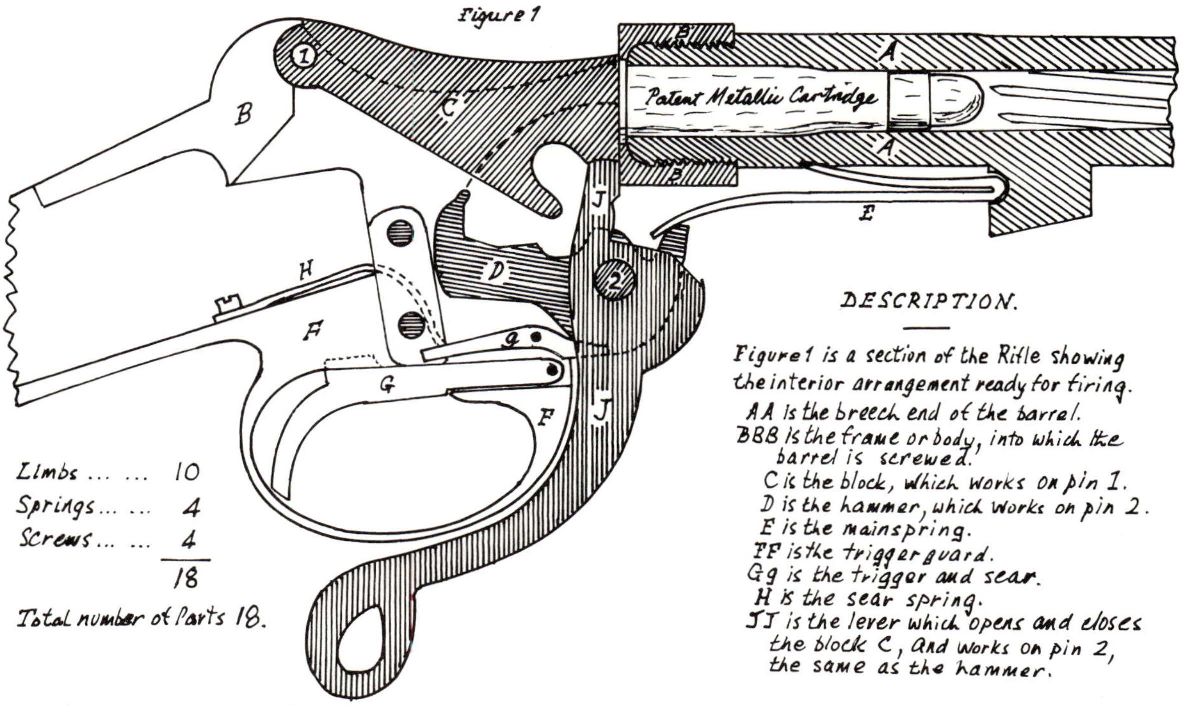

block to work at right angles, so that when the block was dropped into the hollow socket shoe, it formed in itself a valve, thus preventing any escape of gas from the cartridge, or even in firing a loose charge of powder. The breech itself at once formed a valve, and protected the firer completely. As would be seen, on examining the gun, the breech was mounted so that it dropped down into the shoe. It was fitted on the back surface fairly, and the greater the force of the power on the front surface, the tighter became the back joint. It prevented any escape of gas backwards, and the consequence was, if a defective cartridge was used, the column of gas passed out to the front. Being at an angle of 45 degrees the man's face was perfectly safe. But with the breech block falling down in a line with the firer's eye, he thought the breech block in that case was not perfectly secure.He believed that the first principle of a breech mechanism was leaving the man who fired the rifle in a perfectly safe position. The question of rapidity of firing could after all be easily arranged. If the man was in danger, it seemed to him that the breech mechanism was not perfect. He might mention that he maintained the action in his rifle of the ordinary Enfield block, taking the swivel from the breech block. They had the breech block used in the Snider proved to be of a very correct character. They had the extracting action of such a nature that they could get certainty of extraction to gun actions. This had enabled them to gain a speed that he believed had not been gained by any other rifle. In other words, they had fired 60 rounds per minute, and they were prepared to fire at the rate of one per second in the ordinary position. He simply mentioned this to show that the simplicity of the action enabled the firer, at any speed, always to have certainty of action in the rifle.

The chairman enquired how often they had fired taking aim and at what range?

Mr. Soper said that taking aim they had readily fired 30 rounds, producing 29 on the target at 200 yards range. They had repeatedly made scores of 70 to 78 per minute in trials, which had been public trials.

Mr. Bird, Edinburgh, said that in showing the Henry rifle, he thought that one thing he might draw their attention to, was a matter suggested by the opening remarks of the paper namely, the very short movement for the trigger, which he thought was the shortest in any breech-loading rifle. The safety of the rifle, he thought, was acknowledged. It had been fired with loose powder and five or six bullets, and the breech had never moved in any way whatever. As to rapidity, at the great trials the Henry fired the greatest number of rounds in a minute. At Wimbledon it fired 52 shots in two minutes, and put every shot in the target. That was really a public trial, and, of course, it won the first prize, and, in fact, it also won the second prize, there being no rifle that could take a second place beside it. That was at a range of 200 yards. With other advantages there was one which, no doubt, was very important. A man in action was very liable to be flurried. With the Snider and the Martini rifles it was necessary to put the cartridge quite flush in the socket before it could be fired. With the Henry rifle, if the cartridge was as much as 1/16th inch out, in raising the inclined plane the cartridge was forced in. Another thing was in cleaning the barrel from the muzzle. If it had been oiled, the powder which had gathered in flakes was pushed into, and clogged the action. With that gun they could clean the barrel out from the rear, and the fouling falls to the ground.

Mr. Soper said his rifle also cleaned from the rear, and, in reply to the chairman as to whether these were the only two guns that cleaned in that manner, Mr. Westley Richards' representative said their gun also cleaned from the rear.

Mr. Bird, in conclusion, said that in the case of the other rifles they could not lock the action at half cock. In the case of the Henry, this could easily be done. They could go down to half cock while the gun was loaded.

Mr. Greenwood, Leeds, said Mr. Marshall had exactly expressed his own opinion with regard to the mechanical facts of the case. He thought Mr. Marshall had pointed the whole of them out very precisely and accurately. He did not see that anything he (the speaker) could say on the subject would at all add to the information that was before the meeting. He quite agreed with Mr. Marshall's observations and critisisms upon the mechanical movements of the rifles in question.

The chairman said that he thought it would be agreed that the subject before them was of such importance as to warrant the adjournment of the discussion. It was a very wide one, and they would be better prepared for going into the merits of the matter at another meeting. It was one of those questions exciting considerable interest just now, and from a national point of view it was of absorbing interest. It was their duty as mechanical engineers to pay some attention to it. Enough had been said at this meeting to set many minds at work, and he thought that they would gain much by having another discussion on the subject. He proposed, therefore, that they should adjourn the discussion. At the same time he must ask them to thank those gentlemen who had been kind enough to lend specimens of their guns and models, which had illustrated the various inventions so satisfactorily.

A vote of thanks having been accorded on the motion of the President, the meeting closed.

APPENDIX 12.

Being a summary of the reports on the trials of the Martini-Henry Long Chamber rifles, as received from the regiments and presented by the Special Committee on Martini-Henry Breech-Loading Rifles in their first report of 12-7-1870.

Q.1 – What accidents, if any, have occurred? (The majority answered "None", but there were some minor mishaps.)

1. (Aldershot): Rifle No.154 out of order, and sent to be repaired. Found subsequently to have arisen from faulty metal.

11. (Dublin): Small piece of the trigger rest spring broken off. Rifle No.90.

15. (Dublin): The tumbler of rifle No.14 broke after firing 40 rounds, owing to a flaw in metal.

19. (Hythe): The point of the striker of rifle No.137, and the tumbler of No.78 were broken.

21. (Gravesend): None. The trigger axis piece loose in two of the arms.

37. (Ottawa): Tumbler broke in rifle No.64.

40. (Portsmouth): Bent of tumbler of No.54 rifle broken by using force to open the block when the arm was bolted. There appeared to be a flaw in the metal. A new tumbler was made on board Excellent.

Committee's remarks: These accidents do not appear to call for any special remark, as they are none of them peculiar to this construction of arm; and it is distinctly stated in two instances that flaws were found in the broken tumblers, one of which was also broken by the use of unjustified force when the arm was bolted. The looseness of the two axis pins seems to have been an original defect, and is scarcely to be classified under the head of accidents.

Q.2 – What difficulties, if any, have been found in loading? (About half answered "None", but the other half had problems.)

5. (Aldershot): No difficulties have occurred so long as the cartridge is not bent.

8. (Aldershot): If not pressed well home with the thumb, the cartridge does not always explode, though the breech is closed.

11. (Dublin): None, with the exception of 5 cartridges, in which, from being bent, when pressure was used, the cases became creased.

12. (Dublin): None, except in cases of bent or defective cartridges.

13. (Dublin): In some cases the cartridges were found to be too large, about half an inch from the rim; on pressure being applied, they all entered the barrel with the exception of one.

14. (Dublin): Occasionally a cartridge could not be pressed home in a particular rifle, but it was always got off in one of the others. On the last day of firing, the action of lock of No.172 rifle got slightly out of order. The lever had to be depressed three or four times before the spiral spring could be fixed in the firing position.

15. (Dublin): None, except from bent or faulty cartridges.

16. (Dublin): The cartridge when bent would not enter the chamber.

17. (Hythe): With No.26 rifle the paper round the cartridge ruffed up, when putting it into the breech. The paper of the cartridge also stripped with No.137 rifle, and became jammed, preventing the cartridge from entering or being removed from the barrel.

18. (Hythe): Some difficulty, owing to cartridges having been bent.

21. (Gravesend): Several cartridges would not enter. This was apparently caused in a few instances from the base cups being too large; the majority by the paper getting scraped up and jamming the cartridge partly into the chamber, so that the ramrod had to be used.

25. (Portsmouth): Several; consequent on malformation of cartridges; and on the paper rucking up against the edge of the chamber.

26. (Portsmouth): The blank cartridge seems to be too loosely made about the mouth, and there is sometimes a difficulty in placing it in the barrel. With ball, if the cartridge be at all bent, the same difficulty occurs.

27. (Portsmouth): The cartridges fit too tightly into the chamber, especially the blank. They are also apt to become injured by the sharp edge at the entrance of chamber.

28. (Portsmouth): In ten instances the cartridges would not enter the chamber of any of the rifles.

29. (Portsmouth): Frequent difficulties owing to the tight fit of the cartridges.

30. (Portsmouth): In some few cases, principally owing to the ammunition being injured.

32. (Quebec): None, except in rifle No.100.

40. (Portsmouth): Four slight jams in loading. Cartridge forced home by the thumb.

41. (Devonport): On three or four occasions a slight difficulty was found from cartridges getting out of shape.

46. (Quebec): None, except in rifle No.100.

Committee's remarks: It appears from these reports that difficulty in loading has occasionally arisen from the following causes –

1. Cartridges becoming bent
2. Cartridges defective from –
   A. Paper rucking up
   B. Base cups being too large
   C. Body of cartridge being too large; or
3. Sharp edge of chamber causing the paper to ruck up.

With regard to the objections which have reference to the bending of the cartridges, and to the rucking up of the paper, the committee would observe that a remedy has already been provided by the provisional adoption of the short chamber cartridge, which is stronger and has no external covering of paper.

The attention of the Superintendent, Royal Laboratory, will be called to the complaints that some of the base cups were too large. The blank cartridge to be used with the short chamber rifles would be the ordinary service blank as used for the Snider rifles, if experiments should prove that the use of this cartridge is not injurious to the rifling of the arm.

Q.3 – What difficulties, if any, have been found in extracting cartridge cases? (Mostly "None", but about one third of the replies had complaints.)

4. (Aldershot): In rifle No.96 the extractor would not work. Thinks it was owing to rust. Rifle No.157 did not extract blank cartridges easily.

6. (Aldershot): None, except on one occasion, when the base of cartridge was extracted, the case remaining in the barrel.

9. (Aldershot): None; the lever must be depressed sharply to throw out the cartridge case.

10. (Aldershot): None, except in rifle No.68, the extractor apparantly weaker than other rifles.

11. (Dublin): None, except one blank cartridge; base cup torn from the case.

13. (Dublin): The lever must be depressed sharply.

14. (Dublin): When the cartridges missed fire the ramrod had to be used to get them out, the extractor not getting sufficient bite of the base of the cartridge to move the weight of the unfired cartridge.

15. (Dublin): None, except in rifle No.196, the extractor of which was not always certain in its action; in all cases required the application of more force to the lever than in the other rifles.

17. (Hythe): In extracting one cartridge that had missed fire in rifle No.137, the base disc came off, leaving cartridge in the barrel.

24. (Gravesend): None, except when cartridges have jam-

med.

26. (Portsmouth): Very few, and these only when any difficulty has been found in placing the cartridge in the chamber.

29. (Portsmouth): Very frequently the extractor has failed to eject the case, only moving it slightly.

30. (Portsmouth): Some few cartridges stuck at first, but on pushing back the lever a second time they came out.

32. (Quebec): None, except in rifle No.100; extractor had to be worked twice.

35. (Montreal): None, except in rifle No.33; action of extractor bad.

44. (Curragh): Twice during blank firing the paper cases stuck inside, the cap having been ejected by the motion of unloading.

46. (Quebec): None, except in rifle No.100. In most instances the case had to be pulled out with the fingers.

Committee's remarks: It appears from these reports that although in the majority of cases the extraction has been quite satisfactory, there have been some instances in which the extractor failed to work satisfactorily and uniformly.

There is not sufficient information before the committee to show to what this occasional want of uniformity is to be attributed, but it is probable that it has proceeded from one or more of the following causes –

1. Defective cartridges
2. Slight variation in the size of the chambers of the rifles and the form of the extractor, due no doubt to the arms having been made by hand, and not by machinery.
3. Want of experience on the part of the men using the arms.

Q.4 – Has the lever in any case been broken, or so bent as to impede the action? (All answered "No".)

Committee's remarks: None required.

Q.5 – Has rust been found to accumulate about the breech, so as to affect its working? (The majority of answers were "No", with a small number of affirmatives.)

1. (Aldershot): On dismounting rifle No.154 (referred to in Q.1) some rust was found to have accumulated on the sides of the body and on other parts of the breech action.

4. (Aldershot): Rust has accumulated, but not sufficient as to affect the working.

9. (Aldershot): No. Dust has accumulated and influenced the pull off of the trigger.

12. (Dublin): Yes, rust and sand accumulated in the breech, and caused extra friction.

13. (Dublin): No apparently. Sand entered No.66 breech action but the working was not impeded.

14. (Dublin): Rust has accumulated in the breech, but not so as to affect its working. Sand also gets in between the breech block and sides of the lock.

17. (Hythe): Rust has accumulated, but not at present to such an extent as to affect the working.

18. (Hythe): Not sufficiently to affect the working of the breech action.

21. (Gravesend): No, one rifle has not been cleaned, and works perfectly.

23. (Gravesend): No, the breech block of the rifle which had not been cleaned was removed; there was but little rust, although a considerable quantity of dirt, which did not prevent the arm working perfectly. It has never missed fire.

25. (Portsmouth): No, although the rifles were piled in the open air for eight days without cleaning.

37. (Ottawa): Rust has been found to accumulate about the sides of the body of the block, but not sufficient to impede the action. Some dirt got into the lock bolt of No. 83, which prevented the tumbler from acting.

42. (Curragh): A little, but not so as to affect its working.

44. (Curragh): On dismounting one breech action, a small quantity of grit and rust was found.

Committee's remarks: In a few cases rust and dust have entered the breech action, but the working of the breech action has not been affected except in two instances, when it was reported that the pull off of the trigger was affected by the entry of dust; and in another in which the action of the tumbler was interfered with by the entry of dirt.

It is suggested that if the rifle was exposed to wet and dirt the breech would clog. This point was carefully tested in the competitive trials which preceded the recommendation of the arm; and the results then obtained have received strong confirmation from the circumstances that in no case during the present trials is the breech action reported to have become affected by exposure. The committee do not, therefore, attach any importance to the suggestion that the evil might possibly arise.

Q.6 – Has the coil spring been found to become weak or inefficient? (Answers were generally "No", but many were conditional.)

2. (Aldershot): No; unless the misfires arise from this cause.

3. (Aldershot): No; but thinks that misfires were owing to weakness of coil spring.

7. (Aldershot): The coil spring in No.27 rifle is decidedly weaker than it was.

10. (Aldershot): Yes, in all the rifles.

11. (Dublin): Misfires attributed to weak coil springs.

12. (Dublin): Since new coil springs have been put in there have been no misfires.

13. (Dublin): The springs appear to have been originally too weak.

14. (Dublin): The coil springs at first were all rather weak, but since new springs have been put in there have been no misfires.

15. (Dublin): Yes; misfires were frequent and the cartridges invariably exploded on a second blow.

16. (Dublin): In Nos.3 and 196 rifles, the springs were evidently too weak, but since new springs were put in (23rd March) no misfires have occurred.

17 (Hythe): No; unless the misfires are attributable to this cause.

21. (Gravesend): Misfires from one rifle, supposed to be caused by weakness of spiral spring.

23. (Gravesend): Does not think misfires are due to weak coil spring. Captain Drake has fired several hundred rounds himself, and never had a misfire, except with a cartridge that had missed once or twice before.

24. (Gravesend): The same. The new coil spring not so good as the old; decreases the rapidity materially, and by making the pull off bad, impairs accuracy.

25. (Portsmouth): Yes, principally in rifles Nos.7, 8, and 10.

26. (Portsmouth): No; but the springs seemed to have been originally weak in some of the rifles.

27. (Portsmouth): Yes; the springs of some of the rifles were originally too weak, and grew weaker from use.

29. (Portsmouth): Frequent misfires until the new springs were put in. Since then very few.

30. (Portsmouth): The new spring has been found strong enough.

32. (Quebec): Yes, in rifle No.12.

34. (Montreal): The coil springs are all too weak. The misfires are nearly in every case occasioned by the weakness of the springs.

38. (Ottawa): Misfires attributed to weakness of springs.

39. (Ottawa): It is presumed the coil springs in some of the rifles have become weakened.

41. (Devonport): No; unless the few misfires are attributable to that cause.

45 (Ottawa): Not since the long coil spring has been introduced.

46. (Quebec): Not since the new springs have been put in.

Committee's remarks: The general tendency of these reports appears to be to the effect that many of the springs which were issued with these rifles were originally too weak which is corroborated by information which the committee have received from other sources. This subject is treated in another portion of their report.

The evidence from these reports, as far as it goes, tends also to show that by the substitution of stronger springs misfires have been prevented.

In very few cases is it stated that the springs have become weaker with use, and a comparison of the tabulated records on the first pages of the different reports as to the number of rounds fired, and the number of misfires does not bear out these statements. Indeed, if the performance of particular arms be traced through the reports, it appears distinctly that the springs do not become weaker. The committee give a few examples in proof of this assertion —

Rifle	No. of rounds fired	No. of mis-fires	Per cent-age
No.21, 1st trial	575	5	0.86
No.21, 2nd trial	1,663	8	0.47
No.21, 3rd trial.	2,507	8	0.31
No.126, 1st trial	590	44	7.4
No.126, 2nd trial. . . .	1,750	101	5.7
No.126, 3rd trial. . . .	2,658	145	5.4

And it is worth while to notice that the 5 arms, the springs of which are stated in Report No.10 to have all become weaker in use, did, as a matter of fact, give a smaller percentage of misfires in the third trial than in the first, as follows —

Rifle	No. of rounds fired	No. of mis-fires	Per cent-age
Nos.9,68,102,112,180;			
1st trial	2,999	79	2.6
2nd trial	3,000	90	3.0
3rd trial.	2,810	27	0.96

Q.7 – Is the action of the extractor, in throwing out the empty cartridge case, considered too sudden? (All answered "No", but some were conditional.)

1. (Aldershot): No; but it depends on the sharpness with which the lever is pressed down.

5. (Aldershot): The extractor has been found to work well, and its sudden action appears to be necessary, especially in extracting a tight fitting cartridge.

13. (Dublin): The action of the breech action appears to be perfect, and can easily be controlled by opening the breech gradually, which is an advantage in extracting a loaded cartridge.

21. (Gravesend): No; it answers admirably.

23. (Gravesend): No; a man once used to the arm can regul ate the force.

27. (Portsmouth): No; it can be regulated by the quickness or slowness of the action.

30. (Portsmouth): No; provided the soldier does not jerk out with force the loaded cartridge, when wishing to unload his rifle. Should he do so, the cartridge would be injured.

37. (Ottawa): No; but the strength varies considerably with the different rifles.

43. (Curragh): No; very good.

Committee's remarks: The committee have no remarks to make on this subject, which has already been treated under the head of Q.3.

Q.8 – The stock being in two parts, has it remained firm and strong? (All answered "Yes", with two exceptions.)

27. (Portsmouth): Yes. Recommends that it should be tried by slinging the rifle as carried on the march.

33. (Quebec): In one case no. Rifle No.100.

43. (Curragh): Yes, except rifle No.5, fore part became slightly loose.

Committee's remarks: The whole of the answers are in the affirmative, except in two cases in which the butt ends are reported loose.

As doubts have been expressed with regard to the strength of divided stocks for military purposes, the committee think it important to call attention to the fact that the evidence on this point is so far satisfactory, but the test to which the arms have as yet been submitted cannot be considered sufficient fully to determine the point; and the committee think that some special experiments should be made to test the relative strengths of whole and divided stocks.

Q.9 – Has the butt end been found to shrink; or become loose, from the effect of hot dry temperatures? (All answered "No", with some conditional replies.)

6. (Aldershot): Only exposed to cold and damp.

9. (Aldershot): Continuous cold weather.

13. (Dublin): Rifles not been exposed.

15. (Dublin): Rifles not been tested.

17. (Hythe): Too cold for proper trial.

20. (Hythe): No hot weather.

21. (Gravesend): Too cold for proper trial.

27. (Portsmouth): Too cold for proper trial.

37. (Ottawa): No hot weather.

42. (Curragh): No hot weather.

Committee's remarks: The committee have no remarks to make on this point at present, the arms not having been yet subjected to "hot dry temperatures".

Q.10 – Is any inconvenience experienced from recoil? (The majority answered "No", with some affirmative answers.)

1. (Aldershot): No; recoil very slight.

5. (Aldershot): No. Recoil does not appear greater than present rifle.

8. (Aldershot): Yes slightly, with rifle No.27.

9. (Aldershot): No. Recoil insignificant.

11. (Dublin): No; considered by four out of five men less than the Snider.

12. (Dublin): Yes; some men complained of it, but not considered too great.

13. (Dublin): Not more than that of the Snider. The thumb of the right hand should not be placed across the head of the stock as a blow is liable to be given to the firer's face.

14. (Dublin): Not more than from the Snider.

21. (Gravesend): No. The recoil is greater than the Snider, and will probably annoy recruits; it is not sufficient to affect accuracy.

27. (Portsmouth): The difference between the recoil of the Martini-Henry and the Snider is scarcely perceptible.

29. (Portsmouth): Men complained of it when much platoon firing took place, or when ball was fired immediately

after blank.

30. (Portsmouth): Men who do not hold their rifles well in hollow of shoulder feel the recoil greater after twenty rounds.

40. (Portsmouth): No; except when the thumb is placed (as per Musketry Instructions) across the head of the stock, in which case some of the men received a smart blow to the nose, causing it to bleed.

41. (Devonport): No; but greater than the Snider.

Committee's remarks: The reports appear to point distinctly to the conclusion that the recoil is not excessive.

Q.11 – Is the weight of the arm a practical objection on service? (The majority of answers were "No", with some conditional replies; and some in the affirmative.)

1. (Aldershot): No, except when the sword is fixed.

8. (Aldershot): If the arm could be lightened without interfering with its shooting qualities, it would be better.

10. (Aldershot): Certainly, unless soldiers' equipment is otherwise lightened.

11. (Dublin): No, as it is counterbalanced by other advantages.

14. (Dublin): Considered to be rather heavy when the bayonet is fixed.

17. (Hythe): Cannot give an answer at present.

21. (Gravesend): Yes, it tires the men when firing and marching.

23. (Gravesend): Thinks it would be too heavy, especially for engineers.

25. (Portsmouth): It is not objected to by the men.

26. (Portsmouth): The men did not think there was any material difference in the weight.

27. (Portsmouth): No. Considers the weight, with scarcely perceptible increase, more than counterbalanced by the handiness of the weapon, owing to its reduced length.

44. (Curragh): Not for an ordinary man, may be for some of the puny recruits now passed into the service.

45. (Ottawa): No, as far as ascertained.

Committee's remarks: In a few instances the additional weight of the sword bayonet is objected to; but it is clear from the opinions of the greater number of the officers that "there is no practical objection to the weight of the arm on service".

Q.12 – Is the position of the back sight approved of? (About one third of the replies were negative; the rest "Yes".)

1. (Aldershot): Yes; but thinks the V should be deeper.

4. (Aldershot): Inconvenient when trailing arms.

6. (Aldershot): Excellent as regards shooting, but very inconvenient when the arms are carried at the trail.

7. (Aldershot): Thinks it would be better for aiming, and also more convenient when trailing arms, if it were placed nearer the breech. Recommends a deeper V in back sight.

9. (Aldershot): Excellent as regards aiming, but inconvenient when arms are carried at the trail. Recommends that the sight be moved further forward and the V deepened.

10. (Aldershot): No, the V should be deeper.

11. (Dublin): Yes, but recommends a thin platinum wire under notch of back sight.

12. (Dublin): Yes; but recommends the V in notch of back sight to be deeper. Undersighted at long ranges.

13. (Dublin): Yes; recommends a platinum wire on back sight, and rifles to be marked for sighting at every 50 yards.

14. (Dublin): Yes, but the notch should be deeper, still retaining the platinum wire in the centre. The sighting is incorrect, generally undersighted about 50 yards at the long ranges.

15. (Dublin): Yes. A platinum wire inserted in the head of the back sight for distances up to 400 yards would be useful. The rifles are undersighted after 700 yards.

19. (Hythe): Yes, for aiming; but is inconvenient when carrying the rifle at the trail.

21. (Gravesend): No. It is exactly where the rifle balances at the trail. Thinks the sight might be greatly improved; suggests a finer foresight, with a fixed protector so arranged as not to interfere with the sword bayonet, a plain bar for back sight with a square notch and two smaller notches for allowance for wind on either side.

27. (Portsmouth): No. The sighting at all the distances is extremely accurate.

40. (Portsmouth): Yes; but might be improved by having the line on the sliding bar produced up to the top of the back sight to guide the eye when the flap is down.

41. (Devonport): No, it should be placed nearer the breech block.

42. (Curragh): Interferes with the hand when the arm is at the trail, might be moved back with advantage. Recom-

mends a platinum line, like that on sliding bar, be placed on that part of the back sight used up to 400 yards.

44. (Curragh): In present position the arm cannot be carried at the trail unless the hand grips the whole of the back sight and barrel. Recommends a platinum line to be placed below the notch of the back sight, as on the sliding bar; flat sight preferred to V shape on the Snider.

Committee's remarks: The committee think the back sight might be improved; and recommend the adoption of a flat sliding bar with three platinum lines, one long in the centre, and two shorter equally dividing the space on either side.

They also recommend the addition of a platinum wire, at the centre of the V at the end of the flap.

The inconvenience in the position of the back sight when the arm is carried at the trail has been noted; the place where the rifle is held at the trail depends on the balance of the arm, and experiments will be made to determine this point.

Q.13 – How does the sword bayonet answer as a weapon of attach and defence? (The answers to this question were mixed, with a small majority stating "Very well", and a few dissentions. The balance reported "Not been tested".)

1. (Aldershot): Not so well, on account of weight, as present bayonet. The lever is somewhat in the way in bayonet exercise.

2. (Aldershot): Not so well, on account of making the rifle top heavy.

10. (Aldershot): Prefers the ordinary bayonet.

14. (Dublin): Believed to be a superior weapon; but makes the rifle rather top heavy.

15. (Dublin): It appears a most formidable weapon.

25. (Portsmouth): It is much approved of.

27. (Portsmouth): Admirably.

29. (Portsmouth): Prefers ordinary bayonet.

37. (Ottawa): Preferred by men to the ordinary bayonet.

40. (Portsmouth): A special report will be sent.

43. (Curragh): It would probably be effective.

44. (Curragh): Considers it far superior to ordinary bayonet as it could not be gripped like the latter if the thrust failed.

Committee's remarks: The committee find that a very large majority of the regiments approve of the sword bayonet as a weapon for attack and defence. Taking into consideration that a weapon of this description already forms part of the regular equipment of all rifle regiments; that in the absence of any objection it is a distinct advantage to have a weapon that can be used in more than one capacity, and that no valid objection has been shown to exist to the sword bayonet, the committee recommend its adoption. A few of the regiments object to the weight when fixed, as making the rifles top heavy; but the committee would observe that the sword bayonets would not be fixed until the troops were at close quarters, when extreme accuracy of fire had become unnecessary. (See remarks on Q.14.)

Q.14 – Does the sword bayonet answer as an implement, on service, for cutting wood, &c.? (The majority replied "Yes", but some were negative, and some had not tested it.)

2. (Aldershot): Possibly, but thinks soldiers would spoil it.

3. (Aldershot): Thinks not.

5. (Aldershot): No. Length of saw too little, breadth too great.

6. (Aldershot): The saw should be longer. Considers it would very rarely be useful.

9. (Aldershot): Very well; but disapproves of soldiers using their bayonets for cutting wood.

11. (Dublin): Admirably for cutting wood, tolerably well for meat, bones, etc., recommends a few more teeth to saw.

14. (Dublin): It is difficult to cut wood with it.

26. (Portsmouth): Wood easily sawn through, but the saw is rather short.

29. (Portsmouth): Thinks the saw of little practical value, would be improved if the teeth were continued about one inch higher up.

30. (Portsmouth): Yes; it saws branches of trees and bones rapidly.

32. (Quebec): Does not answer for cutting large pieces of wood. The saw is too short, and handle too short and small. It will cut through small pieces of wood easily.

37. (Ottawa): Not very well.

38. (Ottawa): Not sufficient grasp for the hand.

45. (Ottawa): Indifferently.

Committee's remarks: The balance of opinion is decidedly in favour of the saw, a view with which the committee concur.

Several regiments suggest the addition of more teeth, to which the committee sees no objection.

The committee recommend the trial of an experimental sword bayonet, of a construction submitted by Lord Elcho, with the 12 short action rifles now being made for issue to the troops.

Q.15 – Are the cleaning implements (the jag and protector) found useful? (All replies generally "Yes", but some were conditional.)

1. (Aldershot): Yes. Suggest that jag should be smaller at base, to admit of a larger piece of cleaning rag. The rod head is too small.

5. (Aldershot): Yes; but considerable difficulty in working the cleaning rod, especially after blank firing.

6. (Aldershot): Jag excellent, but protector too brittle.

8. (Aldershot): Yes, but the jag is too large when the rag is twisted round it.

13. (Dublin): Jag too large. Protector might be dispensed with, as it is doubtful whether the men would use it.

14. (Dublin): Yes, especially the protector.

15 (Dublin): Yes. The protector becomes brittle in cold weather, and one was broken.

16. (Dublin): Yes, but recommends a piece of sponge tied to a piece of string as preferable to the rag and cleaning rod.

17. (Hythe): Yes, but the jag is liable to become unscrewed by the grooving, and to be left in the barrel.

21. (Gravesend): Yes. Prefers for cleaning to use a wet rag, followed by an oiled rag, in place of pouring water into the barrel, to prevent the liability of water entering the piston hole.

22. (Gravesend): The same. Also disapproves of the mode of fixing the rod into the stock by means of a screw, as it takes time to draw the rod.

23. (Gravesend): Recommends a cord or leather thong with a brush attached in place of cleaning rod.

25. (Portsmouth): Very useful. The men cleaned the rifles with the greatest ease.

27. (Portsmouth): Very useful, and the protector prevents injury to the bore in cleaning.

Committee's remarks: It is quite clear from these reports that the jag and protector are useful, and that they should be retained. The size of the jag should be diminished.

Q.16 – Is the muzzle stopper found generally useful, and is it considered desirable to introduce it? (Mostly "Yes" replies, with the usual few negative answers.)

5. (Aldershot): Yes; but suggests a stopper to go over instead of into the muzzle, to avoid the risk from a damp stopper, and the danger of the stopper becoming broken.

8. (Aldershot): Yes, but stronger metal recommended.

10. (Aldershot): Yes, but considers it dangerous in a breech loader.

14. (Dublin): Yes, especially the protector to the foresight.

21. (Gravesend): No; thinks muzzle stoppers dangerous except when fixed to arms-racks in barrack rooms. The sight protector is difficult to adjust properly, and if put on crooked is likely to injure the sight.

27. (Portsmouth): No, objects to them very strongly. Think they tend to rust the barrel, and to render accidents liable.

28. (Portsmouth): Not desirable to introduce it.

29. (Portsmouth): Yes. To prevent accidents recommends it should not be brought to any parades, except those for guard mounting, or for marching. Approves of the sight protector.

30. (Portsmouth): It protects the foresight, and prevents dust entering the barrel. Objectionable as likely to put the soldier to expense, as the stoppers are sure to be lost.

42. (Curragh): Yes, but recommends stronger metal, and that support (against the barrel) might be given to that part of the stopper which acts as a sight protector.

44. (Curragh): Yes. Since the Snider muzzle stoppers have been discontinued, the men are continually putting pieces of rag in the barrel to prevent damp or rain rusting the grooves.

Committee's remarks: Nearly the whole of the reports are in favour of the introduction of a muzzle stopper of the proposed pattern. Objection is made in one or two instances that a muzzle stopper is dangerous in a breech-loader, and that it tends to rust the barrel at the muzzle. The committee would observe upon these two points –

First, that the danger is greatly diminished by the shape and material of the muzzle stopper, which must attract attention when the rifle is in the firing position.

Second, that the felt on the muzzle stopper having been dipped in a waterproof composition, the rusting of the barrel suggested in this objection can hardly take place.

Q.17 – Has the ammunition been found liable to become broken or damaged in transport, or when carried in men's pouches? (Most answered "No", but there were a few affirmative replies.)

7. (Aldershot): Some were bent, but were straightened and then used.

8. (Aldershot): No, but it has not been carried in the men's pouches.

11. (Dublin): Five rounds were slightly bent.

14. (Dublin): It stands wear as well as the Snider ammunition.

15. (Dublin): Not more than the Snider ammunition.

16. (Dublin): It gets dented and bent, but not broken.

17. (Hythe): No, as far as the trials have gone.

18. (Hythe): Some of the cartridges have become bent and dented owing to several of the packages having been badly packed.

19. (Hythe): Has not been tested by carrying it in the men's pouches.

21. (Gravesend): A few rounds have become bent, but have been easily straightened.

25. (Portsmouth): No. Fifty rounds were carried loose in the men's pouches on guard for fourteen days, and were found perfectly serviceable.

26. (Portsmouth): One hundred rounds of ball cartridge were carried in the pouches of the guard for fourteen days without damage. The cartridges appear in some instances to have been injured by packing.

28. (Portsmouth): Of one hundred rounds carried loose in the pouches for eight days, two were damaged.

30. (Portsmouth): One or two have become bent, probably in the pouches. The length renders them liable to injury.

32. (Quebec): No rounds have been broken in the men's pouches.

34. (Montreal): No pouches suitable for the ammunition have been issued from the Stores Department.

41. (Devonport): Not sufficiently tried, but considers it a weak point.

Committee's remarks: Although the majority of reports are to the effect that the ammunition has not become broken or damaged, it has become so in a few instances; and considering that the trial has not been such as severly to test the cartridges on this point, the committee consider that the adoption of the short chamber cartridge, which is much stronger and less liable to injury, will be attended with advantage.

Q.18 – Has any difficulty arisen from this cause, in loading or extracting? (About one third replied with complaints, but the balance said "No".)

11. (Dublin): With the five rounds before mentioned.

14. (Dublin): Vide answer to Q.2.

15. (Dublin): If bent, the cartridge is difficult to load, but there is no difficulty from this cause in extraction.

16. (Dublin): If dented or bent, it is impossible to load.

17. (Hythe): None, with the exception referred to in Ans.3.

23. (Gravesend): The paper is the weak part of the cartridge as it becomes rucked up and causes the case to jam. The blank cartridge is difficult to load.

25. (Portsmouth): Several cartridges damaged in transport would not enter the chamber, others required force to push them in. No difficulty in extracting.

27. (Portsmouth): Yes, from bent cartridges; 38 out of 2,750 would not enter the barrel, and some others were hard to force in.

28. (Portsmouth): Only the two mentioned in previous answer.

37. (Ottawa): Five cartridges could not be placed in the barrel on account of defective shape.

43. (Curragh): No, except one ball cartridge referred to in Ans.17, which after being straightened was forced home with some difficulty, but after firing was easily extracted.

Committee's remarks: The committee would refer to their remarks on Q.3, adding thereto that they recognise in the absence of paper on the short chamber cartridge another distinct advantage of that construction.

Q.19 – Is the form of cartridge found convenient to use? (Again mostly "Yes" replies, but about one third replied in the negative.)

5. (Aldershot): Too long, liable to become damaged, and entails cumbersome pouches.

6. (Aldershot): Yes, but would be better if shorter.

9. (Aldershot): It may be inconvenient for stowage in pouches.

10. (Aldershot): It is too long.

11. (Dublin): More so than the Snider.

13. (Dublin): Yes; but the blank cartridges are found difficult to draw out from the ball-bag.

23. (Gravesend): Yes, the ball, not the blank cartridge.

30. (Portsmouth): No inconvenience has been noticed.

32. (Quebec): More convenient if shorter.

44. (Curragh): Yes, it is easier handled than the Snider.

46. (Quebec): Yes, if not quite so long.

Committee's remarks: Here again the evidence points to the advantage of a shorter cartridge, such as the short chamber cartridge which has been provisionally adopted.

Q.20 – Have any of the cartridges cut around the base? (The majority answered "No", but some were conditional; and there were a few with problems.)

4. (Aldershot): One (blank).

6. (Aldershot): One.

7. (Aldershot): One.

8. (Aldershot): Five rounds (blank).

11. (Dublin): No actual cutting, but slight escape of gas close to base cup, and where the cap overlaps.

12. (Dublin): No; but slight escape of gas at base, just in front of cup.

36. (Montreal): In two cases whilst firing blank, the extractor forced off the metal base of the cartridge, and the paper had to be pushed out by means of the cleaning rod.

46. (Quebec): Four, easily removed with rod.

Committee's remarks: On this point the evidence is very satisfactory, only seven ball cartridges cut at the base out of a total fired of about 137,308 rounds.

Q.21 – Have any of the caps given way? (Again the usual majority reply of "No", with the usual few complaints.)

2. (Aldershot): One defective cartridge.

4. (Aldershot): No; but two defective cartridges returned.

6. (Aldershot): In most of the misfires the caps seem to have given way slightly. In one instance an anvil was blown out.

9. (Aldershot): In one cartridge there was no cap, another failed to explode.

22. (Gravesend): One cartridge was found in which the head of the cap chamber had not been riveted down, or pierced with touch hole.

35. (Montreal): In three cases the caps have fallen out, in eight cases the caps have been bad and caused misfires.

44. (Curragh): One, that of a blank cartridge.

Committee's remarks: There appears to have been only two instances of caps giving way in the sense intended by this question.

General observations.

1. (Aldershot): States that in accuracy, flatness of trajectory, and penetration, the M-H excels the Snider. The misfires occurred more when the trigger was pressed gently than when pulled more sharply. Thinks the Snider breech action preferable, on account of the interior being more easily examined than that of the M-H. Thinks there may be some chance of accidents from carelessness in observing the indicator and working the bolt. States that the men prefer the M-H to the Snider.

2. (Aldershot): Prefers the M-H greatly to the Snider for shooting. Considers it stronger, and better adapted to resist rough usage. Thinks the position of the lever a great assistance in keeping the right elbow in its proper position when shooting. Recommends that the sling of the rifle should not be permanently fixed.

3. (Aldershot): Rifle much liked by the men, and certainly a good arm. Fears accidents from difficulty in knowing if it be loaded. Fears rust clogging the action.

5. (Aldershot): Thinks a heavier bullet might be used to prevent lateral deviation in wind. Much in favour of the M-H, both on account of its shooting qualities, and the strength and simplicity of the breech action. Thinks the indicator might be made more prominent. Thinks that the trap in the butt would not stand the wear of ordering arms. Considers that the misfires of rifle No.157 were owing to a short piston. Pouches very inconvenient.

NOTE: The springs of these arms have been changed since they were used by the 7th and 23rd Regiments, and with the exception of arm 157, no arms have shown any misfires since the change.

6. (Aldershot): Thinks the M-H very superior to Snider in accuracy, and approves highly of the breech action. Attributes the misfires to the piston being too sharp, and not striking the cap fairly. Pouches very inconvenient, and larger and heavier than necessary.

7. (Aldershot): Thinks the M-H superior to the Snider. The accuracy at long ranges much superior, but at short ranges not so good as the Snider, owing, probably, to the notch in the back sight being very indistinct. Accounts for misfires from weakness of spring, but the piston of No.27 rifle is shorter than those of the others. Nearly all the cartridges exploded when struck a second time. Only three rifles, Nos. 27, 154, and 162 tried by this regiment.

9. (Aldershot): Thinks that misfires are owing to the piston being too pointed, and that the present piston is too slight. Recommends a cover of leather for the breech action. Thinks the bolt more conducive to danger than to safety. A rifle was exploded accidentally, the serjeant handling it believing it to be bolted.

14. (Dublin): Considers the principle of the lock much better than that of the Snider if the spiral springs stand. The chief objection lies in the liability of water and sand to enter between the breech block and sides of the lock.

15. (Dublin): Considers the chief objection to the M-H arm lies in the tendency of the spiral springs to become weak, and the impossibility of preventing water from entering the

breech action. Thinks the Henry barrel combined with the Snider action would provide the service with a better arm.

23. (Gravesend): States that the number of misfires is not so great owing to the men having become used to the arm (vide answers to Q.6). Thinks very highly of the arm, both with regard to the simplicity of the breech action and accur acy of the barrel.

24. (Gravesend): Placed the rifle in the hands of recruit officers without giving them any previous drill. They found no difficulty in using it. Some of them felt the recoil. Rifle No.193 has fired 2,082 rounds of ball, and 1,020 of blank cartridge, without having been cleaned and with only one misfire.

25. (Portsmouth): Reports that the men who have used the rifles are confident that the M-H is superior to the Snider. The position of the lever is inconvenient in the bayonet exercise. The ball bag issued with the rifles not approved of, from the difficulty of putting in and taking out the cartrid-ges.

27. (Portsmouth): Considers the arm very strong, and calcul ated to withstand any amount of rough usage, and can be easily cleaned by the most unskilled man. The shooting was excellent, although the weather was most unfavourable. The scores made on an unfavourable day at 900, 1,000, 1,100 and 1,200 yards excelled those usually made with the Snider at 650, 700, 750, and 800 yards. The rapidity of fire has been about twice that of the Snider. The misfires are a most serious disadvantage, and if not remedied would coun-terbalance all the advantages of the arm. They occur most frequently when the trigger is pressed gently. The men con-sequently stated that they preferred the Snider breech act-ion to the M-H. The cartridges fit too tightly into the cham-ber, but do not swell after emersion* in water. The ball bag not approved of.' (*Viz. – immersion.)

29. (Portsmouth): Considers the M-H superior to the Snider in accuracy and penetration. Prefers the Snider action to that of the M-H, as he thinks the latter cannot be taken to pieces by the soldier for the purpose of cleaning, and also because there is no half-cock. Considers the breech action to be deep and clumsy, the men, when firing, are obliged to place their thumbs alongside, instead of on the head of the stock. Thinks the Henry barrel with the Snider or Henry act ion, a shorter cartridge, and a diminished pull off, together with the back sight more deeply notched and placed nearer the breech, would be a better weapon than the M-H.

30. (Portsmouth): Considers that the M-H surpasses the Snider for accuracy of sighting, lower trajectory, and great-er penetration, but considers that, owing to the recoil, many men will be afraid of it, and make bad shooting, although a good shot will find it easier to shoot with accur-acy.

40. (Portsmouth): Three rifles tried. For the navy the rifle would be more convenient if shorter. States the practice has been carried on at great disadvantage, owing to the bad weather, but the instructor and men expressed themselves very much satisfied with the rifle. The rifles have been great ly pulled about by the men, but none have become injured.

43. (Curragh): Recommends a covering for breech. Remark that the ramrod becomes loose after a few rounds have been fired. Fouling, after firing fifty rounds blank ammun-ition, considerable.

44. (Curragh): Preferred by the men for hardiness and accur acy, and because the painfully tedious position of 'support' would be done away with. Recommends a covering for breech to protect it from weather. Pull off too strong. Thinks the continuous explosion of powder will ultimately wear away the upper end of the grooving, on account of the space between the end of blank cartridge and the grooving, where a quantity of fouling accumulates. Recommends a loop being attached to each packet of ammunition, to enable it to be easily pulled out of the pouch.

48. (Dublin): States that the men using the M-H expressed themselves greatly pleased with it. Found no inconvenience from recoil, which was not greater than that of the Snider. Recommends a thin platinum wire in the bar at the top of flap of back sight. Has observed no impediment in the act-ion of the breech, but thinks that rain and dirt entering it will cause injury. Recommends a leather cover to breech action, and that a damp rag should be used for cleaning the rifle after blank firing, instead of pouring water into the barrel. Thinks the accuracy of the rifle decidedly superior to that of the Snider at the longer, but not the shorter, ranges. Few misfires occurred after the substitution of stronger springs.

49. (Portsmouth): Approves of the reduced length of the arm. The rapidity of loading of the M-H is more than doub-le that of the Snider. The accuracy of the shooting of the M-H is much greater than that of the Snider, and the allow-ance for wind much less. There seems to be no tendency to foul after continuous firing. The manipulation of the breech action is easy, simple, and safe. The lock does not appear liable to injury from rough usage, wear, or weather. The rifles of the 2nd Regiment were piled for a week during the month of January in the open air without cleaning, and were not injuriously affected by the exposure. The cartrid-ges appear strong, and not liable to injury from wet (vide experiments made in 2nd and 99th Regiments). The sword bayonet is a great improvement on the old bayonet. The defects of the arm are as follows: The position of the back sight when the arm is carried at the trail. The sharp edge at the entrance into the chamber. The tight fitting of the cart-ridge in the chamber. The inconvenience of the expense pouch. and the numerous misfires, which appear to be the fault of the arm, not of the ammunition.

Committee's observations: The committee find that the several criticisms contained in the General Observations, which have not been dealt with in the answers to the 21 questions, may be grouped under the following heads, which will be considered seriatim –

I. Misfires. These are attributed to various causes in addition to weakness of coil springs as follows –

A. Trigger being pulled too gently. In three instances is this suggested as a probable cause (Reports 1,22,27). As far as the reports go, it appears that the misfires have almost entirely ceased since the stronger springs have been placed in the arms. It is not probable that with a spring of suitable and sufficient strength any misfires will occur from pulling the trigger gently, an essential to good shooting.

B. Striker being too short. This is complained of in four reports (Nos.4,5,7,21). The objection is applicable to all central fire breech loading arms. There appears to have been some little want of uniformity in the length of the strikers, due probably to the arms having been hand made. There is no reason to anticipate that, when the arms are made by machinery, this defect will occur. The superintendent RSAF is fully alive to the importance of supplying strikers of correct and uniform length.

C. Striker being too sharp. In one report (No.6), this is suggested as a possible cause of misfires. The committee are not inclined to agree with this opinion.

D. Position of anvil in cap. One officer (No.11) suggests this as a cause of misfires. It is a fact that occasional misfires are caused by the anvil having been accidentally placed on one side; but this is a defect in manufacture that very rarely occurs, and the present position of the anvil has been proved to be satisfactory during the long trials with cartridges fired from the Snider and M-H rifles.

E. Indicator screwed too tight. One officer (No.12) has expressed his opinion that the working of the action may be impeded by the too tight screwing of the indicator. The committee, after examination of the breech action, do not understand how the indicator can be screwed too tightly, except by turning the keeper screw the wrong way, but the attention of the Superintendent RSAF will be called to this remark.

F. The action of cold weather on the spring. Although this remark is made by one regiment in Canada (No.34), it is directly contradicted by the results of trials made by another regiment in Canada (No.38); the thermometer in both instances having been below zero. Both these trials were made with the weak springs, and the committee cannot accept the evidence of the trials recorded in Report 34 as conclusive of the effect of cold weather upon the springs.

G. The deterioration of the percussion powder. This is suggested by one officer (No.38) as a possible cause of the misfires; but as the percussion powder in the caps is the same as has been in use for many years, and as the committee are unaware of any complaints having been made of the deterioration of percussion caps, they are not inclined to assign any importance to this suggestion.

Having noticed the various suggestions which have been made to account for the great number of misfires which have occurred with the arms, and having assigned to each of these suggestions as much importance as it seemed to merit, the committee think it proper to observe that there can be no doubt that the main cause of these misfires was the weakness of the spiral spring as originally issued. The concurrence of opinion on this point appears to be decisive (see answers to Q.6), independently of the information which the committee have received from other sources. Indeed, it is admitted that the springs were not so strong as those approved by M. Martini, who states in his letter 14-2-1870, that he employs a spring of 40 lb, but thinks 33 lb will answer. He finds the spring issued in the two arms presented to him from Enfield were only 33 lb.

It also appears that the springs of the 200 experimental arms were not so strong as those of the arms with which the original experiments were made, on the success of which was based the recommendation that the rifle should be adopted. If future springs be made of the strength originally approved by M. Martini, the committee see no reason to doubt that misfires will practically cease.

The committee have made a calculation of the average number of misfires when the 86 rifles mentioned in these reports were fired with the weak springs, and when the same rifles were fired with the stronger springs, and find that with weak springs 163,277 rounds of ball and blank were fired with 3,814 misfires, showing a percentage of 2.34. With strong springs 26,463 rounds of ball and blank have been fired up to the present time with only 9 misfires, or a percentage of .034.

II. Breech mechanism. The following objections are made to the breech mechanism.

A. That accidents may occur in spite of the bolt and indicator. Six reports (1,3,5,8,9,29) contain an expression of opinion that the bolt and indicator are insufficient to afford complete security against accidents.

On this point the committee would make the following observations –

1. The question of the expediency of having the gun at full cock at the moment when the operation of loading is completed is one which has not been overlooked, and the late Small Arms Committee were of opinion that in order to obtain the full advantage of a breech-loader in respect of rapidity, it is desirable to avoid the extra motion of cocking a rifle after loading. In this opinion the present committee concur. The system is not necessarily attended with danger if the soldiers are properly trained.

2. Should it be deemed necessary at any time to carry the arm loaded, the bolt is even more efficient than the half cock, and the operation of bolting the arm safer than lowering the hammer.

3. With regard to the indicator not sufficiently distinguishing whether the arm be cocked or not, the committee would point out that it requires a trained eye to distinguish

between the full and half cock of an ordinary hammer, while the position of the indicator, with reference to the breech pin, is readily distinguishable, not only by sight, but by touch, a point of some importance at night.

B. Difficulty of examining interior. In two reports (1, 29) some exception is taken to the arm on this account. The committee would point out that the dismantling of the breech action is equivalent to the dismounting of the breech action and lock of the Snider rifle; and that the former operation is simple, and requires less mechanical contrivance. The committee do not contemplate that it will be necessary to strip the breech action of the M-H rifle more frequently than it is necessary to dismount the lock of the Snider.

C. Water liable to get into the breech action in washing out. In one case (13) this is complained of. It should be noticed that the instructions issued with the arms direct that in washing out the arm is to be *held muzzle downwards, in order to prevent the possibility of water entering the striker hole.* This operation, however, does not fulfil its object. The committee think that the system of cleaning out after blank firing, which is in use in the RL, might be advantageously tried – viz, to leave the cartridge case of the last round in the chamber until the rifle is washed out.

The fouling after ball firing is so slight, that to clean the rifle a damp rag or tow, followed by an oil rag, will answer perfectly.

D. Piston not large enough to stand wear. In report 9 an opinion is expressed that the piston is too slight to wear well. This opinion does not appear to be sufficiently supported by facts to warrant the committee in attaching importance to it. There is no reason to doubt that the piston of the M-H will wear as well as that of the Snider.

E. Pull off of trigger too strong. There is only one instance (10) in which the pull off is complained of as being too strong previous to the substitution of the stronger springs. There is however, no doubt that the stronger spring has increased the pull off to an inconvenient degree. The attention of the Superintendent RSAF has been called to this point, and he has stated that there will be no difficulty in making the pull off the same as that of the Enfield rifle.

F. Breech mechanism so deep that it renders it difficult for men to place their thumbs over the top when at the "present". One officer (29) raises this objection. The committee conceive that with men with very small hands there may be a difficulty in keeping the thumb in the position laid down by the Musketry Regulations, but they do not think the objection is one to which much imporance need be attached.

G. Position of lever bad for bayonet exercise. In reports 1 and 25 it is stated that the men find it difficult to grasp the rifle at the small of the butt at bayonet exercise. Although only two officers report this, the committee agree that the lever is in the way at bayonet exercise.

H. Trigger too near trigger guard. Report 41 suggests a slight alteration in the position of the trigger, but the committee do not think it advisable to adopt this suggestion.

I. A cover for the breech recommended. This is recommended in six reports (9,42,43,44,48,50). As before observed, the rifle was severly tested in the competitive trials as to its liability to injury by dust and damp, and the committee are of opinion that there is no more need of a cover for this rifle than for the Snider or Enfield rifles, and they consider that there are strong objections to the use of a cover for a military arm.

III. Arm generally objected to as too long.

This objection has been urged in two reports (10 and 40), one of which is from HMS Excellent. It has been stated in the report of the Breech-Loading Committee (p.21), of 11-2-1869, that a barrel of 31 inches, giving a length of arm with short stock of 47 inches, will shoot equally well with the present pattern of barrel of 35 inches, and total length of arm of 51 inches. There can be no doubt that for the naval service a shorter rifle would be preferable, and the committee consider that a rifle of the same length as that in use by the rifle regiments would be more serviceable than a rifle of the present length, for the following reasons –

The rifle will be lighter, better balanced, and handier; on the other hand it will be shorter as a pike, and not so convenient for firing in two ranks standing, objections which do not seem to have caused the rifle regiments to condemn the short rifle, and which the committee do not think sufficient to weigh against the advantages before-named.

IV. Ammunition objected to.

1. Bullet too light. This is only stated in one report (5). The weight and size of the bullet now in use has been decided upon by the former committee after great care and delib eration. The committee, therefore, see no reason to attach weight to this objection.

2. Solid metal cartridge preferred. No.21 prefers a solid metal case to the coiled case. The coiled case was decided on by the previous committee, and this committee see no reason for giving a preference to the solid metal cartridge over that at present in use.

3. Excessive fouling of blank. This objection, in three reports (43,44,50), can only have reference to cleaning the rifle, and has already been met. There is a suggestion in Report 44 that the continuous explosion of powder will tend to wear away the grooving. The committee will note this for trial.

V. Objections to pouch and ball bag, and method of packing ammunition.

The pouch and ball bag are objected to in reports 5,6, 21,25,26,27,44, and 49, on the following grounds – That it is difficult to place the cartridges in the ball bag, and difficult to extract them therefrom; and in the pouch the packets of ammunition sink too low, rendering it difficult to take them out. This remark is found to apply more especially to the packages of blank cartridges. It is recommended in No. 21 that the cartridges should be packed in tens in papier mache cases, and that the ball bag should be soft. In report 44 it is recommended that a loop should be placed on the packages of ammunition to help in taking them from the pouch.

The committee would remark that the subject connected with pouches was not referred to the previous Breech-Loading Committee, and there are no data before them on which to form an opinion. They recommend, therefore, that attention should be directed to these points.

VI. Other objections.

1. Trap in heel of butt not standing wear. In No.5 it is stated that the trap in the butt is liable to become loose and unserviceable through wear. This remark is stated in only one report. The arms have not been sufficiently long in use for the committee to give a decided opinion on this point.

2. Cleaning rods work loose. In reports 21,42, and 43, it is stated that the cleaning rods work loose. The committee recommend that the attention of the Superintendent RSAF should be called to this matter, in order that some better method of securing the cleaning rods be devised.

APPENDIX 13.

Being a summary of the reports on the trials of the Martini-Henry Long Chamber rifles, as received from the various regiments and presented by the Committee on Martini-Henry Breech-Loading Rifles in their final report of 8-2-1871.

Q.1 – What accidents, if any, have occurred? (Most answered "None", but there were a few reports indicating minor problems.)

65. (Hythe): The point of the striker of No.137 rifle was broken. The tumbler of No.78 rifle was broken. Head of tumbler pin of rifle No.11 was broken off; in consequence the indicator is liable to fall off and be lost. Two swivel pins of the top band have been lost owing to their liability to unscrew.

71. (Portsmouth): Rifle No.9 went off once whilst the breech was being closed.

72. (Portsmouth): Two. All the rifles had been dismounted by the armourer-serjeant to the proper pull off. After remounting, rifle No.5 went off twice without a finger near the trigger or the firer ready to fire. In the second instance when the breech was closed the lock was not at full cock, although indicated by both indicator and trigger. After several attempts the lock was put right, but on passing it over to the firer it went off in the air. It was dismounted by the armourer who could not discover the cause, but no accident occurred afterwards.

73. (Portsmouth): The block axis pin of rifle No.1 became loose and dropped out. 40 rounds were fired after this occurred without replacing the pin, and no inconvenience was experienced.

74. (Kinsale): The striker of rifle No.74 broke after firing 280 rounds of ball and 140 of blank cartridge.

88. (Portsmouth): The bent of the tumbler of rifle No.54 was broken by using force to open the block when the arm was bolted; there appeared to be a flaw in the metal; a new tumbler was made by the ship' sarmourer. The cover of the trap of the same rifle was broken off. The point of the striker has been broken in each of the three rifles; this was repaired by the armourer. Suggests that the points of the strikers be strengthened and fitted into the body, and that spare points should be supplied, as this would save time and could be more readily repaired when broken.

89. (Plymouth): In one case the breech axis pin became rusty from fouling, and was broken when being removed. In another case a burr was found in the slot where the tumbler works – it was removed.

91. (Morar): In volley firing, a rear-rank man slipped and blew off the upper band and part of the stock of rifle No. 75 in front of him.

92. (Dum Dum): Owing to the fault of one of the men, rifle No.28 went off on closing the action.

97. (Dugshaie): The tumbler of rifle No.3 broke at practice.

98. (Rawul Pindee): One striker was broken. It was apparently of bad metal.

99. (Lucknow): The block axis pin of rifle No.30 was broken.

Committee's remarks: With reference to the accidents reported as having occurred with rifles Nos.1 and 5 when on trial by the 77th Regiment, it should be noticed that all the rifles issued to this regiment were dismounted by the armourer-serjeant before they were fired. In all probability, therefore, they had not been remounted correctly. This opinion is corroborated by Col. Dixon, Superintendent RSAF, after examination of the arms.

The committee would point to the fact of rifle No.1 having fired 40 rounds without its block axis pin, as a proof that there can be little or no strain on this pin.

One of the tumblers was broken by the use of unjustifiable force when the arm was bolted. Four pistons, one tumbler, and an axis pin have been reported broken, probably owing to faults in the metal. One axis pin was broken owing to force having been used to extract it when rusted in. An alteration will be made to prevent the liability of this pin becoming affected by rust.

With reference to the report from HMS Minotaur, that a rifle hanging fire went off unexpectedly, the attention of the Superintendent RSAF will be called to this rifle when it shall have been returned to Enfield for inspection.

Q.2 – What difficulties, if any, have been found in loading? (About half the replies said "None", but there were some complaints, mostly concerning the cartridges.)

58. (Quebec): None. Rifle No.100 works better than it did.

67. (Portsmouth): Occasionally some difficulty was experienced in forcing the cartridge into the chamber.

69. (Portsmouth): None, except when the rifles had become foul or very dirty.

72. (Portsmouth): One cartridge being bent at the base entered as far as the inner base cup and then stuck. Several slightly stuck at the outer base cup, requiring an extra pressure of the thumb to force them home.

With blank cartridge great delay in firing was caused by the squareness of the front part of the cartridge, the corner of which stuck at the mouth of the chamber.

73. (Portsmouth): In one cartridge the brown paper was so thick that on entering the chamber it peeled back, thereby causing difficulty in loading with blank cartridge.

86. (Channel): Two cartridges would not enter the breech of either of the three rifles.

88. (Portsmouth): None, except with the bent cases, when the extractor had to be used more than once.

90. (Plymouth): There were slight difficulties in loading when the cartridges were bent.

91. (Morar): A few cartridges were found too large at the base for some of the rifles.

96. (Kurrachee): Slight difficulties when the cartridges were bent from being shaken in the ball bag.

98. (Rawul Pindee): There were difficulties when the cartridges became bent or when the base cups were too large.

Committee's remarks: The answers are generally similar to those which have already been reported upon by the committee. Their previous remarks will consequently apply, and it may be observed that the principal objections urged have been removed by the substitution of the short chamber cartridge, which has no external covering of paper.

Q.3 – What difficulties, if any, have been found in extracting cartridge cases? (About half said "None", but there were the usual complaints.)

52. (Aldershot): None, but the lever must be depressed sharply.

53. (Aldershot): None, except in rifle No.68.

58. (Quebec): None. Rifle No.100 has improved.

59. (Quebec): Rifle No.100 very bad.

65. (Hythe): A few cases of the base discs becoming detached, and consequent necessity for using the rod.

67. (Portsmouth): In rifle No.8 an extra jerk was required in many instances to extract the cartridge case.

72. (Portsmouth): The lever must be depressed sharply. In some instances the base discs and cups of the blank cartridge broke off on extraction.

75. (Kinsale): In four cases the base of the blank cartridge was torn off on extraction.

80. (Fermoy): When the rifle is foul an extra jerk is required to extract the cartridge case.

88. (Portsmouth): Twelve slight jams from the cartridges being bent, and in one case from the paper being rucked up; they were all fired except two kept for sample.

90. (Plymouth): None, provided sufficient force is used.

91. (Morar): None. The extractors of all the rifles have worked freely and well.

96. (Kurrachee): Slight difficulties in rifle No.47, which were remedied by the armourer-serjeant.

98. (Rawul Pindee): None, when the men were accustomed to the arm.

99. (Lucknow): No difficulty, except when the breech became rusty.

Committee's remarks: The reports show that in a few cases there has been a want of uniformity in the power of extraction. One report attributes this to rust. In some instances it seems to have arisen from defects in the cartridges, but in general from the inexperience of the soldiers in the proper use of the lever, as no fault in extraction could be observed in any of the rifles which have been returned to Enfield.

Referring to the breaking of the base discs with the blank ammunition, the committee are informed by the Superintendent RL that in future the ordinary service blank ammunition as issued for the Snider rifles can be used in the short chambered M-H, and that no instances have occurred of the breaking of the base discs of this ammunition.

Q.4 – Has the lever in any case been broken, or so bent as to impede the action? (All replied "No".)

Committee's remarks: None required.

Q.5 – Has rust been found to accumulate about the breech so as to affect its working? (About two thirds of the replies said "No"; but of the remaining one third, only a small portion of the replies were really critical of this fault.)

54. (Montreal): Yes. On the 4th, 5th, and 6th of this month there was heavy rain, and the rifles got very wet crossing in the boat to the island. The breech actions became rusted and the pull off was so great that it was almost impossible to move the trigger, and one rifle became useless for the day.

61. (Quebec): No. The rifles have been exposed to all sorts of weather.

68. (Portsmouth): The breech of rifle No.6 became very difficult to open; on examination, the whole of the parts were found clogged with oil, dirt, and rust, apparently of long standing. Remarks that cleaning by an armourer will be occasionally necessary, signs of wear soon appear when the parts are rusted or dry from want of oil.

71. (Portsmouth): During bad weather rust has accumulated quickly, but not so as to affect its working.

72. (Portsmouth): No, except when the rifles were allowed to become rusty from the application of water.

75. (Kinsale): After firing in heavy rain and leaving the rifle uncleaned, No.56 became so rusted as to materially affect its proper working.

77. (Windsor): No. Rust and fibre of cartridge paper in small quantities has been found in the breech action, but not so as to affect its working.

84. (Buttevant): Rust is liable to accumulate between the block and the sides of the lock, but not so as to affect its working.

88. (Portsmouth): Yes. On one occasion rifle No.54 was used for firing throughout a wet day and was put away damp. The rifle was examined 2½ days later, most of the parts of the breech, especially those near the trigger plate, were set with rust, showing that the breech action requires dismounting and cleaning after exposure to wet, in order to insure its efficient action.

90. (Plymouth): Not so as to affect its working, but rust has accumulated about the breech axis pin, and extractor pin, causing much difficulty in removing the breech for cleaning.

91. (Morar): Rust has collected during the rainy season, and the action has become stiff; on opening and closing the breech a few times sharply, its usual freedom of action invariably returned.

93. (Umballa): No. On several occasions during heavy rains the breech mechanism became saturated; water was also poured down the barrel and into the breech block, the coil spring being compressed to allow the water to enter; the rifles were then left for four days, on examination, the inner sides of the breech were covered with rust, but the coil springs and lever were quite free from it owing to the oil upon them, and did not cause any difference in the number of misfires.

94. (Simla): At the commencement of the trial rust affected the action of the piston or striker. The rifle had been exposed to a severe wetting and was left untouched for 48 hours. Misfires at the rate of 80 percent occurred. On taking out the breech block it was seen that owing to the entire absence of oil, much rust was present on the various parts of the action. They were cleaned and oiled, since which time and although the arm has since been exposed to very heavy rain, and has several times been placed under a spout (discharging gallons of water per second) without the breech action having been dried, or even the block taken out, the action has worked perfectly.

98. (Rawul Pindee): No. The rifles were exposed for 42 hours to very heavy rain, dust storms, and sun. 20 rounds of blank were then fired from each arm without a misfire.

99. (Lucknow): Yes. A slight shower of rain caused rust to accumulate in the breech, thereby affecting the action of the extractor. In two instances it was found that the breech block fell too low on the breech being opened, this caused the extractor to protrude so as to prevent the cartridge from remaining pressed home, and the trigger would not act. In other instances the cartridge case was only partially extracted.

Committee's remarks: The remarks of the committee in their former report apply to these answers. In a few instances the action has been impeded by rust, but on the other hand the arms have on many occasions been exposed to very severe trials from wet and dirt, without the working of the breech action being in any way impeded, a result in accordance with that arrived at after severe tests by the committee which recommended this arm.

Any action having a falling block would be equally exposed to injury by rust, whilst the main spring of the Martini action has by its position exceptional protection.

Q.6 – Has the coil spring been found to become weak and inefficient? (Most answered "No", but there were two 'Yes' answers, and some conditional.)

51. (Aldershot): There have been 44 misfires, with one exception the cartridges were all fired the second time. One cartridge after repeated failures in rifle No.187 was fired the first time in rifle No.162.

53. (Aldershot): Not the present ones.

54. (Montreal): No. Only one misfire has occurred since the new springs have been put in.

59. (Quebec): Not the present ones.

65. (Hythe): There have been no misfires since the stronger springs have been put in.

66. (Portsmouth): No. There has not been one misfire during the month.

68. (Portsmouth): Since the new coil springs have been put in no misfires have occurred, and there are no signs of the springs getting weaker.

98. (Rawul Pindee): Yes. Particularly towards the end of the experiments.

99. (Lucknow): Yes. The coil spring is deemed weak, as there were frequent misfires.

Committee's remarks: The evidence of these answers corroborates the opinion expressed by the committee in their previous report to the effect that, by the substitution of stronger springs, misfires have practically ceased.

Q.7 – Is the action of the extractor, in throwing out the empty cartridge case, considered too sudden? (All answered "No", with some qualifying their answer.)

53. (Aldershot): No, it is very advantageous.

73. (Portsmouth): No, it requires the sudden jerk to insure the complete extraction of the cartridge cases.

91. (Morar): No, its suddenness in ejecting the cartridge cases is considered an advantage in quick firing.

Committee's remarks: None required.

Q.8 – The stock being in two parts, has it remained firm and strong? (Most answered "Yes", but there were the usual few dissentions.)

58. (Quebec): No, in rifle No.72.

61. (Quebec): Rifles Nos.34 and 72 have both been screwed up by the armourer-serjeant.

65. (Hythe): Vide answer to Q.9.

77. (Windsor): Vide answer to Q.9.

90. (Plymouth): Vide answer to Q.9.

95. (Poona): Yes, but it has only been exposed to monsoon weather, and not to dry heat.

98. (Rawul Pindee): No. The screw bolt has become loose on several occasions, and when exposed to heavy rain the fore stock expanded, but closed again in a few days.

Committee's remarks: The committee would point out that the evidence on this point is satisfactory. The results of experiments made to test the relative strength of whole and divided stocks, also show that divided stocks are certainly equally strong as whole stocks.

Q.9 – Has the butt end been found to shrink or become loose from the effect of hot dry temperature? (Again mostly "No" replies, but a few had problems.)

58. (Quebec): Rifle No.72 very loose.

61. (Quebec): The butt end does not shrink. Rifles Nos.34 and 72 have both been screwed up.

64. (Hythe): The butt end of one rifle has shrunk a little, but does not appear to be loose.

65. (Hythe): The stock butt of rifle No.78 has become loose, probably from the shrinking of the wood enclosed within the body, and the bolt not fitting the hollow in the butt accurately.

77. (Windsor): The butt end of rifle No.4 was found loose.

88. (Portsmouth): No hot weather.

89. (Plymouth): The stock bolt of rifle No.42 became loose and the head chipped a little.

91. (Morar): No. The rifles were not tested until the hot winds had ceased.

95. (Poona): No hot dry weather.

98. (Rawul Pindee): Yes. The stock bolt screws of several rifles have become loose from the heat of the climate which caused the wood to shrink, and from the continuous ball practice. The screws had to be tightened.

Committee's remarks: The committee would point out that with the exception of a few rifles, all the stocks have stood the wear and tear satisfactorily.

Two of these rifles have been examined by the Superintendent RSAF, the others have not yet been returned to England.

Col. Dixon reports that the stocks of the two rifles were originally badly fitted.

A few reports state that the stock has shrunk away from the shoe. This inconvenience can easily be remedied by the armourer-serjeant.

Q.10 – Is any inconvenience experienced from recoil? (Generally "No", but there were several qualified replies.)

51. (Aldershot): Yes, when the arm is very dirty, and after firing about 50 rounds.

52. (Aldershot): No; but more than that of the Snider.

64. (Hythe): Not after the men became accustomed to the rifle.

68. (Portsmouth): No; more than that of the Snider, but scarcely appreciable.

69. (Portsmouth): It is more than that of the Snider. The men complain of it.

71. (Portsmouth): Yes, especially to those men who are unable to get the butt of the rifle well into the hollow of their shoulders.

72. (Portsmouth): After firing 50 rounds the recoil was very considerable.

73. (Portsmouth): Yes, after the 30th round, especially with quick firing. Attributes it to extreme quickness of rifling twist, increase of charge and the unconsumed powder of previous charge.Considers it greater than that of the Snider.

75. (Kinsale): Yes; more especially when firing with the arms uncleaned.

77. (Windsor): In the standing position the recoil is excessive. Attributes it to the stock being too straight.

79. (Fermoy): Yes, the men complained of it. When the thumb is placed (as per Musketry Instructions) across the head of the stock, the men received a blow on the nose, which has the effect of making them nervous, and putting them off their firing.

80. (Fermoy): The same, but the men do not feel the recoil now.

85. (Palermo): Slight when lying down, none when standing or kneeling.

87. (North America): Yes; the recoil is in excess of that of an ordinary rifle.

88. (Portsmouth): Not since the men have been cautioned not to place the thumb across the head of the stock.

91. (Morar): The recoil is greater than that of the Enfield rifle, though not excessive. More than 100 rounds have been fired out of the same rifle consecutively, and no differ ence in recoil was perceptible.

92. (Dum Dum): Yes, there is a good deal of recoil.

93. (Umballa): No. It is rather more than in the Enfield rifle and is slightly increased when the rifle is dirty.

94. (Simla): The recoil is apparent when 100 or 150 rounds are fired in rapid succession, but it is insignificant for an ordinary number of rounds.

96. (Kurrachee): The recoil is considerable at first to men unaccustomed to the arm.

98. (Rawul Pindee): Yes, though not so great as that of the Enfield. When the thumb is placed across the head of the stock the firer receives a blow on the nose. The arms were not cleaned for a week, during which 120 rounds were fired from each arm, the shooting was as accurate as before, and the recoil not in the slightest degree increased.

99. (Lucknow): Yes, when the rifle is dirty the recoil is very great. Attributed to the shape of the heel plate which does not fit the shoulder.

Committee's remarks: The great majority of the answers state that the recoil is not excessive. This opinion is in accordance with the reports previously received.

Q.11 – Is the weight of the arm a practical objection on service? (Most answered "No", but there were the usual objections.)

52. (Aldershot): Too heavy to make good standing practice.

65. (Hythe): No, but thinks it would be better if 5 ounces lighter.

69. (Portsmouth): In a long march the inconvenience would be considerable.

71. (Portsmouth): Undoubtedly.

74. (Kinsale): Considers it so when fired at the standing position, and when on the line of march.

77. (Windsor): Yes, but thinks that if the weight was more evenly distributed it would not be so.

86. (Channel): Yes, it is much too heavy for seamen, and when the bayonet is fixed, is overbalanced.

87. (North America): The rifle is one pound heavier than the present pattern, to a certain extent this must be considered as an objection.

93. (Umballa): No, for shooting, an improvement.

94. (Simla): The weight of the arm is its only drawback, but does not think it a practical objection.

95. (Poona): Thinks it will be found heavy for the march, and is not well balanced.

96. (Kurrachee): Yes.

Committee's remarks: The great majority of the answers state that the weight of the arm is not a practical objection on service, but the committee have ascertained by trial that the barrel of the M-H may advantageously be lighten ed.

Q.12 – Is the position of the back sight approved of? (There were mixed reactions to this question. The position was generally approved for shooting, but not for carrying at the trail.)

53. (Aldershot): Yes, but inconvenient when trailing arms.

58. (Quebec): Very bad for trailing arms.

65. (Hythe): Inconvenient when the arm is used for bayonet exercise.

69. (Portsmouth): It is too forward, and is inconvenient for trailing arms. The notch has too wide a field of view. Considers the silver mark in the centre very good.

70. (Portsmouth): No. Considers it too far from the eye, and inconvenient when trailing arms.

72. (Portsmouth): No. Inconvenient for trailing arms, and when the left hand is placed for firing.

76. (Youghal): Yes. Recommends a line be drawn down inner side, like that on sliding bar, for distances up to 400 yards.

77. (Windsor): No. It is too far from the firer. The V is too wide. Recommends a platinum line on interior edge of V.

79. (Fermoy): Yes, but owing to the sides of the sight form ing a more obtuse angle, men are liable to get the foresight to one side of the notch.

82. (Limerick): Yes. Considers that quicker and more accur ate aim is obtained with the M-H than with the Snider, on account of the back sight being further from the eye.

83. (Buttevant): Yes. It being further forward on the barrel enables a soldier in shooting to get a firmer hold of the rifle with the left hand. Recommends a white line on centre of head of the flap, similar to that on the sliding bar, as at present it is difficult to get the tip of the foresight exactly in the centre of the notch of the backsight.

90. (Plymouth): No, if placed nearer the breech a better alignment would be obtained, and be more convenient for carrying the arm at the trail.

91. (Morar): It is. All who have fired with the rifle approve of the position of the back sight.

92. (Dum Dum): Yes, it is better placed than that of the Enfield. A deeper V would be preferred. The silver line very soon wears out, recommends the line be continued on the notch of the flap.

95. (Poona): A great improvement on the V shape, and less likely to be affected by the sun.

96. (Kurrachee): Yes, but the foresight appears too blunt for the improved backsight.

98. (Rawul Pindee): No. It is inconvenient for trailing arms. Considers the sight with the flap down too open and shallow, recommends a silver line like that on the sliding bar.

Committee's remarks: The reports approve of the position of the backsight for aiming, but consider that it is inconvenient when the arm is carried at the trail. This objection has been overcome by the difference of balance obtained in the lightened barrel, referred to in the remarks on Q.11.

The form of the bar of the backsight has been dealt with in the Appendix C (ie, in Committee's report).

It has been suggested that the backsight should be more securely fastened onto the barrel (vide Appendix C).

Q.13 – How does the sword bayonet answer as a weapon of attack and defence? (The majority of answers were "Very well", but some did not test it, and there were the usual dissentions.)

52. (Aldershot): It would be too heavy to recover after a lunge forward.

66. (Portsmouth): Preferred to the bayonet now in use in the service.

69. (Portsmouth): Considered superior to the common one, as it can be used as a sword.

73. (Portsmouth): Very well. Recommends the saw be extended to the hilt, and about 1½ inches towards the point.

75. (Kinsale): Preferred to the old bayonet in its particular use, has advantage in forming a separate weapon.

76. (Youghal): Thinks it would act well, but makes the rifle heavy and unweildy.

83. (Buttevant): It seems a much more serviceable and useful weapon than the old bayonet.

88. (Portsmouth): Its adaptability for the naval service has been specially reported on.

91. (Morar): When the sword is fixed, the weight of the rifle at the muzzle is very considerably increased, and in consequence is considered much inferior to the Enfield rifle as a weapon for attack and defence.

93. (Umballa): No means of trying it. It was driven through a door half an inch thick with no evil result.

Committee's remarks: The majority of these answers are in favour of the sword bayonet. A modification of this pattern is now under trial and has been dealt with in the body of the report.

Q.14 – Does it answer as an implement on service for cutting wood? (The answers were mostly "Yes", with three "No", and a few with conditional replies.)

53. (Aldershot): No. Length of saw too little, breadth too great.

58. (Quebec): Not very well.

64. (Hythe): Not been tested.

65. (Hythe): Yes, very well, but thinks the edges, of the inside of the guard and the form of the knob at the end of the hilt, too sharp. Recommends the serrated part be continued an inch further towards the point.

69. (Portsmouth): Could be used for cutting wood, but does not think it would stand hard work.

71. (Portsmouth): Yes; green wood is sawn across rapidly, bones and hard substances can also be cut.

72. (Portsmouth): Yes; it cuts bones better and neater than a butcher's saw. Recommends the teeth of the saw be exten ded to the hilt and one inch nearer the point. The blade cut up meat better than a butcher's knife.

75. (Kinsale): Yes, several bushes of furze were cut down, a 6-inch plank sawn through and chopped, and the rations for three companies were served out by the use of the sword bayonet.

84. (Buttevant): It is useful both for cutting and sawing wood.

85. (Palermo): As a saw it works slowly, and is hard to grasp. It answers well as a butcher's knife.

89. (Plymouth): Yes. It was tried both on and off the barrel on a quarter of beef dressed as a man, by striking with the edge and with the point. The arm was satisfactory in every respect.

90. (Plymouth): Yes, several poles of from 4 to 5 inches in diameter have been sawn through in good time.

91. (Morar): It cuts wood but slowly, seems better adapted for cutting up rations. Thinks that if more teeth were placed in the saw back this defect would be remedied.

93. (Umballa): It will cut small boughs or wood sufficient for firewood, but the saw is not adapted for cutting timber for abbatis, etc.

94. (Simla): Does not think it will, there are too few teeth in the saw. It is heavier by 12 oz than the common bayonet with scabbard, and it seems doubtful whether the supposed advantages of the sword bayonet will be found to counterbalance this increased weight.

97. (Dugshaie): Both as a saw and a chopper, it appears to answer well.

Committee's remarks: The balance of opinion is in favour of the saw.

Q.15 – Are the cleaning implements (the jag and protector) found useful? (All answered "Yes", with some conditional replies.)

51. (Aldershot): Very. Recommends the protector being made of more lasting material.

53. (Aldershot): Yes; but considerable difficulty in working the cleaning rod, expecially after blank firing.

66. (Portsmouth): The jags have not stood the constant use they are subjected to, two having broken and the others not working freely.

67. (Portsmouth): Yes; but the jags have become broken.

88. (Portsmouth): Yes; but very likely to be lost on service. For this reason, it is suggested that the muzzle protector be made of brass, screwed on its inside and fitted to screw on to the head of the cleaning rod when not in use, the cleaning rod having a thread under the head for the purpose of screwing the protector to it. The three protectors supplied to this ship have all been lost.

91. (Morar): Very useful, but the jag is considered too large.

·95. (Poona): Owing to the climate the protectors have all broken to pieces. Recommends they should be made of brass.

99. (Lucknow): Yes, particularly the protector, which is found most useful in protecting the rifling during cleaning.

Committee's remarks: The committee are of opinion, as stated in their former report, that the jag and protector are very useful, and that they should be retained. They recommend a smaller jag for issue, to meet the objections urged.

Q.16 – Is the muzzle stopper found generally useful, and is it considered desirable to introduce it? (Most answered "Yes", some conditionally; and there were four "No" replies.)

51. (Aldershot): Very useful, particularly as a foresight protector.

53. (Aldershot): Yes. Suggests a stopper to go over instead of into the barrel, to avoid the risk of rust from a damp stopper, and the danger of the stopper becoming broken.

68. (Portsmouth): No, and it is not desirable to introduce it; it is of no use, being in the way of the soldier, and not helping to preserve the bore. It would be of great use for sea service.

71. (Portsmouth): Yes, but will entail extra expense on the men by their being lost.

72. (Portsmouth): No. They are liable to become lost or mislaid,and will cause the muzzle to become honeycombed. Thinks the muzzle stopper dangerous, as the rifle might go off by accident, there being no half cock.

75. (Kinsale): Yes, its introduction would be useful in keeping rust from the interior of the barrel in very damp climates.

77. (Windsor): Yes. Thinks the present form is not good, as the bayonet cannot be fixed without removing it. Rifle No. 126 has received injury from the use of it.

80. (Fermoy): Yes, particularly the sight protector, as it prevents the foresight being damaged so as to affect the shooting of the rifle.

83. (Buttevant): Yes. Very useful both for the protection of the barrel and foresight.

85. (Palermo): Yes, but the size of the sight protector might be increased with advantage, so as to diminish the chance of the muzzle stopper being fired away.

91. (Morar): Yes, very useful, and very desirable that it should be introduced. The danger of firing the rifle with the muzzle stopper in is in a great measure remedied by the addition of the sight protector.

92. (Dum Dum): No. It is sure to be lost on service, and any small quantity of dirt that would get into the barrel would do no harm.

94. (Simla): No, it is more than superfluous. It has already slightly corroded the bore of the rifle No.1269/H as far as it has been in contact with the bore.

Committee's remarks: Nearly the whole of the reports are in favour of the re-introduction of muzzle stoppers. Objections have, however, been urged to the pattern issued for trial.

To obviate these, the committee recommend for adoption a muzzle cover as proposed by the Superintendent RSAF, which appears to remedy every fault attributed to the muzzle stoppers, and is besides considerably cheaper in manufacture.

Q.17 – Has the ammunition been found liable to become broken or damaged in transport, or when carried in the men's pouches? (Most replied "No", with two answering "Yes".)

66. (Portsmouth): It is so strong that it is not liable to injury from the ordinary usage in the service.

71. (Portsmouth): Very few cartridges were rendered useless until exposed to very rough usage.

72. (Portsmouth): No. One tied up packet of ball ammunition was steeped in a tub of water and left to dry for 20 hours; two rounds missed fire once, and a third and fourth would not go off at all. The remaining six were left to dry for one week, and they all went off without a misfire. The brown paper remained very damp after drying for 20 hours, which caused difficulty in loading, but after drying for one week no difficulty was experienced.

77. (Windsor): No; but in a few instances the cartridges have become bent.

78. (Windsor): Not been carried in the pouches, but is liable to damage from transport owing to its length.

84. (Buttevant): During the trials five rounds of loose ammunition have been carried in the men's pouches and have not been the least damaged.

85. (Palermo): Not with ordinary usage. Thirty rounds were carried loose in a pouch for six days, the pouch was then trampled upon and thrown from one deck to another; after this very severe test six cartridges were found so damaged as to prevent easy loading.

88. (Portsmouth): A very small percentage (12 in 6,580 rounds) have become bent when carried in pouches.

91. (Morar): A few rounds on opening the ammunition boxes were found bent or otherwise slightly damaged, but the percentage was very trifling. The ammunition does not become damaged by being carried in pouches, and it is not affected by climatic influences.

92. (Dum Dum): A very small proportion has been bulged, but easily made available. One cartridge was found cut round the base but was fired afterwards.

98. (Rawul Pindee): Yes, many of the cartridges became bent in packing; 200 cartridges were carried in pouches, 4 became bent and damaged, but not rendered unserviceable.

99. (Lucknow): Not in transport, but when carried in the pouches they became bent.

Committee's remarks: The same remarks apply as were made in the former report. The great majority of the reports state that the ammunition has not become broken or bent. The shorter cartridge will be found even less liable to injury.

Q.18 – Has any difficulty arisen from this cause in loading or extracting? (Most answered "No", but some were conditional, and there were a few "Yes" answers.)

71. (Portsmouth): When the cartridges were at all damaged, increased difficulty of loading and extracting was experienced, which seems certain to happen so long as the cartridge fits so exactly.

73. (Portsmouth): No. If the base disc becomes bent the cartridge cannot be inserted.

83. (Buttevant): If the cartridge becomes bent the loading is difficult, but there is no difficulty in extracting.

91. (Morar): A few bent cartridges would not fit the breech or press home on this account, but no difficulty has been experienced in extracting any cartridge.

95. (Poona): It is impossible to load if the cartridge is badly bent or the base not placed on square.

Committee's remarks: The answers appear very satisfactory. The committee however, as stated in their former report, recognise in the absence of paper on the short cartridge a very great advantage.

Q.19 – Is the form of cartridge convenient to use? (Most replies were "Yes", but again some were conditional: "No" replies totalled five.)

53. (Aldershot): Too long, is liable to become damaged, and entails cumbersome pouches.

58. (Quebec): Yes, if not so long.

64. (Hythe): The ball cartridge is too long.

69. (Portsmouth): Yes, but would be more convenient if made one half inch shorter.

73. (Portsmouth): Yes. Considers it fits the chamber too tightly, and would be better if shorter.

77. (Windsor): Yes; but recommends cartridges with compressed powder (ie, shorter).

91. (Morar): No; it is too long, and the paper covering occasionally strips and causes slight difficulty in pressing the cartridge home.

Committee's remarks: The same remarks apply as were made in the committee's former reports. The shorter cartridge will probably satisfy the requirements of those who object to the long cartridge.

In report 77 compressed powder is suggested. Uniform shooting has, however, not yet been obtained with powder of this description.

Q.20 – Have any of the cartridges cut around the base? (The majority answered "No", but there were two "Yes" replies.)

72. (Portsmouth): Several blank cartridges cut round the base on extraction, thereby causing delay and difficulty. Vide answer to Q.3.

75. (Kinsale): No, but remarks that in 9 cases out of 10 there is an escape of gas at the base.

78. (Windsor): One, fired from rifle No.151.

Committee's remarks: The reports appear very satisfactory, and with regard to the cutting of some of the blank cartridges round the base, the committee would refer to their remarks on Q.3.

Q.21 – Have any of the caps given way? (Nine replied "Yes", the rest, "No".)

70.(Portsmouth): Yes, in one case.

72. (Portsmouth): Not when the cartridges were in a dry state.

88. (Portsmouth): Three caps appear to have given way, and are forwarded.

91. (Morar): In one instance only; they were generally found good.

Committee's remarks: In reports 77 and 78, 22 instances are reported on caps giving way. This is very exceptional, nearly all the reports stating that there have been no such instances. The committee consider that the giving away of caps in reports 77 and 78 was due to the piston in one of the rifles being either too long or too sharp. The length of piston has now been distinctly laid down, and it is believed that this inconvenience will not again occur.

General observations. (The majority of reports had some comments to make under this heading, but there were 10 that gave no reply.)

52. (Aldershot): States that the firing from 400 to 900 yards was far more accurate than the Snider, but the rifle is rather undersighted at the longer distances. Considers the Snider rifle the best that can be put into a soldier's hands, and fears anything that tends to give rapidity in loading and firing would cause a wasteful expenditure of ammunition. Remarks that even with the Snider it is difficult to keep the fire under control as shown at Arogee and at the capture of Magdala in Abbysinnia.

65. (Hythe): Recommends the stock about two inches in front of the trigger guard to be a little broader and more rounded to enable the left hand to grasp more firmly. The comb of the stock butt is too near the breech block; thinks that if the small be continued 1½ inches further back it would be more convenient. The stock is too short, the firer's nose is often hurt by the recoil. Remarks that the V is too shallow; recommends a vertical line be marked from the centre. States that the accuracy of the M-H in shooting is most remarkable, and their superiority over the Snider more especially marked the longer the distance. The deflect ion caused by high winds is only one half that of the Snider. The penetration of the bullet is very great. Thinks the arm would be perfect if it was made a few ounces lighter, the form of the small where the right hand holds it rendered more convenient by prolonging the lever 1½ inches, reducing the size of the loop, and altering the comb of the stock. Recommends that the side plates be case hardened owing to rust accumulating on them to a great extent. States that the worm of the cleaning rod is liable to be injured or worn.

66. (Portsmouth): Remarks that the pull off of all the rifles (especially rifle No.9) was very irregular. They sometimes required a very heavy and at other times a light pressure. Frequent firing appears to have enlarged the chambers of the rifles.

67. (Portsmouth): The spring and catch of the cover of the cavity in the butt do not appear equal to endure the rough usage of service; two having become unserviceable and the remainder more or less injured.

68. (Portsmouth): Remarks that the arm is capable of enduring any amount of rough usage and exposure to

weather. The immense superiority of the M-H over the Snider, in length of range, power, and accuracy, can hardly be over-rated. The rapidity of fire is twice that of the Snider. Recommends the flap of the trap in the butt to be fitted at an angle of 80 degrees instead of the present 90 degrees. Remarks that considerable amount of play has become observable in the lever, on examination it was found that at the "nose" of the lever, and the step of the block against which the nose works, there was considerable wear. It was probably owing to this that the lever did not always latch itself, but remained about half an inch distant from the catch; no inconvenience was experienced from this. The pull off of two rifles, Nos.6 and 8, have become bad. The black pouch is approved of.

69. (Portsmouth): The M-H is far more accurate at the long ranges than the Snider, but consider the Snider a much more serviceable weapon in the hands of the soldier on account of its simplicity, lightness, little recoil, and facility of repairing any slight damage to lock or rifle.

70. (Portsmouth): The end of the cleaning rod in rifle No. 198 when screwed in tightly, presses against the extractor and interferes with the proper action of the mechanism.

71. (Portsmouth): Considers the M-H superior to the Snider in the following respects; accuracy and flatness of trajectory, position of the backsight, and in having no hammer, although when it is loaded it is more difficult to ascertain whether the rifle is at full cock, but considers it inferior in balance, in the recoil being greater, and the barrel getting almost too hot to hold after ten rounds have been fired, and in the simplicity of the breech mechanism. Considers that on the whole the M-H is not calculated to be a practical arm for the whole service, but an excellent rifle for good shots where employed as sharpshooters, provided the recoil be lessened and the pull off regulated.

73. (Portsmouth): States that 30 rounds of blank cartridge were fired in one minute. Thinks the ordinary "independent" firing quick enough for the soldier; more rapid firing makes the barrel too hot to hold. Considers the M-H a far more serviceable arm than the Snider, especially in accuracy and flatness of trajectory. It is also far superior to the Snider in its higher penetrating power and in the strength and safety of the ammunition and rapidity of fire. States that if pull off could be regulated so as to remain uniform much better practice would be made.

74. (Kinsale): Rifle No.89 was bulged near the muzzle by being fired accidentally in the barrack room with the muzzle stopper in. Remarks that the pull off appears too strong.

76. (Youghal): Thinks the breech action would get out of order if exposed to much rain, but has not proved this by trial. The M-H is much preferred by the men to the Snider.

77. (Windsor): Considers the most objectionable points are –

1. The additional weight
2. The balance
3. Sword bayonet too heavy
4. Muzzle stopper too heavy.

Suggests that the muzzle protector should be converted to a stopper by means of a brass spring lid. Recommends that the foresight should be made of stronger metal. States that with the following alterations the M-H would be the most perfect breech-loading rifle ever placed in the hands of a soldier, viz. –

1. The backsight should be moved further back
2. The V should not be so deep
3. Sword bayonet should be modified in form and weight
4. Muzzle stopper should be made lighter
5. The butt should be more bent, in order to lessen the recoil
6. Preference should be given to a cartridge with powder in a compressed form
7. That a means should be found to obtain waterproof cartridges.

Remarks that the breech blocks in rifles Nos.4 and 193 varied considerably in manufacture. Rifle No.193 has fired 3,159 rounds of ball and 1,020 rounds of blank cartridge without being cleaned, and though the breech action cannot be said to work perfectly, owing to some small defect of the extractor, the arm is in a fairly serviceable condition, and the accuracy superior to that of any of the other four rifles now under trial.

78. (Windsor): The same. Rifle No.193 has now fired 5,079 rounds of ball and 1,020 rounds of blank without being cleaned.

86. (Channel): Remarks that the length from the butt to the trigger is too long for the average seaman without a rest, and great as the advantages of the new arm are in accurate shooting and in detail, considers it inferior to the Snider for seamen if the weight be not reduced to that of the Snider.

87. (North America): Remarks that the simplicity of the loading mechanism would come into full play when firing volleys advancing in charging order. The barrel becomes unbearably hot after firing 20 or 30 rounds quickly, owing, probably, to the thickness of barrel and the nature of the cartridge. The deflection in a strong wind was found less than the Snider.

88. (Portsmouth): Remarks that the rifles have been continually in use, and have had severe trials in bad weather. They have been frequently dismounted for instruction. They are well adapted for naval service, as they have no projections such as hammers, to catch the boat's thwarts, or ropes in going aloft, but would be more convenient if shorter. They have given great satisfaction to both officers and men.

90. (Plymouth): Encloses a report of the comparative shooting of the Snider and M-H rifles from 23-12-1869 to 23-12-1870, which states that 285 men with Sniders against 85 men with the M-H shows an average FoM of 3099.99 against 3903.36. None of the men were picked, but lots were always drawn for the M-H rifles.

92. (Dum Dum): Considers the M-H a very high-class arm, and is much approved by all who have fired it. Thinks that the heavy charge and sharp twist may account for the severe recoil, which may however be the fault of the firer. The barrel is considered too long. The bolt is useless and objectionable and the ball bags bad.

94. (Simla): States that after an exhaustive trial of three months, in regard to accuracy, rapidity of the bullet's flight and power of sustaining that rapidity to long ranges, in simplicity of the breech mechanism, its quickness and ease of manipulation, its strength and safety, its extreme non-liability to get out of order from climate or other influences, the M-H is a military rifle of the highest class, a weapon of terrible efficiency and one compared with which the Snider is a mere toy.

104. (Dum Dum): States that all iron and steel rust very quickly in the Bengal rainy season, during which these arms have been tried, and the test on this point has doubtless been severe. The breech block can, however, be so easily taken to pieces, that accumulation of rust to any extent can be prevented. The coil springs were originally weak, and have been replaced by stronger ones; the misfires have consequently ceased. The re-introduction of the muzzle stopper was advocated to protect the barrel and action in the barrack room and on parade. The recoil is greater than that of the Snider or muzzle-loading Enfield, but only slightly so, and is due to the increased charge and severe twist of rifling; attaches no importance to it in comparison with the other advantages of the rifle, such as flatness of trajectory, range, and penetration, and thinks it partly the firer's fault. Recommends that the barrel be shortened by 3 or 4 inches, as it would be lighter, better balanced, and the accuracy equal, if not better, although the weapon as a pike would be slightly inferior. Considers the form of backsight to be very good for accuracy of aim, and believes it would be approved of by the men after a little practice. Thinks the locking bolt might be done away with, its use being questionable.

105. (Lucknow): Considers that the very complicated nature of the breech action is a disadvantage for a military weapon. The cartridge seems liable to injury, should think the bottle-shaped cartridge would be easier and stronger to carry. The stock does not fit the shoulder so well as that of the Snider, and the pull off of the trigger is very harsh. The rifle was found very accurate, and being so little affected by wind made very good practice at long ranges.

Committee' observations: The committee following a similar course with that pursued in their former report proceed to group the several criticisms not dealt with in the answers to the 21 questions under the following heads --

I – Misfires.

Since the substitution of the stronger spiral springs misfires have practically ceased. Some of the weak springs first issued with the rifles were not replaced when the Indian reports were made out.

II – Breech mechanism.

(A) Pull off of trigger. Several reports mention that the pull off of the trigger has become too strong and irregular since the adoption of the stronger springs. This would arise from the pull off having been originally adapted to the weaker springs. The Superintendent RSAF states that there would be no difficulty in regulating the pull off to any weight that may be required, and when the action is in good order, he sees no reason why the pull off should be less regular than with the ordinary lock.

(B) Side plates. One report, No.65, recommends that the side plates be case hardened. This is a manufacturing question, which may safely be left to the Superintendent RSAF.

(C) Wear of surface levers. One report, No.68, mentions that the surface of the levers of five rifles have become worn through use. Col. Dixon's report, after examination of these arms, expressly contradicts this statement, and therefore what was supposed to have been wear was probably a mere burnishing of the surfaces.

(D) Form of lever. One report, No.65, recommends another form of lever. The committee have recommended a modification of the present form which somewhat resembles that suggested.

(E) Locking bolt. Two reports (92,104) object to the locking bolt, considering it a useless addition to the action. The majority of the reports do not however object to it, and the committee consider its retention desirable.

III – Arm generally objected to as too long.

Two reports (92,104) in addition to those from the navy, recommend a shorter arm. The committee has already expressed their opinion on this subject, viz, that they recom mend a somewhat shorter arm for general service.

IV – Form of stock.

One report, No.65, suggests that the fore-end of the stock in front of the trigger guard should be made broader and more rounded. It also suggests an alteration in the comb of the stock. The committee have recommended the latter alteration, but do not consider the former necessary.

V – Other objections.

(A) Cleaning rods. Three reports (65,70,91) object to the method of securing the cleaning rod, as it frequently works loose. This subject has been dealt with in Appendix C.

(B) Trap in butt objected to. Two reports object to the trap in the butt. The committee recognise the defects in the trap, and have recommended that it be done away with, vide Appendix C.

(C) Barrel becoming too hot. Five reports complain that the barrel becomes too hot to touch after very rapid firing. This is an objection common to all rapid firing arms, but the committee consider that, on service, circumstances would rarely arise when such rapid firing as would make the barrel too hot to hold would be required.

(D) Rifles undersighted at long ranges. Two reports point out this defect. Attention will be given to this point before a pattern arm for final adoption is decided upon.

(E) Chambers become enlarged. One report, No.66, remarks that the chambers of rifles Nos.6, 7, 8, 9, and 10, appeared to have become enlarged by firing, but this opinion is unsupported by actual measurement, the Superintendent RSAF has reported that he was unable to detect any difference of size between these and other chambers. On comparing the casts of chambers taken before and after firing rapidly a thousand rounds of blank cartridge, no difference in size could be detected.

VI – Objections to ball bag and pouch.

One report objects to the ball bag and pouch. The committee in their former report pointed out that this subject was not referred to them, and recommended that attention should be called to it.

APPENDIX 14.

Being a summary of the reports on the trials of the Martini-Henry Short Chamber Rifles as received from the various regiments, and presented by the Committee on Martini-Henry Breech-Loading Rifles in their final report of 8-2-1871.

Q.1 – What accidents, if any, have occurred? (Most answered "None", but four had some problems.)

5. (Aldershot): A rifle went off accidentally whilst at practice, the man not being accustomed to a self-cocking rifle.

6. (Aldershot): The extractor of rifle No.10 was broken at practice. On examination there was found to be a flaw in the metal.

9. (Curragh): The muzzle of rifle No.6 was bulged when received from the 44th Regiment.

12. (Portsmouth): A coil spring has been broken.

Committee's remarks: With reference to the accidents, the committee would remark that none appear to have occurred which can be attributed to any peculiarity in the construction of the Martini breech mechanism.

Q.2 – What difficulties, if any, have been found in loading? (Only one replied with any problem, all others answered "None".)

1. (Aldershot): One cartridge in loading rifle No.6 was caught on the disc by the breech block; states that it was the fault of the cartridge.

10. (Portsmouth): None. The difficulties which occurred with the paper covered cartridge have been entirely got rid of by the substitution of the bottle cartridge.

Committee's remarks: Difficulties that were experienced in loading with the long cartridge appear to have ceased with the short chamber, and consequently shorter cartridge.

Q.3 – What difficulties, if any, have been found in extracting cartridge cases? (About one third of the replies had slight problems with this feature.)

3. (Aldershot): None, unless in hands of awkward men, who have great difficulty in giving sufficient jerk to the lever to throw the cartridge completely out; in this case the block must again be closed, which is difficult after a cartridge has been fired and partially extracted.

8. (Curragh): One cartridge case, being a little bigger in circumference than usual, required a certain amount of force to extract.

9. (Curragh): In one instance there was a slight difficulty in extracting a cartridge case from rifle No.8.

10. (Portsmouth): The extraction of the empty case after firing is neither so easy or certain as with the first pattern rifles, a sharp forcible jerk of the lever is required, and in some cases it has had to be repeated several times. This difficulty appears to occur from the tight fitting of the cartridge after firing, and is not the fault of the extractor. Two cartridges were difficult to extract, owing probably to some fault in the case.

11. (Portsmouth): There was a slight difficulty when sufficient force was not used.

Committee's remarks: It appears from the reports that although the extraction of the shorter case is not so free as that of the long, yet that it is sufficiently so; and the committee believe that any difficulty on this subject will be found to disappear as men become experienced in the use of the arm.

Q.4 – Has the lever in any case been broken, or so bent as to impede its action? (All answered "No", but there was one conditional reply.)

10. (Portsmouth): No, but recommends that the sharp edges of the lever catch should be rounded off.

Committee's remarks: With reference to the observations in report No.10, the committee have recommended that the sharp edges in all parts of the arm should as far as possible be rounded off.

Q.5 – Has rust been found to accumulate about the breech so as to affect its working? (Most replied "No", but there were two answers with problems.)

2. (Aldershot): No; but dust and dirt have accumulated, which would, it is thought, interfere with the working of the breech.

7. (Hythe): Rifle No.3 was accidentally left at full cock; when required the striker was found rusted firmly in the block, so that the lever could not be moved down. This rifle had not been exposed to any bad weather, neither had it been cleaned with water.

9. (Curragh): Yes, once with rifle No.3.

10. (Portsmouth): No. These rifles have been exposed to exceptionally bad weather and constant damp for a month, the breech actions were not dismounted and only cleaned by rubbing with an oily rag; they remained in perfect working order throughout.

12. (Portsmouth): When the lock with the broken coil spring was taken to pieces rust was found to have accumulated in the lock on the spring and various parts of the lock.

Committee's remarks: The committee observe that in the course of the trial at Hythe the striker of rifle No.3 was found on one occasion to be fixed by rust. This rifle has been forwarded to Enfield for examination by the superintendent, together with some remarks on the subject by the IGM. One report mentions that rust had been found on the coil spring and that this coil spring was broken, and this is the only instance, in all the trials of the long and short actioned arms of rust having reached the coil spring.

Q.6 – Has the coil spring been found to become weak or inefficient? (All answered "No", with one exception.)

8. (Curragh): The spring of rifle No.3 was evidently weak, as there were misfires, but were fired on the second trial.

Committee's remarks: There appears no evidence that the springs have become weak or inefficient from use. On this subject the committee would point out that the results of the practical tests to which the arm has been subjected, as well as the evidence which they have received from the mechanical engineers and others, lead to the conclusion that the spiral spring in the Martini breech action is well adapted in all climates to perform with efficiency the work for which it is intended.

Q.7 – Is the action of the extractor in throwing out the empty cartridge case considered too sudden? (All answered "No", one conditionally.)

1. (Aldershot): In some instances the empty cartridge case has not been thrown out with sufficient force.

Committee's remarks: The committee have no remark to make on this subject, which has already been treated under the head of Q.3.

Q.8 – The stock being in two parts, has it remained firm and strong? (All answered "Yes".)

Committee's remarks: The committee would point out that the evidence on this point is satisfactory. The results of experiments made to test the relative strengths of whole and divided stocks show that divided stocks are equally strong as whole stocks.

Q.9 – Has the butt end been found to shrink or become loose from the effect of hot dry temperatures? (All replied either "No", or "No hot weather".)

Committee's remarks: None required.

Q.10 – Is any inconvenience experienced from recoil? (About half said "No", but there were several conditional replies.)

2. (Aldershot): Thinks the recoil is excessive, attributes it to the straightness of the stock.

4. (Aldershot): There is a perceptible increase of recoil compared with the Snider, but does not consider it an objection.

8. (Curragh): The recoil is a little stronger, and the tendency of the muzzle is to throw up greater than the Snider, but the inconvenience is slight.

11. (Portsmouth): No, except by a few nervous men who showed a disinclination to hold the rifle firmly.

Committee's remarks: The majority of the reports state that the recoil is not excessive.

Q.11 – Is the weight of the rifle a practical objection on service? (The majority answered "No", but there were the usual objections.)

1. (Aldershot): It is considered so when the arm is carried at the trail.

2. (Aldershot): No, but recommends that the weight be reduced.

5. (Aldershot): Several men have complained of the weight.

11. (Portsmouth): Considers it too heavy for firing standing but not for carrying on the march.

12. (Portsmouth): Thinks the weight will make a material difference on a long march and in bayonet exercise.

Committee's remarks: The majority of the answers state that the weight of the arm is not a practical objection, but the committee have ascertained by trial that the barrel of the long rifle may be advantageously lightened by 6 ozs, thus making the rifle at least as light as the Snider. The shorter arm of the Rifle Brigade pattern has been proportionately lightened, and may possible be still further lightened in weight.

Q.12 – Is the position of the back sight approved of? (There were mixed reactions to this question, as the sight was generally approved for shooting, but not for carrying.)

1. (Aldershot): It is very inconvenient when the arm is held at the present, more particularly at long range shooting; suggests that it should be moved 4 inches back. Prefers the V to the straight bar and lines, as it is difficult to see the lines when the sun is shining from the front.

2. (Aldershot): Prefers the straight bar for target practice, but for general use considers the V far more preferable.

3. (Aldershot): It is very inconvenient for trailing arms or shouldering from the order. Recommends the flap being reversed. The straight bar and lines much preferred to the V.

7. (Hythe): Yes, for aiming; but it is inconvenient when the arm is carried at the trail. Does not think the straight bar is adapted for general use as the lines cannot be easily seen when the sun is shining and they appear to the soldier to be blurred, so that they cannot tell when they have the fore sight in line. When the rifles have been exposed to the weather the lines have become very indistinct. Thinks the wind gauges too far from the centre line to be of any use.

10. (Portsmouth): Yes, the straight bar is an immense improvement, adding vastly to the ease, quickness, clearness and accuracy of aim. The lines are easily used for allowance for wind. This report enters fully into the reasons for preferring the straight bar to the V.

Committee's remarks: The position of the back sight is generally approved of for aiming, but it is found inconvenient when the arm is held at the trail. This inconvenience is, in a great measure, removed in the balance of the lightened arm. With regard to the shape of the back sight the balance of evidence is in favour of the flat sliding bar, but in some instances the old V shape is preferred. This question has been dealt with.

Q.13 – How does the sword bayonet answer as a weapon for attack and defence? (About one third did not like the bayonet, but the rest approved of it.)

1. (Aldershot): Very well, but the edges on the handle should be rounded off.

2. (Aldershot): Considers it too heavy to be of service when used as a bayonet; and awkward when firing.

3. (Aldershot): Too heavy and unweildy when fixed.

4. (Aldershot): The Elcho bayonet is superior to the old bayonet, but its weight is its drawback.

6. (Aldershot): The Elcho bayonet answers well, combines strength, which is an advantage for cutting and thrusting, and is a very formidable weapon. Recommends that the end of the hilt should have a slight curve on the same side as the edge of the blade.

7. (Hythe): The Elcho bayonet appears an efficient weapon but the knob of the spring of new pattern handle might be reduced, being in the way of the grip, and also the sharp edges might be rounded off.

10. (Portsmouth): Very well, but they are not of the Elcho pattern.

11. (Portsmouth): Considers it too slight.

12. (Portsmouth): Does not consider it could be used with as great dexterity as the present one, owing to the weight of the rifle and bayonet.

Committee's remarks: On the whole the majority of the reports are in favour of the saw backed sword bayonets, although some state that the weight of the arm when the sword is fixed is too great. Three of the reports mention favourably the new pattern Elcho sword bayonet.

Q.14 – Does it answer as an implement, on service, for cutting wood, &c.? (Most answered "Yes", with two conditional replies.)

1. (Aldershot): A piece of seasoned fir 4¾ by 3½ inches was sawn through in less than five minutes.

4. (Aldershot): To a certain extent it might, but not when fixed on the rifle.

8. (Curragh): Yes. A piece of wood 6 inches square was sawn through quite easily. A bone was also sawn through. The ration meat was cut with the blade, which answered very well. Recommends that the teeth of the saw should point both ways.

Committee's remarks: The balance of opinion is decidedly in favour of the saw. One regiment remarks that it would not answer for this purpose when fixed on the rifle. In answer to this the committee observe that it was not intended to be used as a wood cutter when fixed.

Q.15 – Are the cleaning implements (the jag and protector), found useful? (All answered "Yes", with two conditional replies.)

3. (Aldershot): Yes, but the protector is apt to split easily.

4. (Aldershot): Yes, exceedingly; but the material of the protector is too brittle.

Committee's remarks: It is quite clear from these reports that the jag and protector are useful. Two reports state that the protectors are too brittle, the expense of these protectors is so small that if they should break they could readily be replaced.

Q.16 – Is the muzzle stopper found generally useful, and is it desirable to introduce it? (Most answers were "Yes", but some were conditional.)

2. (Aldershot): Yes, more especially the protector as keeping the fore sight from damage.

5. (Aldershot): It is useful to keep out wet and protect the sight, but objectionable as liable to cause accidents.

8. (Curragh): Yes. The rifle cannot be fired without seeing the stopper, so reducing the danger to a minimum. The fact of its covering the sight is greatly in its favour.

11. (Portsmouth): The guard to the foresight is most useful but a stopper is considered dangerous.

Committee's remarks: The committee consider that either a muzzle stopper or cover are desirable.

Q.17 – Has the ammunition been found liable to become broken or damaged in transport, or when carried in men's pouches? (The majority answered "No", with one objection.)

3. (Aldershot): No, but the bullets are too loose, and some have fallen out.

9. (Curragh): No. Packets of ammunition that had been carried in the pouches for 20 days were found to have sustained no damage.

10. (Portsmouth): The brass foil cartridge seems to be more susceptible of injury than the paper covered cartridges previously used. With a little rough usage the seam or fold of the outer metal coil begins to gape; wet reaches the powder more readily than it did with the other pattern.

Committee's remarks: The evidence on this subject appears satisfactory, though the short cartridge does not seem quite so well adapted to resist immersion in water as the long cartridge with paper cover.

Q.18 – Has any difficulty arisen from this cause in loading or extracting? (All answered "No".)

10. (Portsmouth): No. The cartridges can be easily inserted, even when they have been purposely battered about to test them.

Committee's remarks: No difficulty appears to have been found.

Q.19 – Is the form of the cartridge found convenient to use? (All answered "Yes".)

7. (Hythe): Yes, preferred to the long cartridge as it enters the chamber much more easily and is not liable to catch by the brown paper.

8. (Curragh): Yes, being shorter than the old cartridge it is not so liable to become damaged.

Committee's remarks: The short cartridge appears unanimously preferred to the long one.

Q.20 – Have any of the cartridges cut round the base? (All answered "No", with one exception.)

10. (Portsmouth): Yes, in one instance the extractor brought away the head, the cylinder remained firmly adhesive to the chamber and was removed with difficulty with the cleaning rod.

Committee's remarks: On this point the evidence is very satisfactory.

Q.21 – Have any of the caps given way? (All replies "No".)

Committee's remarks: On this point the evidence is satisfactory.

General observations.

1. (Aldershot): Recommends that the stock should have more swell where grasped by the left hand, and also that a felt wad covered with wood be placed over the barrel to protect the fingers from the heat of the barrel.

2. (Aldershot): Recommends that the stocks be made of various angles, the present stock being too straight, and that the fore and back sights be raised on a higher block. States that as the trigger wire is liable to work out, a screw or something immoveable would be better. Recommends the moveable nut, for the socket for cleaning rod, as in Snider, be used, owing to the screw being liable to damage. States that the rifles became extremely hot after firing 10 to 20 rounds rapidly.

3. (Aldershot): The rapid firing has been very successful, but considers that great care should be used to prevent the men from firing away their ammunition too rapidly.

4. (Aldershot): States that men unaccustomed to the M-H rifle were able to obtain double the rapidity with a corresponding degree of accuracy as compared with their present weapon in the independent firing up to 400 yards. The barrel became inconveniently hot after firing 20 rounds rapidly; but no escape of gas at the breech has been observed. No misfires or sticking of cartridges have occurred, nor has the breech action or lever got out of order.The weight of the Elcho bayonet is objected to when fixed on the rifle, and a general wish is expressed for a lighter one of the same description. The position of the lever when the rifle is used as a weapon of attack or defence is found by some to be slightly inconvenient.

6. (Aldershot): Prefers the short-actioned arm to the long one. Objects to the arm as a military weapon on account of the danger of it going off in the hands of a careless soldier. Recommends a mark be placed on the lock plate to show which way the indicator points when the arm is at full cock.

8. (Curragh): Considers the trials very satisfactory. The superiority of the M-H over the Snider as regards accuracy is apparently great, more especially at the long ranges. The motions of loading and extracting are very simple. Considers the arm a safe one, as a man could easily tell in the dark by the indicator whether the rifle was at full cock or not.

Committee's observations.

The committee observe that the general observations in the reports from regiments and districts are extremely favourable to the arms and ammunition in the most important respects. Criticisms which have not been dealt with in the answers to the 21 questions may be grouped under the following heads, which will be considered seriatim.

I – Misfires.

Springs of suitable and sufficient strength having been substituted for the weak springs first issued with the arms, misfires have practically ceased.

II – Breech mechanism.

(A) Observations on the safety of the arm. One regiment recommends that a mark be placed upon the lock plate to show which way the indicator points when the arm is at full cock, to obviate the danger of an accident in the hands of a careless soldier.

The committee would observe that when the arm is at full cock the indicator points at the breech axis pin, therefore it is readily distinguishable not only by sight but by touch.

(B) Trigger wire liable to work out. The attention of the Superintendent RSAF has been called to this. A strong screw will be used in place of the pin.

(C) Escape of gas at the breech. In the report from the 2/22nd Regiment it is stated that "a great escape of gas at the breech was remarked during the last few days firing." The committee observe that in the report from the 2/17th Regiment which subsequently used these arms, no mention is made of any escape of gas. Since the arms have been returned to the RSAF they have been examined and fired by the committee; no escape of gas was perceptible, and they cannot think but that there must be some misconception on this subject.

III – Stock.

With reference to suggestions in some of the reports, the committee have made certain alterations.

IV – Other objections.

(A) Trap in butt. The trap in the butt has been done away with.

(B) Cleaning rods liable to work loose. Some alterations which it is hoped will obviate this defect have been proposed. The shape of the head of the rod has also been altered to make it more convenient to use.

APPENDIX 15.

Being the *Report on the Defects and Irregularities in 65 Long-Action Martini-Henry Rifles returned to RSAFactory, and enumerated in the Reports of Officers of the various Regiments, and in Committee's Letter October 21st, 1870, and on the Appearance of the Arms, together with General Observations on their condition, and Suggestions on Points which appear to call for Special Remarks.*

Q.1 – Accidents.

1/25th Regt: No.9 rifle fired whilst closing the breech.
Remarks: The trigger must have been pulled at the same time.
77th Regt: No.5 went off twice without a finger near the trigger.
Remarks: The armourer is reported to have dismounted these rifles, and omitted in assembling No.5 to place the rest spring under the tumbler, which in consequence did not act.

Q.3 – Difficulty of extraction.

42nd, and 2/2nd Regt: Nos.8 and 68 extracted badly.
Remarks: These two rifles were fired by Col. Fletcher at the RSAF, and no difficulty could be found in extraction.
69th Regt: No.100 extracted badly.
Remarks: This rifle has not arrived from Canada.

Q.8 and 9 – Security of stock and shrinkage of wood.

Rifles Nos.4 and 78 have been screwed up by armourer.
Remarks: These two rifles were badly fitted in the first instance.

Q.16 – Introduction of muzzle stoppers.

2/SFGds: Nos.126 and 89 have been injured by firing them with stopper in.
Remarks: These barrels were bulged at the muzzle.

General observations on certain arms.

2/SFGds: No.193, the extractor is reported to "Catch on face of block in closing".
Remarks: Caused by a slight irregularity in workmanship, but it ultimately righted itself.
1/22nd Regt: Reported fouling to have accumulated about

extractor.
Remarks: Required cleaning.
2/2nd Regt: Pull off of trigger very irregular. Thinks the chamber of barrel worn large, and considerable amount of play observable in levers of rifles, "probably worn".
Remarks: The introduction of the stronger spring would affect the pull off in some rifles, owing to their being hand made. Cannot detect any difference in the size of the chambers. There is no wear observable on the surfaces of the levers or blocks, and the play of the lever is part of the arrangement of the action.
Rifle No.4 cleaning rod screw too far through.
Remarks: Error in manufacture.
Rifle No.102 pulled off at 12 lbs.
Remarks: Caused by the locking bolt being made so thin that it could be shot under the rest when fired, which was done, and then the lever being forcibly wrenched open, the rest could not recede, through the bolt being under it.

The act of forcing the tumbler up the face of the rest has thrown a heavy burr 1/64" high on the top edge of the bearing surface of the rest and tumbler, and the two form like a hook one upon the other, causing the increase of the pull off.

General observations.

The condition of the arms generally is satisfactory, both in respect of the wear and tear, as well as in not exhibiting anything which may be considered as a fault in construction.

I think that the principal objections generally made, viz the want of uniformity in the pull off, can be remedied. It would be better, in order to do this with the best likelihood of a good result, to alter slightly the size of the trigger axis pin, viz, from No.6 to No.5 wire, and to screw the point; this will oblige it to have a head. The pin at present is likely to fall out and be lost.

I would recommend that the trap in the butt be discontinued and the hole in the stock left as small as possible.

From recent experiments I have made, it would seem that the stock bolt should be made of soft steel or iron instead of steel hardened and tempered, and it should also be longer.

I would recommend that the guard and trigger plate, the butt plate, and nose cap should be made of brass.

There is no reason why they should necessarily be made of iron, and on the other hand, it will make a great difference in simplicity and cheapness of manufacture, to make them of brass.

If the cleaning rod was lengthened so that the head stood level with the muzzle of barrel (when screwed home), and the soldier instructed to pass the rod gently down the groove before screwing it home, it is not likely that the rod would become loose through the recoil. The rod might be squared under the head also, and thus give a better purchase for unscrewing and screwing in.

In all other respects the actions of the rifles are very good, showing no wear, although some have been very badly used. Some defects have become apparent owing to hand work and want of gauges, &c. These would not be found in machine made arms.

The barrels show no perceptible wear as the rejecting plug will not enter.

Three of the back sights have become unsoldered, owing to the firing of 140 rounds at one time, the liability of the sights becoming loose through rapid firing can be avoided by screwing them on the barrel, in addition to the soldering process.

The coil springs show no loss of strength, as they are the same length when out of the block as when first supplied, and sustain the proper weight at the position of full cock and bearer.

RSAF Enfield, W.M.H. Dixon,
30-12-70. Col. and Superintendent.

APPENDIX 16.

Being an analysis of the weights of various patterns of Martini-Henry rifles, using the weights of Snider rifles as a standard for comparison.

Description of arm	Weight of arm. lb oz	Weight of barrel. lb oz	Weight of arm w/out barrel. lb oz
Snider –			
Long rifle, Mark I	9 2		
Short rifle, Mark II**	8 12		
Martini-Henry Rifle –			
First model, Type 5	9 7	4 5	5 2
Long chamber, Type 6	9 6	4 6	4 15
Naval pattern, Type 12	8 12		
Shortened, Type 14	8 7½	3 6¼	5 1¼
Service Mark I –			
1st Pattern	8 7½	3 6¼	5 1¼
3rd Pattern	8 12	3 6	5 6
Heavy barrel trials patt.	9 2	3 12	5 6
Service Mark II	8 12	3 6	5 6
Service Mark III	9 0	3 6	5 10

The sources for the quoted weights are –

Snider –
Long rifle: Para. 1327 LoC.
Short rifle: Para. 1407 LoC.

Martini-Henry –
Type 5: Barrel weight, *Engineering*, 19-3-1869. Total weight, Special Committee Supplementary Report, 21-3-1871.
Type 6: RSAF Pattern Book.
Type 12: Special Committee Report, 8-2-1871.
Type 14: Special Committee Supplementary Report, 21-3-1871.

Mark I, First pattern: Special Committee Supplementary Report, 21-3-1871.
Mark I, Third pattern: Para. 2659 LoC.
Mark I, Heavy barrel pattern: Overall Weight, WO Committee Minutes, 9-4-1874.
Mark II: Proceedings of the Committee on Martini-Henry Rifles and Ammunition, 23-4-1884.
Mark III: Para. 3998 LoC.

A brief examination of these weights discloses some interesting points, viz. –

Firstly: The difference in the weight between the late trials and first service pattern arms, and the later service patterns, all using the same basic action. This difference was about 4¾ oz, and some of this would be accounted for by the increase in length of the butts, as a long butt weighed about 2 oz more than a short butt. A slight addition of weight also accrued from the use of the semi-finished stock bolt in lieu of the original fully machined unit, which was waisted in the shank.

Secondly: The decrease in the weight of the barrel of the later service patterns, compared with the late trials and early service patterns, ie, ¼-oz. This may seem to be a rather minor amount to be concerned with, but it was mentioned in the first instance as part of the barrel weight, and of some importance in the overall reduction in weight of the Type 12 rifle. There has been found no mention in later references to any further reduction in the barrel weight, so perhaps the ¼-oz was left off for convenience in the later papers.

Thirdly: The Heavy barrel trials rifle's barrel weight quoted was derived by subtracting the unit weight from the total quoted weight, which gives 3 lb 12 oz. If the Type 12 rifle's unit weight is accepted as 5 lb 1¼ oz, its barrel weight becomes 3 lb 10¾ oz, which is very close to that quoted for the service trials rifle. This indicates that the barrels of those two patterns were probably very similar in form, as mentioned in Chapter 8.

Fourthly: It must be borne in mind that in most instances the quoted weights were taken from measurement of pattern arms; in some instances possibly only one arm was weighed. A sampling of production arms over a period of time would disclose some quite wide discrepancies between their weights and that of the pattern arm.

In the LoC paragraph for the introduction of the Mark III rifle is the statement – *The maximum and minimum weights of the rifle vary as much as 12 oz., according as the stock is made of heart or sap wood. . .*

It will thus be seen that any quoted weight must be taken only as an indication of a possible difference between the various patterns, and not as a specific figure that was unchanging or unchangeable.

APPENDIX 17.

Being a report from Lt.-Col. Catty, OC, 46th Regiment, to the Adjutant-General, Horse Guards, London; dated 19-7-1873, and containing the results of trials carried out by his regiment with the M-H rifle.

46th South Devon Regiment.

Report on the Martini-Henry rifle.

I have the honour to report . . . that the Martini-Henry rifle was received from Enfield, and issued to the regiment on the 20th and 21st March last; up to 12th July 1873, six companies were exercised with the very moderate figure of merit of 58.47. Particulars appended.

This indifferent shooting may be attributed to the following causes –

1. The rifles were not delivered to the regiment in sufficient time to admit of a party of recruits, 41 in number, to be trained with the new arm; and in compliance with orders their drill and practice was performed with the Snider, consequently these men fired with their respective companies at a very great disadvantage.

2. The general novelty of the new arm, and want of practice with it.

3. The disposition throughout the regiment, especially noted in young soldiers, to be afraid of the recoil; this was materially increased by men occasionally seeing others of the same squad with shoulders and faces slightly bruised from the effects of the "kick", and these minor casualties were chiefly observed in the case of men using a rifle with a short butt. A diary has been carefully kept by the officer instructors throughout the annual course, and all defects noted, which are here given seriatim.

1. Accidents – Private Cunningham, F Coy, had his forehead blackened and cut from escape of powder at the moment of firing; the breech remained closed, the base of cartridge was cut, and case remained in the barrel, subsequently removed by armourer-serjeant; number of rifle 3,999. The injury to the man was temporary, and very trifling; cause of accident attributed to cartridge of faulty construction.

2. Has the lever become broken or bent? Not in any case.

3. Has rust been found to accumulate about the breech action so as to affect its working? Not in the slightest degree.

4. Difficulty in extracting cases. Occasional. Lever has to be jerked down with some considerable force several times before the case comes out, but this may be caused by

cartridges of faulty shape and defective construction. It may also result from neglect of soldier to open the breech by a sufficiently strong jerk of the lever.

5. Has the coil spring been found to become weak or inefficient? Eight mainsprings were broken, but notwithstanding this, in four instances the defect was not remarked and the spring compressed in the block worked as usual.

6. The stock being in two parts, has it remained firm and strong? Rifle No.1,872, in possession of Sgt. Trimble. The barrel stud of this rifle gave way and stock shifted up the barrel; cause, apparently, stud not sufficiently brazed. NB – This rifle still remains defective.

7. Recoil. The recoil is certainly greater than in the Snider; still, if the rifle be properly held, and attention given to the men's position at preliminary drill, but little inconvenience will be felt. The long butt is infinitely preferable to the short one; men firing with the latter have had their faces bruised and cut.

8. Minor defects. (A) Forty-three (43) strikers were broken at drill and practice, the majority at the former; but since the adoption of a new and stronger pattern in all the arms, put in by workmen from Enfield on May 26th and following days, only one has been found defective.

(B) Four (4) ramrods were broken and new ones received in exchange.

(C) Three (3) trigger springs gave way, caused probably by slight flaws in steel.

Ammunition. The percentage of misfires and misfitting cartridges has been very small. Cartridges preserved. Invariably when the ramrod has been used to extract the empty case, the same course has been adopted, and all cartridge cases cut round the base or defective in any way, have been carefully kept.

With reference to the general construction of the Martini-Henry rifle as issued to the 46th Regiment, I beg to make the following suggestions and remarks –

1. They should all be made with long butts, as in consequence of the twist and depth of rifling the recoil is somewhat considerable, and men who have had their faces bruised (which is fatal to good shooting) when firing with the short butt, have experienced little or no inconvenience when subsequently using the other. I consider this of primary importance, should the rifle be generally adopted.

2. The thumb piece is too far back; in most cases it is impossible to keep the thumb in the intended position, and at the same time get the forefinger well round the trigger, but this is a matter of minor importance, as the thumb can be easily placed more forward, without in the slightest degree interfering with the arrangement of the sights.

3. Many of the rifles, as far as can be judged, are undersighted from 500 to 800 yards, and the sliding bar has to be raised to the elevation of some 50 yards above the marked distance. The accuracy of the rifle itself, I conceive is perfect when properly sighted, but the thin vertical white sight lines are, in ordinary hands, difficult to aim with, and it is found that when the sliding bar has been reversed the V sight thus secured does not apparently appear to coincide with the centre white line.

4. The keeper screw below the pivot pin on which the breech block works has been found in some instances to turn round, and consequently the pin itself becomes loose, and is likely to be lost.

5. After firing 10 rounds rapidly, as in the volley and independent practices, it is almost impossible to touch the barrel with the fingers, and on a warm day the heat therefrom is still more intensified.

6. The pull off is very unequal and varies by use, on this head complaints are general, so much so, that in the annual course of the last two companies every rifle was carefully tested previous to the commencement of target practice, yet, on the range men have frequently drawn attention to the heavy pull off of their rifles.

In conclusion, I have to state that on the whole the rifles have worked well, and the breech mechanisms fairly stood the test. As soon as men have had a little more practice, and become accustomed to take aim over the plain surface of the backsight, also to overcome their dread of recoil, and if rifles with the long butt were served out to all, the shooting will no doubt be greatly improved.

C. Catty, Lt.-Colonel,
Commanding 46th Regiment.

Return showing the average points, percentages, figure of merit, &c., of the above corps, at target practice 12-7-1873.

Number of companies exercised – 6.
Average points obtained per man in 1st period – 38.40
Average points obtained per man in 2nd period – 26.01
Percentage of third class shots – 17.84
Battalion figure of merit – 58.47
Average points obtained per man volley firing – 11.86
Average points obtained per man independent firing - 12.03
Average points obtained per man skirmishing – 5.35
Percentage of marksmen – 4.81.

APPENDIX 18.

Being an abstract of reports on Martini-Henry rifles, prepared by the Superintendent RSAF, to accompany his minute of 24-10-1873.

For the sake of brevity the regiments reporting will be referred to as –

(A) 1/60th Rifles
(B) 46th Regiment
(C) 2/4th Regiment
(D) SoM, Hythe.

---

1. Block axis pin gets loose.

(A) Yes, several; (B) Yes, a few; (C) Yes, six; (D) No.

2. Cleaning rods break.

(A) Yes, a number; (B) Yes, four; (C) Yes, five; (D) No.

3. Lever catch block liable to have bottom knocked out.

(A) Yes; (B) No; (C) Yes, one; (D) No.

4. Strikers break.

(A) Yes, 26 old pattern; (B) Yes, 43 old pattern, 1 new pattern; (C) Yes, 24 new pattern; (D) Yes, 5 old pattern.

5. Recoil heavy.

(A) No remarks; (B) Greater than Snider; (C) No remarks; (D) More than Snider.

6. Main springs break.

(A) No; (B) Yes, eight; (C) Yes, one; (D) No.

7. Barrel stud comes off.

(A) No; (B) Yes, one; (C) No; (D) No.

8. Trigger springs break.

(A) No; (B) Yes, three; (C) No; (D) No.

9. Thumbrest.

(A) No remarks; (B) Too far back; (C) No remarks; (D) No remarks.

10. Sighting.

(A) No remarks; (B) Under-sighted from 500 to 800 yards; (C) No remarks; (D) No remarks.

11. Barrel heats on firing.

(A) No remarks; (B) Yes; (C) No remarks; (D) No remarks.

12. Pull off irregular in use.

(A) No remarks; (B) Yes; (C) No remarks; (D) No remarks.

13. Butt swivel screws in wood only.

(A) No remarks; (B) No remarks; (C) Yes; (D) No remarks.

14. Butts, long and short.

(A) No remarks; (B) Yes; (C) No remarks; (D) Yes.

15. Stock firm and strong.

(A) No remarks; (B) Yes; (C) No remarks; (D) No remarks.

16. Extraction hard.

(A) No; (B) Occasionally; (C) No; (D) No.

17. Breech action impeded by accumulation of rust or dust.

(A) No; (B) No; (C) No; (D) No.

18. Lever broken or bent.

(A) No; (B) No; (C) No; (D) No.

19. Precision.

(A) No remarks; (B) Indifferent; (C) Bad; (D) Interfered with, until soldier is accustomed to recoil.

20. Sliding bar reversed, V does not correspond with centre white line.

(A) No remarks; (B) Yes; (C) No remarks; (D) No remarks.

APPENDIX 19.

Being the minutes of a conference held at the WO on 24-10-1873, to consider questions connected with the M-H rifle.

Present –

Brig.-Gen. Sir J. Adye, KCB, DoA
Brevet-Col. Jenyns, CB, AAG
Brevet-Col. Radcliffe, CB, Commandant SoM
Lt.-Col. Fraser, RA, Supt. RSAF
Mr. L.W. Engelbach of the WO attended.

Questions connected with M-H arms considered.

The DoA explained the present position of the question, and then proceeded to take the several points as detailed in Col. Fraser's minute of 24-9-1873.

1. Block axis pin.

Col. Fraser thinks trial should be made, and it is agreed that the 4th and 46th Regiments should be supplied with split bronze and steel pins, in equal numbers, and report in a month. A few also to be sent to Hythe. The necessary ammunition to be supplied.

2. Cleaning rods.

Committee think that some should be issued for trial to both regiments, as proposed by Col. Fraser; a few also to Hythe.

3. Lever catch block.

This is of no importance, no change is necessary.

4. Strikers.

Committee propose to call upon colonels of regiments to report carefully on the question of strikers at the end of the month's trial of pins and rods. Snap cap, as suggested by Col. Fraser, to be tried by the two regiments, and at Hythe; 100 to each.

5. Recoil.

Two serjeant instructors from Hythe being in attendance were questioned on this point –

Serjeant-major Davies, 1st Class Serjeant Instructor, Hythe, has had considerable experience with the Snider – also with M-H; has fired 500 rounds at various times. Fires every year in the regular course (90 rounds). M-H beats the Snider, except up to 300 yards. Finds considerable recoil – more than in Snider; it is excessive, and especially for men who begin to fire with the new arm, on whom it has a bad effect. Has not seen any men cut about the face, but hands have been injured. Does not think the men like the new arm better than the Snider. Explains inconvenient position of the thumb piece. The butts (both long and short) are too short – should be an inch longer. Does not like the present grip, the space is too great, as it does not enable his forefinger to get round the trigger. The grip of the left hand is also unsatisfactory; there is not sufficient to lay hold of. The pull off is not good. Sighting tolerably correct. The locking bolt is quite useless.

NOTE – In order to improve the grip of the right hand, the committee propose trial of a small thumb rest outside the body of the arm. A few to be made in the first instance, and sent to Hythe for trial.

Serjeant-Major MacBride, 3rd Class Serjeant Instructor, Hythe, has fired about 1,100 rounds from M-H rifle. Gun very accurate. The breech block is difficult to clean. The position of the trigger renders grip of right hand difficult. Recoil about the same as with the Snider; has found no difficulty from the first. The arm is difficult to clean, owing to chamber being larger than the barrel. Has had no experience with men new to the arm, and therefore cannot say as to complaints of recoil. On the whole, as regards accuracy and rapidity, likes the arm very much. Does not strictly adhere to the Hythe rule as to grip. As to butts, they are too short (even the long one); there is something which makes it inconveniently short. Pull off is variable, sometimes 3 or 4 lb, at others 7 or 8 lb.

The OC 46th Regiment and the IoM of 4th and 46th Regiments were also in attendance, and gave evidence as follows –

Lt.-Col. Catty, Commanding 46th Foot. The regiment is armed with Martini-Henrys. Has not fired much himself. On the whole the men like the arm with certain objections, principally the recoil. Has not read the reports of the Special Committee on Small Arms, and is, therefore, not aware of previous experience. Has just fired 18,000 rounds of new ammunition. Recoil is decidedly greater than with the Snider.

Lt. Newman, IoM, 46th Regiment. Has fired a number of rounds himself. Old soldiers perhaps get accustomed to the recoil. It is specially noticeable with short butts. On the whole the men like the arm. It is more accurate than Snider at long distances, in fact, the M-H is perfect in that respect. The grip is inconvenient, and the present thumb piece is not used.

Col. Catty would certainly like longer butts, and that the present long butts should be the short butts. Pull off very unequal, and during practice.

Lt. Newman states that the new ammunition (No.III) is superior and better made; hardly any misfires or misfits. The recoil funks the young soldiers; several men bruised in the cheeks and fingers.

Col. Catty explains that rust gets into the action, but it does not interfere with the working. Locking bolt is objectionable and useless. New strikers are good. Novelty of the arm, and the small amount of practice is perhaps the cause of the indifferent shooting of the regiment, but recent experience has shown that the shooting has considerably improved. On the whole likes the weapon, and thinks the men like it.

Lt. Newman concurs. As to proportion of butts, he would have it as presently – but the long butts should be the short ones.

Lt. Sharp, IoM, 4th Regiment. Has fired M-H himself, but not much. Has put the regiment through the course. Arm is too short in the stock. The recoil is heavier than the Snider, but not much. The recruits and bad shots complain, but the men get used to it. Nervous men also complain. Grip of the right hand very bad. The men put the thumb to the side. Thinks the proposed side piece to rest the thumb on would be a support, and might be an improvement. Butts certainly too short – had no idea they were as long as the Snider – it would be better if the short butts were abolished and all made long butts, in fact this would be very desirable. Axis pin as at present is objectionable; gets loose. Trigger too rough. The men like the arm on the whole, principally as it is a short arm. With practice, thinks the shooting will be superior to the Snider. There are a number of men in the regiment with black eyes, but no cut fingers. The engraving on the butt plate is useless. Present ammunition is, on the whole, good. Thinks the falling off in the shooting of the regiment is attributable to the short butt and inconvenient grip.

NOTE – The committee deliberated and were confirmed in their previous opinion, that the complaints as regards recoil and uncertain pull off arise chiefly from the supposed short ness of the butts and the inconvenience of grip; and they propose to alter both.

As regards butts – Col. Fraser to report what he proposes, and the expense involved.

6. Mainsprings.

The committee do not consider any change necessary.

7. Barrel studs.

This is of no importance, and no change is considered necessary.

8. Trigger springs.

A manufacturing detail only – no change considered necessary.

9. Thumb rest.

Already dealt with.

10. Sighting.

No change considered necessary.

11. Barrel heating.

Committee propose to try a few leather shields at Hythe, as proposed by Col. Fraser.

12. Pull off.

Committee think that the suggested alterations as to grip and butt will probably remove objections on this head.

13. Butt swivel.

No change considered necessary.

14. Butts.

Committee think it will be desirable to lengthen both sizes an inch, leaving proportions as at present. Proportions of each to be sent to Hythe, 4th and 46th Regiments, for trial. Col. Fraser to report as to expense involved. Engraving on butt plates to be dispensed with, and that on triggers to be modified.

15. Strength of stock.

No change considered necessary.

16. Extraction.

Ditto, ditto.

17. Breech action.

Ditto, ditto.

18. Levers.

Ditto, ditto.

19. Precision.

Ditto, ditto.

20. Sights.

Ditto, ditto.

21. Locking bolt.

Committee quite agree with Col: Fraser, and unanimously recommend its abolition.

APPENDIX 20.

Being a report from Lt.-Col. F. Hamilton, OC, 4th Regiment, to the AAG, Woolwich, dated 17-2-1874, and containing the results of trials carried out by his regiment with improved M-H rifles and components.

With reference to letter 7669/3093, 16-12-1873, I have to report for the information of the C-I-C –

1st. The two experimental rifles with the lengthened stocks are a great improvement on the others.

2nd. With regard to the split block axis pins supplied, 100 rifles were fitted with them, the steel pins stand well, and there were none broken during the trials. The brass pins did not stand so well, and two of them were closed during the trials.

3rd. With regard to the altered cleaning rod, five of them came out during the trial. This has been seen to by the chief foreman from Enfield, who has explained the reason, which was on account of the top band not being sufficiently tightened.

4th. With regard to the leather shields, they are a great improvement in rapid firing; the men can hold the rifle steadily without feeling the heat caused by rapid firing.

5th. With regard to the smooth butt plates, they answer the purpose very well, no difference between them and the roughened ones.

6th. With regard to the modified roughing on the trigger, it is a great improvement, no man has had a cut finger since this alteration (ie, in the two experimental rifles).

7th. With regard to the locking bolt having been removed from the two experimental rifles, it was at all times quite unnecessary.

The whole of the 57,000 rounds of ammunition were fired out of 100 rifles, including the experimental ones, and the test has therefore been a severe one. I have to report that the whole of the rifles stood the test remarkably well.

With regard to the two experimental rifles, they were principally fired at individual firing, the shooting with them was good.

The shooting by volleys was equally satisfactory.

The experiments were conducted under the superintendence of the IoM and Field Officers daily.

2 strikers broke during the above trials (Report 16-2-1874 by IoM, 2/4th). 2 brass split brass axis pins came out in consequence of the split closing.

APPENDIX 21.

Being a report from Major R. Bennet, OC 46th Regiment, to the AAG, Dublin; dated 23-2-1874, and containing the results of trials carried out by his regiment with two new pattern M-H rifles.

I have the honour to report that in accordance with instructions received from Horse Guards by letter 7669/ 3093, C.5129, dated 16-12-1873, a trial has been made of the two new pattern, 1873, M-H rifles at the Pigeon House Rifle Range, Dublin, by a party of the regiment under my command.

The different alterations in the construction of the arm and consequent advantage or disadvantage as contrasted with the pattern now in possession of the regiment, are herewith given in a tabulated form.

1. Stocks. The stocks are 14 and 14½ inches long, instead of 13 and 14. This is a most decided improvement; the necessity of placing the cheek on the head of the stock being to a great extent obviated, and the effect of the recoil as experienced by many men on the face thereby almost nullified.

2. Split block axis pins. These are apparently of steel, and have worked well, remaining firm in their proper position.

3. Cleaning rods. This method of removing the cleaning rod, though preferable to that now in use, by which many have been broken near the swell, is still open to objection. I am of opinion that there would be difficulty in accustoming men to secure the article in question by turning as directed, and consequently the rods would fall out in some cases, and in others be broken, or otherwise damaged by careless manipulation.

4. Leather shield. This has been found completely to answer the purpose of protecting the hand from the heated barrel, but the buckle of the centre strap is objectionable, as it not only interferes with a firm grasp, but the tongue would also be likely, if sharp, to cut or scratch the hand. A little stud or button at each side of the stock might be substituted with advantage.

5. Smooth butt plate. This is apparently a matter of little consequence.

6. Modified roughing on trigger. This is a decided improvement, and if the upper side edges were also slightly rounded it would be beneficial.

7. Locking bolt. The removal of the locking bolt is highly approved of; the manipulation of the bolt itself being considered likely to cause accidents, especially with recruits and careless soldiers. By the act of depressing the lever when loaded, perfect immunity from accidental discharge is obtained, and this course has always been adopted in the 46th Regiment, many of the bolts having been found to require a considerable force to lock the action.

I have also to report that in accordance with instructions dated 12-12-1873, 50 metal and the same number of steel split block axis pins have been placed in rifles now in possession of the regiment by the armourer-serjeant, with a satisfactory result up to the present time; 100 snap caps (dummy cartridges) have also been tested, and they appear to answer the purpose. Five were injured, as follows, viz., three cracked in centre-plug, one misfit, and one wood broken at the end fitting in barrel.

In conclusion I wish to add that the 1873 rifles were subjected to a further test as follows –

Immediately after the expiration of the experimental firing, without being cleaned, 20 rounds were fired as quick ly as possible, the result being very heated barrel, and recoil sensibly increased by accumulated fouling; still the leather shield was found to protect the hand perfectly.

APPENDIX 22.

Being a minute of 25-3-1875 by the Asst.-Supt. RSAF, Lt.-Col. Dyer, RA.

Minute by the Assistant Superintendent Royal Small Arms Factory, relative to the question of the alleged undersighting of the Martini-Henry rifles.

During my recent visit to Aldershot, the question of the rifles being undersighted at ranges of 500 yards and upwards was raised; we have tested the point so frequently here that I availed myself of the proposal of Capt. Thompson, DAAG for Musketry to see some firing on the ranges.

The first trial was at 500 yards; well known shots were selected from different regiments, and the object of the trial explained to the men, and they were specially asked not to attempt to prove their ideas of the rifles being undersighted were true, but to aim fairly each round at the bull's eye, only making allowance for the lateral deviation caused by wind. I have every reason to believe the instructions were carried out as much as possible.

Three rounds were fired by each man with the proper sighting of the rifle. Some of the shots struck the target, but the greater proportion were short.

The sight was then adjusted to about 520 yards range, and the firing repeated with very much better results. I then suggested that each man should fire three rounds with the same adjustment of sight, but with the muzzle of the rifle supported on a sand-bag to eliminate as far as possible any error that might arise from holding the rifle. The bullets then struck as high as they previously had been short, most of them indeed going over the target.

The practice was then repeated at 700 yards with exactly similar results. With the sight at 700 mark all struck low; with the sight raised for a range of about 720 yards – I say about, because this was the mean of all men, some setting the slide for 720 others at 770 – the practice was excellent; but when the sand-bag was used the bulk of the shots went too high.

The result of these trials appears to prove that although the rifle is correctly sighted when the barrel is supported so as to overcome *some disturbing cause* which has a tendency to depress the muzzle at the time of firing, still that for practical purposes it would appear to be better if the sighting were higher.

I am not prepared to offer any opinion as to what is the disturbing cause; it may be the upward pull of the trigger, the balance of the rifle, the way the rifle is held; but whatever the cause, the depression of the muzzle would be so slight that nothing but a delicate mechanical contrivance could detect it, and it would take some consideration to design one.

There appears to be a remarkable unanimity of opinion on the subject, but there is a great divergence of opinion as to the amount of the undersighting, and as it is practically impossible to suit the sighting to every man, it would appear desirable – if any alteration is determined upon – to establish an arbitrary graduation of the sight leaf, as nearly as possible the mean of any number of officers and men that might be determined upon, say, for the sake of illustration, 30 – viz, 10 at Aldershot, 10 at Hythe, 10 at the Curragh – each would be provided with a rifle, the sight leaf of which would be left plain, and each would be asked to graduate the leaf as the results of his own practice at 500 yards and upwards, under varying conditions of wind and weather. When this had been done the rifles should be sent here, and a mean could be readily established by taking all the measurements from the axis of the bore; if when this mean has been obtained it is found to differ so materially from the present graduations as to render an alteration desirable, some simple and inexpensive means can easily be determined on to carry it out.

Enfield Lock. H. Dyer,
25-3-75. Lt.-Colonel, RA.

APPENDIX 23.

Being a precis of reports from regiments in the United Kingdom, on the M-H rifles as first issued. A Special Army Circular of 26-11-1874 had authorised the firing of 10 rounds per man for trial of the rifle. The remarks are given by the Superintendent RSAF.

---

1. 1st Btn. 1st Regt., and Depot 2/1st, Edinburgh, 28-1-75.

Arm generally approved. Lowness of trajectory, accuracy, and celerity of fire great advantages. Many locks (Birmingham arms) too highly tempered. Strikers and tumblers liable to fracture under certain circumstances. Sights too low.*

Remarks:*Reports seem unanimous as to undersighting, but it cannot be discovered at Enfield that it is so. If the trigger is pulled with the lever only partly closed there will always be this liability.

2. 2/5th, and Depot 1/5th Regt., Jersey, 31-12-1875.

An excellent arm as far as can be judged from 10 rounds fired in bad weather. Over 500 yards appeared to be undersighted. Recoil seemed less than that of Snider. Occasional difficulty in extracting, probably from inexperience.* Difficulty in getting second joint of finger round trigger. Slight alteration in sliding bars recommended.**

Remarks:*Difficulties in extraction no doubt due to cause stated. **CO does not seem to be aware that the sliding bar may be reversed.

3. 2/6th, and Depot 1/6th, Geurnsey and Alderney, 30-1-75

Arm approved as being lighter and far more accurate than Snider. Has a much greater range, and is remarkably free from fouling. Loading simple, and no inconvenience from recoil. Is considerably undersighted, however.*

Remarks: *As to undersighting, he has been unable to discover it; but he will make targets with one of the barrels referred to in Report No.4, and from some now making.

4. Depots 64th and 98th Regts, Glasgow, 14-1-1875.

The arm is preferred to the Snider. Five strikers failed to act, and two tumblers broken. Considerably undersighted, and same complaint as 5th Regt, as to imperfect grasp of rifle in certain positions.

9. 2/3rd Regt, Limerick, 6-2-1875.

An excellent arm. Prejudice in regard to recoil seems unfounded, it being little or no greater than the Snider. Arms seem all to be undersighted; but the rifle in all its parts is strong, the mechanism simple, and it most certainly is extremely well made. A few suggestions made as to upper

band, sights,* and rods. Butt swivel useless except in rifle battalions.
NB – The GOC Cork District did not agree with Col. Pearson in all his suggestion as above.

Remarks: *In some of the early trade rifles line on sight was accidentally omitted. Armourers can easily put it on.

10. 2/4th, Depot 1/4th, Depot 43rd Regt, Cork, 13-2-75.

Arm approved. Great improvement on those originally supplied to the regiment. Lengthening the stock has much diminished the kick upwards, although the recoil backwards is not much lessened;* it is not so bad, however, when the rifle is held firmly to the shoulder. Heating of barrel in rapid firing is much modified by increased weight of rifle, caused by thickening the barrel.** Suggestions in regard to the lines on the sight being made of some white metal,† and stock to be thinned a bit where the right hand grasps it.

Remarks: *There must be something exceptional in this regiment, as there are no other complaints as to recoil. **Some mistake here; only 50 barrels have been so made. †Could be done, but appears an unnecessary refinement.

16. 52nd Regt, Depot 85th Regt, Portsmouth, 26-2-1875.

Arm approved as regards shooting powers. Pull off irregular, and extraction in a few cases not satisfactory. Cleaning rods too short. A few cases of cut cheek bones from the thumbnail of right hand on recoil taking place, owing to shortness of stock. Proportions of long and short stocks might be reversed with advantage. Some difficulty in properly grasping the rifle owing to the height of the head of the stock. Remedies proposed. No complaints of excessive recoil.

Remarks: In early manufacture there were exceptional cases of irregular pull off, but can be remedied on the spot. A cartridge case allowed to remain in the gun any time after cooling will always be difficult to extract. The barrel grips the case. The suggestions have mostly been met.

17. 58th Regt., Portsmouth, 23-1-1875.

Arm approved; difficulty in properly grasping the rifle; thumb rest recommended.* Waterproof cover proposed to prevent water getting into the action.** Dummy cartridges required to prevent strikers and tumblers breaking.†

Remarks:*Can be added hereafter if found to be required. **Cover not necessary; no amount of wet will render action unserviceable. †Snap caps now supplied.

20. 1st Btn Rifle Brigade, Windsor, 24-12-1874.

Reloading after firing is more readily affected than with Snider, and the sights are better. Recoil about the same. Pull off in some cases dangerously light. Over 300 yards the arm is rather undersighted. Alteration of sling swivel recommended for rifle regiments, the centre one being done away with, and the lower one placed only one inch from the lever.*

Remarks: *No manufacturing difficulty.

NOTE – The above reports constitute a small proportion only of those received, but as they are mostly in the same style, with the same remarks, as the balance of the reports, they are considered representative enough to warrant excluding the remainder from this study.

APPENDIX 24.

Being the reports from regiments in the United Kingdom on the trials during Nov.-Dec. 1875 of M-H rifles fitted with improved triggers.

For the sake of brevity in the following text, each of the various regiments will be identified by the number allocated to it in the list below. The name of the Officer Commanding each regiment, and the date of report are also shown.

1. 2/Coldstream Gds; Lt.-Col. Lambton. 4-12-1875.
2. 2/Scots Fusilier Gds; Col. Fletcher. 8-12-1875.
3. 102nd Fusiliers; Lt.-Col. Jepson. 8-12-1875.
4. 95th Regt; Lt.-Col. Parkinson. 11-12-1875.
5. 82nd Regt; Major Graves. 11-12-1875.
6. 1/23rd Fusiliers; Lt.-Col. Prevost. 20-12-1875.
7. 2/8th Regt; Lt.-Col. Webb. 21-12-1875.
8. 1/12th Regt; Lt.-Col. Foster. 21-12-1875.
9. 2/17th Regt; Major Boyd. 23-12-1875.
10. SoM; Col. Radcliffe. 28-12-1875.
11. 2/16th Regt; Col. Bancroft. 29-12-1875.
12. 3/Rifle Brigade; Lt.-Col. Maclean. 1-1-1876.
13. 77th Regt; Col. Kent. 1-1-1876.
14. HMS Excellent; Capt. Brandreth, RN. 5-1-1876.
15. 106th Regt; Lt.-Col. Gillespie. 7-1-1876.
16. 2/6th Regt; Major Colthurst. 8-1-1876.
17. 1/15th Regt; Col. Grierson. 8-1-1876.
18. 1/9th Regt; Col. Hawes. 11-1-1876.
19. 2/11th Regt; Major McCausland. 11-1-1876.

REPORTS ON THE NEW COMPONENTS.

1. State the number of rounds fired from each rifle; and, if possible, the number of times the gun has been snapped.

1. Each rifle has been snapped 200 times; 100 with, 100 without snap caps. There have been 50 rounds of ball ammunition fired out of 6 of them.

2. 100 rounds were fired from 46 rifles, 115 from two rifles 409 from two other rifles. Total number of rounds fired 5,648.

Each rifle was snapped without snap cap 1,000 times, besides, of course, occasional snapping.

3. Each rifle fired 20 rounds, and snapped with and without snap cap 20 to 30 times.

4. 20 rounds of ball have been fired from each rifle, and in no instance has a second snap been required.

5. 20 rounds ball, 10 rounds blank. Each rifle was snapped 50 times with the snap cap, and 100 times without the snap cap. 1 round of blank cartridge was fired at the conclusion of the snapping to test the strikers.

6. 10 rounds blank, 20 rounds ball. The rifles were snapped about 60 times.

7. 20 rounds per rifle fired. Snapped about 12 times each.

8. 20 rounds of ball ammunition and 10 rounds blank. Snapped from 50 to 100 times each.

9. 20 rounds ball.

10. 20 rounds of ball were fired from each rifle, and in addition thereto each rifle was snapped at least 1,000 times, viz, 500 with snap caps, and 500 without.

11. 30 rounds of ball and 10 rounds blank. The blank ammunition was first fired as rapidly as possible, and each lock was then examined. The locks were then snapped with and without snap caps for about five minutes.

20 rounds of ball were then fired advancing as skirmishers against targets over 200 yards of distance.

5 rounds by volleys, and 5 rounds independently, of ball were then fired, and when all the firing was over the rifles were examined, and each man asked his opinion as to any improvement of lock or rifle, and about 8 men said they thought the pull off a little stronger than before alteration.

12. 20 rounds of ball cartridge from each rifle, and 20 of blank. The whole of the rifles have been placed in the hands of recruits and 3rd Class shots, and have been snapped over 3,000 times, half with, and half without, the snap cap.

13. 20 rounds from each rifle, 9 men were struck off duty for 8 days, during which they were engaged at position drill three times a day, the 9 rifles being snapped from 80 to 100 times at each drill, so that each rifle must have snapped upwards of 2,000 times during the 8 days.

14. 28 rifles have fired 20 rounds of ball. 54 rifles have fired 20 rounds of ball and 62 rounds of blank, besides being snapped about 100 times. 18 rifles have fired 120 rounds of ball and 20 rounds of blank, besides being snapped about 400 times.

15. 20 rounds of ball and 20 rounds of blank have been fired from each rifle, and every rifle has besides been snapped 1,000 times, half with and half without the snap cap.

16. 10 rounds of ball and 10 rounds of blank. The rifles have been snapped about 600 times.

17. 20 rounds. Each rifle was in addition snapped at least 200 times.

18. 20 rounds each of ball and blank. Each has been snapped about 2,000 times.

19. No firing has yet taken place on account of inclement weather. They have all been snapped innumerable times, several having been in the hands of recruits drilling daily.

2. Describe briefly any special tests you may have applied to the arms, and their results.

1. Several rifles have been placed in sand, afterwards taken out and fired; in no case was the breech injured, or the arms become ineffective.

2. 21 rounds each were fired by good shots in order to test the pull off. 15 rounds were fired by Capt. Willson, IoM, and 15 by Serjeant Wade, Serjeant Instructor. For results, vide (4).

Four rifles were subjected to severe sand and rust trials, and the whole of the rifles were dropped on a board five times from a height of 3 ft 6 ins, to ascertain whether there would be a risk of accidental explosion caused by a jar. For particulars of the experiments, see appendix.

3. (1) rifle being placed at full cock, was dropped butt downwards with a considerable impetus onto a wooden block six times; no accidental discharges and no change in any way observable in regularity of pull off.

(2) breech action well dusted with powdered coal and well worked; no accidental discharge on closing breech, though it worked stiffly.

4. No special tests have been applied except in opening and closing the breech with a vigorous jerk, which the action bore very satisfactorily.

5. No report.

6. (1) Violent hammering of the butts on the ground. (2) Violent and gentle closing of the breech. (3) Filled the lock with earth. Results in each case satisfactory.

7. Striking the butt on the ground with much force, putting dirt and sand into the action. The results were satisfactory in each case.

The blows on the butt of the rifle did not cause the action to move in any way. The sand put into the action rendered the pull off heavier, but did not injure the parts.

8. The arms were all tested in the first instance with a government trigger-tester to ascertain the pull off. 15 rounds were then fired from each rifle, and at the end of each five rounds exertion was made to try to cause the arms to go off, by recocking and then striking the butts violently on the ground, but without effect; a few of the rifles had sand and wet mud inserted into the action, through the interval between trigger and guard, with the view of causing them to go off easier or of their own accord, but without effect.

9. Ordinary practice with ball and blank ammunition. Opening and closing breech sharply, and the reverse. Jumping

and jerking rifle when at full cock. Trying to pull off with spring weighing machine.

10. 30 rifles were piled and exposed in the open air, day and night, during wet weather for six days; water having been poured into the breech action of 12 which were left at full cock during that period.

Two of the same rifles were then subjected to the following very severe test, viz, sand was shaken into the breech action of one, and ashes into the other; water was poured thereon and the rifles placed at full cock in a room for five days. No prejudicial effects were observed except in the last mentioned two rifles, the breech actions of which were clogged and disabled; but on removing the breech blocks and shaking out the accumulated sand and ashes, the blocks being replaced *without any of the parts being oiled,* the rifles became effective.

11. The rifles were tested as follows –

They were struck against the ground, heavily jarred, to see if any tendency to explode existed, but nothing was observed. They were loaded with blank and so tried. The lock was also filled with sand and thus tried, but no rifle went off otherwise than in the proper way on being *fired.* There was also no difficulty in extracting the old cases.

12. No special tests have been applied, but the whole of the altered rifles after being placed at full cock have been violently struck on the ground on the heel plate, without releasing the nose of the sear.

13. Five of the rifles of the men struck off duty were used without snap caps, and the other four with snap caps. This is the only test which has been applied. In one of the nine rifles, after a few day's use, the pull off became very hard, and when snapped without a snap cap, a jar (or painful sensation) was felt by the forefinger. The pull off has also got a "drag" which was not felt at the start. The jar has also been found in one or two of the other rifles.

14. Nil (at present), but there will be by 1st February.

15. In the M-H there was always great danger from accidental discharge from breech action getting clogged with dirt. I have known the mere closing of the lever when the rifle was dirty, cause explosion. I had therefore a quantity of dust thrown into the action of four of these rifles, and the action worked just as well, and odd to say their pull off was affected less than any of the others.

Four rifles with component parts of the old pattern were fired and snapped the same number of times to enable a comparison to be made. The results will be noticed under the headings 4–5.

16. The breech blocks of nine rifles were taken out and the interior of the action sprinkled with fine sand; the blocks were then replaced and the rifles snapped 100 times. The pull off was then found to have increased in 7 rifles, and slightly decreased in 2; it was impossible to discharge any of these rifles either by a sudden jerk, or in the act of closing the breech.

17. Snapping without snap cap about 100 times with highly satisfactory results; no rifle having been injured by the trial.

18. Sand was rubbed around the trigger of one rifle to see if it would work in; it was found not to do so. This rifle was subjected to the same test as the others, the true working of the action remained unimpaired.

19. The butts have been struck on the ground as a test, repeatedly, but the spring has remained firm. The sand test has also been applied, and the rifles have given every satisfaction. They have been snapped frequently with and without snap caps.

3. State whether the alterations have obviated the danger of an accidental discharge of the gun arising from a sudden jar or from dirt having entered between the trigger and lock plate, or from both causes combined.

1. Several rifles have been placed at full cock and the butt dropped from a height of about one foot to the ground; in no case was the spring released.

2. The alterations appear to have entirely obviated the danger of an accidental discharge of the gun arising from a sudden jar, or from dirt or rust.

3. Yes.

4. I am strongly of opinion that the alterations have obviated the danger of an accidental discharge of the rifle, either from a sudden jar or dirt, or both combined.

5. I am of opinion that the alterations have obviated the danger from both causes combined.

6. Yes.

7. The alterations appear to have rendered the danger of an accidental discharge of the rifle almost impossible.

8. I am of opinion that the alterations have quite obviated the possibility of the rifles going off under the above conditions.

The DAAG for Musketry, Cork, reported on the rifles in the hands of A Coy, 12th Regt. on detachment duty at Youghal, viz, – That the alterations had obviated the danger adverted to; and a further test had confirmed him in that decision.

9. There have been no occasions of any accidental discharge from any cause.

10. Yes, apparently so.

11. It appears so; though we never had a case of this sort in my battalion before these alterations were made.

12. The alteration would appear to have modified the risk of an accidental discharge.

13. The trial has been so short that I am unable to form a decided opinion, but I am inclined to think that it is much less liable now to go off than it was formerly.

14. There have been no accidental discharges.

15. They have.

16. The alterations appear to have removed the chances of accidental discharge when closing the breech, and to prevent dirt entering between the trigger and lock plate.

17. The alterations appear to have obviated the danger. Sand was allowed to fall between trigger and lock plate, and on being repeatedly tested, the action was found to have not been injured.

18. Several rifles have been jolted with force on the ground with the action at full cock. In no instance was the spring enabled to free itself.

19. I think so.

4. State whether the alterations have improved the pull off either in regularity or other respects, or have had any prejudicial effect with regard thereto.

1. The pull off in my opinion has been made more regular, and the general effect of the improvement is beneficial.

2. The alterations appear to have improved the regularity of the pull off, and the trigger does not travel as it did when the tumbler rest was used.

3. Pull off greatly improved, being more gradual and regular than in former pattern. Alterations also enable more of the forefinger being placed around trigger.

4. I am of opinion that the pull off is improved in regularity, it being a little heavier (but not too heavy), but decidedly more uniform, and consequently less dangerous.

5. The alterations have much improved the pull off. After the experiments each rifle was tested with regard to the pull off, and it was ascertained that this had not varied to any extent which was appreciable.

6. The result in this case has been on the whole unfavourable, but not in any marked degree.

7. The pull off has been rendered very much more regular and uniform by the alterations made.

8. The pull off requires observation, being very irregular; some pulled as much as 12½ lb at starting, and none were below 8 lb. After firing 30 rounds some pull off about ½ lb less; but those whose pull offs at 12½ lb was first recorded, did not shew any perceptibie diminution in that particular after very severe testing by rapid firing.

The DAAG for Musketry, Cork, also reported on rifles in the hands of A Coy, 12th Regt. – viz, that the alteration had rendered the pull off perfectly regular, and his opinion was confirmed by the result of further tests.

9. The pull off is more regular, but in many cases it has much exceeded 7 lb; in one rifle it is over 12 lb, and in others over 10 lb. This has not apparently affected the practice though, as the pull off is very short in these rifles.

10. In some cases, after being snapped from 500 to 1,000 times, the pull off was considerably raised, varying from 9 to about 20 lb, which appears to have been caused by the trigger pin being too tight; but these, after being exposed to the air as stated in Ans.2 had in the majority of instances regained their normal state.

11. It would seem by the opinion of about one-sixth of those who fired that the pull off has been dragged a little by the alterations made to the lock, without any prejudicial effect to the weapon.

12. The armourer of the battalion is of opinion that the alteration has improved the regularity of the pull off, as actually tested by him. The alteration in the trigger has the further advantage of preventing the pull off being tampered with by the soldier.

13. The pull off of the nine rifles was tested both before and after the drills and the firing took place, and the following is the result –

No. of rifle	Pull off before	Pull off after	Remarks
	lb	lb	
498	9½	12½	No snap cap
90	10	10	ditto
87	8½	10	ditto
169	8½	9	ditto
586	8½	10½	ditto
449	7½	10½	Snap cap
666	9½	11½	ditto
393	9½	12½	ditto
622	9½	12½	ditto

It will be seen from the foregoing that the pull off has increased very much in most of the rifles.

A "drag" has also been felt in some of the rifles which was not felt before commencing drill. I think this was caused by the leverage of the trigger being too long.

14. The pull off of the whole was tested before any firing took place, and again after firing 20 rounds of ball cartridge resulting as under –

Heaviest pull off – 11½ lb
Lightest pull off – 5¾ lb
Average pull off – 7.4125 lb

Differences in pull off (in lbs) –

1:2
1:1½
1:1¼
3:1
9:¾
24:½
19-¼
42:Nil

The pull off is slightly longer, but not to such an extent as to be detrimental to good shooting.

15. Either the trials or the alterations have made the pull off very irregular. The pull off before the trial was 6½ to 7 lb; after, it varied from 8 to 11 lb, the average about 9½ lb.

In the rifles with the old component parts, the pull off fell to 4 lb in one instance, and 6½ lb in the others. A pull off of 4 lb is dangerous, and 6½ lb much too fine for an army weapon, and I consider the increase if not exceeding 9 lb is by no means prejudicial.

16. The regularity of the pull off has been much improved.

17. The alterations have certainly improved the regularity of the pull off, and have had no prejudicial effect whatever.

18. I consider the acute angle of the bent of the tumbler an improvement on the obtuse one of the old pattern, as it renders the pull off more regular.

19. Altogether very much improved. No prejudicial effect noticed.

5. State whether during the trials any strikers have broken, and if so how many, specifying whether in firing, in snapping without a snap cap, or with a snap cap.

1. None.

2. No strikers have broken, although the trials were severe.

3. No strikers broke, or any part of lock damaged.

4. No striker has broken during the trials, or any casualties occurred of any description.

5. None.

6. None.

7. No strikers have broken during snapping, either with or without the snap cap.

8. The rifles stood the test admirably, no single accident of any kind occurring to the rifles, locks, or strikers, though the locks of several, I may say, were filled with sand and dust.

9. None.

10. Two strikers and one lever broken, the former after snapping (with snap cap) about 480 times, the latter after snapping 200 times, the lever being moved backwards and forwards each time.

11. None.

12. As a matter of fact none of the strikers have broken during the trials, but the alteration in itself is not likely to have any effect on that part of the lock.

13. The rifles were used without and with snap caps, and none of the strikers were broken.

14. Three main springs and one indicator keeper screw broken, but no strikers.

15. No strikers were broken in the 50 rifles with the new components, one striker was broken in the 4 fitted with the old parts.

16. None.

17. No strikers broken.

18. No strikers broken during the course of the trials.

19. None.

6. Opinions on the arm generally.

1. In my opinion the arm is now a serviceable and superior weapon.

A note is appended, signed by Capt. Mark Wood, stating that, owing to the exhaustive trials made at Chelsea Barracks by Col. Fletcher, Scots Fusilier Guards, of the improvements mentioned, he has not submitted the whole of the rifles issued to the same trial.

2. The arm works well, and is a good serviceable military weapon. It might be an improvement if the upper surface of the breech block were case-hardened and rendered dull. The men, notwithstanding all cautions, use bath-brick to clean the bright surface, and the dust from the brick penetrates the breech action. The blueing from the trigger guard is apt to come off on the men's coats, and the coats are worn away near the shoulder by the efforts of the men to clean them. Something should be done to remedy this. I consider the alterations in the breech blocks to be a great improvement, and I am borne out in this opinion by Capt. Willson, the IoM, and the armourer-serjeant.

3. Breech action considerably benefitted by alterations, and better shooting has been achieved by bad shots. Thumb piece still appears too high, causing inconvenient stretch between thumb and forefinger. Grip of right hand would be improved by one or more raised ridges on lever close to trigger guard.

4. Most satisfactory – especially with reference to the recent alterations. The sole defect – viz, that of the rifle

going off on closing the breech being entirely rectified.

5. The alterations have *much* improved the arm. The weapon with bayonet fixed is too short. If either barrel or bayonet was lengthened, and some protection offered to the hand when the barrel became heated by rapid firing, I am of opinion that the arm would be very efficient.

6. I think the arm is of too complicated a nature for the army as now recruited. It is difficult to clean and easily gets out of order. I consider these defects might be very serious on an actual campaign.

7. The arm appears good and serviceable, and a handy weapon. Makes good shooting, especially at long ranges.

8. The rifle is a first rate arm, and I am of opinion it would work well on service; but I would respectfully call attention to the want of a uniform pull off.

9. The rifle carries very accurately, and soldiers who were good shots before have made very good practice with it. This has not been the case with ordinary men, who apparently cannot get to understand the sights. The rifle does not balance well when carried at the "slope", and the foresight is liable to injury by the bayonet. I think the lock is still too complicated.

10. Satisfactory, considering the severity of the tests they were subjected to as regards the new components; but the striker is still, I consider, the weak point in the arm, and a most serious defect.

11. It is undoubtedly a good weapon, but perhaps a little complicated for the ordinary soldier; the mechanism of the lock in particular. The bayonet is too short for field service. The great disadvantage of liability to danger from being carried at full cock has not been remedied in the recent alterations.

12. Theoretically speaking, I am strongly of opinion that the alteration will answer the purpose for which it has been introduced, but before expressing a practical decision, a more prolonged trial will be necessary, and this trial should include a drier time of the year, to ascertain whether dust and grit are effectually excluded by the present mechanism.

13. I believe the present alterations to be an improvement, but there are one or two faults which I think ought to be remedied, if it is possible to do so, viz, – 1. The "jar" felt by the forefinger when snapping without a snap cap. 2. The "drag" of the trigger, which is so objectionable in rifle shooting. 3. The pull off which has gone up in some of the rifles from 3 to 4 lbs, the average being 9 lb when first tested, and 11 after the firing.

14. The shooting with it is very good. As it is occasionally necessary for cleansing purposes to strip the action, particularly after firing. it appears to be a great defect to be obliged to employ an armourer for the purpose. If, in accordance with the drill, the flap of the backsight is put down without moving the sliding bar, it is very liable to become bent.

15. As I reported on 23rd October, I considered there were only two defects in the rifle; the undersighting for all distances over 400 yards, and the liability of the action to get clogged with dirt. This last has now been remedied, I think effectually, and also prevented is the continual breakage of strikers and other component parts. I should have included as a defect, the liability of the barrel to get so heated that a man cannot hold his rifle after a few rounds of rapid firing.

16. The alterations reported on have considerably improved the defective lock action, but the weakness of the extractor is still unsatisfactory.

17. The arm is really improved by the alterations.

18. The alteration appears a decided improvement. I consider the M-H thus improved superior to any arm yet introduced into the service.

19. With the present alteration I think the arm almost perfect.

The following is an appendix to the report furnished by Col. H.C. Fletcher, 2nd Battalion Scots Fusilier Guards, 8-12-1875. See answer to Q.2.

---

400 rounds were fired with rifles Nos.87 and 647, with out cleaning, in four days.

These two rifles were afterwards put through the sand test, two handfulls of fine dry sand were poured on the top and bottom of the breech actions, and 3 rounds were then fired, the same again were performed with the breech open, the rifles were then buried in the sand, one with the breech open and the other closed, and afterwards fired 3 rounds, and both rifles were found to work perfectly well. The actions were afterwards taken to pieces by the armourer-serjeant, when it was found that the sand had worked into all the parts of the action, but none had rested on the bent of the tumbler. Two rifles (Nos.26 and 39) were buried in the snow for 24 hours and then fired 10 rounds; handfulls of sand were then thrown on them both with the breech open and shut, 5 more rounds were then fired out of them, and the rifles were found to work perfectly well. The actions were afterwards taken to pieces, and the same result was found as before.

Each rifle was dropped 3 feet 6 inches full cocked, and none were found to jar off except No.420, of which, on examination of the breech action, the trigger spring was found to be broken, this rifle would not have jarred off by the ordinary way of ordering arms. It should be remarked that excepting from the lightness of the pull off there was no means of discovering that the trigger spring was broken, if the rifle was handled in the usual way. If held with the muzzle sloped upwards, the breakage of the trigger spring was shewn by the rifle not coming to the full cock.

When the rifles were fired with great rapidity, and had become extremely hot after about 50 rounds, there was some difficulty in the extraction, but on the rifles cooling everything worked well.

GLOSSARY

Action – The breech mechanism of an arm, using two basic systems, the bolt and the block.
Bolt: One using a sliding piece to close the breech, on the same principle as the ordinary door bolt.
Block: One using a block, generally hinged, to close the breech.
Subdivided as follows –
Dropping: One in which the block is hinged at the top rear at a right angle to and above the axis of the bore. The front of the block drops away from the chamber to open the breech. Eg, Martini.
Falling: One in which the block slides in a vertical slot, and on opening falls away from the chamber. Eg, Henry.
Rolling: (1) One in which the block rotates around a spindle parallel to and slightly below the axis of the bore. The block has a groove on one side, and in operation the block is rotated until this groove comes into line with the chamber, thus opening the breech. Eg, Werndl. (2) One in which the block rotates around a pivot at right angles to, but below the axis of the bore. The block has a flat side, which rolls clear of the chamber when the block is pulled to the rear. Eg, Remington.
Swinging: (1) One in which the block is hinged on a spindle parallel to the axis of the bore, but to one side of it. To open the breech, the block is swung completely out of its housing, leaving the breech clear. Eg, Snider. (2) One in which the block is hinged at the top front at a right angle to, and above, the axis of the bore. To open the breech the block is lifted from the rear and swung forward onto the top of the barrel. Eg, Braendlin.

Adjutant-General – Assisted the C-I-C, and supervised the organisation of the army.

Arm – A rifle or carbine.
Breech-loading: One that is loaded from the rear, by utilising a breech mechanism.
Interchangeable: That in which the component parts of one will exactly replace those of another of the same pattern. The individual parts are made to exact specifications, and are subjected to a rigid examination at various stages of their manufacture. Standard gauges are used, to ensure perfect conformation in form and dimensions.
Magazine: One fitted with a container for several cartridges, but not necessarily a repeating arm.
Muzzle-loading: One that is loaded from the muzzle, the other end of the barrel being closed.
Repeating: One that can mechanically fire several shots from a loaded magazine.

Ball – A bullet. A carry over from the time when the bullet was an actual ball.

Bayonet – An edged weapon for attachment to an arm for offensive or defensive purposes.
Ordinary: In the British service, the common triangular bladed socket bayonet; in effect, the Patt.'53.
Socket: One attached to the barrel of the arm by means of a socket, or tube, which usually engaged the foresight block by means of a zigzag slot to retain it in position.
Saw-back: One with saw teeth on the back of the blade, usually issued to engineers or artillerymen.
Sword: Generally a hilted bayonet with a flat sword type blade. One capable of being used as a sword.
Triangular: One fitted with a tapered triangular or three-sided blade.

Beeswax – Wax secretion of bees, used to construct their cells.

Bore – The interior of the barrel of a firearm.
Large: One of 0.5-inch (12.7 mm) or over.
Polygonal: One in which the bore section takes the form of a multi-sided figure, rather than the usual circle. The intersecting angles of the sides take the place of the grooves in the usual rifled bore.
Relieved: One in which the bore is not parallel for its full length. In a breech-loader the diameter is larger at the breech end, to enable the bullet to gradually assume the rifling, so as to reduce friction of the bullet in the barrel, and thereby increase the muzzle velocity.
Small: One of less than 0.5-inch.

British Service Establishments –
Admiralty: The headquarters of the navy.
HMS Cambridge: A naval shore base, and not a ship, although named as one. This was the navy's "Gunnery" depot, where training and trials concerning all forms of shooting were carried out.
HMS Excellent: Another naval shore base, and major depot for training of recruits, etc.
Hythe: The School of Musketry for the army. A training establishment devoted to producing musketry instructors for the various regiments of the army, and for testing arms and ammunition developed for the army.
War Office: Headquarters of the army.

Bullet – A projectile for a firearm.
Calibre – The diameter of the bore. In rifled arms it is measured across the lands of the rifling.
Cartridge – A self-contained unit for loading a small arm. It consists of bullet, case, charge, and primer.
Ball: One containing a bullet.
Blank: One without a bullet, usually fired for noise effect only.
Bottleneck: One with the case body appreciably larger in diameter than the neck; consequently it has prominent shoulders. It is therefore similar to a bottle in appearance.
Boxer: One made on Boxer's principle.
Case: The main part of a cartridge, its body.
Daw: One made on Daw's principle.
Long chamber: One long in proportion to its bullet diameter, and of straight taper, with a heavy charge. The length is necessary to accomodate the charge.
Short chamber: One short in proportion to its weight of charge, and of bottleneck shape. The shorter but larger diameter case can accomodate the same charge as the long chamber case in the same bore.
Chamber – That part of the bore shaped to accomodate the cartridge.
Long: One that takes a long chamber cartridge.
Short: One that takes a short chamber cartridge.
Charge – The powder load of a cartridge, at that time, black powder (gunpowder).
Compressed: One that is formed under pressure in a mould, thus providing a shaped pellet; or one that is placed loose in the case, and then pressed down to condense it.
Loose: One placed in the case in its natural state, and not compressed in any way.
C-I-C, the Field Marshall Commanding-in-Chief – The officer commanding the British forces.
Council of Ordnance – Sat as required to consider items of ordnance for adoption by the British service.
Director of Artillery and Stores – Originally known as the Director of Ordnance. He co-ordinated the procurement and supply of warlike stores for the armed services.
Fire – To discharge a firearm.
Hang: Delayed ignition of a cartridge after being struck by the firing pin.
Miss: Failure of a cartridge to fire after being struck by the firing pin.
Fixed rest – (Or machine rest) A mechanical contrivance for holding an arm during test firing, to eliminate human error.
Fouling – The residue left in the bore by the burning of the powder charge.
Government manufacturing establishments –
The Royal Arsenal, Woolwich: Manufactured and repaired heavy armaments for the British services.
The Royal Gunpowder Factory, Waltham Abbey: Manufactured most of the gunpowder used by the British services.
The Royal Laboratories, Woolwich Arsenal: Manufactured small arms ammunition, and carried out tests and experiments associated with the development and manufacture of this type of ammunition.
The Royal Small Arms Factory, Enfield Lock: Manufactured and repaired small arms for the British services.
Groove – That part of the rifling cut into the sides of the bore.
Progressive: One that increases or decreases in depth from breech to muzzle. Often used in conjunction with a relieved bore. In the case of a breech-loader the progressive groove would be deeper at the breech (relieved) end of the bore, for the same reason the bore was relieved.
Uniform: One in which the depth remains constant for the full length of the bore.
Inspector-General of Musketry – He co-ordinated the training of the army in musketry and shooting.
Lands – Those parts of the original bore remaining between the rifling grooves.
Leading – Particles of lead left on the interior of the bore by a lead bullet. Caused by excessive fouling and lack of lubrication.
Mark – The progressive pattern, or type, of service stores, usually expressed by a Roman numeral.
Needle-gun – A bolt action breech-loading arm that ignites its cartridge by means of a needle-like firing pin that penetrates the cartridge case, the primer being enclosed within the body of the cartridge.
Ordnance Select Committee – Sat as necessary to recommend items of ordnance for use by the services.
Patent – A government grant of protection for a certain period of time for an invention.
Letters: The patent granted after the elapse of the period of the provisional patent.
Provisional: The first application for patent recognition. Valid for six months to allow investigation or challenge of the patent claim.

Pattern – An early expression for "Mark", but more often a sub-division of one; usually expressed by an Indo-Arabic numeral.
Primer – The igniter of a cartridge. Also called the "cap".
Prize Competition – One with a monetary reward for the winner.
Recoil – The backward thrust of a firearm in response to the explosion of the charge.
Rifling – Spiral grooves cut into the bore, to impart a spin to the bullet to stabilise it.
Progressive: One in which the pitch increases from breech to muzzle. Also known as "gain twist".
Twist: Also known as the "pitch" of the rifling. The grooves are cut in a spiral which is usually measured as one turn in a certain distance; eg, 1 turn in 22 inches (quoted as 1 in 22). Can be found in either right or left hand spiral.
Uniform: One in which the pitch remains constant for the full length of the bore.
Rod – An accessory of the arm, usually carried beneath the barrel.
Cleaning: For a breech-loading arm, it was used for cleaning the bore or driving out cases stuck in the chamber.
Ram: For a muzzle-loading arm it was used to ram home the charge, as well as for cleaning.
Roman numerals – Used to express the Mark of an item of ordnance. A comparison with Indo-Arabic follows –
1 – I
2 – II
3 – III
4 – IV
5 – V
6 – VI
7 – VII
8 – VIII
9 – IX
10 - X
Round – A single cartridge.
Secretary of State for War – The representative of the civilian government concerned with the overall administration of the armed services.
Surveyor-General – He supervised the design and development of equipment for the armed services.
Trajectory – The curve described by a bullet passing from the muzzle to the point of impact.

BIBLIOGRAPHY

Army Orders – British War Office.

A History of the Birmingham Small Arms Company, 1861-1900 – D. Nie (Manuscript).

A Treatise on the Snider – I.D. Skennerton, Margate, Australia, 1978.

Catalogue of the Enfield Pattern Room – British Rifles – Woodend, HMSO, 1981.

Government Papers and Parliamentary Reports, 1867-1887 –
Army Manufacturing Establishments Annual Returns
Reports and Proceedings of Various Ordnance and Small Arms Committees
Royal Small Arms Factory, Enfield Lock –
Pattern Book
Range Book
War Office Minutes.

Gun Digest Treasury – The Gun Digest Company, Chicago 6, USA, 1956.

Instructions for Armourers – Army Circulars, various years – British War Office.

Lists of Changes in War Materiel – British War Office; reprinted I.D. Skennerton, Margate, 1977-79.

Military Breech-Loading Rifles – Majendie and Browne; Royal Artillery Institute, London, 1870.

Patent Specifications – British Patent Office.

Private correspondence between Sir Henry Halford and Mr. W.E.Metford – by kind courtesy of Lord Cottesloe.

Regulations for Musketry Instruction, 1887 – HMSO 1889.

The Boxer Cartridge in the British Service – B.A. Temple, Brisbane, Australia, 1977.

The British Service Lee – I.D.Skennerton, Margate, Australia, 1982.

The Comparative Merits of the Martini Rifle and the Westley Richards Rifle and Ammunition – W.P.Marshall; W. Mitchell & Co., London, 1870.

The Lee-Enfield Rifle – E.G.B.Reynolds; Herbert Jenkins, London, 1960.

The Technical Educator – Cassell, Petter, and Galpin, London, 1871.

Treatise on Ammunition, 5th Edition, 1892 – HMSO 1892.

Treatise on Military Small Arms and Ammunition, 1888 – HMSO 1888.

INDEX